REGIONALIZATION AND GLOBALIZATION IN THE MODERN WORLD ECONOMY

This collection of outstanding essays explores the importance of regionalization and globalization to the world economy. International contributions explore the process of regionalization in the Pacific Area, the Americas, Africa and Europe, and question whether the world economy is characterized by increasing regionalization, rather than globalization. Contributors investigate:

- how the processes of globalization and regionalization, driven by liberalization of trade and capital markets, weaken nationally established monopolies and protected industries;

- whether globalization and regionalization are a challenge to Third World nations and the countries of the former socialist bloc, because they threaten exclusion from the developed industrialized world's free trade blocs;

- the possibility that regionalization creates obstacles for an integrated international economy. Will the world trading system fragment due to Europe, North Amercia and Pacific Asia creating a tripolar economic system?

- *Regionalization and Globalization in the Modern World Economy* makes an important contribution to current debates on development economics.

Alex Fernández Jilberto has been a Fellow of the Universities of Valparaiso (Chile) and Barcelona (Spain). He was a research assistant at the University of Amsterdam (Netherlands), where he is now employed in the Department of Political Science. **André Mommen** has been a Fellow at the University of Brussels (Belgium), a lecturer at the Institute of Labour Problems, Brussels, and now lectures in political science at the University of Amsterdam.

ROUTLEDGE STUDIES IN DEVELOPMENT ECONOMICS

REGIONALIZATION AND GLOBALIZATION IN THE MODERN WORLD ECONOMY

Perspectives on the Third World and transitional economies

Alex E. Fernández Jilberto and André Mommen

London and New York

First published 1998
by Routledge
11 New Fetter Lane, London EC4P 4EE

Simultaneously published in the USA and Canada
by Routledge
29 West 35th Street, New York, NY 10001

Typeset in Garamond by Pure Tech India Ltd, Pondicherry
Printed and bound in Great Britain by Redwood Books, Trowbridge, Wiltshire

British Library Cataloguing in Publication Data
A catalogue record for this book is available from the British Library

Library of Congress Cataloging in Publication Data
A catalogue record for this book has been requested

ISBN 0–415–18192–5

CONTENTS

CONTENTS

LIST OF FIGURES

LIST OF TABLES

LIST OF CONTRIBUTORS

Zehra Gamze Aslancik studied Political Science at the University of Amsterdam and is currently working as a lieutenant in the Dutch Royal Navy in The Hague.

Oscar O. Catalán Aravena is a Lecturer in International Economic Relations at the University of Amsterdam and specializes in economic policies in Central American countries.

Alex E. Fernández Jilberto is a Senior Lecturer in International Relations at the University of Amsterdam. His publications deal with the politics of Latin America and Third World countries in general.

Carolyn L. Gates is a Senior Economist at the Foundation for Indochina Studies (University of Amsterdam) and Fellow of the Institute of Southeast Studies (Singapore). She is currently researching firm behaviour and institutional change in Vietnam.

Barbara Hogenboom is a Research Assistant in the Department of Political Science at the University of Amsterdam and specializes in Mexican politics and regional integration.

Piet Konings is a Senior Researcher at the African Studies Centre, University of Leiden (the Netherlands) and is working on state, labour and class formation in Ghana and Cameroon.

Andrey S. Makarychev is Associate Professor of Political Science at the Nizhny Novgorod State University (Russian Federation).

Henk Meilink is a Senior Economist at the African Studies Centre, University of Leiden (the Netherlands) and is working on structural adjustment programmes, food security issues and Africa's international trade conditions.

André Mommen works in the Department of Political Studies at the University of Amsterdam. He is working on neo-liberal economic reforms in developing and transitory countries.

Alvaro Pinto Scholtbach is working as a policy adviser on foreign affairs for the Dutch Parliament in The Hague.

Vladimir V. Popov is Director of the Centre for Economic Studies at the Academy of National Economy in Moscow.

Batara Simatupang works in the Department of Economics at the University of Amsterdam and specializes in communist economic systems, especially Poland. Nowadays he lectures on structural transformations in South-East Asia.

Miguel Teubal is Professor of Agricultural Economics at the University of Buenos Aires and a researcher at the Centro de Estudios Avanzados at the same university. He has published numerous books on agriculture and poverty in Latin America.

Hans Van Zon is Professor at the School of Social and International Studies at the University of Sunderland (UK) and specializes in Central and Eastern European economic development.

PREFACE

The world at present is facing critical challenges and uncertainties. Forces of global capital remain largely unaccountable to governments. In this book we will try to expose the facts behind the process of globalization and regionalization and study the specificity of the current processes of regionalization in the Pacific Area, the Americas, Africa and Europe. We stress that the process of globalization fosters regionalization and creates a competitive drive within regions that weakens nationally established monopolies and protected industries. Moreover, we argue that the process of globalization and regionalization is a challenge to all nations, especially to those of the Third World and the countries of the former socialist bloc, because it raises the spectre of exclusion from the developed industralized world divided up into free trade blocs. Regional arrangements may spread and become stumbling blocks to a more integrated international economy. Therefore, pessimists predict that the world trading system will fragment and that the multilateral trading system functioning under the aegis of the World Trade Organization (WTO) will disintegrate when Europe, North America and Pacific Asia become 'fortresses' and create a tripolar world system.

Discussion of the 'new world order' prompted by the Gulf War of 1990 and the collapse of socialism in Eastern Europe has reinforced that process of globalism and regionalism. The dynamics of globalization and regionalization, responding to the organization of capital flows, the play of monetary and financial forces and market opportunities, will be the subject of debate in this book.

Globalization and regionalization are also tied in with the failure of state-led socialism and Third World strategies linked to import-substituting industrialization and protectionism. Socialism within one country or bloc became ideologically discredited when it was perceived as an unattractive economic order. This pattern of globalization sharply challenges the North–South normative project that had been affirmed at an earlier stage of world history. Then, the East and South-East Asian states managed to achieve high rates of economic growth even in the face of global recession and 'oil shocks'. That pattern revealed that location in the South was not by itself an explanation for persistent underdevelopment. The movement for a new international economic order was discredited and abandoned. The collapse of the Soviet bloc was seen as confirming claims about the overall economic superiority of capitalism, a view widely endorsed by now throughout the South.

The problem is what to make of the growing need for deeper international economic integration and the apparent decline of national economic policy autonomy. Globalization is usually explained as the result of technological change and productivity growth which brought about a dramatic change in the competitive strength of countries as well as firms and in the creation of a tripolar world system. A new aspect is that North–South relations have changed as diversity and levels of income have widened and globally competitive firms have consolidated their sourcing and production networks all over the world. At present, many governments in the South see globalization as a threat. In the first place, acute indebtedness combined with increased market pressures to serve that debt have obliged all developing countries to make structural adjustments at the expense of the agrarian and urban masses. Meanwhile, they have to pursue these policies in order to become attractive to foreign investors. In this book we will study these devastating effects in combination with pressures exercised by the international financial institutions and the international market forces which are pushing towards economic liberalization and internationalization. Furthermore, we will stress the role of the emerging markets and economies and the formation of powerful trading blocs. All developing countries fear that 'Fortress Europe' and the North American Free Trade Area (NAFTA) will increase regional protection and trade and investment diversion and that protectionist interest groups will slow down the process of multilateral trade liberalization. 'Fortress Europe' threatens the Newly Industrializing Countries (NICs), whose exports compete with those of the European Union (EU) and whose imports of machinery and technology from Japan and the USA limit their ability to take advantage of the potential gains from whatever growth results from the creation of the Single Market.

This book, more than is normally the case with academic enterprises, is the result of a collaborative effort that started many years ago. From the outset we discussed the role of neo-liberal reforms in developing and socialist countries. Liberalization and democratization drives were analysed and discussed in connection with a globalizing economy. Our starting-point for this book was the role of the international economy in driving the transformation of domestic structures in developing countries and in transforming the socialist economies. We asked the authors to consider ways in which globalizing and regionalizing tendencies were shaping a new world order and how states were responding to external threats and opportunities – to competition, economic flows, foreign direct investment (FDI) and political and military pressures. None of the authors have taken our proposals as an unquestionable good. Although some of them are working at the University of Amsterdam they do not form a school of thought or interest. Some of them are very critical of the ongoing process of globalization and regionalization while others adhere to the neo-classical point of view that liberalization and openness are promising mechanisms for a new development strategy. The authors were entirely free to reject or criticize our point of view that the world economy is increasingly regionalizing and that globalism is only a tendency. The following chapters attempt to canvass the evidence for regionalism by analysing changes at country-specific and regional levels of the economy and economic policy.

In contrast to established research groups, which reunite old colleagues, many of us met for the first time on this project. We also have been keenly aware of moving over territory with unsettled frontiers. The debate between 'globalizers' and 'regionalizers' is still going on. Therefore it would be hazardous to synthesize both theoretical approaches. This book seeks to assess the factors determining the regionalization drive. It is not offering an 'alarmist' view on the defensive reactions which lie behind the regionalization drive. The formation of the EU's Single Market or other regional trade blocs are certainly defensive reactions to increased competition. Forms of 'closed' regionalization can lead to trade wars. Trade wars may become a source of international armed conflicts and be a prelude to a new world war. New forms of imperialism may appear and give birth to increased tensions between the centre and the periphery. Lenin, who wrote his essay on imperialism during the First World War, transformed his theory on imperialism into a theory on war. At any rate, our period is increasingly reminiscent of life before the First World War, because commodities traverse the globe with remarkable freedom and speed. Today's global system also looks like a somewhat flexible remix of the nineteenth-century liberal world with enough flexibility in a crisis to manage a bale out. Gone is the idea of competing imperial powers for rare natural resources and markets in a colonial world. Indeed, in our world the system-threatening aspects of *laissez-faire* policies seem domesticated. In our book we will argue that this view is simplistic. Despite all the books on the end of history or the death of the state, we think that states and state institutions are still alive and playing a first-class role in setting the international economic agenda. The World Bank and the International Monetary Fund (IMF) have managed to keep the Third World debt from provoking a global implosion and have forced Third World governments to reform their economies.

For a book of this sort, we had to depend on the scholarly expertise of country specialists. These colleagues have been struggling with 'global issues' at the level of national economies. They have contributed in their own way from different theoretical standpoints to our collective effort to understand the constraints and opportunities that establish the conditions within which states reform their economies when pursuing their global interests. Of course, there are always difficulties when editing papers by authors on different continents and of different scientific backgrounds, from draft form to publication. The contributors to this book, however, have made our task as easy as possible.

Alex E. Fernández Jilberto and André Mommen

1

GLOBALIZATION VERSUS REGIONALIZATION

Alex E. Fernández Jilberto and André Mommen

Since 1945 the globalization of the world economy has made considerable progress. In the critical areas of trade, production and finance, the world has become more interconnected and integrated than ever before. The globalization of financial markets with their volatile effects on national economic management has destabilized and weakened the autonomy of all nation–states. The global market represents a concentration of power capable of influencing national government economic policy and, by extension, other policies as well (Sassen 1996: 39). Market forces and multinational corporations are creating tensions and shaping new patterns of interdependence. Growing corporate interests in foreign investments and exports urge the reduction of traditional trade barriers, while additional pressure arises from regional arrangements. This induces a process of deeper integration and liberalization of foreign trade. Integration refers to the fundamentally political process of policy coordination and adjustment designed to facilitate closer economic interdependence and to manage the externalities that arise from it (Haggard 1995: 2; Keohane 1984: *passim*).

Nation–states adapt to these global pressures or try to resist by joining regional trading blocs within an integrating world economy. Hence, globalization refers to the multiplicity of linkages and interconnections between states and societies which make up the present world. It represents two distinct phenomena: scope (or stretching) and intensity (or deepening). It implies an intensification in the levels of interaction, interconnectedness and interdependence between states and societies. It embraces a set of processes covering most of the globe (McGrew and Lewis 1992: 22) and refers to a profound reorganization of the economy and society in what has hitherto been called North and South, East and West. This division has gone and a 'Triad' configuration has appeared with the emerging industrial economies of Asia as a new gravitational pole of a globalizing economy (Schwartz 1994: 240–258).

A BORDERLESS WORLD?

The concept of 'globalization' has an outspoken liberal connotation. Globalization means the production and distribution of products and/or services of a homogeneous type and quality on a world-wide basis. When referring to globaliza-tion liberals are speaking of the disappearance of trade barriers and state regulation. A *borderless world* is the description many neo-liberal authors give of the future of the globalizing economy (Axford 1995: 94–122). This description focuses on the growth in transnational micro-economic links between the Triad of Europe, the Pacific Rim and North America (Ruggie 1993). It considers the process of globalization as a post-industrial wave (Drucker 1993) and it depicts the growing integration of the world economy from a strongly liberal point of view. According to these views, states and national economies will fade away and give birth to an integrated world market. Financial internationalization has fundamentally under-mined state institutions (Cerny 1996: 91). Robert B. Reich believes that the 'Amer-ican' corporation is becoming disconnected from the USA, because American-owned firms relocate abroad and foreign companies move into the USA. Hence, he thinks that the nationality of a firm's dominant shareholders and of its top executives has less and less to do with where the firm invests and produces its goods (Reich 1991: 119–120). Indeed, American firms employ more and more foreign workers in foreign countries, and overseas capital spending by American firms increased from the early 1980s until the early 1990s. Some of this world-wide activity was nothing more than high-volume standardized production transplanted abroad in order to meet low-cost foreign competitors head-on. According to Reich (1991: 124), the major American company knows 'no national boundaries, feels no geographic constraints' and, although the role of global finance is growing, national savings increasingly flow to whoever can do things best, or cheapest, wherever they are located around the world. This trend is world-wide because national champions everywhere are becoming global webs with no particular connection to any nation (ibid.: 133). Many arguments in favour of this view of a globalizing world economy, because the concept of 'globalization' clearly refers to the process of economic and financial internationalization. Over the past decade, world merchandise exports have roughly doubled, from 10 to 20 per cent. With more and more services being transacted internationally, their share in world trade has risen from 15 to 22 per cent. Operations of the multinationals have expanded and sales by their foreign affiliates may now well exceed total world exports. These statistics all point to globalization – the growing international integration of markets for goods, services, and capital. Globalization is altering the world economic landscape in fundamental ways. It is driven by a widespread push towards the liberalization of trade and capital markets, increasing internationalization of corporate production and distri-bution strategies, and technological change that are rapidly dismantling barriers to the international tradability of goods and services and the mobility of capital (Falk 1995: 172–206). So globalization is creating wider markets for trade, an expanding array of tradables, larger private capital inflows, improved access to technology and, in turn, outward-oriented reforms adopted by developing economies also contribute to globalization. Globalization increases competition between policy regimes. This process of deeper integration requires maintaining a liberal trade and investment regime which contributes to a creeping process of global convergence between all economies. But global capital market integration combined with the volatility of capital flows is making macro-economic management more complex and requires maintaining the confidence of capital owners in developing economies. Thus the internationalization of services will likely lead the next stage of globalization. Tele-communications and information technology will revolutionize the world economy (Humphreys and Simpson 1996: 105–124) with the increasing tradability of services enlarging the scope of firms in developing countries. Declining costs will offer new opportunities to developing countries willing to liberalize their trade and wanting to invest in services. Therefore, globalization has to be understood as a process of suppressing state influence on the economy and of giving private capital hegemony over any investment decision. Moreover, thanks to deregulation, the financial revolution has put the financial sector in a position of hegemony over the real economy at both the international and the national level, undermining not only political auton-omy but the very bases of state authority and democratic legitimacy (Cerny 1996: 91).

On the other hand, we have realists who think that the ongoing process of internationalization and therefore globalization on its own are just reflecting the growth and strength of national companies and the result of the bargaining strength of some powerful states imposing their economic power on weaker states (Kapstein 1991–2: 55–62). Between these two extremes a wide variety of interpretations exists. Some authors discussing the globalization drive argue that globalization only exists in the sector of culture and telecommunications, but that most economies are still 'national' in character. The authors of the French Regulation School reject the contention that the nation–state is *passé* or an accident of history. They argue that the embeddedness of economic institutions is essential for a strong economy and that the nation–state cannot be easily replaced by the market. They state that we do not live in a totally integrated world. Moreover, according to them, globalization is not a totally new phenomenon (Palan *et al.* 1996: 12–31), measured by indicators as the share of exports as a percentage of Gross Domestic Product (GDP) or the share of Foreign Direct Investment (FDI) in total investment flows (Boyer and Drache 1996: 13). Paul Krugman is sceptical about the real character of the globalization of the major economies:

> One might point out that the American economy is not actually that globa-lized: imports are only 13 per cent of GDP, and at least 70 per cent of employment and value-added is in 'non-tradable' sectors that do not compete on world markets.
>
> (Krugman 1996: 18)

Krugman's thesis echoes the Marxist point of view. Marxists think that globalization is real, but also that when globalization is measured by exports as a share of GDP the reality is totally different (see Table 1.1). On that measure, countries are only a little bit more 'globalized' in 1992 than they were in 1913 (Henwood 1996:6). Basing his work on research done by Angus Maddison (1995: 37–39), a Marxist author like Harry Magdoff believes that not trade but the internationalization of finance is the notably distinguishing attribute of the modern globalization drive (Magdoff 1992:

Table 1.1 Exports as percentages of GDP, 1820–1992

	1820	1870	1913	1929	1950	1973	1992
France	1.3	4.9	8.2	7.7	15.4	23.8	22.9
Germany	—	9.5	15.6	12.8	6.2	23.8	32.6
Netherlands	—	17.5	17.8	17.5	12.5	41.7	55.3
UK	3.1	12.0	17.7	13.2	11.4	14.0	21.4
Western Europe	—	10.0	16.3	13.3	9.4	20.9	29.7
Spain	1.1	3.8	8.1	5.0	1.6	5.0	13.4
Russia	—	—	2.9	1.6	1.3	3.8	5.1
Australia	—	7.4	12.8	11.2	9.1	11.2	16.9
Canada	—	12.0	12.2	11.2	9.1	11.2	16.9
USA	2.0	2.5	3.7	3.6	3.0	5.0	8.2
Argentina	—	9.4	6.8	6.1	2.4	2.1	4.3
Brazil	—	11.8	9.5	7.1	4.0	2.6	4.7
Mexico	—	3.7	10.8	14.8	3.5	2.2	6.4
Latin America	—	9.0	9.5	9.7	6.2	4.6	6.2
Japan	—	0.0	2.4	3.5	2.3	7.9	12.4
China	—	0.7	1.4	1.7	1.9	1.1	2.3
India	—	2.5	4.7	3.7	2.6	2.0	1.7
Indonesia	—	0.9	2.2	3.6	3.3	5.0	7.4
Korea	—	0.0	1.0	4.5	1.0	8.2	17.8
Taiwan	—	—	2.5	5.2	2.5	10.2	34.4
Thailand	—	2.1	6.7	6.6	7.0	4.5	11.4
Asia	—	1.3	2.6	2.8	2.3	4.4	7.2
World	1.0	5.0	8.7	9.0	7.0	11.2	13.5

Source: Maddison 1995: 38.

44–75). In reality, the economies of small countries acquire more openness when successfully industrializing, because they can get proportionately bigger benefits from international trade than large countries (Maddison 1995: 38) (see Table 1.1). Because integration in the world market almost automatically implies open economies, it is said to sharply restrict nations' capacity to autonomously design their own political economy. Nations are all shedding the protectionist measures that once upheld their respective welfare state systems (Esping-Andersen 1996: 1–31). With respect to this phenomenon, Samir Amin (1997: 5) argues that globalization via the market is a reactionary utopia which has to be countered by developing an alternative humanistic project of globalization consistent with a socialist perspective and a global political system which is not in the service of a global market, but which defines its parameters in the same way as the nation–state historically represented the social framework of the national market and not merely its passive field of deployment.

Robert Wade thinks that 'globalization' is a 'buzz word' and that therefore one has to become sceptical about the globalization process, because the world economy is more international than global. Most multinational enterprises have a national home base and populations are much less mobile than goods and finance. Most national economies produce more than 80 per cent for domestic consumption (Wade 1996: 61). However, national economies have become more interconnected than ever before and they are integrated through FDI and international trade. National borders have become permeable and protectionism is no longer a guarantee of economic stability. Trade has steadily grown faster than output and FDI has grown even faster than trade. FDI flows grew three times faster than trade flows and almost four times faster than output (ibid.: 63). Firms have become involved in international networks and alliances, creating joint ventures for research and production of trade. Multinationals now control one-third of the world's private sector assets and 30 per cent of private Gross National Product (GNP) in the major European countries. Wade argues that finance, more than production, has been internationalized. Liquidities are rapidly exchanged across borders because of the deregulation of the financial sector. In the 1960s and 1970s exchange controls hampered financial expansion abroad, but since the 1980s the 'financial derivatives' have added a new dimension to world finance and made governments powerless to control finance. Integration was advanced by the spread of new technologies and by firms wanting to protect their innovations by marketing their patents. The degree of internationalization of the exploitation of patents grew substantially higher than the degree of internationalization of trade. The share of trade in GDP is the highest in the small economies of Asia and Europe. But exports account for only 12 per cent of GDP or less for the USA, Japan and the single-unit Europe. Overwhelmingly, world production and trade are nationally oriented and controlled by big national capital. FDI goes mostly to the developed world and is only secondarily invested in a developing country in the same region (ibid.: 62–66).

Accelerated FDI followed widespread financial liberalization and the pursuit of new strategies of investment and productive organization on the part of multinational firms. Growth of world flows of FDI by multinational firms has exceeded the rates of merchandise exports since the mid-1980s. In many developing countries FDI constitutes the principal source of foreign capital and integrates them into the globalizing and regionalizing economy. The pattern of FDI is extremely complex, because FDI flows are concentrated within three poles of attraction: the USA, the EU and Japan. FDI flows towards the developing countries are concentrated and directed to just ten developing economies of which the Asian 'tigers' and China form the bulk. A large number of developing countries, mainly in Africa, are excluded from these benefits (Robson 1996: 33–44).

Moreover, with a share of 84 per cent in 1989, intra-regional trade was mainly concentrated among the northern industrialized nations. Wade argues that North–South trade is extremely regionalized and not globalized. EU trade concentrates on Eastern Europe, the Middle East and Africa, while Japan and the USA are the major trading partners of the emerging economies of Asia and Latin America (see Table 1.2). After the lowering of the trade barriers during the 1980s from an Organization for Economic Cooperation and Development (OECD) average of about 25 per cent to 5 per cent in the 1990s, non-tariff barriers have become more important. It

Table 1.2 Shift of regional weights in trade, 1985–94

	1985	1990	1991	1992	1993	1994
EU's trade						
within EU	53.5	59.2	59.7	61.1	59.9	60.4
with NAFTA	10.5	8.4	8.3	8.1	8.9	8.9
with Asia(*)	4.1	4.9	5.4	5.7	7.1	9.3
NAFTA's trade						
with EU	17.7	19.3	18.8	18.0	15.9	14.9
within NAFTA	38.0	36.9	37.2	37.9	40.2	42.7
with Asia(*)	12.0	15.3	16.2	17.0	17.4	21.4
Asia's trade						
with EU	12.4	14.9	14.4	17.1	15.4	14.5
with NAFTA	22.0	20.2	19.1	18.9	19.0	26.3
within Asia(*)	25.6	31.9	34.5	36.9	36.5	48.5

Source: Shin Yong-dai, Kim Jeong-hong and Lee Hang-koo (1996: 88).
Note: Asia's data for 1994 include the Oceania region.

could be argued that North–South trade is frustrated by quotas and 'voluntary' trade restraints.

Changes occurred in the North–South trade pattern. North–South trade has fallen as a proportion of total trade, a process of marginalization that was due to the decline of the share of raw materials in global trade. Falling oil prices after 1985 and a fall in the terms of trade for primary product exports determined southern decline. However, exports of manufactures from the South to the North increased. In 1989 manufactured exports from the South accounted for only 16 per cent of total trade and half of these exports go to the USA. The NICs import a small proportion of their imports from the South and their share of global industrial output also remains relatively small (see Table 1.2).

According to Fouquin, regionalization is a 'natural phenomenon' (1995: 37) embracing the Americas under the aegis of the USA, the Pacific Rim with Japan as leading trading partner and, finally, the EU which had been constructed around the Paris–Bonn axis. In contrast to the USA, Japan did not construct a free trade area along the lines of NAFTA. Within the EU the Germany–France tandem is dominant and is a pivotal force linking German influence in Eastern and Central Europe with French predominance in Northern Africa and the Mediterranean area (see Table 1.3). Fouquin argues that free trade unions do not necessarily favour increasing trade exchanges between the member states. EFTA is perhaps the best example of a less successful free trade area set up by developed countries. The failure of EFTA to stimulate trade between the member states was due to the fact that the small economies of EFTA had to look for export opportunities in the much greater European Community (EC) and therefore neglected intra-regional EFTA trade. Finally, EFTA members applied for EC membership. The EC started in 1957 with six members and progressively opened its membership to other European

Table 1.3 Trade directions of the four most important exporting countries

US	Japan	France	Germany
5.8 Mexico	2.9 Other Asian NICs	3.6 Northern Africa	3.6 Austria/ Switzerland
5.5 Canada	2.7 China	2.9 Belgium/ Luxemburg	2.5 Central Europe
3.3 Venezuela/ Ecuador	2.5 Asian NICs	2.9 South Africa	2.3 Belgium/ Luxemburg
2.2 Other Latin American countries	2.4 Indonesia	2.5 Italy	2.2 Netherlands
1.9 Brazil	2.0 Indochina	2.3 Sub-Saharan Africa	2.0 Italy
1.8 Japan	1.9 USA	2.0 Mediterranean Europe	2.0 Russian Federation
1.6 Australia/New Zealand	1.8 Australia/New Zealand	1.8 Germany	1.9 France
1.4 Asian NICs	1.3 South Africa	1.6 Britain	1.8 Scandinavian countries
1.1 South Africa	1.1 Other Asian countries	1.5 Switzerland/ Austria	1.6 Mediterranean countries
1.1 Other Asian NICs	1.1 Gulf States	1.3 Middle East (except OPEC states)	1.6 South Africa

Source: Fouquin (1995: 39).
Note: The trade direction measures relative exchanges between countries in relation to their total world trade.

countries. In 1995 the European Union (EU) had fifteen members with at least ten members in the waiting-room (ibid.: 40–42). Andrew Gamble and Anthony Payne (1996: 250) think that the globalization and regionalization process is not the outcome of state projects, but the combination of historical and emergent structures. States remain major players in the construction of free trade areas and some of them are setting the pace of the globalization process when designing new trade regimes. According to Ruigrok and Van Tulder (1995: 289–290), 'the international restructuring race led to a "regionalization" within the Triad regions (Europe, Japan plus the Asia Pacific), and the alleged "globalization"'. The question remains whether and to what extent this regionalization should be considered a premonitory symptom of increasing globalization and absolute competition among firms.

THE REGIONALIZATION PHENOMENON

Globalization conditioned the build-up of protectionist regulations, including calls for competitive devaluations, as well as the spread of regional trading blocs. Regionalism is almost 'by definition' discriminating against non-members of a trading bloc (Sander 1996: 17–36). Regionalization can be defined as an integration process on the regional level with the help of governments. Regionalization appears here as an aspect of a process towards the liberalization of markets and FDI regulations. These regional arrangements appear to be the direct result of governmental actions instituting regional trade regimes and creating deeper integration of separate economies on the regional level. Regionalization is a recent phenomenon. After the sharp reduction in world trade flows in the 1930s and 1940s, and the slowness with which the governments reopened their markets to global trade in the 1950s and 1960s, regionalization was the result of US multinational firms investing in production units overseas. These multinationals shifted a good part of their production units into relatively closed markets and sometimes they integrated their operations globally. Regional integration processes were fostered by FDI and economic cooperation or integration policies initiated by post-war governments in Western Europe. The Soviet Union created its own economic trade area. Everywhere, regional integration was a matter of political and military policies and intervention implemented by coalescing nation–states. In Latin America the so-called complementary agreements were preferential arrangements between countries closely linked by geographical proximity or common interest that provided for the apportionment of the manufacturing of various parts and components used in the same production process. These arrangements involved the danger of establishing monopoly positions by giving preferential treatment to selected industries. The Latin American Regional Market proclaimed that regional markets had to be competitive in character, but in later declarations it proposed postponing the reduction of tariff barriers for commodities that would face intra-area competition. The difficulties of readjustment and the possibility of bankruptcy were often cited as a reason for less competition (Balassa 1962: 21–56).

In the developing world, the former colonial countries created free trade areas but the uneven levels of industrialization between the member countries made regional integration through trade liberalization unlikely to be effective without an explicit framework of measures designed to ensure an equitable allocation of new complementary investment. Positive discrimination in favour of the less advantaged countries had to be implemented in order to foster complementarity. External trade traditions persisted. The bulk of trade still went to the industrialized world. Under the Lomé Convention, African states acquired privileges to export to the EC market under national quotas at prices usually higher and more stable than prevailing world market rates. In addition, all developing states were suffering from the shortage of foreign exchange because they had to pay for capital goods imports in hard currency. The result was that investment programmes were held back and that most of their manufactures remained uncompetitive in international markets. Free trade areas in the developing world wanted to forge links to create genuine and equitable regional integration and wanted to mobilize resources to promote import-substituting industrialization policies.

The regionalization process in the Asia Pacific area is fundamentally different from these previous attempts. Asia Pacific regionalization builds on the powerful use of opportunities for international specialization in production within a frame-work of intensifying economic ties within the region. With no formal, inter-governmental structures for promoting intra-regional trade and specialization and no region-wide trade discrimination, intra-regional trade shares are higher than those within the EU. This unusual phenomenon of high regional concentration of trade with neither official trade discrimination, nor formal institutional support, challenged old ideas of regional development, and inspired a new debate on the concept of regionalism. The defining concept of Asia Pacific and Latin American regionalization is 'open regionalism', which encompasses integrative processes that contain no element of exclusion or discrimination against outsiders (CEPAL 1990; 1994). Pacific Rim countries campaign for reduction of barriers to trade, such as tariff and non-tariff barriers (NTBs), and other obstacles such as transport and transaction costs. They favour an open world trading system in the pure WTO spirit. These countries adopted strategies based on export-led growth, while Europe developed a form of inward-looking regionalization. The concept 'open regionalization' grows naturally out of the themes of market integration, and government support for public goods that facilitate international trade within the region. 'Open regionalism' is the product of market-driven mechanisms. It encompasses regional cooperation on mutual reduction of trade barriers and agreements on trade liberalization, extended to others on an unconditional non-favoured-nation basis. 'Open regionalism' has come up against support in the Americas for concepts of 'discriminatory regionalism'. Most preferential trading arrangements in the developing world adopted free trade schemes with intra-regional trade liberalization which discriminates against outsiders. Some free trade schemes initiated by the USA in recent years also had an ingredient of internationalization of protectionism.

None the less, regionalization refers to the development of intra-regional trade and investment, each inducing a process of 'deeper' behind-the-border industrial integration. The reason for this is clear: potential for gain within regional arrangements can be considerable. First, there is always an advantage of scale. The formation of regional markets without internal barriers makes advantages of scale available. A second major gain is the benefit from combining existing national markets. Small firms within each national market may grow within a larger market. Regional coordination of export promotion strategies may permit the establishment of facilities (financial institutions, marketing firms, freight forwarders, special technical services) (Garnaut and Drysdale 1994: 1–7).

Within this process of regionalizing economies liberalization is seen as a force that helps channel the resources of economies and people into activities where they are most likely to excel. Regionalization appears as a force that softens the effects of globalization by pooling governmental policies and also compensates for the loss of national policy sovereignty. Yet regional arrangements may undermine liberalization when they divert trade and investment (Lawrence 1996: 2) or they may also become a complement or supplement to liberalization under the multilateral trading system.

THE FDI AND THE LOW-WAGE CHALLENGE

The rapid growth and impact of global finance went hand in hand with the appearance of monetary instability and new information technologies. Financial markets globalized and financial operators became as powerful as the governors of central banks who lost sovereign control over the value of currencies. This incited central banks and governments to create monetary stability by establishing regional accords on exchange fluctuations and to integrate production capabilities within each of the three major regions. The rapidly growing strength of Japanese, Korean and European firms in global markets compelled US firms to compete in all world markets and to break up their home-based monopolies. This competitive drive forced multinational firms to redeploy to developing countries and NICs, which outstripped trade growth and contributed to growing unemployment in the developed world, notably in Western Europe. In the developed world firms were pleading for deregulation and flexibility of the work-force, and in order to help these firms some governments lowered wages and invented tax holidays.

FDI by multinational firms increased spectacularly and redeployed production on the principle of comparative advantage. This micro-economic phenomenon plays an important role in the globalization and regionalization drive and is at the very roots of the crisis of the Western 'Fordist' system of industrial production (Ruigrok and Van Tulder 1995). Furthermore, regionalization becomes a policy instrument and a vehicle for cross-border regulations between countries with the same historical background or geographical proximity. Therefore, regionalization is a process controlled by states and political forces and may become a tool for regional protectionism. Multinational firms with a strong regional base may become interested in regional protectionism while others may become more interested in reduced inter-regional trade barriers. In general, the weaker firms will feel threatened by globalization and, in turn, they are more likely to choose bloc regionalization and regional protectionism. In this case, regionalization is a negative reaction to globalization. But bloc regionalization may stimulate competition among firms within a region and reinforce the microdynamic drive to globalization. FDI, cross-border trade and migratory movements accompany the process of globalization and regionalization. With trade, FDI is just one of the powerful levers of deeper economic integration and when these levers reinforce the regionalizing trend they create the need for political arrangements. For instance, Japan is not only exporting a third more to Asia than it does to America; it is making a fifth of its FDI in Asian countries. In terms of size, the Japanese economy represents almost two-thirds of the entire East Asian economy if China is excluded. As the largest exporter and provider of aid, Japan is able to greatly influence, if not dictate, Asia's regional future (Ahn 1996: 5–23). Hence, globalization and regionalization trends are not necessarily antagonistic or antithetical. The two processes are likely to reinforce each other when the same micro-economic forces drive them, because both disrupt and dilute the powers of oligopolies and special-interest groups. But the general form of the global economy is one in which regional players are jockeying for position, and where both protectionism and defensive bilateralism can increase (Axford 1995: 120–122).

Today, three major regional FDI poles – Europe, North America and Asia Pacific – have emerged. These FDI regional poles constitute a challenge to the developing countries of South Asia, the Middle East, sub-Saharan Africa and the former socialist bloc. Because of their economic weakness, the economies of these regions are confronted with a process of globalization they can hardly influence or discuss from a position of strength. The importance of 'global localization' has increased, because international firms are increasingly looking for flexible production in a period of competitive strength. International diffusion of technology and services is boosting the FDI regionalization drive. Therefore, the traditional 'Fordist' and 'Taylorized' big industrial producers are confronted with new players on their home markets who oblige them to react in the same way by internationalizing their production. At the same time they are feeding protectionist pressures in the USA and in Europe.

Meanwhile, numerous firms have run away to low-wage countries in developing or newly industrializing countries or they have invested in production facilities in Central Europe where wages are low and markets are still developing. These 'low-wage export platforms' are an important feature in the globalization and regionalization drive. Much of their output is destined for Europe and the USA. This trend is reinforcing the regionalization process because the production and sourcing networks are operating just across the border. The FDI of European firms in Central Europe and of US firms in Mexico is sustaining this regionalization drive. Other developing or former socialist countries are trying to join this regionalization move and establish 'export platforms' within their own country or region and connect them to the capitalist core. They want to follow the Asian NICs down that path and are turning to export-oriented industrialization strategies in the hope that their 'export platforms' will serve global markets or join regional sourcing networks and markets.

Though the importance of low wages for high-tech production has diminished and emerging economies are trying to follow the example of the East Asian NICs, comparative advantage remains a factor, as is shown by China's export push. Therefore, firms are looking for flexible production facilities in low-wage countries and this means that redeployment from high-wage countries to low-wage countries still occurs. This explains why financial markets foster the globalization and regionalization of production and sourcing networks (Helleiner 1994: 146–168; Reinicke 1995: 39–56). Therefore, becoming a member of a sub-regional grouping is vital for all developing countries in order to develop inter-firm ties and boost FDI. Human resources requirements and infrastructure are necessary too, but they represent heavy investment burdens which are often beyond the financial capabilities of many a developing country. Again, these investments require foreign aid on soft conditions and the import of technology. In order to finance these structural changes, the developing countries are forced to open up their local financial markets and to create a stock exchange market, and to privatize their state-run

11

telecommunications and transport enterprises if they want to pursue the policy of outward-oriented industrialization. In addition, they will have to find markets for their manufactured exports and acquire direct access to Western markets in a period of increased competition between Third World countries.

THE TRIAD BLOCS

In the 1930s and during the Second World War most parts of the world were divided into imperial and quasi-imperial spheres surrounded by barriers to trade and investment. Memories of that inspired the USA to combat discriminatory trading blocs after 1945. Meanwhile, decolonization has produced a slow erosion in formal trading blocs.

The regionalization process started as early as the 1960s in the form of a gradual elimination of all economic barriers, without eliminating the fragmentation of the region into national markets. Most of these regional agreements remained within the concept of free trade areas and most of them were based on a multilateralization of bilateral agreements or unions. The mushrooming of initiatives gave birth to many treaties and institutions of economic integration which still exist, but never were a success, because regional areas were conceived as likelier sites for import-substituting industrialization than small national markets. Few of these regional groupings were successful in furthering freer trade or deeper economic integration between partners. In the developing world regional agreements were seen as a means of reducing dependence on economic ties with the capitalist core region (Kahler 1995b: 19–27).

External pressure was clearly important in provoking the initial movement to liberalization in most countries. Between 1986 and 1991, thirty developing countries undertook unilateral liberalization and today a number of developing countries have more open trade policies, when measured by the level and dispersion of tariffs and the prevalence of quantitative restrictions, than the USA and the EU. Moreover, trade negotiations have begun to affect sovereignty as well as the historical framework of societies at a time when international commodity agreements to stabilize or increase prices for primary commodities have attracted less interest. Developing countries became active participants in the GATT/WTO and individually and as members of coalitions they were committed to the Uruguay Round. Regional arrangements provided external credibility for their own programmes of trade and investment liberalization, as well as wider market access, particularly in the protection-prone industrialized capitalist world.

Western Europe

For a long time Western Europe was considered the model for regional economic integration. The distinguishing feature of the EU's economic integration is its 'depth' with its far-reaching liberalization of factor markets. Yet the factors that drove the integration process of the EU were predominantly political (i.e. not market-driven): economic and military neutralization of Germany and containment of Soviet communism (see Chapter 7 by Alvaro Pinto Scholtbach; Grimwade 1996: 150–191).

Out of these political goals arose a set of institutions, beginning with the European Coal and Steel Community (ECSC). These structures provided a framework for formal integration and within this framework, once established, informal integration was fostered. The European Economic Community (EEC) moved rapidly to a *dirigiste* agricultural regime in a period when the European market was characterized by trade between semi-autonomous national economies and national companies ('champions'). In the 1970s and 1980s the EC was pushed towards deeper integration as a consequence of technological change and increased competition with the newly industrializing countries. Meanwhile, economic and political pressures driving integration have increased now that German reunification and American decline have raised questions about the role of the nation–state and the loss of government autonomy in a highly institutionalized EU (Streeck 1996: 299–315). The privatization of many state-owned European enterprises, partly in response to the EU's 1992 Single Market programme, was intended, among other goals, to reduce the scope of subsidy and buy-at-home distortions. None the less, many of these market-liberalization projects were subject to the idea that the large national champions had to be restructured with the help of the state in order to make them profitable.

The EU's future now depends on the organization's ability to impose the fulfilment of the Maastricht criteria on all members in order to introduce a common currency in 1999. Monetary union will obviously remove exchange rate and national monetary policy from the list of flexible government policies in response to recessions. The Economic and Monetary Union (EMU), in the form implied by the 1991 Maastricht Treaty, will also impose restrictions on fiscal policy. Governments may run budget deficits of no more than 3 per cent of GDP a year in the run-up to EMU. And if Germany gets its way, countries using the single currency will be confined to budget deficits of no more than 1 per cent of GDP over the cycle. This means they must run balanced budgets and embrace the holy principles of monetarism. If Germany succeeds in imposing strict fiscal limits on other single-currency countries, all the burden of adjustment in a recession will fall on output and jobs. The only policy instruments then left to national governments will be micro-economic ones (i.e., structural changes to labour markets). Advocates of the single currency state that the EMU would eliminate the cost of foreign-exchange transactions and exchange-rate hedging. However, it is not obvious that the benefits of economic integration in the sense of liberalization of product and factor markets cannot be obtained without monetary union. For governments, it would help to stabilize the international currency markets. For the EU's single market, inaugurated at the end of 1992 to allow the free movement of people, capital, goods and services, it would end 'competitive' devaluations, within the monetary union. Notwithstanding these promising prospects, many European citizens believe that increased competition and monetarism will provoke a decline of their national welfare state in an ever expanding EU.

13

In May 1992 the European Free Trade Association (EFTA), which is a grouping of smaller European nations, joined with the EC to form the European Economic Space (EES). It was stipulated, at the EC's insistence, that the EFTA nations would individually adopt the same competition policy regimes as those within the EC. The main problem is still that the EU was conceived as a unified internal market with strong protectionist characteristics and that a further regionalization of the Western European economies can only take place within the institutional and political framework of the EU. EFTA nations who want to join the EU are compelled to give up an important part of their sovereignty. Furthermore, liberalization of the EU's trade could only be realized through bilateral agreements and a complicated system of preferences and quota systems. The EU, with its Common Agricultural Policy (CAP), its role in the Multifiber Arrangement (MFA) and its use of NTBs to protect its steel and textile industries has also from the outset constituted an exercise in the internationalization of protectionism. There is still some anxiety in the rest of the world that the EU may yet turn into 'Fortress Europe'. Although the EU is a full member of WTO, very few of its trading partners receive most favoured nation treatment, but many developing countries are eligible for the EU's Generalized System of Preferences (GSP), which allows exemptions or reduced duty rates for the developing countries (see Chapter 7).

The USA and Latin America

Because Latin America has received little new international lending since 1982, the Latin American governments have had to pay their interest bills on foreign debt by running large trade surpluses. The debt crisis was therefore also a major factor in the deterioration of the US trade balance, as Latin America has cut imports and raised exports to the US markets. The $US1.3 billion US trade surplus with the region in 1980 became a $US14.1 billion US trade deficit with the region by 1987 (Sachs 1989: 17). Obviously, the debt crisis of the 1980s obliged Mexico and the larger South American countries to implement economic reforms, which were centred at first on stabilizing prices and the balance of payments. Then a new wave of reform resulted in government attacks on traditional trade and investment barriers, a process of privatization of state-owned enterprises, and regulatory reforms. The Latin American countries with their protectionist regimes had become increasingly vulnerable to bilateral pressure from the USA and when trying to solve severe balance-of-payments problems had to put a premium on attracting foreign investment. This gave a larger role to the international financial institutions who all urged liberalization and privatization of the economy. In the 1990s virtually all Latin American countries launched reforms aiming at integrating their economies into free trade. These policy reforms meant more or less frontal assaults on the interests of groups rooted in import-substitution activities.

In Mexico, NAFTA was at the core of the liberalizing programme that broke with traditional economic interventionism (see Chapter 11 by Alex E. Fernández Jilberto and Barbara Hogenboom). The agreement was also a means of guaranteeing access to the US market, threatened by increasing use of administrative trade remedies and anti-dumping legislation (Ruigrok and Van Tulder 1995). How NAFTA, with its incorporation of Mexico within the US protective system will damage the trade of other countries remains to be seen. That is the reason why other Latin American countries (Chile, Colombia, Venezuela) are in NAFTA's waiting-room. NAFTA can facilitate a restructuring of the hegemonic position of the US economy with respect to the Latin American continent and definitely eliminate the formal Latin American free trade associations. The Common Market of the South – or Mercado Común del Sur (MERCOSUR) – founded on 26 March 1991, was inspired by a neo-liberal substratum underpinning the idea that a liberalized regional market could boost the activities of regional firms. As a result of this liberalization drive the average tariff charged by Latin American nations to outsiders dropped in 1993 to 15 per cent, from 56 per cent in 1985 and this opening made Latin America the world's fastest-growing market for goods made in the United States. But half of Latin America's trade is now with the USA, and Latin American countries with traditional trade links with Western Europe, such as Brazil, Argentina, and Uruguay, are re-orienting their exports to North America. Because free trade associations may include more and more Latin American countries, it is important to establish whether several sub-regional free trade associations might expand or coalesce. The main problem these Latin American countries are concerned with is the liberalization policies announced by NAFTA. In the case of the poor and weak economies of Central America, joining NAFTA has become a hot item because membership of NAFTA can offer them more possibilities for their agricultural and manufactured products. On the other hand, the USA may push for signing bilateral agreements with the Central American states which will make them more dependent than before upon North American goodwill (see Chapter 12 by Oscar Catalán Aravena).

Although they are discriminatory, regional trade agreements can be consistent with WTO, so long as most sectors are liberalized. Preferential lowering of market access barriers inevitably causes diversion of trade.

The Asia Pacific region

Asia Pacific is emerging as the most dynamic economic region where China, Japan, the USA, the Russian Federation and more countries are contending economically and strategically. But the Asia Pacific region is quite different in several aspects from the European–Atlantic area where regionalism has been most successful. Inter-state relationships are primarily bilateral and are not grouped in common institutions or alliances like the EU or NATO. In response to the EU and NAFTA and after the Uruguay Round, interest in regionalism increased in this area. But what this region is still lacking is a common political and security identity. Economic imperatives are pressing for interdependence, open economies and open regionalism as shown by the successful launching of the Asian-Pacific Economic Cooperation (APEC) and the deepening networks of firms and trade. In comparative terms, the former is state-driven and the latter market-driven. In order to accomplish effective regionalism, it is necessary that the economic imperatives spill over and prevail over military and political imperatives. There are two options when attempting to build regional integration. The first option is to group all Asian countries, excluding the Americas and Oceania, on common Asian values. Countries like Malaysia, China and some Japanese nationalists are in favour of this option. Another option is to build on an alliance with the USA and Oceania in order to preserve security ties. South Korea and the small NICs, with their traditional links with the USA, are in favour of this option. They are joined by Australia, Japan and Canada (Ahn 1996: 6–8).

Regionalization in Pacific Asia is a *de facto* process, because of complementarities between Japan, the NICs and the ASEAN countries and China in terms of their technological capabilities, factor endowments, and wage and income levels. Even as the region's exports to countries outside the region have doubled over the last decade, intra-regional trade has tripled, rising to about 40 per cent of total trade from about 33 per cent in the middle of the 1970s. Since the 1970s the Asian economies have undergone considerable trade liberalization, particularly in East Asia. The rapid growth of East Asia's economies is also reflected in its trade performance. East Asia's newly industrializing countries recorded the highest growth rates in both exports and imports. They have been catching up with Japan in terms of total imports and exports. Interdependence among themselves has increased because of rising intra-regional trade and foreign direct investment. Their economic growth is no longer dependent on the US business cycle. The Asian economies are increasingly integrating and showing a growing ability to generate demand from within the region. The key features of the region's integration are: first, a tradition of market-led economic growth; second, the large stake that many of the nations in the region place on the multilateral trading system; third, the weak incentives that exist for concluding large, formal free-trade agreements in East Asia alone; and finally, the transfer of industries, particularly manufacturing industries, from early starters to latecomers. Unlike the economies of the EU, this interdependent growth was achieved without a formal integration network in a process of market-led economic integration. Self-sustaining economic growth was favoured by the integration of the socialist Asian countries and the relative decline in US economic power. For several reasons this induced rising trade friction between nations on both sides of the Pacific (Stubbs 1995: 785–797), but trade liberalization since the mid-1980s was mostly non-discriminatory and unilateral, and sometimes influenced by the multilateral disciplines of GATT. The main exceptions, sometimes temporary, have favoured the USA, following pressure from Washington to reduce bilateral trade imbalances.

The Asia Pacific economy is the most dynamic economic region and consists of countries with levels of economic development ranging over a very wide spectrum. These differences in economic structure have strong implications for the pattern of economic growth and integration and interdependence. Economic changes in the more advanced countries have influenced the spread of industrialization from Japan and the NICs (Korea, Taiwan, Hong Kong, Singapore) to the other ASEAN

16

countries. The ASEAN group of countries was from the very beginning not based implicitly or explicitly upon an import-substitution strategy (Krueger 1980: 38). It was the first regional trading arrangement based upon an outward-looking trade strategy. The ASEAN countries have very open economies reflecting their development strategy of relying on free flows of goods and capital. Furthermore, the region has emerged as a top trading region with China and the ASEAN countries catching up from behind. ASEAN's trade initiative, ASEAN Free Trade Area (AFTA) founded in January 1992 pursues regional economic cooperation, because, post-Cold War, the organization needed a new *raison d'être*. Preferential tariff reductions will be extended to fifteen selected industrial product groups in which all internal tariffs will be abolished over fifteen years. The conclusion of the AFTA agreement served an important symbolic purpose for ASEAN as an organization, because ASEAN feared isolation in a world of increasingly protectionist regional trading blocs. It was estimated that ASEAN would lose 4 per cent of the value of its 1988 exports to North America from the trade-diverting effects of NAFTA, and 8 per cent of the value of its exports to the EU from trade diversion caused by the conclusion of the Single Market (Schlossstein 1991: 292–4) (see Chapter 13 by Batara Simatupang and Chapter 14 by Carolyn Gates).

The AFTA agreement was a defensive move, motivated by an increasingly regionalized world economy. But positive experiences of economic liberalization in Indonesia, Thailand and Malaysia encouraged governments to cooperate on the regional level. Trade liberalization combined with economic growth in the late 1980s to generate confidence in the neo-classical arguments defended by the Bretton Woods institutions. The advent of export-oriented industries brought about a serious rift between highly competitive exporting groups and those producing for the protected domestic market. By adhering to the AFTA agreement, the ASEAN governments were locked in a regime of lower tariffs. Liberalization of intra-regional trade opened up the door to production for a region-wide market and the high rates of growth in manufacturing induced a rapid change in the composition of intra-ASEAN trade. By 1993 manufactures constituted three-quarters of intra-ASEAN exports, up from less than one-third in one decade. New regional complementaries were emerging and intra-industry trade in manufactures grew significantly, which reflected the regionalization of production networks.

Like the EU, ASEAN now faces the dilemma of how to 'deepen' cooperation, while its membership is 'widening'. Of course, nobody is talking about a monetary union or a common agricultural policy yet. Moreover, trade disputes may call into question ASEAN's cohesiveness. AFTA's aim is to reduce tariffs on almost all items of intra-ASEAN trade to below 5 per cent by 2003, and to remove most NTBs to imports. Some 'sensitive' agricultural items will be allowed protection until 2010, because in many Asian countries cultivation of rice is seen as a strategic industry. In the Asia Pacific region free trade is integrating since the six ASEAN countries and Australia, Japan, Korea, New Zealand and the USA founded the APEC forum in 1989. Since then, membership has been enlarged to include China, Hong Kong and Taiwan and more recently Mexico, Papua New Guinea and Chile. The APEC committed themselves on 15 November 1994 in Bogor (Indonesia) to creating a free trade area stretching from the USA to Thailand and from Chile to China. The objective is economic integration, freeing product and factor markets from official and unofficial resistance. But this ambitious goal set out in what will now be known as the Bogor Declaration, is expected to be reached only by 2020 and stipulates that developed nations should achieve 'free and open trade' by 2010 and developing nations by 2020 but the difference between developed and developing nations is not defined. Moreover, the Malaysian government managed to attach an addendum to the declaration stipulating that the date of 2020 is not binding and the Japanese and Korean governments are muttering about excluding agriculture from APEC's discussions. Paul Keating, the Australian Prime Minister, and Bill Clinton argued that tariff cuts made under APEC could go further and faster than those already agreed under the GATT, but other countries (Japan and Thailand) emphasized that they wanted the WTO to set the pace. Japan in particular stressed that liberalization must not hurt APEC's poorer states, whereas other developed states supported the idea that falling trade barriers in Asia may create extra jobs back home. The APEC will avoid negotiated tariff cuts and encourage each country to reduce tariffs unilaterally. These considerations explain why APEC had very humble beginnings and was considered with scepticism. Furthermore, the diversity of APEC's membership is striking, with member nations on both sides of the Pacific.

APEC is on the way to becoming an inter-governmental institution, with a ministerial council and a secretariat. It is planning to extend liberalization initiatives to various fields of functional cooperation. APEC looks like following in the footsteps of the EU, with the risk of similar pitfalls. But APEC's regional trade liberalization can also provide a non-confrontational, high-level forum. For instance, China wants to be a member of the WTO, thus including a fifth of the world's population in a new liberal trade regime. Although China has promised to do much to bring down tariffs, as well as to phase out most quota restrictions by 1999, it remains highly illiberal over imports. Foreign firms must still deal with a state trading cartel and many trading regulations go unpublished. This might be about to change soon since China announced in November 1995 an impressive range of trade-liberalizing measures when President Jiang Zeemin attended the APEC summit in Osaka, Japan. The US presence in Asia also helps allay Asian concerns about Japanese hegemony in the region. Bilateralism has always been the reserve weapon in the US economic foreign policy, particularly in the Pacific, where regional institutions have been weak and global rules seem permissive. Here the USA has regularly turned to bilateral pressure backed by trade sanctions. But the most controversial issue in APEC remains formal trade liberalization, though APEC was the reaction of several nations aware of the danger of a world divided into blocs that discriminate against outsiders. Because APEC is itself a regional arrangement, it has the paradoxical mission of combatting preferential regionalism. Therefore its members have explored ways in which to develop forms of open regionalism and trade facilitation as well as liberalization.

REGIONALIZING THE CAPITALIST PERIPHERY

Africa and the Middle East

In Africa national economies could not achieve economic growth by seeking to increase their production of tradable agricultural commodities because of the low demand elasticity for tropical agricultural products. Many African countries could not break out of low-demand growth commodities into agricultural products for which demand was increasing more rapidly (Easterly 1996: 19–30). Governments played a central role in the development process and did not consider private entrepreneurship essential to development. They doubted whether international trade would be a source of growth for agricultural economics and they preferred to trust the state as the major economic player. Protection was to be achieved through tariffs and quantitative restrictions. In the 1980s rapid economic reform and a near universality of trade liberalization of market-based approaches to development were introduced in Africa. In a majority of African countries the old framework was dismantled and replaced by liberal, market-based approaches to growth and a high degree of openness to international trade was gradually enforced by the international organizations (Lofchie 1994: 145–83). Economic decline and political instability hampered any form of regional economic cooperation. Several sub-regional organizations still exist in Africa, but they are of no importance for their development or self-reliance. Given the low level of development of the African economies and their economic unimportance to the advanced industrial world, these issues have not been salient. African economies still heavily rely on multilateral and bilateral aid and this makes them subject to external policy scrutiny from the EU and the international financial institutions and banks (Dixon *et al.* 1995: 1–15; Clapham 1996: 161–266). Many of the African countries are for many reasons (cultural, political, geographical) under French influence. France continues to enjoy a special, if conflictual, relationship with the Maghreb and sub-Saharan Africa, moreover, France is their main point of access to Europe (Alden 1996: 11–25). Beyond that, all African countries will have to exert pressure to make the Western world live up to its rhetoric about free trade and free capital movement, because if the export-oriented development model now being adopted across many countries turns out to be successful, the USA and the EU will have to open up their markets (Griffith-Jones 1993: 33–50). None the less, African leaders are convinced that Africa has no other choice than to pursue regional integration in order to transcend its growing marginalization, though all previous regional integration schemes (Maasdorp 1996: 1–16) in the aftermath of independence have failed to produce a positive effect (see Piet Konings and Henk Meilink in Chapter 6). The obstacles to regional integration in Africa remain formidable and hamper the implementation of a regional cooperation scheme based on the European model of integration. Therefore, existing regional organizations in Africa will not survive if they do not contribute to economic development and only serve political concerns.

The economic difficulties of the 1980s curtailed much of the freedom the Maghreb countries had enjoyed during earlier years but this urged them to work more effectively together at the regional level. The renewal of diplomatic relations between Morocco and Algeria in 1988 finally removed barriers to renewed cooperation, this time to include Mauritania, as well as Libya. After a first meeting of all five of the region's leaders in Algeria in June 1988, the Arab Maghreb Union (AMU) Treaty was signed on 19 February 1989 (see Chapter 9 by André Mommen). Maghreb's relations with the EU are characterized by the region's continuing economic dependence on its northern neighbours. Far from increasing overall European trade with the Maghreb, the gradual phasing out of restrictions on the entry of Maghreb's exports to Europe has led to a decrease of overall European trade with the Maghreb from 2 per cent of its total in 1977 to 1 per cent by the late 1980s. Many other countries, especially those of the Eastern Mediterranean, are confronted with similar problems. That is why they are moving beyond the traditional emphasis on trade in goods to a deeper economic integration involving trade in services, free flow of capital, and the adoption of common institutions and rules governing their economies. They all want to be associated with the EU or are pleading for preferential access to the EU markets for their industrial and agricultural products. In practically all cases these economies have a large state sector and high unemployment rates, which create social and political instability and feed religiously inspired radical movements and terrorism. The most striking example of this contradictory development is provided by Turkey's road to further economic and political integration into the EU (see Chapter 8 by Zehra Gamze Aslancik).

Countries of the Maghreb and the Middle East are more developed than their sub-Saharan counterparts. None the less, they have experienced adjustment difficulties similar to those undergone in Latin America. There is an economic reason for doubting that the EU will do all that much for its southern regions. These southern regions export mainly farm products, textiles and low-technology goods, which tend to compete with the output of EU members, Spain, Portugal and Greece. That is why access to the EU's markets is still governed by tariffs and quotas and why Morocco's most successful export to the EU is *cannabis*, a so-called 'illicit crop'. Moreover, the EU members differ both among themselves and about the role of the Mediterranean. Spain and France vie to present themselves as the leaders of the region, while Germany is more concerned about Central and Eastern Europe than the Mediterranean Countries. The agreement signed in Barcelona in November 1995 talks of phasing in free trade in 2010 and eliminating barriers to trade in manufactures. By contrast, trade in agriculture will be liberalized only as far as the various agricultural policies allow, i.e. the EU will continue to keep out many North African crops. None the less, EU farm policy is gradually being liberalized and, by 2010, it may no longer be the daunting barrier to trade it is now. The EU has signed trade-and-aid-promoting 'association agreements' with several Mediterranean countries. The new aid will encourage the North African and Middle Eastern countries to increase their trade with each other, which is now, on average, less than 5 per cent of their total foreign trade. That will not only make them more attractive to outside investors, it will also, under the EU's cumulative rules of origin, give them access to more EU markets (see Chapter 9 by André Mommen).

Central and Eastern Europe

The end of the Cold War was the result of a capitulation by one side. The disintegration of the Soviet state and the withdrawal of Soviet power from Eastern and Central Europe went hand in hand with the rapid closing down of regional conflicts which had been kept going by superpower patronage and provoked thorough-going changes in the international political system. First, it reopened the question of national self-determination, and the possibility of legitimate secession. Second, it left the winning side (capitalism) in possession, however spuriously, of the ideological high ground: there was now only one large-scale picture of modernity, i.e. how societies everywhere should allegedly be organized and governed.

When the Soviet 'empire' collapsed, it fell into its constituent parts. Some national elites, such as those in the Central Asian republics, inherited the state even though they had been beneficiaries of the old order. In Central Europe, nationalists or post-communist social-democrats came to power. Twenty new states were rapidly created but most of them remained dependent on one-sided trade with Russia (see Chapter 3 by Hans Van Zon). In Central Europe and the states of the former Soviet Union reforms of external trade regimes and the removal of barriers to a rapid and successful transition to a market-based economy and the growth of external trade have been mostly domestic. Although reforms have progressed in just a few years, it now appears that catching up with other countries will take decades, because all the states of the former communist bloc have inherited a heavy burden of long functional isolation from the world markets, a distorted structure of production and prices, backward technology, and a large shortfall in the institutional infrastructure, tradition, and culture of a market economy. These economies are highly industrialized, but in a way that is very different from the pattern in most capitalist economies. Distortions are making a successful and rapid integration into the world economy doubtful. The existence of large industrial sectors and a skilled labour force would seem to preclude a policy of 'starting from scratch'. The difficulty is that these transitional economies are still unable to attract enough foreign capital to modernize their industry and official assistance is exclusively directed to the refinancing of old debts.

Parts of Central Europe are enjoying a process of economic and political stability after having suffered from a sharp decline in industrial output and high inflation rates. The former Soviet and the former Yugoslav republics remain in considerably greater turmoil. Except for the three Baltic states, the former Soviet republics are still struggling to create a stable commercial environment. To some degree, in all former Soviet and Yugoslav republics, nationalism stepped into the political vacuum left by the breakdown of communism, the collapse of the currency and the withering away of ideology. Restoration of capitalism in combination with nationalist regimes was the outcome of *perestroika* in the Soviet Union and the Yugoslav road to socialism. After the demise of communism the emphasis on building a solid anti-communist economic bloc in Western Europe disappeared, which posed the question of further integration of the Central and Eastern European countries within the EU. Many ideological and economic reasons favoured such further integration (peace-keeping, strengthening of democratic institutions, economic and social modernization, ecological protection). Both EU and EFTA signed association agreements with the countries of Central Europe and this provided them with the more favoured trade relations by reducing tariffs below the levels that apply to other countries. The agreements include special provisions for several sensitive sectors (agricultural products, apparel, iron and steel, chemicals) in which these transitional economies have significant export potential, but in which the EU is saddled with excess capacity.

The irreversible collapse of the intra-socialist neo-barter trading system (CMEA) made the need to find alternative partners for external trade of the utmost urgency for all ex-communist countries (see Chapter 3 by Hans Van Zon). For the smaller ex-communist countries the potential trading partners were the EU and the EFTA countries because of the insolvency of the Soviet Union and its successor states, however, free access to these markets was denied. 'Fortress Europe' was only interested in imposing selective restrictions on trade and in imposing trade and payment liberalizations according to GATT principles. Furthermore, the EU adopted administrative, product- and resource-specific impediments to the import of goods from Eastern Europe. Iron, steel, chemicals, fertilizers, cement, footwear, aluminium, textiles, heavy machinery, meat, and agricultural products are exports of low-technological standards the governments in Eastern Europe could use to improve their balance of trade. Eastern European firms can take advantage of cheap labour and undemanding environmental protection rules and they are able to export at any price because of their soft budget constraint. The economic cyclical–structural recession the eastern economies have been faced with during and after the communist collapse has been reinforced by the fact that imports from the West are gradually wiping out much, if not most, of the industrial economy inherited from communism, generating more unemployment and social instability, and upsetting trade and payment balances. Barriers to imports of agricultural products and other consumer goods have been erected everywhere. However, the most important problem remains the position of Russia within this context of internationalization. Liberal reformers in Moscow are countered by groupings of 'raw materials lobbies' and '*compradores* elites' interested in commodities trade with the West, while 'industrialists' are stressing the necessity of a reconstructed regional market of a Soviet type. Russia is still struggling with the loss of its superpower status, while the country shows a strong tendency to divide itself up into semi-independent regions. Market forces introduced by liberal reformers liberated decentralizing forces in the Far East who prefer intra-regional trade with China, South Korea and Japan (see Chapter 4 by Andrey S. Makarychev). Market forces have been hampered by inconsistent shock therapies failing to achieve macro-economic stabilization and imposing greater costs than in the Baltic or Central European states. But the main problem remains the uncertainty concerning the Russian road to market capitalism. According to Vladimir Popov (see Chapter 5), world-market integration of the Russian economy will depend on a choice being made between the European or Asian development patterns or a combination of both. Will FDI solve the problem of Russia's declining investment capacity?

CONCLUSIONS

Regional economic integration has to be understood as one of the key factors in the process of globalization, because the process of regionalization is creating the institutional and political framework accompanying the process of deeper integration of markets and the removal of trade barriers. Furthermore, the process of world-wide economic integration and globalization of capital accumulation is a matter of national economies integrating around regional gravitational poles and facilitating closer cooperation and deeper integration when removing trade barriers. These growing patterns of regional market integration can be considered a step towards the rapid globalization of an open international political economy. None the less, this process towards increasingly integrated regions can induce growing competition between trade blocs and economic giants. The latter hypothesis is feeding a crucial debate between those who argue that international cooperation between the most powerful states in a post-hegemonic world is possible and likely, and those who predict growing competition between the major economic powers. Although this debate is echoing the old imperialism debate once animated by the Russian bolsheviks, the advocates of both opinions have centred the debate on examinations of changing trade flows and the trends in intra-as opposed to inter-regional trade, while other analysts prefer stressing the importance of flows of foreign direct investment across and within regions in an attempt to determine how economic links will develop over the next decade. Much research has been done on the growing power of economic blocs on competing currencies. The argument here is that each of these dimensions of regional integration is influenced by the form of capitalism that is characteristic of the three main economic areas of the developed world: North America, the Asia Pacific region, and Western Europe. To elaborate our arguments, we focused discussion on the process of regional integration and on some inter-related dimensions which are particular to the economics of liberalization, globalization and regional integration. Both the EU and the NAFTA are essentially defensive responses to the threats and opportunities of globalization. NAFTA was born out of a sense of growing weakness on the part of the USA and a loss of faith in the liberalizing power of GATT. Increasing integration of developed economies with developing countries will not occur without provoking adjustment costs for industrialized countries, especially for those labour-intensive industries employing low-skilled workers. The reallocation of resources that this structural change entails will inevitably generate friction. So there is a risk that protectionist pressures will arise when the industrialized countries fail to soften the social costs of adjustment and/or cannot facilitate the reallocation of resources through the creation of more flexible markets.

BIBLIOGRAPHY

Ahn, B. (1996) 'Regionalism in the Asia-Pacific: Asian or Pacific community?', *Korea Focus on Current Topics* 4(4): 1–23.

Alden, C. (1996) 'From policy autonomy to policy integration: the evolution of France's role in Africa', in C. Alden and J.-P. Dalloz (eds) *Paris, Pretoria and the African Continent: The International Relations of States and Societies in Transition*, Basingstoke and London Macmillan: 11–25.

Amin, S. (1997) *Capitalism in the Age of Globalization: The Management of Contemporary Society*, London: Zed Books.

Axford, B. (1995) *The Global System: Economics, Politics and Culture*, Cambridge: Polity Press.

Balassa, B. (1962) *The Theory of Economic Integration*, London: George Allen & Unwin.

Barnett, R. J. and Cavanagh, J. (1995) *Global Dreams: Imperial Corporations and the New World Order*, New York: Simon & Schuster.

Bosworth, B. P. and Ofer, G. (1995) *Reforming Planned Economies in an Integrating World Economy*, Washington, DC: The Brookings Institution.

Boyer, R. and Drache, D. (1996) 'Introduction', in R. Boyer and D. Drache (eds) *States Against Markets: The Limits of Globalization*, London and New York: Routledge: 1–30.

CEPAL (1990) *Transformación económica con equidad*. Santiago de Chile: Naciones Unidas.

CEPAL (1994) *El regionalismo abierto en América Latina y el Caribe. La transformación ecónomica al servicio de la transformación productiva con equidad*, Santiago de Chile: Naciones Unidas.

Cerny, P. G. (1995) 'Globalization and collective action', *International Organization* 49(4): 595–625.

Cerny, P. (1996) G. 'International finance and the erosion of state policy capacity', in P. Gummet (ed.) *Globalization and Public Policy*, Cheltenham and Brookfield: Edward Elgar.

Clapham, C. (1996) *Africa and the International System: The Politics of State Survival*, Cambridge: Cambridge University Press.

Dixon, C., Simon, D. and Näman, A. (1995) 'Introduction: the nature of structural adjustment', in D. Simon, W. Van Spengen, C. Dixon and A. Närman (eds) *Structurally Adjusted Africa: Poverty, Debt, and Basic Needs*, London and Boulder, CO: Pluto Press: 1–14.

Drucker, P. F. (1993) *Post-Capitalist Society*, New York and London: HarperBusiness and Butterworth-Heinemann.

Easterly, W. (1996) 'Why is Africa marginal in the world economy?', in G. Maasdorp (ed.) *Can South and Southern Africa Become Globally Competitive Economies?*, Basingstoke and London: Macmillan: 19–32.

Ehrenberg, R. G. (1994) *Labor Markets and Integrating National Economies*, Washington, DC: The Brookings Institution.

Esping-Andersen, G. (1996) 'After the golden age? Welfare state dilemmas in a global economy', in G. Esping-Andersen (ed.) *Welfare States in Transition: National Adaptations in Global Economies*, London: Thousand Oaks and New Delhi: Sage Publications: 1–31.

Falk, R. (1995) *On Humane Governance: Toward a New Global Politic. The World Order Models Project Report of the Global Civilization Initiative*, Cambridge: Polity Press.

Fouquin, M. (1995) 'Mondialisation et régionalisation', in R. Bistolfi (ed.) *Euro-Méditerranée. Une région à construire*. Paris: Publisud: 37–55.

Gamble, A. and Payne, A. (1996) 'Conclusion: The new regionalism', in A. Gamble and A. Payne (eds) *Regionalism and World Order*, Basingstoke: Macmillan: 247–264.

Garnaut, R. and Drysdale, P. (1994) 'Asia Pacific Regionalism: The Issues', in R. Garnaut and P. Drysdale, *Asia Pacific Regionalism: Readings in International Economic Regionalism*, Pymble: Harper Educational Publishers.

Garrett, G. and Lange, P. (1995) 'Internationalization, institutions, and political change', *International Organization* 49(4): 627–56.

Gilpin, R. (1993) 'The debate about the new world economic order', in D. Unger and P. Blackburn (eds) *Japan's Emerging Global Role*, Boulder, CO and London: Lynne Rienner Publishers: 21–36.

Griffith-Jones, S. (1993) 'Economic integration in Europe: implications for developing countries', in D. Tussie, and D. Glover, *The Developing Countries in World Trade*, Boulder, CO and Ottawa: Lynne Rienner Publishers and International Development Research Centre: 33–50.

Grimwade, N. (1996) *International Trade Policy: A Contemporary Analysis*, London and New York: Routledge.

Haggard, S. (1995) *Developing Nations and the Politics of Global Integration*, Washington, DC: The Brookings Institution.

Helleiner, E. (1994) *Regionalization in the International Political Economy: A Comparative Perspective*, Toronto: Joint Centre for Asia Pacific Studies, University of Toronto and York University.

Helleiner, E. (1995) *States and the Reemergence of Global Finance: From Bretton Woods to the 1990s*, Ithaca and London: Cornell University Press.

Henwood, D. (1996) 'Post what?', *Monthly Review* 48(4): 1–11.

Humphreys, P. and Simpson, S. (1996) 'European telecommunications and globalization', in P. Gummett (ed.) *Globalization and Public Policy*, Cheltenham and Brookfield: Edward Elgar: 41.

Ickes, B. W. (1994) 'The dilemma of privatization', in J. Serafin (ed.) *East-Central Europe in the 1990s*, Boulder, CO, San Francisco and Oxford: Westview Press: 107–36.

Jara, A. (1993) 'Bargaining strategies of developing countries in the Uruguay Round', in D. Tussie and D. Glover (eds), *The Developing Countries in World Trade*, Boulder, CO and Ottawa: Lynne Rienner Publishers and International Development Research Centre: 11–32.

Jones, R. J. B. (1995) *Globalisation and Interdependence in the International Political Economy*, London and New York: Pinter Publishers.

Kahler, M. (1995a) *International Institutions and the Political Economy of Integration*, Washington, DC: The Brookings Institution.

Kahler, M. (1995b) 'A world of blocs. Facts and factoids', *World Policy Journal* 12(1), 19–27.

Kapstein, E.B. (1991–92) 'We are us: the myth of the multinational', *National Interest* 26 (Winter): 55–62.

Keohane, R. O. (1984) *After Hegemony: Cooperation and Discord in the World Political Economy*, Princeton, NJ: Princeton University Press.

Krueger, A. O. (1980) 'Regional and global approaches to trade and development strategy', in R. Garnaut (ed.), *ASEAN in a Changing Pacific and World Economy*, Canberra, London and Miami: Australian National University Press.

Krugman, P. (1996) 'Stable prices and fast growth: just say no', *The Economist* 31 August–6 September: 17–20.

Kwan, C.H. (1994) *Economic Interdependence in the Asia Pacific Region: Toward a Yen Bloc*, London and New York: Routledge.

Lawrence, R. Z. (1996) *Regionalism, Multilateralism, and Deeper Integration*, Washington, DC: The Brookings Institution.

Lofchie, M. F. (1994) 'The new political economy of Africa', in D. E. Apter and C. G. Rosberg (eds), *Political Development and the New Realism in Sub-Saharan Africa*, Charlottesville and London: University Press of Virginia: 145–83.

Maasdorp, G. (1996) 'Overview: avoiding Karginalisation', in G. Maasdorp (ed.) *Can South and Southern Africa Become Globally Competitive Economies?*, Basingstoke and London: Macmillan: 1–18.

McCormick-Adams, R. *et al.* (1993) *Limits to Competition: The Group of Lisbon*, Lisbon: The Gulbenkian Foundation.

McGrew, A. G. and Lewis, P. (1992) *Globalisation and the Nation States*, Cambridge: Polity Press.

MacIntire, A. J. and Jayasuriya, K. (eds) (1992) *The Dynamics of Economic Policy Reform in Southeast Asia and the South-west Pacific*, Singapore: Oxford University Press.
Maddison, A. (1995) *Monitoring the World Economy 1820–1992*, Paris: OECD (Development Centre Studies).
Magdoff, H. (1992) 'Globalization – To what end?', in R. Miliband and L. Panitch (eds) *Socialist Register*, London: The Merlin Press: 44–75.
Oman, C. (1994) *Globalisation and Regionalisation: The Challenge for Developing Countries*, Paris: OECD (Development Centre Studies).
Palan, R., Abbott, J. and Deans, P. (1996) *State Strategies in the Global Political Economy*, London and New York: Pinter.
Polhemus, J. (1994) 'Still South Africa's hostage? The RCS states in a changing Southern Africa', in F. B. Rich (ed.) *The Dynamics of Change in Southern Africa*, New York: St Martin's Press.
Reich, R. B. (1991) *The Work of Nations: Preparing Ourselves for 21st-Century Capitalism*, New York: Vintage Books.
Reinicke, W. H. (1995) *Banking, Politics and Global Finance: American Commercial Banks and Regulatory Change, 1968–1990*, Aldershot and Brookfield: Edward Elgar.
Robson, P. (1996) 'The changing international economic system', in G. Maasdorp (ed.) *Can South and Southern Africa Become Globally Competitive Economies?*, Basingstoke and London: Macmillan: 33–44.
Ross, R. J. S. and Trachte, K. C. (1990) *Global Capitalism: The New Leviathan*, Albany: State University New York Press.
Ruggie, J. (1993) 'Territoriality and beyond: problematising modernity in international relations', *International Organization* 47(1): 149–174.
Ruigrok, W. and Van Tulder, R. (1995) *The Logic of International Restructuring*, London: Routledge.
Sachs, J. D. (1989) *New Approaches to the Latin American Debt Crisis* (Essays in International Finance, no. 174), Princeton, NJ: Princeton University, International Finance Section, Department of Economics.
Sander, H. (1996) 'Multilateralism, regionalism and globalisation: the challenges to the world trading system', in H. Sander and A. Inotai (eds) *World Trade after the Uruguay Round: Prospects and Policy Options for the Twenty-First Century*, London and New York: Routledge: 17–36.
Sassen, S. (1996) *Losing Control? Sovereignty in an Age of Globalization*, New York: Columbia University Press.
Scherer, F. M. (1994) *Competition Policies for an Integrated World Economy*, Washington, DC: The Brookings Institution.
Schlossstein, S. (1991) *Asia's New Little Dragons: The Dynamic Emergence of Indonesia, Thailand, and Malaysia*, Chicago: Contemporary Books.
Schwarz, H. M. (1994) *States versus Markets: History, Geography, and the Development of the International Political Economy*, New York: St Martin's Press.
Shin Yong-dai, Kim Jeong-honh and Lee Hang-koo (1996) 'Korea's choices in dealing with worldwide regionalism', *Korea Focus on Current Topics* 4(4): 86–94.
Sobell, V. (1990) *The CMEA in Crisis: Toward a New European Order?*, New York: Praeger.
Streeck, W. (1996) 'Public power beyond the nation–state: the case of the European Community', in R. Boyer and D. Drache (eds) *States Against Markets: The Limits of Globalization*, London and New York: Routledge: 227–249.
Stubbs, R. (1995) 'Asia Pacific regionalization and the global economy', *Asian Survey* 35: 785–797.
Wade, R. (1996) 'Globalization and its limits: reports of the death of the national economy are greatly exaggerated', in S. Berger and R. Dore (eds) *National Diversity and Global Capitalism*, Ithaca and London: Cornell University Press: 60–88.
Wallace, W. *Regional Integration: The West European Experience*, Washington, DC: The Brookings Institution.

2

EXTERNAL PRESSURES SHAPING REGIONALISM

A critical assessment

André Mommen

Allowing market forces to operate is a central aspect of regionalization. It supposes a political willingness to allow the market to provide information and incentives, to reward and punish, to force efficiency upon many unwilling and willing actors. In this chapter I will try to explain how states have adapted to the international environment in the light of external pressures. I will argue that domestic policies shape the regionalization process when sufficient opportunities are offered to states in order to gain the required comparative advantages for a successful shift to outward-oriented economic policy. The regionalist trend received its original impetus from multinational companies interested in delocalizing their production units in order to lower their production costs. Multinational firms established branches in developing countries and started global assembly lines. But these branches in foreign countries also bought most of what they sold in the region of the products' final sale, rather than transferring from the home base. This attracted the interest of multinational firms in cross-border activities and encouraged international finance to operate on a world scale. International finance reinforced this process by financing international trade and Foreign Direct Investment (FDI). As a consequence of these cross-border activities in developing countries, their share of world FDI inflows jumped from 23 per cent in the mid-1980s to more than 40 per cent in 1992–94. Structural change in developing countries contributed to greater international capital market integration and deregulation, liberalization of markets, asset diversification, and the operations of the multinationals contributed to this drive. Thus, what matters here is understanding these connected drives towards globalization and regionalization and the underlying internal and external pressures caused by these drives exercised on regimes adapting their economies to global constraints (Ruigrok and Van Tulder 1995: 237–238).

An important factor in this move was that the globalization and regionalization drives received political support from hegemonic players on the international scene. These hegemonic players forced down regimes and governments who were dependent on import-substituting industrialization (ISI) with the help of the Bretton Woods institutions. ISI was replaced by outward-oriented industrialization policies when developing countries adopted Structural Adjustment Programmes (SAPs). SAPs opened a Pandora's box because of the substantial costs of liberalization imposed on domestic interest groups. They required a complex bargaining strategy between the state and its international creditors, on the one hand, and the state and its domestic political groups, on the other. National interest groups influenced the timing of the policy reforms and their scope, while international actors pressured the state to adopt even more radical reforms (Lehman 1993: 102). A second victory followed when the USA launched its new arms race ('Star Wars') which left the Soviet Union without a response. Finally, in 1989 the Soviet empire broke down and was replaced by a set of capitalist economies. The breakdown of the communist and the ISI regimes was caused by their poor economic performance. Their inward-looking industrialization drive was disastrous, because domestic industries turned out to be either economically too small or too large and were developed in a highly protectionist environment and were set up as monopolies. The combination of all these factors meant that such inefficient domestic industries became a vested interest supporting ISI policies based on tariff barriers, overvalued exchange rates and inefficiencies. As these inefficiently operating industries grew larger, the growth rate slowed down and reforms became more and more difficult. ISI policies and decreasing export earnings also provoked high inflation rates. Short-term measures were taken in order to combat these difficulties, but the underlying economic structural problems were not attacked.

BREAKING WITH IMPORT SUBSTITUTION

Three historical stages can be distinguished in the growth to an outward-oriented economic policy. In the first period (1945–72) most developing countries opted for inward-oriented industrialization combined with an outward-oriented export mix of raw materials, agricultural products and basic industrial commodities. In the second phase (1973–1982), these countries sought to stabilize their economies in order to adjust them to declining export returns and increased crude oil prices. Balance-of-payments problems became a common feature of those countries with non-competing national industries supplying the domestic market. Their overvalued currencies cut them off from any export opportunity. In the third phase (1982–present) international institutions have moved in and compelled governments to adopt structural adjustment policies. Developing countries were pressed to adopt a policy mix of privatization, liberalization and outward-oriented growth (Krueger 1992: 1–58; Haggard 1990: 51–190). This increased openness to the world market was determined by balance-of-payments problems and the necessity of attracting FDI. Historical and geographical factors also played a role when foreign companies decided to invest in services and industries (delocalization) in developing countries. The regionalist trend grew out of this process of delocalization.

During the 1970s the newly industrializing countries (NICs) of the Pacific Rim began to come in line. South Korea and Taiwan tried trade liberalization after having trusted ISI. These countries were leaders in a flying-goose formation

(Inoguchi 1989: 48). Thus, dependency within regional production hierarchies may facilitate increased productivity (Bernard and Ravenhill 1995: 171–209). Some Asian countries hesitated to liberalize their economies and were reluctant to attract FDI. Later on, under pressure of debt-servicing difficulties most developing countries shifted from ISI to varieties of outward-oriented policy reforms. Sometimes these reforms were nothing but pious statements of intention but in other cases, they were half-hearted and intended to convince the Bretton Woods institutions to continue conditional foreign aid. The Bretton Woods institutions attacked ISI policies on the grounds that they led to a misallocation of resources. High levels of protection take away any incentive for industry to become more efficient and oblige local consumers to pay unnecessarily higher prices than in the developed world. Their criticism was that ISI discriminated against other sectors of the economy, especially agriculture, but also exporting industries.

The crucial problem is that infant industries fail to grow up. In many developing countries these industries have little prospect of being able to sell on the world market and thus to reap economies of scale. In order to reduce the relative costs of inputs needed by this industry exchange rates have to be kept overvalued, which makes exports expensive. Inefficiencies increase when state-owned companies are compelled to give employment to school leavers and to provide cheap services to the fast-growing urban population. Loss-making state firms are a drain on the national budget, leading to asphyxiation of other sectors, especially agriculture. This explains why in some poor African countries de-industrialization started (Chazan et al. 1992: 227–322). In the 1980s the Bretton Woods institutions started applying their SAPs to developing economies. These SAPs included efforts to attain stabilization through demand-side measures, an increase in tradables, the liberalization of the domestic and international sectors, a reduction in the scope of the public sector with cutbacks in expenditures and investment, plus encouragement of privatization.

The Bretton Woods institutions pressed for policy reforms based on SAPs and this meant a break with ISI. These policy reforms were in line with the financial interests of the international banks and the developed world who were the major creditors of the developing world. Since then a considerable amount of economic literature has emerged about the role of international finance in connection with SAPs, the importance of exchange rate policies, the role of external and internal factors in bringing about the need for reform, plus the impact of inflation and macro-economic imbalances on government policies. Countries reforming their economic structures focused their attention on packages which varied over time for many reasons, because their initial circumstances differed significantly or because discussion about policy reform packages only arose when there were serious economic difficulties. The inability to service external debt was the common feature of such a crisis. Alteration of policies stimulated private sector activities. In most developing and socialist countries regulation of wages and social insurance benefits was changed. Financial regulations, often resulting in severe credit rationing, were revised and firms had to reform when price controls were abolished and control over access to needed inputs was relaxed in order to spur economic growth. Reformers became natural agents of change and urged governments to defeat popular resistance against the abolishment of state regulation. Since the early 1980s global commercial banks have stopped financing the middle-income developing countries. Private flows from commercial banks and FDI declined sharply because of the Latin American debt crisis of 1982. Export credits, too, collapsed in net terms. Capital markets took over the role of commercial banks as the dominant force in development financing.

THE ROLE OF INTERNATIONAL FINANCE

External pressures exercised by international institutions and capital markets were of crucial importance in the 1980s when the debate on the liberalization of developing economies was launched. The role of international finance in particular came to the fore when in 1982 the US banking system was near to collapse and when the private financial sector was not inclined to assume the risk of additional lending to the developing world. The way out of the debt crisis was conversion of bad debts into equity with a view to recapturing lost asset value at some future date. Expanding FDI through debt conversion became an attractive idea but debt conversion is unlikely to bring additional FDI flows and may, in fact, even detract from them. There is much more scope for applying debt-for-equity conversions to portfolio FDI. But even in this respect there are limiting constraints: e.g. the relative backwardness, inefficiencies, and small size of local capital markets; the ease with which these markets can be manipulated by a few large individual or institutional players; the absence of well-run publicly listed companies needed for the organization of a stock exchange market; and the adjustment pressures being exerted by the Bretton Woods institutions to keep devaluing the currencies of the indebted countries. Of course, regional capital markets can alleviate these constraints but not in the short term. Regional capital markets can only develop when governments feel compelled by external agents to adopt policy reforms in the direction of greater openness and when they are convinced that by doing so they will yield fruitful results, progress towards significant expansion in foreign investment flows, and better access to foreign capital markets. However, developing countries face two unpalatable realities. First, they represent a higher risk for foreign investors. Second, official capital flows are limited because of budget constraints in the industrialized countries. Therefore the developing countries are compelled to lessen reliance on external finance and to increase both the quantity and use-efficiency of domestic savings. Achieving this purpose depends on the rate of institutional development and the possibility of having access to foreign markets for their exports. Policy change in domestic financial sectors and in resource mobilization and allocation is also necessary. All developing countries were obliged by the World Bank and the IMF to change the balance between public and private investment and expenditure, because the public sector was deemed to have failed to perform satisfactorily when running productive enterprises and mobilizing resources (Krugman 1993: 32–48).

Concerns about misallocation of resources and adverse effects on the development of domestic capital markets have led international lending institutions to explore alternatives to subsidized administered credit controlled by public sector agencies as a means of distributing development funds. One of the most promising of these alternatives was development credit auctions. By 1993 auctioning of development credits had already started in Chile and Bolivia, where the experience had been highly positive in terms of improved efficiency and competitiveness, reduced transactions costs, and increased government share of the rents. Auctions do not retard development of security markets and include transparency in lending, competitiveness, fairness, price discovery, reduced transaction costs, and a virtual elimination of rent-seeking activities. Chile began to allocate credit via discriminatory pricing sealed bid auctions in June 1990, using funds from the World Bank and from the Inter-American Development Bank. Separate auctions have been held for banks and leasing companies. The auctions have elicited prices fairly close to the opportunity cost of capital and the participation of leasing companies and banks has significantly enhanced competitiveness.

This world-wide financial revolution was prepared by the failure of the West European and Japanese governments to create a more closed financial order (Eichengreen 1994: 54–59; Walter 1991: 195–239). In fact, the early 1970s was a turning point in the globalization of financial markets. The extensive liberalization initiatives throughout the advanced industrial world in the 1980s granted international banks and financial operators considerable autonomy. In May 1989 the Organization for Economic Cooperation and Development (OECD) agreed to extend its Code of Liberalization of Capital Movements to cover all international capital movements, including short-term financial transactions. The financial liberalization drive can be explained as a consequence of the increased mobility of financial capital caused by several liberalization decisions taken by the USA, Japan and Britain in combination with the sudden emergence of Japan as a financial power and as the largest creditor of the USA. The US deregulation movement was driven by foreign capital inflows financing the growing external current account deficit that accompanied the rapid expansion of the US economy after 1982. The US dollar rose because of an overfinancing of that deficit and the unique depth and liquidity of US financial markets, combined with the global importance of the US dollar in attracting Japanese surplus savings. US financial markets were deep enough to absorb the enormous pool of petro-dollars as well. The issue of anonymous US capital bonds after 1984 provoked capital flight from Latin America, which in turn hindered full recovery of these economies from the 'debt crisis' of 1982.

Japan's creditor position eased its decision to endorse financial liberalization. As Japanese companies and financial institutions accumulated government bonds, they demanded and received in 1977 the right to trade them in a secondary market for portfolio management purposes. This was the beginning of a liberalization drive boosted by domestic competition among banks and their desire to escape from domestic regulations. In response, they started international activities. British domestic financial markets were integrated with global markets by the opening up of the London Stock Exchange to foreign securities firms in October 1986 (the 'Big Bang'). Liberalization reforms had to make the City more attractive to foreign capital in order to preserve London's position as an international financial centre. Once again, the mobility of capital encouraged a competitive deregulation movement as the British authorities felt compelled to join the US deregulation dynamic. When one state starts to deregulate and liberalize its financial markets, other states are forced to follow its lead in order to attract foreign capital or to hold onto their own savings (Helleiner 1994: 167). After the 'Big Bang' in London, financial deregulation was decided in the European Union (EU), Scandinavia, New Zealand, Canada and Australia.

EXTERNAL PRESSURES

Governments react to external and internal pressures for change. The first major problem is the magnitude and speed of responses to the economic reform programme on the part of the economic participants. The longer-term aftermath of reforms depends on the evolution of the political and economic process in the immediate post-reform period. When the short-run economic impact of reform is highly negative, political support for the programme will erode and the reformers will be ousted from government. This occurred in Poland and Russia where the ultra-reformers were soon sacked after having lost their credibility (Bates and Krueger 1993: 1–26). When the impact of reforms is positive and the government is able to reach a consensus on its reform policy, the outcome will be the establishment of an outward-looking economic regime.

The second major problem is *how* countries react to external pressures and how much room they have to manoeuvre. External pressures can be very strong in the case of an acute balance-of-payments crisis. In that case governments have to invite international banks and institutes in to keep their economy afloat. The power of the international institutions means that a clear-cut process of global homogenization of domestic rule is under way and that the nation–state increasingly faces problems in controlling economic and financial exchanges which in turn challenge the state's ability to provide security for its citizens (Huysmans 1995: 471–487).

The third major problem is that internationalization affects countries and regions in a different way because of the unevenness of their development and strength and because of the disparities in their interconnectedness. Some countries are more powerful than others. Weak states have less possibilities than strong states to influence the global economy, and at the domestic level weak governments will face difficulties when implementing changes imposed by international fora and institutions. Strong or hegemonic states exercise hegemonic power over other states and oblige them to compromise or to change their regimes or institutions. (Hegemony means a state that enjoys a comparative advantage in the production of high value-added goods, a significant lead in technology over other economies, and a privileged access to raw materials and to markets for its produce.) Here the role of management and leadership in international financial and trade systems has to be emphasized. This requires a surplus of savings over domestic investment require-ments which allows the other countries to have access to its large and efficient capital markets. Globalization and regionalization are cross-border processes driven by capital flows and technological economic changes controlled by large industrial-ized economies (Ostry and Nelson 1995: 79–112). Thus the latter are creating a new kind of interconnectedness depending on a variety of political and economic resources which most of the developing countries are lacking. This new intercon-nectedness is regulated by the great powers of the Triad and their multinational firms. Most of the benefits of the globalization drive flow to these actors, because they possess the greatest capacity to absorb and adapt to the newly created inter-national environment (Hurrell and Woods 1995: 457). The Triad-based global competitiveness urges multinational corporations to interact with governments in order to secure their sustainable competitive advantages. Within the Triad new multinationals have already emerged in the Asian economies. Generally, Triad multinationals prefer FDI because they can conserve their proprietary advantages. In the case where governments are weak, multinationals may reduce them to the status of *compradores* governments. Though the globalization process is happening to them, developing countries have, at least to some extent, the power to open or close themselves to world or regional markets. But relative autarky is punitive since the competing centre of power (Soviet Union) has disappeared. Only a handful of countries (North Korea, Cuba, Iran, Libya, Iraq) have remained outside the global-ization process in this way. Over the past decades all other developing countries have tried to integrate themselves, more or less, into the capitalist world system.

Though a successful breakthrough of market–liberal economic policies may boost economic growth, in turn economic openness can reinforce illiberal patterns or fuel assertive foreign policies. That is why a liberalizing Mexico is different from a liberalizing Brazil, India or China. In Algeria, Afghanistan, Turkey and Iran, rejectionist Islamic movements are opposed to powerful homogenizing pressures coming from the world market. In the successor states of the Soviet Union rejectionist movements adhere to right-wing extremist ideologies. Although the liberalization drive facilitated the transplantation of liberal institutions and values across the world, the transmission of these values and institutions is uneven because liberalization skews political power in favour of a new elite of the very rich. Coalitions of 'losers' may rise against increased international competition and the subsequent privatization drive. In Western countries rapid internationalization of production in connection with growing economic interdependence came into con-flict with the national welfare state which had strengthened its role in the domestic economy. This is in contradiction with the increased internationalization of produc-tion because objectives such as maintaining full employment and price stability conflict with external objectives such as the liberalization of capital movements and trade. A decisive factor in all these reform processes is the role of the Bretton Woods institutions and the donor agencies of bilateral aid progammes. They became extremely active in the period of crisis when balance-of-payments difficul-ties appeared or when they had to provide additional resources to secure the reform efforts. During the debt crisis of the early 1980s in particular, international institutions and official creditors played a major role in determining comprehensive economic policy reforms. The debt crisis was a key event because of its negative impact on the developing world's economy. The same scenario was applied in 1989 when the communist economies collapsed. The reforms that ensued were thoroughgoing, because the authorities were constrained to fundamentally revise their economic policies and institutions.

Finally, the most important question with respect to policy changes is to identify the 'losers' of the reforms, because they may constitute powerful opposition groupings to any kind of economic adjustment. At any rate, in all countries, these opposition groups encompass the industrial working classes employed in state-owned factories and services and the older people fearing for their pensions. When large factories are shut down and unemployment rates rise, the urban masses may rise against the government and the 'winners'. The 'winners' are always the new entrepreneurs, the (corrupt) bureaucrats, the owners of exporting industries and services, and the emerging class of technocrats, managers and middlemen. In Eastern Europe the 'losers' reintegrated as the reformed Communist parties operating under the flag of social-democracy. In Third World countries they trusted the old populist parties in order to defeat the new course. But all populist or ex-communist formations collecting the vote of the 'losers' were unable to resist external pressures from a globalizing and regionalizing economy or to solve the problem of the heavy external debt burden. Once they formed governments they had to endorse reform programmes that did not differ that much from the liberal project which the parties of the 'winners' were pleading for. In Argentina the Peronist Carlos Menem took a liberal stance. In Mexico the ruling Partido Revolucionario Institucional (Institutional Revolutionary Party, PRI) complied to the demands of multinational capital and the international banks, while in Chile the post-Pinochet regime did not break with export-led growth (see Chapter 11 on Mexico and Chile).

THE ASIAN MODEL

Questions regarding external pressure urging economic reforms and trade liberalization abound (Gilpin 1993: 36). When in the 1980s ISI policies had to be abandoned due to pressure from the international financial institutions and communism was defeated, developing countries became interested in the Asian model of outward-oriented industrialization (Gourevitch 1989: 8–23). The economic success of South Korea in particular attracted much attention (Byung-Nak Song 1994: 1–2). The debate on the Asian 'miracle' revealed that two competing paradigms existed: the neo-classical economists of the Bretton Woods institutions presented the East Asian 'miracle' as the outcome of wise economic policies, while their opponents paid more attention to the crucial role of the strong Asian state in guiding economic growth (Chowdhury and Islam 1993: 42–56). However, both approaches admitted that, apart from an abundant labour force and low wages, the economic success of the Asian states came about when these states developed an internal capital market controlled by the government. Because the state allocated credit to priority sectors and exporting industries, the government preferred consensus-building with a powerful private sector supporting the idea that domestic economic fortunes were closely linked to export growth (Wade 1989: 71–76). Institutional reforms followed when the growing economy required trade liberalization and financial reforms. The question of whether the politics the East Asian high performers adopted were conducive to stimulating economic growth is not discussed here (see World Bank 1993; Wade 1990; Amsden 1989). It is important, however, to know that with the exception of the Philippines (Wurfel 1988) – a Latin American country in Asia – some Asian countries have already achieved income levels comparable to the poorer European countries. In these Asian economies a virtuous circle emerged, with exports financing the imported inputs and capital equipment needed for additional growth. Exposure in world markets to new products and techniques spurred even greater growth. The expansion of trading activities by the Pacific Basin developing countries was accompanied by dramatic changes in the commodity structure of their trade. A pronounced shift occurred in their exports towards manufactured goods and other high-value-added activities. Hong Kong and Singapore specialized in labour-intensive manufactures at an early stage in their development. Then they were followed by South Korea and Taiwan. Later on, in the mid-1980s the ASEAN-4 (Association of South-East Asian Nations) countries who had abundant natural resources – Thailand, the Philippines, Malaysia, and Indonesia – began specializing in manufactures at a later stage in their development.

In Asia certain common features emerge in this process of export-led growth and regional integration (Bernard and Ravenhill 1995: 171–209): first, successful exporters have surmounted their lack of technical, managerial, and marketing know-how and their lack of knowledge of world markets by finding ways of combining local productive capacity with foreign expertise. Second, successful exporters have provided a policy environment that ensures that domestic firms compete with foreign firms on an equal footing. This means adequate short-term trade financing at world market conditions, unrestricted access to imported intermediate goods at world market prices, the avoidance of currency overvaluation, and adequate access to the capital goods and investment finance necessary for efficient production and expansion. In the case of the NICs and the natural resources-based Asian countries, gradual reforms to improve financial intermediation were undertaken in order to promote greater integration into world capital markets. As a part of the liberalization effort, Korea, which is a member of the International Monetary Fund (IMF), accepted Article VIII in 1988, and announced plans to fully open its financial services sector to foreign participation by 1992. Reforms are also under way in Indonesia and Thailand. Indonesia accepted Article VIII in 1988 and deregulated its financial sector. Thailand followed in 1990 and is in the process of dismantling existing capital controls. Finally, the newly idustrializing countries (NICs) have generally avoided the currency overvaluation that has plagued many other developing countries. The NICs have tended to maintain undervalued currencies which were the source of international economic friction. Asian countries specializing in the exports of manufactures continue to prosper handsomely and to make increasing inroads into industrial country markets for an ever-widening range of products (Haggard 1989: 129–141). The less developed countries that have followed suit have almost succeeded to some extent in increasing the quantity and proportion of foreign exchange earnings derived from manufactured exports. In almost all these 'successful' countries, manufacturing for export has become the fastest-growing sector of the economy, although – especially for the larger economies – it typically remains small in relation to agriculture and manufacturing for the domestic market. But export manufacturing's contribution to the balance of payments is typically much greater than its contribution to total output or employment. Although the range of products has changed and includes more capital-intensive and high-tech goods, labour-intensive manufactures remain the most typical and widespread exports. Many of these modern and capital-intensive industries were set up to serve both domestic and foreign markets. The most important manufactured export from developing countries is still textiles but the importance of textiles is declining. In Mexico and in Eastern and Southern Asia electronics and automobiles have become very important. Today, the Asia Pacific region is now the world's largest source of, and the largest market for, electronic parts, components, and supplies.

Comparative assessment is an important tool in evaluating a country's performance. The experience of the Asian 'tigers' shows that annual growth rates of 10 per cent a year can be sustained for many years. South Korea is now growing at almost 8 per cent, even though its Gross Domestic Product (GDP) per head is now more than $US10,000. Singapore's GDP per head is now almost the same as that of the USA and its economy has lately been growing at rates of up to 10 per cent a year. Indonesia (Hill 1996) aside, the old and new 'tigers' are relatively small countries closely allied to the USA. This alliance has helped these small states apply economic reforms as the USA backed their autocratic governments and allowed them to alter the class base of their regimes. Furthermore, the USA generally consider the growing prosperity of the 'tigers' in its own strategic interest in the region. As a result, the USA has been inclined to open its markets to goods produced by these allies. Moreover, moves towards democracy helped bolster US support for South Korea and Taiwan. The USA backed democratization in the Philippines in 1986 as well.

The question remains whether growing exports from Asia hurt the interests of the industrialized world. Increased imports from Asia may spur the USA and 'Fortress Europe' to impose non-tariff barriers (NTBs) on imported manufactures, but one may argue that the entry of more developing countries into export-manufacturing industries does not necessarily hurt older producers. As incomes and costs rise in the NICs and they open their domestic markets, more opportunities are offered to less developed countries to supply them with cheap manufactures. Multinational firms wanting to relocate production from industrialized

36

countries, especially in high-tech industries, will prefer investing in the NICs because of their superior skills and their supporting industries.

Although protectionism is harming the economic chances of developing countries, protection may favour the spread of export manufacturing among more developing countries. A good example here is the US textile quotas against Hong Kong and voluntary export restraints and other restrictions against Japan, South Korea and Taiwan which encouraged these countries to relocate their investment in the textile industry to other Asian countries or to Mexico near the US border. Asian low-wage countries such as Thailand and Indonesia are looking for back-door access to the giant US market. A quarter of the employment created by the *maquiladoras* – assembly plants that have preferential tax and tariff treatment – comes from Asian firms (*The Economist*, 24–30 August 1996: 55). The same now occurs in the Asian automobile industry. In 1996 Thailand produced 560,000 vehicles, almost all of them sold at home. By 2000 Thailand is set to produce more than 1 million cars, 10 or 20 per cent for export. Thailand, which has never had a national car industry, has welcomed foreign investors with open arms. By 2000 Thailand will be the biggest car market in South-East Asia as well as its biggest car maker. Big foreign manufacturers are building whole cars rather than just assembling kits. Thailand's car industry started in July 1991, when the government reduced tariffs on imports of kits. The Philippines are looking for large-scale FDI in car production too. FDI is attractive when labour costs are low (which is especially appealing to Japanese firms coping with a strong yen), there is an established network of suppliers of components and services, a friendly tax and tariff regime, a reliable infrastructure, and a skilled workforce. Car makers are developing global networks. Local producers of components who do not meet international standards will not be integrated into that global network. The World Trade Organization (WTO) is backing this strategy, because by 2000 local-content provisions have to be eliminated. The ASEAN, which is moving towards an Asian free trade area is also in favour of full liberalization of markets. Malaysia and Indonesia, both members of ASEAN and car-producing countries, have also promised to open their markets. Both countries hope that technology will be transferred and local content gradually increased when producing a national car with the benefit from some tariff protection for a while. Prospects for expanded export manufacturing in developing Asian countries have improved. The appreciation of the yen and of the European and Asian NIC currencies, combined with the depreciation of most developing country currencies (even against the US dollar), have increased the competitiveness of developing countries' manufactured exports against major industrial economies and NICs. As the case of the Malaysian and Indonesian car industry shows, export manufacturing and production for local markets can be combined and fuel economic growth (Lim 1996: 19–51). FDI can boost this industrialization drive. But manufacturing plants located abroad have been largely of two different types: first, those that produce for local markets, frequently with government encouragement and protection, that is, 'import substitution' (for example, the early establishment of motor vehicle and equipment firms in Argentina, Brazil, and Mexico); and, second, those that supply Western and Japanese markets from so-called 'export platforms' (for example, the manufacture of electronic components in Malaysia and Thailand). The latter were usually labour-intensive, relying upon the availability of substantially cheaper supplies of unskilled, but trainable, labour in the host country.

Today, many Asian and Western firms are re-examining their investment strategies, because many countries have reduced their protection levels and opened up their markets to stiffer international competition. For example, the import-substituting factories no longer represent essentially independent production points, but are viewed as parts of much larger regional or international production systems (Machado 1992: 169–202). FDI flows may have an impact on the development of this kind of regionally organized internationalized production system. The Asian NICs expanded their investment in other Asian countries and are now looking for direct investment opportunities in Latin America. South Korea's *chaebols* invest in car-making and television set-making plants in Brazil. Latin American politicians visited China hoping for trade expansion. Chile's trade with Asia will overtake its trade with the USA. Asian investment is going into commodities. China has invested in Peruvian mining and Asian timber firms have acquired rights in Guyana and Surinam.

POLICY RESPONSES TO EXTERNAL PRESSURES

Until now developing countries have failed miserably in their pursuit of the NICs' export-led growth strategy and have not been able to organize high-tech product lines. This failure stems from several factors, among them being the hostility of the West with its discriminatory trade policies. Current trade policies in developed countries already discriminate against developing countries. The MultiFiber Arrangement (MFA), which regulates world trade in textiles and textile products, is the most blatant example. Voluntary export restraints and other NTBs against specific products from individual countries still exist but other reasons can be discerned. Successful export-led industrializers are rather small economies, while until recently the larger economies remained domestic market-oriented. When the larger economies became interested in export manufacturing it was mainly to earn foreign exchange to invest in ISI activities destined to serve their potentially huge domestic market. The rulers tended to favour import protection for domestic market monopolies and a low-waged, underemployed labour force. Their problem was that they remained relatively inefficient producers of non-standard and less competitive products. This maybe explains why these countries lagged behind the NICs and their world trade and economic growth relatively declined. For instance, India's ranking as an industrialized nation slipped between 1950 and 1986 from the 10th to the 26th position in the world (Swamy 1994: 23). China's regression in the world economy was conspiciously less than that of India. Nowadays, China has decisively overtaken India in almost all respects.

During the 1980s those developing and socialist countries experiencing balance-of-payments crises and a period of accelerating inflation were compelled to launch stabilization programmes. During this period political forces began to impinge on economic policies and shifts in policies tended to solidify new coalitions. Thus adaptations to external shocks were mediated by political processes leading to changes in political and economic regimes. Some states responded to these shocks aggressively, others postponed structural reforms. But when stabilization programmes failed and foreign banks became reluctant to increase lending or extend credit, these countries had to completely change their economic policies (Haggard 1990: 9–48). Apparently, successful reforms required the empowerment of strong regimes with reformist technocracies responding to external pressures.

These external constraints play a powerful role in pushing a government towards policy changes. Crises are always an important stimulus to reform the economy. With the abolition of tax barriers and the reallocation of capital, the rate of return on investment increased (Tanzi 1995: 90–122). Therefore, it may be useful to study why policy reforms differed so dramatically from country to country (Chan and Clark 1992: 1–26). China, India, Mexico, Brazil and Chile illustrate how domestic forces constrain economic policy and shape state responses to the external environment. As these countries with ISI regimes turned towards global markets, a paradoxical consequence was an increase in pressure towards increased regional integration. The growth records can be used to argue that authoritarian forms of government are more efficient at achieving economic growth and equity than democratic forms of government. Although most Latin American countries had a large state sector, their economic performances were disappointingly low. Most of these countries experienced military rule, or, as in the case of Mexico, a mitigated one-party system. In India the Congress Party long dominated the political landscape, trusting ISI policies, but Indira Gandhi's authoritarian rule did not necessarily bring high economic growth or macro-economic stability (Kapuria-Foreman 1992–93: 25–40). As the case of China shows, authoritarian rule is an instrument in order to bring about policy changes when economic stagnation makes reforms urgently needed (Chi Huang 1992: 125–146).

China

Until the 1980s China was an insignificant participant in international markets for goods and capital. China was not a borrower from international financial organizations and did not receive foreign aid from bilateral development agencies or FDI (Rugman 1993: 97–99). Responding to external pressures Socialist China had to reverse its traditional Maoist emphasis on self-reliance and ISI (Hussain 1994: 11–30). Since then, China's rapidly rising economic star has attracted world-wide attention (Shang-Jin Wei 1995: 73–104). Today, FDI is transforming the economic structure of the coastal provinces of mainland China. By the early 1990s China's role in the international economy had been changed. In 1992 China had already become the world's tenth largest exporter (Lardy 1994: 2). FDI, foreign aid and borrowing on the international capital market finance China's industrialization drive and data suggest that FDI will continue to rise over the next decade. During the 1980s several devaluations reduced the degree of overvaluation and a secondary market for foreign exchange provided funds for decentralized trading in goods and services. China effectively unified its dual exchange rate system in 1994 and prepared for convertibility of the yuan for trade transactions. Relaxed controls on capital flows favoured capital outflows. On 1 December 1996 the yuan became convertible.

From 1978 to 1993 China's real Gross National Product (GNP) expanded at an average rate of over 9 per cent a year and real output almost quadrupled in that period. China's rate of growth was more than twice the average of all developing countries and even exceeded that of all Asian NICs.

The growth of FDI has been exponential. By 1991, the total amount of realized FDI in China was already $US4.37 billion. FDI increased from $US11.2 billion in 1992 to $US25.71 billion in 1993. Since then even more capital has poured in. The realized FDI thus increased exponentially. China has been highly dependent on FDI to generate manufactured exports. Most of China's manufactured exports are produced by FDI firms or by Chinese firms with close connections with foreign capital. Most of these enterprises mushrooming in townships and villages specialize in export processing. By the end of 1993, the total number of foreign firm or joint ventures had reached 167,500 (Shang-Jin Wei 1996: 77–105). State-owned firms, which in 1992 accounted for about half of manufactured goods output, have been only modest contributors to the expansion of exports. Thus China was not as successful in linking the rapidly growing FDI export industries with the more traditional state-owned sector. Some of the factors that were crucial to the growth of the 'tigers' are also available in China, e.g. high savings and investment rates. At 40 per cent of GDP, Chinese savings rates are even higher than in the Asian 'tiger' economies. The fact that Asian governments consume a relatively small share of GDP is seen as being important to economic growth. The Chinese government's share of GDP is small: in 1995 it was just 11.6 per cent of GDP, compared to around 20 per cent in the Asian 'tigers'. China's enormous labour reserve force means that it will take much longer to experience upward pressure on wages as a result of labour shortages. A final parallel with the 'tigers' is to what extent China's economic growth is due to successes in manufactured exports. China is following the East Asian 'tiger' pattern by increasing productivity and embracing international standards in technology and product development. In 1978 China's exports totalled a mere $US9.9 billion, but by 1994 they were $US121 billion, making the country the eighth largest exporter of manufactured goods in the world. Though Chinese export growth figures compare well with that of the 'tigers', the country is unusually dependent on foreign investors to make them. Foreigners account for 30 per cent of China's exports, while they account for just 2 per cent of the country's manufactured output. Will the efficiency of foreign investment rub off on domestic producers? This does not seem to be happening in China, because export industries are concentrated in enclaves. Two big and related difficulties have still to be overcome: a financial system which is not yet run on market lines, and the huge number of 100,000 loss-making state-owned enterprises employing two-thirds of the urban workforce. Almost half the state-sector firms are making losses and that proportion is rising instead of declining. State banks are under pressure to keep those loss-making firms afloat in order to avoid mass unemployment in the cities. This mass of unpaid debts is undermining the financial system and makes the country vulnerable to bouts of inflation (27 per cent in 1993). However, in March 1995 China's first central bank legislation came into effect and charged the People's Bank of China with conducting the country's monetary policy (Walter 1996: 41–45). None the less, the private sector is growing so fast that the state's share of production and employment is falling steadily. The number of workers employed by state firms has fallen by 10 million to 90 million in 1995 alone, while employment in private firms in the townships and villages (companies set up by local governments but run on market lines) is expanding (Mackerras et al. 1994: 78–89). China's immense size is complicating its political and economic development strategy. Great disparities of income divide the rich coastal regions from the poorer inland provinces. This makes the Communist rulers reluctant to liberalize the regime for fear of losing control over the coastal provinces. But the more growth widens the disparities, the greater the dilemma (Ngai-Ling Sum 1996: 231–236; Gong 1994: 29–43).

The Tiananmen Square upheavals in 1989 were a clear indication that the post-1978 reforms had provoked discontent arising from relative deprivation unleashed by the economic reforms. Inequalities in income distribution and market pressures had victimized parts of the population, above all, the intellectuals (Hsiung 1992: 74). The Tiananmen Square incident was at least partially the result of a growing contradiction between the vibrant market and stagnant state sectors. Reforms had divided the Communist Party as well, because it remained unclear whether the Party was willing to give up its monopoly of political power. The ruling faction of the party elite could remain in power because economic growth legitimized its political course in a period when other communist regimes were falling (Simai 1994: 160–163). Obviously, China is preparing itself for the role of a major political and economic actor with key interests in the region. This view accords with the reality that Mao's policy of 'self-reliance' had to be buried. Policy responses to the challenge of the future global and regional balance, therefore, required an upgrading of China's economic capabilities, through internal restructuring and by becoming a part of the Asia Pacific Rim. China has clearly become a major participant in the regional Asian economy and it is virtually certain to become even more important in the future because of its dynamic growth and continuing economic reforms. Central government has in effect lost control over the process of capital accumulation (Womack and Guangzhi Zhao 1994: 168–173) and regional authorities have become increasingly assertive in promoting and protecting their local interests. They are critical about decisions made by the central government and are reluctant to pay taxes to it (Cook and Li 1996: 302).

India

The history of India's recent liberalization policies is a chronology of internal pressures. India's objective after gaining independence was to achieve economic self-sufficiency under a planned economic system in which the state had a key role to play. But self-sufficiency remained elusive because ISI failed to make India an economic giant. Inefficiencies, stagnation and corruption became common features of India's economic system (Agrawal 1984: 375–392; Lewis 1991: 367–389). Torn by inner contradictions within the ruling classes, the state succumbed to external pressures and abandoned whatever was left of ties to its earlier semi-autonomous model of development. Under the pressure of globalization, a significant section of the business class was 'compradorized'.

The first phase began with an IMF loan in 1980. Policy changes favoured privatization and FDI, which enhanced the role of market forces at the expense of the public sector. Finally, the economy was recomposed in tune with the process of globalization (Cable 1995: 209–231). India, together with Bhutan, Bangladesh, the Maldives, Nepal, Pakistan and Sri Lanka, joined the South Asian Regional Cooperation Council in 1983. Subsequently, a new policy regime took shape. The main features were: deregulation of industries, decontrol of prices, liberalization of imports, tax reductions and increase in deficit spending. Rajiv Gandhi, on taking power in 1984, tried to overcome the bureaucratic approach to economic policy. His team encompassed representatives of the rising professional and managerial elites, most of them classmates from the Doon School and former managers of foreign multinationals or technocrats from the IMF and the World Bank (Swamy 1994: 188). The implemented liberalization measures met resistance from domestic pressure groups when several industrial products were freed from pricing and distribution controls and import restrictions were changed from quotas to tariffs. But reforms did not run deeply or widely enough to provoke serious resistance from mighty lobbies such as industrialists or organized labour in the private or public sector (Ahluwalia 1995: 233–259). The main resistance came from the ruling bureaucracy and the cadres of the Congress Party, who feared to lose rents accruing to powers of patronage. Liberalization was felt to be a shift in emphasis in the government's agenda from the lower economic strata to the upper strata.

When assuming power in 1984 the newly appointed Rajiv Gandhi administration tried to establish better contacts with the ASEAN states. When aligning its foreign policy to economic liberalization Commerce and External Affairs Ministries were brought under one umbrella. The liberalization of imports and the decline in the exports, particularly of engineering goods, made the stress on productivity increases and cost efficiency imperative. India adopted a regional approach to trade and investment and opened offices and had Trade Fairs in Singapore and Kuala Lumpur. Promoting economic cooperation with the developing nations has been one of the key issues of India's foreign policy since independence. This search for cooperation has taken place at both the multi-lateral and bilateral levels. India proposed the establishment of an Asian Clearing Union, Regional Trade Liberalization and the funding of an Asian Reserve Fund but the ASEAN states were sceptical about these initiatives. The Asian Clearing Union was viewed as a duplicate of the Asian Development Bank and the more developed ASEAN countries refused to make sacrifices in favour of the poorer countries. Despite the stress India put on mutual economic cooperation, these relations remained of little significance because of India's inward-oriented economic policy. This ISI policy left little room for imports from ASEAN countries. India saw FDI as a form of export promotion. Foreign investment in India had to be in advanced technology and due to this condition there was hardly any scope for ASEAN countries to invest in India in that period. This changed during the 1970s when India tried to develop closer economic ties with the ASEAN states by encouraging joint industrial projects in a period when the North–South talks were deadlocked. But ASEAN resolutely kept the Indian dialogue off its agenda. The real issue evidently was not economic complementarity but the lack of convergence on political issues. Indian firms failed to win contracts in Malaysia for none other than political reasons (Sridharan 1996: 200). But in the Middle East India made progress because of its pro-Arab stance. Moreover, Japan's economic reach in the South-East Asian region increased because of its ability to provide aid or credit facilities which India was unable to give. Therefore India's economic ties with the ASEAN states tended to remain underdeveloped.

At the end of the 1980s India was in the throes of a deepening economic crisis. When during the Gulf War India experienced an acute foreign exchange crisis it was forced to contract emergency loans from the IMF. The IMF imposed its prescriptions and in 1991 the newly appointed Rao administration moved to macro-economic liberalization and stabilization measures. It appeared that the first phase of modest liberalization had weakened India's economic capacity to withstand external shocks. None the less, the preconditions for export orientation had been shaped. The second and decisive phase only started in 1991 with the first Structural Adjustment Loan (SAL), and Structural Adjustment Credit (SAC) provided by the World Bank. The economic measures initiated in 1991 under the IMF and World Bank supervision constituted the second phase of a coherent programme designed to restructure the economy. Prime Minister Narasimha Rao undertook bold initiatives to reinvigorate the moribund economy and to make the Indian economy progressively market-oriented and integrated into the globalizing economy (Singh 1994: 1–16). He led India to embark on a more liberal trade, investment, monetary and fiscal regime in order to transform the inward-looking economy into an outward-looking one. Rao devalued the rupee by 18 per cent in order to strengthen India's export position. Deregulation became characteristic of India's investment policy. FDI over a wide area received automatic approval and fiscal and monetary reforms included deregulation of the financial sector and the announcement that the rupee would become convertible within five years (Agrawal et al. 1995: 159–203). The total value of exports steadily increased (Desai 1994: 227–234). Industrialists who were technologically and organizationally well positioned to take advantage of the new regime, either by investing in core activities or by entering into joint ventures with foreign capital, were able to expand their businesses but many industrialists feared the invasion of foreign capital and increased competition in their home market. Anti-trade reformers acted against the signing of the Draft Final Agreement (DFA) of the Uruguay Round Talks on the General Agreement on Tariffs and Trade (GATT) and gained support from the agrarian interests who foresaw lowering of agricultural subsidies and the payment of royalties for the use of multiple generations of patented seed varieties. The slow pace of reforms dictated by the impact of anti-reform campaigns weakened the ruling Congress Party which lost power in many states of the Union. Since the 1991 balance-of-payments crisis India has moved towards greater integration into the world economy. Foreign companies were invited to build new roads and harbours or electric power stations. The stock market of Bombay was made accessible to foreigners via the 'India funds'. The technocratic elite finds the economic successes achieved by the South-East Asian countries inspiring. Therefore, India is determined to exploit its competitiveness in labour-intensive export manufacturing and to attract FDI from South-East Asian firms willing to invest in textile plants along the coastal areas of Orissa and Madras. This liberalization policy shows how India's internal distribution of power is changing. But the Indian government has done virtually nothing to build broad-based support for the policies it has unleashed. The rural poor do not believe that their life may be better via changing economic policy. The urban working classes fear privatizations because they will inevitably lead to job losses on a scale never before seen in India. India's public sector provides job security to tens of millions of Indian workers. Statutes prevent firing of workers in private businesses. The main reason for the high costs of Indian products lies in the rigid (oligopolistic) commercial and (feudal) social relations in the economy which have also undermined the benefits of a sheltered market and import substitution. Although the ruling Congress Party provided stability, this long rule turned into corruption. Over the years, the Congress Party became a personality cult built around the Gandhi family. This situation has now come to an end. The Bharatiya Janata Party (BJP) and the United Front (UF) offer two different alternatives. The BJP is a nationalist party based on Hindu chauvinism and small businessmen, while the UF is a loose coalition of leftist and centrist parties with strongholds in several states of the Union and a following among the rural poor (Kohli 1996: 122–127).

When one compares India's economic performance with the other Asian countries, the FDI figures are glaring. FDI going to India during 1994 reached just $US1 billion, while during the same period China received $US22 billion and Indonesia over $US18 billion (Clad 1996: 108). India is slowly preparing for liberalization and FDI, but is still a prisoner of its traditional bilateral fixations and of the size of its economy. India's neighbours understandably view potential Indian economic hegemony with suspicion, and see in expanded commerce a possible increase of India's power in the region. Until now, the South Asian Association for Regional Cooperation (SAARC) has remained the prisoner of the Indo-Pakistan conflict. A better impetus for India's regional integration is coming from the ASEAN which aims at modest but tangible lower tariff reciprocity by 2005 through AFTA. India's liberalization measures made ASEAN states enthusiastic because of India's vast market. Contacts have been made between the ASEAN leaders and the Indian government. This committee on joint sectoral cooperation discussed the modest level of improvement in the two-way trade between India and ASEAN and the opportunities opened up in the wake of ASEAN Free Trade Area (AFTA). India's overall trade with ASEAN is insignificant and Singapore and Malaysia have remained India's major ASEAN trading partners. Products from the NICs have slowly replaced the imports from India in the region. ASEAN states adopt a strictly one-to-one relationship with India. The most far-reaching exchanges have occurred between India and Singapore when Rao liberalized his economy and preferred the 'Singapore connection' because of Singapore's strength in high value-added capital goods and services. Moreover, ASEAN countries improved their bilateral economic ties with India, but bilateral trade and investment activities do not make India and the ASEAN economies mutually indispensable to one another as economic partners. Clad (1996: 110) asserts that South-East Asia's special advantage is the mobility of capital within the region while in South Asia intra-regional capital flows remain tiny and trade payments constitute less than 3 per cent of the total aggregate trade receipts of India and Pakistan. In fact, the 1996 South Asia Preferential Trade Agreement (SAPTA) points the way in a region where open frontiers and free cross-border contacts still meet distrust.

Latin America

Mexico

After the debt crisis of 1982 Latin American countries had to pay out more than they were receiving, while levels of export prices declined. Latin American countries had to cut imports and living standards and they diverted production to exports in order to achieve a surplus on their trade balance. This brought a deep recession in a period when capital export continued. Despite populist opposition to continued debt repayment, Latin American governments did not break with the international financial order. The debt crisis was one of the reasons for the fall of the military regimes, but none of the parliamentary successor regimes made an attempt to repudiate the old debts. Instead, these successor regimes complied with the requests of the international banks and institutions. The debtor countries did not respond tamely to the demands of international finance, but in general they engineered a deliberate transformation of their economy and its international orientation. The result was the adoption of liberal reforms which contrasted sharply with the former periods of inward-oriented industrialization (Grugel 1996: 131–168). Mexico broke with its pattern of state-led capitalist development and joined GATT and the North American Free Trade Agreement (NAFTA) (see Chapter 11 on Mexico and Chile) and Mexico's financial sector was rapidly liberalized. Private sector pressure was indirect, reflecting the power structure of capital. Privatization was part of a larger plan to restore growth with new inflows of capital (Maxfield 1997: 92–119). The new orientation responded to the interests of a narrow domestic and international coalition who wanted to attract FDI in manufacturing and cover the balance-of-payment deficits in the future. Privatization, wage cuts and liberalization prepared Mexico for entry to NAFTA. The Mexican government hoped that liberalization plus access to the USA and Canadian markets would make the country a globally competitive site for FDI. By the end of 1991 the bulk of the privatization programme had been completed. All these reforms, however, were carried out by the PRI elite against widespread popular protest and overt revolts in the South.

Brazil

Like Mexico, Brazil after 1982 lost access to foreign loans and had to cut imports. The government provided fiscal and financial incentives for exporting firms in order to create a balance of trade surplus but successive stabilization programmes, drafted by the civilian governments of Sarney and Fernando Collor, failed. President Fernando Collor's neo-liberal course ended up in a political crisis when the Brazilian Parliament removed him from office. Collor was replaced by Vice-President Itamar Franco, a well-known opponent of liberalization. Meanwhile, Brazil's economy experienced a slump with no recovery in sight; FDI was diverted to Mexico and other liberalizing Latin American countries. In these circumstances, by the end of 1992 Brazil was forced to adopt a liberalization programme that reduced tariffs from an average of 32 per cent to under 15 per cent in 1993. Under pressure from the external environment Brazil moved firmly to an open economy. After a decade of false starts the country had fallen into liberalization by default, as a last resort (Cammack, *et al.* 1993: 310). The difference between Mexico and Brazil was that the Mexican state, with its *de facto* one-party regime was able to 'avoid the policy immobilism' characteristic of Brazil and Chile, and to make policy decisions – even unpopular ones – when they were deemed necessary (Collier and Collier 1991: 589).

In Mexico the state had to co-opt dissident factions. Furthermore, the Mexican government had shaped powerful mass organizations mobilizing workers and peasants that served as interlocutors and conciliators. Mexico successfully implemented stabilization plans, thus illustrating the policy-making capacity of the integrative, hegemonic regime (Buendía 1996: 566–591). Thus, unlike Brazil, where governments in a weak political position were not able to adopt austerity programmes as all interest groups fought to maintain income shares, the Mexican authorities had the resources with which to form a coalition for an austerity policy imposing serious costs in the short run, but promising gains to all in the long run. The Brazilian party system was much weaker, fractionalized and of post-war origins; they were just loose groups of politicians without a viable political centre. According to Lal and Maxfield (1993: 37–40), opposition to stabilization and liberalization programmes originated in the industrial workers, and industrialists opposed tight money policies. Brazilian industry was dependent on state-subsidized credit and opposed to internal and equity financing and this made industry vulnerable to cuts in subsidies and rising interest rates. Another reason for the failure of Brazilian stabilization programmes is the state institutions. Brazil had no central bank able to effectively control the money supply and the public sector expenditures. Spending departments had strong supporting constituencies and underwent electoral pressure.

Chile

More than Mexico and Brazil, Chile completed a process of liberal reforms and acquired relative stability with respect to its fiscal and external balances. During the past decade its GDP annual growth rate averaged 5–6 per cent and its exports diversified. In 1995 per capita GNP was $US4,355. Slowly Chile has moved back to democracy but the Chilean experience remains controversial (Stallings and Brock 1993: 78). Before the Augusto Pinochet *coup d'état* Chile had, more than in other Latin American countries, strong political parties with a clear class character. After the coup in 1973 the military discouraged the political activities of the conservative National Party and outlawed the Socialist, Communist and Christian Democratic parties. When the economic and financial crisis of 1982 erupted and the Bretton Woods institutions had to provide structural adjustment loans, the traditional Right reappeared as a political force of importance for the ruling military bureaucracy. Previously the military had broken with ISI and protectionism. Then Chile's economy slowly moved away from copper towards non-commodity products. Firms were urged to export, while declining industries went bankrupt. The political question of interest is to what extent the Pinochet regime could rely on a new coalition of economic 'winners' and defeated 'losers'. Because the government discouraged political activities and the middle classes were still terrified by the memory of the Popular Front, the 'losers' were outpaced by the 'winners'. The trade unions were powerless; they lost members and lacked a tradition of effective political leadership.

The economic downturn and balance-of-payments crisis of 1982 threatened the very existence of the military regime in Chile. Many local businesses had obtained dollar loans and the banks were insolvent. The Banco de Chile and the Banco de Santiago, leaders of two conglomerates, were in the greatest difficulties. The government dismantled the conglomerates and sold off their affiliated companies. A devaluation combined with higher tariffs stabilized the economy; banks were subsidized and bad loans were purchased by the Central Bank. Holders of dollar debts received a preferential exchange rate and the government guaranteed a part of the privately contracted foreign debt. The macro-economic model worked out by the new Finance Minister, Hernán Büchi was aimed at a moderate rate of economic growth and low inflation through investment and export promotion. He gradually depreciated the peso and lowered tariffs to a flat 15 per cent in order to boost exports and investment. Non-traditional exports continued to grow, while imports remained depressed since a growing trade surplus was needed to service the still high external debt. Because privatizations had contributed to reduce the budget deficit and sectoral changes were occurring, the regime could survive. Büchi started selling a large number of the enterprises the government had inherited from the conglomerates and introduced forms of 'popular capitalism'. Several firms were purchased by foreign investors using discounted debt paper. The role of the IMF was crucial during the whole experiment of economic liberalization and privatization of the Chilean economy as it generally reinforced these policies and helped

47

open the doors for external finance and private bank loans, which were crucial in enabling the government to finance the trade deficit until 1982. Apart from the international actors, the military had acquired enough political autonomy to implement economic reforms. Firms and trade unions opposed to trade liberalization in its extreme forms had lost any influence during the first decade of the Pinochet dictatorship. Open non-discriminatory import tariffs were lowered and become as low as 11 per cent on average.

However, the disastrous 'crash' of 1982 had weakened the Pinochet regime and democratic reforms had become necessary when a gradual dismantling of the authoritarian regime was underway. But the democratic institutions did not affect economic policies. When the Aylwin government came to power in 1989 it supported the trade, exchange rate, and macro-economic policies of the previous military regime. The pillars supporting this policy were maintaining a macro-economic equilibrium, achieving integration into the international economy, and fostering long-term growth and attracting FDI. The Christian Democrats of Aylwin and prominent economists of the Left adhered to these policy goals. Investor confidence made Chile move into the category of a low-risk country (*Financial Times*, 14 March 1997). Thus Chile's rate of FDI increased to 4 or 5 per cent of GNP, which was among the highest in the world. Two years after the transition to democracy a broad national consensus clearly existed to maintain all the structural reforms implemented by the former military regime. This consensus was cemented by the global ideological context, because similar changes were implemented across Latin America and Asia. Meanwhile, export diversification progressed and the share of copper export in total exports decreased from 80 per cent in 1980 to merely 32 per cent in 1995. Chile signed bilateral trade agreements with Argentina, Bolivia, Colombia, Ecuador, Mexico, Venezuela, and Canada. Chile joined the Asia Pacific Economic Cooperation (APEC) forum, is interested in membership of the Mercado Común del Sur (Common Market of the South – MERCOSUR) and wants to become a member of NAFTA (Arriagada Herrera and Graham 1994: 242–289).

CONCLUSIONS

Fifty years after the end of the Second World War, regionalism is emerging as a compromise between globalism and protectionism, between internationalization and ISI. The growing importance of 'open' regional agreements obliges countries to cooperate and to join networks of interdependence (Jones 1995: 103–163). But external pressures oblige regimes to change their institutional framework by adjusting their economies and opening their frontiers to international competition and because of these external pressures many countries believe that they may realize greater economic gains from regionalism than from existing multilateral systems. The driving force behind regionalism is international competition. Since starting out in Europe regionalism has spread to the Americas and Asia. The former socialist countries of Eastern Europe, which adopted externally oriented market economic systems also prefer regional approaches to gain access to advanced markets. Many developing economies are taking their first steps towards creating an open regional market integrated into the international exchange of goods, capital and labour. Economies are becoming increasingly open to contacts with neighbouring countries. New commercial and institutional structures are emerging, encouraging integrative processes in the region. Governments are promoting the deepening of these links and elaborate systems of special state guarantees and incentives for foreign investors in key industries. They open their borders when implementing structural reforms and are breaking with ISI policies. It should be stressed that the process of regionalization is the combined result of global and domestic changes and that the ongoing process of regionalization is shaped by policy changes which are the outcome of internal struggles and confrontations. It is clear that the debt crisis of 1982 was a major event leading to structural changes in world politics and that the international players started a liberalization drive that ended up in increased interconnectedness of national economies. Developing economies had to give up their ISI policies and were forced to adhere to forms of open regionalism in order to foster FDI and find outlets for their outward-oriented industries. As a result of this regionalization drive three dominant regions ('triadization') came to the fore, representing the three major economic powers of the world. Other regions on the globe were excluded from this global restructuring process, but these regions are now pressing for an alliance with one of the 'triads'. India and China want to join the Asia Pacific Rim. The countries of Latin America want to apply for NAFTA in order to have access to the North American Market. Eastern Europe is looking for an association agreement with the EU, while many non-oil states in Africa and the Middle East are knocking on Europe's door.

Popular notions of globalization run counter to the possibility of increasing regionalization within the international system. The question remains as to the ultimate compatibility of opposing patterns, of further globalization in combination with increasing regionalization. The tension between both is obvious and highlights the wider issue of a deterministic versus a voluntaristic point of view, because globalization suggests that the remorseless advance of international capital and pressures to open up national economies will signify the end of the nation–state and national identities. Though contemporary liberals think that the steady pressures of economic opportunities and competition pave the way to a liberal world order, the road to a globalizing and regionalizing world order still remains a matter of political decisions. States try to influence international economic relations by using existing patterns of international interconnectedness in accordance with their domestic economic programmes and interests. Hence, politics still play a key role in the shaping of regionalism. The main question here concerns the balance between the political and the economic if we assume that states may be pivotal to economic development nationally and internationally in both the short and the longer terms. Moreover, international institutions and banks are exercising pressures which depart from the political principle that weak states have to be turned into a web of interconnected external relations. But international pressures do not mean that states will disappear from the international scene, political actors can be identified and they play an important role in the process of regionalization. Their relative strength is reflected in the decisions that are taken or the divisive reactions they provoke and which set the pace of the regionalization process.

BIBLIOGRAPHY

Agrawal, A. N. (1983) *Indian Economy: Problems of Development and Planning*, New Delhi: Vikas Publishing House.

Agrawal, P., Gokarn, S. V., Mishra, V., Parikh, K. S. and Sen, K. (eds) (1995) 'India: crisis and response', in P. Agrawal, S. V. Gokarn, V. Mishra, K. S. Parikh and K. Sen, *Economic Restructuring in East Asia and India*, Basingstoke: Macmillan: 375–392.

Ahluwalia, I. J. (1995) 'New economic policies, enterprises, and privatization in India', in R. Cassen and V. Joshi (eds) *India: The Future of Economic Reform*, Delhi: Oxford University Press: 233–259.

Amsden, A. (1989) *Asia's Next Giant: South Korea and Late Industrialization*, Oxford and New York: Oxford University Press.

Arriagada Herrera, G. and Graham, C. (1994) 'Chile: sustaining adjustment during democratic transition', in S. Haggard and S. B. Webb (eds) *Voting for Reform: Democracy, Political Liberalization, and Economic Adjustment*, New York: Oxford University Press: 242–289.

Bardhan, P. (1984) *The Political Economy of Development in India*, Oxford: Oxford University Press.

Bates, R. H. and Krueger, A. O. (1993) 'Introduction', in R. H. Bates and A. O. Krueger (eds) *Political and Economic Interactions in Economic Policy Reform: Evidence from Eight Countries*, Oxford and Cambridge, MA: Basil Blackwell: 1–26.

Bernard, M. and Ravenhill, J. (1995) 'Beyond product cycles and flying geese: regionalization, hierarchy, and the industrialization of East Asia', *World Politics* 47 (2): 171–209.

Buendía, J. (1996) 'Economic reform, public opinion, and presidential approval in Mexico, 1988–1993', *Comparative Political Studies* 29 (5): 566–591.

Byung-Nak Song (1994) *The Rise of the Korean Economy*, Hong Kong: Oxford University Press.

Cable, V. (1995) 'Indian liberalization and the private sector', in R. Cassen and V. Joshi (eds) *India: The Future of Economic Reform*, Delhi: Oxford University Press: 209–231.

Cammack, P., Pool, D. and Tordoff, W. (1993) *Third World Politics: A Comparative Introduction*, Basingstoke: Macmillan.

Chan, S. and Clark, C. (1992) 'Changing perspectives on the evolving Pacific Basin: international structure and domestic processes', in S. Chan and C. Clark (eds) *The Evolving Pacific Basin in the Global Political Economy: Domestic and International Linkages*, Boulder, CO and London: Lynne Rienner Publishers: 1–26.

Chazan, N. *et al.* (1992) *Politics and Society in Contemporary Africa*, Boulder, CO and London: Lynne Rienner Publishers.

Chi Huang (1992) 'Leadership change and government size in East Asian authoritarian regimes', in S. Chan and C. Clark (eds) *The Evolving Pacific Basin in the Global Political Economy: Domestic and International Linkages*, Boulder, CO and London: Lynne Rienner Publishers: 125–146.

Chowdhury, A. and Islam, I. (1993) *The Newly Industrialising Economies of East Asia*, London and New York: Routledge.

Clad, J. (1996) 'India in 1996: steady as she goes', *The Washington Quarterly* 19(4): 103–114.

Collier, R. B. and Collier, D. (1991) *Shaping the Political Arena: Critical Junctures, the Labor Movement, and Regime Dynamics in Latin America*, Princeton, NJ: Princeton University Press.

Cook, I. and Li, R. (1996) 'The rise of regionalism and the future of China', in I. G. Cook, M. A. Doel and R. Li (eds) *Fragmented Asia: Regional Integration and National Disintegration in Pacific Asia*, Aldershot: Avebury: 200–219.

Desai, R. G. (1994) 'Dunkel Draft and its implications in a developing economy', in G. S. Batra and N. Kaur (eds) *New Economic Policies in Developing Countries*, vol. 2, *Foreign Trade and Export Policy*, New Delhi: Anmol Publications: 227–234.

Economist, The, 24–30 August 1996: 55.

Eichengreen, B. (1994) *International Monetary Arrangements for the 21st Century*, Washington DC: The Brookings Institution.

Financial Times, The, 14 March 1997.

Gilpin, R. (1993) 'The debate about the new world economic order', in D. Unger and P. Blackburn (eds) *Japan's Emerging Global Role*, Boulder, CO and London: Lynne Rienner Publishers: 21–36.

Gong, G. W. (1994) 'China's fourth revolution', *The Washington Quarterly* 17(1): 29–43.

Gourevitch, P. A. (1989) 'The Pacific Rim: current debates', in P. A. Gourevitch (ed.) *The Pacific Region: Challenges to Policy and Theory, The Annals of the American Academy of Political and Social Science*, 505: 8–23.

Grugel, J. (1996) 'Latin America and the remaking of the Americas', in A. Gamble and A. Payne (eds) *Regionalism and World Order*, Basingstoke and London: Macmillan: 131–168.

Haggard, S. (1989) 'The East Asian NICs in comparative perspective', in P. A. Gourevitch (ed.) *The Pacific Region: Challenges to Policy and Theory, The Annals of the American Academy of Political and Social Science*, 505: 129–141.

Haggard, S. (1990) *Pathways from the Periphery: The Politics of Growth in the Newly Industrializing Countries*, Ithaca and London: Cornell University Press.

Helleiner, E. (1994) *States and the Reemergence of Global Finance: From Bretton Woods to the 1990s*, Ithaca: Cornell University Press.

Hill, H. (1996) *The Indonesian Economy Since 1966: Southeast Asia's Emerging Giant*, Cambridge: Cambridge University Press.

Hsiung, J. C. (1992) 'China in the twenty-first century global balance: challenge and policy response', in S. Chan and C. Clark (eds) *The Evolving Pacific Basin in the Global Political Economy: Domestic and International Linkages*, Boulder, CO and London: Lynne Rienner Publishers: 67–82.

Hurrell, A. and Ngaire, W. (1995) 'Globalisation and inequality', *Millennium: Journal of International Studies* 24 (3): 447–470.

Hussain, A. (1994) 'The Chinese economic reforms: an assessment', in D. Dwyer (ed.) *China: The Next Decade*, Harlow: Longman: 11–30.

Huysmans, J. (1995) 'Post-Cold War implosion and globalisation: liberalism running past itself', *Millennium: Journal of International Studies* 24(3): 471–487.

Inoguchi, T. (1989) 'Shaping and sharing Pacific dynamism', in P. A. Gourevitch (ed.) *The Pacific Region: Challenges to Policy and Theory, The Annals of the American Academy of Political and Social Science*, 505: 46–55.

Jones, R. J. B. (1995) *Globalization and Interdependence in the International Political Economy*, London and New York: Pinter Publishers.

Kapuria-Foreman, V. (1992–93) 'Comparative growth in India and the People's Republic of China 1950–1988: a reappraisal', *Comparative International Development* 27(4): 25–40.

Kohli, A. (1996) 'Can the periphery control the center? Indian politics at the crossroads', *The Washington Quarterly* 19(4): 115–127.

Krueger, A. O. (1992) *Economic Policy Reform in Developing Countries* (The Kuznets Memorial Lectures at the Economic Growth Center, Yale University), Oxford and Cambridge, MA: Basil Blackwell.

Krugman, P. (1993) 'Changes in capital markets for developing countries', in P. H. Baker, A. Boraine and W. Krafchik (eds) *South Africa and the World Economy in the 1990s*, Cape Town and Johannesburg: David Philip, Washington, DC: the Brookings Institution: 32–48.

Lal, D. and Maxfield, S. (1993) 'The political economy of stabilization in Brazil', in R. H. Bates and A. O. Krueger (eds) *Political and Economic Interactions in Economic Policy Reform: Evidence from Eight Countries*, Oxford and Cambridge, MA: Basil Blackwell: 27–77.

Lardy, N. (1994) *China in the World Economy*, Washington, DC: Institute for International Economics.

Lehman, H. P. (1993) *Indebted Development: Strategic Bargaining and Economic Adjustment in the Third World*, New York: St. Martin's Press.

Lewis, J. P. (1991) 'Some consequences of giantisme', *World Politics* 43(3): 367–389.

Lim, L. Y. (1996) 'ASEAN: new modes of economic cooperation', in D. Wurfel and B. Burton (eds) *Southeast Asia in the New World Order: The Political Economy of a Dynamic Region*, Basingstoke: Macmillan: 19–35.

Machado, K. G. (1992) 'ASEAN state industrial policies and Japanese regional production strategies: the case of Malaysia's motor vehicle industry', in S. Chan and C. Clark (eds) *The Evolving Pacific Basin in the Global Political Economy: Domestic and International Linkages*, Boulder, CO and London: Lynne Rienner Publishers: 169–202.

Mackeras, C., Taneja, P. and Young, G. (1994) *China Since 1978: Reform, Modernisation and 'Socialism with Chinese Characteristics'*, New York: St. Martin's Press.

Maxfield, S. (1997) 'Capital mobility and Mexican financial liberalization', in M. Loriaux *et al.* (eds) *Capital Ungoverned: Liberalizing Finance in Interventionist States*, Ithaca and London: Cornell University Press: 92–119.

Ngai-Ling Sum (1996) 'The NICs and competing strategies of East Asian regionalism', in A. Gamble and A. Payne (eds) *Regionalism and World Order*, Basingstoke and London: Macmillan: 207–245.

Ostry, S. and Nelson, R. R. (1995) *Techno-Nationalism and Techno-Globalism: Conflict and Cooperation*, Washington, DC: the Brookings Institution.

Rugman, A. M. (1993) 'Drawing the border for a multinational enterprise and a nation–state', in L. Eden and E. H. Potter (eds) *Multinationals in the Global Political Economy*, Basingstoke: Macmillan: 84–100.

Ruigrok, W. and Van Tulder, R. (1995) *The Logic of International Restructuring*, London and New York: Routledge.

Shang-Jin Wei (1995) 'The open door policy and China's rapid growth: evidence from city-level data', in T. Ito and A. O. Krueger (eds) *Growth Theories in Light of the East Asian Experience*, Chicago and London: The University of Chicago Press: 73–104.

Shang-Jin Wei (1996) 'Foreign direct investment in China: services and consequences', in T. Ito and A. O. Krueger (eds) *Financial Deregulation and Integration in East Asia*, Chicago and London: The University of Chicago Press: 77–106.

Simai, M. (1994) *The Future of Global Governance: Managing Risk and Change in the International System*, Washington, DC: United States Institute of Peace Press.

Singh, P. N. (1994) 'Globalising Indian economy: the environment', in G. S. Batra and N. Kaur (eds) *New Economic Policies in Developing Countries*, vol. 1, *Globalisation Strategies and Economic Liberalisation*, New Delhi: Anmol Publications: 1–16.

Sridharan, K. (1996) *The ASEAN Region in India's Foreign Policy*, Aldershot: Dartmouth.

Stallings, B. and Brock, P. (1993) 'The political economy of economic adjustment: Chile, 1973–90', in R. H. Bates and A. O. Krueger (eds) *Political and Economic Interactions in Economic Policy Reform: Evidence from Eight Countries*, Oxford and Cambridge, MA: Basil Blackwell: 78–122.

Swamy, D. S. (1994) *The Political Economy of Industrialisation: From Self-Reliance to Globalisation*, New Delhi, Thousand Oaks and London: Sage Publications.

Tanzi, V. (1995) *Taxation in an Integrating World*, Washington, DC: The Brookings Institution.

Wade, R. (1989) 'What can economics learn from East Asian success?', in P. A. Gourevitch (ed.) *The Pacific Region: Challenges to Policy and Theory*, *The Annals of the American Academy of Political and Social Science*, 505: 68–79.

Wade, R. (1990) *Governing the Market: Economic Theory and the Role of Government in East Asian Industrialization*, Princeton, NJ: Princeton University Press.

Walter, A. (1991) *World Power and World Money: The Role of Hegemony and International Monetary Order*, New York: Harvester Wheatsheaf.

Walter, N. (1996) 'Inflation and growth in a country in transition', in M. Guitian and R. Mundell (eds) *Inflation and Growth in China*, proceedings of a conference held in Beijing, China, 10–12 May 1995, Washington, DC: International Monetary Fund: 41–45.

Womack, B. and Guangzhi, Z. (1994) 'The many worlds of China's provinces: foreign trade and diversification', in D. S. Goodman and G. Segal (eds) *China Deconstructs: Politics, Trade and Regionalism*, London and New York: Routledge: 131–176.

World Bank (1993) *The East Asian Miracle: Public Policy and Economic Growth*, Policy Research Report, Washington, DC: World Bank and Oxford University Press.

Wurfel, D. (1988) *Filipino Politics: Development and Decay*, Ithaca and London: Cornell University Press.

3

CENTRAL AND EASTERN EUROPE

Catching up or marginalization in the European free trade zone?

Hans van Zon

In this chapter the consequences of trade liberalization for the associated countries in Central and Eastern Europe[1] as foreseen in the association agreements with the European Union (EU) and their position in the international division of labour are discussed, especially in relation to the eventual emergence of new regional economic blocs. First, the heritage of the socialist past upon present international economic relations of associated countries is analysed. Until the late 1970s leaders of the socialist countries believed in the system of two competing world markets and the growing share of their socialist countries in the world economy and fast expanding mutual trade. The 'socialist world market' functioned on different principles from the 'capitalist world market'. International economic relations between socialist countries were planned and based mainly upon clearing arrangements, i.e. in practice, barter trade. They were channelled and controlled through the central state apparatus, mainly foreign trade organizations. Enterprises usually did not know their suppliers and customers abroad. International economic relations were mainly confined to trade in tangible commodities. Trade in services, Foreign Direct Investment (FDI) and international capital flows were negligible. Although there were international specialization agreements within the Commission for Mutual Economic Assistance (CMEA), specialization within the CMEA was weakly developed. Related to this, the share of intra-industry trade was very low. Within the CMEA, international economic relations were above all centred on the Soviet Union as the dominant power in the CMEA. One unique aspect of the Soviet Union was that it was less developed economically than some of its satellite states. Trade between the smaller CMEA countries was on a very low level (see Table 3.1) and trade with the developed market economies was, on average, about 30 per cent of foreign trade turnover.

This system of international relations increasingly showed signs of stress from the early 1970s onwards. Since the first oil price shock (1973), within the CMEA prices of fuels and raw materials, the so-called hard goods that could be traded at the (capitalist) world market as well, began to follow world market prices, based

54

Table 3.1 Central and Eastern Europe: direction of exports

	1980	1985	1987	1989	1991	1993	1995
Transition economies	50	50	53	47	30	23	20
Former SU	27	28	30	25	18	10	9
Central and Eastern Europe	19	16	18	16	8	7	8
Other socialist countries	4	5	6	5	4	5	4
Developed economies	36	36	35	43	60	65	71
Developing countries	14	14	12	11	10	13	9

Source: Economic Commission for Europe (1996: 191).
Note: Central and Eastern Europe (former European CMEA countries, except the Soviet Union and the countries of the Former Soviet Union – FSU).

on five-year averages. This fundamentally changed the terms of trade within the CMEA, initially to the benefit of the Soviet Union, the major provider of oil and raw materials within the CMEA. Also, the delivery of fuels and raw materials began to slow down as growth of output began to slow down and as the Soviet Union, from the early 1980s onwards, began to prefer sales to the West, for higher prices. Thus the smaller CMEA states had to adjust to a situation of non-assured growth of delivery of fuels and raw materials. This was especially problematic as the CMEA system of international relations was geared to distribution of incremental production, due to the system of barter trade and long-term trade agreements.

Due to these developments, there was a mounting pressure to import from the West.[2] Increasingly, imports that used to come from the East were imported from the West. This was partly related to stagnation phenomena in each of the member countries. Lack of quality and uncertain delivery conditions increasingly became a problem for those enterprises that wanted to enhance quality and output of production. The result was that long before the collapse of communism the mutual system of international economic relations had begun to disintegrate. Also, mutual trade between the smaller CMEA member states began to decrease. During the 1980s even a customs war between these countries developed as relative scarcities in each of the countries differed and smuggling became very profitable. For example, the Poles used to shop to a great extent in the better supplied shops in the German Democratic Republic (GDR) and Czechoslovakia, with the result that the native populations, especially in border areas, were increasingly confronted with scarcities.

NEW TRADE PATTERNS

With the collapse of communism in Central and Eastern Europe mutual trade between the CMEA countries collapsed as well (Van Brabant 1993). During the Sofia meeting of the CMEA (1 January 1991) it had been decided to conduct all trade transactions in convertible currencies but, actually, this was only a formalization of an already existing situation. In a very short time mutual trade disappeared (see Table 3.1). With the abolition of central planning, the planning of CMEA relations disappeared as well. Generally, enterprises in the countries of Central and Eastern Europe preferred to buy inputs, as far as they had the money to buy, in the West. Western inputs were of better quality and with better delivery conditions. Share of trade with the West increased, especially for the Visegrad countries, while share of trade with the East plummeted. In the first phase of transition the total volume of trade diminished considerably, also related to the fact that then all post-socialist countries were faced with a dramatic decline in demand. By mid-1997, all Central and Eastern European countries, except Bulgaria, have entered a growth phase. Seven years after the beginning of transition, patterns of international economic relations exhibit more stable patterns. Bulgaria, Romania, Albania, Latvia and Lithuania, the least performing countries that witnessed the largest production decline and that have a low level of economic development, still have a relatively large share of foreign trade with the other post-socialist countries.

The Visegrad countries, Slovenia and Estonia, the best performing economies among the associated countries, have most of their trade with the EU. Their share of trade with the Former Soviet Union (FSU) and other former CMEA member countries has become very low.[3] It is remarkable that these countries' share in total Western trade with Central and Eastern Europe has increased enormously. For the Visegrad group alone the share in total Eastern trade (including the FSU) with the EU increased from less than one-third in 1985 to about 50 per cent in the mid-1990s (see Table 3.2).

Here it should be said that the share of East–West trade in total foreign trade is generally not large for Western countries. Moreover, exports of the former European CMEA member states to the Organization for Economic Cooperation and Development (OECD) as a share of total non-OECD imports of the OECD decreased from 13.1 per cent in 1990 to 11.3 per cent in 1995.

The geographic patterns of foreign trade of Central and Eastern European countries is highly asymmetric. In the Central and Eastern European countries,

Table 3.2 Share of the Visegrad group in total
ex-CMEA trade with the EU

Main trading partners	Exports	Imports
1985	24.7	30.7
1988	31.7	34.9
1989	32.0	36.3
1990	37.1	41.6
1991	41.4	47.8
1992	46.3	51.2
1993	62.0	52.4
1994	64.6	52.9
1995	48.8	44.1

Source: Inotai and Stankovsky (1993: 6); *Eurostat.*

Table 3.3 Imports of OECD states from Central and Eastern Europe, 1982–94
as percentages of total imports

From	OECD imports					
	1982	1985	1987	1990	1994	1995
OECD	66.5	70.5	74.6	77.7	73.3	74.7
non-OECD	33.5	29.5	24.9	22.3	26.7	23.8
CMEA-Europe	3.2	2.8	2.2	2.9	2.6	2.7

Source: Author's calculations on the basis of OECD, *Monthly Statistics of Foreign Trade.*

exports to the EU had a share of about 50 per cent in total exports in 1993, while in
the EU's total exports, the Central and Eastern European countries only accounted
for about 2 per cent (see Table 3.3). Whereas for the Central and Eastern European
countries there was a fundamental shift in trade orientation from the former Soviet
Union towards the EU, this shift has not been felt very much by the countries of the
EU, except for particular industries.

Table 3.4 Volume of export trade of European countries compared, in dollars per capita

Size of country	Western Europe		Central and Eastern Europe	
larger than 50 mn	Germany (81.1)	4,480	Russian Fed. (148.9)	295
	UK (58.3)	3,109		
	France (58.1)	3,357		
	Italy (57.9)	2,911	Ukraine (51.9)	123
countries 35–50 mn	Spain (38.9)	1,500	Poland (38.5)	364
countries 20–35 mn			Romania (22.8)	215
countries 10–20 mn	Netherl.(15.4)	8,366	Belarus (10.3)	71
	Greece (10.5)	761	Czech Rep. (10.3)	999
	Belgium (10.1)	10,310	Hungary (10.1)	871
countries 5–10 mn	Portugal (9.9)	1,563		
	Sweden (8.8)	5,617		
	Switzerland (7.1)	10,597		
	Austria (7.98)	4,919	Bulgaria (8.6)	484
	Denmark (5.2)	719	Slovak Rep. (5.4)	579
	Finland (5.1)	4,536		
	Portugal (9.9)	4,536		
countries 1–5 mn	Norway (4.3)	7,348	Croatia (4.8)	
	Ireland (3.6)	8,024	Moldovia (4.4)	40
			Lithuania (3.7)	186
			Latvia (2.6)	177
			Slovenia (2.0)	2559

Source: Author's calculations, based on figures from Economic Commission for Europe.
Note: Number of inhabitants in millons shown in brackets.

This asymmetry in relative significance of trade flows can be understood by comparing trade intensity. Central and Eastern European countries have a low trade intensity compared with West European countries (see Table 3.4). They have a peripheral position in world trade flows. Also, the composition of foreign trade flows changed drastically with the change-over to a market economy. Under socialism, exports to the socialist world, that accounted on average for about two-thirds of total exports, exhibited the typical pattern of developed industrial countries. Exports to the OECD region, however, exhibited patterns that are typical for Third World countries. After the collapse of the socialist world in 1989, exports have been mainly to the OECD region. The composition of trade flows with the West did not change much, however. It means that the overall export pattern of the countries of Central and Eastern Europe changed from that of typically industrialized countries to that of less developed countries. Exports from Central and Eastern Europe to the EU proved to be rather stable in terms of composition. Trade reorientation did not mean trade diversion.[4] Exports to the EU are above all in products that are 'sensitive', i.e. subject to various forms of protection on the EU side. Conspicious in trade in textile products is outward processing trade.

FOREIGN DIRECT INVESTMENT FLOWS

The share of trade of specific macroregions in total trade of each of the associated countries only gives a partial picture of the emerging pattern of international economic relations. Other factors are FDI, capital flows and trade regimes (see Table 3.5).

Table 3.5 FDI in Central and Eastern Europe, cash basis, end 1995, cumulative total since 1988 and FDI per capita

	Level (mn $) June 1995	FDI per capita
Poland	2751	71
Czech Republic	5881	569
Hungary	11391	1107
Slovakia	704	132
Slovenia	530	266
Albania	201	57
Croatia	273	58
Bulgaria	362	43
Romania	967	42
Macedonia	16	7
Estonia	638	420
Latvia	587	227
Lithuania	113	30
Ukraine	699	13
Belarus	33	3
Moldovia	76	17
Russia	5118	35

Source: Economic Commission for Europe (1996: 151).

FDI is less compared with the high expectations at the beginning of the transition process. It did not appear to be a trigger for industrial development. FDI flowed in those regions that were economically and politically stabilized and could offer prospects for growth. These were also the regions that were most open to the market. Often, FDI served to open markets for the respective post-socialist countries rather than serving as a base for exporting.

One of the most conspicious features is the high concentration of FDI. It is highly concentrated in a few territorial niches in the Czech Republic, Hungary and Poland. It is no coincidence that FDI flows to those regions in Central and Eastern Europe that were already economically most developed before the socialist experiment began. The perceived attractiveness of FDI in countries that are less open to the market and liberalized and desperately need capital, may itself be a major factor to push these countries towards further marketization and liberalization. But foreign investors often do not favour free trade arrangements. Car manufacturers, like Volkswagen in the Czech Republic, negotiated temporary protection measures to boost their market shares. The pattern of capital flows involves, apart from FDI, loans by international financial institutions, debt repayments, donations and capital flight. Despite the assistance efforts of the G7 countries, and especially the EU, in the first years of transition, net transfer of resources in a lot of Central and Eastern European countries appeared to be negative. In the early 1990s capital actually left the area; international banks withdrew short-term funds and these economies were unable to raise much new long-term capital. Sizeable volumes of funds began to flow back to the region only in 1993 (Economic Commission for Europe 1996: 142).

One element in international capital flows is revenues from illegal exports. This kind of foreign trade sometimes constitutes more than half of the total estimated exports (Lithuania, Bulgaria). This situation is typical for countries in which the state has little grip upon economic processes. This is often related to the weakness of the state in combination with high taxation. In these countries liberalization often means more scope for illegal activities, especially in the area of foreign trade where easy money can be earned. This illegal foreign trade exacerbates the problem of structural balance-of-payment deficits which faces practically all transitional economies. These balance-of-payments deficits lead to increasing indebtedness. High indebtedness leads international financial institutions to have a greater say in economic policy formulation and this contributes to further liberalization.

ASSOCIATION WITH THE EU

Each of the countries under review has signed an association agreement with the EU, according to which the EU will abolish trade barriers for industrial products and will give various concessions with regard to trade in agricultural products within a time span of six years, while the associated countries liberalize trade with the EU within ten years. However, quotas for a lot of sensitive products remain in place on the EU side. EU protectionism in agricultural markets is not affected by the new trade regime with the associated countries. Besides this, the associated countries have the option of becoming members of the EU and to this end they are in the process of adapting institutions and laws to EU norms (Commission of the EU 1995). For each of the associated countries the main foreign policy option is to become a member of the EU as soon as possible.

However, as time proceeds, the disadvantages of membership at an early stage become apparent, for both sides. For the EU there is the problem that the institutional infrastructure, conceived for six member states, is not geared towards a Union with more than fifteen member states. The Amsterdam Intergovernmental Conference in June 1997 has not solved this problem and the institutional reform of the EU that was to enable enlargement has been postponed. Moreover, there is the problem of costs associated with the membership of a number of poor associated countries. For example, the present Common Agricultural Policy (CAP) and Cohesion Policy are unsustainable with an enlargement to the East. With the present EU institutional structure, the cost of admitting Slovenia would be, according to Barta and Richter, for Slovenia ECU0.2 bn, for the Czech Republic ECU2 bn, for Slovakia ECU0.9 bn, for Hungary ECU2.3 bn, for Bulgaria ECU2.3 bn, for Poland ECU9.3 bn and for Romania ECU9.3 bn (Barta and Richter 1996: 8). However, Barta and Richter point out that the costs of protracted integration or non-enlargement might also be very high:

> All in all, the general pattern of a broad calculus of the cost of Eastern enlargement to the EU will be a movement from static adjustment costs before enlargement, followed by short-term direct (budgetary) costs at the moment of enlargement, to cumulative (though relatively small) long-term dynamic economic benefits accompanied by high non-economic (political and security) benefits in the longer run after enlargement.
>
> (ibid.: 12)

These authors conclude that the 'main interest of the EU lies in the utilisation of emerging opportunities to penetrate new markets rather than in long-term industrial co-operation', (ibid.: 10).

On the part of the associated countries, one gradually begins to realize that the time schedule of the present association treaties is rather tight, given the slow adjustment process of industry, especially heavy and machinery industry. With respect to membership, one begins to realize that one has to deal with a moving target, i.e. the *Acquis Communautaire*, that is expanding each year. Many industries cannot compete on EU markets and these are not only the high-value-added industries, for instance, in recent studies on the Polish steel and sugar industries, it was predicted that in both industries many enterprises could not compete with EU enterprises if trade barriers were abolished now or in the near future (Van Zon 1996). The question is whether Central and East European industries will be able to compete in the EU free trade area, without government subsidies. Nowadays it is very difficult to identify branches that may become competitive world-wide as full transparency has not yet been attained, due to deficiencies in price formation, hidden subsidies for enterprises, inter-enterprise debt, etc. An additional problem for the Central and Eastern European countries is the lack of institutional infra-structure, especially in the first phase of transition. As explained above, the post-socialist countries inherited economies and societies that were not internationalized to any large extent compared to the developed market economies. Enterprises were in most cases not accustomed to conducting business abroad, marketing was unknown to them and export promotion schemes were non-existent. Often exports were taxed. In many cases domestic production was taxed so heavily that foreign competitors could easily compete, due to absence of taxation. Often imports were promoted rather than exports.

Another problem is the lack of finances that prevents Eastern producers coming to market while their Western competitors have marketing funds. Moreover, some-times Western products have been sold in Eastern markets much cheaper than in their domestic markets.

The lack of internationalization of society and the economy is also reflected in the lack of language proficiency, the lack of knowledge about international business practices, and the lack of institutions supporting domestic companies abroad, such as foreign affiliates of banks and international chambers of commerce. A weak financial infrastructure severely hampers the selling of products abroad. For ex-ample, in the aviation industry it is not usual to pay cash for planes but to lease them or use borrowed money. Most Eastern aircraft producers have to ask for payment in cash with the result that few customers can be found. The system of after sales services is also not well developed. Due to all these factors, Western competitors have a big comparative advantage, even when they offer products of comparable quality. Then there is the problem of competition of subsidized food products on the part of the EU that is not solved in the framework of the association agree-ments. There is a long way to go before Central and East European countries become members of the EU and accession is mainly dependent on institutional reform with the EU and political willingness on the part of EU member states. For a long time associated countries will remain in limbo. In the best scenario the EU may be an integrating and stabilizing force. In the worst scenario the Central and Eastern European countries may again move away from the EU. There will be mounting pressure by powerful interest groups to ease the provisions of the association agreements in favour of protection. The degree of external liberalization is the result of a specific configuration of interest groups and this configuration may change over time.

REGIONAL FREE TRADE ZONES

In Central and Eastern Europe several initiatives have been taken to further economic cooperation between sub-groups of post-socialist countries or groupings of West and East European countries. The most significant initiative has been the Central European Free Trade Zone (CEFTA), established under strong pressure from the EU. The four Visegrad countries constituted an ideal sub-group within Central and Eastern Europe to create a free trade zone as these countries were the

61

first to sign association agreements with the EU and they were the most advanced on the path of transition. However, the advantage of such an initiative has not been seen by each of the participating countries. Czech Prime Minister Václav Klaus repeatedly has stated that the CEFTA has mainly served the cosmetic goal of pleasing the EU. Although the aim is to abolish all trade barriers, it appears that there are still a large number of trade barriers that are reflected in the low level of intra-CEFTA trade.[5] Between 1985 and 1992 intra-CEFTA trade almost halved, from between 8.4 and 9.4 per cent to between 4.5 and 6.7 per cent.[6] Since 1993 the share of intra-CEFTA trade increased but in mid-1995 was still much below the levels attained during the 1980s under the CMEA regime (*Economic Bulletin for Europe* 1995: 45). It is interesting to note that Slovenia, which was early in 1997 not yet a CEFTA member but has signed free trade agreements with all four CEFTA members, has broadly the same share of its trade with CEFTA as has Poland (ibid.: 45). It should be taken into account that the Visegrad countries have competing export structures. These countries never had high shares of mutual trade. Another free trade arrangement in the region is the Baltic Free Trade Agreement that came into force on 1 April 1994. This agreement has not boosted trade in the region. The share of exports of the Baltic states to the Baltic states as a share of total exports declined from 1994 to 1995 from 11.1 per cent to 10.3 per cent. Respective figures for imports are 5.4 and 5.5 per cent (ibid.: 68). However, exports to Finland, Sweden and Germany increased from 16 per cent in 1994 to 27 per cent in 1995 (ibid.: 69).

CONCLUSIONS

Integration of the associated countries of Central and Eastern Europe with the EU is proceeding much faster than integration processes within the region. Within Central and Eastern Europe, a clear dividing line is emerging. On the one hand, there are the Visegrad countries, Slovenia and Estonia, that have a higher level of economic development, are more open to the market and have higher economic growth rates. They successfully diverted foreign trade from the former Soviet Union to the EU and they attracted the bulk of FDI into the region. This group of countries will probably be the first group of Central and East European countries to enter the EU. The second group consists of the remaining countries, i.e. Romania, Bulgaria, Lithuania and Latvia. These countries face the risk of becoming further marginalized in the wider European Economic Space. The first group of countries saw their exports to the EU booming. But they increased exports mainly in markets that are non-dynamic and could be easily penetrated through low prices. For each of the Central and Eastern European countries, the export base to the EU, the most important market, consists of a few agricultural and industrial products, the latter including clothing, steel products, chemicals, footwear and wood products. The commodity concentration in exports to the EU is high for each of the Central and East European countries. Some products could be exported profitably due to low input prices and related to distorted price structures. Therefore, increased trade with the EU rests upon a rather fragile basis. A further diversification of exports oriented to higher value-added products and based upon a deeper integration with the EU industrial structures is necessary. A deepening of integration within Central and Eastern Europe may further this process. To this end, an international economic policy is required, both on the side of the Central and Eastern European countries as well as on the side of the EU, that goes beyond the option of free trade. If the future, enlarged EU is mainly a common market, i.e. a wider European free trade area, the chances of marginalization, above all for the weaker Central and Eastern European countries, will be greater.

NOTES

1 The countries of Central and Eastern Europe are defined in this chapter as the associated countries, i.e. the Baltic states, Poland, the Czech Republic, Slovakia, Hungary, Slovenia, Romania, Bulgaria and Albania, plus Croatia, Serbia, Bosnia Herzegovina, and Macedonia.
2 This does not automatically mean a rising share of trade with the West as Table 3.1 shows. This is not congruent with the widespread view that with liberalization of foreign trade during the 1980s, East–West trade boomed.
3 For example, in 1994 5.4 per cent of Polish exports were to Russia, whereas 6.8 per cent of Polish imports came from Russia (Hausner 1995).
4 Exports of textiles, footwear and miscellaneous manufactures increased from ECU2.9 bn (22.3 per cent of total exports) in 1990 to ECU9.8 bn in 1994 (28.9 per cent of total exports). The exports of wood, articles of stone and bare metals increased from ECU3.2 bn (24.6 per cent of total exports) in 1990 to ECU8.5 bn in 1994 (25.1 per cent of total exports). Exports of chemicals and plastic products decreased from ECU1.3 bn in 1990 (10 per cent to ECU3.0 bn in 1994, 8.8 per cent). Of agriculture and food products from ECU2.2 bn in 1990 (16.9 per cent) to ECU2.6 bn in 1994 (7.7 per cent) (*Europe Weekly Selected Statistics*, 30 October 1995). The share of all these product categories together in total exports to the EU decreased slightly, from 73.8 per cent in 1990 to 70.5 per cent in 1994.
   The combined share of machinery, electrical equipment, optical and photographic instruments, vehicles, aircraft and transport equipment rose from 40.5 per cent of total EU exports to Central and Eastern Europe in 1990 to 41.5 per cent in 1994. Exports of textiles, footwear and miscellaneous manufactures rose from 15.7 per cent in 1990 to 17.9 per cent in 1994.
5 Respectively, 8.6 per cent of total exports and 6.6 per cent of total imports for Hungary. Respective figures for Poland are 5.4 per cent and 5.9 per cent (1994) (*Economic Bulletin for Europe* 1995: 45).
6 For Hungary the share of trade with the other Visegrad countries as a share of total foreign trade decreased from 9.1 per cent in 1985 to 4.5 per cent in 1992. For Czechoslovakia these figures were 9.4 per cent and 6.7 per cent, for Poland 8.4 per cent and 4.8 per cent (Fogarassy and Sass 1993).

BIBLIOGRAPHY

Barta, V. and Richter, S. (1996) *Eastern Enlargement of the European Union from a Western and an Eastern Perspective* (Research Reports 227), Vienna: The Vienna Institute for Comparative Economic Studies.
Commission of the European Union (1995) *White Paper on Preparation of the Associated Countries of Central and Eastern Europe for Integration into the Internal Market of the Union*, Brussels: COM (163 final).

Europe Weekly Selected Statistics, 30 October 1995.

Fogarassy, G. and Sass, M. (1993) *Economic Integration of the Visegrad Countries, Facts and Scenarios*, Budapest: Institute for World Economics of the Hungarian Academy of Sciences.

Hausner, J. (1995) *The Polish Industry*, Gelsenkirchen: Institute of Work and Technology.

Inotai, A. and Stankovsky, J. (1993) *Transformation in Progress: The External Economic Factor* (Research Reports 200), Vienna: The Vienna Institute for Comparative Economic Studies.

United Nations Economic Commission for Europe (1995) *Economic Bulletin for Europe*, Geneva: UN.

UN Economic Commission for Europe (1996) *Economic Survey of Europe 1995–1996*, Geneva and New York: UN.

Van Brabant, J. (1993) *Industrial Policy in Eastern Europe: Governing the Transition*, Dordrecht: Kluwer.

Van Zon, H. (1996) *The Future of Industry in Central and Eastern Europe*, Aldershot: Avebury.

4

ECONOMIC REFORM AND NEW PATTERNS OF POST-SOVIET REGIONALISM

Andrey S. Makarychev

Within the framework of political and scholarly discussions concerning the future of the Russian Federation one of the central categories is expressed by the term 'regionalism'. In today's Russian political science, perhaps, no other issues are as important as a complex of problems connected with regionalization. Absolutely unknown contradictions are emerging on the political and economic arenas, and the future of the country will to a great extent depend upon their resolution. The vast changes that have occurred in the ex-Soviet geopolitical space over the past decade bring us face to face with the opening of a new era in contemporary history, one in which peoples themselves have rejected totalitarianism and are seeking to restore civil society through the introduction of democratic regimes. Taking into account the recent political developments within the Commonwealth of Independent States (CIS), it does not seem necessary to underline the fact that the above subject is of an ever growing importance for the future of this area, which, by its sheer geographical extension and demographic weight, is undeniably destined to exert a considerable impact on the rest of the world. That is why the different manifestations of regionalism are of crucial importance for post-communist Russia.

DEFINING REGIONALISM

The first problem discussed in this chapter is related to the very notion of region. What indeed is the region and how ought it to be conceptualized? All debates on regionalism should primarily be based on comprehending the region as a complex and very controversial phenomenon. It seems obvious that there is no universal definition of region. In fact, this is one of the most elusive and vague notions in modern political science. To illustrate this point let us dwell upon different – and sometimes mutually exclusive – interpretations of region.

Region is frequently used in foreign policy connotation. Thus, in the American political parlance, 'regional problem' touches a whole geopolitical area – for example, such as Northern Africa or South-East Asia. There is also a philosophical interpretation. For Braudel in the Mediterranean, 'region' might be an analogy of the 'world' of a peculiar mentality. There are also historical viewpoints. In the Middle

Ages, 'region' roughly corresponded to diocese. For example, in Latin America the macroregions had been formed on the basis of viceroyalty or one or two audiences; these were generally the areas that became nation–states after the Wars for Independence. The microlevel usually corresponded to a parish, municipality or an urban *barrio* (Mörner 1993: 7).

There are scores of geographical definitions. Several quotes will suffice to illustrate: 'Regions are those areas that show within their boundaries essential uniformity in dominant physical conditions and consequently in dominant life responses'; 'Region is a complex of land, air, plant, animal and man regarded in their special relationship as together constituted a definite, characteristic portion of the Earth's surface' (Markusen 1987: 251).

There have been some attempts to synthesize different approaches. Ann Markusen proposed the following definition: 'A region is an historically evolved, contiguous territorial society that possesses a physical environment, a socioeconomic, political, and cultural milieu, and a spatial structure distinct from other regions and from the other major territorial units, city and nation' (ibid: 17).

This brief survey shows the futility of any efforts to find a definition suitable for everybody. According to Christopher Harvie, 'ambiguity of the term means that it straddles several schools of interpretation, without integrating them' (Harvie 1994: 5). Perhaps we should agree with Walter Isard who formulated his attitude in the following way: the region disappears when we engage in pure spatial theorizing, only to reappear as a concept to be tolerated in order to validate our doctrines. To put it in other words, only 'the region is defined by the research problem' (Isserman 1993: 5–6). Despite a certain simplification, this 'relativist' (or functionalist) approach might be applicable to our study. Moreover, in the political practice of most developed countries 'region' is not defined in precise terms to allow more flexibility and accommodate more diversity in practical regional policy issues.

Provided that the definition of region depends on the matter of the problem under consideration, we ought to distinguish between two dimensions of the word 'regionalism'. First, it could be used to depict a way of associating adjacent and neighbouring territories due to economic, cultural, political or defence concerns. For Karl Deutsch, a 'region is a set of countries that are more markedly interdependent over a wider range of different dimensions ... than they are with other countries' (Deutsch 1981: 3). Thus, regionalism in this sense might be equated with regional integration.

Second, there are patterns of dissociative regionalism. This understanding of the notion usually is mentioned in combination or in conjunction with other terms such as 'decentralization', 'regional autonomy', 'localism', 'territorial identity', and so on. Under the dissociative version of regionalism one of the critical problems is that of accommodation: internal diversity, be it economic, political or ethno-religious in character, can weaken liberal democracy. This is certainly the case when local interest groups and national minorities set their sights on greater independence.

Both types of regionalism exist in a very competitive and highly conflictual domain of Russian politics. These issues as a rule are subjects of collisions and clashes between different factions of political elites. Let us scrutinize now how these two dimensions of regionalism reveal themselves in the political life of the Russian Federation.

ASSOCIATIVE REGIONALISM: USSR–CIS – WHAT NEXT?

The trend towards regional integration in the post-Soviet area is a reflection of the world-wide tendency of creating supranational political institutions whose prerogatives exceed those of nation–states. It is known that Western liberalist thinking calls for reliance on the widening role of intergovernmental institutions as channels for cooperation and on creating and managing a workable and peaceable secure world. This strategy is based on the emergence of common interests and the growing role of interdependence in the world. In Russia, however, regional integration represents an intrinsically heterogeneous trend consisting of quite different visions of future political, economic and security arrangements surrounding Russia.

There are a great number of attitudes to the prospect of reintegration of the post-Soviet geopolitical area. They can be divided into several categories. Let us start with the right flank of the political spectrum. Russian liberals as represented, for example, by the Democratic Choice of Russia party are often accused of rejecting the very sense of integration and propagating the idea of Russian economic self-sufficiency. Such a criticism was partly justified since the party leader Yegor Gaidar had left the government in early 1994 under the formal pretext of his disagreement with the plans to foster closer economic cooperation with Byelorussia. He feared that taking on too serious commitments would be burdensome for the weakened Russian economy. Boris Fiodorov, the former Minister of Finance, also shared similar views. However, later the liberals were forced to rethink their initial positions. From 1995 Yegor Gaidar has advocated a more balanced approach. He came to recognize that the demise of the USSR has turned out to be a big economic problem. Consequently, economic integration with ex-Soviet republics is seen by him as one of Russia's vital interests. According to Gaidar's view, integration should be pushed forward by fast economic growth and further liberalization: 'what the European Union has been doing for forty years, Russia could realize for three to four years, provided that our own market reforms do not fail' (Gaidar 1995a: 18). On another occasion he repeated: 'Europe could not be united by tanks, it was the viable market that fulfilled that task. Similarly, former USSR nations could be united on the basis of strong rouble' (Gaidar 1995b: 43).

Alexey Uliukaev, another leading figure among liberal intellectuals, stated that integration should be seen as a result of the

> gradual erecting of the civil society and common socio-economic, judicial and cultural environment. First we need a free trade area, a customs union, unification of legislation, economic restructuring and democratic changes. Afterwards one can expect to have double and multilateral citizenship, creation of the common market for goods, capitals and services, fostering

economic union, a common security area and common international political initiatives.

(Uliukaev 1995: 43)

Liberals, as we see, perceive integration closely linked to economic liberalization and the development of effective institutions of civil society.

The second group of politicians who have publicly announced their stand with regard to reintegration are those representing the left-centre, namely, socialists and social democrats. The leader of the Yabloko Party, Grigory Yavlinsky, for quite a long time had been considered a defender of economic integration since he had been working with Mikhail Gorbachev on the Union Treaty until 1991. Yavlinsky never questioned his pro-integration position, but starting from 1995 within the Yabloko leadership other voices were raised. When the Treaty on fostering cooperation between Russia and Byelorussia was about to be signed, Yavlinsky hinted that there was no clear profit for Russia in precipitating this process since economic reforms in Byelorussia were moving slower than in Russia. Later Yavlinsky's team labelled the regime of Byelorussian President Alexander Lukashenko authoritarian and overtly anti-democratic. This shift in Yabloko views could be partly explained by purely political considerations: on the eve of the June 1996 presidential elections Yavlinsky played the role of the chief democratic opponent of Boris Yeltsin, the task which predetermined his scepticism with regard to Yeltsin's policy.

Another political stream within the left-centre is represented by several pro-socialist parties. The prospects of reintegration are better articulated in the platform of the Socialist People's Party established in early 1996 by Martin Shakuum. Socialists realistically recognize that no common economic 'space' within CIS countries exists, for the present. Conclusion of the Treaty on Cooperation between Russia and Byelorussia is seen as a step towards fostering economic integration. As one of the presidential contenders in the 1996 elections, Martin Shakuum sharply criticized some of the liberals' assumptions.

> Our liberal reformers postulated that they can create an effective economy and a viable statehood on the territory of Russian Federation which is but a stump artificially separated from the Soviet Union. In the meantime they did not take into account dense economic, political and human contacts within the post-Soviet area.

Accordingly, the prospect of erecting a 'national market' limited by the scope of the 'national state' is treated as unfeasible.

Left-centrists usually refute the argument that the state of the Byelorussian economy is inferior to the Russian one. Minsk seems to be a reliable partner for them. They think, however, that the prospects of the post-Soviet regional arrangements will basically be dependent on what the Russian scale of priorities will look like since for reintegration to be a success, Moscow must assume the functions of the leader promoting and fuelling the whole enterprise.

Let us turn now to the government elite. Sometimes it is compared with the Eurobureaucrats who sympathize with strong supranational bureaucratic institutions. The Russian 'party of power', however, is in no way monolithic and consists of several factions. First, there is a 'raw materials lobby', or a 'comprador elite', as it is sometimes called by the leftists. They are interested in a pattern of economic openness which could assist them to increase the oil and gas exports. Hence, the alliance with Byelorussia and some other neighbouring republics is seen through the prism of eventually obtaining privileged tariffs on gas and oil export to Western Europe via ex-Soviet republics.

Second, the so-called 'industrial lobby' advocates the necessity of fostering the mechanisms of integration in order to restore cooperation with ex-USSR nations, to stop the industrial decay and return Russian goods to the markets of the CIS countries. Industrialists deny the applicability of purely monetarist tools to stabilize the Russian economy and rely heavily on governmental protectionism which is to help them in the foreseeable future to secure their presence in the markets of CIS countries (*Politicheskiy Protsess* 1995: 36). The combination of these two competing and simultaneously complementary versions of reintegration greatly influenced the decision of Boris Yeltsin to start moving towards closer union with Byelorussia in spring 1996.

On the opposite flank we may find two quite different interpretations of the future of regional integration in the territory of former Soviet Union. The ultra-nationalist Liberal Democratic Party of Russia (LDPR) is obsessed with the idea of rebuilding the Russian Empire by means of absorbing the post-Soviet states and subsequently granting them the same status as territorial units constituting Russia. This is how Vladimir Zhirinovsky, LDPR leader, explains his standpoint:

> Why do we need the CIS? We keep it at our cost. Everything is done at our expense. We should help nobody. We are merely squandering our riches. Our state is Russia. We do not need either the USSR or the CIS. Those who would like to join us voluntarily, could be accepted as parts of indivisible Russia.
>
> (*Politicheskiy doklad na VII sjezde LDPR* 1996: 8)

The Communist Party of the Russian Federation (CPRF) claims to be the leading political force seeking to restore the unity of the country abrogated in 1991. However, there are certain contradictions in the CPRF stand with regard to reintegration. Thus, on the one hand, they repeatedly stress that Boris Yeltsin has started *rapprochement* with Byelorussia under communist pressure. On the other hand, the communist press sharply criticizes the President and the government for torpedoing the alliance with the former USSR republics. It remains unclear whether communists strive to restore the Soviet model of statehood or are ready to applaud a purely economic alliance.

These are the basic political platforms reflecting different attitudes to the future of post-Soviet reunification. Now let us examine the practical course of events. Starting in 1994, Russia had chosen two 'vectors' of reintegration. First, it initiated the process of assembling the slavic nations who shared similar cultural, religious and ethnic features. The 1996 Treaty on cooperation with Byelorussia could be viewed as the first step in this direction, thus challenging Ukraine to make her own long-term choice. Second, Russia, rightly enough, did not wish to confine her commitments purely to the slavic environment. Being a multi-ethnic country, Russia cannot distance herself from the neighbouring Asian nations, since they are of significant economic interest and could threaten domestic stability within non-Russian ethnic regions. Initial stages of integration with Kazakhstan and Kirghizstan were undertaken in spring 1996 and demonstrate that Moscow is ready to be cooperative and accommodating with the Islamic world. One should bear in mind that the ex-Soviet states of Central Asia could hardly be separated from each other by means of fixed and clearly delineated borders. That is why Russia's *rapprochement* with the two 'K's might involve also Tajikistan and Uzbekistan in the process of erecting common economic structures. In fact, a rather flexible Russian-led scheme of regional integration with different options and different speeds has appeared: one is free to choose between the CIS, the Treaty of Four on Customs Union and the Russian-Byelorussian model of cooperation.

To a certain degree, fixing the 'special relations' with Bielorussia and, to a lesser extent, with the two Central Asian republics, Kazakhstan and Kirghisztan, in early 1996 was due to the inadequate 'softness' of the CIS structures as established in 1991. Existence of national currencies, the widespread practice of blocking Russian TV programmes in some CIS countries, fortification of national borders and customs, striking gaps in economic legislation, growing orientation of post-Soviet republics towards economic cooperation with foreign countries – all these factors led to Russian dissatisfaction with the possibilities of the CIS. Almost all CIS members were attempting to treat the very nature and spirit of cooperation quite differently, depending on changing political circumstances. As Viacheslav Nikonov, President of 'Politika' Foundation explains, that was the Russian reason for choosing the way of deepening integration with concrete governments ready to undertake necessary political measures (*Rossiyskaya Gazeta*, 6–12 April 1996).

Byelorussia became Russia's special partner not by mere chance. Its independence in 1991 was rather the result of general political conjuncture than of struggle with the Union centre. No broad political movement towards independence was characteristic of Byelorussia in early 1990s. On the contrary, the referendum of May 1995 signalled that about 75 per cent of its population was in favour of closer contacts with Russia. What is more, Byelorussia was the only ex-Soviet country where nationalists exemplified by the People's Front never gained political power. In economic terms, Byelorussia among all the former USSR republics is one of closest linked to Russia.

What are the basic Russian incentives to get involved further in the integrative process? First, there are economic considerations. Among the major advantages for Russia in allying itself more closely with countries like Byelorussia are:

- minimization of the rent to be paid for stationing Russian troops in the 'Near Abroad'. This is true with regard to Armenia, Georgia and Azerbaijan as well.

- the much needed possibility of controlling transit tariffs. There are some signs that Russian capital is interested in penetrating, for example, Byelorussian oil refineries in Mozyr and Novopolotsk. These installations are relatively well equipped and located close to the western border, the fact that facilitates oil supply to Europe.

- to aid economic recovery, Russian manufacturers need to regain the consumers in the former Soviet republics since most Russian production is not yet competitive enough to conquer the Western markets. By the same token, it could be supposed that the former Russian banking and commercial companies might take over weaker firms from Byelorussia or elsewhere. In this sense we can assume that the Russian-Byelorussian confederation might become the incarnation of the financial and industrial interests of the major lobbying groups who have put their stakes on the Yeltsin–Lukashenko integration plans.

- Also important is access to the mineral resources which lie outside Russia (deposits of non-ferrous metals). This is the case with the Caspian Sea and Kazakhstan oil. Apart from these reasons, some very important communication networks connecting Russia with abroad go through the 'Near Abroad': sea ports, railroads, highways, etc., for example, the Yamal–Western Europe gas pipe goes through Byelorussia.

Second, of no less importance, are the geopolitical reasons. As Sergey Karaganov, member of the Presidential Council, put it, after having signed the Treaty with Minsk, Russia is able to solve three tasks simultaneously: first, to secure direct access to Europe; second, to facilitate her presence in Kaliningrad; and third, to prevent Ukraine from becoming a buffer state with anti-Russian inclinations (*Vek*, 14, April 1996).

To restore her status and prestige as a great power, Russia is seeking to exert more influence on her neighbouring countries. Not by chance does the 1996 Treaty with Byelorussia stipulate the coordination of foreign policies, interaction in the security domain and elaboration of common approaches in military policy. That could mean that Russia might avoid building a new defence system on its Western borders (Smolensk and Briansk *oblasts*) and keep under her control a number of strategically important radar stations.

Military stations in Kazakhstan are also important for Russian security since Russia on her own is unable to erect powerful defence structures. Moreover, integration with neighbouring countries will remove Russian external borders and simultaneously provide better communication with most important European and Asian countries, including India, China and others.

Third, there are clear political circumstances linked, however, to the economic integration. President Alexander Lukashenko of Byelorussia is a very comfortable partner for Russia to deal with. He did not support the 'Trilateral Accord' to dismantle the Soviet Union in late 1991, and after being elected, the President declared that *rapprochement* with Russia will be top priority for his government. He promised to 'rectify the historical mistake of 1991'. The authoritarian style of

Lukashenko's leadership, as well as that of Nursultan Nazarbaev, suits Russia since there are no other viable actors in Minsk and Almaty to be negotiated.

However, some very significant problems arise in the domain of Russia's integration with her regional partners. First, the Commonwealth countries are very different in terms of their economic development. It will almost inevitably force Russia to subsidize other areas (for example, underdeveloped Southern Kazakhstan). Agreements signed in April 1996 mention the creation of the so-called structural funds for that purpose. It is foreseeable that such kinds of arrangements could hardly be acceptable to both Russian public opinion and the budget. Estimates show that CIS countries owe Russia about $US 9 milliards. This debt could be written off in the case of further integration.

Integration with Byelorussia has also met some criticisms from the 'strongest' Russian regions. It is indicative of these resentments that, for example, Nizhny Novgorod governor Boris Nemtsov was the first regional leader of the Russian Federation to criticize Moscow's support for Alexander Lukashenko's regime in November 1996. According to Nemtsov, closer union with Byelorussia is too costly for the Russian federal budget and might deprive Russian regions of access to federal monies. He said that the only way Byelorussia could be integrated would be on the condition that no special privileges were granted to this republic in terms of customs service, regulations of trade and commerce, banking and financing, as well as political indulgence compared with the other Russian provinces. Nemtsov's *démarche* was the first sign of growing preoccupations within Russian regional elites with regard to draining Russian finances to deepen the CIS integration.

Second, erection of a workable free trade area could be hindered by the inconvertibility of local currencies. It precludes the CIS member states from genuine labour division even within the framework of the 'Alliance of Four' since barter or semi-barter deals still prevail. Russia mostly provides energy products, while receiving from other countries grain, food, cotton, etc. In January 1997 Boris Yeltsin signed a decree that fosters the creation of the so-called 'Payment Union' within the CIS. It is aimed at the settlement of the procedure of mutual accounts between Russia and Ukraine, Byelorussia and Kazakhstan (*Rossiyskaya Gazeta*, 10 January 1997).

Third, even more troubles are to be expected with the mechanism of the customs union. Obviously, it requires unification of tariff rates, but that can be reached only by means of hurting somebody's interests. For example, Bielorussia, where the local automobile industry is minor in comparison to Russia, gains no profit from establishing strict customs barriers for foreign cars imported to its territory, meanwhile Moscow will keep insisting on such protectionist measures.

Fourth, there are political circumstances that might question *rapprochement* with some post-Soviet regimes, at least in the public mind. This is for instance the case of Byelorussia whose President Alexander Lukashenko starting in autumn 1996 took a confrontational and authoritarian stand in solving institutional conflict with his parliament. Since Lukashenko's unwillingness to comply with democratic procedures became obvious, some Russian liberals have declared that integration with

Byelorussia is dangerous for Russian interests. The same attitudes apply to Georgia whose leadership advanced claims to receive a share in the division of the Black Sea Fleet.

Of special importance is Ukraine. This country is nowadays the third largest recipient of American foreign aid after Israel and Egypt, the fact that demonstrates that the United States is ready to engage in the struggle for future Ukrainian foreign policy orientation. It is obvious by the same token that the countries of Western Europe will continue to be reluctant to recognize Ukraine coming closer to the Russian economic interests. Olexander Potekhin, Director of the Ukrainian Centre for Peace, Conversion and Conflict Resolution Studies, distinguishes four basic options for his country in terms of its foreign economic perspectives: (a) the 'Finnish' model of pro-Western orientation with political and economic stability but military neutrality; (b) a Ukraine increasingly re-orienting its economy towards Russia; (c) a Ukraine whose eastern areas have joined Russia and whose western areas are independent; (d) deep political and economic reintegration with Russia (Potekhin 1996: 187–188). Another expert on Ukraine, Alexander Motyl, forecasts that his country will follow the 'Austrian' model of economic and political development (Motyl 1993: 193–194).

In general, we can assume that the most likely scenario for the post-Soviet states in the next five years is a Russian-led association based on a variety of bilateral and multilateral ties, including separate loose alliances between Russia and some of the other CIS members. Some countries, like Ukraine, will insistently strive to reduce their dependence on Russia in terms of oil and gas supply. This strategy will require diversification of their foreign economic contacts. Other CIS countries will keep counting on Russia in the domain of security, looking for protection against outbursts of violence in neighbouring areas (this is the case of the Central Asian governments of Uzbekistan, Tajikistan, Kyrgyzstan and Turkmenistan). A great deal of flexibility will be needed on the Russian side in relations with countries like Georgia, Moldova and Azerbaijan whose leaders will make a condition of their membership of CIS structures on Russian recognition of their territorial integrity.

ECONOMIC ASPECTS OF REGIONALISM

During the Soviet period, all fifteen republics were integrated into one economy and one planning system. The union was treated as one country by the central planners in Moscow and central planning fostered a high level of economic integration under Russian dominance. Just before the dissolution of the Soviet Union trade between the republics was composed of a high share of each republic's output, between 40 and 70 per cent of net material product (NMP). Only Kazakhstan had a low trade ratio. Many republics depended on Russia for their energy supplies and in return provided Russia with light industry and agricultural products. But there was also a net flow of goods and subsidies to the socialist periphery which asphyxiated the Soviet economy. Therefore, well before the Soviet Union collapsed in 1991, inter-state trade with its system of distorted relative prices, mostly in the form of low energy prices, was already in a process of revision.

After the formal dissolution of the union in 1991 and the liberalization of prices in the Russian Federation inter-state trade collapsed (see Table 4.1). Moreover, Russia and the other CIS states suffered sharp declines in production and high inflation rates. The negative consequences of the disintegration of the Soviet Union were reinforced by the Russian big-bang price liberalization of January 1992. Industrial production declined by about 40 per cent. All Russia's neighbours experienced an economic crisis that was influenced by the separation from Russia.

Table 4.1 International and inter-republic trade, 1990–93 ($US millions)

		1991		1993	
	Republic	Exports	Imports	Exports	Imports
	Russia	80,900	82,900	43,900	33,100
	Ukraine	13,390	15,907	6,300	4,700
	Kazakhstan	1,777	3,250	1,529	1,269
	Belarus	3,438	5,256	737	777
	Uzbekistan	1,390	2,217	1,466	1,280
	Azerbaijan	725	1,413	351	241
	Georgia	515	1,543	222	460
	Lithuania	679	1,543	696	486
International Trade	Moldovia	405	1,432	174	210
	Latvia	304	1,642	460	339
	Armenia	109	855	29	188
	Kyrgyz Republic	89	1,298	112	112
	Tajikistan	609	655	263	374
	Turkmenistan	195	523	1,156	749
	Estonia	198	592	461	618
	Russia	146,185	95,802	55,355	34,109
	Ukraine	60,348	71,841	17,628	35,294
	Kazakhstan	13,993	24,810	7,863	11,788
	Belarus	27,660	28,740	12,144	13,739
	Uzbekistan	11,327	18,818	4,100	5,243
	Azerbaijan	8,213	7,300	1,555	1,526
Inter-republic trade	Georgia	5,168	7,608	573	1,321
(at explicit exchange	Lithuania	7,213	12,082	1,548	1,852
rates)	Moldovia	4,984	8,442	1,203	2,417
	Latvia	6,516	8,302	978	1,082
	Armenia	3,509	5,477	583	999
	Kyrgyz Republic	3,250	5,120	814	1,175
	Tajikistan	2,760	5,375	292	611
	Turkmenistan	4,603	4,042	2,734	2,717
	Estonia	3,289	5,257	568	543

Source: Bosworth and Ofer 1995: (116–117).

Inflation in Russia only started to decrease in 1994. Ukraine and Belarus, who had postponed serious economic reforms, registered low declines in output during the first year of independence, but later on inflation rates soared. Trade between the former Soviet states and with the rest of the world declined dramatically. Russia reduced its energy exports to the other former socialist countries and former Soviet states in combination with rising energy prices in order to stabilize its balance of payments and its own energy household. Turkmenistan, which had only started exploiting its vast gas fields, managed to increase its exports and imports but the other Central Asian countries faced severe economic decline, which reflected the problems they had when integrating their economies into the global economy.

Despite the formal dissolution of the Soviet Union, the former empire continued to exist in the form of a monetary union based on the Russian rouble. All the newly established states in Central Asia stayed within the rouble area. The consequence was rampant inflation in the rouble countries because of the chaotic economic environment and the inflationary pressures and monetary overhang. In the middle of 1992 Russia decided to protect itself against the importation of higher inflation from the periphery, and to control its subsidization of the other CIS states. The most important action was to limit the issue of rouble credits by other republics to finance their imports from Russia. Special correspondence accounts were established between the central banks obliging them to exert tight credit control. Rouble creation was limited, but the result of this monetarist intervention was the appearance of various types of non-convertible parallel currencies ('coupons'), which suffered from even higher inflation rates than the Russian rouble. None the less, the Russian rouble continued to play the role of the main medium of trade.

The CIS countries had to develop the institutional and service structures required for foreign trade. Therefore they needed to change the composition of production. In reality, the states of the former Soviet Union are struggling to create, almost 'from scratch', the regulatory structures required by their infant market economies and the introduction of an externally convertible currency. In Russia and the other former Soviet republics the initial decline in domestic trade inflicted great damage on the level of production, more than that caused by the collapse of inter-state Council for Mutual Economic Assistance (CMEA) trade, because they were ill prepared for independence. Radical economic reforms without coordination at the CIS level hampered economic recovery. Gradual withdrawal from state trade and liberalization of retail trade ensured that local monopolies lost power, but in general their decline was slowed by governments, and mafioso organizations controlling retail shops and restaurants appeared in the cities. Initially, internal trade liberalization boosted 'kiosk' trade in the Russian cities, but since then spacious stores and wholesale markets have developed. In combination with this free retail trade local governments have created better opportunities for local businessmen but they also frustrated the creation of a national market by imposing taxation on economic activities and intra-state trade and they negotiated deals with the central government in Moscow concerning export rights and imports. Moreover, they enacted their own laws and imposed their own local taxes. As a result of all these interventions markets became fragmented and internal trade declined (see Table 4.1). Declining trade among the CIS republics caused serious damage to the former Soviet economies. Before the collapse of communism in 1991 inter-state trade with Ukraine and Kazakhstan represented about one-third of NMP. Russian trade with the other republics was rather low (18 per cent) but the smaller republics were almost entirely dependent on their trade with the Russian economy. Of all the former Soviet republics, Russia was the largest importer of food and industrial products. Russia continues to have the largest internal market. Observers think that with western expertise and financial help Russia will be able to develop its own industries in order to meet the demands of its population for consumer products because the country depends to a lesser extent on global trade. Its large energy and raw materials reserves can help finance necessary imports once the modernization of these sectors has been brought about.

Ukraine, the second largest state of the Soviet Union, has a large Russian minority. After the demise of Leonid Kravchuk, the newly elected president Leonid Kuchma in 1994 initiated closer political and economic relations with Russia. Kuchma negotiated an International Monetary Fund (IMF) loan promising the implementation of economic reforms. Although Ukraine's economy is rather similar to the Russian economy, but compared with Russia, Ukraine lacks significant energy resources and its industry is rather old-fashioned, its export capacity to the West is limited. The other Slavic republic Byelorussia is as over-industrialized as Ukraine, but poorer in agrarian and energy resources, but it used to produce a wide range of food and consumer goods based on inputs imported from Russia and the other former Soviet republics. Belarus was the 'assembly line' of Russia. Of all the other Soviet republics it depended on Soviet trade the most. Byelorussia was reluctant to declare independence and in 1994 the newly elected President Alexander Lukashenko started his campaign for the reunification of Byelorussia with Russia. Byelorussia's foreign policy was largely influenced by its dependency on Russian energy imports. The Russian Federation is Byelorussia's main export market for its agricultural and industrial products. In 1997 a federation treaty with Russia was ratified satisfying the overwhelmingly Russian-speaking population of Byelorussia. Some liberal intellectuals proposed the idea of a loose economic federation with the Baltic states or membership of the Visegrad Group (Poland, Hungary, Slovakia, and the Czech Republic). Neither proposal met any sympathy from the Byelorussian population.

When Russia imposed tough conditions on any CIS state staying in the rouble zone, these CIS states had to give up their independent monetary policy and to join Russia's economic liberalization policy together with a variety of Russian controls. Only Tajikistan accepted these harsh conditions. The others CIS members left the rouble zone. In most cases the other currencies were allowed to fluctuate in relation to the rouble. Today, all the former Soviet states still carry the heavy heritage of a long functional isolation from the world markets, a structural distortion of prices and backward technology. Most of the states are highly industrialized but integration into the world economy will be very painful. It will need a reorientation of the economy from the production of heavy machinery and metalworking to light industries.

THE RUSSIAN MODEL OF DISSOCIATIVE REGIONALISM

Now we turn to another dimension of the regionalist problematic, namely, the process of Russia's internal decentralization and devolution of powers to her subnational units. The problem of regional dissociation sprung up in the final period of the existence of the USSR. In 1990 Mikhail Gorbachev recognized that 'many options are available for the country: confederation, associate relations, etc. The Union is so heterogeneous that we must apply different tools to keep it: some of its constituent parts will be held by collar, some others – by short lead, the rest – by long rein, etc.' (*Soyuz mozhno bylo* 1995: 95). A number of different and not always well balanced proposals had been advanced at that time. There is evidence that certain Politburo members discussed the plans for splitting up the Russian Soviet Federative Republic into six or seven large regions and equating their judicial status with that of one of the other fourteen Soviet republics (ibid.: 139). But the idea of decentralization was in vogue basically among the first-wave democrats: one of their first leaders, Gavriil Popov, was known as an advocate of the division of USSR into about forty independent states. Even Boris Yeltsin initially considered the variant of creating seven Russian states instead of one. Later he recognized that such a view was a serious mistake.

The period 1990–91 was one of the most complicated and controversial in terms of regional decentralization. In fact, two main options were debated. The first was confined to the destruction of the old Union, and stipulated that the independent republics would voluntarily form a new kind of association. The second scheme was based not on dismantling the structures of the Union but on their reforming and renovating. That was the stance of Gorbachev and, to a certain degree, of the Kazakh leader Nursultan Nazarbaev. They thought that sovereignty and self-government did not contradict the principles of 'New Federalism'.

The implementation of the first option has been further complicated by the position taken by some republics within the Russian Federation. Thus, Tatarstan insisted on joining the new Union Treaty as its signatory, as opposed to being merely a part of the Russian Federation. Due to such claims the Treaty on the Union of Sovereign States drafted in July 1991 stipulated that 'the constituent states form the Union directly or as parts of other states'. Such an ambiguity predetermined the weakness of that document which had never been adopted.

In October 1991, after the aborted coup, another attempt to reconstruct the Union was undertaken. This time the new federal structure was proposed under the label of the Union of Free Sovereign States but this initiative began to give clear signs of strain very quickly. Some governments advanced unacceptable conditions, for example, Azerbaijan's President Ayaz Mutalibov agreed to sign the document only if the new Union would provide him with 'sufficient forces to contain the aggression of Armenia'.

Later the new name was invented, the Union of Sovereign States. Gorbachev understood quite well that the Russian Federation would play the decisive role in its ratification. The Soviet President argued that such a Union is of crucial importance for Russia if she wants to keep her influence, since direct leadership could be unacceptable to Russia's neighbours.

The pivotal problem that undermined the new Union was its internal structure. Yeltsin, Nazarbaev and the Byelorussian leader Shushkevich insisted on confederation while Gorbachev was ready to accept only federation. Discussions on that issue put an end to the prospects of integration. On 7–8 December 1991 the leaders of Russia, Ukraine and Byelorussia signed the treaty which in fact abolished the Soviet Union.

The last attempt by Gorbachev to prevent the disintegration was his appeal of 18 December 1991 to speed up the process of creating a new union which this time was proposed to be named the Commonwealth of European and Asian States. However, the leaders of four already independent republics – Russia, Ukraine, Byelorussia and Kazakhstan – decided to sign a four-sided treaty without waiting for the reform of the USSR.

Confusion and the rapidity of regional self-assertion and self-identification raised a great number of questions with regard to the future of domestic regionalization in Russia herself. The basic points of discussion were: should the process of decentralization which has killed the Soviet Union be supported within the Russian Federation? Could liberalization be achieved in such an intrinsically varied and multi-ethnic society as Russia? Could the liberal reforms be implemented on the regional level, or are the initiatives from the Centre indispensable?

The adherents of classical Western-style liberalism, represented by Yegor Gaidar's party, The Democratic Choice of Russia, defended the conception of fully fledged federalism, first of all in terms of strictly defining the financial rights and responsibilities of the regions. Liberals believe that the well-being of the regions ought to be dependent basically on how the market reforms are promoted by their regional political elites. Gaidar's colleagues are convinced that all cases of separatism stem from the ineffective economic strategy of the central government. The liberals themselves often compare their parliamentary voting behaviour on regional issues with the European right.

The Party of Russian Unity and Consent (PRES) led by Sergey Shakhray is treated as the 'party of regions'. It favoured the federalization of the country based on the traditions of regional aggregation and self-assertion. Starting in the Constitutional Assembly of 1993, Shakhray advocated the devolution of powers to regions on a step-by-step basis provided that the territorial integrity of the federation should not be questioned. Close to them was the Civic Union (a by-product of the Scientific and Industrial Union) chaired by Arkady Volsky. Gravitation towards analogous attitudes was strong among some parliamentary factions such as 'New Regional Policy', 'Stability', 'Russia', 'New Names', etc. It is true that often they have been accused of relying too strongly on purely bureaucratic instruments for the implementation of their ideas and of being in too close an alliance with the government.

The Democratic Party of Russia (former leader, Nicolay Travkin) have contributed to the practice of regionalism by proposing that political rights should be given not to the subjects of the Federation, but to the local authorities. Comparable, but slightly more radical, positions were shared by the Russian Movement for Democratic Reforms. The tiny 'Dignity and Mercy' party insisted on special attention being paid to those regions which have suffered from natural catastrophes, serious technological accidents, and so on.

The Yabloko party, led by Grigory Yavlinsky, was and still is in favour of dismantling all inter-regional trade barriers, making more transparent the allocation of subventions to certain regions by the parliament, thus avoiding 'special privileges' to regions on an individual basis. In future the 'Yabloko' legislators would prefer to see Russia composed of several large-scale regions ('lands') with common historical roots and significant potential for becoming powerful and autonomous economic actors. All these 'lands' should be provided with absolutely equal status since the bulk of the ethnocratic elites' claims addressed to the federal centre are illegitimate, according to Yavlinsky's aid Viktor Sheinis. This position is also shared by a significant number of other political and economic actors, among them 'The Business Roundtable of Russia' and the 'Reforms – New Course' movement led by Vladimir Shumeiko.

The ideas developed by other parties are quite different and stand in sharp contrast to those expressed by the democratic camp. The Liberal Democratic Party of Russia is overtly against federalism, moreover, in its asymmetric version. Its slogan is 'Russia United and Indivisible'. LDPR leader Vladimir Zhirinovsky propagates the idea of the liquidation of national or ethnic republics (such as Tatarstan or Chechnia) and introducing pre-Revolutionary *gubernii*, based on the purely territorial principle of Russian regional structure (*Politicheskiy doklad* 1996). Nationalists claim that no reform in Russian history was ever generated on the regional level. They say that currently federalism has given certain advantages only to the regional barons. Communists and their allies from the Agrarian Party do not have clear ideas about regionalism and federalism. In public they prefer to avoid discussing this burning issue but in fact they aim to restore the old communist system with the hegemony of one party which rules out even the slightest possibility of regional autonomy.

If we turn to the practical course of events, some very important questions arise. First, there is a growing suspicion in society that the only beneficiaries of the new model of 'market' federalism have been the regional elites. The very structure of regional governance in Russia is frequently depicted by political scientists in terms of 'regional authoritarianism'. It means that in the regions the local executive leaders are in a position of almost complete control over the political process. Most governors are ardent supporters of federalism in their relationship with the Centre, but at the same time are strong 'centralists' in dealing with their subordinates in local and/or municipal administrative bodies.

That kind of situation predetermines a sort of 'special relationship' between the regional chief executives (Governors or Presidents of Republics) and the Federal

President. According to the Constitution, the supreme bodies of the Russian Federation constituent entities are vested with the right of legislative initiative. However, the regions, territories and autonomies prefer to use direct bargaining tactics with the President to lobby their interests in promoting construction, social sphere, the level of supplies, etc.

It is understandable that this executive level in Russia is stronger than the legislative one and is usually perceived as more effective. There are numerous factors that hinder the activity of regional lobbyism in the parliament. First of all, lengthy parliamentary procedures require a lot of time and patience. There are also some problems with the Duma structure. On the one hand, the bulk of the work in drafting, evaluating and securing the passage of bills rests with the committees. At the same time, the principal issues of the Duma's work are tackled by the State Duma Council, where only the chairman of the Duma and the leaders of factions have the right to vote, while committee representatives' votes are merely advisory.

Next, due to usual lack of time prior to the hearings, law-makers find themselves unprepared for serious debate. But most important is the lack of established channels of interaction with public structures in the regions where the MPs come from.

Of course, not all regional dealings with the federal authorities have been success stories. For example, in 1991 the leaders of more than 150 administrative units of the Russian Federation appealed to the presidential apparatus to allow the mass creation of the so-called 'free economic zones'. Although the bulk of Russian territories have failed to implement this idea due to their economic weakness, most leaders of regional administrations involved in bargaining tactics with the President have later succeeded in shifting some important budget, fiscal and even foreign economic policy prerogatives from Moscow Kremlin into their hands.

Second, the new source of conflicts and collisions within the federation relates to the clashes of different regional interests. It is understandable that the importance of the regions depends on the level of their industrial development. That is why Moscow, St Petersburg, Yekaterinburg, Nizhny Novgorod and other huge military–industrial conglomerates are among the leaders of regional lobbyism. Yet the interests of different regions do not always coincide with each other and can be reconciled.

What are the most important types of regional lobbies in Russia? One might distinguish the agrarian lobby which very often solicits credits for individual regions (central Black Earth zone, etc.) and more protectionism (increasing government prices for agricultural products, reduced rates for credits, favourable taxation, import limitations). Agrarians defend the well-being of the poorest regions which have a significant concentration of the rural population (the Volga region, the Russian South 'Belt', etc.). They have their defenders in the Agrarian Party of Russia.

The fuel and energy complex represents, unlike the above-mentioned one, the interests of the most economically safe regions whose export of the raw materials is of great importance for the state budget (Tiumen, Yakutia, Karelia, Komi Republic, Murmansk, Magadan, and Arkhangelsk regions). They advocate increasing the export of gas and oil and obtaining privileged tariffs for that. That is why they need further liberalization and total cancellation of export taxes.

Next, the financial and commercial lobby which had been formed in the late 1980s dominated such political parties as the Economic Liberty party, the Entrepreneurial Political Initiative, the Civic Union, etc. for quite a long time. Some of them were represented in the State Duma committees. They represented such regions as Nizhny Novgorod, Samara, Yekaterinburg, Perm', Cheliabinsk, Krasnoyarsk, Tomsk, etc. In particular, the financial and commercial lobby is interested in passing legislation favourable to foreign investments. Another illustration is the automobile lobby which can act on behalf of the workers of major enterprises and the residential neighbourhoods of many cities.

Third, there is a problem of an ethno–political nature with regionalization. The acute contradictions between 'rich' and 'poor', or 'industrial' and 'agrarian' regions do not correspond to the opposition between the so-called 'national republics' and ethnically Russian territorial units. Russia has the formal institutional basis to allow different territorial identities and to accommodate different regional interests, sometimes with an ethnic or religious background. But here, however, lies a sharp contradiction: certain manifestations of ethno-cultural regionalism are hardly compatible with the emerging structures of the civil society. More concretely, constitutionalism is built upon the principle of equality (in terms of rights, opportunities, patterns of representation, division of tasks inside that institution), while territorial phenomena are always based on the spirit of inequality. Indeed, every region, every community with a specific composition of its ethnic population is trying to emphasize its special distinguishing features in contradistinction to others (neighbouring regions, adjacent territories, etc.). In this sense, everything that happened in Chechnya turned out to be a strong blow against the mass perception of federalist ideas in Russia. To some extent, all patterns of decentralized authority unfortunately are being perceived by many Russians as leading to elitism, separatism and nationalism.

Still under Gorbachev, the pioneers of 'sovereignization' (Tatarstan, Yakutia, Checheno-Ingushetia) passed their first Declarations of Sovereignty. Availing themselves of the weakness of the federal Centre, they in fact discontinued their payments to the central budget. Consequently, the burden of federal taxes was shared mostly by the most ethnically advanced Russian regions. Some of them (for example, Vologda and Sverdlovsk regions) reacted by announcing their intention to declare themselves 'republics' in order to elevate their formal status within the framework of the federation.

Tensions were exacerbated by the political leaders of some 'domestic' republics (Kalmykia, Dagestan, Chechnya) who started advancing territorial claims to neighbouring regions. The territorial dispute between Northern Ossetia and the Ingush Republic provoked local armed conflict. All this explains the acuteness of tensions between different groupings of Russian regions. Spontaneity and the rapidity of market liberalization have created multiple problems for the process of regional identification in Russia and have led to instability in the regional set-up. Against the weakening background of the federal centre, regional elites are becoming more actively involved in federal affairs and making their economic and political demands more dynamic. The optimum balance has not yet been found, either between the federal centre and the regions, or in region-to-region relations. This process will to a significant degree be influenced by a possible regrouping of the Russian regional landscape.

MIXED FORMS OF RUSSIAN REGIONALISM

The transition to the market economy has encouraged numerous forms of regional arrangements which combine the features of its associative and dissociative models. Thus, there is a tendency to assemble economic alliances between the subjects of the Russian Federation ('Big Volga' Association, 'The Siberian Accord', the hypothetical Ural Republic and the Far Eastern Republic, etc). Yet not all of them have been success stories.

In the Far East the sentiments favourable to inter-regional cooperation were quite vocal until 1993. By that time it had become clear that Kamchatka, Magadan, Sakhalin, Khabarovsk and Vladivostok were incapable of reaching a compromise with each other. Apart from that, these are underpopulated areas unable to achieve economic self-sufficiency by avoiding strong ties with other parts of the country. The Trans-Baikal regions are also lacking common ground to form a strong economic cluster, for example, Chita *oblast* gravitates towards cooperation with southern parts of Eastern and Western Siberia, while the more dynamic Buriat republic and the Irkutsk *oblast* are eager to establish closer links with Mongolia and China. The Southern regions of Western and Eastern Siberia started to form their internal industrial market. In March 1992 the first attempt was made to create a political structure to tackle common problems, The Siberian Accord. Delegates from the Ural regions were invited to attend. However, after 1994 the Siberian cooperation had lost its initial impetus since many inter-regional contradictions have appeared (for instance, the conflict between Novosibirsk and Tomsk with regard to the tender on oil extraction). The European regions of Russia (the Black Earth zone, the Volga regions, the Russian South) are traditionally oriented to Moscow and have no strong feelings of inter-regional cooperation. The Russian North however, was, showing a trend towards mild economic insulation from Moscow, claiming to have the rights to sell the mineral resources to foreign markets without binding regulations from the Centre.

Increasing numbers of experts have voiced their dissatisfaction with the state of Russian regionalism and advanced some far-reaching proposals. Thus, according to Vladimir Pastukhov, there are at least three disadvantages in the present fragmented model of Russian regionalism. First, the bulk of regions lack material resources that would prevent them being subject to manipulation by the federal centre. Second, there exists tremendous economic inequality between the regions. Third, there is political inequality between the subjects of the federation, the fact that makes some of them struggle to keep their privileges, while others are forced to gain them to survive (Pastukhov 1996: 67).

As Pastukhov and numerous other experts suggest, there is a need for integration and amalgamation of the subjects of the federation. Integrated regions would really become powerful players in the Russian political and economic scene. Merging of several regions would equalize the status of all of them and make the whole system of federal governance in Russia easier. Besides, the joining of different 'small' regions into 'big ones' would lead to the redistribution of the resources inside the new subjects of the federation, yet not through the federal centre as happens nowadays, but by new regional authorities themselves. This might significantly 'unload' the federal centre.

It is interesting that starting in the autumn of 1996 another model of inter-regional cooperation appeared. It was caused not by territorial proximity and economic complementarity, but rather by the fact of being members of the so-called 'club of donors'. The most economically viable regions of the Russian Federation, namely, those who are making the biggest contributions to the federal budget, initiated the sophisticated pressure campaign on the central authorities. In November 1996 their leaders made clear moves to fix their special status in the federation. Some of these ten regions (for example, the Moscow federal district) requested special tax privileges. Others (like Nizhny Novgorod) favoured creating such conditions that would stimulate other regions to become 'donors' and start filling federal budgets.

So we see how mobile and fluid the new forms of in-Russia regional clusters are nowadays. The norms and the procedures of inter-regional cooperation are still not settled, and this inconstancy brings new elements of instability to the Russian method of liberalization.

CONCLUSIONS

Liberalization of the economic processes has provoked a 'shake-up' of the spacio-territorial foundations of Russian politics. We are witnessing a restructuring and regrouping of the Russian regions, a fact that, in combination with CIS evolution, resembles very much the post-modernist notion of 'fragmegration'.

In fact, Russia has reaffirmed the world-wide tendency of the dual and ambiguous nature of relations between liberalization and regionalization. Liberalization brings about two different processes. On the one hand, market transition and the introduction of liberal economic rules foster regional fragmentation. Gorbachev's politics of openness, 'New Thinking' and *glasnost* had eroded the foundations of the USSR and finally caused its desintegration. Simultaneously, the promotion of liberal economic policy in the Russian Federation has resulted in the necessity of regional decentralization. This trend has created deep regionalization inside the Russian Federation. On the other hand, market imperatives necessitate the search for some forms of regional aggregation. Market transition might lead to the creation of both smaller and larger territorial units with more or less defined internal political structures.

These two tendencies go hand in hand, though the first one appeared earlier and is easier to discern. Political and economic liberalization provokes very complex and sometimes overlapping patterns of regionalization. It took a short while to turn Russia to a 'country of regions'. It will take much longer to build up long-term and cohesive alliances with other interested post-Soviet republics.

Both versions of post-Soviet regionalism, depicted above, have demonstrated their advantages as well as their natural limitations. It is obvious that the aforementioned processes are aimed at 'unloading' the state and depriving it of a significant number of traditional functions that are being transmitted to the smaller and/or bigger political structures. It remains to be seen, however, how far this process is going to advance. The dependence of political regionalization on the nature and pace of liberal reforms will, however, remain strong and a long-term factor in Russian political life.

The obvious preponderance of politics over economics in both associative and dissociative models of regionalism constitutes Russia's specificity. Purely political considerations dominated at the time of the dissolution of the Soviet Union and of the growing insistence by the Russian regions on new privileges and prerogatives in trading. Sharp conflict between the President and the Supreme Soviet in 1993 was accompanied by multiple attempts to win regional elites over to both opposing sides. Again, political motivations shape the current debates over Russian relations with Byelorussia, Kazakhstan, Ukraine and other neighbouring states with some potential for integration.

BIBLIOGRAPHY

Bosworth, B.P. and Ofer, G. (1995) *Reforming Planned Economies in an Integrating World Economy*, Washington, DC: the Brookings Institution.

Deutsch, K.W. (1981) 'On nationalism: world regions and the nature of the West', in P. Torsvik (ed.) *Mobilization, Center–Periphery Structures and Nation-Building: A Volume in Commemoration of Stein Rokkan*, Bergen, Oslo and Tromsö: Universitetsforlaget.

Gaidar, Y. (1995a) *Besedy s Izbirateliamy* (Talks with voters), Moscow: Eurasia Publishers.

Gaidar, Y. (1995b) *Zapiski iz Zala* (Notes from the hall), Moscow: Eurasia Publishers.

Harvie, C. (1994) *The Rise of Regional Europe*, London and New York: Routledge.

Isserman, A.M. (1993) 'Lost in space? On the history, status and future of regional science', *The Review of Regional Studies* 23(1): 5–6.

Markusen, A. (1987) *Regions: The Economics and Politics of Territory*, Totowa, NJ: Rowman and Littlefield.

Mörner, M. (1993) *Region and State in Latin America's Past*, Baltimore, MD: Johns Hopkins University Press.

Motyl, A. (1993) *Dilemmas of Independence: Ukraine after Totalitarianism*, New York: Council on Foreign Relations Press.

Mroz, J.E. and Pavliuk, O. (1996) 'Ukraine: European linchpin', *Foreign Affairs* May/June: 52–62.

Pastukhov, V. (1996) 'Paradoxalnye zametki o sovremennom politicheskom rezhime' (Paradoxical notes on today's political regime), *Pro et Contra* 1(1): 67.

Payn, E. (1994) 'Separatism y federalism v sovremennoy Rossii' (Separatism and federalism in contemporary Russia), *Kuda idyot Rossia?* (Where is Russia heading?), Moscow: Interprax.

Politicheskiy doklad na VII sjezde LDPR (1996) (Political report at the VII LDPR Congress), Moscow.

Politicheskiy Protsess v Rossii: sovremennye tendentsii i istoricheskiy kontekst (1995) (Political process in Russia: current trends and historical context), Moscow: Centre for Comprehensive Social Studies and Marketing, Business Roundtable of Russia.

Potekhin, O. (1996) 'A Ukrainian perspective', in *Visions of European Security*, Stockholm: report from a project organized by the Olof Palme International Centre: 187–188.

Regiony Rossii v perekhodniy period (1993) (Russian regions in the period of transition), Moscow: Russian Union of Industrialists and Entrepreneurs, Expert Institute.

Rossiyskaya Gazeta, various issues as shown.

Soyuz mozhno bylo sokhranit (1995) (The Union could be preserved), (The White Book. Documents and facts about Mikhail Gorbachev's policy toward reforming and maintaining the multinational statehood), Moscow: Gorbachev Foundation.

Uliukaev, A. (1995) *Liberalism i politika perekhodnogo perioda v Rossii* (Liberalism and politics of transition in Russia), Moscow: Eurasia Publishers.

Vek, 14, April 1996.

5

PREPARING THE RUSSIAN ECONOMY FOR WORLD MARKET INTEGRATION[1]

Vladimir V. Popov

INTRODUCTION

The Russian (and the Commonwealth of Independent States, CIS) path of economic transformation, though not so much by design of the policy-makers, but rather due to the flow of events, has proved to be very different from both the shock therapy treatment adopted by most East European countries and by the Baltic states, and the gradual approach adopted by China. The former managed to achieve macro-economic stabilization (and bring down inflation) shortly after the immediate deregulation of prices, whereas the latter kept inflation under control while liberalizing prices gradually. In contrast, Russia and the other CIS states deregulated prices instantly, but failed to proceed with macro-economic stabilization. The Russian reform path may thus be described as inconsistent shock therapy, which implies that Russia tried, but has not succeeded in carrying out conventional 'big bang' policies. At the same time the economic transformation in Russia has proved to be associated with greater costs than elsewhere. The recession has been in force for seven years (1990–96) already and has caused a reduction of Gross Domestic Product (GDP) of nearly 50 per cent. Worse indicators were observed only in some Former Soviet Union (FSU) states and in countries affected by wars. In the East European countries the recession lasted for three to four years causing the reduction of output by 20 to 30 per cent, whereas in China and Vietnam reforms led to an immediate increase in output.

True, real incomes and real consumption, after plummeting in January 1992, when prices were deregulated, recovered afterwards. Though there is considerable uncertainty over the measurement problems, it appears that in 1995–96 real incomes of the Russian population were *on average* comparable with the level of the mid-1980s. However, because income inequalities increased tremendously – and much faster than in the East European countries – for the absolute majority of the Russians living standards deteriorated substantially.

Together with the rise in crime rates, the increase in mortality, the reduction of life expectancy and other unfavourable developments (which, again, were more pronounced in Russia that in other economies in transition), this caused wide-spread feelings of social discontent. According to public opinion polls, most Russians feel that they are now worse off than before the reforms. Strong support for the pro-communist and pro-nationalist candidates in the December 1995 parliamentary elections (42 per cent and 12 per cent of seats in the Duma, respectively) and in the summer 1996 presidential elections (over 40 per cent of the votes for the communist candidate in the runoff) is another indicator of the high costs of Russian transition.

Whereas the progress in creating a market-oriented economy in recent years has been indeed remarkable and, in many cases, no less substantial than in the East European countries, Russia has had to pay a greater price for economic transition. Why? The answer depends, of course, on the theory adopted. Shock therapists argue that much of the cost of Russian reforms should be attributed to the inconsistencies of the policies followed, namely, to the inability of the government and the Central Bank of Russia (CBR) to fight inflation in 1992–95. On the other hand, the supporters of gradual transition state exactly the opposite, blaming the attempt to introduce conventional shock therapy package for all the disasters and misfortunes.

Shock therapists point to the example of the East European countries and the Baltic states, most of whom managed to reduce inflation to below 50 per cent annually in the year following the liberalization of prices and are now enjoying economic recovery. Gradualists cite the example of China, arguing that the lack of recession and high growth rates is the direct result of the step-by-step approach to economic transformation.

While debates between shock therapists and gradualists continue, less attention is being paid to the actual outcome of transition. What kind of economic system is emerging out of transition? In what respects is it different from the existing and emerging market economies? What are the feasible options for the policy-makers to change unfavourable patterns of development? These relatively less discussed questions are dealt with in this chapter. To be more precise, the aim of this chapter is to examine the trends that are shaping the contours of the future Russian economic system, to speculate in what directions it is going to develop, to set out the limits of liberalization and internationalization and to discuss possible options for long-term growth. It is argued that although it may be tempting to characterize the emerging Russian (and the CIS) market structure as one that combines the features of both the European and the Asian model this is not really the case. A closer look reveals that this kind of description may be no more than a general negative statement: evolving Russian capitalism is not going to be compatible with either the European, or with East Asian patterns.

The closest analogue may probably be found in some of the commonest Latin American archetypes of the 1970s – very high wealth and income inequalities, strong social tensions and poor consensus in the society about reforms, large unreformed *latifundias* in agriculture, non-competitive sectors in industry supported by government subsidies, economically and politically weak government whose commitments are stretched beyond its financial abilities, which results in numerous cases of government failure, outbursts of inflation and capital flight, discouraging savings, investment and growth.

This is a rather pessimistic, but yet the most probable scenario based on extrapolation of the existing trends. To change this scenario into a more favourable one, non-cosmetic reforms are required: restructuring of government services (public goods and social transfers) so as to make them smaller, but efficient and financially sustainable; sound industrial policy supporting competitive export-oriented industries rather than non-competitive inward-looking industries; a strategy to promote savings and investment (maintaining low exchange rate of the rouble, reforming the pension system, increasing government investment and attracting Foreign Direct Investment (FDI) into resource projects); strong social policy which may be the only chance to build consensus under the conditions of high wealth and income inequalities. Political feasibility of such a scenario does not seem to be high, though some moves in this direction are likely.

EMERGING RUSSIAN-STYLE CAPITALISM

It seems natural, at least on the intuitive level, to believe that the East European countries and the Baltic states are heading in the direction of the market models that currently exist in Western Europe. Even more so, that they are aiming at becoming members of the European Union (EU), which requires them to harmonize their policies and institutions with those of the EU. It is also natural to assume that China and Vietnam are developing a type of market economy that is broadly consistent with the existing regional patterns: ASEAN countries and South Korea may show China and Vietnam their immediate future, while Japan could indicate a more distant future. With regards to Russia (and the CIS) the future patterns of development are less clear. Factors dealing with economic culture may prove to be crucial in shaping the contours of emerging Russian capitalism as fixed capital, human capital, traditions and stereotypes of economic behaviour are inherited by the new system from the old one and thus link the future economic development to the past. Comparisons of economic culture in Russia, other former Soviet republics, the East European countries, and China lie evidently beyond the scope of our analysis. However, it may be appropriate to mention some widely accepted conclusions about cultural differences, which emerged not only from the Soviet, but also from pre-Soviet history. Overall, Russian public opinion seems to be more polarized than in the East European countries and the Baltic states, where a wider agreement on major economic reform issues exists. Communist ideals are deeply rooted in Russian history; geographical, ethnic and economic diversity contributes to contradictions between major regional and industrial elite groups. Besides, law and order traditions seem to be relatively weak in Russian society, which results in a higher crime rate, a larger shadow economy, widespread corruption, etc. Finally, egalitarian and collectivist feelings are more pronounced in Russia – there is a less tolerant attitude towards income inequalities and a much stronger emphasis on preservation of employment in times of recession.

On the other hand, Russia does not have the same traditions of business and work ethics as the East Asian countries. Individuals' links to the community are weaker than in East Asia: Russian labour mobility, for instance, even in the Soviet era was much higher than in Japan (and even higher than in Europe), while social services provided by companies (health care, apartments, recreation, etc.), although substantial, were never as extensive as in China. Pessimists claim that the Russian tragedy is that Asian-type responsibility of individual to the community has been already destroyed (partly before and partly after the 1917 Revolution), whereas the new European-type responsibility to the society (state) has not yet emerged. Optimists see this as a source of Russian strength, claiming that it allows them to combine the best of both worlds.

More than a century-old debates between Westerners and Slavofiles are now revitalized as Russia is struggling to define its new identity and to find its new role in the world economy and politics. The contours of the future Russian economic model are now being shaped within the framework of these debates: the most frequently used 'yardsticks' for comparison are the USA and Germany in the West, but also Japan, China, Korea and the Association of South-East Asian Nations (ASEAN) economies in the East. Below I focus on some likely options for the development of basic features of the 'Russian-style' market.

Privatization and ownership

The drama of privatization in post-communist economies is driven by the huge gap between the demand for and the supply of assets. The approximate supply of assets – the book value of property to be privatized, however uncertain the estimates of the book value are – is comparable to the size of annual GDP; the approximate domestic demand for assets is equal at best to several per cent of GDP because it is financed from the limited pool of national savings, which altogether usually amount to between 20 and 30 per cent of GDP and are absorbed by investment, the government budget deficit, and current account surplus. Hence the supply of assets exceeds the demand by at least ten times and perhaps even a hundred times.

Theoretically, proceeds from sales of state property may be used to replace tax revenues of the state: by lowering taxes the government may yield room for private investors to spend more on acquiring shares of state enterprises. In practice, however, savings and taxes are not substitutes and the ability of the government to boost savings rate through lowering taxes is at best limited. Only the inflow of foreign capital can make a difference and can contribute substantially to the higher demand for assets, especially in small countries. Until now it was significant only in China and Hungary (accumulated FDI of 30 per cent of GDP), but not significant enough to compensate for the low domestic demand for assets.

Due to this discrepancy between the supply of and the demand for property, under all fast privatization programmes (carried out in several years) assets are greatly underpriced – their market value tends to be ten and more times lower than their book value. Since book value in economies in transition cannot be measured

Table 5.1 1994 market capitalization per unit of production/production capacities, in dollars

Industries	North America	Western Europe	Eastern Europe	RUSSIA	
				March 1994	Dec. 1994
Telecommunications (unit: access line)	1637	848	2083	69.97	105
Electricity (unit: MW)	372,000	650,000	448,000	2,260	21,000
Oil (unit: barrel of proven reserves)	7.06	3.58	n/a	0.17	0.08
Tobacco (unit: '000 cigarettes)	5.61	4.07	7.35	2.42	4.18
Cement (unit: tons)	144	162	40	1.92	8

Source: The Economist, 14 May 1994; *Russian Capital Markets* 1994, CS First Boston, p.63.

properly (because it is based on prices established by the planners, which do not reflect replacement costs), the market value of privatized companies is usually compared with annual sales, production capacities, stocks of mineral deposits, etc. In all cases, however, the result is pretty much the same: relative (unit) capitalization of companies in transition economies is usually ten and more times lower than that of their Western counterparts (see Table 5.1). This is hardly surprising since even in Western countries privatization of large state companies may disrupt the stock market if carried out too quickly. Ways of privatization, of course, matter a great deal. In fact, two of the three major privatization schemes used in post-communist countries (giving away assets to employees free or at token prices and distributing property through vouchers) were so popular in most of them exactly because of this reason: they did not allow the stock prices to be too depressed by artificially boosting the demand for assets and thus bridging the gap between limited demand and huge supply.

The third major privatization method – marketing of assets to the highest bidder – has the most depressing effect on stock prices and was more or less successful only in countries that managed to attract large amounts of foreign capital: the former German Democratic Republic (GDR), Hungary and Estonia who used this kind of privatization model (see Table 5.2) are all at the very top of the list of countries ranked by the ratio of FDI to GDP (EBRD 1997: 12). Poland, where concessions to work collectives and the use of vouchers were relatively modest, and even more so, China, proceeded with privatization more slowly than other countries, so that the pressure of the excess supply of property on stock prices was not that pronounced.

Giving away state property to employees (allowing them to get shares free or to buy them at low prices) or to citizens (through distributing vouchers) does not depress stock prices and thus contributes to the development of the securities markets. It is quite significant that state revenues from privatization in Czech Republic, where only a very minor part of the total property was actually sold on

Table 5.2 Privatization methods for medium and large enterprises, end 1995

Country	Sale to outside owners	Management employee buyout	Equal access voucher privatization	Restitution	Other	Still in state hands
Czech Republic						
By number	32	0	**22**	9	28	10
By value	5	0	**50**	2	3	40
Estonia[a]						
By number	**64**	30	0	0	2	4
By value	**60**	12	3	10	0	15
Hungary						
By number	**38**	7	0	0	33	22
By value	**40**	2	0	4	12	42
Lithuania						
By number	< 1	5	**70**	0	0	25
By value	< 1	5	**60**	0	0	35
Mongolia						
By number	0	0	**70**	0	0	30
By value	0	0	**55**	0	0	45
Poland						
By number	3	14	6	0	**23**	54
Russia						
By number	0	**55**	11	0	0	34

Source: World Bank (1996: 53).

Notes: [a] All management buyouts were part of competitive open tenders.
[b] Percentage of total shown, end of 1995, numbers in bold show the dominant method in each country.

the market (see Table 5.2), were as high as in Hungary, which sold nearly all assets at auctions and enjoyed the highest inflow of foreign capital (over 3 per cent of GDP annually in the first half of the 1990s). Similarly, direct privatization income in Lithuania that used the voucher scheme on a widest scale and Estonia that followed the German model and carried out the Treuhand-type privatization (see Table 5.2) was roughly the same (0.4 per cent of GDP annually in 1993–95) (Sutela 1996).

Another reason why giving property away and voucher-based privatization can be characterized as 'stock market friendly' is that they lead immediately to the widest dispersion of shares and to the emergence of millions of individual shareholders. The other privatization model – marketing of shares to the highest bidder – leads to the emergence of strategic outside investors; they are mostly stakeholders rather than shareholders, i.e. share ownership is highly concentrated; and these are banks and other financial institutions that are often best suited to take the position of strategic investors.

Two distinct features of Russia's privatization model were high speed and large concessions to work collectives. By the beginning of 1996, only three years after mass privatization started, Russia had managed to privatize fully or partially over 120,000 enterprises (including over 20,000 large enterprises, i.e. those with more than 200 employees). Together with hundreds of thousands of private businesses that emerged from scratch, in 1995 they accounted for 62 per cent of total employment (over 80 per cent were in industry, agriculture, construction, trade and public catering) according to official estimates. In terms of speed of privatization at least, Russia therefore, together with the Central European countries, became one of the leaders of the transitional economies.

The privatization scheme, however, was different from that of the East European countries in that the workers were entitled to get a large share of the total assets nearly for free. About half of all small enterprises (mostly in trade, public catering and personal services) were leased to work collectives with the provisions to buy them out later at discount prices (the other half were mostly sold at auctions and investment competitions at market prices), whereas in most large enterprises work collectives received considerable blocks of shares (up to 51 per cent) at prices well below the market level (the rest of the shares were sold at market prices for vouchers and money). The World Bank estimates that 55 per cent of large and medium-size enterprises in Russia were privatized through management–employee buyouts, whereas the comparable ratios for other economies in transition were typically below 14 per cent (except for Estonia – 30 per cent – where such buyouts were part of competitive, open tenders) (World Bank 1996: 53).

Post factum, it looks like this was the most feasible way to privatize state property, although the Russian model was certainly a compromise between economic and social goals. The demand for assets was extremely low in Russia, partly because of the lack of domestic savings, partly because of the poor investment climate which suppressed foreign investment. As a result, the book to market ratio for companies subject to privatization was somewhere in the range of 50:1 to 100:1, i.e. the actual value of assets in current prices was about 50 to 100 times higher than the market price of companies, shares (see Table 5.1). In the first two years of the reforms the Russian stock prices remained mostly unchanged in nominal terms, which meant their real value decreased by about a hundred times. Consequently, there was no chance to sell enterprises at prices more or less close to their book value. The actual choice was between selling assets to whoever was willing to pay the highest price, but still at a great discount (most likely, to Russian *nouveaux riches* and to foreign investors), or giving them away in a more or less fair way to citizens, workers, and/ or managers.

Choosing from the different ways of privatization (marketing assets to the highest bidder; distributing vouchers and selling property for vouchers; giving away assets to work collectives/managers), the government finally suggested a plan involving considerable concessions to the opposition and managed to pass it through the parliament.

The first method of privatization (auctioning property for money) was preferable on economic grounds: it gave control over enterprises to efficient owners – strategic investors, either domestic or foreign, willing to proceed with restructuring; besides, it allowed the state to get some proceeds into the budget. The second method of privatization (auctioning property for vouchers) was virtually as good as the first in

economic terms (except that the government did not receive any additional revenue), and was even better on social grounds, allowing a fair distribution of property
among citizens free of charge. The third method of privatization (giving away
property to work collectives) was inferior to the first in economic terms (because
work collectives normally were not efficient owners), and inferior to the second
method in social terms (because assets per worker and profitability of particular
enterprises varied enormously, whereas teachers, doctors and research fellows did
not receive any property at all).

However, it is exactly this third method of privatization that was largely supported by existing managers – 'the red directors' by workers in profitable industries
for obvious reasons, and even by the workers in unprofitable enterprises (partly due
to misunderstandings, partly because work collectives by getting a large stake in
their enterprises were able to control or at least to influence managers). Democrats,
or those who advocated shock therapy treatment, supported the first and the second
methods of privatization, opposition forces, or proponents of the gradual transition,
the third method.

By accepting the idea of giving away up to one half of total assets to the workers
nearly free of charge, the government managed to increase prices for another half
and, more importantly, to avoid accusations of 'selling off the motherland to the
new millionaires and to foreigners'. The major issue of privatization, who gains
control over the enterprises – outsiders (new rich or foreigners) or insiders (management and work collectives) – was resolved in favour of the insiders: they established
control over nearly all large enterprises and over about a half of small enterprises. A
random survey of 439 enterprises conducted by the World Bank in 1994 revealed
that workers and managers were dominant owners in 70 per cent of all non-state
enterprise or in 84 per cent of all non-state privatized enterprises (excluding new
firms that had emerged from scratch) (EBRD 1995: 132).

The costs of insiders' control are well known. Slow restructuring, reluctance to
fire employees and to pay back debts in due time are often blamed on insiders'
control. As compared to their East European counterparts, Russian enterprises
proved to be extremely reluctant to restructure by firing employees: the unemployment rate grew slowly in Russia and still remains relatively low. However, the
benefits of the chosen privatization model are obvious as well: privatization was
carried out in record time and there is evidence that strategic investors are already
emerging, at least in the largest and most attractive enterprises.

The banking system

With regards to banking and the financial system, the crucial choice for reforming
economies is between the American-type system and the Japanese-type one (the
European system is in between the two), or, to use a different expression, between a
market-based and a bank-based financial system.

In the American model, the banking sector is not concentrated and banks do not
enjoy a position of strength *vis-à-vis* non-financial corporations. The latter rely

mostly on internal sources of financing (undistributed profits and depreciation), whereas external sources are less important and include mostly sales of securities, not bank credits. Hostile take-overs and leveraged buy-outs reflect the absence of insiders' control on management and are common in the USA (Pohl *et al.* 1995).

In contrast, the Japanese (European) model implies that several major banks (the 'big three', the 'big five', or whatever) control the major part of total credits and are in a position to influence the investment decisions of non-financial companies. While in the USA 50 per cent of common stock is owned by individuals, in Japan and Germany only 22 per cent and 17 per cent respectively belong to individuals, while companies/institutions control over 60 per cent of all stocks (banks alone control 19 per cent and 10 per cent, respectively) (Blasi *et al.* 1996: 211). In addition to being large shareholders (stakeholders) of non-financial corporations, large banks provide them with the cash needed to finance investment: external sources of financing are by no means negligible as compared to internal funds, and bank credits account for a good portion of external financing. Both models have their advantages and limitations: the American model is usually perceived as a more competitive one, whereas the Japanese model is the one that allows a reduction of risk, bankruptcies and instability.

In market economies bank credits and equity financing complement rather than substitute for each other: normally, the larger the bank credits, the higher is market capitalization (see Figure 5.1). Nevertheless, it is significant that in Japan and in most West European countries market capitalization is two and more times lower than total bank credits, whereas in the USA, the UK, the Netherlands and Switzerland, as well as in some developing countries (Malaysia, Singapore, South Africa, Chile, the Philippines) market capitalization is roughly comparable with total domestic credit provided by the banking sector (see Figure 5.1).

In centrally planned economies securities markets virtually did not exist and banks were the only existing financial institutions at the time when the transition to the market started. As a result, despite all their structural weaknesses, banks enjoyed some obvious advantages in managing financial flows from the very beginning. In most post-communist countries, even though periods of high

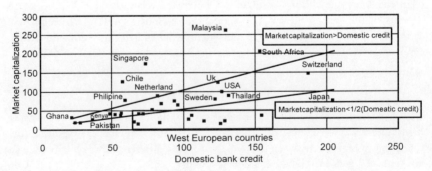

Figure 5.1 Market capitalization and bank credit as a percentage of GDP, 1995
Source: World Bank (1997: 240–42, 268–70).

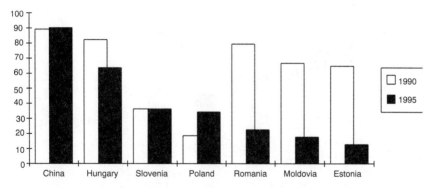

Figure 5.2 Bank credit as a percentage of GDP in selected transition economies, 1990 and 1995
Source: World Bank (1997: 240–242, 268–270).

inflation have led to a marked demonetization of national economies and the real volume of bank credits have fallen drastically (see Figure 5.2), banks have remained a relatively more important source of capital financing (as compared to securities markets) during transition: market capitalization normally stays now at a level of below 10 per cent of GDP, whereas bank credits amount to several dozen per cent of GDP (see Table 5.3 and 5.7).

The Russian banking sector, however, seems to be the weakest among all those economies in transition. Back in Soviet times total bank credit to enterprises exceeded half of GDP, with long-term credits alone amounting to 12 per cent of

Table 5.3 Relative size of bank credit and concentration of banking assets in some transition economies, 1994

Country	Outstanding bank claims as a percentage of GDP	Share of top 5 banks in total banking assets, per cent	Share of largest[a] banks in total assets, per cent
Belarus		75	88
Czech Republic	95	65	71
Estonia	30[b]	75	
Hungary	63	63	68
Latvia	44[b]	57	
Lithuania	29[b]	71	
Poland	33	66	71
Romania	21	74	79
Russia	13	33	43
Slovak Republic	63	79	79
Slovenia	32	70	89
Ukraine	18	70	82

Source: Transition Report (1995); EBRD (1995: 161–2); data for Baltic states are from, Hansson and Tombak (1996).

Notes: [a] Banks with individual asset share of over 3 per cent.
[b] Total bank assets, mid-1995.

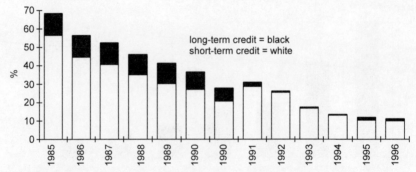

Figure 5.3 Bank credit outstanding USSR and Russia as a percentage of GDP
Source: Goskomstat.

GDP. After deregulation of prices in 1992 the demonetization of the economy proceeded surprisingly quickly: total bank credits outstanding fell to about 10 per cent of GDP by the end of 1996, while the long-term credits shrank to less than 1 per cent of GDP (see Figure 5.3). When the possibility of the bank crisis was discussed in summer 1996 the frequently made argument was that the total bank assets are so small when compared to the size of the economy that even the collapse of major banks would not be a disaster.

True, in Russia, as well as in other post-communist economies banks became one of the few growing sectors – they expanded even in the midst of the transformational recession, hiring new employees and opening new offices. The GDP created in banking, finance and insurance grew by 57 per cent in 1991–94, while the total GDP decreased by a good 35 per cent.[2] However, this increase was largely due to the growth of operations other than issuing credits to the enterprises. First, banks became more focused on individuals rather than on enterprises: the share of personal deposits in M_2 stood at 50 to 60 per cent in the 1980s (partly this was monetary overhang), decreased to below 10 per cent in late 1992, but then increased to over 40 per cent by the end of 1996. Enterprises' cash and bank deposits went down from the highest point of 28 per cent of GDP in late 1992 to only 4 per cent of GDP by the end of 1996 (World Bank 1991: 130; *Expert*, 13 January 1997: 12–13).

Second, currently bank operations with enterprises are focused mostly on processing payments, not on issuing credits. Initially, in 1992–94, newly created banks were very weak and survived only because they were able to get huge credits from the CBR (see Table 5.4). Commercial banks formed out of regional branches of specialized banks in fact acted as 'channel banks': a good part of their liabilities were credits from CBR intended for specific industrial enterprises. To be eligible for such a centralized (CBR) credit an enterprise was supposed to apply to the respective industrial department that in its turn applied to Inter-Agency Commission on Credits. If the application was approved, the CBR issued credit to the commercial bank from which the enterprise wanted to get this credit. Normally these were ex-specialized banks providing services to that particular enterprise before transition and continuing to do so afterwards.

Table 5.4 Balance sheet of commercial banks in 1992, billion roubles

Assets	1 Jan.	1 May	Liabilities	1 Jan.	1 May
Credits: short-term	395	850	Founding capital	43	76
Credits: long-term	40	50	Deposits (roubles)	315	475
Inter-bank credits	15	25	Deposits (foreign currency)	3	390
Cash	5	7	Loans from banks[a]	190	460
Correspondent accounts	130	110	Government loans[b]	45	110
Foreign currency	5	445	Others	34	154
Precious metals	0	10			
Others	40	168	Total	630	1665
Total	630	1665			

Source: *The Economist*, 18 July 1992.
Notes: [a] Mainly from CBR and Sberbank.
[b] From republican and local authorities.

In late 1992, CBR credits to commercial banks amounted to between 30 and 40 per cent of total credits outstanding to enterprises, and, perhaps, to over 50 per cent of total credits of 'channel banks'. For the 'channel banks' these CBR credits were more important sources of funds than deposits of companies and households and inter-bank credits.

On the asset side of the balance sheet, the most surprising disproportion was the share of total assets invested in hard currency (at that time the rapidly growing exchange rate of the dollar in roubles provided greater returns than interest rate on credits). Unlike Western banks, Russian commercial banks were mostly borrowing long term and lending short term: long-term loans constituted only a very small portion of their total assets (see Table 5.4).

Later, the CBR stopped issuing credits to companies through commercial banks, inflation slowed down and the share of assets invested in hard currency decreased. However, these changes only revealed the real structural weaknesses of the Russian banking sector. It turned out that bank services to companies are based not on accepting deposits and issuing credits, but on processing payments. As Table 5.5 suggests, the lion's share of activity of Russian banks has to do with processing payments, which is in sharp contrast to the operations of the Western banks.

Correspondent accounts, which in American banks constitute only less than 1 per cent of total assets/liabilities, in Russia amount to 18 per cent of liabilities and 33 per cent of assets (the latter is largely due to the requirements of correspondent Western banks which do not trust their Russian counterparts much); the share of liabilities in the form of processed payments in Russian banks is over two times higher. Banking operations *per se* – accumulating deposits and issuing credits – are only a small visible part of the iceberg, whereas about 70 per cent of total liabilities and about 50 per cent of assets are engaged in auxiliary operations of clearing payments. Data in Table 5.5 are for the end of 1994, more recent information on the consolidated balance sheet of the banking sector unfortunately is not available.

Table 5.5 Structure of assets and liabilities of Russian and American banks, end of 1994; percentage of total

Liabilities	Russia	USA
Cheap (low or no interest) liabilities Liabilities	70.1	32.5
Current accounts	29.1	24.6
'Loro' correspondent accounts	18.4	0.9
Payments processed	16.7	< 7
Expensive (high interest) liabilities	17.1	58.5
Deposits	2.2	49.4
Inter-bank credits received	13.2	8.1
Non-working (non-interest-bearing assets) Assets	50.5	13.1
'Nostro' correspondent accounts	33.1	0.8
Cash, reserves in the central bank, fixed capital, other	17.4	12.3
Working (interest-bearing) assets	49.5	86.9
Credits to non-financial sector	31.4	58.1
Government securities	4.3	22.1
Inter-bank credits issued	11.0	2.6
Non-government securities	1.0	3.0

Source: Dmitriyev *et al.* 1996.

It is safe to assume, however, that one major change that has occurred in the last two years is the increase in the share of government securities in total bank assets (estimates put it at 17 per cent of net assets in April 1996) at the expense of the reduction of the share of bank credits to businesses. The share of bad loans, meanwhile, rose from 32 per cent in 1994 to 37 per cent in 1995 and to 45 per cent in the first quarter of 1996 (Belousov *et al.* 1995; *Finansoviye Izvestiya*, 14 June 1996).

Last, but not least, the concentration in the Russian banking sector is much lower than in other economies in transition. As Table 5.3 suggests, in all economies except Russia, the share of the largest five banks in total banking assets is within the range of 57–79 per cent, whereas in Russia it is only 33 per cent. By the beginning of 1997 the average bank had only two branches (if Sberbank with over 30,000 branches all across Russia is excluded) and the registered capital (equity) of less than $US500,000. There are no 'big three' or 'big four' nation-wide banks. The largest Russian bank – Sberbank (the former state Savings bank still controlled by the CBR) – accounts for 13 per cent of total credit outstanding (and its share is falling rapidly), while the ten largest banks account for only one-third of total credits (see Table 5.6). Only two Russian banks had assets of over $US5 billion and capital of over $US500 million by early 1997. Even the largest Russian banks compare very poorly with their Western counterparts: with the exception of Sberbank, their assets do not exceed several billion dollars – less than 1 per cent of GDP each.

Table 5.6 Assets, registered capital and credits of the ten largest Russian banks, 1 January 1997

Bank	Assets, trillion roubles	Registered capital, trillion roubles	Credits outstanding*, trillion roubles	Share in total credit outstanding[a], percentage
Sberbank	256.5	15.3	31.9	13
Vneshtorgbank	27.9	6.1	8.1	3
Inkombank	22.2	2.0	7.7	3
ONEXIMbank	20.6	2.9	10.6	4
Mosbiznesbank	17.7	1.0	3.1	1
Rossiyskiy Credit	16.3	1.2	2.5	1
Tokobank	14.5	1.1	3.3	1
Stolichniy Bank Sberezheniy	13.9	1.3	2.5	1
Menatep	12.2	1.0	7.8	3
Natsional'niy Reservniy Bank	11.2	1.6	2.2	1
Total	413.0	33.5	79.7	33

Source: *Finansoviye Izvestiya*, 13 February 1997; Goskomstat.
Note: [a] In hard currency and in roubles, excluding inter-bank credits.

Why did Russia adopt a decentralized banking system, whereas most other economies in transition, including radical reformers, adopted a more conservative Japanese-European type highly concentrated model of the banking sector? The immediate reasons are well known and are associated with the fight between the Russian and the all-Union governments (between Yeltsin and Gorbachev) for the distribution of powers in 1991: banking was chosen to be one of the battle-grounds, when the Russian government declared all branches of all-Union banks on Russian territory independent from Gosbank, with the result that nearly a thousand new banks emerged overnight. In early 1991 Russia transformed all 900 regional branches of specialized banks on its territory into independent banks, and the banking business became the first fully-fledged market with a competitive structure. By 1 February 1991, the number of independent banks had increased to nearly 1,400, and they accounted for over 40 per cent of total credit outstanding. By 1 September 1991, over 1,500 banks controlled 64 per cent of total credit outstanding. By 1 December 1991 there were 1,616 independent banks, including 155 co-operative banks. By the beginning of 1992, 1,300 banks accounted for 93 per cent of total credit in Russia, whereas in all Soviet republics the total number of commercial banks exceeded 2,000. By the end of 1996 in Russia alone there were over 2,600 banks (about 500 of them were not operating, however).

Nevertheless, it is difficult to say whether these immediate reasons represent a particular fundamental pattern or should be viewed as a mere coincidence of events. Other former Soviet republics were also leading 'banking wars' against the Union, but seem to have adopted a more European-type of banking system after-wards.

Corporate financing and control

With respect to corporate financing and control, the outcomes of the Russian transition, perhaps surprisingly, seem to be more in line with the liberal (shock therapy) approach than in East European countries. In the transitional economies with poorly developed capital markets most industrial companies are not really able to sell their shares and bonds, which is an argument in favour of the Japanese model ('only large banks can mobilize resources for capital investment'). Indeed, so far capital markets in most ex-socialist countries have been developing in the direction of the Japanese (European) model. In most of these countries market capitalization is normally at a level of several per cent of GDP, whereas bank credits amount to several dozen per cent of GDP (see Tables 5.3 and 5.7). In Czech Republic, for instance, nearly 80 per cent of total capital investment in 1993–94 was financed by bank credit to enterprises, whereas several investment funds managed about one half of the shares of individual investors.

Table 5.7 Stock market capitalization and volume of annual trade in stocks in 1995

Country	Market capitalization (listed and unlisted stocks)		Volume of trade (listed and unlisted stocks)		Ratio of volume of trade to market capitalization
	billion $	*Percentage of GDP*	*billion $*	*Percentage of GDP*	*percentage*
China	42.1	6.0	49.8	7.1	116.3
Czech Republic	15.7	35.0	3.6	8.1	33.6
	(20.3)	(45)	(10.4)	(23)	(51)
Slovakia	1.2	7.1	0.8	4.8	71.5
	(6.3)	(36.2)	(3.0)	(17.2)	(48)
Poland	4.6	3.9	2.8	2.4	72.7
	(6.8)	(5.8)	(13.8)	(11.7)	(203)
Hungary	2.4	5.4	0.4	0.8	17.7
	(3.8)	(8.7)	(2.5)	(5.7)	(66)
Russia	15.9	4.6	0.3	0.1	2.0
	(50)	(13)	(13)	(3)	(26)
Estonia	(0.4)	(10.0)	(0.24)	(5.9)	(60)
Croatia	0.6	3.2	0.05	0.3	8.6
Slovenia	0.3	1.6	0.4	1.9	77.0
Lithuania	0.2	2.0	0.04	0.5	37.2
Bulgaria	0.06	0.5	0.005	0.0	7.7
Armenia	0.003	0.1	0.002	0.0	66.7

Source: World Bank (1997: 134–6, 240–2); Johnson *et al.* (1997: 15).

Note: World Bank data (figures without brackets) are for 1995 and presumably do not include the OTC trading. Figures in brackets were collected by OECD, include OTC trading, and were computed by annualizing the data for March–August 1996 which are compared to 1995 dollar GDP. For Russia estimates are for 1996 as a whole and are taken from press reports.

The notable exception, however, is Russia, where banks virtually stopped the financing of capital investment. Total bank credits outstanding in relation to GDP declined steadily; in 1992 they ensured the financing of only 10 per cent of total capital investment, in 1993 – even less – 6 per cent. No less important, long-term credits (over 1 year term) amount to only 5 per cent of total bank credits and do not play any significant role in the financing of capital investment. In late 1996, when inflation was already largely under control, interest rates on bank credits to industry still stood at a level of about 100 per cent, higher than the rates on inter-bank credits, the CBR rate (about 50 per cent), the returns on GKOs – government Treasury bills (30 per cent), and much higher than the rates of return in industry itself (10–20 per cent) (*Expert*, 13 January 1997: 14–15).

Markets for corporate securities are only emerging, and it is only large companies that can resort to equity and bond financing. Nevertheless, it seems that these sources of investment financing for large companies are already more important than bank credits. Total volume of trade in shares in 1995 (mostly over-the-counter, OTC) was estimated at about $US5 billion – 1–2 per cent of GDP or 25 per cent of market capitalization (*Finansoviye Izvestiya*, 2 February 1996; World Bank 1996: 108). And market capitalization as well as the volume of trading increased threefold in the second quarter of 1996 after stock prices soared on the eve of the presidential elections, and twofold in late 1996 to early 1997 after Yeltsin recovered from heart surgery (see Figure 5.4). Estimates for 1996 put the total market capitalization at between $US50 and 55 billion (13 per cent of GDP) and the volume of trade in shares at 40–70 million a day, or $US13 billion annually (3–4 per cent of GDP) (*Expert*, 13 January 1997: 21). By mid-1997 market capitalization was presumably at a level of about 25 per cent of GDP, whereas the volume of trading – over 5 per cent of GDP, which made Russia one of the leaders of stock market development together with China and Central European countries (see Table 5.7).

The Russian stock market in 1993–97 definitely outperformed the stock markets of the East European countries. In summer and autumn 1994 the demand for shares of major Russian companies increased greatly (mostly due to the inflow of foreign capital), so that their stock prices skyrocketed (jumping up by about ten times). Later the stock market remained sluggish due to the Chechen war and political uncertainty, but in April–June 1996 stock prices increased about three times in real and dollar terms anticipating and then welcoming Yeltsin's victory in the presidential elections (see Figure 5.4).

Overall Russian stocks grew from December 1992 to mid-1997 eight times in dollar terms, whereas Hungarian stocks – less than three times and Polish stocks – less than two times over the same period (see Figure 5.4). Among the various factors that influenced the performance of the stock markets the inflow of foreign capital was clearly a very important one: it explains why Hungarian stocks, despite the privatization model which was least favourable to the growth of the stock market, did better than Polish and Czech stocks. However, it may well be that the similar performance of stock markets in Czech Republic (which managed to privatize ·more assets than other economies in transition) and Poland (where

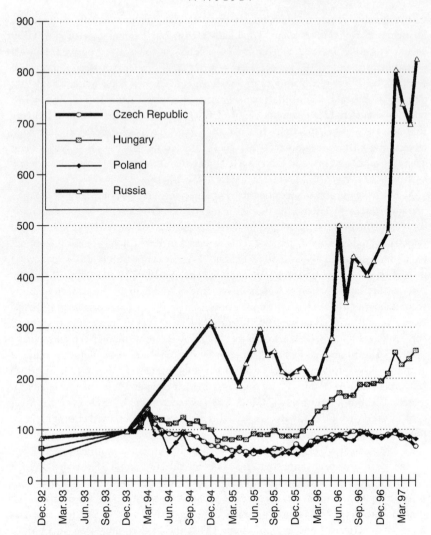

Figure 5.4 Dollar stock prices indices, December. 1993 = 100 per cent
Source: *The Economist* (1993–97).
Note: For Russia in 1992–93 = authors' estimates.

privatization proceeded relatively slowly) is explained by the more 'securities friendly' nature of the Czech privatization. Also, the outstanding performance of the Russian stock market, despite the relatively weak inflow of foreign investment, is quite significant.

In the largest and most attractive Russian companies with high market liquidity outside investors by now own more shares than workers and managers, and this pattern is likely to emerge in other companies, whose shares are not yet traded on the market and that are still controlled by work collectives. While in the large, but not the largest, privatized Russian companies in 1996 outsiders owned only 31 per cent of the share, with 59 per cent of the shares belonging to insiders and 9 per cent to the state, in the 100 largest Russian companies outsiders owned on average 57 per cent of all shares (insiders = 22 per cent, the state = 21 per cent) (Blasi *et al.* 1996; Blasi 1997).

The future role of institutional investors is still an open issue. Until recently banks were not the major owners of shares of non-financial companies; and mutual, pension and insurance funds are just starting to emerge.[3] Even in the largest Russian banks investment in non-government securities amounted in the beginning of 1995 to only 1 per cent of total assets – less than in the largest American banks (3 per cent), not to speak of other Western countries (see Table 5.5).

There was a lot of speculation in the press that this pattern may have changed after the 'shares for loans' auctions – sales of the most lucrative pieces of government property to the highest bidder that started in late 1995 and did not involve any concessions to the work collectives. Several major banks received – as a collateral for credits issued to the government – large blocks of shares of non-financial companies (Menatep Bank won 78 per cent of shares of Yukos – the second largest oil producer, Oneximbank got 38 per cent of the shares of Norilsk Nickel, etc.).

By the end of 1996 the newspapers were writing about the group of five–seven banks that control a good half of the Russian economy.[4] The largest group, Oneximbank, reportedly controls banks with assets of some $US5 billion and industrial enterprises with sales of about $US9 billion; the second largest, Menatep, has banking assets of about $US2 billion and holds control over enterprises with sales of about $US6 billion (*Expert*, 2 December 1996: 19). This is obviously a significant proportion of the national economy (1995 GDP was $US364 billion), but still just about several per cent.

Moreover, as a recent survey shows (Blasi 1997), in large privatized state enterprises financial institutions (holding companies and financial–industrial groups, investment funds and banks) control only 10 per cent of all shares. In the 100 largest Russian corporations the share of stocks owned by financial institutions is somewhat higher – 18 per cent, but the proportion of stocks belonging to outsiders is also higher, so that the share of financial institutions in total outsiders' ownership is approximately the same for large and largest companies – about one-third.

Overall, at least for the time being, Russia seems to be the only country among the transition economies that is developing a truly market-based system of corporate financing and control. The distinct character of Russian privatization – large concessions to workers and managers coupled with the high speed of the process – definitely contributed to the dispersion of shares to millions of individual shareholders and did not allow financial institutions to become major stakeholders of non-financial companies. On the other hand, the weak and decentralized banking sector is the single most important reason that predetermined the development of the Russian financial system along the lines of the British-American model. In other post-communist countries with 'securities-friendly' modes of privatization, but without decentralized banking, the German/Japanese model emerged (see Table 5.8).

Table 5.8 Types of financial systems emerging in transition economies

	Type of banking system	Concentrated	Decentralized
Type of privatization	Vouchers and give away of property	German/Japanese type financial system	American-type financial system
	Marketing of property to the highest bidder	German/Japanese type financial system	

One way or the other, more liberal financial markets may be a sign of the 'wilder' nature of emerging Russian capitalism: as in other areas, it may turn out that, although the Russian transition was not so radical, its outcome would be more radical than elsewhere, leading to the creation of a quite liberal economic system.

Asset and income distribution

Though data on the distribution of wealth in Russia in recent years are lacking, there are reasons to believe that this distribution has changed dramatically recently and is now extremely uneven. The initial accumulation of capital in the late 1980s to the early 1990s proceeded under conditions of unbelievable opportunities for enrichment. First, the fortunes of the new Russians were built in external trade, in commodity exchange business and in banking and finance; in virtually all cases it was the difference between state-regulated prices and the free market (domestic or foreign) prices that laid the foundation of these fortunes.

According to some very rough estimates (Aslund 1996), in 1992 alone benefits from cheap state credits issued to companies at 10–25 per cent interest rate (at times when inflation was 2,500 per cent) amounted to 30 per cent of GDP, whereas revenues derived from export operations (due to the difference between government-regulated domestic prices and world market prices for resources) and import operations (due to subsidized exchange rate used by importers of food) amounted to 30 per cent and 15 per cent, respectively – overall, a staggering 75 per cent of 1992 GDP. Even if these estimates are upward-biased several times, the magnitude of the redistribution process is still quite impressive. Even more so considering that the subsidization of credit and import operations did not come to an end until 1993, whereas export licences and quotas (which allowed government bureaucrats to ask for bribes) continued well into 1994.

The redistributed revenues were more than enough to purchase all the shares traded on the market at that time – market capitalization in 1992–93 stood at just several per cent of GDP. While part of these new fortunes left the country (capital flight), another part was used to establish new businesses and to acquire existing companies in the course of privatization. The share of managers in total shareholders equity is said to have increased from 8 per cent right after the end of the voucher privatization (mid-1994) to about 20 per cent currently, whereas in newly established companies managers controlled over 50 per cent of the shares already in 1994.

Greater than in other economies in transition, income inequalities contributed to the widening of disparities in wealth distribution. It is reasonable to predict that high income inequalities will persist in the foreseeable future: even if the government adopts a strong social policy, it has only limited abilities to fight illegal incomes, the major source of income differentiation, to collect taxes (especially personal income taxes), and to increase expenditure on welfare.

Gini coefficient grew by a good half in just four years, while decile and pentile ratios increased more than three times (see Table 5.9), which is an exceptional record for economies in transition. As available evidence suggests (Cornia 1996), increases in inequalities in the East European countries were significantly smaller than in Russia: Gini coefficient grew from a level 19–27 per cent in 1989–90 to about 23–35 per cent in 1993–94, while decile ratio grew from 2.0 to 3.4 times to 2.7 to 4.3 times only. Partial analogues of the rapid growth in income inequalities in Russia may be found only in Bulgaria, the Baltics, and some other former Soviet republics: these countries are already surpassing OECD levels of Gini coefficient and are catching up with the Latin American levels.

Table 5.9 Income distribution and some social indicators, 1990–96

	1990	1991	1992	1993	1994	1995	1996
Income shares of the population:							
first pentile	9.8	11.9	6.0	5.8	5.3	5.5	6.5
second pentile	14.9	15.8	11.6	11.1	10.2	10.2	10.9
third pentile	18.8	18.8	17.6	16.7	15.2	15.0	15.5
fourth pentile	23.8	22.8	26.5	24.8	23.0	22.4	22.4
fifth pentile	32.7	30.7	38.3	41.6	46.3	46.9	44.7
Pentile ratio	3.34	2.58	6.38	7.17	8.73	8.53	6.88
Decile ratio	4.4	4.5	8.0	11.2	15.0	13.5	13.0
Gini coefficient, percentage		26.0	28.9	39.8	40.9	38.1	37.5
Average income as a percentage of subsistence level	352	303	210	219	238	202	211
Average pension as a percentage of average wage	33	33	26	34	34	38	38
Average pension as a percentage of average income	47	40	38	44	37	35	39
Spending on pensions as a percentage of GDP	6.2[a]			6.3[b]			
Spending on family benefits as a percentage of GDP	1.7[a]			0.4[b]			

Source: Goskomstat; data for social transfers are from Milanovic (1995: 32, 41).
Notes: [a] 1987–88.
　　　　[b] 1992–93.

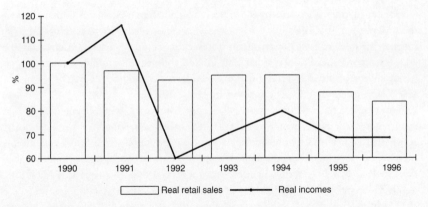

Figure 5.5 Real incomes and real retail sales per capita, 1990 100 per cent
Source: Goskomstat.

Because the share of the top 20 per cent high income families in total income increased from 31 per cent in 1991 to 47 per cent in 1995 (see Table 5.9), the assumed reduction of average income of total population by 12 per cent (see Figure 5.5) was very unevenly distributed: whereas for the top 20 per cent average income increased by over a third, for the remaining 80 per cent of the population real average income declined by a good third. Besides, due to higher price increases for food goods than for other commodities, the ratio of average income to subsistence level (which consists mostly of the cost of the basket of food goods) declined from 3.5 in 1990 to 2 in 1995 (see Table 5.9), and nutrition standards, according to the statistics of the consumption of food products, deteriorated considerably.

The greater reduction in living standards of the majority of population was caused by some objective reasons, such as the greater magnitude of the Russian recession, the larger productivity gap between industries, which contributed to higher wage differentials among industries, etc. But whatever the reasons for this impoverishment, the government was supposed to intervene in order to at least neutralize the outcomes of these unfavourable developments, if the roots of the problem were beyond its reach.[5]

While for the younger people such deep temporary decreases in real incomes were, perhaps, manageable, senior citizens and especially pensioners considered them absolutely unacceptable. When faced with an option of losing one-third of real income in the next five to ten years, but regaining this income later, they rejected this option on the basis of absolutely rational considerations and resisted reforms by all possible means. The only way to ensure the support of the elderly for reforms was to guarantee that their real income was not going to fall: such a policy could have contributed greatly to building consensus for reforms, not to speak of moral considerations.

Unfortunately, the Russian government failed to meet this challenge: it did much less than the East European countries who pursued shock therapy policy, despite the obviously greater magnitude of the problem. Poland was the only country that succeeded in increasing the real income of pensioners during transition, but in other Central European countries the ratio of average pension to average wage either increased (Hungary, Slovenia) or did not fall considerably (Czech and Slovak Republics) (Milanovic 1995). In Russia this ratio fell markedly in 1992; its increase in subsequent years is misleading because it occurred under the conditions of rapid decline of the share of wages in total income: if compared to average per capita incomes, average pensions declined by nearly 30 per cent in 1990–95 (see Table 5.9).

Spending on pensions stayed at a level of about 6 per cent of GDP during transition (see Table 5.9), whereas in the East European countries on average it increased in the same period from 7 to 10 per cent, not to mention spending on family allowances, which decreased greatly in Russia, but remained constant (2.5 per cent of GDP) in the East European countries (ibid.: 1995). Share of income transfers in total income increased in Russia only slightly – from 12.8 per cent in 1989 to 15.6 per cent in 1993–94, whereas in Central European countries it either stayed constant at a much higher level (in Hungary 26–28 per cent) or increased considerably (in Slovenia from 11 per cent to 20 per cent, in Poland from 21 per cent in 1989 to 34 per cent in 1991–92) (Cornia 1996).

All in all, it looks like the Russian government in the field of social policies followed a more shock-oriented path than most East European countries, though the need for income redistribution in favour of the disadvantaged groups of the population was greater than elsewhere. By allowing the previously strong system of social guarantees to weaken and disintegrate the Russian authorities missed a chance to build up support for the reforms and to weaken social tensions. Uneven income distribution (flow) will continue to contribute to the inequalities in the distribution of assets (stock) with the result that the rich will get richer and will have more opportunities to become major shareholders. With large disproportions in wealth distribution Russia is unlikely to develop a system of corporate financing and control based on institutional rather than on individual investors.

In short, Russian capitalism with regard to wealth and income inequalities and the market for corporate control may resemble more that of the 'robber barons' days in the USA rather than a consensus-based Asian model or a state-regulated European one. As one of the Russian parliamentarians put it: 'This is not the wild West, this is the wild East.'

Given the famous Russian (and Soviet) intolerance towards social inequalities, strong social policy is a must for consensus building, especially in view of the much needed unpopular measures, such as withdrawal of subsidies to inefficient industries, promoting savings and investment at the expense of consumption, etc. but, unfortunately, the ability of the government to raise funds for such a policy is in question.

Role of the state

In European countries the role of the government is extensive in all areas: creating institutions and regulatory framework, providing public goods (education, health care, infrastructure, etc.), and carrying out social transfers. In contrast, in East Asian economies, while government regulatory functions are sometimes even stronger than in European countries, the size of the government, as measured by its revenues and expenditure in relation to GDP, is considerably smaller (1.5 to 3 times) than in Europe, which means that the state involvement in providing public goods and especially social transfers is quite limited.

As the data in Table 5.10 suggest, tax revenues as a proportion of GDP decreased markedly in most transition economies. However, Central European countries and Estonia managed to arrest the decline, while Russia (together with Lithuania, Latvia, and several South-East Europe and Central Asian states) experienced the greatest reduction. Chinese government revenues as a percentage of GDP fell by over two times since the late 1970s, but it looks more like a conscious policy choice rather than a spontaneous process (authoritarian regimes always have better power to collect tax revenues, if they choose to do so, as did all governments in the Centrally Planned Economies (CPEs) before the transition).

Given the limited ability of the government to arrest the reduction of budget revenues, progress in reducing the deficit naturally depended to a large extent on the ability to cut expenditure, which in turn required a minimum consensus on how to do that and, by its very nature, turned out to be a slow process. Defence expenditure was cut dramatically (to 3 per cent of GDP in 1996, according to official estimates); the financing of health care and education (which were still provided mostly free of charge) declined markedly as a proportion of GDP; the share of social transfers in GDP also fell, though less markedly. Finally, in 1995–96 the deficit was reduced to about 3 per cent of GDP and the market for government treasury bills was created, so that the major part of the deficit was financed in a non-inflationary way.

However, the reduction of the government expenditure occurred in the worst possible way – it proceeded without any coherent plan and did not involve the reassessment of government commitments. Instead of shutting down some government programmes completely and concentrating limited resources on others with an aim to raise their efficiency, the government kept all programmes half-alive, half-financed, and barely working. This led to the slow decay of public education, health care, infrastructure, law and order institutions, fundamental R&D, etc. Virtually all services provided by the government – from collecting custom duties to regulating street traffic – are currently the symbol of notorious economic inefficiency. There were numerous cases of government failure which further undermined the credibility of the state.

The model that emerges in Russia seems to be based on minimal government involvement in all areas of economic life. In the former Soviet Union not only government regulations were pervasive, but also the financial power of the state was roughly the same as in European countries (government revenues and expenditure amounted to about 50 per cent of GDP, see Table 5.10). This allowed the state to provide the bulk of public goods and extensive social transfers.

In post-transition Russia (and other CIS countries) the state found itself deprived of its former vast resources and powers. On the one hand, it turned out

108

Table 5.10 Total revenues of consolidated government budgets including some off-budget funds as a percentage of GDP in some transition economies

Year/ country	1989	1990	1991	1992	1993	1994	1995	1996[a]
Central European countries[c]	**51.8**	**51.6**	**47.4**	**49.1**	**49.0**	**48.8**	**48.1**	**45.1**
Czech Republic	61.7	60.2	52.2	49.5	51.4	51.2	49.6	44.5
Slovak Republic					43.6	46.4	46.8	44.6
Hungary	59.1	53.9	52.1	56.1	55.4	53.9	49.6	47.0
Poland	44.1	42.9	41.5	44.1	47.6	45.5	—	—
Slovenia	42.4	49.3	43.7	46.5	47.1	47.1	46.2	44.4
Baltic states[c]	**47.2**	**41.8**	**38.3**	**31.4**	**35.2**	**33.5**	**33.4**	—
Estonia	39.5	35.7	36.4	34.6	39.6	41.2	40.7	—
Latvia	52.0	46.0	37	27.4	35.8	34.2	34.9	—
Lithuania	50.0	43.7	41.4	32.1	30.2	25.1	24.6	—
European CIS countries (excluding Russia)[c]				**32.1**	**33.0**	**35.7**	**33.5**	**32.0**
Belarus	—	56.8	47.5	44.0	43.6	48.4	43.2	41.0
Moldovia	—	—	—	20.2	13.0	23.1	23.9	23
Ukraine	58.2	—	—	—	42.3	—	—	—
USSR (1988–90)/RUSSIA (1992–95)[b]	**43.5**	**47.2**	—	**28.0**	**29.0**	**28.2**	**26.1**	**23**
South East Europe countries[c]	**52.3**	**47.0**	**36.6**	**33.5**	**36.0**	**39.9**	**37.8**	**31.2**
Albania	47.8	47.1	30.9	25.6	34.6	33	24	17.8
Bulgaria	58.0	53.3	42.3	32.4	37.2	40.2	36.0	—
Croatia	—	—	34	34	33.6	43.8	50.6*	—
FYR Macedonia	—	—	—	38.0	41.0	51.0	45	44.5
Romania	51.1	40.5	39.3	37.6	33.6	31.4	33.5	—
Caucasian states[c]			**32.9**	**31.4**	**33.4**	**18.9**	**10.8**	—
Azerbaijan	—	—	35.7	49.2	47	21.2	13	16
Georgia	—	—	30.0	13.6	19.8	16.6	8.5	—
Central Asian countries[c]	**35.2**	**38.8**	**35.6**	**24.9**	**25.9**	**28.9**	**21.6**	**20.0**
Kazakhstan	35.4	32.8	25.0	24.6	23.5	17.2	16.5	15.3
Kyrgyzstan	38.0	38.6	35	17	23	20.8	15.6	—
Tajikistan	—	—	33.2	26.6	27.1	45.5	19.3	12.3
Turkmenistan	32.4	—	—	—	13.4	—	—	—
Uzbekistan	35.0	44.9	49.1	31.4	42.6	32.3	35.1	32.3
Asian non-CIS countries[c]	**32.2**				**26.4**			
China[d]	35.1	34.0	33.9	33.3	20.8	18.8	—	—
Mongolia	48.6	—	—	—	36.2	—	—	—
Vietnam	14.8	—	—	—	22.3	—	—	—

Source: Transition Report Update, April 1996; EBRD (1996: 24–48); Transition Report Update, April 1997; EBRD (1997: 35–59); *Economic Systems*, 19(2), June 1995: 103; Goskomstat; De Melo *et al.* (1995, table 8); State Statistical Bureau (1995: 223).

Notes: [a] Estimate.

[b] Excluding revenues of the off-budget social insurance funds. If these revenues are included, total government revenues amounted to about 36 per cent in 1993 and 1994.

[c] Unweighted average.

[d] Data are from the Chinese national statistics and include off-budget funds, which constitute about half of all revenues and are not taken into account in World Bank publications (16.5 per cent and 11.7 per cent in 1989 and in 1993, respectively).

that government regulatory activities have only limited efficiency due to difficulties in enforcing regulations since the authoritarian regime was replaced by the weak democratic one (in contrast to Central Europe, where strong democratic regimes emerged). On the other hand, government revenues plummeted after the CPE was dismantled, falling below 30 per cent of GDP (including off-budget funds) in 1996. This is still more than in East Asian countries on average, but much less than is needed to finance government commitments – still very large agricultural and housing subsidies, mostly free education and health care, and a universal pay-as-you-go system of social insurance.

Unless the government is prepared to radically reassess its commitments, so as to make them financially sustainable, it is safe to predict that many government activities in providing public goods and social transfers will slowly die. Since they can only partly be replaced by private and semi-private businesses, this would probably be the worst option and a clear-cut case of government failure.

Industrial structure and international specialization

In addition to some common patterns of structural change in the economies in transition (rapid growth of the service sector, especially of trade, banking, and financial services; reduction of the share of investment in GDP and greater emphasis on consumer goods; conversion of defence production, etc.), Russian restructuring is associated with the reallocation of resources from secondary manufacturing into raw materials industries, which is pretty unique for the economies in transition at least on the scale it is currently happening in Russia.

The need to reallocate resources results from the huge gap in efficiency and competitiveness between different sectors of the Russian economy. While the fuel and energy sector, steel and non-ferrous metal industries are most efficient and competitive, agriculture, machinery and equipment (with some minor exceptions) and light industry are least efficient and competitive. The Russian resource sector (fuel and electric energy, steel and non-ferrous metals) employed only three million workers in 1995, but produced nearly as much output as machine building, light industry and agriculture together with a total employment of 17 million workers. Labour productivity in the resource sector was over five times higher than in machinery and equipment and in agriculture, and, surprisingly, even capital productivity was slightly higher (see Table 5.11). The actual productivity gap should be even greater than suggested by the data in current prices presented in Table 5.11, because domestic fuel and energy prices in 1995 were still only about 70 per cent of world prices.

Before the radical reforms the inefficient sectors of the Russian/Soviet economy were subsidized directly and indirectly (through different price structures). Because of the magnitude of the problem, it was unrealistic to eliminate subsidies at once: agriculture, machine building and light industry employed over 20 million workers, nearly 30 per cent of the total workforce. The actual policy of gradual removal of

Table 5.11 Employment, capital stock and output in major industrial sectors, 1995

Industries	Employment, annual average, million	Fixed capital stock, trillion roubles[a]	Gross output, trillion roubles	Labour productivity	Capital productivity
				per cent of national average	
Resources (fuel, energy, metals)	3.0	2319	418	326	72
Machinery and equipment and light industry	6.7	1265	175	61	56
Agriculture	9.9	1805	276	65	60
Total economy	67.1	11504	2870[b]	100	100

Source: Goskomstat.

Notes: [a] After revaluation of January 1, 1996. Breakdown by branches of industry (energy, fuel, etc.) is estimated from 1994 data.
[b] Estimate derived from the ratio of gross output to GDP in 1994 (1.73) and GDP for 1995 (1659 trillion R).

subsidies to inefficient industries was thus, if not optimal, then the best feasible option. However, the form in which those subsidies were provided (price subsidies, not direct subsidies to producers for restructuring) was anything but optimal.

Now, Russian domestic prices seem to be approaching world price proportions and the first part of the restructuring, associated with the reduction of inefficient production, has already largely occurred. Due to changes in relative prices favouring resource industries, their output was falling in recent years more slowly and their exports increased in a number of cases. As a result of price and output shifts, the share of resource industries (fuel and energy, steel and non-ferrous metals) of total industrial output increased from 24 per cent in 1991 to 51 per cent in 1996 at the expense of the reduction of the share of secondary manufacturing, mostly machinery and equipment and light industries (see Table 5.12).

The resource sector in fact has already become the backbone and the most important staple of the Russian economy. It accounts for 75 per cent of total exports to far abroad (50 per cent – fuel and energy, 25 per cent – metals and diamonds) and for an even greater share of exports to near abroad. The share of fuel and energy sector alone in total capital investment in goods producing industries increased from 20 per cent in 1991 to about 40 per cent in 1995 (see Table 5.13). Gas and oil industry workers enjoy the highest wages in the country: about $US400 a month as compared to about $US200 in banking and insurance, $US100 on average, $US80 in machine building, $US55 in light industry, and below $US50 in agriculture in 1995.[6]

Gazprom – the largest Russian company producing about 600 billion cubic meters of gas (worth around $US50 billion at world prices) and heavily criticized for not paying enough taxes, in fact contributed in 1995 $US4 billion in taxes to the government budget, or about 4 per cent of consolidated budget revenues, whereas

Table 5.12 Reduction of output by industry and the structure of industrial output at current prices

Industries	Volume of output (1990 = 100) per cent				Share of particular industries in total output, percentage				Price index in 1994 (1990 = 1)
	1992	1994	1995	1996	1990	1992	1995	1996	
Fuel	87	69	68	66	8.0	19.4	17.6	19.0	5434
Electric energy	96	83	81	79	4.2	6.8	13.4	16.7	6071
Steel	77	54	59	57		8.6	10.1	9.5	3292
Non-ferrous metals	68	54	55	52	12.0	9.1	7.0	5.9	2088
Construction materials	78	47	43	32	3.1	2.4	3.6	3.5	2032
Food	76	57	52	47	11.7	9.4	11.3	10.7	1975
Chemicals	73	44	48	43	7.6	8.8	8.2	7.2	2889
Petro-chemicals									2344
Wood	78	44	41	32	5.3	4.4	4.9	3.6	1752
Machinery and equipment	77	45	40	37	30.8	20.4	17.7	15.8	2017
Light	64	26	18	13	12.1	7.1	2.4	1.8	875
Other	—	—	—	—	5.2	3.6	3.8	6.3	—
All industry	75	51	48	46	100	100	100	100	2484
Agriculture	86	73	67	62	—	—	—	—	365

Source: Goskomstat.

Table 5.13 Capital investment by industry, percentage of total (excluding investment into residential construction and social sector)

Industrial complexes	1989 USSR	1991	1993 Russia	1994	1995
Fuel and energy	22	20	38	32	38
Steel and non-ferrous metals	4	5	7	7	8
Machine-building	12	10	5	6	6
Chemical and wood industries	5	5	4	4	4
Construction and construction materials industry	9	9	6	8	5
Agro-industrial sector (agriculture, food and light industry)	29	32	19	18	8
Transportation and communication	13	14	14	21	26
Other	6	5	7	4	5

Source: The Economist, 1993–1997.

the share of the company in total employment is less than 0.5 per cent. Taxes paid by Gazprom provided 26 per cent of all federal budget revenues in 1996, while taxes paid by energy sector were 69 per cent (as compared to only less than 20 per cent in

1990) (*Segodnya*, 31 May 1997). Taxes in oil and gas production and in oil refining already amount to over 50 per cent of gross output, whereas in the USA the comparable figure is 25–30 per cent (*Finansoviye Izvestiya*, 20 June 1996; *Segodnya*, 31 August 1996).[7]

On the other hand, machinery and equipment and light industries are rapidly losing their share of the domestic market to foreign competitors. The share of machinery and equipment in total Russian exports decreased from 17.6 per cent in 1990 to 3.7 per cent in 1995. In 1994 alone output in machine building and light industry fell nearly by a good half and now they produce only less than 40 per cent and less than 15 per cent respectively of what they used to produce in better times before the recession (see Table 5.12). Whereas employment in resource industries increased by nearly half a million (15 per cent), employment in machine building and light industry declined by over 5 million (nearly 2 times) in 1990–95.

Russian restructuring, however, is far from being complete. As Russian domestic fuel prices are finally catching up with the world level, the previous industrial policy by default (together with the oddest fuel price subsidies) is coming to an end. The agenda for the new sound industrial policy is now twofold: first, redirect subsidies from inefficient to efficient industries; second, replace remaining price subsidies by direct income subsidies (or, in hopeless cases, by labour force and welfare programmes).

The most heavily subsidized sector is agriculture: in 1995 it received about $US2 billion from the federal budget and another $US3 billion from regional budgets – the amount equivalent to the monthly wages of agricultural employees (about $US50 per employee a month). If tax concessions and government and CBR's credits (which are never paid back and periodically written off) are taken into account, the total amount of transfers to agriculture increases to over $US14 billion, or nearly one-fourth of gross revenues of the whole sector (*Segodnya*, 31 July 1996). Because the bulk of all transfers goes to former collective and state farms that in 1995 produced just slightly over half of total agricultural output (peasants' households accounted for another 43 per cent of output, and independent farms for 2 per cent), it turns out that value added in large agricultural enterprises is close to zero, if not negative.

On the other hand, there are a few pretty competitive, or potentially competitive secondary manufacturing industries (i.e. those that can quickly become competitive with reasonable investment), which account for only a tiny part of government subsidies. The aerospace industry, especially the production of defence aircraft, is, perhaps, the most notable example. In 1995–96 Russian exports of armaments, after plummeting to below $US2 billion in 1994, increased to over $US3 billion a year according to Russian official statistics ($US4 billion according to Stockholm International Peace Research Institute, and $US6 billion according to the US Congressional Research Service) and it is estimated that half of this export consists of aircraft and parts. The leading fighter models, MIG and Sukhoy, account for nearly one-third of all defence aeroplanes used in the world (USA, CIS, and China excluded); several dozen of these fighters are exported annually. Russia also exported in 1995 seventy out of seventy-six produced helicopters (the production capacity is estimated at around 300).

Civil aircraft producers seem to be less competitive – exports in 1994 amounted to $US200 million only and production here nearly came to an end after Russian air companies stopped buying planes because of the shortage of funds. Hopes for the breakthrough are now linked to several joint projects with major Western aviation companies.

In the area of space technology Russian producers so far have managed to penetrate the market for commercial satellite launchers (about twenty are expected to be launched in 1997) with the most reliable 'Proton' carrier and have managed to ensure some financing from the USA for the joint Alfa project which allows Russia to continue its development of the spacelab.

Unfortunately, the Russian aerospace industry is not really getting any kind of special treatment from the government. Programmes to support conversion are coming to an end, whereas other budgetary sources of financing of restructuring are simply not available. Direct subsidies to both defence and non-defence aircraft producers seemed to be in the range of $US100 million in 1995 and could not make a substantial difference. Instead, the State Committee on Machine Building (*Roskommash*) was working hard to organize domestic production of goods that used to be imported from former Soviet republics and from far abroad: production capacities for forty-six such items, including commuter trains, buses, mini-tractors, pulp and paper machinery, magnetic tomographs, has recently been created, and the special programme with a significant name 'Import substitution' calls for establishing the capacities for another fifty-seven items not produced in Russia currently (*Fiansoviye Izvestiya*, 5 July 1996).

In the late 1920s, when the New Economic Policy (NEP) that allowed the existence of the market economy was about to be rolled back, there were debates between two schools of planners – genetics and teleologists. The former suggested that planning should be indicative rather than directive, that it should conform to the market, following trends identified by the market itself, that industrialization should start from light industry and proceed gradually as savings generated in a natural way would become available. The latter argued that planners should not feel constrained by the objective laws and potentials of the economy, that they should not rely on the slow and obsolete market, but should speed up the development by mobilizing savings through price controls and directive planning in order to quickly create the non-existent heavy industry that would allow industrialization of the country.

It is this latter view that became the official policy with the result that industrialization of the 1930s and later became a major isolationist import substitution experiment: from that time on the share of exports in Soviet GDP did not increase until large-scale fuel sales abroad started in the 1970s. The huge perverted industrial structure created without any regard to costs and prices of the world market proved to be stillborn and non-viable in 1992, when it finally faced foreign competition after half a century of artificial isolation.

Today Russia is choosing once again between export-oriented growth and protection autarky. On the one hand, there is the example of the East Asian countries that managed to rely on export as a locomotive of economic growth: in China, for instance, the share of export in GDP increased from 5 per cent in 1978 to 23 per cent in 1994, while the GDP itself was growing at an average rate of about 10 per cent. On the other hand, there are much less appealing examples of 'the champion of isolationism' – North Korea – and other socialist countries, of many developing countries of socialist orientation, who were creating their own heavy industries following the advice and the assistance of the Soviet Union, of India (where the share of export in GDP remained frozen at a level of 6 per cent from the 1950s to the 1980s) and many Latin American countries.

The option of promoting export-oriented growth would require massive and rapid industrial restructuring, mostly in favour of resource-based industries, but also in favour of some competitive high-tech sectors (aerospace) and, perhaps, particular capital- and labour-intensive industries at the expense of agriculture and most secondary manufacturing industries. Similar to the restructuring of government services, it is more efficient to make the needed cuts at once (and to support people through social and manpower programmes instead of subsidizing non-competitive companies) rather than to extend them over time forcing inefficient industries to die gradually. Rapid growth of the resource sector may provide rent (partly appropriated by the resource sector itself, partly by the government) for much needed investment to restructure some few still promising secondary manufacturing industries and enterprises (Gazprom and major oil companies are already trying to diversify by buying fuel equipment producing companies). This radical option, however, may not prove to be completely feasible politically since the inefficient sectors suffering from the competition of imported goods (agriculture and machine building) account for a much larger share of total employment than efficient sectors and exercise a good deal of influence in the corridors of power.

The other option – continuing support to major non-competitive industries – is a slower and more costly way of restructuring, implying the preservation of subsidies to and protection of weak producers. Paradoxically, this option, despite the intentions of those who propose it to stop the de-industrialization of the country, may lead to exactly the opposite: poor performance of the resource sector will not generate enough revenue to support all the non-competitive industries with the result that even the few still competitive or potentially competitive secondary manufacturing industries will fail to get necessary support and will slowly disintegrate.

CAPITAL ACCUMULATION AND LONG-TERM GROWTH

If the Russian economy starts to grow in 1997 at an average rate of 5 per cent a year, it would take till 2007 to achieve the pre-recession 1989 level of GDP (see Figure 5.6). Even 5 per cent annual growth may be quite an optimistic scenario, however, since most economies recovering from transformational recession did worse than

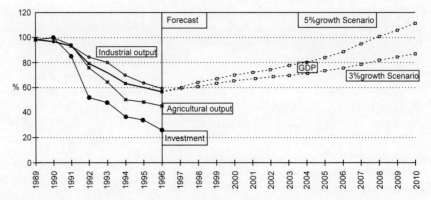

Figure 5.6 GDP, investment, industrial and agricultural output, 1989 = 100 per cent
Source: Goskomstat.

that. The crucial prerequisite for steady long-term economic growth – the solid flow of investment – is nearly completely missing from the current Russian economic scene.

Whereas previously investment/GDP ratios in the CPEs were among the highest in the world and comparable with the East Asian economies, they declined substantially during transition and are now more in line with Latin American countries (see Figure 5.7). The brighter part of the story is associated with the inevitable increases in capital productivity (which was extremely poor in CPEs) but these increases can materialize mostly through the restructuring of the existing capital stock, which also requires new investment.

Meanwhile, Russian investment in 1995–96 was nearly four times lower than in pre-recession 1989 and did not even compensate for the retirement of capital stock. In 1995 Russian investment/GDP ratio even fell below that of many East European countries and Baltic states (see Figure 5.7), where it increased markedly during recovery and where the magnitude of the needed restructuring is somewhat less dramatic than in Russia.

With regards to the availability of savings for financing investment, the future does not look encouraging either. Business profits and depreciation funds are low; personal savings, though high, are made mostly through accumulating hard currency (financing capital flight, not investment), whereas the rouble savings are falling (see Figure 5.8); the government runs a sizeable budget deficit, no less than half of which is financed through domestic borrowing (the bulk of the rest through international borrowing); the inflow of foreign direct investment is weak, so that a substantial trade surplus and international borrowing are barely enough to cover debt service payments and capital flight.

The prospects for increasing savings and investment and for achieving high growth rates thus seem to be pretty bleak, unless something is done to revert existing trends. Several measures seem to be especially promising in this respect. As in other areas, the feasibility of these measures depends largely on the

116

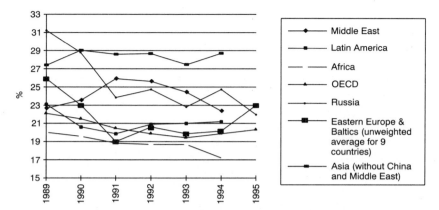

Figure 5.7 Percentage of share of investment in GDP
Source: EBRD (1996, 1997) for Eastern Europe and Baltics; Goskomstat for Russia; IMF for the rest.
Notes: For economies in transition = investment in fixed capital only, since changes in inventories were affected by high inflation.

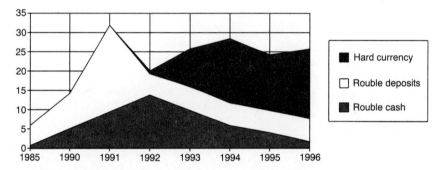

Figure 5.8 Personal savings as a percentage of personal disposable income

ability to build consensus and the confidence to carry out politically difficult decisions.

Exchange rate of the rouble

The necessary component of the growth strategy is the low exchange rate of the rouble. Undervaluation of domestic currency is a necessity for all developing countries since they usually need to earn a trade surplus to finance debt service payments and capital flight. Unlike mature market economies, most poorer countries keep the exchange rates of their currencies low as compared to Purchasing-power parity (PPP) (see Table 5.14), which allows them to limit consumption and imports and to stimulate exports, investment, and growth (more details in Popov 1996). This used to be the strategy of Japan, Korea, Taiwan and Singapore some time ago, when those countries were still poor and were catching up with high

117

income states. This is currently the strategy of many new emerging market economies, especially that of China, which continues to keep the exchange rate at an
extremely low level (five times lower than PPP rate) by accumulating foreign
exchange reserves at a record pace.

For resource-rich countries, however, there is a danger of 'Dutch disease', which
arises because resource export is so profitable that it earns a trade surplus even
under the overpriced exchange rate. Thus, Middle East countries (mostly oil
exporters) are the only major group of states in the developing world with the
exchange rate close to PPP (see Table 5.14). The threat of 'Dutch disease' is real for
Russia, since by 1996 the exchange rate of the rouble approached some 70 per cent
of the PPP. The previously high export growth rates slowed down substantially
(from 20 per cent in 1995 to 8 per cent in 1996 for total exports, and from 25 per
cent to 9 per cent, respectively, for exports to non-CIS states). Needless to say, it
was Russia's already weak export of manufactured goods that was most affected by
the appreciation of real exchange rate. In 1996 among the economies in transition
Russia (together with Slovenia, by far the richest country, experiencing recovery
from 1993) had the smallest gap between domestic and international prices (see
Table 5.15).

An appropriate exchange rate for the rouble is now the crucial issue of macro-
economic growth strategy. Economists and policy-makers tend to disagree on what
kind of exchange rate policy is best for economies in transition. While some stress the
importance of maintaining the stable *nominal* exchange rate by fixing it and using it.

Table 5.14 Ratio of actual exchange rate of national currencies in $US to PPP for selected countries in 1993[b]

Countries/regions	Ratio, percentage	Countries/regions	Ratio, percentage
OECD[a]	116	Transition economies[a]	81
Germany	126	Central Europe[a]	54
Japan	165 (179)	Slovenia	69
U.S.	100 (100)	Croatia	65
Portugal	73 (79)	Hungary	62 (65)
Developing countries[a]	44	Poland	48 (58)
Asia[a]	36	Slovak Republic	37 (51)
China	22 (19)	Czech Republic	36 (43)
India	24 (25)	Romania	31 (34)
Korea	72 (86)	Bulgaria	30 (31)
Turkey	54 (48)	USSR[a]	91
Africa[a]	37	Russia	26 (53)
Latin America[a]	46	Ukraine	18
Mexico	58 (39)	Moldovia	13
Middle East[a]	83	Belarus	9

Source: Russian Statistical Yearbook (1995: 474); *Finansoviye Izvestiya*, 10 November 1995; World Bank (1997: 248–50).
Note: [a] 1990.
    [b] Percentage figures in brackets for 1995.

Table 5.15 Ratio of the actual exchange rate to the PPP rate of the dollar for selected transition economies (range of monthly averages)

Country/year	1990	1991	1992	1993	1994	1995	1996
Slovenia	0.9–1.4	1.0–1.7	1.4–1.6	1.4–1.6	1.3–1.6	1.1–1.3	1.3–1.3
Hungary	1.9–2.4	1.9–2.0	1.7–1.8	1.6–1.8	1.6–1.8	1.5–1.6	1.7–1.8
Poland	2.1–3.9	1.6–1.9	1.8–2.0	1.8–2.0	2.1–2.3	1.8–2.0	1.8–1.8
Czech Republic	2.5–3.8	3.5–3.1	2.7–3.1	2.5–2.6	2.2–2.5	2.0–2.2	1.9–2.0
Slovak Republic	2.9–3.9	3.0–3.6	2.9–3.0	2.6–2.8	2.4–2.7	2.1–2.3	2.1–2.2
Lithuania	—	—	—	—	2.4–3.2	1.8–2.3	1.7–1.8
Romania	1.8–2.6	1.6–5.0	2.8–4.2	2.2–3.1	2.1–2.6	2.1–2.5	2.4–2.6
Bulgaria	3.3–5.1	2.9–10.9	3.0–4.7	2.3–2.8	2.3–3.1	1.8–2.2	1.9–2.8
Ukraine	—	—	—	—	—	1.8–2.5	1.3–1.7
Russia	—	33.0–131.0	10.2–45.7	2.5–8.0	2.4–2.8	1.4–2.4	1.4–1.5

Source: PlanEcon.

as a nominal anchor to fight inflation, others claim that *real* exchange rates are supposed to be kept stable (which implies constant devaluations, if inflation is higher than elsewhere) so as to ensure that the actual rate is substantially below PPP rate in order to stimulate export and growth (See Hosino *et al.* 1995 for more details). The Czech Republic, Estonia, Latvia, Mongolia in 1991–94 and more recently Russia, tried to keep stable the nominal exchange rate despite the continuation of rather high inflation, thus allowing the real exchange rate to appreciate. In contrast, in Poland, Romania, Slovakia, Slovenia, Croatia, Ukraine and Belarus the real exchange rate was more or less stable in 1991–94 while the nominal exchange rate depreciated considerably.

Each approach has its own advantages: while the first one may prove to be useful for fighting high inflation quickly (wherever it is possible) at the initial stages of macro-economic stabilization, the second one may be better suited for overcoming transformational recession and promoting economic recovery by facilitating the transfer of resources from domestic demand to exports, which is the pressing need in all economies in transition (Sato 1995).

The conventional shock-therapy approach to macro-economic stabilization recommends using the pegged exchange rate as a nominal anchor while pursuing an anti-inflationary policy. There is certainly reason in such an argument: a high rouble increases import competition and helps to hold down inflation, in fact this was the case in Russia in the second half of 1995. However, the desirability of the continuation of the strong rouble policy is highly questionable because it puts pressure on the export sector and increases foreign debt, forcing Russia to maintain high interest rates to slow down the capital flight at a time when exactly the opposite is needed.

There is a difference between a stable and a strong currency: whereas the former is highly desirable for all countries, the latter may prove to be an unaffordable luxury for economies in transition, like Russia, trying to overcome the transformational recession. It may well be therefore that the CBR and the government were right to establish a sort of a crawling peg for the rouble, but were wrong in choosing to peg it at a pretty high level.

By pegging the rouble at a lower rate and continuing to build up foreign exchange reserves, the CBR could have killed more than two birds with one stone: Russian exports and trade surplus would increase, domestic interest rates would fall, there would be additional stimulus for the dedollarization of the Russian economy and for the inflow of foreign direct investment. A weaker rouble, to put it another way, may be the device that would allow the maintenance of higher saving rates without high interest rates, the creation of additional stimuli for production, investment and exports, while limiting consumption and imports.

Although personal savings rate was high in Russia in recent years, the rouble savings rate (i.e. the proportion of Personal Disposable Income – PDI – invested in rouble cash, rouble bank accounts and other rouble-denominated financial assets) declined from about 20 per cent in 1992 to 6 per cent in 1996, while investment in hard currency (capital flight) as a percentage of PDI increased from 1 to 20 per cent (see Figure 5.8). In late 1995 Russian citizens and businesses, according to available estimates, were holding some $US43 billion in foreign currency, mostly US dollars ($US10 billion in domestic bank accounts, $US15 billion in cash and another $US18 billion in accounts outside Russia),[8] which was equivalent to over 10 per cent of Russian $US364 billion 1995 GDP at actual exchange rate. Despite the stability of the rouble in 1995 and much higher rouble interest rates (as compared to dollar interest rates), there was no noticeable decrease in purchases of hard currency (see Figure 5.8). While a low rouble policy may not immediately cause the reduction of purchases of hard currency, it may at least make it easier for CBR to limit the growth of rouble money supply through making the capital flight more expensive (as more roubles will be needed to buy hard currency).

Another good reason for keeping the exchange rate low and building up foreign exchange reserves is the new vulnerability of the rouble with respect to short-term capital flows. Foreign investment in rouble-denominated government treasury bills was recently allowed by authorities and quickly increased to some 15 per cent of the $US40 billion market for government treasury bills in 1997. Restrictions for foreign investment in GKO are to be completely removed by 1998 (*Segodnya*, 26 July 1996; *Fiansoviye Izvestya*, 10 April 1997). Foreign investment in those securities is definitely desirable to lower abnormally high domestic interest rates that hinder investment, but it requires high foreign exchange reserves as a protection from the balance-of-payments crisis.

With an appropriate monetary policy (at least partial sterilization of increases in the money supply caused by foreign exchange reserves build up), the inflationary pressure may be dealt with, as shown by the example of many emerging market economies. Money-based stabilization (as opposed to exchange rate-based stabilization) was successful in quite a number of countries (Albania, Slovenia, Croatia, Macedonia) and there is no evidence that it is an inferior strategy to pegging the exchange rate for fighting inflation (Zettermeyer and Citrin 1995). Exchange rate is far too important to use it only for fighting inflation. Even more so now that Russia currently seems to be pretty close to achieving macro-economic stability and looks forward to economic growth.

While the technicalities of managing a low exchange rate are not discussed here, it may be appropriate to mention that such a policy has one important practical advantage. Unlike other measures to promote growth, it may be implemented relatively easily since it favours the interests of all the powerful industrial groups (creating a stimulus for the export-oriented resource sector, as well as providing protection from import competition to secondary manufacturing and agriculture), whereas costs of such a policy (limits on consumption) are paid by unorganized and politically non-influential consumers.

Reforming the pension system

A promising way to increase domestic savings is to reform the current pension system. The debate over whether the transition from the current pay-as-you-go system to the mandatory/voluntary fully funded pension plans can raise domestic savings or not, cannot be dealt with in this chapter, even more so since the evidence on the issue seems to be mixed (Schmidt-Hebbel *et al.* 1996: 87–117). Irrespective of the debate, however, it is pretty obvious that the current Russian pay-as-you-go system is extremely inefficient and should be reformed.

The existing system is based on mandatory contributions to the off-budget Pension Fund by employers (28 per cent payroll tax) and employees (1 per cent). The share of pensioners in the total population is only 16 per cent, whereas the share of employees is 45 per cent, which means that the average pension should approach 80 per cent of the average wage ($45 \div 16 \times 29$ minus administrative costs), whereas in reality it amounted only to 38 per cent in 1995 (see Table 5.9). Though the share of wages in GDP in 1995 fell to a record low of 30 per cent, if payroll taxes were fully collected, the share of pensions in GDP was supposed to be at a level of at least 9 per cent (30×0.29 plus pension taxes paid on non-wage incomes), whereas in reality it was only 6 per cent. Even so, the Pension Fund is unable to make the ends meet, still fails to pay pensions in time, accumulates pension arrears, and is lobbying for increased rates of pension contributions.

To put it another way, the pension system is apparently not working properly, the major reason being the unwillingness of employers to pay very high social security contributions (altogether over 40 per cent of the wage fund: 28 per cent for pensions and the rest for medical, disability and unemployment insurance) and the extreme inefficiency of the authorities in collecting these (and other) taxes. This is the fundamental reality of the Russian economic situation: there is no short-term solution to the tax evasion problem and hence, it is the pension system (and government spending in general) that has to be adjusted to the financial abilities of the state, not vice versa.

Steps to reform the pension system have been modest so far. In 1997 the government planned to start transition (which would require three to five years) to the so-called 'individualized pension accounts', in which all contributions made by employers and employees will be personified. Two laws were drafted by the government in February 1997 envisaging that pensions in future would consist of two parts: the base pension equal to 80 per cent of the subsistence minimum for pensioners; and the additional sum dependent upon the size of the pensioner's former salary and the length of time he or she contributed to the Pension Fund. Though it is not exactly clear what the link would be between the amount of accumulated contributions and pension levels, such a system (provided there would be at least some links), once implemented, is likely to make employees interested in checking how accurately their employers make payments to the Pension Fund. More radical plans – a transition to the Singapore-type mandatory fully funded pension systems – seem to find supporters among academics and in the government.[9] If the ability of the government to gather taxes remains weak in the foreseeable future, it may well be that the pay-as-you-go system is an unaffordable luxury for Russia.

Promoting foreign and domestic investment

One of the major missed opportunities of recent years was the failure to attract foreign direct investment into resource projects. Overall, in 1989–96 Russia received some $US5 billion of FDI, which is equivalent to about 1 per cent of its annual GDP, as compared to 30 per cent of GDP in Hungary and China, and 5–15 per cent in Albania, the Czech Republic, Estonia, Latvia, Poland (EBRD 1997: 12; World Bank 1996: 64). The reasons for poor Russian performance in this area are well known: political instability, high inflation and unstable currency (until recently), incomplete and frequently modified legislation, poor infrastructure, etc. Nevertheless, the fact is that Russia failed to use its 'resource advantages' to bring in foreign capital: the huge rent in resource industries provides compensation for political and economic risks, so foreign investors are less sensitive to economic, political and legal uncertainty. Oil-rich Azerbaijan, for instance, in 1989–96 managed to attract $US0.9 billion of foreign direct investment (equivalent to over 20 per cent of GDP even under conditions of the ongoing war), while resource-rich Kazakhstan and Turkmenistan managed nearly $US3 billion and $US0.5 billion, 13 per cent and 11 per cent of GDP, respectively (EBRD 1997).

In contrast, Russia in recent years has failed to prevent the reduction of investment and output even in competitive resource industries (oil and gas included), which should be viewed as a major failure of government policy. Some major resource projects have debated for nearly a decade with little practical progress, while the crucial law on the list of projects eligible for the production-sharing agreement was discussed for two years by the parliament and still not approved at the time of writing (mid-1997). The major reason is probably the old-type mentality – better not to use the resources at all, than to sell them at a 'low' price, the belief that the policy-makers know better than the international market the 'real' price of resource projects and joint ventures, and the unwillingness 'to allow the foreigners to get rich on Russian resources'. However, investments were needed yesterday and are needed now – every day of delay with major resource projects slows down Russian economic recovery.

Another way to stimulate investment is to increase government investment in infrastructure – even at the expense of financing them through government borrowing. As available evidence suggests, public saving does not crowd out private saving one to one, but, rather, private sector offsets each dollar of public saving by not saving only $US0.25 to $US0.50 (Schmidt-Hebbel *et al.* 1996: 87–117). Very fast growing economies of East Asia normally keep government investment high, despite relatively low ratios of total government expenditure to GDP, so that the share of capital expenditure in total government outlays is much higher than in other countries (Sachs and Warner 1996). To put it another way, even debt-financed government investments pay off by increasing the national saving and investment rates.

Unfortunately, Russia was not able to increase government investment in recent years, in fact, it was falling at the same rate as private investment. According to Goskomstat, the share of state-supported investment (excluding investment of state enterprises, but including that financed through off-budget funds and cheap state credits) in total investment stood at a level of just over 30 per cent in 1992–95, whereas the share of investment directly financed from federal and regional budgets decreased from 26–33 per cent in 1992–93 to 21–24 per cent in 1994–95. As a proportion of GDP, budgetary financed investment declined from 4.5 per cent in 1992 to 3.8 per cent in 1994 (EBRD 1995: 72). In 1995 the Ministry of the Economy developed a mechanism for selecting and supporting promising investment projects (20 per cent of total investment financing is to be provided by the government, 80 per cent by the private investor), but the mechanism is not working because of lack of funds.

CONCLUSIONS

As mentioned in the beginning, the aim of this chapter was not to discuss the advantages and disadvantages of shock therapy versus gradual transition strategy, but rather to examine the trends that shape the basic features of future Russian capitalism and to evaluate some possible scenarios of economic development. Major conclusions are summarized below.

1. In carrying out privatization – the most important institutional reform – the Russian government has given work collectives larger concessions than the governments in the East European countries did. By doing that it emphasized political feasibility over equity and economic efficiency. It seems, however, that the game was worth a candle: massive and quick privatization became socially acceptable and politically feasible at the cost of establishing control of the

insiders (former managers and work collectives) over most privatized enterprises. As shares are traded, strategic investors from the outside gain control over enterprises and start restructuring.

2. Decentralization of the banking system and the emergence of millions of individual shareholders due to the extremely 'worker-friendly' nature of Russian privatization facilitated the development of the American-type (market-based) system of corporate financing and control: banks and other financial institutions are not normally stakeholders in non-financial companies, nor do bank credits account for a substantial portion of investment financing. Nevertheless, the usual advantages of such a system are not really visible in Russia: shareholders do not seem to exercise efficient control over management, whereas small markets for corporate securities cannot compensate for the lack of bank credits.

3. While the magnitude of the Russian recession and the large increases in income inequalities have led to a considerable reduction of living standards for the majority of Russians, the government has done less to mitigate these unfavourable developments (and thus to strengthen the support for its reforms) than in Eastern Europe. In a sense, in the area of social policy, Russia was more shock-oriented than the East European countries, though the need for sound social policies in Russia was greater than elsewhere.

4. Taking into account objective difficulties in bringing down inflation, the recent Russian experience with macro-economic stabilization (massive reduction of the deficit and tightening of monetary policy) should be viewed as moderately successful. However, the inability to properly handle the downsizing of the government (poorly designed cuts in expenditure without the reassessment of commitments to provide public goods and social transfers) remains an obvious policy failure. The role of the state in recent years has declined substantially not only in terms of the reduction of state property, state revenues and expenditure (which was inevitable and planned), but also in terms of its ability to efficiently provide public goods and a regulatory framework (which was neither planned, nor desirable).

5. It was unrealistic to proceed with the elimination of all subsidies because the inefficient machine building industry and agriculture were so large and so much behind efficient resource industries in terms of productivity. However, the actual Russian policy in the field was largely a failure, partly because it took the most inefficient form of price subsidies (instead of direct subsidies), partly because it did not succeed in either supporting investment in competitive resource industries, or in allocating funds to those few high tech industries (aerospace) that had good prospects of becoming competitive.

6. Granted that a quick exchange rate-based stabilization was not used in Russia anyway, it probably made sense to keep the exchange rate considerably undervalued to encourage exports, restructuring, and growth, while fighting inflation through tight fiscal and monetary policy (sterilization of increases in money supply caused by the growth of foreign exchange reserves), not through highly priced national currency. The crawling peg established for the rouble from mid-

1995 proved to be an important device in fighting inflation in the second half of 1995, but Russian domestic prices were rapidly approaching world levels and there is now a danger that a strong rouble will undermine exports and economic recovery.

If current trends continue, emerging Russian capitalism is not likely to copy European or East Asian patterns of development, but instead may resemble somewhat the Latin American model. Poor traditions of complying with laws and regulations and of low tax revenues; highly uneven distribution of wealth and income and strong social tensions; government failure to provide public goods and social transfers and to restructure the economy through supporting the winners rather than the losers; poor investment climate, capital flight, growing foreign debt, low savings, investment, and growth – this bleak picture is the most probable option if the government does not carry out major reforms.

The brighter scenario, on the other hand, implies that the government would adopt a growth strategy based on:

- downsizing part of the government, while making the remaining part more efficient;
- sound industrial policy favouring export-oriented industries;
- efforts to build consensus through strong social policy;
- measures to stimulate savings and investment (through low exchange rate, pension system reform, increased government and foreign investment).

While quick progress in adopting such a growth strategy does not seem to be politically feasible, some steps in this direction are more or less inevitable, especially in the longer term.

NOTES

1 This chapter is partly based on a paper 'A Russian puzzle. What makes the Russian economic transformation a special case', WIDER/UNU, RFA 29, 1996.

2 *Finansoviye Izvestiya*, 29 September 1995. Data are from the report of the Joint Committee of Goskomstat and the World Bank, which recalculated Russian GDP to account for the previous understatement of the growth of the service sector. Later these data were accepted as official.

3 During voucher privatization there emerged over 650 'voucher investment funds' – close-ended mutual funds which accumulated the vouchers of about 25 million people. Their investments are mostly in shares of loss-making and low profitable companies that are not traded on the market; dividends that these funds pay on their own shares do not even compensate inflationary losses (in 1995, when inflation stood at 130 per cent, dividends provided returns of only 70 per cent). As a rule, these funds did not emerge as powerful institutional investors.

4 See, for instance, *The Financial Times*, 1 November 1996. The usually named banks are Oneximbank (headed until recently by V. Potanin), Menatep (headed by M. Khodorkovsky), Stolychniy Bank (which recently acquired Agroprombank, headed by A. Smolensky), Most Bank (headed by V. Gussinsky), Alfa Bank (headed by P. Aven and M. Friedman). Another company often mentioned together with these banks, Logovaz

(headed until recently by the outspoken B. Berezovsky) is not a bank, but a dealer for the major VAZ autoplant.

5 The share of compensation of employees in total monetary income decreased from 74 per cent in 1990 to 40 per cent in 1995, while the share of property, entrepreneurial and other income grew from 13 per cent to 44 per cent in the same period (the rest is accounted for by social transfers). This shift may be only partly explained by the changing social structure of the Russian society, since in most mature and emerging market economies the share of labour income is much higher than the 40 per cent registered in Russia. The major reason for the dramatic increase in business and other incomes at the expense of labour compensation is the ability of employers to hide a good part of wages from taxation by showing it as entrepreneurial and other incomes in bookkeeping in order to avoid high social insurance payments (calculated as a percentage of the wage fund) and high excess wage tax (effective in 1992–95). The ratio of average wage to per capita GDP in 1994 in Russia was only 60 per cent as compared to about 100 per cent in most East European economies, and about 120 per cent in the USA.

6 These industries are just extreme examples. Differences in efficiency and competitiveness of other industries seem to follow this same general pattern: high in primary manufacturing and low in secondary manufacturing. For instance, with regards to chemicals, fertilizer production seems to be efficient and competitive, whereas pharmaceuticals do not. The only major exception is the relatively efficient aerospace industry.

7 After the deregulation of prices in January 1992, fuel and energy prices were controlled directly and later indirectly (through export quotas and export taxes), but nevertheless were allowed to increase from 3 to 5 per cent of the world price level in January 1992, to between 30 and 40 per cent of the world level in 1994, and to about 70 per cent in late 1995. Export taxes on resource goods were gradually lowered and finally abolished on 1 April 1996 (export tariffs for oil were eliminated from 1 July 1996), whereas prices for fuel exports to near abroad increased to 75 per cent of the world price for gas (40 per cent for oil and coal) in 1994, and to about 70–80 per cent in 1995.

8 *Business MN* 1995: 43. Total capital flight from Russia has reportedly been at a level of $US7 to $US16 billion annually from 1992 to 1996, amounting to perhaps as much as 5 per cent of GDP and one-third of private savings, and roughly equal to annual external borrowings (*The Financial Times*, 9 April 1997; *Finansoviye Izvestiya*, 1 April 1997).

9 The plan for such a new pension system was outlined by the expert of the Moscow Carnegie Centre and the idea was supported by the Deputy Minister of the Economy (*Segodnya*, 17 July and 14 August 1996).

BIBLIOGRAPHY

Aslund, A. (1996) 'New Russian enriched through three main sources', *Finansoviye Izvestiya*, 20 June 1996 (in Russian).

Barr, N., Flanders, S. *et al.* (1996) *From Plan to Market. World Development Report*, Oxford: Oxford University Press.

Belousov, A. *et al.* (1995) *Economic Monitoring of Russia: Global Trends and Business Conditions in Industry*, Moscow: Institute for Economic Forecasting, July 1995: 39–42 (in Russian).

Blasi, J., Kroumova, M. and Kruse, D. (1996) *Kremlin Capitalism: Privatizing the Russian Economy*, Ithaca and London: Cornell University Press.

Blasi, J. (1997) *Russian Research Project*, New Brunswick, NJ: Rutgers University Press.

Cornia, G.A. (1996) 'Transition and income distribution: theory, evidence and initial interpretation', paper prepared for the conference 'Transition in Eastern Europe: current issues and perspectives', Dresden, March 1996.

De Melo, M., Denizer, C. and Gelb, A. (1995) 'From plan to market: patterns of transition' (Policy Research Working Papers, 1564), Washington, DC: The World Bank.

Dmitriyev, M., Matovnikov, M., Mikhailov, L., Sycheva, L., Timofeev, Y. and Warner, A. (1996) *Russian Banks on the Eve of Financial Stabilization*, St. Petersburg: Norma (in Russian).

EBRD (1995, 1996, 1997) *Transition Report*, London: EBRD.

Economic Systems 19(2): 103, June 1995.

The Economist, various issues as shown.

Expert, 13 January 1997: 12–13, 14–15.

The Financial Times, various issues as shown.

Finansoviye Izvestiya, various issues as shown.

Hansson, A. H. and Tombak, T. (1996) 'Banking crises states: causes, solutions and lessons', paper prepared for the 'Second Dubrovnik conference on transition economies', Dubrovnik, June.

Hosino, S. *et al.* (1995) *Current State of and Goals for the Russian Economy* (proposals on Economic Reforms in Russia), Tokyo: Japanese State Institute for Economic Research, June 1995 (in Russian).

International Monetary Fund (1996) *International Financial Statistics* 6, Washington, DC: IMF.

Johnson, L. D., Neave, E. H. and Pazderka, B. (1997) 'Financial systems in transition economies', paper for the European Public Choice Society Annual Meeting, Prague, Spring 1997.

Johnson, L. D. and Pazderka, B. (1995) *It's No Gamble: The Economic and Social Benefits of Stock Markets*, Vancouver, BC: Fraser Institute.

Khozyaistvo SSSR (National Economy of the USSR) (monthly publication), Moscow: Goskomstat (various years).

Milanovic, B. (1995) *Poverty, Inequality and Social Policy in Transition Economies*, Washington, DC: World Bank.

Pappe, Y. (1996) *Institutsional'niye Izmeneniya v TEK Rossii i ikh Vosproizvodstvenniye Osnovaniya (1992–96 gg.)*, unpublished paper, Moscow.

Plan Econ Report (various years) Washington, DC: Plan Econ Inc.

Pohl, G., Jedrzejczak, G.T. and Anderson, R.E. (1995) *Creating Capital Markets in Central and Eastern Europe*, Washington, DC: World Bank.

Popov, V. (1996) 'Growth strategy', *Segodnya*, 14 March 1996 (in Russian).

Rossiysky Statistichesky Yezhegodnik (Russian Statistical Yearbook), various years, Moscos: Goskomstat.

Sachs, J. and Warner, A. (1996) *Achieving Rapid Growth in the Transition Economies of Central Europe*, Cambridge, MA: Harvard Institute for International Development, January.

Sato, T. (1995) 'Adjusted concepts of transformation policies: some cordial suggestions', a paper presented at the International Workshop 'Reevaluating economic reforms in Central and Eastern Europe since 1989', Budapest, September 1995.

Schmidt-Hebbel, K., Serven, L. and Solimano, A. (1996) 'Saving and investment: paradigms, puzzles, policies', *The World Bank Research Observer* **11** (1) (February): 87–117.

Segodnya, various issues as shown.

State Statistical Bureau (1995) *China Statistical Yearbook*, Beijing: China Statistical Publishing House.

Sutela, P. (1996) *Privatization in the Countries of Eastern and Central Europe and of the Former Soviet Union*, Helsinki: UNU/WIDER, 1996.

A Study of the Soviet Economy (1991), Washington, DC: IMF, World Bank, OECD, EBRD, 3 vols.

UN International Comparison Programme (1995) *Russian Statistical Yearbook 1995*, Moscow: Goskomstat: 474.

World Bank (1997) *World Development Indicators*, Washington, DC: World Bank.

Zettermeyer, J. and Citrin, D. (1995) 'Stabilization: fixed versus flexible exchange rates', in D.A. Citrin and A.K. Lahiri (eds) *Policy Experiences and Issues in the Baltics, Russia, and Other Countries of the Former Soviet Union*, Washington, DC: IMF.

6

REGIONAL ECONOMIC INTEGRATION IN SUB-SAHARAN AFRICA

Piet Konings and Henk Meilink

INTRODUCTION

Since the attainment of political independence, African leaders have repeatedly expressed their commitment to regional integration, mainly for political and economic reasons. One result is that Africa now has the largest number of regional integration arrangements in the world. Unfortunately, our historical review of these schemes will provide ample evidence that most of them have remained ineffective or dormant.

The issue of regional integration has acquired a new relevance and urgency in Africa of late due to wide-reaching changes globally and nationally. For various reasons, contemporary Africa has been forced to operate in a far more hostile external context than a decade ago. Among these are the demise of the Soviet communist ideology and the opening up of markets in Eastern Europe. African leaders have become deeply concerned that such changes will further diminish aid and capital flows to Africa. Moreover, the past years have witnessed a decisive move towards the formation of regional trading blocs – Europe, the Americas, and East Asia – which pose a severe threat to Africa's trading prospects. Africa's situation has become all the more alarming as its national economies are experiencing a deep and prolonged economic crisis. That is why virtually all African states have been compelled to implement IMF and World Bank-mandated Structural Adjustment Programmes (SAPs) in one form or another. SAPs are intended to tighten up government expenditures in order to reduce the budget and balance-of-payments deficits. Their central demands include elimination of subsidies; dismantling of price controls; 'rationalization' of the state sector through privatization, layoffs, wage cuts and closures; liberalization of the economy, guided by 'market forces' domestically and 'comparative advantage' internationally; promotion of commodity exports and foreign investment; and currency devaluation (Daddieh 1995).

By all accounts, African leaders have become more convinced than before that Africa has no choice but to pursue regional integration if it is to transcend its growing marginalization in the global economy and its severe economic crisis. Their renewed commitment to regional integration was clearly expressed during the June

1991 Organization of African Unity (OAU) summit meeting at Abuja, Nigeria. On that occasion, they signed a treaty to establish an African Economic Community (AEC) by the year 2025, complete with an Africa-wide monetary union.

In this chapter we wish first to review the various regional integration schemes that came into existence in the aftermath of independence, and then to try to explain the reasons for their relative failure. Finally, we will examine the consequences of Africa's rapidly changing position in the global economy for regional integration.

THE EMERGENCE AND DEVELOPMENT OF REGIONAL INTEGRATION SCHEMES IN SUB-SAHARAN AFRICA

Regional economic integration schemes in sub-Saharan Africa (SSA) seek as elsewhere to expand intra-regional trade and, eventually, to create economic unions between member states. There are typically four stages in the process of creating such a union: the establishment of a preferential or free trade area by reducing or eliminating barriers to trade between member states; the creation of a customs union involving free or preferential trade between members plus the creation of a common external tariff on imports from non-member states; the initiation of a common market where capital and labour join goods and non-factor services in a free flow between member states; and the realization of an economic union when common fiscal and monetary policies (the latter implying a single central bank) are added to the common market (Martin 1992; McCarthy 1995). The economic argument in favour of integration essentially rests on the potentials which a larger market size will create (Aghrout 1992). It would enable African firms to benefit from the advantages of the 'economies of scale' principle, allowing them to optimize their production capacities and thus reduce their production costs to (internationally) competing levels. Furthermore, the pooling of scarce resources through cooperation and integration would increase the efficient use of available economic and social means of production, at the same time serving the goal of lower production costs. Integration would also trigger increased trade between partners which in turn would enhance regional inter-industry linkages and induce production growth in individual countries.

In addition to the predominant economic rationale for regional integration, several factors have furthered the proliferation of these schemes in Africa (Lancaster 1991; Daddieh 1995). First, regional economic ties have a long history in Africa. Long-distance trade throughout Africa existed before the Europeans arrived. While colonialism undoubtedly disrupted and even altered some patterns of interaction, it did not completely destroy all such ties. Moreover, the colonial powers even organized some economic activities – trade, finance, monetary affairs, administrative responsibilities, transport and communication networks – on a regional basis. A number of these arrangements survived into the independence period, including the monetary unions between francophone countries and France, and the East African Common Services Organization comprised of Kenya, Uganda, and Tanzania.

Second, African states gained independence at a time when regional integration was popular among developing countries and other parts of the world. Latin American states, supported by the Economic Commission for Latin America, were experimenting with their own schemes of regional cooperation, including the Central American Common Market and the Latin American Free Trade Area. Asian states soon followed with the creation in 1967 of the Association of South East Asian Nations (ASEAN). The European Economic Community (EEC), initiated with the signing of the Treaty of Rome in 1957, was already functioning, and it provided a model for groups of developing countries wanting to create their own regional integration schemes.

Third, African leaders brought with them to independence their own aspirations towards continental or regional unity. One group, the Panafricanists, favoured political integration as a prerequisite to economic integration. Its members (Kwame Nkrumah, Sékou Touré, Modibo Keita, Cheikh Anta Diop) advocated the immediate and total integration of the African continent, and the setting up of a single continental government with common institutions. Another group, the Gradualists or Functionalists, anxious to preserve the African states' recently acquired sovereignty, favoured a more gradual approach to African integration. This group (Félix Houphouét-Boigny, Jomo Kenyatta, Léopold Senghor) held that economic integration should precede political integration. Its members championed loose cooperation in non-controversial areas (technical and economic issues) and viewed regional institutions as a stepping-stone towards the increasing political and economic unification of the continent. In the end, the Panafricanists had to accept major revisions to their original vision to enable a continental interstate organization, the OAU, to be born in May 1963. Significantly, this organization was not given the authority to make decisions that were binding on member states. Regional cooperation among African governments centred thenceforth primarily on economic objectives.

Fourth, given the small size of African markets and the difficulty, if not impossibility, of gaining access to markets of the industrialized world, many African leaders and the Economic Commission for Africa (ECA) perceived regional integration as a means to effect import-substituting industrial growth. Regional integration, in fact, was to provide the necessary protection and training ground for industrial development:

Regional integration in this way becomes an inward-looking instrument of industrial development, diverting trade from cheaper sources in the rest of the world to higher cost producers within the union. Aligned to this argument for protection, but viewed from the opposite end of the spectrum, is the view that the larger protected market could serve as a training ground within which long-protected domestic industries can cut their competitive teeth in the larger regional market before being exposed to the harsh conditions of the global market-place.

(McCarthy 1995: 215)

Fifth, regional integration has often been projected as the most appropriate strategy to cut the heavy dependence of African states on international trade and to realize collective economic self-reliance. For instance, the Lagos Plan of Action (LPA), adopted by African Heads of State at the OAU meeting at Lagos in April 1980, proposed an African Economic Community aiming at 'the promotion of collective, accelerated, self-reliant and self-sustaining development of member states' (Danso 1995).

Finally, regionalism has been difficult to resist politically. There is a general recognition on the part of African leaders of a need to act in concert in order to enhance their bargaining position *vis-à-vis* foreign governments, international institutions and multinational corporations.

Regional Integration in Africa

It is interesting to observe that regional integration efforts in post-colonial Africa initially were based on regional integration schemes introduced by the former colonial powers. We want to briefly discuss here three such initiatives. One of the first attempts was the creation of the 'Union douanière et économique de l'Afrique centrale' (UDEAC) on 8 December 1964. This union, comprising the Central African countries Cameroon, the Central African Republic, Chad, the Congo, Equatorial Guinea, and Gabon, revamped the Equatorial African Customs Union (UDE) created by France in 1959. Though the objective of the UDEAC was the creation of a common market, it has made very little progress since. Several reasons can explain why UDEAC member countries have failed to achieve any significant economic integration. They include heavy dependence on export of primary commodities to the industrialized market economies, restriction of free trade movement of resources among member countries due to government regulation of economic activity or competitive nationalism, and French dominance of the economies of UDEAC countries, resulting in French influence on the patterns and direction of their trade.

The next serious attempt at economic integration in Africa was the establishment of the East African Community (EAC) by Kenya, Tanzania, and Uganda in December 1967, which was based on various forms of cooperation during the British colonial period. The community began with a shared currency, a regionally coordinated infrastructure, harmonized economic policies, a system of common institutions, and unrestricted labour mobility. However, this promising scheme collapsed within a decade because of dissatisfaction with the distribution of the benefits of integration. Tanzania and Uganda felt the arrangements worked to the benefit of Kenya, the most industrially developed country of the three. The emergence of General Idi Amin as President of Uganda soured its relationship with Tanzania and also disrupted the meeting patterns of the Community. Ideological differences between capitalist Kenya and socialist Tanzania made cooperation difficult. Moreover, the community members all maintained strong trade relations with Britain, further diminishing the chances for integration.

Another important integration scheme was the 'Communauté économique de l'Afrique de l'Ouest' (CEAO) established in April 1973. It was the successor organization to the 'Union douanière et économique de l'Afrique occidentale' (UDEAO), a free trade area set up within the framework of the former French West African Federation. Its membership included seven francophone West African states, namely Benin, Burkina Faso, Ivory Coast, Mali, Mauritania, Niger and Senegal. Like UDEAC member states, CEAO members were also part of the franc zone system and its affiliated institutions. The World Bank declared in 1989 that the CEAO has been the most successful among Africa's market integration schemes (World Bank 1989). While this may be the case, the organization has certainly also experienced various problems and difficulties. First of all, there has been little or no progress towards implementing the measures of positive integration required to establish an economic entity. The common external tariff, scheduled for January 1985, was not implemented. In addition, most member states continued to operate certain trade restrictions in defiance of the Treaty provisions. Furthermore, the absence of a regional industrial policy resulted in duplication of industrial efforts. In fact, the industrial development of the CEAO countries was heavily dependent upon investment by foreign (French and American) multinational corporations (Martin 1992: 76–77).

Following these and other tentative beginnings, there have been several renewed attempts to forge regional integration. There is no space to fully discuss all these schemes (see Aly 1994). Here we will review only the foremost current ones. These can be divided into two broad groups: those that fit into the historic 1980 LPA, and those that emerged outside the LPA.

The LPA sought to promote Africa's long-term industrialization and development through the creation of larger, sub-regional markets and, eventually, of a continent-wide market by merging the sub-regional markets. The ECA sponsored the setting up of three regional arrangements which covered the following SSA sub-regions: West Africa, East and Southern Africa, and Central Africa. West Africa was to be served by the Economic Community of West African States (ECOWAS), with sixteen member states. ECOWAS actually pre-dated the LPA, having been established in 1975, and it served as a model for subsequent integration schemes within the framework of the LPA. East and Southern Africa was to be served by the Preferential Trade Area (PTA), established in 1981 but put into operation in 1984, with nineteen member states. In 1993, the PTA was superseded by the Common Market for Eastern and Southern Africa (COMESA). Central Africa was to be served by the Economic Community of Central African States (ECCAS), with ten member states. Though the treaty establishing ECCAS was approved back in 1983, its implementation is still under negotiation. Together with the Arab Maghreb Union (AMU), established in 1989, with five member states, these arrangements were expected to bring about an all-African common market by the year 2000.

These LPA schemes were clearly over-ambitious. They appear to have been motivated first and foremost by political considerations: the introduction of large trading blocs enabled the OAU to give expression to its Panafrican ideal. They did not sufficiently take into account the various economic problems facing regional integration in Africa. In fact, they were simply superimposed upon the already existing integration arrangements. This created the problem of overlapping memberships and conflicts of divided loyalty. Little wonder that none of them have achieved their integration targets within the timetables adopted. ECOWAS has perhaps been the most visible and certainly the most closely studied one (Asante 1986; Okolo and Wright 1990; Lancaster 1991; Martin 1992). Its experience shows the negligible progress these schemes have made in economic terms and their eventual exploitation for political and diplomatic ends.

ECOWAS

ECOWAS was established on 28 May 1975 mainly at the initiative of Nigeria, which strove to counter French influence in the region and to enhance its own. This was the first regional attempt to integrate French, English and Portuguese-speaking African states with a combined population of over 185 million and a GDP of $US123 billion. Economic union of the sixteen member states (Benin, Burkina Faso, Cape Verde, Gambia, Ghana, Guinea, Guinea Bissau, Ivory Coast, Liberia, Mali, Mauritania, Niger, Nigeria, Senegal, Sierra Leone and Togo) was planned to come about in three stages. In the first two-year period, members were to freeze their tariffs on primary products produced by other members and on manufactured goods eligible for preferential treatment in intra-ECOWAS trade. The second period, which was to last eight years, was to culminate in the elimination of import duties on intra-ECOWAS trade. The final stage would last five years and involve the imposition of a common external tariff. For products to qualify for tariff concessions within the community, a local ownership rule required eventual 51 per cent local ownership, as well as 35 per cent local value added.

To compensate the poorer members of ECOWAS for the costs of participation in the community, a Fund for Cooperation, Compensation, and Development was set up. ECOWAS members were to contribute to the fund on the basis of their relative income levels and their gains from new investments in the community. Finally, a West African Clearing House was set up in association with ECOWAS to facilitate the use of local currencies in financing intra-ECOWAS trade.

While institution building has proceeded apace, no significant progress has yet been made towards positive integration in ECOWAS. Intra-community trade has remained low, amounting to only 5 per cent of the total trade, and has even shown a steady tendency to decline. Indeed, trade liberalization has made little progress: no common external tariff has yet been established, the 1981 deadline for the freezing of tariff rates was not met, and little has been done towards implementing the new timetable.

The less developed ECOWAS member states also fear that the support and compensation arrangements will prove inadequate in the face of the dominant position of Ivory Coast, Nigeria and Senegal. Furthermore, ECOWAS's rule of product origin has become a source of serious disagreements. The rule bolsters indigenous manufacturers but restricts exports from Ivory Coast and Senegal (since their industrial plants are considered foreign investment) and discourages foreign investment. More critically, the pattern of trade has not altered. Ivory Coast and Nigeria still dominate the export of manufactured goods. Instead of progress on labour mobility, there was a setback: in 1981 and 1983, Nigeria expelled more than 1 million Ghanaian migrant workers.

There is no movement of capital within the region because capital markets remain underdeveloped. Lack of progress in the payments system is due to the failure of ECOWAS (notwithstanding its declared long-term commitment) to establish a single monetary zone, with a common currency and a pooling of foreign exchange reserves. Non-compliance of member states includes a failure to contribute their full agreed payments to the community budget and their capital contribution to the fund. ECOWAS integration efforts have been further complicated by several other economic and political factors. Its sixteen members also belong to the Lomé Conventions: thus, 70 per cent of ECOWAS's principal exports go to Europe, and indeed, the latter was the largest source of foreign aid for all but two of the ECOWAS states in 1987. Internal cohesion has been undermined by the chaotic sociopolitical landscape typified by civil wars in Liberia and Sierra Leone and political instability in Gambia, Togo and Nigeria. Internal cohesion has also been affected by France's economic and political dominance over its former colonies, creating problems of conflicting memberships and loyalties. Some have attributed ECOWAS's slow pace of integration to the so-called Nigerian factor, which refers to the fear of domination by Nigerian political and economic power in the region. Despite these multiple problems, most heads of state continue to attend the annual meetings, vociferously reaffirm their commitment to the goals of the organization, and frequently approve new and often ambitious schemes for ECOWAS to undertake. According to Lancaster (1991), two benefits, both of them political, derive from ECOWAS's annual meetings. One is the exposure heads of state receive in their own media and in the media of other West African states by participating in a meeting with a large number of other heads of state. But probably more important are the opportunities offered by these annual meetings for the political leadership of West Africa to deal with regional issues of importance to them which would not readily be dealt with in the much larger annual meetings of the OAU or at the bilateral level. ECOWAS thus appears to be becoming a regional political or diplomatic organization, and this evolution may sustain it even in the face of its failure to realize its formal goals of economic integration.

Other regional integration schemes

Turning to the group of integration arrangements that came about outside the LPA, there are two important ones which are associated with the Communauté Financière Africaine (CFA) franc, UEMOA and CEMAC. Within the ambit of ECOWAS there is the West African Economic and Monetary Union (UEMOA), whose members – Benin, Burkina Faso, Ivory Coast, Mali, Niger and Togo – share a common central bank, the Central Bank of West African States (BCEAO). And within the ambit of ECCAS there is the Economic and Monetary Union of Central Africa (CEMAC) – Cameroon, Central African Republic, the Congo, Gabon, Chad, and Equatorial Guinea – with its central bank, the Bank of Central African States (BEAC). Within the geographical area of COMESA there are the Southern Africa Customs Union (SACU), with its associated monetary union, the Common Monetary Area (CMA), and the Southern African Development Community (SADC).

SACU – with South Africa, Botswana, Lesotho, Namibia, and Swaziland as members – is a well-established customs union that currently operates under the terms of an agreement concluded in 1969, but which as an operating unit goes as far back as 1910. SACU is an exceptional integration scheme in the African context in the sense that it has common external tariffs. SADC started out as the Southern African Development Coordination Conference (SADCC), set up in 1980 as a nine-member organization of the Frontline States – Angola, Botswana, Lesotho, Malawi, Mozambique, Swaziland, Tanzania, Zambia, and Zimbabwe. The political aim of SADCC was to bring independence and majority rule to Zimbabwe, Namibia, and South Africa. Its economic aim was to reduce the dependence of its member states on South Africa and the industrialized countries through cooperation on specific projects in priority areas such as transport and communications, food, security, and energy. SADCC's relative success as a regional cooperation organization was partly due to its focus on action rather than on institution building. In the early 1990s, the achievement of Namibian independence and the imminent demise of apartheid in South Africa challenged the very existence of SADCC. In August 1992 the Treaty of Windhoek was adopted, launching the SADC. Whereas SADCC was structured on the basis of regional cooperation, SADC, like COMESA, has an integration agenda, albeit one with an enabling nature without a fixed framework of target dates moving towards the establishment of a common market. Besides regional integration, SADC also aims at cooperation in the areas of security, peace, democracy, and conflict resolution. South Africa became the eleventh member of SADC in November 1994, Namibia having joined its forerunner at independence in 1990 (McCarthy 1995; Mistry 1995).

Failure of regional integration schemes

Trade figures are a painful reminder of the failure of most African integration schemes to achieve their primary goal of promoting regional trade expansion. The World Bank (1989) estimated that official trade among Sub-Saharan African countries amounts to a paltry $US4 billion, or only 6 per cent of total African trade. This share of intra-regional trade in total trade is conspicuously low compared with Western Europe (72 per cent), Eastern Europe (46 per cent), Asia (48 per cent) and North America (31 per cent) (McCarthy 1995: 219). It is, however, important to emphasize that a substantial volume of intra-regional trade in SSA continues to take place through informal channels which are often subject to varying degrees of official interference and harassment. Such informal exchanges across Africa's permeable borders are partially re-establishing the extensive pre-independence network of trade in goods and the associated migratory patterns.

There are various reasons for the failure of most regional integration schemes in Africa. Some of these have already been touched on above. First, integration arrangements demand a high level of political commitment and administrative expertise, which is often lacking in Africa. When the creation and strengthening of national identity are in full swing, as in many African countries, governments are naturally loath to sacrifice national sovereignty and control over economic policies. Moreover, African leaders are often divided on major political and ideological issues.

Second, political will is also affected by gains and losses from integration. One of the basic problems of regional integration schemes is that the economic *costs* of participation for member states can be immediate and concrete, while the economic *benefits* typically accrue only after a long period, are uncertain, and are often unevenly distributed among member states. The costs include, first, a decrease in government revenues when tariffs are reduced. Another cost may be the collapse of local firms as they find themselves unable to compete with firms in other member countries, resulting in a loss in national income, production and employment. This is the polarization effect of economic integration. The poorer members of the economic union often perceive that they are losing opportunities for industrialization and they demand compensation.

Third, institutional proliferation is bedevilling African regional integration schemes. To a large extent, the activities of these schemes overlap and are not coordinated, resulting in a duplication of functions and multiple membership. In Southern Africa, for example, Lesotho and Swaziland are members of SACU, CMA, SADC, and COMESA. In West Africa, Benin, Burkina Faso, Ivory Coast, Mali, Niger, Senegal and Togo are members of UEMOA and of ECOWAS. Mauritania is a member of both ECOWAS and AMU. Such multiple membership inevitably leads to problems of incompatible and potentially conflicting objectives, and raises the issue of divided loyalties and primary allegiance; it also stretches to the limit the African countries' already scarce human, administrative and financial resources.

Fourth, there is the deficiency in infrastructural provisions, such as transport and telecommunication services and fifth, the play of extraregional politics is another factor seriously affecting the cohesion of African regional integration schemes. In particular, France's continuing economic and political dominance over its former colonies is a permanent irritant and a major obstacle to the progress of integration arrangements in West and Central Africa.

The sixth and paramount problem, however, is that the present economic situation in Africa is not conducive to integration and expansion of intra-regional trade. There is a great diversity in size and level of economic development. And, above all, African economies are not complementary, many of them producing the same range of primary commodities exported to the industrialized countries, leaving little room for trade among themselves. Most of these economies also lack the capacity to develop complementary sectors; consequently, a sound base for growth in intra-regional trade through inter-industry trade does not exist.

Structural Adjustment Programmes

Some authors also point out that some aspects and objectives of the Structural Adjustment Programmes (SAPs), which are in the process of being implemented in several African countries, may actually militate against regional integration (cf. Asante 1991; Daddieh 1995; Mistry 1995). They argue that the present SAP measures may have serious repercussions on regional integration, at least in the short term, as they are typically nationally oriented. The emphasis of SAPs on achieving immediate increases in export earnings has triggered competition among African states in their efforts to maximize exports of the same primary commodities. This has a deleterious impact on prices and thus on the net earnings from exports. African countries find themselves in a competitive situation which tends to undermine the cause of cooperation. Furthermore, the SAP reform of macro-economic policies in national contexts also clashes with the need to regionally harmonize these types of policies (in particular exchange and trade policies). SAPs are averse to forms of positive discrimination, for example, reciprocal preferential tariffs or selective non-tariff barriers (as practised in PTA and UDEAC), which seek to foster trade within the area of integration. SAPs' goal of trade liberalization opens the door for relatively cheap imports of manufactured goods. This quickly out-competes fragile African industries and threatens to remove any basis for regional industrialization programmes in the future. Dramatic budget cutbacks as mandated by SAPs are in conflict with the necessity to contribute financially to regional development plans. As a consequence of the (SAP-related) retrenchments in the public sector, the capacity to provide state personnel for the implementation of regional integration plans is also diminished. Finally, SAPs bring about a reduction of domestic effective demand (due to a drop in consumer purchasing power). This will very likely discourage imports from partner states, which again is not compatible with the required process of African integration and cooperation. Confronted by what they perceive as an increasingly hostile international environment and the severe crisis of African economies, African heads of state recently reaffirmed their commitment to regional integration. In their meeting at Kampala in May 1991 they concluded that the only viable way out of the development crisis facing Africa is the redoubling of efforts towards early, effective continental integration. On that occasion, the former Nigerian Leader, General Olusegun Obasanjo, did not mince his words: 'While the world is grouping into blocs to strengthen national economies, Africa remains fragmented and drifting, and is therefore in danger of being completely marginalised' (Daddieh 1995: 259). One month later at the OAU summit meeting at Abuja, Nigeria, African heads of state signed a new treaty for the establishment of an African Economic Community (AEC) and an Africa-wide monetary union by the year 2025. The AEC will seek the elimination of custom duties, the abolition of quantitative and administrative restrictions on trade, the establishment of a common tariff and a common commercial policy, the removal of obstacles to the free movement of persons, services and capital, the harmonization of agricultural, environmental, monetary and industrial policies, the promotion of community solidarity, the creation of a compensation fund (Danso 1995).

AFRICA IN THE CHANGING GLOBAL ENVIRONMENT

Meanwhile, rapid developments in the global trading system have led to the establishment of a few powerful trading blocs, which are likely to present an immediate challenge (or threat) to Africa's trade prospects. These emerging economic groupings include the North American Free Trade Agreement (NAFTA), integrating the USA, Canada and Mexico; the Asian Free Trade Area (AFTA) in South-East Asia, signed in 1994; and the EC whose countries moved closer to unity after the Treaty of Maastricht (1992) and the signing of the European Single Act of 1993. In particular, the EU Single European Market (SEM), enlarged with Mediterranean, Nordic and Eastern European countries, will profoundly reshape Europe–African relations in the near future, including those arrangements made under the Lomé Conventions (Tibazarwa 1994).

Furthermore, the opening up of markets in Eastern Europe following the demise of the Soviet communist system will provide new opportunities for investment in and trade with the EU member countries on the part of the Eastern European countries. It is expected that both the enlargement of the EU trading bloc and the growing attention for Eastern Europe will gradually lead to further EU disengagement from the African continent (Daddieh 1995).

The completion of the Uruguay Round of trade negotiations in December 1993 and the subsequent creation of the World Trade Organisation (replacing GATT) has triggered another significant change in the international economic setting. Sub-Saharan Africa is expected to be adversely affected by a gradual erosion of trade preferences previously granted to African, Caribbean and Pacific (ACP) countries under the Lomé Conventions. It is feared that increased global competition, accompanied by further tariff liberalization, will ultimately cause Africa to lose ground in EU markets. The more competitive Asian Newly Industrializing Countries (NICs) are likely to squeeze out African exporters.

In short, in the context of the new global realities, Africa has to operate in a far more hostile external environment than a decade ago. Africa is rapidly losing ground, in fact, in the global economy. Its share of world GNP and world trade has sunk to insignificant levels. SSA's proportion of world exports which stood at an already low 2.4 per cent in 1970, further sagged to a mere 1 per cent in 1992. Africa's share in world cocoa production fell from 70 per cent in 1970 to 51 per cent in 1991 and its share in coffee production plummeted from 33 per cent in 1970 to 19 per cent in 1991 (UNCTAD 1993). Private direct investment, now mounting world-wide to \$US200 billion per annum, has also largely bypassed African economies. In 1992 less than 1 per cent of this flow reached SSA countries (Adedeji 1993). Moreover, the composition of Africa's exports has scarcely changed: primary agricultural products (cocoa and coffee) still account for a major proportion of total export earnings, just as they did some thirty years ago.

The basic problem is that SSA remains excessively dependent on a few non-manufactured exports for which world market prices continue to fall due to the limited growth in global demand. Recent expansion in world trade has been in manufactured goods and services, not in raw materials. Africa's tragedy is that it has failed to move away from its primary agricultural commodities, enlarging the manufacturing component in its export structure. Manufactured goods amount to just 5 per cent of total SSA exports. In other words, SSA has painfully failed to diversify its exports base. Related to this problem, has been the serious deterioration in SSA's terms of trade (import/export price ratio) during the 1980s and into the 1990s. The resulting sharp drop of around 25 per cent in the 'purchasing power' of export earnings at the end of the 1980s has undermined SSA's capacity to import the goods and services crucial to maintaining its production levels. To continue the list of unfortunate events, SSA countries have also not been able to benefit from the preferential trading relationship with the EU laid down in the Lomé Conventions. In 1975, ACP countries accounted for 20 per cent of the total of imports from developing countries into the EU. But even though most ACP exports could be imported duty-free, this dropped to only 11 per cent in 1990 (Betz 1994; Global Coalition for Africa 1995).

In the light of the worrisome external trade performance of SSA countries, the question of how the Uruguay Agreement and the Single European Market will affect SSA countries' trade prospects becomes paramount. Not enough time has passed yet to empirically assess the outcomes for SSA countries, nor for other developing regions. The few studies carried out thus far have therefore applied econometric models (usually neo-classical partial or general equilibrium analytical frameworks) to predict quantitative outcomes of the new global trade arrangements.

The principles and assumptions underpinning these models are in many cases irrelevant or even misleading, when it comes to the real economic and social characteristics of specific countries, which are obviously extremely difficult to incorporate into such models. Consequently, the outcomes of quantitative estimates of 'gains and losses' resulting from further trade liberalization must be handled with great caution (for a critical view, see Walker 1994). If we keep this in mind, it is not surprising that outcomes for SSA countries vary from one study to another depending on the model and methodology applied. For example, the OECD calculated (in 1993) a global gain of \$US195 billion resulting from a 50 per cent reduction in world-wide trade restrictions. Developing countries as a group were to see their exports grow to a total of \$US50 billion. Most of this gain was to go to Asia (\$US31.6 billion) and Latin America (\$US9.6 billion). SSA was also to gain, but to a very modest degree: \$US2.2 billion, amounting to just 4.4 per cent of the total gain for developing countries.

Sharply contrasting with this, however, are the conclusions drawn in two other recent studies which forecast a loss, rather than a gain, for SSA countries once the Uruguay Agreement is fully implemented (Yeats 1995; Davenport 1995). The basic reasoning here is that SSA countries stand to lose from the Uruguay Agreement because their extensive tariff preferences in the OECD markets will disappear as a result of the overall lowering of trade barriers (tariff and non-tariff types) following the agreement. Trade losses will be incurred by those countries which see their 'preference exports' replaced by exports from third, non-preference countries. Theoretically, of course, export gains resulting from the general lowering of tariffs could more than offset the losses from the disappearing preference exports but this is not likely to happen.

To gain more insight into the fate of SSA during trade liberalization, one needs to identify the destination markets of SSA exports and see how these markets will implement trade liberalization. Yeats found that (in 1988) about 78 per cent of SSA exports went to industrialized countries, including 47 per cent destined for the EC and 24 per cent for North America. Japan only attracted 3 per cent of SSA exports and less than 10 per cent went to other African countries (the remaining 16 per cent were scattered around the globe).

Clearly the conclusion is that the EC and, to a lesser extent, North America's handling of trade liberalization is of prime interest to SSA prospects. Analysing the types of products in SSA exports, as a next step, reveals the importance of 'raw materials and non-temperate zone foodstuffs' (cocoa and coffee), and the insignificance of manufactured goods, in the export structure of SSA (except oil exports). OECD tariffs and other trade barriers are relatively high for manufactured goods but low or nil for the primary products of the type SSA is exporting. This means that SSA will gain little from tariff cuts, since they apply to an unimportant category of products from the point of view of SSA. Of more significance to SSA is what happens to the preferences now enjoyed by African exporters to the EC. It is known that no less than 97 per cent of each African country's exports now enter the EEC duty-free. This is in sharp contrast to the conditions for countries in Asia, for example, only 4 per cent of Taiwan's exports are duty-free, the rest being subject to tariffs averaging 7 per cent.

How large would the replacement of African exports be in the event of a complete EU liberalization of duties? Yeats used a World Bank trade projection model known as Smart (what's in a name!) and found that African annual trade losses would amount to $US250 million. This represents about 2 per cent of the total current value of SSA exports to OECD countries. Among the heavy losers are Ivory Coast, Cameroon, Kenya, Senegal and Zimbabwe. It was calculated that in Japan losses will amount to $US14.3 million and in the USA a gain of $US89 million can be reaped, meaning that the combined result in the three OECD markets would amount to about $US203 million losses annually. Taiwan and Korea, by contrast, will gain substantially from complete tariff liberalization in the EU, to the tune of $US2.3 and $US2.4 *billions* (!) respectively. The overall conclusion is that SSA countries will continue losing ground in the international trade flows as the Uruguay

Agreement moves forward. In the second study (Davenport 1995), a partial equilibrium model was used to estimate SSA losses in export earnings resulting from 'preference erosion' compared to the year 1992. Davenport's conclusion is that tariff liberalization on tropical (agricultural) products and fish will cost African ACP countries $US156 million in lost export revenues. Coffee, tobacco and cocoa are the main losers, and the countries most adversely affected are: Cameroon, Ivory Coast, Ghana, Kenya, Malawi and Zimbabwe. Moving to the industrial category of metals, minerals and wood products, we find estimated losses of $US176 million. Countries most affected are those where metals form a key export product, such as the Congo, Ghana, Guinea, Zaïre and Zambia. Adding to this a loss of $US173 million in export revenues from 'temperate agricultural products' brings the total to $US505 million in lost revenues (ibid.). This represents around 1.1 per cent of Africa's total export earnings in 1992. These outcomes may not seem dramatic, but one must realize that for individual countries which in most cases are dependent on a few export products, losses may be far-reaching. The five African countries that will lose a relatively large share of their export earnings are Mauritius, Zaïre, Malawi, Mauritania and Madagascar.

It should be emphasized that the chosen methodology of estimating the effects of trade liberalization allowed only the calculation of so-called 'static losses'. The dynamic effects generated by future investment decisions and government policies have not been taken into account. According to Davenport, these could substantially increase the losses.

It should be noted that both observers, after acknowledging that SSA countries will be adversely affected by increased global trade liberalization and increased global competition, hasten to emphasize that 'internal deficiency factors' have also reduced SSA's export supply to OECD markets. Reference is made to such factors as inadequate infrastructure, the lack of entrepreneurial skills, insufficient investment funds, inadequate incentives, the hostile climate for foreign investors and the lack of an appropriate policy framework. All such factors are crucial to achieving a level of industrialization which would make possible an increase of manufactured exports into OECD markets (ibid.). In his suggestions for 'offsetting policies' to combat trade losses, Yeats stresses the important contribution SSA countries themselves could (and should) make: an 'aggressive liberalization' of their own high-tariff trade barriers. Such a reform could clear the road for increased intra-African trade.

This brings us back to the problem of SSA's increased marginalization in the world economy. Probably the only way to halt and reverse this process is a firm commitment to the establishment of well-functioning regional groupings, which could eventually grow to become genuine competitors in world markets. A positive note is that trade liberalization in OECD countries is expected to generate a rise in world income which will probably also increase the demand for SSA exports. In order to survive, a more united sub-Saharan Africa must seize these new opportunities. It must succeed in recapturing lost market shares in the future world economy.

141

CONCLUSIONS AND PROSPECTS

Notwithstanding the deepening economic and political crisis in a large number of SSA countries in the 1990s, governments continued their efforts towards greater regional integration on the continent. An example is the creation of the 'African Economic Community' (although not yet functional) in May 1994 as a follow-up of the 1991 Abuja Treaty.

In recent years a change in the approach to integration is clearly emerging. The current trend is away from trade arrangements *per se* and towards broader regional project and sectoral coordination, policy harmonization and the creation of regional infrastructural and institutional frameworks. The basic idea is that in order to facilitate the trade integration process, a sound regional policy environment is a *sine qua non* but achievements are not yet encouraging.

In West Africa the revised ECOWAS Treaty was signed in 1993. Ratification progressed very slowly, however. In 1995 only nine out of the sixteen member states had actually ratified the new ECOWAS. Equally disappointing has been Nigeria's decision to reverse the trade liberalization reforms it had begun in 1986. This country has always been suspicious of the Franc Zone membership of its fellow ECOWAS partners.

In Eastern and Southern Africa the PTA was transformed in 1993 to COMESA, the Common Market for Eastern and Southern Africa. This new arrangement aims at the creation of a customs union and enhanced coordination of monetary and financial policies, including full currency convertibility and a fair distribution of integration benefits among its member states. In the same area we already mentioned SADCC's transformation into SADC (Southern African Development Community) in 1992. Whereas the old SADCC focused on project and sectoral coordination, the new SADC's intention is to move to greater trade liberalization through tariff and non-tariff barrier reduction (Aryeetey and Oduro 1996). The fact that these two organizations now have similar objectives and a large overlap of membership (SADC incorporates several COMESA member states) make the co-existence of the two arrangements questionable and is already creating rivalry for financial resources. COMESA's prospects were weakened after South Africa joined SADC in November 1994. This last event may have drastic implications. Initially both the former SADCC and PTA were set up to diminish dependency on apartheid South Africa. With the emergence of a new South Africa in 1994, Southern African economies find themselves in an entirely new economic and political era and more dependent on South Africa then ever before. This country will undoubtedly increasingly set the terms for future integration efforts in the region (Mistry 1996). This chapter has attempted to demonstrate that the present domestic and international context has become remarkably different from what it was a decade ago. Contemporary Africa is confronted with an increasingly hostile external environment as well as with a dramatic crisis of its national economies, and this has led to the widespread adoption of SAPs. Anxious to forestall a further marginalization of the continent, African leaders have regularly reaffirmed their commitment to regional integration. Given the disappointing achievement of previous regional integration schemes in SSA, however, one cannot avoid the following question: how can the chances of success for a renewed commitment to regional integration be enhanced?

As discussed above, there are formidable political and economic obstacles to regional integration in Africa. That is why a growing number of scholars and development institutions advise African leaders to adopt a more pragmatic and flexible approach to regional integration which views market integration as a long-term objective (McCarthy 1995; World Bank 1989). This approach requires the designing of incremental but comprehensive steps to regional cooperation and integration, the strengthening of specific functional forms of cooperation – involving collaboration between independent countries or agencies on identified projects or schemes – and the creation of an enabling environment for the free movement of goods, services, labour and capital. To this end, resolute leadership is needed to overcome parochial and entrenched interests and to ensure that benefits are shared equitably. A more active role by governments and the OAU will be critical in this respect.

SADCC, one of the most successful regional cooperation schemes in Africa, exemplified such an approach. It promoted regional cooperation in the form of sectoral development (for example, project cooperation in sectors such as transport and communications, water and electricity). Such forms of regional cooperation could lay the foundation for eventual market integration and the acceptance of loss of sovereignty that this will entail.

This does not imply that the current regional schemes, based on the model of market integration, should be abandoned. The importance African leaders attach to the creation of common markets even excludes such a possibility. However, the political and economic realities of Africa caution against the creation and preservation of over-ambitious integration arrangements. Meanwhile, one important step towards improving the functioning of existing schemes would be to discontinue multiple memberships in arrangements which have more or less the same objectives. Our historical review of regional integration schemes in SSA provides ample evidence that such multiple memberships have often given rise to conflicting interests, thus impeding the advance of regional integration efforts.

BIBLIOGRAPHY

Adedeji, A. (ed.) (1993) *Africa Within the World: Beyond Dispossession and Dependence*, London: Zed Books.

Aghrout, A. (1992) 'Africa's experiences with regional cooperation and integration: assessing some groupings' *Afric/ Instituto Italo-Africano* 47(4): 563–586.

Aly, A. A. H. M. (1994) *Economic Cooperation in Africa: In Search of Direction*, Boulder, CO and London: Lynne Rienner Publishers, Inc.

Aryeetey, E. and Oduro, A. D. (1996) 'Regional integration efforts in Africa: an overview', in J. J. Teunissen (ed.) *Regionalism and the Global Economy: The Case of Africa*, The Hague: FONDAD: 11–49.

Asante, S. K. B. (1986) *The Political Economy of Regionalism in Africa: A Decade of ECOWAS*, New York: Praeger Publishers.
Asante, S. K. B. (1991) *African Development: Adebayo Adedeji's Alternative Strategies*, London: Hanz Zell Publishers.
Barratt Brown, M. and Tiffen, P. (1992) *Short Changed: Africa and World Trade*, Boulder, CO and London: Pluto Press.
Betz, J. (1994) 'The new international Environment and EC-ACP cooperation', in S. Brune, J. Betz and W. Kuhne (eds) *Africa and Europe: Relations of Two Continents in Transition*, Munster: Lit Verlag: 123–139.
Coussy, J. and Hugon, P. (eds) (1991) *Intégration régionale et ajustement structurel en Afrique subsaharienne*, Paris: Ministère de la Coopération et du Développement.
Daddieh, C. (1995) 'Structural Adjustment Programmes and regional integration: compatible or mutually exclusive?', in K. Mengisteab and B. I. Logan (eds) *Beyond Economic Liberalization in Africa: Structural Adjustment and the Alternatives*, London and Atlantic Highlands: Zed Books Ltd: 243–268.
Danso, K. (1995) 'The African Economic Community: problems and prospects', *Africa Today* 42(4): 31–55.
Davenport, M. (1995) 'The Uruguay Round Agreement and the effects of the erosion of preferences on African ACP states', paper prepared for the Workshop on the Implications of the Uruguay Round for African Commonwealth Countries, Harare, Zimbabwe.
Global Coalition For Africa (1995) *Africa Faces the Future: An Issue Paper*, Document GCA/Plenary/No.2/11/1995, Maastricht, The Netherlands.
Johnson, O. E. G. (1991) 'Economic integration in Africa: enhancing prospects for success', *The Journal of Modern African Studies* 29(1): 1–26.
Lancaster, C. (1991) 'The Lagos three: economic regionalism in Sub-Saharan Africa', in J. W. Harbeson and D. Rothchild (eds) *Africa in World Politics*, Boulder, CO: Westview Press, 249–267.
McCarthy, C. (1995) 'Regional integration: part of the solution or part of the problem?', in S. Ellis (ed.) *Africa Now: People, Policies, and Institutions*, London: James Currey/Portsmouth: Heinemann: 211–231.
Martin, G. (1992) 'African regional cooperation and integration: achievements, problems and prospects', in A. Seidman and F. Anang (eds) *Twenty-First-Century Africa: Towards a New Vision of Self-Sustainable Development*, Trenton, NJ: Africa World Press/Atlanta: ASA Press: 69–99.
Mistry, P. S. (1995) 'Reviving the economies of South Africa and Southern Africa: the role of regional economic cooperation', *Africanus* 25(1): 36–45.
Mistry, P. S. (1996) 'Regional dimensions of structural adjustment in Southern Africa', in J. J. Teunissen (ed.) *Regionalism and the Global Economy: The Case of Africa*, The Hague: FONDAD: 165–289.
Mukisa, R. A., and Thompson, B. (1995) 'Prerequisites for economic integration in Africa: an analysis of the Abuja Treaty', *Africa Today* 42(4): 56–80.
Okolo, J. E. and Wright, S. (eds) (1990) *West African Regional Cooperation and Development*, Boulder, CO: Westview Press.
Rimmer, D. (1989) 'Africa's economic future', *African Affairs* 88(351): 175–185.
Robson, P. (1993) 'La Communauté européenne et l'intégration économique régionale dans le tiers-monde', *Revue Tiers Monde* XXXIV(136): 858–879.
Tibazarwa, C. M. (1994) 'European African relations: challenges in the 1990s', in S. Brune, J. Betz and W. Kuhne (eds) *Africa and Europe: Relations of Two Continents in Transition*, Munster: Lit Verlag: 25–42.
UNCTAD (1993) *Handbook of International Trade and Development Statistics 1992*, New York: United Nations.
Vadcar, C. (1995) 'La constitution de zones de libre-échange et l'Afrique', *Afrique Contemporaine* 175: 31–42.

Walker, L. (1994) 'The Uruguay Round and agriculture: how real are the gains?', *Review of African Political Economy* 4(62): 539–558.

World Bank (1989) *Sub-Saharan Africa: From Crisis to Sustainable Growth*, Washington, DC: World Bank.

Yeats, A.J. (1995) 'What are OECD trade preferences worth to sub-Saharan Africa?', *African Studies Review* 38(1): 81–101.

7

THE EUROPEAN UNION AND ITS EXPANDING EASTERN AND SOUTHERN BORDERS

Alvaro Pinto Scholtbach

INTRODUCTION

Technological changes and increased competition with Newly Industrializing Countries have obliged all governments in the industrialized world to reconsider their position *vis-à-vis* the globalizing economy and to mobilize their economic and intellectual resources to manage the embryonic international order. Regional integration has occupied a central place in this management. The distinguishing feature of Europe's regional integration is its long-standing and gradually expanding record; its 'depth' with its far-reaching liberalization of factor markets and the proclaimed path towards further integration in political areas. This 'Europe' is, on the other hand, part of an era when the East–West and North–South divides are undergoing thoroughgoing changes and the emergence of free trade areas is making the West European model of regional integration less attractive because of its institutional constraints. The same changes in the world stage underline at the same time the priority being given by the major political actors in Europe to the completion of the ongoing process. The radical internationalization of the global economy and the impact of the collapse of communism have inevitably made the European Union a main international player with all the costs and benefits these changes bring. The autonomous changes in the world require policies of accommodation within the EU as well as regarding its relations with its main (extra-)regional partners. On the political field, the strategic changes of the post-Cold War age have revived the old ambitions of the key players in Europe to once again become leaders in international politics. The first, though cautious, step to address this political ambition was taken in 1992 with the adoption of the Treaty on European Union, the Maastricht Treaty. Crucial in this respect was, and still is, the question regarding the future relationship with the United States. The issue has reappeared on the agenda, partly because of the geopolitical changes provoked by the 1989–91 revolution, partly as a consequence of the ongoing politics of international trade. The latter is not totally new, but it has certainly received a major boost from the current globalization *Zeitgeist*. The issue at stake regards the USA remaining a natural European partner or becoming a strong competitor in the world stage and the consequences this might have for the political cohesion within the transatlantic framework. Yet the major accommodation, in terms of both the nature of future economic and political integration and the institutional framework on which both will depend, will be forced from the transformation of the current European Union (EU) of fifteen member states into a new kind of regional integration consisting of as many as twenty-five countries in the next century. The challenge will be to incorporate the transitional economies of Eastern Europe into an institutional framework primarily designed to enable cooperation between well-developed Western European economies. The European Union will be forced also to redefine its relationship with the developing countries.

On the economic field, the process of internal accommodation started in 1986 with the Single European Act and its further development, through the creation of the internal market, is now intended to reach its final step in Economic and Monetary Union (EMU). Since the mid-1980s, economic integration has moved forward and thanks to institutional changes has achieved a relatively stable frame-work to project the Single European Market and, perhaps in the near future, even a single European currency. The social framework, however, has deteriorated sub-stantially, with unemployment rates reaching unprecedented levels.

The search for answers to the open questions is taking place under hardly favourable conditions. The EU finds itself, because of the difficulties involved in the process of accommodation to the above-mentioned external constraints, in a stage of increasing competition with national reflexes and preferences. The experi-ment of forging a federalist Europe, the idea of a 'United States of Europe', is more than ever under siege. Europe as a functional response to the needs of modern capitalism is going out of fashion. The contest between political parties in the national arenas is taking on more and more the character of a struggle about who is the champion defender of national interest. And as has been the case for almost all periods of Euroscepticism during the short history of European integration, the way to become the champion is by stressing the alleged contradiction between national and supranational sovereignty. The nation–state, the fundamental unit of sovereignty according to its most fervent defenders, reappears as a useful tool, and strange enough, not only to nationalist conservatives, but also to some forces on the progressive side of the political landscape. Under these conditions, the political structures at the supranational level are under attack. Reinforcement of them is perceived, not only by the most virulent, insular Europhobes, as a frontal assault on state sovereignty. In this chapter we shall discuss the process of European integra-tion in the light of the current domestic changes and its implications for the external policy of the EU towards its peripheries in Central and Eastern Europe and the Mediterranean.

THE DIALECTICS OF INTEGRATION

The West European model of regional integration has for a long time been con-sidered an example of how things ought to be done. The region's capacity to satisfy

147

most of the socio-economic demands of its citizens and maintain at the same time an historically unprecedented record of peaceful relations between democratic states are generally recognized as the main achievement of its postwar integration process. This image has been an important driving force behind the transformation of Central and Eastern Europe after 1989.

The nature of the process, however, has been highly debated. According to the most dominant view, which has been held for a long time, conceptualized by the functionalist or neo-functionalist scholars and extensively propagated by federalist politicians during the booming years of European cooperation, economic integration was a process that almost inevitably would lead to political integration. The logic of the European project was its self-reinforcing nature, its expansion from one sector to the other, and the emergence of supranational authorities that gradually would overshadow pre-existing national particularisms (Haas 1958: 16). In this setting, the emergence of European authority structures would come at the expense of national ones, leading ultimately to the disappearence of the nation–state as the centre of political authority.

Intergovernmentalists, on the other hand, although sharing the assumption that European integration has been primarily driven by economic added value, rejected the allegedly evolutionary dynamic of integration stressed by functionalists. Integration was conceived to be merely the result of interstate bargains. National governments were and would remain the crucial actors in this game. According to this school of thought, the European Community (EC) (and the European Union as it has been known since 1992) is better described as an experiment in pooling sovereignty, not in transferring it from states to supranational authorities.

'Europe', deliberately or not, has satisfied both neo-functionalist and inter-governmentalist spectators. In the course of time, many policies which initially were announced as merely economic accommodations, have generated substantial and quite unique political and institutional changes. Supranational institutions have arisen (the European Commission, the European Parliament, the European Court of Justice) and from time to time, the topic of political integration has come to the fore. Closer cooperation has moved forward without affecting national identities. The basic reason behind the evolution of this 'mix' has been the acceptance of the alleged inseparability of economic and political strategic interests. After World War II, economic cooperation and the adoption of common policies assisted the political aim to rescue the nation–state; regional integration provided the safe framework to reaffirm its place in the new European order (Milward 1992: 44). The basic trade-off was Germany's acceptance of French political leadership in the European Community in return for a strong German role in economic matters. On strategic issues, Germany became tied to the West through American leadership within the North Atlantic Treaty Organization (NATO) (Kissinger 1994: 821). Moreover, the model of cooperation chosen by the European players, which neither reflected the ideal of American federalism nor Washington's preference for external liberalization and multilateralism (Tsoulakis 1991: 15), reflected the universal consensus prevailing on state interventionism. Economic emphasis came on the elimination of intra-EC trade barriers and provisions for competition policy, side by side with state intervention at the national level. The main exception, in terms of a truly common policy regime, was agriculture. For social and political reasons (20 per cent of the labour force in the EC countries worked in this sector), liberalization of this sector was a bridge too far. The Common Agricultural Policy (CAP) incorporated in the EEC treaties envisaged the Europeanization of agricultural protection and became the most prominent symbol of European integration (Milward 1992: 224–317). But the most striking feature of this period, as Tsoulakis has pointed out, was the continuous strengthening of the mixed economy and the welfare state. The role of the state became increasingly pronounced at both the micro- and the macro-economic levels. The economic crisis of the 1970s marked the turning point in terms of the political consensus about national and European policies (see next section).

In institutional terms, the period stemming from the Treaty of Rome (1957) and the establishment of the European Economic Community (1958) was characterized by the dominance of intergovernmental bargains and the steady increase in the European executive bureaucracy. Gradually, 'Europe' turned out to be synonymous with 'Brussels'. Steps towards deepening of the integration process took place through the creation of two intergovernmental systems, in 1971 the European Political Cooperation (EPC) for foreign policy issues and in 1979 the European Monetary System (EMS). The Single European Act (SEA) of 1986 marked a turning point for two reasons. In the first place because it ended the period of stagnation of the integration process of the 1970s by presenting a visionary project, the single market and its magic date of completion, '1992'. Its implementation was accompanied by a steady process of both deregulation and privatization, but also with substantial incrementation of legislative activities and institutional reforms. The place of the European Commission and 'Brussels' in general were strengthened as managers of the increased EC budget. The SEA marked at the same time the transition from the centralized state model expanded in the 1950s from national states into the Community, to a model based on three levels of government: Community, state and region (Bianchi 1992; Caporaso 1996). The effect of the SEA and the accompanying measures taken at the national and Community levels was twofold: a shift in power from states to markets and gradually also from national governments to local and regional authorities. The impact of the latter accentuated further the tendency to restructure the balance of power between central, regional and local authorities in some states. Following the SEA, the reform of the Structural Funds in 1988 and the establishment of the Council of Regions in the Maastricht Treaty (1992), regional authorities became actors with a great amount of confidence in their powers of decision-making. The regions forced their way into circles which long had been the exclusive domain of national governments. At the Community level, the EU evolved into an institution of economic and political mediation between the member states, resembling what could be called an international regulatory state (Caporaso 1996: 29–52). This policy shift served to legitimize the role of 'Brussels', but offered at the same time a convenient scapegoat to political forces eager to denounce the 'attack' on the nation–state directed from 'Europe'.

THE NEW STAGE

One of the glories of post-war Western Europe was its ability to absorb the vast majority of its working population. Economic growth and increasing employment in manufacturing industries compensated the decrease in the rural sector, making it possible to maintain through much of the 1950s and 1960s average unemployment rates below 2.0 per cent. Moreover, real wages experienced an enormous increase and served as a solid basis for the foundation of an expanding consumer society. The crisis of the 1970s marked the turning point. The large increase in oil prices after 1973 and the relatively high labour costs led to a worsening of the terms of trade affecting the competitiveness of the EC member states in markets inside and outside the Community. From then on, the EC entered a period in which modest economic growth has been accompanied by rising unemployment. From the oil crisis of 1973 onwards, unemployment has been rising from rates of 4 per cent in the 1970s to 9 per cent in the 1980s and more than 11 per cent in the 1990s. The most severe decrease was in industrial employment, which between 1973 and 1991 dropped by more than 15 per cent (*Economic Outlook* 1996: 59). The most striking consequence of the external economic shocks of the 1970s, and the one that later would bring the European countries together again in the search for a 'common sense of direction', was the fall of intra-EC trade. As a percentage of total trade its decline reached almost 10 per cent between 1972 and 1981 (*Eurostat Yearbook* 1995). The decline was particularly concentrated in strong demand sectors, reflecting the growing import penetration from Japan and the Asian Newly Industrializing Countries (NICs). Initially, national responses to the new international economic environment differed considerably and were accompanied by a widening of regional inequalities within the Community. After the second increase in oil prices in 1979, the situation deteriorated even more. Unemployment rates kept rising and the share of EC goods in world markets kept shrinking.

Of crucial importance for the shift to a new common policy was the European Round Table of Industrialists (ERT). Established in 1983, the main aim of the ERT was to find a common response to the deteriorating competitiveness in relation to the USA and Japan through the development of European policy instruments to strengthen the industrial capacity and generate support for the idea of the Single Market. Together with the European Commission, the ERT laid the basis for several programmes in the field of intra-European research and development. Its greatest influence was, however, in the field of a more general policy reformulation towards supply side measures and deregulation, and the emergence of a new consensus on restrictive monetary policies and budgetary conservatism with the latter reflecting the wide acceptance of the German policy approach during the previous years. In the new approach to European integration, the European Commission emerged as the most effective agent of deregulation of the markets. In

June 1985, the European Council approved the White Paper on the completion of the Single Market. Its main feature was the supply side nature of the measures and a timetable for their adoption. Measures for greater policy coordination and policy centralization were deliberately kept outside the framework by being politically unacceptable.

The launching of the internal market reflected the political impact of the crisis of the 1970s. The member states had become increasingly dependent on intra-EC trade to find a way out of the economic recession and their growing unemployment. The external economic shocks had not only put an end to the years of continuous economic growth, full employment, rising productivity and rising wages. It also gradually marked the end of the consensus on the existing model of regulated capitalism. Its main feature, the non-market allocation of resources for the numerous arrangements of the welfare state, on which social and political stability after 1945 had been founded, came under attack. The changes in the production structure, accompanied by the liberalization of national regulatory restrictions after the collapse of fixed exchange rate systems and the Bretton Woods system, accentuated the perception that national authorities were losing ground to the forces of globalization. Their pivotal role in financial and monetary areas decreased considerably, while in terms of social and welfare protection, the legitimacy of the state lost its axiomatic character. And this was not only among the political forces of the Right. For the parties of the Left, post-war Europe as a system showed itself capable of delivering economic growth, as well as social prosperity in a politically democratic environment. Economic growth and full employment were necessary and demonstrations of economic and social justice. From the 1970s onwards, growth and redistribution, the implicit contract between the political forces in Western Europe, entered a stage of renegotiation. As Sassoon put it,

> In the 1970s and 1980s, the 'new positional warfare' – to use Gramsci's expression – was over the role of the state in the reorganization of capitalist relations. The Left tried to expand the prevailing regulatory regime even further. The Right advocated a substantial retrenchment of the state and liberalization of a market expanded by privatization. By the early 1990s, the Left had been comprehensively defeated.'

> (Sassoon 1996: 446)

Since then, anti-welfare views have gradually become commonplace, even within the social-democratic parties. The political shift did not come out of the blue. The demonstrable effect of the failure of Mitterrand's government in the early 1980s to pursue a Keynesian policy of public spending and nationalization to regulate the market and control interest rates, put pressure on all Left forces to change their policies. The socialist government in Spain was perhaps the most striking example of it, but it was not the only one.

For social democrats and, to a certain extent, also Christian democrats, Europe became the arena to compensate for the loss of regulatory powers at the national level. The leading figure in this post-national regulation effort was Jacques Delors, who before being appointed as head of the European Commission had been in charge of the Ministry of Finance in the second government of Mitterrand and was responsible for the revision of the previous economic policies. His main achievement was the internal market and the progressive elimination of barriers. His main goal was the transfer of macro-economic policy to the Community level. Macro-economic policy, as Delors conceived it, was a task that unavoidably needed to be fulfilled at the Community level in order to prevent the emergence of 'savage capitalism'. The idea was to extend the powers of the Community to those areas, particularly social policy, in which an effective regulation of intra-Community capitalist production and accumulation could be enforced.

HETEROGENEITY

The idea of building a 'social dimension' was born in the more advanced economies of Western Europe, with the exception of Margaret Thatcher's Britain, with the aim of protecting them from the competition and investment attraction of the less developed economies of Southern Europe. The fear was that, because labour markets were less integrated than capital markets, the removal of barriers would lead to businesses moving to low-wage countries like Spain, Greece and Portugal. The move would exert pressure on the social system of the wealthier northern countries, downgrading the level of wages and social security arrangements. Policy competition, because of the lack of policy coordination, would finally be detrimental to the more developed welfare economies. The crucial problem with the social dimension of the European Community that Delors wanted to develop, was that the same socio-economic heterogeneity within the Community, the 'North–South' divide, prevented a common understanding of policy coordination. Harmonization of social and labour policies through general upgrading to the northern level would have meant that the southern economies were taking away its main asset for economic convergence. The transfer of powers to European institutions in the field of social policy was also strongly opposed, on ideological reasons, by Britain.

The final result of the intergovernmental bargain, not surprisingly, rested on the lowest common denominator. The social dimension of the Maastricht Treaty and its Social Charter of 1992, a basic framework, offered mainly minimal norms on working conditions. Britain, champion of neo-liberal orthodoxy, saw even this meagre step as a socialist measure to control the market and decided to 'opt out'. In essence, the salient feature of the Maastricht Treaty was the reaffirmation of the new belief in anti-inflationary policies as the only method available to national governments to recover economic growth. The treaty reaffirmed at the same time the very logic of the European enterprise of the 1980s, namely, that it was about market integration and that its policy-shaping process was largely dominated by strong organized business interests. Social policy remained in the hands of the member states; a centralized European effort was limited to the Structural Funds created following the SEA to close the gap between the richest and the poorest regions. In so far as one can speak of a common sense of direction regarding social issues, it has been the one indirectly enforced through the Maastricht criteria on the EMU, since all member states have followed to a certain extent the same pattern of socio-economic deregulation (see next section).

The recovery of European economies after the mid-1980s has been attributed in many countries to the implementation of the new economic panacea. Gradually, a new policy consensus has emerged on the need to limit the role played by governments, both at the national and the Community level. The emphasis put on de-involvement in the post-Maastricht era is clearly visible in the behaviour of the European Commission under the presidency of Jacques Santer. After several failures to get political and financial support from the member states for (Delors's) action plans to tackle economic rigidities and stimulate the creation of employment, Santer's Commission has assumed a cautious, almost timid attitude. Its role has changed from the one of initiator of grand legislative projects as under Delors's presidency to a mere enforcer of Single Market regulations.

The notorious intergovernmental state of mind of the 1990s has prevented the design of a common policy to foster positive integration, i.e. the adoption of supranational rules to achieve greater coordination of policies side by side with the current negative integration, the ongoing policy of market deregulation. The underlying reasons for this are the persistent socio-economic asymmetries among the member states, notwithstanding the relative convergence achieved in the 1980s. As can be seen in Table 7.1, disparity in incomes in real terms within the EU remains considerable, notwithstanding the fact that during the period 1984–94 Spain, Ireland and Portugal have moved closer to the European average. The favourable economic performance of Spain and Portugal in the 1980s was attributable largely to foreign investment and the existence of substantial unexploited resources, mainly an abundant supply of cheap labour (Larre and Torres 1991: 195). But intra-country differences persisted and they can be expected to increase even further after the entry of the transition economies of Central Europe into the EU.

TRANSITION ECONOMIES AND THE EU

The collapse of communism in Central and Eastern Europe (CEE) has generated a general shift to trade dependency on Western Europe. Commercial relations between CEE countries have declined substantially, despite efforts like the Central European Free Trade Association (CEFTA) and the Commonwealth of Independent States (CIS) to retain something of the regional cooperation of the past. In general, the focus of foreign trade relations is the EU, which has become their major trading partner, taking between 50 and 70 per cent of their exports and accounting for a similar proportion of imports. Within the EU, Germany has the lead, accounting in 1995 for a share of 30 per cent in exports and 23 per cent in imports. The same EU-driven pattern, with Germany occupying a central place, has been visible in the inflows of capital into the region, consisting of a wide range of types of

153

Table 7.1 Basic indicators of EU and EA countries, 1985–94

		GNP per capita		PPP estimates of GNP per capita	
			Average annual growth (%)		$US = 100
		$US 1994	1985-94	1987	1994
EU	Luxemburg	n.a.	n.a.	n.a.	n.a
	Denmark	27,970	1.3	76.6	76.8
	Germany	25,580	n.a.	n.a.	75.3
	Austria	24,630	2.0	72.8	75.6
	Sweden	23,530	−0.1	76.1	66.2
	France	23,420	1.6	75.9	76.0
	Belgium	22,870	2.3	74.6	78.3
	Netherlands	22,010	1.9	70.0	72.4
	Italy	19,300	1.8	70.9	71.3
	Finland	18,850	−0.3	72.1	62.4
	Great Britain	18,340	1.3	70.7	69.4
	Ireland	13,530	5.0	40.6	52.4
	Spain	13,440	2.8	50.2	53.1
	Portugal	9,320	4.0	41.3	46.3
	Greece	7,700	1.3	42.1	42.2
Eastern Europe Countries	Slovenia	7,040	n.a.	33.1	24.1
	Hungary	3,840	−1.2	28.9	23.5
	Czech Republic	3,200	−2.1	44.1	34.4
	Estonia[a]	2,820	−6.1	29.9	17.4
	Poland	2,410	0.8	21.4	21.2
	Latvia[a]	2,320	−6.0	24.1	12.4
	Slovak Republc	2,250	−3.0	n.a.	n.a.
	Lithuania[a]	1,350	−8.0	33.8	12.7
	Romania	1,270	−4.5	22.7	15.8
	Bulgaria	1,250	−2.7	23.5	16.9
Mediterranean EU-candidates	Malta	n.a.	n.a.	n.a.	n.a.
	Cyprus	n.a.	n.a.	n.a.	n.a.
	Turkey	2,500	1.4	20.9	18.2

Source: The World Bank (1996).
Note: [a] Preliminary estimates.

capital, from foreign direct investment (FDI), through portfolio investment to medium and long-term bank credits (*Economic Survey of Europe in 1995–1996* 1996: 6, 110).

Economic performance in the region, although being driven from the same direction, shows a pattern of considerable differences among states. After the overall economic decline after 1989, differences have become increasingly marked in the record of recovery shown up in the last years, with the highest growth rates concentrated mainly among the members of CEFTA: the Czech Republic, Hungary,

Poland, Slovakia and Slovenia. Economic performance in the Baltic States and the CIS has lagged far behind the average record of CEFTA. Within the latter, the core of economic recovery has comprised the politically viable candidates for EU membership (the Czech Republic, Hungary and Poland), which have accounted for nearly 90 per cent of net capital flows into Eastern Europe (ibid.: 6). Aggregate flows of FDI into Central and Eastern Europe and the Baltics has shown the same tendency, and the same holds for the operations of the European Bank for Reconstruction and Development (EBRD) established in 1991 to foster the transition towards open market-oriented economies. Besides the Russian Federation, which for mainly political reasons has absorbed the largest portion of EBRD resources, the three feasible EU candidates have undertaken large-scale privatizations involving the highest levels of foreign investment flows into the region (EBRD 1996: 13, 19).

Economic performance in these countries has improved considerably in accordance with the increased access of their exports to the EU, and is expected to continue improving if further trade liberalization takes place. But unemployment has risen to unprecedented levels, accompanied by inflationary pressures. The volume of actual investment, notwithstanding the improvement registered in the last years, has been relatively low, demonstrating that the process of economic recovery, because of the persistence of legal and institutional impediments, will last for a relatively long time, with all its consequences for the date and nature of their accession into the EU. Probably, differentiation regarding EU policy regimes, including the Single Market, will be needed even after their accession, since none of the eventual new members have economies able to stand the strain of the EU's strict rules regarding competition policy. Efforts to prevent such a differentiation determine current EU policy towards Central and Eastern Europe. The EU, to whom the G7 in 1989 delegated the coordinating role in the market conversion of CEE countries, and who since then has provided more than three-quarters of total financial assistance, has recently shifted its policy towards a more clear pre-accession strategy.

This policy shift, adopted at the Essen Summit of 1994, is mainly centred on the preparation of the European Agreement countries for their future accession to the EU. This 'Essen strategy' is composed of a structural dialogue on a wide range of political and economic issues and the implementation through the Poland and Hungary Action for Restructuring of the Economy (PHARE) programme (initially created for Poland and Hungary and later extended to other CEE countries) of several measures, ranging from industrial and agricultural modernisation to reforms in the field of education and the environment, needed for the adaptation of their economies to the requirements of the Single Market. With a budget reaching 6 billion ECU for the period 1996–99, PHARE is the largest assistance programme for the transition economies. The same holds for TACIS, the programme of technical assistance to the CIS countries. TACIS differs from PHARE in that it lacks the emphasis on pre-accession measures.

Regarding the integration of CEE countries into the EU, its nature and its consequences for the EU will depend on which countries are involved.

Negotiations, starting in 1997, will take several years and will be handled on a bilateral basis reflecting the differences, in terms of political and economic feasibility, within the European Agreement countries, the hard core being the Czech Republic, Hungary and Poland. All three can expect to be admitted somewhere in the first decade of the next century.

Nevertheless, the widening of the EU, even if it is limited to this group, will alter the picture of the EU in several ways, particularly regarding the position of the southern EU countries. To them, the integration of the transition economies will be a far from painless task. Given the similarities between the two groups of countries, with both mainly concentrated in traditional and agricultural activities, a loss of competitiveness and comparative advantages can be expected for the southern member states, while the benefits of enlargement will be concentrated mainly in Northern Europe, given its economic complementarity with Central Europe (Padoan 1994: 340–342). This asymmetry has been reflected in the already preponderant economic role played by Germany (and other northern economies) but has been compensated, at least temporarily, through several safeguard provisions built into the European Agreements and the maintainance of relatively high EU tariffs on products of particular interest to the southern economies (food, textiles, chemicals and steel). Moreover, escape clauses in the European Agreements explicitly keep open the possibility of a return to managed trade in case of sectoral difficulties or economic deterioration in a region of the EU (Kol 1995: 117). Nevertheless, trade liberalization towards CEE countries has increased considerably and is planned to lead to the opening of the EU markets through the elimination of import tariffs and quantitative restrictions in 1998. Removal of trade barriers on the side of the CEE countries will have to be completed, following a differentiated schedule per country, within a transitional period of ten years. The final objective is the establishment of a free trade area around the year 2003. The only EU market to remain partly protected will be agriculture, at least for the time being, since the EU will have to reform the Common Agricultural Policy (CAP) following the rules agreed by the World Trade Organization (WTO). The reform will be gradual and will comprise in particular the reduction of price guarantees, through a shift from income support to decoupled subsidies, as in the USA, in order to reduce the volume of subsidized exports. Quantitative limitations on imports will be transformed into tariffs. Reform of the CAP will have the positive effect, together with the fact that it would mean the adoption of a policy more in accordance with the WTO, that liberation of financial resources needed for the integration of new EU member states will be permitted. The CAP cannot be applied integrally to the new entrants; extension of the existing price guarantees enjoyed by EU farmers, aside from being contrary to the agenda of the WTO, would generate enormous inflationary pressures on their economies. In addition, their level of development indicates that for the time being, they will not be able to absorb EU regional and social expenditures to the same extent as the Union's less developed economies. But even if they could, for the net contributors to the Union, direct payments reaching amounts of billions per year are inconceivable under the present conditions of popular discontent and austerity programmes to meet EMU criteria.

Successful integration of the transition economies into the EU will require more access of their exports to the EU market in the pre-accession period. Their ability to compete after entry will depend on their capacity to adapt their economies to the qualitative rules (environmental and veterinary) of the Single Market. If this happens, they can be expected to become strong competitors. Measures to compensate for or decrease adjustment costs for the weaker southern economies, such as an increase of the Structural Funds created in the light of the Single Market or the creation of a new system to close the regional gap within the EU, are difficult to conceive, given the current pressure on national and community budgets. Economic convergence, if it ever happens, will be mainly brought about by monetary unification and the economic policy it envisages. But here, too, the costs of monetary alignment will be asymmetrical, since the weaker economies will have to give up a policy instrument which is used to defend their intra-regional competitiveness. The entry of these countries into the EMU under the favourable conversion rate of their currencies would compensate to a certain extent the loss of the monetary instrument, but preferential treatment within the EU will remain necessary, economically and politically. Otherwise, the fear of Southern Europe of being displaced by Central Europe from its status of first periphery of Northern Europe to a second rate status, could become a major obstacle to the widening of the EU.

ECONOMIC AND MONETARY UNION

One of the most significant steps taken at the end of the 1970s to get the Community out of its period of 'fatigue' was the establishment of the European Monetary System (EMS) in 1979. The EMS was a pragmatical response by the Six after several failed attempts, mainly because of British reluctance, to create a comprehensive Economic Monetary Union in the early 1970s. It was a response to the newly emerging foreign exchange market, the first to globalize in the mid-1970s as controls were lifted and new technology created new opportunities for arbitrage. The EMS, a joint Franco-German initiative launched initially by German Chancellor Helmut Schmidt, aimed at reducing exchange rate instability among EC currencies and strengthening the EC economically and politically *vis-à-vis* the United States. The direct reason for the EMS was the continued instability in exchange markets, mainly resulting from the continuous sinking of the US dollar, and its consequences for the export-led EC model, and more specifically for the German economy, which became severely constrained by the overvalued D-mark. The EMS served at the same time as an instrument of anti-inflationary policies by putting pressure on governments to follow the policy mix established in Frankfurt. It provided for a tighter Exchange Rate Mechanism (ERM), a mechanism designed to impose exchange rate stability, with fluctuations among pegged but adjustable exchange rates (contained within a narrow band) and compulsory and unlimited central bank interventions when currencies reached this margin. Until the crisis of

1992, the ERM proved to be an effective mechanism. Inflation rates and exchange rates remained under control. Moreover, the ERM served to consolidate central bankers' increasing margin of manoeuvre and independence in relation to governments. The system was in fact run by central bankers, with finance ministers becoming actively involved only in times of currency alignments (Tsoulakis 1991: 176).

The disadvantage of the system, as shown in the exchange rate crises in 1992 and 1993 affecting the strong overvalued pound sterling, the French franc and the Spanish peseta, and in 1994–95 once again the Italian lira, was that it was merely about convergence of inflation rates and not about real economic performance. The collapse of the ERM in September 1992, provoked by the financial transfers in Germany after unification and market speculation against overvalued currencies, underlined the fundamental impossibility of maintaining pegged exchange rates among economically divergent countries. The fiscal burden of German unification required the Bundesbank to raise German interest rates to control inflation at a time when the rest of Europe was in deep recession and unemployment was rising. In countries like Britain and France, the high level of unemployment made higher interest rates politically untenable.

The collapse of the ERM illustrated, moreover, the vulnerability of pegged but adjustable exchange rates to speculative attacks even when governments insisted, as the British and French actually did, that their monetary policies were consistent with current exchange rates. Economic inequalities, coupled with the expectation that political authorities would not be able to resist the pressure to devalue, permitted, as has been explained by 'Mister speculation' George Sörös, the market to 'react and adjust' (Sörös 1996: 9). This adjustment proved to be highly profitable and let the Sörös Quantum fund make 1 billion dollars on Black Monday by helping to push sterling out of the ERM. For the other weak currencies, a new band of fluctuation was introduced with a maximum of 15 per cent. The lessening of the band meant in practice the end of foreign intervention to support these currencies. The reason behind this policy shift was in accordance with the main lesson learned from the ERM crises, i.e. that no amount of intervention would be able to work if the economic fundamentals are wrong. Moreover, the shifted balance of power between central banks and the market had made interventions extremely costly and almost ineffective. In the early 1970s, the reserves of the central banks in industrial countries were eight times larger than the daily foreign exchange trading; in the 1990s, the relation was totally reversed, with foreign exchange trading amounting to twice the size of currency reserves (*The Economist*, 7 October 1995).

Since the ERM crises, exchange rates have behaved quite stably within the new wider bands, speculation has become non-profitable since central banks are no longer forced to intervene and in general, the countries that have left the ERM or devalued have been able to lead economic recovery, thanks to lower interest rates and better export conditions. The ERM crises left Europe as a whole about 15 per cent more competitive against the USA, Japan and other trading partners (Johnson 1994: 71). Within the EU, on the other hand, the devaluation of some currencies, particularly the Italian lira, has caused problems to the export sector of countries where no devaluation has taken place, particularly France. Within the internal market, devaluation in country A damages the competitiveness of country B, since the advantage of a lower exchange rate of A cannot be neutralized by higher import tariffs in B. In other words, economic integration through the internal market is too deep to allow floating rates. This, in short, is the basic economic motive behind the monetary union. The choice of the type of monetary union, between a weak one consisting of fixed exchange rates based on the D-mark or a strong one implying a single currency, is, on the other hand, political.

The political decision taken in Maastricht to establish the EMU responded to the shared conviction, particularly in France, that something ought to be done in order to reaffirm Germany's commitment to European integration after its reunification. It reflected at the same time the desire, especially in the countries with an almost complete alignment on German monetary policy, to shift the prevailing Bundesbank-centred system to a more collective form of monetary management. None the less, its further elaboration as the new 'consensual idea', and the successful efforts to cope with the initial scepticism expressed by the leadership of the Bundesbank, would have been difficult to conceive of without the role played by the Committee of Central Bankers. Its collective understanding of the EMS crisis, in essence reflecting the German interpretation of it and the belief in the need for tight monetary and fiscal policies, is nowadays the major engine behind the single currency. Central bankers have shown themselves able to 'persuade' governments, as functionalists would argue, to 'change their national preferences' and accept the rule of depoliticized money; political calls for lower interest rates and an anti-cyclical fiscal policy to cut unemployment have been successfully rejected as being incompatible with the goal of price stability.

The first stage of the EMU was the creation of the internal market in 1990 and the achievement of complete freedom of capital movement throughout the European Union. The second stage, which began in 1994, consisted of the establishment of the European Monetary Institute in charge of the technical preparations for the introduction of the single currency and the European system of central banks. The third and final stage is planned to start in January 1999 when the participating currencies (which ones will be decided mid-1998) will be pegged to each other; the Euro will be in circulation by 2002.

The way the EMU has been conceived since the Maastricht Treaty reflects two views resulting from the ERM crises: first, a tight monetary policy cannot be accompanied by a loose fiscal policy; and second, foreign exchange rate intervention must be kept to a minimum in order to discourage speculators.

To enforce a tight fiscal policy before entering the third stage of the EMU, the Maastricht Treaty stipulated the criterion that government deficits should be reduced to a figure close to 3 per cent of GPD and that general government debts should move in the direction of 60 per cent of GDP. Regarding the other criteria, concerning exchange rates, long-term interest and inflation rates, the assumption was, rightly as has been proved by the developments of the last years, that convergence would be achieved without major problems and would be fostered once the Euro enters circulation. With the adoption of the Stability Pact at the end of 1996, the emphasis on a tight fiscal policy has been reiterated.

Convergence between the EU member states regarding the policy mix envisaged in the Maastricht Treaty has been significant. All sixteen states have moved in the same direction concerning inflation and interest rates (*Voortgang naar Convergentie* 1996: II). The main currencies have also rejoined the ERM, including the Italian lira, and all sixteen states have followed policies to reduce government deficits. The current financial situation of the EU members suggests, nevertheless, that virtually none of them (the exception being the smaller countries) will be able to meet a narrow reading of the Maastricht criteria, particularly the requirement of a deficit below 3 per cent of GDP, without paying the price of social unrest. In Germany and France, unemployment has reached unprecedented levels, while in Italy, the adjustment measures needed to achieve a sustainable reduction of the government deficit, mainly through a drastic reform of the system of pensions, are politically difficult. Exclusion of Italy, on the other hand, would induce an attack on the lira in currency markets, leading to devaluation and higher interest rates to cope with it. Higher interest rates would depress the economy and make the fiscal deficit (less tax revenues, more welfare payments) even worse; the possibility of Italy entering the EMU in the near future would disappear. Under these conditions, the scenario of monetary unification limited to a 'hard core' of countries (Germany, France and the Benelux countries), with Italy being the only big country staying outside, has become highly likely. A definitive postponement of the single currency is, on the other hand, unacceptable to France, since it would mean a perpetuation of the leading role of Germany, with the D-mark acting as the anchor for a renewed EMS. For France, the goal is to limit Rome's room for manoeuvre to devalue and destroy even further the competitiveness of the French economy. A goal, which at first sight is difficult to reconcile with Germany's official pronouncements, namely, that a narrow reading of the 3 per cent GPD rule is a condition *sine qua non* for a strong and healthy monetary union. Nevertheless, the Germans themselves are also having problems following this rule. In other words, as a blessing in disguise, Germany's inability to follow its own decrees (*'drei ist drei'*) has given France and Italy room to manoeuvre to advocate a more flexible interpretation of the criteria. The other option would be postponement of the EMU, which also for the Germans would not be attractive. Abandonment of the single currency would require amendments to the Maastricht Treaty and would presumably generate a major financial crisis. The outcome of the latter could be a revaluation of the D-mark, with all its negative consequences for the German economy.

CLOSER COORDINATION

The acceptance of the Stability Council, an informal meeting of the ministers of finance of the EMU countries, although lacking a formal institutional framework, was the result of strong pressure, particularly from France, to guarantee a more balanced relationship between monetary and fiscal policies than the one envisaged in the Maastricht Treaty. Formally, the latter has remained unchanged, since in terms of its institutional structure, it remains based on a combination of strong monetary and weak fiscal policy; monetary policy will be run on a centralized basis, the European Central Bank, while fiscal policy will remain decentralized, i.e. in the hands of the national governments. Nevertheless, the creation of the Stability Council indicates that eventually a greater coordination of national fiscal policies will arise, and in that framework, political management, i.e. a more flexible inter-pretation of the Maastricht and Stability Pact constraints on budgets, is possible. The reasons for this are clear. The Maastricht Treaty and the Stability Pact set limits on government deficits and the accumulation of government debt, not on the rate of unemployment. It neither resolved the question of what kind of fiscal stabiliza-tion policy would apply in cases when the economic situation deteriorated. The EMU's main objective is price stability and low inflation. The facts prove, none the less, that the costs of low inflation, on which the success of the EMU largely will depend, are not just a loss of output but also of employment. That the EMS period coincided with the highest level of unemployment in Western Europe, can hardly be rejected as a mere coincidence. If the European Monetary Authority in charge of EMU follows the kind of zero inflation policy advocated by the Bundesbank, the result could be an even more serious aggravation of the problem. But the magnitude of the impact will not be uniform. Despite all the success of the internal market, a 'European' economy as such is non-existent. Despite all the convergence induced by the advent of the EMU, the EU is still composed of divergent national economies, in terms of economic growth, unemployment rates, inflation rates, labour relations, disparities in cost levels and productivity, etc.

An EMU comprising the great majority of EU member states would simply freeze the existing differences, given the lack of room to manoeuvre of govern-ments to pursue adjustment after the disappearence of monetary variables. By abandoning exchange rate adjustments, the task of adjusting for competitiveness and relative prices could be transferred to the labour market. But given the rigidity of it in most of the countries, the price of adjustment would predominantly be in terms of losses in output and employment. Substitutes for the loss of the exchange rate as an adjustment instrument also cannot be expected in labour mobility within the EU or in inter-regional budgetary transfers, since both are perceived to be politically undesirable. Labour mobility, because of the already high social tensions caused by migratory workers in the EU, intra-regional budgetary transfers because of the lack of support for increasing the EU budget and the necessity of liberating financial resources to support the future expansion of the EU with Central and East European countries. Paradoxically, the EMU can be the answer to sustain cohesion between North and South within the EU, and, at the same time, make possible its enlargement with the East. The integration of the Southern economies into EMU can represent a package deal; if accompanied by major reallocations of the EU budget, meaning the gradual abolition of the cohesion funds and substantial reduc-tions of the expenditure for the Common Agricultural Policy, together accounting for almost 90 per cent of the total EU budget, enough financial resources can be liberated to both permit a looser fiscal policy to support economic growth in the South and the integration of CEE countries in the EU. Such an approach would need greater coordination of economic and fiscal policies, and political management of the centralized monetary policy in the hands of the future European Central Bank. Signs that the new panacea for European integration will indeed be co-ordination were revealed recently with the muted welcome given to the Dutch proposal launched in May 1997 to design a Marshall Plan for Central and Eastern Europe. In order to disguise its financial implications, the Plan has been explained primarily as an effort to achieve greater coordination of public and private invest-ment in the region.

The second lesson learned from the crises in the ERM is that foreign exchange rate intervention must be kept to a minimum in order to discourage speculators. The issue concerns in particular the future regulation of exchange rates between the Euro and the currencies staying outside the EMU within a new EMS. One of the main features of the current EMS has been its asymmetry, combined with a three-tier structure, with Germany occupying the first tier, the aligned countries occupying the second tier, and those remaining outside the EMS in the third tier (Tsouklalis 1991: 184). The same multi-tier pattern can be expected to characterize the relation-ship between the 'ins' and 'outs' of EMU after the creation of the single currency. The 'outs' would then be regrouped in a modified monetary system, an EMS II, connected to the EMU group by means of a fixed but adjustable peg to the Euro. The new exchange rate mechanism of this EMS II would rest on wide margins of fluctuation and additional security measures against direct intervention. The intention, mainly because Germany is not expected to offer exchange rate guarantees, is to rely on the voluntary cooperation of the 'outs' to go forward with convergence programmes before entry to the inner group. German officials have reiterated that the Euro should stay in the centre of a future EMS-II, which should be a modified 'more asymmetrical' system than the existing EMS. In their view, the responsibility for stabilizing the currencies of the non-participants in EMU must be undertaken primarily by the non-participants themselves in the final stage (Istituto Affari Internazionali 1996: 37). A similar approach has been taken by the European Monetary Institute in its reports to the EU Ministers of Finance. In essence, the proposals of the EMI are designed to keep currency intervention to a minimum after 1999; from then on, no formal obligation or multilateral target would exist concerning narrow bands of fluctuation between the prevailing currencies and the Euro. A broader and more flexible exchange rate mechanism of this kind would allow the 'outs', including the future members of the EU from Central Europe, to follow a policy of gradual progression to the EMU.

An EMU for all would be, as Dornbusch has put it, like a marriage between partners of very unequal assets (Dornbusch 1996: 117). Reality shows that the EU already is a marriage between partners of very unequal assets. Intra-country differ-ences have been and will when necessary be taken into account, particularly through a more flexible approach to fiscal policy. Political management of monetary policies is therefore necessary. The EMU, on the other hand, can be expected to deliver a strong Euro, increasing its demand in European and world markets and leading to a diversification from dollars by investors and central banks. With the single currency in force, European central banks would be forced to hold more Euros in reserve instead of dollars, since trade and financial transactions would be more and more invoiced in the new currency. According to some calculations (*The Economist*, 19 October 1996), this shift would leave European central banks with excess dollar reserves of perhaps $US70 billion. In addition, central banks outside Europe can be expected to be attracted to the Euro as an international currency for invoicing world trade, intervention and investment, increasing the demand for the new European currency even more. In other words, the world would move from a single dominant currency towards a multiple-currency system, with the Euro becoming a stronger reserve currency than the D-mark, which already invoices approximately 15 per cent of total world exports (UN 1996). The decisions taken in Maastricht to integrate more deeply in areas hitherto in the hands of the member states, were taken in response to the collapse of communism in Eastern Europe and the reunification of Germany. They were the expression of a grand, although unsatisfactory and incomplete political strategy, and not of the demands of citizens, as was demonstrated later by the difficulties encountered by many governments in ratifying the treaty. Maastricht incorporated the idea of a European citizenship, and sought to decentralize the level of policy decision-making through the concept of sudsidiarity and the role of regions, yet its ratification crisis, with Danish and French referenda almost getting out of control, showed that the top-down method was getting exhausted and that popular scepticism about the course set for Europe was growing. The political nationalism of the electorate, fed by xenophobic sentiments and social fragmentation, has, so to speak, come up against the official nationalism of its political elites. Opposition to 'Europe' is merely the manifestation of discontent about the fading away of the 'status quo', the fear of the welfare state being destroyed by the advent of the EMU, rather than the expression of an articulate new political programme. The perception of growing civic disillusionment with politics, together with the public recognition of the constraints of multilevel governance in the European Union, and the resurgence of exclusive nationalisms in Eastern Europe, have understandably turned the attention to issues like identity and loyalty as crucial to explain the viability of the process of integration. No one would deny, indeed, that the politicization of integration and its expansion into sensitive political spaces are inseparable from questions of Community-building and the affective dimension of integration. The current crisis in Western Europe, the manifestation of civic discontent with the ongoing decline of wealth, has none the less introduced an element of incalculability into each country's public life and into the relations of nations with each other (Maier 1994: 63). The domestic constraints on European policy have grown. The EMU will have to accommodate these constraints. If it succeeds, this move towards supranational policy-making will certainly have a spillover into other areas of policy besides monetary issues. It will lead to a closer coordination of fiscal and economic policy.

THE EU AS A REGIONALIZING FORCE

Further integration of Western Europe through the EMU is expected to increase its economic power. At a time when foreign policy is increasingly driven by the politics of international trade, Europe's growing economic power is bound to be accompanied by some sort of political protagonism on the world stage. The European Union already has a population of more than 360 million people and a GDP of more than 6.2 billion ECU, one fifth higher than the USA and a third higher than Japan (European Commission 1995: 105). The EU is in addition the principal provider of foreign direct investment (FDI), holds more than 35 per cent of global financial reserves and is responsible for almost 20 per cent of world trade, excluding intra-EU trade (UN 1996). Moreover, the EU's free trade area is gradually being extended to the whole of Europe and is intended to reach at some point even North Africa, reflecting a package deal between German and French geopolitical priorities.

The first is being achieved through the creation of the European Economic Area (EEA), which includes the last three remaining members of the European Free Trade Area (EFTA), Norway, Iceland and Switzerland, after the incorporation of Austria, Sweden and Finland into the EU. Their accession expressed the fundamental weakness of EFTA, when compared to the EC (now the EU). Founded in 1960 on the initiative of Britain as a loose intergovernmental body whose goal was free trade rather than economic and political integration, EFTA proved to be merely a marriage of convenience (McCormick 1996: 56). Tariffs between EFTA members were cut, but this did not prevent several of them increasing their trade with the EC, and finally becoming members of the EU. Current EFTA members have been forced by popular opposition to remain outside the EU, but can be expected to apply for membership once this opposition vanishes, Iceland and Norway, in particular, since their economies have become extremely dependent on access to the EU markets.

Further cooperation with the transition economies is being pursued through the European Agreements covering several Eastern European countries. As mentioned earlier, trade liberalization is gradually being implemented, but has been of considerable importance for their economic recovery. According to the European Agreements, the EU is committed to phase out import tariffs and quantitative restrictions, improve market access for agricultural products and extend anti-dumping rules to these countries. A free trade area is planned to be established at the end of a transitional period before the year 2003. Free trade agreements are also expected to be signed in the future with the countries of the former Soviet Union. The EU has additionally taken the lead in providing economic and technical assistance to Eastern Europe and it is the main trading partner of the former Soviet Union. Regarding the former Yugoslavia, the EU has assumed the prime responsibility for financial support and to a certain extent for even conducting the process of reconstruction of Bosnia Herzegovina.

The extension of the EU's free trade area to North Africa is expected to take place at the beginning of the next century, depending on the results achieved in the framework of inter-regional cooperation agreed at the Euro-Mediterranean Conference held in Barcelona in 1995. The EU declared the region of strategic importance and agreed to work towards a Euro-Mediterranean partnership through the development of a long-term programme in economic and political areas with Algeria, Cyprus, Egypt, Israel, Jordan, Lebanon, Malta, Morocco, Syria, Tunisia, Turkey and the Palestinian Autonomous Territories. Regarding Malta and Cyprus, the EU policy follows a pre-accession strategy since both have applied and *de facto* have been accepted for EU membership. However, negotiations with both countries remain frustrated, because of political obstacles stemming from their demands for selective integration into the EU, as in the case of Malta, and the Turkish occupation of northern Cyprus. *Vis-à-vis* Turkey, which also has applied to join the EU but whose membership for economic and political reasons remains a *fata Morgana*, policy emphasis resides on the implementation of the European-Turkish Free Trade area established in 1996, reflecting the European recognition, under severe pressure from the USA, of Turkey's strategic position with regard to the Balkans, Central Asia and the Middle East. Greater access to the EU market, none the less, has been postponed or placed in a web of time-consuming negotiations, reflecting the ambiguous attitude of the EU to Turkey, whereby the geopolitical importance of the region is recognized, with the politics of Islam and the fear of large migrations playing a central role together with the vital EU interest of having uninterrupted access to oil supplies. Towards the other non-European Mediterranean countries, policy emphasis, because EU membership is excluded, is directed to achieving a say in their domestic politics in exchange for a steady liberalization of trade policies.

The expansion of the EU through the establishment of free trade areas involving its peripheries, however remote they all may be in practice, raises the question of the nature of this process; whether it will lead to bloc formation and a further fragmentation of the world economy in protected areas. According to some studies (Kol 1995: 181–182), the policies designed and implemented by the EU with trade partners ouside the region, with a clear distinction for the Common Agricultural Policy, are in general characterized by liberalization and deregulation. Evidence, indeed, shows that together with the dynamic expansion of Europe's regional economic area through the model of associationism, the European Union has become in recent years a main, tough resigned player in the multilateral system. Under strong pressure from the USA, the EU has been forced to accept reforms of its agricultural policy and to open up its market to competition from outside in areas ranging from telecommunications and electronics to textiles and clothing. Against all odds, and along with the United States and Japan, the EU has become a key player in world trade negotiations and in the ongoing discussions about the future agenda of the World Trade Organization. This activation of its multilateral standing has been accompanied by an increasing involvement in a web of negotiations with Latin America and Asia, both being emerging markets of vital importance for

Europe. In general, the EU has shifted its traditional policy of protection of its markets to penetration of others. The new associationism of the EU, together with its multilateralism, has revived the discussion about the old associationism and development assistance being given to the former colonies in the framework of the Lomé Convention. Established in 1975 and succeeding earlier agreements of cooperation between EC members and their former colonies, the Lomé's striking feature was its non-reciprocity and special treatment covered by special protocols carrying elements of price indexation and export guarantees, and the inclusion of the System for the Stabilization of Export Earnings (STABEX) to guarantee export revenue stability of the associated countries of Africa, the Caribbean and the Pacific (ACP). Lomé was a defensive EC policy, designed to secure supplies of raw materials to European industry in the uncertain times generated by the process of decolonization; the oil crisis of 1973 had demonstrated that Europe was the industrial area most exposed to the threat of action by commodity producers. The former colonies were expected to supply the raw materials and maintain close political relations with Europe. As Grilli has argued, Lomé reflected the purposes of European associationism, i.e. to protect the interests of the Community through the maintenance of a certain political stability and the perspective of economic development in the newly independent states of Africa, and by giving Europe a measure of political influence in the bipolar world of the Cold War (Grilli 1993: 40). Lomé's stagnation in the 1980s has been attributed (ibid.: 42) to the fact that, with the waning of the defensive dimension, European associationism ceased to develop and adapt to the changing world; in other words, it lost its momentum of the 1970s. One could argue, however, that the stagnation of Lomé is precisely the consequence of the development of a new version of the defensive dimension of European associationism; the focus has changed, not the principles and purposes. The new European associationism is directed towards Central and Eastern Europe and the Mediterranean countries, and this has indeed affected Lomé. Whether this will lead to the death of Lomé is, on the other hand, hardly conceivable; it would mean a loss of international status for the EU and the ACP countries. The continuity of the Convention against all odds, notwithstanding the debates being held between the EU and the ACP countries about its adaptation to a policy regime in conformity with the rules of the WTO, indicates that both parts still attach importance to its political aspects. On the EU side, reflecting mainly the political interests of France, the aim is to politicize the relationship, on the ACP side to receive special treatment once Lomé is transformed into a more traditional tool of development assistance.

EUROPEAN POWER

The EU and the USA

In the transatlantic setting, the division of labour was quite clear; the Community was a civilian power under the military leadership of the USA. European acceptance of it responded to the political logic of European integration, namely, French–

German relaxation and the prevention of Germany becoming once again a military power. German rearmament was launched at the end of the 1940s and the crucial question for Western Europeans was to find a political framework to regulate it. The way to address the issue, without implications for France in the sense of a loss of sovereignty over its military power, was restricting Germany in the NATO alliance. The French were reluctant to sacrifice their national defence to an integrated Western defence including Germany, given that it would mean putting in German hands the defence of France, while constricting at the same time France's ability to pursue its own colonial wars (Kissinger 1994: 515). This was the main cause of the defeat of the idea of a European Defence Community in 1954. Germany entered NATO in 1955 and became militarily dependent on the USA. France pursued a semi-independent policy by being politically inside NATO, but militarily outside its integrated structure.

The end of the Cold War and the growing economic power of the EU are bound to be accompanied by changes in the transatlantic relationship. The creation of the common currency will strengthen Western Europe's bargaining position *vis-à-vis* the United States. Both the EU and the USA will have to accommodate this new situation. The final result will be relatively greater European autonomy from the USA; a reflection of a more equal distribution of dependence. For the time being, the relationship will remain slightly the same. The collapse of communism and the reunification of Germany have created new conditions, but not of the magnitude initially expected, at least not regarding their consequences for the projection of the framework provided by the Pax Americana. Maastricht established for the European Union an intergovernmental third pillar, a Common Foreign and Security Policy, and the place to show it could work was the former Yugoslavia. Events showed that it did not. The third pillar turned out to be an obstacle to action, a useful alibi for the European powers to retreat from the use of military force and assume the consequences of the previous policy of recognition of the partition of Yugoslavia. An end, temporarily, to the Yugoslavian (and European) drama was put by the USA. Washington intervened and confirmed, as the leading figure behind the peace agreements of Dayton has argued, that the USA remains a *European power* (Holbrooke 1995). For the time being, the *only* European power.

The emerging context of European security is once again largely dictated by the Pax Americana; the security and defence policy dimension of European integration remains a matter of transatlantic engineering. After a short *intermezzo* between 1991 and 1995, the question of whether the EU will or will not build up its political and security standing will be answered in Brussels, the seat of NATO. After the Yugoslavian drama, Western Europeans, including the French, have realized that military action is inconceivable without American political and logistical support. The USA has also taken the lead in the process of accommodation of the Alliance to the demands of the Europeans, particularly the French, concerning the reinforcement of the European pillar within NATO. The result of this is a weak connection between the Western European Union (WEU) and the European Union, and the definite abandonment, at least for decades to come, of European pretensions to an independent defence policy. The policy of enlargement of NATO by the Central European countries and the deal concluded with Russia about its position in the new European security order have also been US-driven. The 'Founding Act on Mutual Relations, Cooperation and Security between NATO and the Russian Federation', signed in Paris in 1997, revealed once again the contours of the emerging European security map, in that it reaffirmed that, notwithstanding the fact that for the coming decades Europe will be a mix of several military arrangements, its axis will be NATO under US leadership.

The transatlantic alliance will remain in place, and it will change into a more diffuse arena for extra-regional bargaining on strategic issues not only concerning security and defence matters. The main feature of this process will be the internalization of the USA in the determination of policy in the EU and the difficulties it will cause to the maintenance of cohesion within the ranks of the EU. Steps towards internalization have already been taken. Since the Transatlantic Declaration signed in November 1990 by the EU and the USA, joint consultations have been taking place in areas ranging from foreign and security policy to trade, terrorism and drugs. Moreover, an agreement has been reached on the convocation of half-yearly summit meetings to discuss issues of common political and economic interest. Another step was taken at the Madrid Summit in December 1995 with the signing of an Action Plan to translate common goals into concrete joint measures to intensify political consultation and to promote commercial cooperation. A more ambitious idea to inject new life into the transatlantic relationship, launched in 1995 by the German Foreign Minister, Hans Kinkel, regarded the creation of a Transatlantic Free Trade Area (TAFTA). Kinkel's TAFTA, which in his view would be a pragmatic response to the fact that no further global liberalization of trade can be expected to take place in the near future, would become a lever to open markets world-wide and reflect the political will in the EU and the USA to pursue 'open regionalism', since it would be about dropping trade barriers and it would be open to third countries willing to join. The idea, as expected, has been given only a muted welcome both in Europe and the USA. The basic reason for this lack of support resides in the persistence, notwithstanding the recent *rapprochement* between the EU and the USA on economic issues, of major EU–US disagreements, as has recently been highlighted by the controversy surrounding the US anti-Cuba Helms-Burton Act. Moreover, an agreement of the kind of TAFTA would mean that the USA would get a direct say on a number of EU practices. A greater internalization of the USA in the EU, offering Washington the possibility to exert even more pressure than it already has exerted on EU policies (such as on the reform of the Common Agricultural Policy, the reform and enlargement of NATO), would be, certainly for France, unacceptable.

France and Germany

The central issue for the future of European integration is the development of the Franco-German relationship. France is now facing the new reality of a reunified

Germany; Bonn's overpowering voice on economic and political matters is becoming evident. The USA, parallel to this, has become Bonn's major ally, reinforcing Germany's position *vis-à-vis* France even more. The enlargement of the European Union with the Central European countries will have the same effect. But France and Europe as a whole have no other alternative than to accept this reality. As Garton Ash has argued, if Germany wants to be a normal country like Britain, France or America, it will need to have Western neighbours to its east (Garton Ash 1994: 81). To find lasting inner equilibrium, the reunified Germany will have to assist in the westernization of the new democracies in the east and bring them into the structures of Western and European integration. To find lasting inner equilibrium in Europe, France's geopolitical interests in the Mediterranean and the Middle East will have to be incorporated into the agenda of the EU. The extension of the EU through the creation of free trade areas involving its eastern and southern peripheries underlines this political imperative. Towards the East, the short-term objective is to manage the consequences of the collapse of communism and prevent unregulated migration; the long-term objective is to prevent the emergence of a new *Mitteleuropa* under the umbrella of Germany. Bonn, paradoxically, is the main engine behind the rapid integration of Central Europe into the EU and NATO as a way to prevent such a scenario becoming reality. Paris, making successful use of this paradox, is the main engine behind Europe as a regionalizing force towards the Mediterranean.

CONCLUSIONS

European integration is a continuous bargaining process. Its strength resides in its capacity to build up internal cohesion through the articulation of a collective interest. Essential to it has been the Franco-German equilibrium. In terms of economic policies, the package deal has been the liberalization of the market for industrial goods and the Europeanization of the market for (French) agriculture. In institutional terms, the equilibrium has been reflected in the combination of federalism and intergovernmentalism. Efforts to depart from this pattern and place new policy areas within the supranational framework of the (economic) European Community proved to be unsuccessful at the time of the SEA and once again in Maastricht. The latter produced treaties on the European Union and Economic and Monetary Union, but with them, it made the institutional system even more complicated than it already was. Moreover, the EMU was launched without the creation of the European Political Union demanded by Germany. Maastricht followed the old bureaucratic method, but instead of creating the necessary conditions for the EU to solve the problems that states unilaterally are unable to solve, it created the conditions for collective inertia. Bosnia was the clearest example of this. The Amsterdam Summit of 1997, convocated to simplify and democratize the system, and fill the gaps left by Maastricht, maintained the EU in limbo. Major steps forward were not achieved, nor a clear plan for the way the enlargement would be approached. Measures to accommodate the EU to the reality of geographical expansion were postponed to the date of no return, somewhere in the first decade of the new millennium. Amsterdam, none the less, delineated the contours of the future EU and made clear that its shape will scarcely resemble the current one. The introduction of the concept of flexibility was its major achievement. Its adoption made at least clear that, among European leaders, a consensus was emerging on the need to pursue a more differentiated path. A shared recognition of the remoteness of a European federal state, because of the future reality of growing divergences in an extended EU, and the persistent old reality that British and French national preferences are and will remain tempted to limit, rather than to strengthen the powers of supranational arrangements. Under these conditions, regional integration in Europe will be a mixture of greater coordination of domestic policies and new associationism regarding external policies. Forced by external circumstances and the internal policy to maintain the Franco-German equilibrium, the EU will need to open its markets and expand its borders through the creation of free trade areas involving its peripheries in the South and the East.

BIBLIOGRAPHY

Bertram, C. (1995) *The Future of European Security and the Franco-German Relationship*, The Hague: Netherlands Scientific Council for Government Policy.

Bianchi, P. (1992) 'What economic scenario for Europe?', in C. Crouch and D. Marquand (eds) *Towards Greater Europe?*, Oxford: Blackwell Publishers: 64–90.

Caporaso, J. (1996) 'The European Union and forms of state: Westphalian, regulatory or post-modern?', *Journal of Common Market Studies* 34(1): 29–52.

Dornbusch, R. (1996) 'Euro Fantasies', *Foreign Affairs* 75(5): 110–124.

EBRD (1996) *Annual Report*, Basel and London: European Bank for Reconstruction and Development.

Economic Outlook (yearbook) (1996) Economics and Statistics Dept., Paris: OECD.

Economic Survey of Europe in 1995–1996 (1996), Geneva: United Nations Economic Commission For Europe.

The Economist, various issues as shown.

Employment Outlook 1996 (1996) Paris: OECD.

European Commission (1995) *European Economy, 1995 Broad Economic Policy Guidelines*, Brussels: European Commission, Directorate-General for Economic and Financial Affairs.

Eurostat Yearbook 1995 (Dutch version) Brussels: EGKS-EG-EGA.

Fursdon, E. (1980) *The European Defence Community: A History*, London: Macmillan.

Garton Ash, T. (1994) 'Germany's choice', *Foreign Affairs* 73(4): 65–81.

Gilpin, R. (1987) *The Political Economy of International Relations*, Princeton, NJ: Princeton University Press.

Grilli, E. R. (1993) *The European Community and the Developing Countries*, Cambridge: Cambridge University Press.

Haas, E. (1958) *The Uniting of Europe: Political, Social and Economic Forces, 1950–1957*, Stanford, CN: Stanford University Press.

Hoffman, S. (1989) 'The European Community and 1992', *Foreign Affairs* 68(4): 27–47.

Holbrooke, R. (1995) 'America: A European Power', *Foreign Affairs* 74(2): 38–51.

IGC-Benelux Memorandum (1996) The Hague: Ministry of Foreign Affairs.

Istituto Affari Internazionali (ed.) (1996) *Revision of Maastricht: Implementation and Proposals for Reform: A Survey of National Views*, Roma: Istituto Affari Internazionali.

Kissinger, H. (1994) *Diplomacy*, London: Simon and Schuster.

Kol, J. (1995) *Bloc Formation: Fragmentation and Stability in the World Economy*, The Hague: Netherlands Scientific Council for Government Policy.

Larre, B. and Torres, R. (1991) *Is Convergence a Spontaneous Process? The Experience of Spain, Portugal and Greece*, Paris: OECD.

McCormick, J. (1996) *The European Union: Politics and Policies*, Oxford: Westview Press.

Maier, C.S. (1994) 'Democracy and its discontents', *Foreign Affairs* 73(4): 48–64.

Main Economic Indicators (1995) Paris: OECD.

Milward, A.S. (1992) *The European Rescue of the Nation–State*, London: Routlege.

The New Transatlantic Agenda, Joint EU-US Action Plan (1995) Brussels: European Council.

Padoan, P.C. (1994) 'The changing European political economy', in R. Stubbs and G.D.R. Underhill (eds) *Political Economy and the Changing Global Order*, London: Macmillan: 336–351.

Risse-Kappen, T. (1996) 'Exploring the nature of the beast: international relations theory and comparative policy analysis meet the European Union', *Journal of Common Market Studies* 34 (1): 53–80.

Sassoon, D. (1996) *One Hundred Years of Socialism*, London: I.B. Tauris.

Sörös, G. (1996) 'Can Europe work? A plan to rescue the Union', *Foreign Affairs* 75(5): 8–14.

Tsoukalis, L. (1981) *The European Community and its Mediterranean Enlargement*, London: Allen and Unwin.

Tsoukalis, L. (1991) *The New European Economy*, Oxford: Oxford University Press.

United Nations Centre on Transnational Corporations (1996) *World Investment Report: Transnational Corporations as Engines of Growth*, New York: United Nations.

United States Security Strategy for Europe and Nato (1995) Washington, DC Department of Defense, Office of International Security Affairs.

Voortgang naar Convergentie (1996) Frankfurt am Main: Europees Monetair Instituut.

Wallace, H. and Wallace, W. (1995) *Flying Together in a Larger and More Diverse European Union*, The Hague: Netherlands Scientific Council for Government Policy.

171

8

A REGIONALIZING MIDDLE POWER

Turkey's role between Europe and Asia

Zehra Gamze Aslancik

Turkey is unique for many reasons. It is an Islamic country which has embraced Western institutions and a Latin alphabet. In the 1920s the country carried out a national revolution from above, modernizing its political and social institutions. In the immediate post-war years, Marshall Aid was granted to Turkey and in 1952 the country became a member of the Organization for European Economic Cooperation (OEEC), thus promoting Turkey's ties with the West. Turkey obtained membership of NATO and established close contacts with Europe. For several decades Turkey was America's closest ally against the Soviet Union in the Caucasian region. Therefore Turkey joined several anti-Soviet regional organizations. In the early 1990s, after the fall of the Soviet Union, when defining Turkey's international role in a globalizing and regionalizing world, President Turgut Özal spoke about 'establishing a hegemony from east to west, from the Adriatic Sea across Central Asia to China'. Prime Minister Süleyman Demirel spoke in a similar way: 'The achievement of independence by these countries [of Central Asia] is an embodiment of the age-old Turkish dream and ... [Turkey] is prepared to do everything possible to help them implement political and economic reforms' (Smolansky 1994: 203).

The 'awakening' of this imperial idea designated Turkey's leadership in a region where China, Russia and the European Union (EU) meet and where political instability has grown. Will contemporary Turkey be able to fullfil these imperial aspirations?

TURKISH LEADERSHIP

Turkey is a regional power that, in relation to the newly emerged Caucasian and Central Asian republics, has regained some influence in this region. Common ethnical, linguistic and cultural ties may serve as common ground for the establishment of a Turkish-dominated economic and political regional integration process that could serve Turkey's expansionary policy. Of the twelve states that were created after the disintegration of the Soviet Union, six are Muslim countries and a majority of their population consists of Muslims. These are: Kazakhstan, Uzbekistan,

Azerbaijan, Tajikistan, Kirghizia and Turkmenistan. Each one of them is poor; they are all landlocked countries and their economic dependence upon others is bound to be their permanent feature. Some of them are strategically well placed, which is bound to help them to play some role in regional affairs. Kazakhstan and Kirghizia are situated between China and Russia. Tajikistan, Uzbekistan and Turkmenistan lie on the Afghan borders. Armenia and Azerbaijan lie on the borders of Iran. All these countries are situated in the midst of Muslim countries, but they share with Turkey the secular nature of the state, which is probably communism's enduring legacy, and the failure of Iran to influence them.

Since the 1960s Turkey, Iran and Pakistan have sponsored the Economic Cooperation of the Middle East (ECO). For the Central Asian states this opened up the possibility of transferring exportable goods to international waters. Founded in 1964 as the Regional Cooperation for Development, the ECO was intended to foster economic growth and development between Turkey, Iran and Pakistan. This US initiative in the region was intended to form a bulwark against the Soviet Union. But in 1979 this alliance collapsed after the Islamic Revolution in Tehran and in 1985 the organization was revived as the ECO. In 1992, the three founders invited the newly independent states of Central Asia and the Caucasus to a conference to be held in Tehran. All the countries attending the conference expressed a desire to strengthen ECO (Smolansky 1994: 291). The first ECO conference held in a Central Asian republic met in Ashkabat (Turkmenistan) in May 1992 and was attended by the three founders plus Turkmenistan, Uzbekistan, Kyrgyzstan, and Kazakhstan. Tajikistan and Azerbaijan did not participate because of internal political problems. The conference agreed on the idea of a free trade area and the completion of the Mashhad–Sarakhs–Tajan railroad. A highway was to link Istanbul with Alma Ata via Tehran.

The landlocked nature of the new Muslim countries is bound to enhance their political and economic dependency upon others (Lipovsky 1996: 211–224) and Turkey may be in a position to exploit such a situation. Turkey has historic ties with all Central Asian states, except Tajikistan, which is a cultural continuation of Iran. Turkey has sponsored trade with the Central Asian states. By and large, the Turkish model of political and socio-economic development is attractive to the Muslim republics. Throughout 1991–92, nearly all Central Asian leaders confessed they saw Turkey as a model to follow (Hunter 1996: 137). Relations with Central Asia have also become institutionalized in the context of regular 'Turkic summits'. Essentially, Turkey adopted a strategy that aims to mobilize its cultural, ethnic and linguistic ties with the Turkic republics in Central Asia. Turkey is in a position to offer more than Iran. But in Central Asia, and there are several reasons for this, Russia has remained a major player. Since 1993, Russia has expressed its concern over what have been described as efforts to create a pan-Turkish alliance. This criticism fuelled a Russian-Turkish rivalry. A pan-Turkish alliance could antagonize Russia, Iran, and China, who see pan-Turkism as a threat to their own territorial integrity and security. In Turkey itself, Pan-Turkism did not survive the Kemalist revolution from above. As an ideology, Pan-Turkism seems more remote

173

today than its fellow nineteenth-century phenomenon, Pan-Slavism (Pettifer 1997: 197–211).

In my opinion, Turkey cannot play the role of a major regional leader in the Caucasus and Central Asia. A Turkish confederation of Central Asian States is not the future. The weakness of the contemporary Republic of Turkey has to be traced back to the times when the Ottoman Empire collapsed and the nationalist social and political forces tried to modernize and reconstruct a regime based on import-substituting industrialization. Turkey never could become a pole of economic attraction for its neighbours. Therefore this chapter will describe the progress Turkey has made from a pre-modern mode of governance and of production to the contemporary Republic. This description is necessary in order to explain the current political and economic situation in the region and, more specifically, the Turkish position in this.

THE OTTOMAN HERITAGE

The structures established in the Ottoman era, such as the Ottoman way of governance, the Asiatic mode of production and of social relations have to be explained in order to understand the current structures in Turkish society. I will call these concepts the Ottoman legacy (or heritage), because of their impact on contemporary Turkey. It is, however, important to keep in mind that the Ottoman society was not an Islamic society as such, but was rather a 'contingent feature of the necessary intermediation in tributary forms of rule and appropriation, and hence relates to the use made of Islam by historically specific social forces' (Bromley 1994: 39–40).

Between 1280 and 1453 a form of tributary society emerged. It was a society which had a structure of agrarian surplus production, linked to an urban, tributary form of appropriation, involving centralized taxation of the peasantry and direct political regulation of urban production and trade. All land, with the exception of religious lands, was the patrimony of the sultan. Peasants with rights of access to the land formed the main units of production and consumption. In this so-called Asiatic mode of production land is the means of production and, unlike feudalism, the method of surplus appropriation is achieved through taxation by the central state.

Another important feature of the Asiatic mode of production is the 'despotic state', a ruling class which consists of the state and military bureaucracy, and the religious institutions. The state did not derive power from the control of public works but from its ability to appropriate almost the entire surplus in the form of taxes.

There were three areas of surplus appropriation for the state. These were agriculture, industry, and trade. In the area of agriculture the state was the legal owner of landed and manufactured property. The second source of revenue was the urban surplus obtained by means of taxes imposed on craft industry and trade. The craft industry was subject to rigid state control, the craft guilds paid high taxes and therefore lost a lot of their surplus.

The third and last source of revenue, trade, had a somewhat different standing. Merchants were relatively free from rigid control and tax payments. The surplus of trade was not as important as the agricultural surplus because the surplus of trade was a smaller amount. Above that, the merchants were in the fortunate position of being the creditors of the tax farmers. The profits the merchants earned were in addition to those which were earned from international trade and the marketing of rural surplus (Alatas 1993: 475–476).

The profits of both the tax farms and the guilds went to the urban-based intermediaries of the state and so the state became the legal owner of landed and manufactured property. These intermediaries were formed by the Ottoman state and the *ulema* (or theologians). The initial power of the state is explained by the gathering of tribal military power. It was this tribal military power that established a new dynasty and represented it in areas which did not have large-scale public works. When one talks about the 'despotic state', one should raise the issue of the source of state power in the Asiatic mode of production (ibid.: 475).

The theory of bureaucratic despotism applies to Ottoman Turkey. This could be called the pre-capitalist Islamic (Islamic because in the religious way of thinking all land belonged to God, not to mankind) form of state. It was this above-mentioned urban location and tributary form of surplus appropriation that did not contain a dynamic long-term improvement of the forces of production of the kind unleashed by the establishment of the capitalist mode of production. For the ruling class it was urban consumption, not productive innovation, that was the driving force to make the peasants pay taxes (Gills and Frank 1992). However, due to the tributary character of the society, little impetus was left for agricultural or industrial improvement. During the sixteenth and seventeenth centuries the only way revenue was provided was by external accumulation (conquest of land). The danger of this situation was that the state was too powerful and fixed to cope with external (economic or political) factors which could upset the balance. This became clear when the influx of gold and silver from the New World into the Mediterranean in the sixteenth century created a 'price revolution' and especially when the rerouting of international trade routes became apparent. The problems became more acute when the Ottoman territorial expansion was blocked by Europe (Ahmad 1993: 22). Surpluses could only be raised by an increased resort to tax farming, which led to a growing pressure on the peasantry.

To deal with the rivals of the Ottoman Empire, the Europeans who were forging ahead, the Ottomans continued to reform and adapt their institutions to meet the internal and external challenges. At first the Ottomans thought that military reorganization as sufficient to meet the European expansion. External accumulation was necessary in order to provide revenue for the state, and the Ottoman society had little means of internal renewal (Bromley 1994: 48–49). Of course, all the modernizations in the army required, increases in the taxes, and consequently an increase in tax farming. These developments abroad and within the empire required fundamental changes within Ottoman society, but the conservative powers, supported by the *ulema* and the janissary army, refused to go along with the reforms. The sultan, then, stood alone because there was no force in society to whom he could turn for support (Ahmad 1993: 23).

Finally in the nineteenth century the men at the Porte realized that true westernization meant that the Ottoman Empire needed classes based on secure property rights who could prosper without fear of having their wealth confiscated by the state (ibid.: 24). The restructuring of Ottoman society was a development which was in fact the need of the *state* for revenues after a period of decline. The Tanzimat reformers were convinced that the only way to survive was to participate within the expanding world economy and to allow industrial Europe access to the Ottoman economy. This was the so-called Tanzimat Mentality. The Tanzimat Mentality is today again the prevailing view in the making of Turkish economic policy.

The *ulema* who lost their financial independence, lost more than that: they lost their monopoly on education, judicial and administrative affairs to the different Ministries. 'Agreeable' *ulema* were co-opted into the bureaucracy. In 1875 the failure to generate sufficient growth and revenue resulted in bankruptcy of the state. This meant a new era for Ottoman history. After this event the European domination really expanded, both in political and economic spheres. European influence in the economic sector in particular had a determinant character.

European domination of the economy was a mixture of: an invasion of foreign currencies, foreign control over public revenue and expenditure and foreign merchants who came to control large parts of commerce and finance (Bromley 1994: 56). After 1815 the trade balance with Europe first deteriorated and then remained in deficit until the First World War. All these developments meant that the Turkish economy would become a dependent economy and all (industrial) development would be dependent development.

In 1908 the Hamidian regime had been overthrown by the Young Turk revolution. The Young Turks were young army officers and bureaucrats for whom the army was their chief beneficiary. This Young Turks movement was a reaction to the continuing loss of territory. The movement was divided into two principal groups: the Liberals and the Unionists. The former were supporters of the constitutional monarchy controlled by high bureaucrats. They thought that Turkey's salvation was to be found in the world economy system. The latter (members of the Committee of Union and Progress, the CUP) were also constitutionalists, but they saw the overthrow of the autocracy as the first step towards social and economic transformation. They no longer had confidence in the *laissez-faire* policies, inspired as they were by the German and Japanese experiences (Ahmad 1993: 36–38). The Young Turk revolution of 1908 was followed in 1913 by the coup of the CUP. The members of the CUP were dissatisfied with the deterioration in Ottoman society and economy. But the First World War changed everything. It destroyed the Ottoman Empire, however, it also liberated the Turks (for the time being) from the immediate influence and control of the Europeans. The CUP was able to carry out its programme of reform and in this era the foundations of the new nation–state were founded. The Turks, under the leadership of Mustafa Kemal Pasha, started the

War of Independence in 1919 against the Greeks. In 1923 the modern Republic of Turkey was declared. It meant the beginning of the process of state-building.

The War of Independence was a nationalistic struggle by a national movement, which was built on the organizational foundations of the CUP. It used the term *millet* for its description of nation, nationalist and national (ibid.: 48). Because the nationalists had an image of atheists who were waging war against the caliph, religious people refused to join the movement (ibid.: 48). In 1923 the secular Republic was established with Mustafa Kemal as its first president and Ankara as its new capital. Kemal was an authoritarian ruler and when he reached a position of national political power, he did not hesitate to take measures against those in the military who could form a threat to himself or his programmes. The abolition of the Caliphate was the second important feature of the Ottoman past Kemal thought was necessary in order to protect Turkey from a counter-revolution. Kemal refused to use Islam as an extending ideology. On the other hand, he used the clergy to legitimize political movements when necessary. So Kemal managed to marginalize both the military and the religious conservatives from the political scene (Ayata 1996: 40–56).

REVOLUTION FROM ABOVE

The pre-revolutionary structures proved to be difficult to change, even the Kemalist revolution (1919–23) could not transform the social, political and economic circumstances of the mass of the Turkish peasantry (Keyder 1995: 193–212). So the Kemalist revolution could only be a revolution from above. Obviously, the impasse of the traditionally dominant social structures faced with the new ones (initiated by Kemal Atatürk during the Kemalist revolution) created a situation where the introduction of change did not involve a stimulation of popular forces (Cox 1983: 166).

Many scholars have defined the concept of revolution, as 'the dispossession of an exploiting class that destroys the old ruling class' (Bromley 1994: 162). Theda Skocpol makes a contrast between social revolutions and what she calls political revolutions. The latter do transform state structures but they do not transform social structures, and they are not necessarily accomplished by class conflict (Skocpol 1979: 5). Ellen Kay Trimberger and Robert Cox have defined the concept 'revolution from above'. The uniqueness of the Kemalist revolution lies in the fact that it contains several different features of different concepts of 'revolutions from above' (Bromley 1994: 161). The Kemalist revolution was a revolution that was initiated by the military and had the nationalist features Trimberger mentions. But the pre-revolutionary military was not a homogenous group. The next feature Trimberger describes is the nationalist character of the revolution. The nationalist aspect of the Kemalist revolution is, indeed, one of great importance.

Robert Cox also examined the concept of 'revolution from above', but he put it in a complete context of social transformation. Cox used the Gramscian analogy to conceptualize transformation of functional relationships. In his description of the emergence of different kind of states in an era (or, rather, a world order) of rival imperialisms (Cox 1987: 151–210), he also explains the revolution in Russia. In Russia a redistributive party-commanded state emerged out of the crisis of the old-regime agrarian–bureaucratic state. This form of state has a redistributive mode of production which is carried on under the leadership of a revolutionary party with a monopoly of state power (ibid.: 198). This explains several aspects of the Kemalist revolution, because there are many similarities in the process of creation and implementation of the new state forms between Russia and Turkey at that time.

However, the most substantial difference is the fact that the Bolsheviks had a communist ideology, whereas the Kemalist revolution's ambition was to create a 'western' capitalist mode of production which would be able to enter the world system in a competitive way. The similarities are the pre-revolution conditions such as the form of social and production relations, and the pre-revolutionary strong, coercive state which had no base in civil society.

Following Gramsci's analogy of the war of movement and the war of position (a slowly but surely built class-based counter-hegemony in a civil society (ibid.: 204)) for a successful (socialist) revolution, the war of movement is best suited to explain the internal developments prior to and during the Kemalist revolution. The absence of a hegemonic civil society (accompanied by an undeveloped capitalist mode of production) and the tradition of a strong state, formed the background for the war of movement in Turkey. This war of movement was necessary in order to provide the space for the transformation the Kemalists wanted. The coincidence of the war of movement with a 'real' war (the War of Independence) smoothed and eased the process of the war of movement: the actual destruction of the Ottoman state form. The fact that this transformation was 'led' by the state is of the utmost importance for the concept of 'passive revolution'. Namely, the state replaced the social groups (or forces) in leading the struggle of renewal (or transformation).

After the war of movement, the Kemalist revolution became a 'passive revolution' ('passive' stands for the inability to realize a complete or 'social revolution' or transformation of society). The Kemalist revolution contained a new set of political ideas which implied a new set of social (that includes the economic) and political relations. But the new set of relations could not be implemented by the Kemalists.

The Gramscian concept of the 'passive revolution' incorporates more concepts of the construction of a political society. An example of such an implication is the concept of hegemony. In the Gramscian context hegemony means more than just domination by coercion. In short, hegemony is a combination of consent and coercion, whereas the amount of consent determines if hegemony predominates. Gramsci enlarged his concept of the state, together with the elements of government (administrative, executive and coercive apparatus): 'the notion of the state would also have to include the underpinnings of the political structures in civil society' (Cox 1983). These underpinnings are all the institutions which construct 'the certain modes of behavior and expectations consistent with the hegemonic social order' (ibid.: 164). The hegemony of the ruling class is, broadly, based on consent and the acceptance of certain modes of expectations and behaviour. This last aspect has a twofold character, it applies to both the state and the civil society.

In Turkey's case (including the Ottoman Empire), it can be said that a civil society never emerged. The heritage of the deficiency of a civil society, combined with the tradition of a strong state, made it almost impossible for the Kemalists to make way for the emergence of a civil society and a certain level of retreat of the state. The transformation from an Asiatic mode of production to an 'obliged or imported' western capitalist mode of production had to be accompanied by a form of 'socialization'. At that time the prevailing social relations were based on a rural, Asiatic mode of production. 'Socialization' increases the mutual dependence of people and the semblance of their dependency across classes (a process in the establishing of the hegemony of the capitalist mode of production). It transforms and reintegrates traditional communities into new units and in addition transforms the mental outlook and world view, in order to function within the capitalist mode of production (Van der Pijl 1989: 16). This process of 'socialization' did not properly take place in Kemalist Turkey. This stage of development of a state is typical for what Kees Van der Pijl calls the 'Hobbesian state': a strong, effective state where a 'broad identity between state, ruling, and governing class' exists, the ruling class is a permanent state class (ibid.: 19). The prevailing difference between a 'Hobbesian state' and a 'Lockian state', is that the latter is a 'self-regulating' society, whereas the former controls and regulates the social relations. The civil society in the 'Lockian state' plays the key role in the state–society relationship where the state has withdrawn. In Gramsci's words this means that in a 'self-regulating' society, hegemony over the historical development belongs to the private forces, to the civil society. The functions of the state are limited to the safeguarding of public order and to respect for the laws (Gramsci 1971: 261). In Turkey, where no bourgeois class or any other social institution or association existed, a civil society could not develop. Moreover, there was no tradition of civil participation and emancipation. What must be stressed here is the fact that the indigenous people in the Ottoman Empire, and later in the republic, were not familiar with participation in the political sphere. Civil participation and emancipation require a level of education or 'socialization' and, moreover, confidence. Confidence is a necessity for both the state and the people to develop a civil society.

EXPORT ORIENTATION WITHIN A NEO-LIBERAL PACKAGE

With the transition to a multiparty system after 1945, an essential element of the preceding regime was retained, to the extent that the army remained secondary to the established civilian authority. In the 1950s, the anti-etatist Demokrat Partisi [Democrat Party (DP)] took power from the, until then, monopolistic Cumhurivet Halk Partisi [Republican People's Party (CHP)] led by Ismet Inönü. But after the massive crop failure of 1954, the country turned to import substitution. Licensing was required for all imports, with many import commodities transferred to the quota list. A system of mutiple exchange rate was introduced. Tariff rates were increased considerably. US aid to Turkey in the immediate post-war period was concentrated on agriculture and infrastructure. This aid was consistent with an inward-oriented industrialization scheme and contributed to Turkey's reliance on capital imports. Productivity of public enterprises remained relatively low. The investment in agriculture and the subsequent reliance on price support for the sector did pose an unbearable burden for recurrent expenditure. In 1958, Turkey had to agree on a stabilization programme prepared by the International Monetary Fund (IMF). The Turkish lira was devalued and the multiple exchange rate abandoned. Import programmes became the major instrument of import control. During the 1960s state planning was introduced and industrialization was fostered by an inward-oriented development strategy through high protective tariffs, restrictions, regulations, quotas and overvalued exchange rates. In 1960 the military took power and deposed Prime Minister Adnan Menderes. The DP was legally dissolved and its leaders executed. In 1961 the military returned to their barracks. The elections of 1961 were won by Ismet Inönü's CHP. He formed a government that relied on the military. The DP remained dissolved but Süleiman Demirel's Adalet Partisi [Justice Party (AP)] emerged as its successful successor party. In 1965 the CHP lost the parliamentary elections and the AP formed a majority government. The military did not oppose this change of the political guard, because the CHP had shown its inability to form a stable government with the help of the minor parties.

During the 1960s and 1970s, all imports into Turkey were regulated by annual import programmes and this import regime remained in force until the 1980s. Since the adoption of the first five-year development plan in 1963, Turkey has used a complex system of export incentives. Domestic investments were encouraged through investment allowances, tax deductions, low-cost credits, tariff reductions, and exemptions on imported machinery and material inputs. Until 1980, domestic production was assisted by import licensing and these measures discouraged exports. To counteract these adverse effects, incentives were provided to exports (Önis and Riedel 1993: 18–38).

Turkey's interest in membership of the EC dates back to the early 1960s. In 1963 Turkey signed an Association Agreement with the European Community (EC). Turkey's application for association and then for membership was mainly inspired by political considerations. The wide disparity in living standards between Turkey and Western Europe made the country's application for full membership unrealistic. In the 1960s agriculture still was the backbone of Turkey's economy as its industrial base was very weak and its integration into the world economy was very limited. But the orientation of its exports was towards Europe. Hence, an incentive existed to ensure that markets in the EC were not lost through the EC trade discrimination.

Although the EC had become Turkey's main trading partner, the country failed to prepare its economy for full EC membership (*Turkey* 1984: 8–11). Turkey failed to take advantage of preferential access to the EC market. Protectionist tariffs against the import of industrial products were not abolished. Moreover, the Association Agreement was inadequate for the task of preparing Turkey for full membership, given the fact that the tariff preferences for industrial products could only have a limited impact on Turkey's economy. By 1971 the EC had extended preferential treatment to other developing countries under the General System of Preferences (Müftüler-Bac 1997: 53–106).

During the 1970s Turkey failed to adjust to the oil shocks and the country was faced with a large trade deficit, heavy indebtedness and rampant inflation. The government borrowed imprudently to mitigate the growth-retarding impact of the first oil shock but could not borrow its way out of the second shock. Foreign private lenders started to cut off credit to Turkey after a debt crisis in 1977. Other financial inflows decreased as workers abroad reduced their remittances and exports declined. By 1979 Turkey's economy was bankrupt (Hine 1996: 131–154). Political instability increased, wildcat strikes spread and political violence weakened the centre-left coalition government led by CHP leader Bülent Ecevit. In November 1979 a centre-right government led by Süleyman Demirel took over. Demirel brought in a team of technocrats led by a former economist of the World Bank, Turgut Özal, in order to reform the economy now that Turkey was forced to reschedule its debts to Western governments and foreign banks. It was clear that a serious effort to change the economy would involve the introduction of tight money control, a reduction in the losses of the state companies, reduction in the magnitude of public investments, and devaluation of the Turkish lira. A precondition for rescheduling Turkey's foreign debt was the acceptance of the IMF's Structural Adjustment Programmes (SAPs) implemented on 24 January 1980. But the strikes and political violence continued. The unions were angry because they were excluded from the design process. This motivated the military to intervene once more (Krueger and Turan 1993: 348–357).

The military regime, which took over in September 1980, crushed the left opposition and dissolved all political parties. The military supported the Özal programme of social stabilization and export-led economic growth, involving structural adjustment and economic liberalization (Aktan 1996: 177–197) but the military had only a vague economic vision. The economic programme designed by Özal (who was kept in office by the military) involved a switch from import-substitution to export-orientation within the neo-liberal reform package, such as devaluation, privatization of state-owned enterprises, and abolishing large-scale subsidies. In addition to the usual stabilization measures, the government intended to liberalize the economy and to rely on market forces instead of state intervention. In 1982, after a bankers' crisis, Özal and his team were removed from the government. In November 1982 a new constitution was adopted by referendum and a year later the military restored democracy (Hale 1994: 246–275). Özal with his newly founded Anavatan Partisi [Motherland Party (ANAP)] re-emerged as prime minister after the elections of November 1983. He immediately liberalized the investment regime.

Özal's economic policy has been rather successful. GNP growth showed a 5.4 per cent annual increase in 1980–88 compared with 3.3 per cent in 1975–80. Exports had to become a major engine of growth (Taskin and Yeldan 1996: 155–

176). State intervention in export promotion, however, did not conform to the neo-liberal logic. Export subsidies in the forms of low interest credit, exchange rate policy, export tax rebates, and duty free imports had been utilized until the GATT abolished them in 1988 (Önis 1993: 83). Direct payments to exporters of manu-factures in the form of tax rebates became forbidden. But exchange rate policies still provided incentives to industrial exporters without violating the GATT rules. The export-orientation policy was initially a success. Export growth during the first part of the decade was remarkable and was engineered by domestic firms with domestic finance. Export successes were obtained through a consistent export-promotion policy relying on three instruments: exchange rate policy, which affects every tradable good, and credit policy and fiscal incentives, both of which tend to produce biased sectoral effects. By the 1980s, Turkey's current account deficit was a manage-able $US1 billion. The balance of payments turnaround during the 1980s was achieved largely by dramatic improvements in exports, which increased from $US2.9 billion in 1980 to $US13.6 billion in 1991 (Önis 1995: 107–129).

Agriculture's share of exports fell from 58 per cent in 1980 to 20 per cent in 1988. The share of textiles doubled to 27 per cent and steel increased from 1 to 13 per cent. In 1987, 47.8 per cent of Turkey's exports went to the EC. Turkey's textile industry benefited from closer integration with the EC involving a mutual reduction of trade barriers, and confidence existed about the ability of Turkish industry to compete in the EC market. However, many distortions caused by import protection and export incentives made a general appreciation difficult. Some industries regarded as symbolic of economic progress would not survive unrestricted com-petition. Foreign investment did not contribute much to the export growth. Exter-nal finance, from the World Bank, accompanied the SAPs of the 1980s.

The major factors in this export success were trade liberalization measures, the exchange regimes and heavy reliance on import subsidies. In January 1980 the Turkish lira had been devalued and eleven mini-devaluations followed within sixteen months. From 1 May 1981 onwards the exchange rate was adjusted on a daily base. All these reforms had made exports more attractive to domestic producers and import substitution less attractive. The export-led growth accomplished an import-ant transformation in the composition of Turkey's exports and promoted resource allocation from agriculture to industry. But the necessary level of diversification did not lead to the hoped-for industrial product exports. Traditional industrial products continued to account for the bulk of exports. So economic growth stagnated by the end of the 1980s, because the rapid growth of the economy had not accomplished an export deepening. Manufactured exports were concentrated in the traditional sec-tors, such as textiles, food processing, and iron and steel. The distinguishing characteristic of the Turkish export performance during the period was that it rested on the extraction of resources for exports by suppressing domestic demand through wage reductions and currency devaluations. This surplus was exported with the provision of generous subsidies and led to increased profits. Unfortunately, these exports had limited resource-pull effects on the rest of the economy and could not lead to a rapid absorption of unemployment (Önis 1991: 27–53).

A successful implementation of the neo-liberal package requires more than just economic measures. The development of political institutions in which neo-liberal policy can be formulated and accepted also became necessary (Bill and Springborg 1994: 448). But the government failed to produce a policy, together with private business, to encourage key sectors or markets to develop. The large domestic market and the firms producing for this market were neglected. Real wage repression ended when democracy was restored. This resulted in the increase of domestic demand but it conflicted with the export-orientated policy. A programme of (export) growth also needs to be built upon a 'broader programme of macro-economic management and industrial restructuring' and needs the 'social and political consensus which can no longer be assumed as automatically given or imposed from the above as in the exceptional setting of the early 1980s' (Önis 1993: 93). The Turkish government failed to minimize the conflict of interest involving the rapid growth, and also failed to incorporate the demands of the large internal market within the export- and market-oriented policy. Coupled with an overall decline in the share of physical investment in traded goods, Turkey's export expansion based on wage reductions and price incentives hit its political limits in the late 1980s and began to falter. Industrial growth was not investment-led. The adjustment programme relied on the assumption that financial liberalization would stimulate private savings and investment. Moreover, the growth rate for the 1980s remained lower than the average 5.6 per cent achieved between 1960 and 1980 (Önis 1996: 155–178).

Foreign borrowing and foreign debt increased considerably in the second half of the 1980s while investment rates declined. Employment growth was sluggish. The fight against inflation was given priority in the adjustment programme. During the first year of the programme, inflation rose to 110 per cent, but with the help of restrictive monetary and fiscal policies, inflation fell. Although inflation was lowered, successes in this sector remained short-lived.

Efficiency did not increase sufficiently to make the Turkish economy really competitive. Turkey is still missing an efficient fiscal system and has to finance a loss-making public sector (Uygur 1993: 215–238). Although the private sector has grown, it owed its initial growth to high tariffs and government procurement and incentives. Moreover, it suffers from a lack of domestic capital and industry has to rely first on state banks, then on private banks and foreign capital. In 1991, the state sector still provided 46 per cent of gross fixed investment. The loss-making state sector was designed to provide the private sector with cheap goods and services, which it did inefficiently and at high costs. The state sector remained corrupt and an instrument for political patronage. High cotton prices paid to Turkish peasants deprived the Turkish textile industry of its competitive edge on the world market. Total farm subsidies appear to be below those provided by the EU, although in some cases (wheat) they are approaching those of the EU. Agricultural price support is an inefficient (but politically necessary) way of achieving income distribution and a source of inflationary pressure, because subsidies are financed by printing money (Mango 1994: 54–63).

183

In 1987 Turkey applied for full membership of the EC. Although the EC indicated the eligibility of Turkey for eventual EC membership, this will not occur in the near future. Turkey may, of course, be able to establish closer links with the other Black Sea economies and the countries of Central Asia, but these markets are not comparable in size with those of the EU. Whether or not Turkey will attain full membership of the EU is a much-discussed issue. The question is, would membership of the EU be of greater attraction to foreign firms than a Turkey outside the EU? One may presume that regional integration will promote foreign direct investment because of the enlarged markets, growth in incomes and the scope and scale economies it promotes. Regional integration offers location advantages and regional incentives to foreign firms. Turkey possesses a comparative advantage in the export of labour-intensive goods, especially textiles, clothing and shoes. These and other exports are subject to non-tariff barriers in the EU. Turkey is cited in many an anti-dumping case by the EU. Thus Turkey inside the EU is likely to attract larger volumes of foreign direct investment than Turkey outside the EU and to reinforce the process of export-led industrialization. However, until now the desired diversification of manufactured exports has not been achieved. Textile products, with about 40 per cent of total manufactured exports, continue to be the major export item. Only a limited amount of diversification was obtained through growth in the share of iron and steel products with 15 per cent of total industrial exports. Hides and skin products (7 per cent), chemical products (6 per cent) and electrical machinery and equipment (4 per cent) are lagging behind. None the less, these five items constituted about 70 per cent of the total industrial product exports by 1990, compared with a share of 56 per cent in 1980. Industrial expansion was concentrated in labour-intensive branches (textiles, clothing and leather), but new export industries gained some importance (iron, steel, chemicals). Summing up, the new strategy of export-led growth had favoured the development of new industries, but did not last long enough to lift the economy onto a sustainable growth path (Taskin and Yeldan 1996: 174). Although liberalization was begun and incentives distributed to foreign firms have served to arouse the interest of foreign firms in Turkey, foreign direct investment remained insignificant, notwithstanding Turkey was generously distributing investment incentives to foreign investors in the Free Port Zones (Balasubramanyan 1996: 112–130).

After 1986 policy uncertainty hit the most vulnerable variable, namely, private productive investment. Manufacturing productivity was growing too slowly while exports stagnated after 1989 as a result of the real appreciation of the Turkish lira. The liberalization of imports caused a net increase in the imports of consumer goods and the capital account liberalization contributed to the real appreciation of the lira. Further liberalization measures occurred in a period of real exchange appreciation and caused a growing trade and current account deficit. It became clear that the Turkish economy was near to collapse.

After 1987 the popularity of Özal and his ANAP declined rapidly although Özal was elected in 1989 to the presidency (Önis and Webb 1994: 128–134). Meanwhile Demirel had reappeared on the political scene with his conservative Dogru Yol Partisi [True Path Party (DYP)]. When Özal was elected President of the Republic in 1989 he was succeeded by Yldirim Akbulut and after the 1991 elections by Mesut Yilmaz as Prime Minister. But Yilmaz lost the parliamentary elections held in November 1991. Demirel's DYP formed a coalition government with the Sosual Demokrat Halk Partisi [Social Democratic Populist Party (SHP)], but political instability increased. When in 1993 Demirel was elected President of the Republic after the death of Özal, Tansu Çiller's DYP and Erdal Inönü's SHP did not break the coalition, although this coalition government had to combat high inflation rates, a declining lira, an external debt of about 72 per cent of GNP and a sizeable public sector borrowing requirement amounting to 16 per cent of the country's GNP.

The DYP reshaped the country's agenda after the accession to power of Tansu Çiller as the party leader. The SHP merged with the CHP and took the name of the CHP. The new CHP elected Deniz Baykal as its new president. This change in the left-wing partner led to a break-up of the coalition with the DYP in late September 1995. Çiller's attempt to form a coalition with the right-wing ANAP failed and led to early elections in December 1995. The political crisis was provoked by the rise of Necmettin Erbakan's pro-Islamist Refah Party [Welfare Party (RP)] which succeeded in winning the municipal elections in March 1994. The rise of the RP was due to chronic voter discontent. An overwhelming majority of the urban settlers were dissatisfied with the political stalemate and blamed the political parties for being out of touch with the needs of the people. Just before the elections of 1995 the DYP/ CHP coalition achieved a major foreign policy goal by signing a customs union agreement with the EU. In order to capitalize on this success Prime Minister Çiller took a clear pro-western stand against the RP anti-western campaign. Çiller targeted modern segments of Turkish society, specifically women voters, by attacking the RP and she underlined the need to deepen the market reforms through privatization combined with political reforms. But Erbakan's low-key campaign created for him an image of the protector of the poor shantytown dwellers. The RP narrowly won the elections (see Table 8.1). Its success not only signalled the end of the traditional centre–right politics but it also brought, for the first time in Turkish history, a party which openly challenged the secular basis of the Kemalist state (Heper 1997: 32–45). With the RP controlling 28.7 per cent of the seats, the parliament that resulted from the election on 24 December 1995 was unable to produce a stable government. After six months the DYP/ANAP minority coalition government broke down, because at the same time the ANAP was supporting parliamentary investigations of corruption against the DYP leader Çiller. Çiller who ran a clear anti-Islamist ticket, formed a RP/ DYP coalition government on 28 June 1996 with Erbakan as its new Prime Minister. Many have interpreted this move by Çiller as an opportunist decision in order to stop investigations of corruption against her.

The RP wants to transform itself from a small party into a mass centre-right party. Erbakan thinks that his long-term goal of directing Turkey into a pro-Islamic country can be attained. He is willing to accept, in accordance with this view, short-run compromises. Although the military are influencing Turkey's foreign and military policy, Erbakan chose Iran as the destination of his first foreign official trip. Amid explicit US warnings Erbakan also did not hesitate to finalize a $US20

Table 8.1 Turkish general election results

Parties	Seats			
	1946	1950	1954	1957
Republican People's Party	395	63	31	178
Democrat Party	64	420	505	424
Nation Party	—	1	5	4
Freedom Party	—	—	—	4
Independents	—	3	1	—
Total	459	487	542	610

Parties	1961	1965	1969	1973	1977
Justice Party	158	240	256	149	189
Republican People's Party	175	134	143	185	213
National Salvation Party	—	—	—	48	24
Democratic Party	—	—	—	45	1
Reliance Party	—	—	15	13	3
Republican Peasants Nation Party	54	11	—	—	—
Nationalist Action Party	—	—	1	3	16
Nation Party	—	31	6	—	—
New Turkey Party	65	19	6	—	—
Turkish Worker's Party	—	15	2	—	—
Unity Party	—	—	8	—	—
Independents	—	—	13	6	4
Total	450	450	450	450	450

Parties	1983	1987	1991	1995
Motherland Party	121	292	112	132
Populist Party[a]	117	—	—	—
Social Democratic Populist Party	—	99	91	—
Nationalist Democracy Party[b]	71	—	—	—
True Path Party	—	59	179	135
Democratic Left Party	—	—	61	76
Welfare Party	—	—	61	158
Republican People's Party	—	—	—	49
Total	450	450	450	550

Source: Hale (1994: 343–334).
Notes: [a] Merged with Social Democrat Party in 1985, to become Social Democrat Populist Party.
[b] Dissolved in 1986.

billion natural gas project during his visit to Tehran in 1996. Moreover, the RP wants to change the direction of Turkey's foreign policy towards the Middle East impeding the defense industry cooperation agreement with Israel. There are no signals that the RP wants to end the free market economic policy (Çarkoglu 1997: 86–95). In short, Turkish politics are rapidly changing and have entered a new phase of increasing religious consciousness and rising demands for responsive and accountable politics. In the meantime, the military are closely following Erbakan's pro-Islamic policy. The Constitutional Court also studies the activities of Erbakan's RP and its connections with radical Islamic groups and sects (*tarikats*).

MIDDLEPOWERMANSHIP IN THE CAUCASUS

When the Soviet Union fell apart in 1991, the traditional approach of Turkey's foreign policy changed. The Turkish government initiated an active foreign policy in search of economic and political ties with the nearly 45 million ethnic Turkic people living in Central Asia and the Caucasus. Turkish companies and business-men were offered an opportunity to climb out of the internal economic impasse and the stagnation of exports. Turkey's geographical location provided the room to enter new key markets and to benefit from trade with Central Asia and the Caucasus. Turkish businessmen relied on the Turkic sentiments of kinship, cultural ties, and common language with the Central Asian and Caucasian partners to establish long-term and profitable economic relations. The Turkish government also played an active role in establishing economic and political ties with the newly emerged Republics. The first Turkish visit, under Özal, to the Republics was in March 1991. In March and April 1992 a new delegation toured the Republics. During this tour 10,000 scholarships were provided for students to study at Turkish universities, $US1.5 billion worth of credits were distributed with $US650 million in soft loans for food and $US600 million in commercial and credit guarantees (Dannreuther 1994: 58). Trade with the Turkic republics increased from $US276 million in 1992 to $US640 million in 1994. Private investment also increased and amounted in 1994, to $US2.5 billion. But when in 1995 an international consortium was formed in order to invest in the exploitation of the 'early oil fields' in Azerbaijan, only a relatively small Turkish oil company obtained a small stake of 1.75 per cent in it (Debergh 1996: 124; Bolukbasi 1997: 80–94).

Hitherto, Turkey has not been able to enlarge its exports of manufacturing products to the Caucasus. There are several reasons for this inability to increase exports, which can be found at the international level of developments in particular. But what I want to stress is the national situation of Turkey that obstructed the aims of the government to become a political and economic 'hegemony' in the region. Özal led the initiative concerning the establishment of the Black Sea Economic Cooperation, and the emphasis on the potential leadership of Turkey in the Turkic world. He re-examined the Kemalist policy of non-interference in the affairs of neighbouring states and based Turkey's foreign politics on pragmatic considerations rather than on ideological ones (Sayari 1992: 15).

After the Bolshevik Revolution there was no initiative to seize Russian territory. The Kemalists saw it as an imperialist vision belonging to the past. But after the collapse of the Soviet Union apparently defunct ideologies reappeared. A chain of Turkic or partly Turkic populations of about 42 million people created independent states through the Caucasus (Azerbaidjan, Dagestan and Tajikistan) and beyond. Turkey became involved by proxy in the conflict between Armenia and Azebaijan over the enclave of Nagorno-Karabakh, because the Turkish military advised the Azerbaijani army. But in the war between Russia and the Chechen rebels, Turkey played only a passive role. Russian and Turkish intelligence services discussed these matters of mutual interest, because Moscow feared the use of Turkish territory by Chechen rebels.

Obviously, the new Turkic republics are looking for new partnerships. In the late-Soviet era these republics were notoriously nepotistic and corrupt, but most of them are oil-rich. The discovery of vast natural gas and oil reserves in Azerbaijan is a dramatic factor dominating regional politics. The republic of Turkmenistan also has huge gas reserves. But Turkey's foreign policy with the Caucasus and Central Asia is not only concerned with oil and gas politics, Turkish trade interests are pushing for ventures with local groups. Therefore, Turkey is involved in strategic infrastructural projects in the region, such as the modernization of the telecommunication sector and satellite television. New air and bus routes have been opened. The Central Asian states are all in urgent need of capital and hard currencies but Turkey is itself a highly indebted country with serious structural problems. Turkish private business has little experience in setting up joint ventures abroad. Moreover, the markets in the new Turkic republics are small and do not constitute a consumer market because large parts of the population are pastoralist tribes. All Central Asian republics have kept strong economic and military links with Moscow. None the less, after 1989 Turkish engineering firms conquered market shares in the Turkic republics and observers saw Turkey as a bridge between east and west. But in the 1990s trade stagnated and more attention was paid to the oil issue and the transport of oil from the Caspian fields to the Black Sea.

What is problematic is Turkey's foreign relations with the nationalities in the Caucasus. Over twenty nationalities live here, speaking more than fifty languages and dialects. Some are still fighting civil or regional wars financed out of oil revenues or illegal trade. Even in these small local wars Turkey was unable to play the role of a regional power in Central Asia or the Caucasus. In many respects the chaos and violence in the Caucasus – in 1996 there were at least five separate wars – present Turkey with a lot of problems. The advantages of economic penetration in the east have to be set against the increased risk of military and political instability. In the question of cultural and religious affinity the Turkish bourgeoisie thinks that there are already too many 'primitive' people invading the big cities.

The main reason is, again, the lack of internal (or social) hegemony based on a historic bloc. In Turkey the traditional historic bloc (a co-optation based on compromise rather then on consent) consisted of state-institutions and bureaucracy. This co-optation was no longer effective after the change in economic policy in the direction of neo-liberalism. The bureaucracy lost its close links with the state structures. In the 1980s the army officers wanted to break down the traditional connections between the bureaucracy and the CHP, for they, the army officers, were strong supporters of the private sector. This resulted in the alienation of the bureaucrats from the state (Bill and Springborg 1994: 275). But a new historic bloc has not been constructed, because of the absence of one ruling class in society. The historic bloc which fits best in the neo-liberal era, the government and private business, failed to achieve social hegemony in the 1980s. Internal division and conflict as the result of several circumstances concerning Turkish identity in the 1990s, such as the human rights problem, made it difficult to develop a historic bloc. On the other hand, the 'active' foreign policy of Turgut Özal did, temporarily, create a consensus and confidence among the population. But state authority in social questions remained, especially after the Kurdish problem became more prominent. This problem could not be resolved, and escalated in the use of the military force. Neo-Ottomanism was seen as a possible solution to the domestic problems, the Kurdish problem and as a way of creating a context for Turkey's foreign policy for the Balkans and the former Soviet Union within a new cultural and political setting (Dagi 1993: 75).

All these characteristics of Turkish society combined with the specific features of governance made the goals of the Turkish private sector and state difficult to realize. But also the role of Turkey in the context of the (world) hegemonic order played a part. What initially was a positive outcome for Turkey's incorporation into the post-war world order, namely, Turkey's geopolitical situation, is now determining its role as a third, mediating party.

The Turkish government and the economic actors represent what Cox has called the 'middle power' within the hegemonic world order. They initiate and create the different conditions and structures in the Caucasus and Central Asia in order to incorporate the republics into the world system. The Turkish actors became the mediators for the western actors who were interested in the region. The different interests of the various actors are illustrated by the developments concerning the trans-Caucasian oil pipeline. The importance of the energy sector in particular within the economic potential of the region makes several western and local companies and political entities want to establish long-term commitments. That is the reason why the consortium of several oil companies, which will develop the trans-Caucasian pipeline, consists of both commercial and state companies. The twofold route the pipeline will follow, an Azerbaijan–Georgia–Turkey option and an Azerbaijan–Russia option, shows the current political and economic relations in the region. In 1995 the Azerbaijan government opted for the so-called 'two-pipeline solution', at least for the first flow from the fields. This provides for a pipeline through Russia, and also through the Caucasus to a terminal in south-east Turkey. The preferred Russian route also runs through Bulgaria and therefore requires a terminal in northern Greece. Meanwhile, the oilfields of Azerbaijan will be a source of enormous wealth once the problem of oil transport is solved. But oil prices are low and the leading oil producers want to prevent new producers from entering into the market. The solution proposed by the Azerbaijani International Oil Consortium in which the Western oil companies participate, is to take a limited quantity of 5 million tons a year in order to bring some revenues to Azerbaijan and to start to introduce their oil on the world market. But Turkish interests are protesting against this proposal, as it would be uneconomic to build a pipeline to transport so little oil. Moreover, Turkey wants the pipeline carrying Azerbaijani oil to the West to cross

Turkish territory and thinks that this oil should benefit Turkey and the neighbouring Turkic countries. But a conflict with Russia has to be avoided, because Russian gas has a monopoly in Turkey and powers much of Turkish industry. Today, the excitement about Azerbaijani oil has evaporated (Bolukbasi 1997: 8–94). In 1996 a new railway linking the landlocked Central Asian republics with Iran and the Indian Ocean was opened. Iran is offering an outlet to the sea for Central Asia. Although Iran is competing with Turkey in the region, both countries have common interests. In 1996 the Turkish Erbakan government signed a major gas deal with Iran. Erbakan's proposal of a $US20 billion business deal with Iran was viewed as an affront to the United States.

CONCLUSIONS

By the late 1970s, the import-substitution model previously followed was in crisis. In 1980 an outward-oriented growth model was tried against a background of real depreciation of the Turkish lira. Although Turkey had experienced high growth rates during the early 1980s, increasing economic difficulties demonstrated the country's weakness as a regional economic power. In the 1980s Turkey under Prime Minister Özal was seen as a model of Western economic development, with high growth rates, a liberal and open economic policy based on good inflow of foreign investment and developing stock markets. But since the early 1990s, serious doubts have begun to emerge about some aspects of this apparent progress and modernization, partly as a result of the rise of Islam as a political force in Turkish society. The Turkish economy is crippled by high inflation and unemployment and burgeoning public debt. The war with the Kurds is undermining the country's political stability and costs billions of dollars. Ever-expanding cities are adding to this instability. On every border Turkey has difficulties. To the south, relations with Iraq and Syria are problematic. To the east and north, the demise of the Soviet Union did not bring serious economic advantages and, to the west, the European Union seems as far away as ever from offering full membership, despite the Customs Union agreement in 1995–96. Turkish troops joined the United Nations force in the Balkan peace-keeping operation and established close relations with Macedonia. Turkey's role concerning the Caucasus is one of mediator between the western partners and the Turkic republics, not of a hegemonic force. Turkey can only provide economic and political insights, figures, information and cooperation to the Western investors and companies, based on Turkey's cultural and ethnic ties.

To the outside world, it seems as though Atatürk provided modern Turkey with an identity that it did not have before, that he made it a modern nation–state. But the Ottoman heritage is present below the surface, powerful and difficult to overcome.

The limitations on Turkey becoming a regional 'hegemony' are found within Turkey itself. The Turkish government and the economic actors initiated and created the different conditions and structures in the Caucasian and Central Asian republics in order to incorporate them into the world system, not in the 'Turkic hegemonic' system. In conclusion, one can say that in the Turkish society no 'civil society' emerged, and the strong position of the state continued. The ruling class was a permanent state (or state-related) class, and despite the efforts 'from above' no real 'self-regulating' society with a bourgeois class emerged. Social production relations were not able to construct a 'hegemonical' historic bloc. So if such a historic bloc was not able to develop in Turkish society, it is almost impossible for Turkey to fulfil a leading (or hegemonic) role at an international level.

BIBLIOGRAPHY

Ahmad, F. (1993) *The Making of Modern Turkey*, London: Routledge.
Aktan, O. H. (1996) 'Liberalization, export incentives and exchange rate policy: Turkey's experience in the 1980s', in S. Togan and V. N. Balasubramanyan (eds) *The Economy of Turkey since Liberalization*, Basingstoke and London: Macmillan: 177–197.
Alatas, S. F. (1993) 'The Asiatic mode of production and the formative Turkic and Iranian states in modern times', *Central Asian Survey* 12(4): 473–496.
Ayata, S. (1996) 'Patronage, party, and state: the politicization of Islam in Turkey', *The Middle East Journal* 50(1): 40–56.
Balasubramanyan, V. N. (1996) 'Foreign direct investment in Turkey', in S. Togan and V. N. Balasubramanyan (eds) *The Economy of Turkey since Liberalization*, Basingstoke and London: Macmillan: 112–130.
Bill, J. A. and Springborg, R. (1994) *Politics in the Middle East*, New York: HarperCollins College Publishers.
Bolukbasi, S. (1997) 'Ankara's Baku-centered Transcaucasia policy: has it failed?', *The Middle East Journal* 51(1): 80–94.
Bromley, S. (1994) *Rethinking Middle East Politics*, Cambridge: Polity Press.
Çarkoglu, A. (1997) 'The Turkish general election of 24 December 1995', *Electoral Studies* 16(1): 86–95.
Cox, R. W. (1983) 'Gramsci, hegemony and international relations: an essay in method', *Millennium: Journal of International Studies* 12(2): 162–175.
Cox, R. W. (1987) *Production, Power and World Order: Social Forces in the Making of History*, New York: Columbia University Press.
Dagi, I. D. (1993) 'Turkey in the 1990s: foreign policy, human rights, and the search for a new identity', *Mediterranean Quarterly: A Journal of Global Issues* 4(4): 60–77.
Dannreuther, R. (1994) 'Creating new states in Central Asia', *Adelphi Paper* 288 (March): 3–83.
Debergh, J. P. (1996) 'De Turkse invloedssfeer na de implosie van de Sovjetunie', in P. de Meyer, E. Franckx, J.-M. Henckaerts and K. Malfliet (eds) *Oost-Europa in Europa. Eenheid en Verscheidenheid. Huldeboek aangeboden aan Frits Gorlé*, Brussels: VUBPRESS: 113–130.
Gills, B. K. and Frank, A. G. (1992) 'World system cycles, crises and hegemonical shifts, 1700 BC to 1700 AD', *Review*, 15(4): 621–687.
Gramsci, A. (1971) *Selections from the Prison Notebooks*, ed. by Q. Hoare, G.N. Smith, New York: International Publishers.
Hale, W. (1994) *Turkish Politics and the Military*, London and New York: Routledge.
Heper, M. (1997) 'Islam and democracy in Turkey: toward a reconciliation?', *The Middle East Journal* 51(1): 30–45.
Hine, R. C. (1996) 'Turkey and the European Community: regional integration and economic convergence', in S. Togon and V.N. Balasubramanyan (eds) *The Economy of Turkey since Liberalization*, Basingstoke and London: Macmillan: 131–154.
Hunter, S. T. (1996) *Central Asia since Independence*, Westport, CONN and London: Praeger.

Keyder, C. (1995) 'Democracy and the demise of national developmentalism. Turkey in perspective', in A. K. Bagchi (ed.) *Democracy and Development: Proceedings of the IEA Conference held in Barcelona*, Basingstoke and London: Macmillan.

Krueger, A. O. and Turan, I. (1993) 'The politics and economics of Turkish policy reforms in the 1980s', in R. H. Bates and A. O. Krueger (eds) *Political and Economic Interactions in Economic Policy Reform: Evidence from Eight Countries*, Cambridge, MA and Oxford: Basil Blackwell: 333–386.

Lipovsky, I. P. (1996) 'Central Asia: in search of a new political identity', *The Middle East Journal* 50(2): 211–224.

Mango, A. (1994) *Turkey: The Challenge of a New Role*, Westport, CONN and London: Praeger.

Müftüler-Bac, M. (1997) *Turkey's Relations with a Changing Europe*, Manchester: Manchester University Press.

Önis, Z. (1991) 'Political economy of Turkey in the 1980s: anatomy of unorthodox liberalism', in M. Heper (ed.) *Strong State and Economic Interest Groups: The Post-1980 Turkish Experiment*, Berlin and New York: Walter de Gruyter: 27–53.

Önis, Z. (1993) 'The dynamics of export-orientated growth in a second generation NIC: perspectives on the Turkish case, 1980–1990', *New Perspectives on Turkey* 9: 75–100.

Önis, Z. (1995) 'The political economy of export-oriented industrialization in Turkey', in Ç. Balim, E. Kalaycoghu, C. Karatas, G. Winrow and F. Yasamce (eds) *Turkey: Political, Social and Economic Challenges in the 1990s*, Leiden, New York and London: E. J. Brill: 107–129.

Önis, Z. (1996) 'The state and economic development in contemporary Turkey: etatism to neo-liberalism', in V. Mastny and R. Criag Nation (eds) *Turkey Between East and West: New Challenges for a Rising Regional Power*, Boulder, CO: Westview Press: 155–178.

Önis, Z. and Riedel, J. (1993) *Economic Crisis and Long-Term Growth in Turkey*, Washington, DC: The World Bank.

Önis, Z. and Webb, S. B. (1994) 'Turkey: democratization and adjustment from above', in S. Haggard and S. B. Webb (eds) *Voting for Reform: Democracy, Political Liberalization, and Economic Adjustment*, Oxford: Oxford University Press: 128–184.

Pettifer, J. (1997) *The Turkish Labyrinth: Atatürk and the New Islam*, London: Viking.

Pijl, K. van der (1989): 'Ruling classes, hegemony, and the state system', *International Journal of Political Economy* 19(3): 7–35.

Sayari, S. (1992) 'Turkey: the changing European security environment and the Gulf Crisis', *Middle East Journal* 46(1): 9–21.

Skocpol, T. (1979) *States and Social Revolutions: A Comparative Analysis of France, Russia, and China*, Cambridge: Cambridge University Press.

Smolansky, O. M. (1994) 'Turkish and Iranian policies in Central Asia', in H. Malik (ed.) *Central Asia: Its Strategic Importance and Future Prospects*, Basingstoke and London: Macmillan: 289–310.

Taskin, F. and Yeldan, A. E. (1996) 'Export expansion, capital accumulation and distribution in Turkish manufacturing, 1980–89', in S. Togan and V. N. Balasubramanyan (eds) *The Economy of Turkey since Liberalization*, Basingstoke and London: Macmillan: 155–176.

Turkey and the European Community: Summary Report (1984), Deutsche Orient-Institut im Verbund der Stiftung Deutsches Übersee-Institut.

Uygur, Ercan (1993) 'Trade policies and economic performance in Turkey in the 1980s', in M. R. Agosin (ed.) *Trade and Growth: New Dilemmas in Trade Policy*, Basingstoke and London: Macmillan: 215–238.

Winrow, G. (1995) 'Regional security and national identity: the role of Turkey in former Soviet Central Asia', in Ç. Balim, E. Kalaycoghu, C. Karatas, G. Winrow and F. Yasamce (eds) *Turkey: Political, Social and Economic Challenges in the 1990s*, Leiden, New York and London: E. J. Brill: 22–41.

9

MOROCCO'S ECONOMY BETWEEN THE MAGHREB AND EUROPE

André Mommen

Je me pose soudain la question: la corruption est-elle un délit de droit commun ou un délit politique?

(Tahar Ben Jelloun 1994: 133)

Morocco's trade policies have, since 1983, developed in a direction progressively based on the principles of the multilateral trading system and reforms embarked upon in the 1980s have pushed Morocco to a new stage of development. Morocco's government stands ready to throw open its markets to free trade from the rich north and to establish closer economic ties with its developing neighbours, especially oil-rich Algeria and some African countries south of the Sahara (Nigeria). Morocco's location south of Europe has brought a number of comparisons with the relationship between the USA and Mexico. Today, the European Union (EU) absorbs about 65 per cent of Morocco's exports and provides the country with about 54 per cent of its imports. This explains why the Moroccan government is negotiating the creation of a free trade area comprising the five Maghreb countries and the EU.

Morocco's recent 'economic successes' are usually attributed to the country's successful structural adjustment reforms implemented under the aegis of the International Monetary Fund (IMF) and the World Bank. In this chapter we shall see that optimism about fast and successful export-oriented industrialization has to be tempered. Morocco is just like any other heavily indebted economy looking for export opportunities and just like any other developing country it was forced to leave its import-substituting industrialization (ISI) policies in order to embark upon Structural Adjustment Programmes (SAPs) initiated by the World Bank. In 1993, for the first year, the country did not have recourse to the use of IMF resources, debt relief or other exceptional financing. Budgetary and monetary policies advised by the IMF prepared Morocco for fiscal, monetary and exchange rate reforms which in turn contributed to a deeper integration of the country in the world economy. Morocco was able in 1993 to establish the convertibility of the dirham for current account transactions. Opportunities offered by the Arab Maghreb Union (AMU) are rather scarce while the impact of the EU on the AMU's and

Morocco's chances of further economic development is overwhelming (Blin and Parisot 1990: 57–90).

AN EMERGING ECONOMY AND DEMOCRACY?

Although recent publications have depicted Morocco as an 'emerging' (Abdaimi 1994) economy or as an African 'dragon' (Leymarie and Tripier 1993), from 1990 to 1994 Morocco's Gross Domestic Product (GDP) grew by 4.4. per cent a year and its exports by merely 2.5 per cent. These figures prove that Morocco was at that time by no means comparable to an Asian 'dragon'. In 1994 Morocco's GDP increased by 11.6 per cent but GDP decreased in 1995 by 7.6 per cent (see Table 9.1). These results were obtained in a two-year period of extraordinary drought causing a fall in agricultural output of 46 per cent (Bank Al-Maghrib 1995: 19; L'Opinion, 28 February 1996). Moreover, Morocco still is at the mercy of inflationary pressures. In December 1995 sharp price increases occurred of up to 1.3 per cent for industrial products and up to 11.1 per cent for agricultural products (Bank Al-Maghrib 1995: appendices). New waves of price increases in January and February 1996 were said to be caused by the effects of price adjustments and the financial law of January 1996 (L'Opinion, 18 February 1996).

Instead of having the characteristics of an 'emerging' economy, Morocco has many characteristics of a less-successful developing country: 16 per cent of its urban workforce is jobless and unemployment in the agrarian areas is much higher, largely hidden and structural (Libération, 1–2 January 1996). Observers think that Morocco's resources will give the country the potential to become an industrial and agricultural 'tiger' (The Agro-Based 1990), because they see the country taking advantage of irrigated agriculture (which is rapidly developing) (Seddon 1989b: 175–189; Swearingen 1987: 143–192).

In the case of Morocco it is clearly true that the development of state enterprises entrenched a set of patron–client relations that underpinned the authoritarian monarchy headed by Hassan II. This cemented a web of social, political and economic relationships that led to extensive corruption and enormous inefficiency as decisions were made on political rather than economic criteria. The state system itself remained rather weak and personalized around Hassan II as monarch and

Table 9.1 Morocco: basic economic data (in $US million)

	1988	1989	1990	1991	1992	1993	1994	1995
Real growth (per cent)	10.4	2.5	3.7	6.9	−4.0	−1.0	11.6	−7.6
Exports ($mn)	3,608	3,312	4,210	4,277	3,956	3,850	4,013	4,734
Imports ($mn)	4,360	4,991	6,282	6,253	6,692	6,820	7,188	8,573
Current account	467	−790	−200	−396	−427	−690	−750	n.a.
Intern. Res.	547	488	2,066	3,100	3,504	3,410	4,622	4,012
External debt ($bn)	21.1	22.1	22.5	22.9	23.2	22.5	22.5	22.3
Debt service ratio (per cent)	26.1	33.1	21.9	27.6	26.6	33	33.3	30.0

Source: MacDonald et al. (1995: 81); World Bank (1996: 216–222); Bank Al-Maghrib (1995: annexes).

Commander of the Faithful (Waterbury 1970: 144–158). The king succeeded in combining forms of political democracy with a form of Prussian authoritarianism. He managed to suppress any form of opposition to the fundamentals of his regime in a period when Morocco had clearly moved in the 1970s from economic stagnation to crisis. Pressure exercised by international institutions and the EU finally forced Hassan II to democratize his regime and to rally the opposition parties to his economic policy. Hassan II agreed that the new Constitution should be submitted to a referendum. But the Chamber of Representatives adopted the new electoral law in spite of a boycott by the opposition Bloc Démocratique (*Al Koutal*).

As governments liberalize the economy, they usually reform themselves (Balta 1992: 130–136) but in Morocco political pluralism and civil liberties are progressing very slowly. Hassan II revised the Constitution and gave more power to the parliament. In the meantime he also emphasized his royal prerogatives. Ministers had to be chosen by a Prime Minister appointed by the king. However, Hassan has reaffirmed his commitment to human rights. On 4 September 1992 the new Constitution (the fourth since independence) was endorsed by a referendum with 99.96 per cent of the vote in which 97.25 per cent of the 11 million registered voters had participated. The results of the parliamentary elections held on 25 June 1993 were unfavourable for Hassan II. The opposition Bloc Démocratique increased its representation from 59 to 91 seats, but failed to conquer a majority (Ghazi 1995: 124–126). In January 1995 Hassan II tried to form a coalition government including the Bloc Démocratique but the opposition withdrew when Hassan II refused to sack his almighty Minister of Home Affairs, Driss Basri. Again, Hassan II formed a government of the Right. In a speech broadcast on 20 August 1996 Hassan II announced that he wanted to reform Morocco's parliamentary system (*L'Opinion*, 22 August 1996). Again, a referendum held on 13 September 1996 gave an impressive majority (99.5 per cent) in favour of Hassan's proposal for a new constitution establishing a bicameral system and a responsible government.

Since the 1960s Hassan II has postponed any thoroughgoing reform of the agricultural sector. Between 1966 and 1980 the state sold about 305,000 hectares of land to the peasantry, but the owners of large estates remained in possession of the best land. In 1995 new legislation on landed property was passed in order to combat a further cutting up of property. According to the most recent agrarian survey (1973–74), about 88.5 per cent of all farms were smaller than 10 hectares (see Table 9.2). In order to slow rural migration to the cities the government is planning a partition of a part of the 445,000 hectares of cultivable land belonging to the crown.

Although Hassan II is reluctant to democratize, he is concerned about the potential for social unrest. Hassan II has only managed to survive popular protests by controlling political life by a judicious mixture of 'stick and carrot' – the former against the clandestine political groupings and the latter for the official political parties. Centre-right loyalist parties always predominated and held the majority of seats in most elected assemblies and councils, with the exception of some of the larger cities, such as Casablanca. Hassan's general strategy in the political sphere was

Table 9.2 Structure of the Moroccan farming sector

Size (ha)	Percentage of total number of farms	Percentage of total cultivable land
> 5	73.5	24.4
5 > 10	15.0	20.9
10 > 20	7.8	21.1
20 > 50	3.0	16.7
50 > 100	0.5	7.2
< 100	0.2	9.7

Source: *L'Economiste. Hebdomadaire économique marocain*, 4 January 1996: 27.
Note: Figures are based on a survey made in 1973–74 by the Ministère de l'Agriculture et de la Mise en Valeur Agricole (MAMVA).

to consolidate the support of the opposition parties in order to permit these parties to express different opinions on economic and social matters without disapproving of the fundamentals of his regime. Regularly, the king announces a series of amnesties and pardons, designed to undermine any criticism of the government's harsh treatment of political opposition (Branciard 1994: 56–59; Zartman 1987: 1–33).

Morocco's civil society is much better organized than those of its African neighbours. Strong trade unions and political parties organize the urban classes and ensure that the Islamic religion is less attractive to the urban poor than elsewhere in North Africa. But all post-colonial regimes are likely to be resistant to a radical strategy entailing a fundamental break with external economic and financial controls over the region in a quest for economic efficiency. With the collapse of the Soviet empire socialist populism has lost its attraction. So the main focus of interest has shifted towards the twin themes of liberalization and democratization.

REMOVING THE CONSEQUENCES OF MOROCCO'S ISI POLICY

Economic patterns established by the French during the period of the protectorate still exert a strong influence on the economic structure of contemporary Morocco. Under the French an intricate mosaic of private, public and semi-public corporations had been developed. Much as in France monopolies were established. The phosphate deposit monopoly dates back to 1923 (Stewart 1964: 162–205; Tiano 1963: 165–283). After independence the development strategy was based on heavy investment in irrigation and agriculture, the development of 'forward linkages' in the phosphate sector, and the build up of a natural infrastructure (Zartman 1964: 119–152). Since then the Moroccan economy has combined a vibrant modern industrial sector and a dualistic agricultural sector (Miège 1950: 66–118; Bonnefous 1991: 62–63), i.e. which is, at the same time, a modern and yet a subsistence farming economy. Morocco's exports reflect its diversified economy. Phosphates, textiles, electronic goods, handicrafts, citrus fruits, vegetables, canned and frozen fish, tourism and remittances from many Moroccans working in Europe are the main sources of currency earnings. Although the economy is well diversified, the country's export earnings still come in large part from the export of rock phosphates. Morocco, with a 63 per cent share of the world's known reserves is, after the USA and the USSR with an 11 per cent share of the world market, the third biggest rock phosphate-exporting country in the world. An increasing share of its production of phosphoric acid is processed domestically. But many developing countries have built new production capacity and while Morocco is losing its Third World markets, the developed world has invested in labour-saving techniques which have depressed prices for phosphate on the world market (Leymarie and Tripier 1993: 185–198). Since the 1970s Morocco's phosphate industry has lost its comparative advantages, notwithstanding heavy investment in downstream activities. The manufacturing sector produces a wide range of goods, including leatherwear and mechanical and electrical products. The agricultural sector, which employs 44 per cent of the labour force, is predominantly oriented toward food production and livestock. Irrigated agriculture accounts for about 10 per cent of total arable land but contributes over half of the sector's value added (citrus, vegetables, and sugar) as well as two-thirds of its exports. But inadequate rainfall continues to be a significant problem and requires heavy investment in additional irrigation capacity. Once an exporter of wheat, Morocco has been a substantial importer since 1975. The heavy costs of food imports have contributed to continued merchandise trade deficits. The growing fishery sector may become an important source of export earnings, but its natural outlet has been cut off by protectionist measures taken by the EC when in the 1980s Spain and Portugal joined the Community.

Another important feature of Morocco's economic development is the dominant role played by the public sector (Kadmiri 1988: 16–26). Morocco's economic development was based on the role of the state for the mobilization of resources. In 1985 the state sector represented 90 per cent of the mining and power sector, 70 per cent of all financial institutions, 50 per cent of transport and communication, 25 per cent of manufacturing and 3 to 4 per cent of agriculture and trade, or 17 per cent of GDP and 80 per cent of realized total value added. The Moroccan economy was dominated by 32 large state firms (Bédhri 1991: 25). This explains the failure of the private sector as the engine of economic development. Public sector expansion was necessary to maintain growth above the pace of population growth (on average 2.5 per cent over 1965). Public consumption and investment increased during the 1960s and 1970s, while private consumption declined to as low as 67 per cent in 1981. The excess demand of public consumption and investment spilled over into the trade sector and made imports grow from 22 per cent of GDP in 1970 to over 30 per cent in the 1975–1984 decade, while exports remained a fixed proportion of GDP. Food production did not keep pace with demand, which necessitated substantial increases in food imports (Laraki 1989: 6–7). Because of low wages paid in industry and services, food subsidies were necessary too, while the abundant labour supply kept wages low and gave Morocco's exports a comparative advantage in international markets, but caused slow growth of the internal market for consumer products.

The mining sector still remains Morocco's major source of public revenues and accounts for almost 20 per cent of the country's export earnings. Phosphate remains an important although declining source of revenue. Morocco has minimal energy resources and depends on the import of crude oil. Its production of local energy is based on hydro-electrical power plants. Its coal production covers only 20 per cent of total consumption. Crude oil imports make the country dependent *vis-à-vis* OPEC. Price increases of crude oil may cause balance-of-payment difficulties. The effects of the first 'oil shock' in 1973 on the balance of payments were largely compensated by important price increases of phosphate the country was exporting at ever larger quantities. The second 'oil shock' of 1979 occurred in a period when prices of rock phosphate had declined to the pre-1973 level. In 1981 the economic growth rate turned negative in the wake of a drought-induced recession.

During the 1960s Morocco's development strategy was based on state investment in agriculture (Guerraoui 1986: 177–216) and a restrictive monetary policy. The government had chosen liberalism instead of socialism, although liberalism was not extended to foreign trade. Tariff protection was increased and a programme of ISI was set up. The parastatal sector (Ali 1987: 117–131) grew by taking over foreign property and enterprises. The alliance between the monarchy and the rural *notables* (Waterbury 1970: 61–143; Ali 1989: 56–60) was based on a model of agricultural development (Tuluy and Salinger 1989) and ISI (Leveau 1985: 61–100). This strategy dated back to colonialism when the French had invested in capitalist large-scale agriculture and food-processing industries. The Moroccan bourgeois class also profited from protectionism and high tariffs. The result of this policy was slow growth and economic stagnation during the years of drought. Inflation was kept down and exports increased at the same rate as imports. Poverty drove many families to the expanding cities at the coast in a period when social mobility was favoured by the massive departure of Europeans and Jews (Swearingen 1987: 143–192). In the early 1970s growing latent discontent and two aborted *coups d'état* led to a decisive change in strategy. The Economic Plan of 1973–77 emphasized state investment in industry and expenditure on education, health and the social sector. Monetary and budgetary laxity accompanied this change in development strategy and an ideological campaign against foreign capital owners was achieved with the Moroccanization of enterprises and the distribution of land from coloniza-tion. Land distribution slowed the rural influx to the cities and the Moroccanization of foreign enterprises was to the benefit of the Moroccan bourgeoisie (entrepren-eurs and higher civil servants) and Hassan II (Diouri 1992: 44–49). Moroccanization of the economy aimed at restraining foreign investment in combination with a policy of ISI. The basic assumption of the Economic Plans was that export-oriented growth was expected to result primarily from domestic processing of the country's principal resource, rock phosphate, as well as from traditional agricultural exports, which in turn necessitated increased imports of capital goods and technology. It was thus evident that Morocco had chosen a new development strategy beginning in 1973. A tripling of the real phosphate price from 1973 to 1974 and a fivefold increase of the export value had a considerable impact on fiscal policy, the domestic price structure and productive structure. The state embarked on an ambitious investment programme (irrigation and infrastructure) doubling the investment rate. Public investment increased by a factor of 8.6 between 1973–77. This strategy was endorsed by major donors, such as the World Bank and the United States Agency for International Development (USAID) (Seddon 1989b: 179). The state expanded its parastatal sector (Kadmiri 1988: 103–125). The phosphate boom contributed to an overvalued exchange rate and an inflationary push but in 1975 phosphate prices plunged and by 1976 the world price had dropped to the 1973 value in real terms, which contributed to a large external account and budget deficits. For technical reasons the government was unable to cancel its ambitious investment projects. For the first time these deficits were financed by recourse to heavy foreign borrowing (floating-rate loans) without adopting strong stabilization measures. Then the government instituted restrictive credit policies, raised import duties, tightened quantitative import restrictions, and cut public expenditure, particularly on capital goods. For political reasons it would have been very difficult to make sharp reductions in civil service salaries and in food subsidies. This provoked a large budget deficit in 1976 and the following years. Meanwhile growth rates remained high (9 per cent a year), but it was growth on credit. Finally, the sharp rise in the budget and current account deficits obliged the goverment to undertake a Stabilization Programme in 1978. It included measures aimed at reducing the basic disequilibrium by limiting imports, and maximizing the inflow of hard currencies from tourists and from Moroccans abroad. The Stabilization Programme had to be abandoned in 1979 because of bad crops due to drought, the second 'oil shock', price rises for primary products and social disturbances. The salaries of civil servants and workers were increased, while food subsidies increased by a factor of 3.7 from 1978 to 1980 because of rising import prices. The state continued to finance its expansionary investment programme by loans. Growth picked up to 4.2 per cent a year in 1979–80, but at the cost of a growing disequilibrium. By 1979, external debt had grown from $US953 million or 24 per cent of Gross National Product (GNP) in 1970 to $US9.9 billion or 64 per cent of GNP, while total debt service reached 23 per cent of exports. The current account deficit reached 12.5 per cent of GDP in 1981–82 and the fiscal deficit attained 14 per cent of GDP. Notwithstanding this disastrous evolution of the macro-economic indicators, the goals of the ambitious 1981–85 Economic Plan that called for a further expansion in public investment were not cancelled (Seddon 1989a: 234–265; Mateus *et al.* 1988: 4–5; Malki 1989: 163–177).

In 1978, USAID drew attention to the rise in food imports (cereal imports rose from 17,792 quintals in 1980 to 27,229 quintals in 1984), the stagnation of the non-irrigated sector of agriculture and the growing rural exodus (Seddon 1989b: 179). About 75 per cent of the total land consisted of farms of 5 hectares or less and these farmers did not respond to the incentives provided by the government to produce more for the market. For the smallholders drought remained the principal problem. A World Bank report of 1978 stressed the necessity of a total restructuring of the public sector combined with privatization. The World Bank promised to finance this operation with a loan worth $US240 million and six state firms in different sectors (water, railroads, oil refineries and distribution) were chosen to be restructured. In 1980 the Jouahri Report was submitted to the government (Rousset 1987: 269–282). Inspired by the famous French Rapport Nora of 1967, Abdellatif Jouahri pleaded for structural reforms, larger autonomy for state enterprises and eventually privatization (Brachet 1992: 73; Bédhri 1991: 47–52).

THE MOROCCAN ECONOMY UNDER IMF AND WORLD BANK INFLUENCE (1983–93)

Morocco's economy was prepared for more openness during the period 1983–93 when the Bretton Woods institutions became involved in carrying out SAPs and fiscal reforms. SAPs constituted a radical change in comparison with the previous development strategies. Containment of public expenditure and a reduction of state budget deficits were combined with a rescheduling of interest payments and a restructuring of Morocco's huge foreign debt (Roe et al. 1989: 1–33). The World Bank became involved with structural adjustment loans (SALs). All these measures were aimed at reducing the anti-export bias, a reduction of effective protection and a reduction of the bias against savings and employment (Horton 1990: 109). Import liberalization and tariff reduction programmes were combined with increases in indirect taxes and transfers from the phosphate company Office Chérifien des Phosphates (OCP) to compensate for state revenue losses. Higher interest rates, price deregulation and reforms of the financial sector were implemented. Stabilization adjustment had considerable domestic costs. Cuts in private and public capital formation prevented the realization of the government's ambitious growth and development objectives (Khader 1995: 38–48). Consumer purchasing power decreased sharply, which on several occasions prompted social unrest and food riots in the big cities. During the entire adjustment period, Moroccan society was threatened by conflicts of interest, since the government imposed the adjustment costs on some social groups and classes (Seddon 1989b: 175–189; Khrouz 1993: 80–98). National unity had to be strengthened because of the threat implied by these conflicts. The war in the Western Sahara played this unifying role, even if it proved very costly.

DEBT MANAGEMENT

The 1978–79 Stabilization Programme hoped that export growth would come mainly from phosphates and their derivates, although the prices of phosphates had recently plummeted. The government thought that the current account deficit could be more effectively reduced by restricting imports, a policy that would enhance protection of the new industries created in the wake of the 1973 investment boom. On the budgetary front, the deficit was reduced by revenue enhancement and expenditure compression. Consumption subsidies in order to stabilize retail prices of certain basic commodities were not cut because they were considered politically essential. This programme was supported by the IMF although the Fund thought that the budget deficit was attributable not only to excessive capital expenditures but also to the substantial growth of consumer subsidies and defence outlays. The IMF stressed the need to raise domestic savings and appropriate tax, expenditure and interest rate policies. But the improvements obtained by the Stabilization Programme were transitory. In October 1979, the price of crude oil doubled, which put further pressure on the external account and budget deficits. By 1980 the budget deficit was expected to increase to 13 per cent of GDP (Horton 1990: 31–34; Mateus *et al.* 1988: 6–7). The government requested IMF support for a three-year Extended Fund Facility (EFF) loan worth Special Drawing Rights (SDR) 810 million in order to embark upon growth-oriented structural adjustments (see Table 9.3) (Horton 1990: 34–36). Because of a variety of reasons demand could not be adequately controlled. The government's reaction was to minimize price increases which then led to higher budgetary subsidies. Moreover, the rise of the US dollar aggravated the situation.

In the early 1980s Morocco was regarded as a troubled debtor (see Table 9.3). Some 45 per cent of the population then lived below the poverty threshold of $US238 per capita and the deepening crisis had already provoked the violent demonstrations in 1981 over increases of food prices caused by a total removal of subsidies on most dairy products and price increases for the most important staples (soft wheat, vegetable oil, and sugar powder). In two days of clashes in Casablanca over 600 people were killed by troops (Gallissot 1989: 29–39). Faced with such opposition to the austerity measures tentatively introduced, the Moroccan government hesitated to push ahead, thereby incurring the disapproval of the IMF and the World Bank. By the end of 1982 external debt had risen to almost 78 per cent of GDP and debt service amounted to 40 per cent of exports (see Table 9.4). In March 1983 a foreign exchange crisis – the external debt reached $US6.9 billion – obliged the government to solicit emergency financial assistance from the foreign banks in the form of new loans and the rescheduling of existing debts owed to commercial banks and official debitors. In August 1983 a SAP was initiated, involving a 10 per cent devaluation, fiscal and credit restraints, cuts in public expenditure and reductions in the level of food subsidies (Azam and Morrisson 1994: 97–99). Price increases of between 20 and 35 per cent produced immediate popular revolt.

The IMF entered into a stand-by arrangement for SDR300 million and generated pledges of about $US500 million for balance-of-payments assistance. In 1983, the real GDP growth slipped to 2.1 per cent and unemployment reached around 30 per cent. The general elections were postponed until September 1984 and a caretaker government of national unity was formed by Hassan II. Pressed by the World Bank and the IMF, the government introduced SAPs in 1984 and was able to reschedule its debts towards the end of 1985. The principal elements of SAPs involved a shift to outward-looking trade and exchange rate policies, far-reaching reforms of price, credit, tax and regulatory policies to remove institutional and other obstacles to efficient mobilization and use of resources in key productive sectors of the economy. The Moroccan government had little alternative but to acquiesce (Horton 1990: 41–43).

Table 9.3 Stand-by and Extended Arrangements approved during 1980–92, and related purchases under the Compensatory Financing Facility

Effective date	Type	Expiry date	Duration in months	Acess	Total annual	Amount	Amount drawn	Date of drawing CFF	End of shortfall year	Purchases (mm SDRs)	Purchases as percentage of quota
10.08.80	EFF[a]	10.07.83	36	540.0	180.0	810.00	147.00	04.29.82[e]	March 1982	236.40	105.00
03.09.81	EFF[b]	10.07.83	31	363.0	140.5	817.00	136.50	09.17.85[e]	June 1985	115.10	37.54
04.26.82	SBA	04.25.83	12	125.0	125.0	281.25	281.25				
09.16.83	SBA	03.15.85	18	133.3	88.9	300.00	300.00				
09.12.85	SBA[c]	02.28.87	18	65.2	43.5	200.00	10.00				
12.16.86	SBA[d]	03.31.88	16	75.0	56.3	230.00	230.00				
08.30.88	SBA	12.31.89	16	68.5	51.0	210.00	210.00				
07.20.90	SBA	03.31.91	9	32.6	43.5	100.00	48.00				
11.13.92	SBA	03.31.93	15	30.0	24.0	91.98	18.40				

Source: Nsouli et al. (1995: 9).

Notes: [a] Arrangement was cancelled in March 1981 and replaced by another extended arrangement.
[b] Arrangement was cancelled in April 1982.
[c] Arrangement was cancelled in December 1986.
[d] Arrangement was extended to 30 April 1988.
[e] Combined export and cereal purchase.

Table 9.4 Morocco's total external debt, 1975–93

	1975	1980	1985	1989	1990	1991	1992	1993
Total debt in $US billion	1.7	9.7	16.4	20.8	23.3	21.6	21.6	21.4
Debt/export ratio as percentage	67.4	223.8	366.7	315.0	280.3	259.7	242.4	251.3
Debt/GNP as percentage	19.4	56.2	125.1	94.4	94.3	81.0	78.9	81.7
Debt service in $US billion	0.15	1.4	1.1	2.1	1.8	2.1	2.1	2.6
Debt service/export as percentage	6.3	32.4	26.8	32.8	21.0	25.2	23.7	30.7

Source: World Debt Tables 1990–91, 1994–1995.

In 1985 Morocco negotiated a new arrangement with the IMF, but the government failed to achieve the IMF targets in 1986. Meanwhile the 'Paris Club' of the government creditors and the 'London Club' of the creditor banks agreed to reschedule debt repayments. Despite good harvests in 1985 and 1986, and the fall of oil prices, the trade balance deteriorated and at the beginning of 1986 the World Bank expressed its concern about the underlying structural weakness of the Moroccan economy (Brachet 1992: 105–107). Thereafter Morocco gradually abandoned its economic policy of ISI and started with reductions in public expenditure and food subsidies. The IMF cancelled its stand-by arrangements when the government hesitated to change its economic and fiscal policy. In 1986 and 1987 Morocco was obliged to make a firm commitment to a radical reform of the economy and to adopt trade liberalization, privatization of the state sector and encouragement of private investment. In September 1987 the World Bank declared that Morocco was 'well poised' for economic success, as a result of its stabilization efforts and SAPs. The World Bank subsequently increased its lending, to make Morocco the Bank's third largest recipient after Turkey and Pakistan (Azam and Morrisson 1994: 107–115; Horton 1990: 44–47; Payne 1993: 148–155; Kingdom of Morocco 1990).

In August 1988 the IMF approved a stand-by credit of SDR210 million in spite of the slow pace in the reduction of food subsidies (see Table 9.3). With greater success, the government restricted demand, especially of public expenditure and combined these schemes, under IMF auspices, with supply-side adjustment programmes financed by the World Bank in order to obtain greater efficiency of resource allocation in the tradables sector with special reference to export promotion. Meanwhile the 'Paris Club' of creditor countries agreed to reschedule payments on external debt worth $US940 million in October 1988 and September 1990. In December 1988 the World Bank approved a new SAL in order to assist the country with debt management. Negotiations over the rescheduling of Morocco's commercial debt with the so-called 'London Club' occurred regularly. IMF stand-by arrangements which expired were regularly replaced by new arrangements. In 1989 negotiations for the rescheduling of $US1,900 million owing to the commercial banks of the 'London Club' were started and would continue until April 1990 when an agreement was reached on a rescheduling of about $US3,200 million of medium-term debt over a period of twenty years (Nsouli *et al.* 1995: 50–52).

Finally, the external current account and overall budget deficits improved substantially as a result of the combined effects of declining world oil prices, better harvests, debt rescheduling, etc. and by 1989, the external current account showed a surplus, while the budget deficit declined to about 6 per cent with an inflation rate of merely 2.5 per cent. All of this had been achieved with an inflation rate that never exceeded 15 per cent per year. Meanwhile the IMF continued its pressure to reduce the budget deficit especially when in 1989 the recovery abruptly halted and the current account and fiscal deficits suddenly increased. In 1990 the government reacted by reducing investment expenditure and devaluing of the dirham by 9.25 per cent in the hope exports would pick up and money transfers of Moroccans working abroad would increase (Santucci and Benhlal 1990: 720). The 'Paris Club' agreed that the official development aid would be repaid over twenty years, and other credits over fifteen years. A stand-by credit from the IMF worth $US134 million had to float the government's economic and financial programme.

Stand-by credits from the IMF eased the implementation of economic reforms aimed at promoting investment and increasing productivity, at strengthening the budgetary position and reorienting credit towards the private sector, at an annual GDP growth of 4 per cent, at a decline of inflation to 5 per cent a year and at a reduction in current account deficit. The overall budget deficit was reduced from 3.1 per cent of GDP in 1991 to 2.2 per cent in 1992. This monetary policy had to encourage the provision of private-sector credit. Trade barriers were removed by restructuring the tariff system. High priority was now given to the development of the capital and financial markets.

By 1992 Morocco had received more than $US6,000 million in loans. The World Bank planned a loan worth $US1,600 million for the implementation of new projects. Bilateral debt owed to Saudi Arabia and other Gulf states, estimated at around $US3,600 million was cancelled in the aftermath of the Gulf War in which Morocco participated on the side of the USA and Kuwait against Iraq. Soft World Bank loans and Saudi Arabian financial assistance helped Morocco to balance its current accounts and to reduce its budget deficits. Gulf Arab largesse came from the Arab Fund for Economic and Social Development and the Kuwait Fund for Arab Economic Development. These Funds helped in financing irrigation works and road projects. The World Bank granted in 1991 a loan of $US300 million for the restructuring of the mining and sugar industry. Budget deficits steadily reduced from around 12 per cent of GDP to under 2 per cent in the same period and nowadays Morocco's foreign debt of $US22 billion (or 80 per cent of GDP) is fairly under control. But over the same period real value of its outstanding debt has risen from 42 to 65 per cent of its face value. In January 1993 the government informed the IMF that the dirham was convertible, except for capital transactions. Morocco's acceptance of IMF Article VIII in May 1993 was an important step to full convertibility of the dirham. Although exchange control was not entirely abolished, the government gave up the right to impose any control on current payments for trade and capital transactions or set up discriminatory currency arrangements. In June 1993 Moroccan banks or private enterprises were allowed to raise credits with foreign financial institutions to finance imports without prior authorization. By 1992 Morocco's foreign debt seemed to be under control. Foreign debt was $US21,305 million, of which the 'Paris Club' states accounted for $US10,549 million, the 'London Club' $US3,525 million, the international financial institutions $US5,700 million and the different Arab funds and countries $US1,531 million. With $US8,008 million credit France was the biggest lender (Abdaimi 1994: 122–130). The cost of servicing this debt remained a heavy burden with repayments in 1994 equivalent to 4.2 per cent of GNP. Although in 1993 SAPs under supervision of the IMF were ended and foreign debt was under control, the growing spending deficit still remained too high (5 per cent of GDP over 1995) (Tuquoi 1995: 2; Nsouli et al. 1995: 50–52).

LIBERALIZATION POLICIES

Hermetic tariff and non-tariff protection to foster industrialization had been the government's policy since 1973 but many arguments were advanced in favour of import liberalization. First, industry should provide goods to national consumers at world prices or lower and the government should not reserve the domestic market for domestic producers. Second, the creation of rents for import licence holders was undesirable and also one of the factors generating demands for rents in other sectors. Third, free trade had to provide a natural disincentive to the build-up of excessive capacity compared with demand. Fourth, free trade could be a weapon against the highly monopolized internal market (Eussner 1992: 187–8; Chevassu 1987: 195–217). In order to compete, Morocco needed to liberalize imports; to reduce import duties and their surrogates (special import taxes, the stamp tax, and special import duties); to pursue a flexible exchange rate policy, devaluing if necessary to make up for past appreciation of the real exchange rate; to remove other policy-induced anti-export biases, including administrative impediments to exports; and to sharply ameliorate the domestic regulatory framework. In 1983 the IMF obliged Morocco to revise its investment and export code. Profit abatements and exemptions were reduced, except for export-related profits. Incentives were increased for the use of labour-intensive technologies. Exporters received a 100 per cent tax holiday for five years after investment and duty-free imports of inputs for export production. The year 1983 therefore marks a watershed in the evolution of Morocco's trade policy because it was the end of protection of the infant industries (*The Kingdom of Morocco 1989* 1990: 11–43).

Rather than attempt to revive the SAL, which had already been suspended in 1981, the World Bank decided to approach Morocco's needs for far-reaching structural reforms through a series of several adjustment operations in industry, finance, education, agriculture and public enterprises (Khrouz 1993: 90–93). Sectoral approaches were politically more acceptable to the government than the SAL's across-the-board approach. In January 1984 the World Bank assisted Morocco with an Industrial and Trade Policy Adjustment Loan (ITPA1) worth $US150,4 million (Horton 1990: 64–69). ITPA1 would contribute to a real boom in manufactured exports over the period 1983–86. The central idea of ITPA1 was undoubtedly the reform of trade policy and production incentives for exports and the home market. The top priority was to reduce the anti-export bias in the structure of incentives and to increase the domestic supply of foreign exchange from economically efficient exports and import substitutes. In July 1985 ITPA2 which was in line with ITPA1 disbursed $US200 million (Horton 1990: 67–101). Two Agricultural Structural Adjustment Loans (ASAL1 and ASAL2), an Education Loan and a Public Enterprise Restructuring Loan (PERL) worth $US790 million followed between October 1985 and June 1988.

Liberalization policies imposed by the IMF and International Bank for Reconstruction and Development (IBRD) concentrated on removing import restrictions. The maximum import tariff was brought down in several steps from 400 per cent in 1984 to 45 per cent in 1986. In 1987 Morocco joined the General Agreement on Tariffs and Trade (GATT). The list of goods that were prohibited to import was abolished and the list of products requiring a licence before importation was considerably reduced. Already in 1983 the reformed investment code permitted foreign majority ownership in some industrial sectors. Much of the so-called Moroccanization decree of 1973 was abolished by the end of 1989. Initially, the Moroccanization decree aimed at bringing industrial enterprises and real estate under the majority control of Moroccan citizens but it was also a source of corruption (*The Kingdom of Morocco 1989* 1990: 11–20).

In total value of external trade, transactions in relation to GDP rose from 29.4 per cent in 1964 to 38.3 per cent in 1988 despite the successive upheavals in the world economy. Foreign trade liberalization led to an improvement in the performance of the foreign trade sector and the strengthening of its role in the economy without any reduction of imports. Traditional exports (citrus fruits and phosphate) only accounted for 11.5 per cent of total exports in 1993 against 19.4 per cent in 1988 and 36.4 per cent in 1982. This relative reduction was mainly due to the fall in exports of phosphates, but it was more than compensated for by the increase in sales of fertilizers and phosphoric acid during the same period (see Table 9.5).

In 1991 a new foreign trade law was discussed in order to reduce protection of existing industries and establish a higher degree of transparency. Total liberalization of domestic prices was not foreseen before 1996. At the end of 1995 sugar prices were liberalized and grain prices were to follow in May 1996. But the Office National Interprofessionel des Céréales et des Légumineuses (ONICL) would regulate the grain market by intervening in price formation and grain storage. Domestic agricultural prices moved closer to world market prices and offered less protection. Although these steps represented an opening of the Moroccan economy to competition, tariffs are still protecting final products and prevent a more complete liberalization (Bernoussi 1993: 237–261).

Today, all regulations apply equally to all industrial investments regardless of the nationality of the investor. Foreign exchange becomes much easier for investors,

Table 9.5 External trade balance (in million dirhams)

		1992	%	1993	%	1994	%	1995	%
Imports c.i.f.	Crude oil	8,007	12.75	6,693	10.81	6,902	10.46	6,721	9.22
	Chemicals, fertilizers	3,515	6.60	3,771	6.09	2,937	6.52	4,534	6.22
	Iron and steel	869	1.38	996	1.61	1,116	1.69	1,784	2.45
	Industrial equipment	16,365	2.091	6.682	26.95	1,207	24.49	15,742	21.60
	Wood	1,666	2.65	1,400	2.26	1,734	2.63	1,964	2.70
	Wheat	2,736	4.36	3,267	5.28	1,491	2.26	3,997	5.49
	Sulphur	1,829	2.91	1,071	1.73	1,126	1.71	1,585	2.18
	Fabrics	1,194	1.90	1,117	1.80	1,428	2.16	1,587	2.18
	Plastics	1,459	2.32	1,484	2.40	1,943	2.95	2,297	3.15
	Agricultural equipment	415	0.7	365	0.59	832	1.26	515	0.71
	Total (incl. others)	62,805	100	61,908	100	65,963	100	72,869	100
Exports f.o.b	Oil products	n.a.	–	n.a.	–	770	2.20	886	2.20
	Phosphates	2,621	7.72	2,416	7.30	2,515	6.79	2,426	6.03
	Phosphoric acid	3,425	10.01	3,256	9.47	3,987	10.77	4,699	11.68
	Fertilizers	2,446	7.20	2,895	8.42	2,496	6.72	3,076	7.64
	Clothing	4,137	12.18	4,012	11.67	3,804	10.28	3,640	9.05
	Crustaceans and molluscs	2,501	7.36	2,924	8.51	3,521	9.51	4,310	10.71
	Citrus fruits	1,461	4.30	1,443	4.20	1,384	3.74	1,716	4.71
	Hosiery	2,406	7.09	2,731	7.95	2,708	7.32	2,856	4.26
	Canned vegetables and fruit	885	2.61	790	1.92	845	2.28	1,308	7.10
	Canned fish	1,360	4.00	1,354	3.94	1,440	3.89	1,542	3.83
	Fresh fish	871	2.56	738	2.15	742	2.00	762	1.89
	Total (incl. others)	33,959	100	34,366	100	37,012	100	40,240	100

Source: Lawless (1996: 781–2).

because the investment code guarantees free transfers of profits, dividends and capital without limits. Although the dirham is not yet entirely convertible and restrictions are maintained for Moroccan nationals when travelling abroad, the foreign exchange black market has disappeared. The value of the dirham is determined on a trade weighed basis, reflecting a basket of currencies of the most important trading partners (Abdaimi 1994: 276–307). Meanwhile, Morocco is thinking of a Euro-Maghreb Monetary Union when Maghreb currencies would be made convertible.

PRIVATIZATION OF STATE FIRMS

In October 1986 Hassan II announced in parliament that a commission would study the privatization problem. The French investment bank Lazard Frères was discreetly invited over for an audit of the state enterprises. On 8 April 1988 Hassan II declared in parliament that the state should retain sole control of six strategic industries [Office National de l'Eau Potable (ONEP), Office National de l'Electricité (ONE), Office National des Chemins de Fer (ONEF), OCP, Royal Air Maroc (RAM), Office National des Postes et Télécommunications (ONPT)] contributing to the state budget, but should sell off the remainder, including sugar refineries, bus companies and subsidiaries of the six strategic state firms. Moreover, the debt owed by state enterprises was equivalent to about one-third of the total public debt. According to the government privatizations should bolster 'popular capitalism' and broaden the regime's support by creating a larger middle class (Rousset 1987: 267–282). In May 1989 the government proposed to transfer the majority of state enterprises to the private sector, and in October 1989 a Ministry of Privatization was created (Belghazi 1993: 235–236). The law on privatization came into effect in January 1990. Privatizations met fierce resistance from the Left which rejected the withdrawal of the state from the key sectors of the economy. The Moroccan bourgeoisie was frustrated because privatization would advantage foreign investors eager to convert Morocco's foreign debt into shares of enterprises. The opposition argued that privatizations had to be decided by acts of parliament. The unions feared dismissals and uneven regional economic development when state enterprises were privatized. The government answered with the promise that no jobs would be lost and that the weaker regions would receive all support (Benlahcen-Tlemçani 1990: 63–9).

The privatization programme aimed at selling off seventy-five state enterprises and thirty-seven hotels. Privatization was seen as the major means of attracting capital and technology from overseas and of opening public monopolies to private investors. The first group of ten companies selected in 1992 for privatization included the Cimenterie de l'Oriental, the Complexe Textile de Fès, Chelco, the Société des Dérivés du Sucre, Industrie Bonnetière de la Vallée (IBOVAL), Vêtements du Nord (VETNORD) and the Hôtel Malabata. In 1994 the selling of the Société Nationale d'Investissement (SNI), which had holdings in forty companies and Sofac-Crédit was prepared and executed.

In September 1994 the Minister of Privatization announced the sale of five major state companies: the Société Nationale de Sidérurgie (SONASID), the Société des Industries Mécaniques et Electriques de Fès (SIMEF), the Société Marocaine de Stockage (SOMAS), the Société Chérifienne de Distribution et de Presse (SOCHE-PRESS) and the Banque Marocaine du Commerce Extérieur (BMCE) and in December 1994 it was announced that the two main oil refineries Société Marocaine de l'Industrie du Raffinage (SAMIR) and the Société Chérifienne des Pétroles (SCP) were to be privatized. In spring 1995 the government announced privatizations in the mining sector and the phosphate industry (a sector previously excluded from privatization). By the summer of 1996, twenty-five state companies and seventeen hotels had already been sold or privately divested, among them the SNI and Shell Oil.

The sale of the BMCE in April 1995 raised 1,500 million dirhams, but for SONASID no serious bid was received when it was offered for sale in February 1995. SONASID required considerable investment to make this steel firm competitive. This failure made it clear that problems may arise in the future as the government proceeds to sell its lame ducks. In 1993 it was reported that all four- and five-star hotels would be sold to international companies as a package deal. With its 700 enterprises and conglomerates the public sector was relatively well developed in services, textiles, clothing and the agro-industry. Therefore the Ministry of Economic Affairs and Privatization was created. During the previous years public companies had been privatized without any plan or economic strategy. The withdrawal of the state from industry and agriculture was described as an attempt to attract foreign capital and local savings to the Bourse des Valeurs de Casablanca (stock exchange). But the privatization process was rather slow, because the public had to be convinced that the operation was not against the national interest and that the ruling class was not manipulating the stock market. Traditionally, Moroccan private capital prefers family ownership and/or management structures and mistrusts foreign capital. Because public development companies and holding companies dominate the Bourse des Valeurs de Casablanca they [especially the Office pour le Développement Industriel (ODI), the Banque Nationale pour le Développement Economique (BNDE), SNI and the Caisse de Depôt et de Gestion (CDG)] became easily involved in privatization schemes which they saw as part of the standard portfolio management, and not as privatization operations (Seddon 1996: 765). A familiar divestiture, especially for larger state holdings, was the sale to a hard core of shareholders, by direct negotiation or tender to provide management expertise and possibly a subsequent offering of shares to employees.

In July 1991 the World Bank approved a $US235 million loan to the financial sector in order to develop Morocco's domestic financial markets and to invest in private export-oriented industries, services and tourism. The Moroccan banking sector is still highly regulated (Lahrichi 1987: 219–246) and dominated by three big investment banks (the BNDE for industry, the Caisse Nationale de Crédit Agricol (CNCA) for agriculture and the Crédit Immobilier et Hôtelier (CIH) for housing and tourism). Although the fifteen commercial banks – of which the BMCE is the most important – are mostly private, the state holds a minority stake in each of them (Moore 1987: 247–265). But the government wants to increase competition in the banking sector and to attract the savings to state savings banks in order to bring interest rates down and to break the informal cartel of the banks. The Bank Al-Maghrib, Morocco's Central Bank, controls the commercial banking sector and is associated with the six special credit institutions with sectoral responsibilities. In order to attract the savings of Moroccans working abroad, the government founded in 1989 the Bank Al-Amal. This investment bank had to become involved in the funding of new businesses in Morocco. In 1994 the Minister of Privatization, Abderrahmane Saaidi, announced the sale of most of the state's 50.39 per cent holding in the BMCE, partially on the Bourse des Valeurs de Casablanca and partially as international tender, half restricted to local non-bank investment institutions and half to all bidders. The new shareholders include the Royale Marocaine d'Assurances, Morgan Grenfell (London) and Morgan Stanley (New York). In October 1994 the Compagnie de Transports du Maroc – Lignes Nationales (CTM-LN) was also sold on the Bourse des Valeurs de Casablanca. In 1995 the government announced that a large stake in the ONTP would be sold to a strategic international player and that the remaining shares would be sold to the public (Seddon 1996: 775–777). The financial law of 1996 foresaw privatization of the three important firms SAMIR, SONASID and BNDE which had to bring in some 4 billion dirham. These privatization schemes drafted by the Citibank were accompanied in January 1996 by the introduction of 8 per cent interest-bearing vouchers which had to be sold to a broader public with no financial expertise. With these vouchers one could buy shares of state firms which were on the stock market to be privatized. Apparently, it was the government's intention to create a broad class of small capitalists and to activate the still sleepy Bourse des Valeurs de Casablanca. Therefore the Casablanca stock exchange was privatized in 1993.

The vouchers are convertible into shares of any forthcoming privatizable firm and have priority over subscription in cash. The first issue in January 1996 was a great success and raised almost 2 billion dirhams ($US248 million) in revenue. Almost half the subscriptors had never participated in a privatization scheme before. Although an overwhelming number of individuals subscribed for between three and fifty vouchers, nearly three times as many bonds were allocated to individuals demanding over fifty bonds (Khosrowshahi 1997: 246). In fact, the vouchers were, in the end, filling state coffers immediately. The public offering of SAMIR shares in March 1996 mobilized 3 billion dirhams for 6 million shares. Although the price valuation of the SAMIR shares was too high, two-thirds of the voucher holders converted their vouchers to shares. Obviously, these small shareholders were hoping to realize high short-term capital gains. As speculators began to sell their shares rapidly a tremendous downward pressure on price occurred. Meanwhile a shortage of vouchers in circulation obliged the government to issue more vouchers in May 1996 when the market was saturated and investors were disappointed with the outcome of the SAMIR privatization. Many considered this operation a pure swindle. After this disaster the subsequent share offering of

SONASID in July 1996 was only slightly oversubscribed despite a generous discount.

From the beginning, the slow pace of privatization had disappointed those who called for faster, more in-depth change. The firms on the privatization list represented a cross-section of the clear 'winners' with little overemployment. This calls into question what theoretically should have been the main goal of privatization, namely, the elimination of inefficiencies created by public ownership and management. The mining, transport and telecommunications state monopolies, which were run as personal fiefdoms, were missing from the list. Despite its call for total divestiture, the state has quietly maintained 'golden shares' in several privatized firms. The Société de Financement d'Achat à Crédit (SOFAC), a consumer credit company sold in April 1994, underwent a little-publicized capital increase before privatization. As a result, the state's share was not 52 per cent at privatization but 55 per cent, and state holding companies retained a share of the company after disvestiture. State ownership of BMCE went up from 13 per cent to 20 per cent after privatization when a Spanish investor pulled out. In 1996 the state took a 70 per cent stake in Morocco's only television company.

LOOKING FOR FOREIGN INVESTMENT

The low labour costs and the relative proximity to the main market, the EU, favoured the inflow of foreign capital. The abolition of the 1973 'Moroccanization' decree and the relaxing of foreign exchange controls accelerated foreign and domestic investment. The response of foreign investors to these changes was an increase in their investment of 7 per cent annually in the 1982–88 period (*The Kingdom of Morocco 1989* 1990: 111). The state-run Office de Commercialisation et d'Exportation (OCE), which monopolized farm produce and processed food exports was dismantled in 1986. The new investment code contained many tax holidays and custom exemptions which are differentiated according to the size and the type of the investment and the region where it is invested. These reforms met serious opposition from import-substituting firms producing solely for the domestic market who feared that liberalization would ruin them. But import liberalization was seen as a means of compelling import-substituting firms to become more competitive *vis-à-vis* foreign products in terms of price and quality.

Morocco's accession to GATT membership enhanced the country's image. In 1990 the government organized an international conference on free trade zones in order to attract foreign investors from the Far East, America and the Gulf states. As a result of greater financial stability and liberalization of the capital market, foreign banks became interested in Morocco's economy. In 1993 the first commercial loan to the country in over ten years was conceded by European banks. In the same year the Banco Exterior de España became the first foreign banking group to acquire sole ownership of its Moroccan subsidiary. Before, European or American groups had only held a substantial minority stake in their former Moroccan subsidiaries.

This was the case with the Algemene Bank Nederland Amro and its Algemene Bank Marokko (ABM), the Arab Bank Ltd and its Arab Bank Morocco, the Deutsche Bank and its Banque Commerciale du Maroc (BCM), the Banque Nationale de Paris (BNP-Internationale) and its Banque Marocaine du Commerce et de l'Industrie, the City Bank with the City Bank Maghreb, the Crédit Lyonnais with the Crédit du Maroc, Paribas International with the Société de Banque et de Crédit, the Société Générale with the Société Générale Marocaine des Banques, Paribas and Worms with the Société Marocaine de Dépôt et de Crédit (Tangeaoui 1993: 291).

Between 1985 and 1990, the current account deficit was reduced from 7.7 per cent of GDP to 1.6 per cent and foreign exchange reserves increased covering almost three months of imports. By 1990 the rise in investment had produced a more optimistic outlook, because foreign investment was expected to help cover the current account deficit and to create about 80,000 jobs a year. World market integration further developed. Textile and clothing industries in particular boomed so that in the beginning of the 1990s 25 per cent of exports were made up of textiles, clothes, leather, shoes, and carpets and only 20 per cent by phosphates. Foreign Direct Investment (FDI) increased now that export-oriented textile and clothing companies took advantage of the improved policy environment. Italian and Spanish textile firms moved in (Seddon 1996: 771) and made of the Tangier-Tétouan region an important textile centre (Branciard 1994: 139). But threats of protectionist measures coming from the expanding EU were not likely to reassure foreign investors and made Morocco's situation somewhat precarious as a potential export base. Morocco attracted less FDI than other emerging economies of comparable size and per capita income because foreign investors complained about administrative difficulties, the lack of transparency of the capital market, the inconsistencies of the administrative procedures and corruption (Blin and Parisot 1990: 77–79). Moroccan partners were only interested in short-term profits. Delocalization investment in Morocco was concentrated on the textile sector because of low labour costs and access to the European market, not enough in high-performing electronic industries – only SGS Thomson and Daewoo moved in. Delocalization of investment to Morocco was certainly not encouraged by the EU, which prefers investment in its own poor regions instead of promoting investment in its periphery. Moreover, it was reported that the Pakistani and Indian textile and garment industry was nibbling Morocco's market share (Tuquoi 1995: 2).

Finally, in June 1993 Hassan II outlined his future development goals. His objective was to create additional investment incentives and to reduce the bureaucratic delay of new investment; to reform the financial system, in particular the banks and the Bourse des Valeurs de Casablanca; to quicken the pace of privatization; to establish proper and transparent business practices. The Comité de Suivi et d'Impulsion des Investissements (CISI) was established in 1994 to speed up foreign investment in close partnership with the Moroccan commercial banks and the Central Bank. Economic liberalization measures succeeded in attracting FDI and were in line with the ambitious privatization programme intended to bring stock capital of 112 state companies to the stock market for which the government expected to collect

$US2.2 billion by the end of 1996. At the same time the government began selling back to their original owners the oil companies which had been nationalized in 1973 and Shell, Total and Mobil Oil agreed to buy back their former Moroccan subsidiaries. In July 1994 Prime Minister Abd al-Latif Filali promised that strategic enterprises, such as ONE, OCP and RAM would be included in the privatization programme. In April 1996, the first private power project, and one of the largest concession contracts in the world, was signed between the ONE and two Western companies for $US1.6 billion. Despite the vehement opposition of local representatives, in March 1996 the city of Casablanca outsourced the provision of water, electricity and sanitation to the French firm Lyonnaise des Eaux.

Because of the recession in Europe foreign investment outside the privatization process remained modest. In a White Paper published in autumn 1995 by the strong arm of the government, the Minister of Home Affairs, Driss Basri, it was argued that a financial and economic strategy for the mid-term was needed in order to join the club of 'emerging economies' (Tuquoi 1995: 2). A few weeks later a World Bank study ordered by Hassan II was leaked to the media. This study repeated the World Bank's pleas for more economic openness. Priority was to be given to the private sector. This report provoked tensions between the different circles of the bourgeoisie supporting the government. It appeared that the report was approved of by the modernizers campaigning for more transparency in business and financial transactions. Moroccan banks were encouraged to extend their international activities. In 1993 the BMCE took a stake in the Banco Exterior de España and opened a branch in Madrid. Although Morocco's Central Bank remained cautious in licensing foreign banks, the Banco Central Hispano-Americano (BCA) was allowed in 1993 to buy a 15 per cent stake in the BMCE. Meanwhile Tangier, where in the time of the International Zone a free trade area existed, became the first 'offshore banking zone' offering international banks tax holidays for fifteen years. The new zone is intended to compete with other offshore zones in the area.

PREPARING FOR A GREATER MAGHREB

The problems the Moroccan government had to face during the 1980s were not exceptional and all Maghreb countries were subject to economic crises obliging them to liberalize their economies and to democratize their regimes (Bédhri 1991: 93–118). The Maghreb countries were heavily indebted (see Table 9.6). The creation of an Arab Maghreb Union (AMU) could be the response to the threat of the even more radical changes which the liberalizing regimes of North Africa feared. In 1987 the ruling Neo-Destour Constitutionalist Socialist Party of Tunisia removed Habib Bourguiba from power but the country was by no means out of the woods yet. The widespread riots that shocked Algeria indicated the limits of the regime's ability to contain discontent and in 1989 President Chadli Bendjedid promulgated a new constitution guaranteeing many civil and political liberties and scrapping all references to socialism and the leading role of the Front de Libération Nationale (FNL) and the army. This did not prevent the rise of the Front Islamique de Salut (FIS)

A. MOMMEN

Table 9.6 Total foreign debt of the five Maghreb countries (in $US million)

	1985	1990	1991	1992	1993
Algeria	22,912	27,858	28,199	26,813	25,757
Morocco	16,234	23,532	21,567	21,599	21,430
Tunisia	5,931	7,691	8,250	8,543	8,701
Libya	4,759	4,922	–	–	–
Mauritania	1,528	2,143	2,236	2,138	2,203

Source: Alaoui (1994: 56); *World Debt Tables* (1994–1995).

which gained considerable popularity due to its focus for opposition to the corrupt and ineffectual regime. In Morocco Hassan II promised to liberalize his semi-parliamentary regime.

In Mauritania the military regime collapsed and in July 1991 a referendum was held to approve a new constitution instituting multi-party politics. Moreover, Libya was interested in joining a new Maghreb bloc because Colonel Gadhafi feared complete isolation in the region. Political changes appeared to have brought all governments back from the brink of very serious political problems and provided an opportunity to address the region's social and economic dilemmas. But historical rivalries were still dividing the Maghreb countries. Algerian opposition to Moroccan claims to the Western Sahara (Bistolfi 1992; Vergniot 1989: 386–418) not only reflects the ideological differences of the two regimes – socialism or a planned economy versus a *laissez-faire* monarchy – but also the long-standing rivalry between the two countries for domination of Northwest Africa (Leveau 1989: 269–280). Similarly, Tunisia walks the line between its two oil-rich neighbours Libya and Algeria. Morocco and Tunisia are friends of the West, while in the past Algeria and Libya were Soviet clients when buying their weaponry. Moving beyond the purely military side, however, the picture was more complicated. The Soviets bought eight times what the Americans did in the Moroccan marketplace and they were heavily involved in the phosphate and fishing sectors there, while France and the USA held prominent positions in the Algerian economy. The end of the Cold War and the collapse of the Soviet empire also meant the end of East–West rivalry in the region.

The most important problem, apart from the position of the Gadhafi regime in Libya, is the problem of the Western Sahara dividing Moroccan and Algerian foreign policy. Algeria backed the Polisario Front fighting for an independent Sahara Republic. But in May 1987 *rapprochement* between Morocco and Algeria removed the political obstacles to regional unity, especially when Morocco reiterated its commitment to Maghreb unity and Algeria was confronted with declining oil revenues. Diplomatic relations between both countries were restored in 1988, but never became particularly good.[1]

Due to historical reasons the economic structures of the five Maghreb countries are different. After independence Algeria put a strong emphasis on ISI and embarked upon an ambitious programme of building steel factories and petrochemical complexes (Branciard 1994: 129–134). Tunisia gave its agricultural sector

214

priority and invested in water-supply programmes. Tunisia is rich in oil, gas and phosphates, but also developed traditional crafts and industries. The textile sector became one of Tunisia's most important sectors, generating 30 per cent of the country's export earnings. Although Tunisia's external debt and its unemployment rates are high, they are well below those of Algeria and Morocco. Libya's oil exports account for 99 per cent of its export earnings and its economy is less diversified. Mauritania's economy is very weak too, because of its large traditional stock-breeding sector and its cyclical iron ore exports. Morocco and Tunisia opted for closer association with the EC from the outset because both economies are dependent for their exports and imports from Europe.

Fear inspired the Maghreb leaders to join forces when creating the AMU, which reflected the aspirations of the region. The creation of the AMU in 1989 was a response to the decision of the EC to choose 'deeper integration' after having accepted Spain and Portugal as new members. The creation of the AMU was prepared by the *rapprochement* between Morocco and Algeria in May 1987 at a summit meeting attended by Hassan II and the Algerian President, Ben Djedid Chadli, under the auspices of King Fahd of Saudi Arabia. The two leaders promised to settle various disputes, because the other Maghreb nations regarded the conflict in the Western Sahara as an obstacle to regional unity (Malki 1988: 214–219; Deeb 1993: 189–203; Jaidi 1987: 343–359; Spencer 1993).

The first Maghreb summit, held in June 1988, decided to create a Greater Maghreb with Algeria, Libya, Morocco, Tunisia and Mauritania. Hassan II insisted that the movement towards an AMU did not preclude Morocco's ambition to join the EC. Finally, in February 1989 at a meeting of North African heads of state in Marrakech, the AMU grouping of these five states was inaugurated (Alaoui 1994: 115–184). The newly created organization aimed to promote unity by allowing free movement of goods, services and labour and by promoting intra-Maghreb trade which was at a very low level (see Table 9.7). Morocco and Algeria, with populations of about 27 million each, are the dominant states of the AMU, while Tunisia with about 8.8 million and Libya with 5.2 million are small powers. Mauritania is a desert state with a bedouin population of about 2.2 million, with an economy dependent on iron ore export (Balta 1990: 252–268).

Table 9.7 Inter-Maghreb trade as a part of total foreign trade (as a percentage)

	1964		1970		1977		1988	
	exp.	*imp.*	*exp.*	*imp.*	*exp.*	*imp.*	*exp.*	*imp.*
Algeria	1.16	2.4	1.5	2	0.01	0.3	1.60	0.95
Libya	–	–	–	–	–	–	0.25	2.86
Morocco	2.46	2.07	4	1.7	0	0	4.40	1.20
Mauritania	–	–	–	–	–	–	0.80	1.80
Tunisia	7.89	2.06	14.2	0.9	1.2	0.01	3.90	3.90

Source: Alaoui (1994: 92).

The treaty of 17 February 1989 (*Arab Maghreb Treaty* 1989), giving birth to the AMU, created a structure reminiscent of the institutions of the EC. Apart from a Presidential Council of heads of state and a Committee of Ministers of Foreign Affairs, the structure comprises a General Secretariat, a Consultative Council and a Judicial Institution. The first thing the AMU had to undertake was to destroy existing economic barriers (exchange control, import restrictions, custom duties) and foster economic integration. Indeed, the AMU started discussing food, oil, security, economic affairs, human resources and infrastructure. In 1989 and 1990 ministerial and sectoral committees were set up to study food, human resources, economic and security affairs and infrastructure (Blin and Gobe 1989: 382–383; Le Troquer 1990: 588; Alaoui 1994: 118–121). The major feature of AMU exports is that they are heavily concentrated on one economic region (EU) and exports to this region are basic and processed agricultural products, consumer goods – mainly textiles and clothing – and minerals. Tariff and non-tariff obstacles concerning agricultural and agro-industrial exports make it difficult to diversify outlets. The AMU countries are small trading economies in global terms. Trade is an important and growing element and in view of their high debt burden, the link between trade, money, finance and development is particularly important. Improved access to export markets together with increased availability of external financing is urgent. All AMU countries are vulnerable to changes in the external trading environment, given their limited export base and the fact that they are small suppliers in most of their export markets. Trade barriers and other trade-distortive measures exist in AMU's export markets for such products as textiles, clothing and citrus fruits or canned fish. This explains why the AMU did not achieve great economic gains during the first years of its existence (Bistolfi 1990: 17–25).

In 1990 a committee was created to coordinate oil prices. Plans were drafted for a common identity card. In 1990 the Moroccan parliament endorsed two agreements with Algeria, one for the establishment of joint ventures for the creation of a second gas pipeline from Algeria through Morocco to Spain and one for closer economic and industrial integration of both economies. Ties between Morocco and Tunisia and Libya were increased. Because of the Gulf War and its aftermath Hassan II did not attend the third meeting of the AMU in March 1991 in Libya where the Ministers of Foreign Affairs decided on the creation of a Maghreb Bank for Trade and Investment and closer cooperation between the four countries. But at the fourth conference of the AMU held in September 1991 in Casablanca, Hassan II succeeded in gaining support for a Middle East peace conference (Chtatou 1993: 266–287).

In 1991 the Moroccan government permitted the Société Nationale des Auto-routes du Maroc to study the construction of the Maghreb Unity Highway linking Mauritania with Benghazi in Libya. Sections of the highway are already under construction in Morocco. The European Investment Bank (EIB) agreed to cover the costs of this $US430 million project with a long-term loan, while Japan's Overseas Economic Cooperation Fund and the World Bank cover the costs of modernizing Moroccan roads throughout the country (Lawless 1996: 757, 761). But soon divisions in the AMU surfaced when in August 1990 Iraq invaded Kuwait and King Hassan II vehemently condemned the invasion (Le Troquer 1990: 590–593). Relations between Morocco and Algeria lacked any form of cordiality and mutual distrust poisoned the discussions about the creation of a free trade area in North Africa. The civil war in Algeria and the problem of Islamic fundamentalism were two factors which hampered the process of political and economic liberalization. Although agreements were reached on the building of the Maghreb Unity Highway, of the fifteen conventions signed since the inauguration of the AMU, none had as yet been fully implemented. This made the Moroccan Minister of Foreign Affairs, Abd al-Latif Filali announce in February 1993 that a pause in the development of deeper integration of the five Maghreb countries had been decided at a recent meeting of the Ministers of Foreign Affairs of the AMU countries. Because of increased tensions with Algeria about the Western Sahara in December 1995 Morocco threatened to freeze its AMU acitivities. The Moroccan government condemned a meeting in January 1996 between Tunisian and Mauritanian foreign ministers with the Algerian President Liamine Zéroual, who was the AMU president. In fact, in 1996 the AMU was practically dead.

Establishing a free trade area with the southern Mediterranean region became the centrepiece of the EU's new Mediterranean strategy. The EU's strategy includes Algeria, Egypt, Israel, Jordan, Lebanon, Morocco, Syria, Tunisia, Cyprus, Malta, Turkey and the successor states of the former Yugoslavia. In the late 1970s the EC had already launched the idea of a free trade area but cooperation agreements of unlimited duration were signed and allowed tariff-free entry to the EC for manufactures and provided limited tariff preferences for agricultural exports. The agreements foresaw financial assistance by the EIB. But despite growing trade between the two regions, bilateralism remained predominant. Between 1970 and 1994 the EU accounted for about half of the imports of the Mediterranean countries, but these countries accounted for less than 3 per cent of the EU's total exports and imports. The EU is also the principal trading partner of all the Maghreb states (Khader 1995: 129–140). Algeria, Tunisia and Morocco solicited closer cooperation and a gradual reduction of restrictions on exports of agricultural and industrial products to the EU (Balta 1991: 29–38). Intra-Maghreb trade did not progress because of this dependency on exchanges with Europe, for instance, in 1994 only 4 per cent of Morocco's global transactions took place with the AMU countries. Even Morocco's trade with the Arab countries declined from 16 per cent of total trade to 10 per cent in 1994. Against this background, the Lisbon European Council called for a 'global policy in the Mediterranean'. In November 1995 the Barcelona Declaration was adopted, spelling out the new EU strategy. The EU renewed emphasis on a multilateral framework and advocated more open trade policies by the EU with respect to agricultural imports (Nsouli et al. 1996: 14). Three sets of final objectives were spelled out in Barcelona: first, engendering political stability and containing political tensions arising from immigration; second, encouraging balanced and sustainable growth; and finally, dealing with a number of challenges that require EU cooperation, such as environmental protection. Guided by this framework, the EU wanted to sign bilateral agreements with each of the Mediterranean countries with five sets of intermediate objectives and instruments:

1. Creating a free trade area between the EU and the Mediterranean countries over 12–15 years.
2. Increasing investment flows into the Mediterranean countries.
3. Fostering Mediterranean intra-regional links.
4. Establishing institutional fora for dialogue.
5. Providing performance-linked financial support from the EU (Oualalou 1996).

RAPPROCHEMENT WITH THE EU

Since independence Morocco has continually sought more favourable trade agreements with the EU (Zartman 1971). A five-year agreement conferring 'partial association' was negotiated in 1968 and signed in January 1969. In October 1972 the EC drafted its Global Mediterranean Policy in harmony with the Community's perspective of a larger EC. A new cooperation agreement for an unlimited period was signed on 27 April 1976 with Algeria, Tunisia and Morocco allowing most of their industrial and agricultural products to enter the EC and organizing a broader integration of the three Maghreb countries and the EC. The object of this agreement was to promote economic and trade cooperation between Morocco and the EC, taking account of their respective levels of development, and to provide a firm basis for such cooperation, consistent with their respective international obligations (Alaoui 1994: 34–53). The problem is that the bulk of Maghreb's export consists of products that are subject to import restrictions such as voluntary restraints on textile products and tariff and non-tariff measures, including reference prices, for agricultural products (Badiane 1993). Restrictions on several important products were not removed. Olive oil, citrus fruits, wine, textiles and refined oil products were refused free access (Berramdane 1992: 327; Branciard 1994: 155). (In early 1987 most of these restrictions were gradually reduced, the notable exception being textiles.)

In 1984 Morocco applied for full membership of the EC. The EC's answer was a new quotas agreement signed in January 1985. Morocco expressed its concern about EC's protectionism and the inadequacy of the EC's arrangements. Because of SAPs Morocco tried to institutionalize its exchanges with the EC.

The third enlargement of the EC with Portugal and Spain in January 1986 closed all doors to Europe for Moroccan agricultural exports now that the EC had become self-sufficient in practically all agricultural and industrial products, and now that the EC was on its way to an accelerated construction of a 'green Europe', the institutionalization of a 'blue Europe' (fishery) and a harmonization of its currencies. The European authorities were well aware of this problem, but their Global Mediterranean Policy seemed to be working more to generate rhetorical statements than what it was orginally designed for (Bahaijoub 1993: 235–240; Berramdane 1990: 39–55; Mahiou 1990: 27–37; Balta 1991: 29–220).

In the hope of gaining wider European support for its foreign policy (Western Sahara) and improved trading links, Hassan II applied to join the EC in July 1987. In October 1987 the EC rejected this second application for full membership, because the conditions of the Treaty of Rome – being a democratic regime and a European country – were not fulfilled. In 1987 negotiations on a new fishing agreement were held with the EC, as Spain had joined the Community in 1986. The accord signed on 25 February 1988 replaced the earlier Spanish-Moroccan accord concluded in 1983 and allowed the EC to fish 120,000 tons in Moroccan waters if they paid financial compensation worth ECU281.5 million. In March 1992 Morocco signed a new trade agreement with the EC and in May 1992 – after long talks – a new fishery agreement allowed Morocco increased compensation of ECU102 million per year (Seddon 1996: 767). The financial compensation the EC granted Morocco was aimed at diversifying the country's agricultural output in order to make Morocco less dependent on food imports and to reinforce its economic ties with Europe. Spanish fishing holds most of the fishing licences for Moroccan waters. Clashes between Moroccan and Spanish fishermen broke out. Morocco's export of canned fish is mostly to the EU, although the export of sardines to the EU is limited to 17,500 tons a year. The Moroccan government pressed for a reduction in the number of vessels allowed to fish in Moroccan waters and signed in 1991 a fishery accord with the Soviet Union giving Moroccan canned fish preferential treatment on the Soviet market. In 1995 fishing agreements with the Russian government were renewed (*Le Matin du Sahara et du Maghreb*, 30 December 1995). Morocco had become an important producer of canned fish (especially sardines) (Leymarie and Tripier 1993: 157; Alaoui 1994: 63–86). Meanwhile, on the advice of the World Bank and Ernst & Young, Morocco decided in 1996 to modernize its fishery fleet by investing 20 million dirham and investing in port facilities and canneries.

Morocco contacted the EC about a new relationship based on a free trade zone in a period when diplomatic relations with the EC had deteriorated because Amnesty International had issued a list of political prisoners still held in Morocco (Santucci and Benhlal 1990: 715–719). The European Parliament voted in 1992 against a four-year programme of aid, worth ECU438 million (see Table 9.8) in protest against human rights abuses. Hassan II reacted by closing his famous prison of Tazmamart and freeing political prisoners and members of the Polisario Front. In the meantime Hassan II upset the opposition parties when during the municipal elections his police arrested many opposition candidates on charges of being implicated in drug traffic. This item had moved to the fore when the EC heavily criticized Morocco for its illegal export of cannabis to Europe. In December 1992 Morocco signed an agreement with the EC on the eradication of cannabis growing and a relief programme for its poor cannabis-growing peasants in northern Morocco. More-over, European countries are concerned about illegal Moroccan immigration (Khader 1995: 161–165). About 700,000 Moroccans already work in the EU. Morocco argues that the EU should help modernize its agriculture in order to increase the country's living standards and to stop migration to Europe.

In December 1992 the European Commission approved loans worth $US590 million to Morocco. Generally, the EU backed debt-reduction and liberalization measures and SAPs introduced by the World Bank and the IMF. The EIB made a loan available to modernize the telecommunication sector. In March 1993 the EC

A. MOMMEN

Table 9.8 EU financial aid to Maghreb countries (in million ECUs)

		Budget	EIB loans	Total
First protocol	Algeria	44	70	114
(1978–1981)	Morocco	74	56	130
	Tunisia	54	41	95
	Total	172	167	339
Second protocol	Algeria	44	107	151
(1981–1986)	Morocco	109	90	199
	Tunisia	61	78	139
	Total	214	275	489
Third protocol	Algeria	56	183	230
(1986–1991)	Morocco	173	151	324
	Tunisia	93	131	224
	Total	322	465	778
Fourth protocol	Algeria	70	280	350
(1992–1996)	Morocco	218	220	438
	Tunisia	116	168	284
	Total	404	668	1072

Source: Slim (1993: 135).

announced that a free trade zone with Morocco could be discussed. In July 1993 the EU proposed an annual increase of 3 per cent in quotas of citrus fruit, orange juice, fruit and vegetables from Morocco in 1997–2000 and in December 1993 the EU started negotiating with Morocco on a new association agreement. Meanwhile Morocco was pushing for closer cooperation with the EU and had hosted in October 1994 a multilateral conference in Casablanca where thirty countries of the Middle East and North Africa met in order to discuss closer economic cooperation and trade. When in February 1994 negotiations were opened for a new agreement with Morocco, European-Moroccan relations were established on four pillars: first, political dialogue on security problems; second, economic, scientific, social and cultural cooperation; third, the gradual introduction (within twelve years) of a free trade area for industrial products; and finally, financial cooperation. The Moroccan government insisted on the necessity of increased financial support and the establishment of a free trade area (Branciard 1994: 156). In January 1995 Morocco signed an agreement with the EU to bring agricultural trade relations close to the provisions of GATT. Under the new agreement, Morocco's preferential status in tomato exports to the EU is reduced, but exports will be allowed to maintain their traditional level and a minimum price is imposed for the winter months. Finally, on 26 February 1996 an association agreement and a fishery agreement for four years were signed between the EU and Morocco. The association agreement was based on the principles of reciprocity, partnership and respect of democratic and human rights as discussed at the first Euromediterranean

Conference held in Barcelona on 27 and 28 November 1995 (Naïm 1995; Tuquoi 1995) and on the 'four pillars' of Moroccan-European relations (*L'Opinion. Quotidien national d'information*, 28 February 1996). The fishery agreement foresaw a gradual reduction of the EU's fishery fleet and an ECU355 million compensation for Morocco (Bank Al-Maghrib 1995: 23–24). Further negotiations on free trade in agricultural products are expected to start in 2000.

FRANCE AND SPAIN

France remains Morocco's most important creditor and trading partner (see Table 9.9), accounting for about 25 per cent of Moroccan imports and 33 per cent of its exports. Exports to France contracted during the 1980s when France reduced its imports of phosphate and fertilizers by 40 per cent. Capital goods comprise about one-third of imports from France. Morocco remains dependent on French support when negotiating with the EU. French agrarian interests delayed any progress on the road to Morocco's integration into the EU. French diplomacy only wants to mediate between Morocco and the Polisario Front over Western Sahara and prevent Moroccan Islamist fundamentalism from operating from France (Seddon 1996: 773). None the less, Morocco remains France's true ally and a military cooperation agreement was signed between the two countries when Prime Minister Filali visited Paris in October 1994. In turn, France promised to support Morocco in its negotiations with the EU on a new partnership agreement and pressed the EU to increase economic aid to the Maghreb countries. France stood at the cradle of the Club financier méditerranéen founded in November 1990 in Aix-en-Provence. In October 1990 France initiated discussions on the creation of a Conference on Security and Cooperation in the Mediterranean (CSCEM), a cooperation group of the AMU states, Malta, Spain, France, Italy and Portugal in order to discuss technical problems such as pollution, desertification and food problems. Italy and Spain proposed that one-quarter of 1 per cent of the combined GNP of the EC

Table 9.9 Exports by countries of destination in percentages of total exports

	1987	1988	1989	1990	1991	1992	1993	1994	1995
EU	61.3	56.6	64.6	65.0	62.4	64.0	60.0	64.4	62.1
Bel./Lux.	4.0	3.7	5.7	3.9	3.4	3.5	2.9	3.3	3.1
France	29.5	26.0	29.3	31.5	31.8	32.8	31.7	32.1	29.7
Germany	6.2	5.6	5.3	5.3	4.9	4.7	4.3	4.3	4.1
Italy	5.5	5.6	6.3	6.9	6.2	5.6	5.7	5.8	5.7
Netherl.	3.5	3.0	3.4	3.2	2.5	3.1	2.9	2.9	2.4
Spain	6.8	7.2	8.3	9.2	8.8	9.0	9.3	9.3	9.4
UK	2.7	2.9	3.9	3.3	2.7	3.3	3.9	3.8	4.5
Japan	4.3	4.6	4.6	3.9	5.2	4.9	6.6	6.7	7.7
USA	1.6	2.1	2.2	1.9	2.5	3.7	3.5	3.5	3.4
India	5.4	9.2	2.0	4.6	7.0	6.0	6.4	5.9	6.6

Source: Nsouli *et al.* (1995: 115); Bank Al-Magrib (1994 and 1995).

states be allocated to a development fund for the Maghreb. In return, the Maghreb states would agree to restrict immigration to the EC (Vasconcelos 1993: 12–15). A multilateral investment bank was foreseen (Basfao and Henry 1990: 3–13; Slim 1993: 113–136; Branciard 1994: 157).

With French President François Mitterrand relations had been strained, but with France's newly elected president Jacques Chirac they improved immediately when the latter visited Rabat in July 1995. In May 1996 Hassan II was received with the 'highest honours' in Paris. President Chirac had already shown his preference for Tunisia and Morocco and his distrust of the regime of Liamine Zeroual in Algeria (Simon and Tuquoi 1996: 4). In January 1996 France signed several economic agreements with Morocco. France promised to pay FF345 million for the modern-ization of Morocco's railroads and the development of its water supply and capital goods sector. Paris knocked FF1 billion off Morocco's foreign debt to France (out of a total debt worth FF25 billion). In turn, Morocco bound itself to invest the equivalent of FF400 million in northern Morocco where cannabis growing is concentrated. The remaining part of the debt, FF600 million, was destined for French firms wanting to participate in Morocco's privatization scheme. A treaty regulated French investment in Morocco and repatriation of profits and capital (*Le Monde*, 16 January 1996).

Since the 1970s Spain had been interested in developing its fishing industry but the agreement which was signed with Morocco in 1977 was not ratified. Finally, a temporary agreement for 1979–83 was signed. Joint ventures could be established and funds for the improvement of the Atlantic ports were provided. The idea of building a bridge or a tunnel between Gibraltar and Tangier was revived. Funds for the project had to come from the EC. The fast economic growth Spain enjoyed after joining the EC enabled the government in Madrid to open a credit line worth FF67 billion. Spain was now Morocco's second trading partner after France. Spanish FDI increased and in the same period Spain signed similar agreements with Tunisia and Algeria (Gobe 1990: 97–106). In June 1988 a bilateral trading agreement with Spain was signed and discussions were started over the installation of an electrical cable under the Straits of Gibraltar. In September 1988 an agreement was signed for the construction of a pipeline across Moroccan territory connecting the oil fields of Algeria with Europe. Quarrels between Spain and Morocco over the Western Sahara surfaced when Spain voted in the UN against Morocco. In turn, Morocco wanted to discuss the future of the Spanish enclaves, Ceuta and Melilla but Morocco could not afford this quarrel and in September 1989 an agreement was signed on defence cooperation, technology transfers and on the holding of bilateral summits (Lawless 1996: 755–756).

Spain became an even more important partner for Morocco after King Juan Carlos' visit to Rabat on 4 July 1991 when a treaty of friendship was signed and both countries decided to cooperate in military affairs. Finally, Spain promised to reschedule official debt within Morocco's 'Paris Club' agreements and to open up a new credit line. Total debt to Spain was estimated at $US1,012 million. In December 1992 Spain agreed to provide a new five-year credit programme worth

$US1,056 million and in February 1995 Morocco received a new credit line of $US1.125 million as signed in 1994. Spain no longer seemed concerned about the fate of its former colony in Western Sahara. Spain overtook France as the principal investor in Morocco and on 30 April 1991 signed an agreement with Morocco and Algeria on a second gas pipeline linking Algeria to Spain. Metragaz (Société pour le Pilotage de la Construction du Gazoduc Maghreb-Europe) was founded, with its headquarters in Casablanca. For this pipeline the EU was to lend Morocco – together with funds for structural adjustment and EIB loans – a total of ECU438 million between 1992 and 1996. But Spanish opposition to improved access to the EU for Moroccan agricultural products strained mutual relations. Morocco countered with demands for drastic cuts in EU fishing quotas, which largely affected Spain's fishing industry. Spain holds most of the fishing licences for Moroccan waters. Again, the Moroccan government criticized Spain because of the statutes of autonomy for the two enclaves Ceuta and Melilla. Relations with Spain improved in the beginning of 1996 when the EU signed a fishery agreement and when Felipe Gonzalez signed in Rabat a financial deal worth $US1.2 billion (150 billion pesetas of which is a soft loan worth 60 billion pesetas). Spain signed an agreement with Morocco to build a tunnel under the Straits of Gibraltar for which $US4.5 billion had to be levied on the capital market.

Relations with the other Iberian country, Portugal, were improved following a visit by Prime Minister Anibal Cavaco Silva in May 1994 to Rabat. Portugal also offered support for Morocco in its negotiations with the EU. Morocco made efforts to diversify its export markets. Apart from Eastern Europe and the Maghreb countries, Japan and India became important trading partners.

CONCLUSIONS

Morocco has achieved a certain momentum in the economic reform process that differentiates it from most African and Middle Eastern countries, such as Algeria, Zaïre and Nigeria. Its economic and political stability has been recognized as two factors determining its fast economic recovery since the 'lost decade' of the 1980s. In Morocco balance-of-payment deficits are being controlled through a reduction of the money supply and a mobilization of savings. To reduce protectionism and orient industry toward exports, Morocco has adopted a policy of trade liberalization, price reforms and privatizations (Leveau 1993: 245–256). Although Morocco created an environment for rapid economic development, its economy is moderately complementary with those of its African neighbours. The complementarity of the AMU economies is rather theoretical. Mutual trade with its AMU neighbours does not exceed 2 per cent of total trade, and with 65 per cent the EU is by far the most important trading partner of the Maghreb countries. Earning of hard currencies gained top priority in spite of the necessity of realigning their economies because of their mutual interests.

Though the country did not emerge as a real new 'tiger' by the end of the 1980s, its economic transformation was not a disaster and its economy was well prepared for world-market integration. Relatively high growth and low inflation rates were obtained. The country's external accounts have become more manageable and foreign exchange reserves have increased. But much of Morocco's economic growth came from the expanding informal sector of the economy, especially in the textile industry. Rapid expansion in this sector was fuelled by the low costs of production and the absence of workplace regulations. The abandonment of ISI strategies has greatly reduced the burden of external debt, most of which was owed to official debtors. The gradual pace of reform did not provoke major disruptive effects on the economy. The road to a convertible dirham was long and painful. The privatization programme which was originally approved in 1989 had to raise a substantial amount of revenue for the state. The Moroccan government firmly believes that durable industrial growth requires internationally competitive production in terms of price and quality and that the economy has to be considered as a whole and not as artificially partitioned into import-substituting and export-oriented sectors. First, SAPs sponsored by the World Bank compelled Morocco to liberalize its imports, to devalue its currency, to deregulate its domestic price and distribution system, to increase its interest rate, and to reform its banking system. The role of the private sector was changed and transformed into the motor of economic development. The ISI strategy was gradually abandoned. Since the country implemented major economic reforms, real economic growth rates have picked up with an average of 4.5 per cent over the period 1985–94. In a country where half the population is at subsistence levels, drought remains a threat to economic and political stability. Morocco's liberalization programme has been relatively slow to develop. Liberalization of imports is implemented along a medium-term schedule which provides sufficient time for adjustment and reorientation in accordance with private sector representatives.

Second, Morocco's location south of Europe has brought a number of comparisons with the relationship between the USA and Mexico. Economic liberalization is expected to make a new 'tiger' in Europe's southern cone. Morocco's 'tiger factors' include the sequence of economic reforms, political stability, a gradual improvement in the country's technological development, and the diversification of the economy. Largely driven by its close economic ties to Europe, Morocco has the potential to become a new 'tiger', but 'Fortress Europe' is hampering this development. As an associate of the EU Morocco tries to have access to the European Single Market. The foreseen free trade area between Morocco and the EU in combination with the World Trade Organization (WTO) liberalization drive will produce a shake out among Morocco's infant and small industries (*L'Opinion*, 25 February 1996).

Third, the regional Maghreb arrangement is likely to have a more limited and neo-functional form. Within the constraints of the SAPs instigated by the World Bank, it is possible that closer patterns of regional economic and trade cooperation will be generated. Much will depend on the quality of the democratization process and the degree to which a continuous political momentum can be maintained on the issue. The pay-offs are likely to be important given a global order that is going to be determined by the rise of regional trade blocs. The external demonstrable effect of regionalizing economies and trading blocs will in some degree facilitate the integration of the Maghreb countries. None the less, as a region of relatively weak state structures, low purchasing power and limited market opportunities, it will also face strong obstacles and diverging state interests.

Fourth, Morocco's infrastructure is old-fashioned; the gap between the rural population living in a subsistence economy and the urban population is widening; corruption is growing in all levels of the administration; education is poorly organized and illiteracy is spreading. Unemployment rates are high among university graduates. In a country with a high birth rate economic growth has to exceed 7 per cent a year when an economy wants to 'emerge' from underdevelopment.

NOTE

1. In 1992 Mohamed Boudiaf, who had been in exile in Morocco for more than twenty years, became Algerian head of state and he urged the Polisario Front to make peace with Morocco. But following the assassination of Boudiaf, diplomatic relations worsened and the frontier was closed again. In 1993 ambassadors were exchanged and the border was re-opened. However, in 1994 relations deteriorated again after mutual accusations of sponsoring terrorist activities on each other's territories.

BIBLIOGRAPHY

Abdaimi, M. El (1994) *Maroc: Pays émergent? Bilan et perspectives d'une transition financière*, Marrakech: BEREPIE.

The Agro-Based Industries in Morocco: Key Characteristics and Rehabilitation Issues, United Nations Industrial Development Organization, 12 March 1990 (*Studies on the Rehabilitation of African Industry*, No. 9), New York: UN.

Alaoui, M. B. H. El (1994) *La coopération entre l'Union Européenne et les pays du Maghreb*, Paris: Nathan.

Ali, D. B. (1987) 'Etat et reproduction sociale au Maroc: le cas du secteur public', *Annuaire de l'Afrique du Nord* 26: 117–131.

Ali, D. B. (1989) 'Changement de pacte social et continuité de l'ordre politique au Maroc', *Annuaire de l'Afrique du Nord* 28: 51–72.

'Arab Maghreb Treaty' (1989), *Africa Research Bulletin* 26, 2, 31 March.

Ashford, D. E. (1965) *Morocco-Tunisia: Politics and Planning*, Syracuse, NY: Syracuse University Press.

Azam, J.-P. and Morrisson, C. (1994) *The Political Feasibility of Adjustment in Côte d'Ivoire and Morocco*, Paris: OECD.

Badiane, O. (1993) 'The common agricultural policy and the African countries', in I. W. Zartman (ed.) *Europe and Africa: The New Phase*, Boulder, CO and London: Lynne Rienner Publishers: 75–94.

Bahaijoub, A. (1993) 'Morocco's argument to join the EEC', in G. Joffé (ed.) *North Africa: Nation, State, and Region*, London and New York: Routledge: 235–246.

Balta, P. (1991) 'L'UMA et le défi de la CEE', in B. López García, G. Martín Muñoz and M. N. de Larramendi, *Elecciones, participación y transiciones políticas en el Norte de Africa*, Madrid: Agencia Española de Cooperación Internacional, Instituto de Cooperación con el Mundo Arabe: 29–38.

Balta, P. (1992) 'A l'heure du multipartisme', *Confluences méditerranées* 3: 130–136.

Balta, P. and Rullean, C. (1990) *Le grand Maghreb. Des indépendances à l'an 2000*. Paris: Editions la Découverte.

Bank Al-Maghrib (1991–95) *Rapport annuel.*

Basfao, K. and Henry, J.-R. (1990) 'Introduction. Le Maghreb, l'Europe et la France', *Annuaire de l'Afrique du Nord* 29: 3–13.

Bédhri, M. (1991) *Privatisation et réforme des entreprises publiques dans les pays de l'U.M.A.,* Casablanca: Afrique Orient.

Belghazi, S. (1993) 'Approches de l'industrialization et politique industrielle au Maroc', in *Abderrahim Bouabid et la question économique. Actes de la journée d'études de l'A.E.M. Mohammédia, 31 janvier 1993*, Rabat: Publication des Annales Marocaines d'Economie, Association des Economistes Marocains: 231–236.

Benlahcen-Tlemçani, M. (1990) 'Les risques de la privatisation du secteur public au Maroc', *Economie et Humanisme* 313: 63–69.

Bernoussi, A. (1993) 'La stratégie de mobilisation des financements extérieures au Maroc', in *Abderrahim Bouabid et la question économique. Actes de la journée d'études de l'A.E.M. Mohammédia, 31 janvier 1993*, Rabat: Publication des Annales Marocaines d'Economie, Association des Economistes Marocains: 237–261.

Berramdane, A. (1990) 'Le Maroc et l'Europe: un destin commun', *Annuaire de l'Afrique du Nord* 29: 39–56.

Berramdane, A. (1992) *Le Sahara occidental enjeu maghrébin*, Paris: Editions Karthala.

Bistolfi, R. (1990) 'La politique Maghrébine de la Communauté: quels développements?', *Annuaire de l'Afrique du Nord* 29: 17–25.

Bistolfi, R. (1992) *Le Sahara occidental, enjeu maghrébin*, Paris: Editions Karthala.

Blin, L. and Gobe, E. (1989) 'L'Union du Maghreb Arabe: Un bilan de l'intégration économique', *Annuaire de l'Afrique du Nord* 28: 377–384.

Blin, L. and Parisot, B. (1990) 'Les relations économiques entre la CEE et les pays du Maghreb', *Annuaire de l'Afrique du Nord* 29: 57–96.

Bonnefous, M. (1991) *Le Maghreb: repères et rappels*, Paris: C.H.E.A.M.

Brachet, P. (1992) *Corruption et sous-développement au Maroc*, Paris: L'Harmattan.

Branciard, M. (1994) *Le Maghreb: au cœur des crises*, Lyon: Chronique sociale.

Chevassu, J.-M. (1987) 'Le rôle de l'état marocain dans la croissance: le blocage et la restructuration du secteur industriel', *Annuaire de l'Afrique du Nord* 26: 195–217.

Chtatou, M. (1993) 'The present and the future of the Maghreb Arab Union', in G. Joffé (ed.) *North Africa: Nation, States, and Region*, London and New York: Routledge: 266–287.

Deeb, M.-J. (1993) 'The Arab Maghribi Union and the prospects for North African unity', in I. W. Zartman and W. M. Habeeb (eds) *Polity and Society in Contemporary North Africa*, Boulder, San Francisco and Oxford: Westview Press: 189–203.

Diouri, M. (1992) *A qui appartient le Maroc?*, Paris: L'Harmattan.

Eussner, A. (1992) 'Private industry response to structural adjustment and deregulation in Morocco', *Internationales Afrikaforum* 28(2): 181–195.

Gallissot, R. (1989) 'Les émeutes, phénomène cyclique au Maghreb: rupture au reconduction du système politique', *Annuaire de l'Afrique du Nord* 28: 29–39.

Ghazi, A. (1995) *Les lignes de force d'une monarchie constitutionnelle authentiquement marocaine*, s.l.

Gobe, E. (1990) 'Autour du Forum Méditerranéen: valses hésitations et enjeux', *Annuaire de l'Afrique du Nord* 29: 97–105.

Guerraoui, D. (1986) *Agriculture et développement au Maroc*, Paris: Editions Publisud.

Guerraoui, D. (ed.) (1993) *Ajustement et développement. Maghreb, Afrique subsaharienne, l'Europe de l'Est*, Casablanca and Paris: Editions Toubkal and L'Harmattan.

Habeeb, W. M. (1993) 'The Maghribi states and the European Community', in I. W. Zartman and W. M. Habeeb (eds) *Polity and Society in Contemporary North Africa*, Boulder, San Francisco and Oxford: Westview Press: 204–220.

Horton, B. (1990) *Morocco: Analysis and Reform of Economic Policy*, Washington, DC: World Bank (EDI Development Policy Case Studies. Analytical Case Studies no. 4).

226

Jaidi, L. (1987) 'Etat-Nation et intégration économique arabe: vers un nouvel espace régional', *Annuaire de l'Afrique du Nord* 26: 343–359.

Jelloun, T. B. (1994) *L'Homme rompu*, Paris: Editions du Seuil.

Kadmiri, A. (1988) *Economie et politique industrielle au Maroc*, Casablanca: Les Editions Toubkal.

Khader, B. (1995) *Le Grand Maghreb et l'Europe. Enjeux et perspectives*, Paris and Ottignies: Editions Publisud and Editions Quorum.

Khosrowshahi, C. (1997) 'Privatization in Morocco: the politics of development', *The Middle East Journal* 51(2): 242–255.

Khrouz, D. (1993) 'De l'endettement à l'ajustement', in D. Guerraoui (ed.) *Ajustement et développement au Maghreb en Afrique subsaharienne, et en Europe de l'Est*, Casablanca: Editions Toubkal: 80–98.

The Kingdom of Morocco 1989. Trade Policy Review (1990), Geneva: General Agreement on Tariffs and Trade.

Kingdom of Morocco: Sustained Investment and Growth in the Nineties, Main Report (1990), no. 8417 – MOR, Washington, DC, Nov. 1990.

Lahrichi, N. B. (1987) 'Etat et système financier au Maroc: mutations et adaptations', *Annuaire de l'Afrique du Nord* 26: 219–246.

Laraki, K. (1989) *Food Subsidies: A Case Study of Price Reform in Morocco*, Washington, DC: The World Bank (LSMS Working Paper no. 50).

Lawless, R. I. (1996) 'Morocco: history', *The Middle East and North Africa* (Regional Surveys of the World), London: Europa Publications Limited, 42nd edn: 748–764.

Le Troquer (1990) 'Chronique internationale', *Annuaire de l'Afrique du Nord* 29: 555–599.

Leveau, R. (1985) *Le fellah marocain, défenseur du trône*, Paris: Presses de la Fondation Nationale des Sciences Politiques, 2nd edn.

Leveau, R. (1989) 'Eléments de réflexion sur l'état au Maghreb', *Annuaire de l'Afrique du Nord* 28: 269–280.

Leveau, R. (1993) *Le sabre et le turban: l'avenir du Maghreb*, Paris: Editions F. Bouvin.

Leymarie, S. and Tripier, J. (1993) *Maroc: Le prochain dragon? De nouvelles idées pour le développement*, Casablanca: Editions EDDIF.

MacDonald, S. B., Hughes, J. E. and Crum, D. L. (1995) *New Tigers and Old Elephants: The Development Game in the 1990s and Beyond*, New Brunswick and London: Transaction Publishers.

Mahiou, A. (1990) 'Le Maghreb et la CEE: entre la crainte et l'espoir', *Annuaire de l'Afrique du Nord* 29: 27–37.

Malki, H. El (1987) 'L'interventionnisme de l'état marocain à l'épreuve de l'ajustement', *Annuaire de l'Afrique du Nord* 26: 284–298.

Malki, H. El (1988) 'Le Maghreb économique entre le possible et le réalisable', in A. Claisse and G. Conac, *Le Grand Maghreb, données socio-politiques et facteurs d'intégration des Etats du Maghreb*, Paris: Economica: 211–219.

Malki, H. El (1989) *Trente ans d'économie marocaine 1960–1990*, Paris: CNRS.

Mateus, A. *et al.* (1988) *A Multisector Framework for Analysis of Stabilization and Structural Adjustment Policies: The Case of Morocco*, Washington, DC: The World Bank (World Bank Discussion Paper 29).

Miège, J.-L. (1950) *Le Maroc*, Paris: Presses Universitaires de France.

Moore, C. H. (1987) 'Les enjeux politiques des réformes bancaires au Maghreb', *Annuaire de l'Afrique du Nord* 26: 248–265.

Naïm, Mouna (1995) 'Pays européens et méditerranéens tentent de redéfinir leurs relations', *Le Monde*, 28 November.

Nelson, H. D. (1986) *Morocco: A Country Study*, Washington, DC: The American University, 5th edn.

Nsouli, S. M. *et al.* (1995) *Resilience and Growth through Sustained Adjustment: The Moroccan Experience*, Washington, DC: International Monetary Fund (Occasional paper, International Monetary Fund no. 117).

Nsouli, S. M., Bisat, A. and Kanaan, O. (1996) 'The European Union's new Mediterranean Strategy', *Finance and Development* 33(3): 14–17.

L'Opinion, various issues as shown.

Oualalou, F. (1996) *Après Barcelone... le Maghreb est nécessaire*, Casablanca and Paris: Les Editions Toubkal and L'Harmattan.

Payne, R. (1993) 'Economic crisis and policy reform in the 1980s', in I. W. Zartman and W. M. Habeeb (eds) *Polity and Society in Contemporary Africa*, Boulder, San Francisco and Oxford: Westview Press: 139–167.

Roe, A, Roy J. and Sengupta J. (1989) *Economic Adjustment in Algeria, Egypt, Jordan, Morocco, Pakistan, Tunisia and Turkey*, Washington, DC: The World Bank.

Rousset, M. (1987) 'Etat et secteur public au Maroc. Une nouvelle approche de l'intervention économique de l'Etat', *Annuaire de l'Afrique du Nord* 26: 267–282.

Sadik, A. (1989) *Intégration et systèmes économiques comparée. Le Grand Maghreb Arabe. Essai de synthèse*, Casablanca: Afrique Orient.

Santucci, J.-C. (1985) *Chroniques politiques marocaines (1971–1982)*, Paris: Editions du CNRS.

Santucci, J.-C. and Benhlal, M. (1990) 'Chronique Marocaine', *Annuaire de l'Afrique du Nord* 29: 715–719.

Seddon, D. (1989a) 'The politics of "adjustment" in Morocco', in B. K. Campbell and J. Loxley (eds) *Structural Adjustment in Africa*, New York: St Martin's Press: 234–265.

Seddon, D. (1989b) 'Morocco in the 1980s', in S. Commander (ed.) *Structural Adjustment and Agriculture: Theory and Practice in Africa and Latin America*, London: Overseas Development Institute: 175–189.

Seddon, D. (1996) 'Economy', in *The Middle East and North Africa (Regional Surveys of the World)* 42nd edn, London: Europa Publications: 764–778.

Simon, C. and J.-P. Tuquoi (1996) 'Au Maghreb, la France privilégie le Maroc et la Tunisie', *Le Monde*, 24 January.

Slim, H. (1993) 'Le codéveloppement. Un nouveau modèle de la coopération Euro-maghré-bine', in A. Vasconcelos (ed.) *Européens et Maghrébins. Une solidarité obligée*, Paris: Editions Karthala: 113–136.

Spencer, C. (1993) *The Maghreb in the 1990s: Political and Economic Developments in Algeria, Morocco and Tunisia*, London: The International Institute for Strategic Studies.

Stewart, C. F. (1964) *The Economy of Morocco 1912–1962*, Cambridge, MA: Harvard University Press.

Swearingen, W. D. (1987) *Moroccan Mirages: Agrarian Dreams and Deceptions 1912–1986*, Princeton, NJ: Princeton University Press.

Tangeaoui, S. (1993) *Les entrepreneurs marocains: pouvoir, société et modernité*, Paris: Editions Karthala.

Tiano, A. (1963) *La politique économique et financière du Maroc indépendant*, Paris: PUF.

Tuluy, H. and Salinger, B. L. (1989) *Trade, Exchange Rate, and Agricultural Pricing Policies in Morocco*, Washington, DC: The World Bank (World Bank Comparative Studies, The Political Economy of Agricultural Pricing Policy).

Tuquoi, J.-P. (1995) 'Les déconvenues marocaines d'un libéralisme mal assimilé', *Le Monde*, 28 November.

Vasconcelos, A. (1993) 'L'impératif de la connection', in A. Vasconcelos (ed.) *Européens et Maghrébins. Une solidarité obligée*, Paris: Editions Karthala: 7–25.

Vergniot, O. (1989) 'La question du Sahara Occidental. Autodetermination et enjeux référendaires (1956–1989)', *Annuaire de l'Afrique du Nord* 28: 386–418.

Waterbury, J. (1970) *The Commander of the Faithful: The Moroccan Political Elite – Study of Segmented Politics*, New York: Columbia University Press.

World Bank (1994–95) *World Debt Tables. External Finance for Developing Countries, Volume 2, Country Tables*, Washington, DC: The World Bank.

World Bank (1996) *World Development Report*, New York: Oxford University Press.

Zartman, I. W. (1964) *Morocco: Problems of a New Power*, New York: Atherton Press.

Zartman, I. W. (1971) *The Politics of Trade Negotiations Between Africa and the European Economic Community: The Weak Confront the Strong*, Princeton, NJ: Princeton University Press.

Zartman, I. W. (1987) 'King Hassan's new Morocco', in I. W. Zartman (ed.) *The Political Economy of Morocco*, New York: Praeger: 1–33.

10

REGIONAL INTEGRATION PROCESSES IN LATIN AMERICA

Argentina and MERCOSUR

Miguel Teubal

INTRODUCTION

Important social and economic transformations have been taking place in recent years. The end of the Cold War and the triumph of neo-liberalism have not led necessarily to a fully fledged 'open' world economy as might have been expected. While the promotion of multilateralism is the proclaimed objective of public policy in many countries and by international organizations, the emergence and consolidation of regional trade and economic blocs have also become a significant trend in the new world scenario. This is probably more a sign that increased intercapitalist rivalry, as between the main centres of world capitalism and with regards to the interests prevailing in each, continues to influence international developments now that the East–West divide of the Cold War has been set aside.

The formation and strengthening of regional trade blocs in the European Community (EC), the Far East Association of South-East Asian Nations (ASEAN) and the North American Free Trade Agreement (NAFTA) and Common Market of the South (MERCOSUR) seem to reflect these trends. Important areas of the Third World have become associated with one or another of these trade blocs. Increasingly, decisions previously pertaining to the nation–state are being 'internationalized' and/or transferred to regional economic blocs. Nevertheless, as explained below, certain elements of these integration processes are contradictory to what could be expected regarding the development of a completely 'open' world economy and the liberalization policies predicated by the IMF and World Bank.

While the EC was in the making for several decades, it now emerges as one of the main world economic blocs, probably much more fortified than ever before. NAFTA can be seen as a response to this new scenario, reflecting the need the USA has to enhance her own power base. NAFTA has tended to cater mostly to the main corporate interests of the USA, and to a lesser extent, Canada and Mexico. Finally, in the Far East, though not always formally institutionalized, a series of trade and economic groupings associated with Japan or Japanese interests are also greatly influencing regional developments.

230

These trends have been operating despite – or maybe because of – the impact of globalization, that complex process that is exerting a substantial influence on the domestic economies of Latin American countries. Globalization has been associated with 'structural adjustments' of which the liberalization processes affecting trade and foreign investments, particularly in matters concerning world finances and large transnational corporations, constitute an important part. As one author puts it:

> globalization as commonly discussed refers to the explosive growth in the past twenty-five years of huge multinational corporations and vast pools of capital that have crossed national borders and penetrated everywhere. This globalization is seen as largely the result of a parallel technological explosion in computerization, telecommunications, and rapid transportation.
>
> (Tanzer 1995:1)

Notwithstanding the above, economic integration is also on the rise in the 1990s after a brief sojourn in the 1960s. The formation of trade and economic blocs in the Americas are undoubtedly influencing the restructuring of trade and investment flows and production processes. The overall influence of both globalization and regional integration is difficult to assess. Whether they are contradictory processes in themselves or are complementary to each other is another matter to be considered. What will be the characteristics of economic integration in the Americas as a consequence of the present globalization process? Which sectors or social actors will be the main beneficiaries of these processes? What alternatives, if any, are being put in the context of regional integration for other sectors of civil society? What is the probable impact of this process for the main sectors of civil society, and for the development of trade union and social movements in South America? The course of action to be developed in the future will undoubtedly depend on a myriad of factors, some of which are presented in this chapter.

NAFTA AND MERCOSUR

With the establishment of NAFTA and MERCOSUR, regional integration in the Western Hemisphere has forcefully been put on the agenda of international relations.

NAFTA, which includes the USA, Canada and Mexico, is probably the first preferential and reciprocal trade arrangement between two developed countries and a developing country. Having formally begun to operate in 1994, NAFTA is looked upon as an institutional setting which is to favour a series of mostly US corporate interests via the expansion of their trade and investment opportunities (Buxedas 1995). So far it is no more than a free trade area; the establishment of a common external tariff, and the coordination of institutions and policies leading to a Common Market, have yet to be considered. As a matter of fact, while the free mobility of capital is one of the main objectives of NAFTA, the movement of labour, in particular of Mexican labour to the north, remains an important stumbling block in Mexican–USA relations. Nevertheless, according to some authors, NAFTA will eventually go well beyond the trade agreements signed by its member countries at present, to include commitments on trade in services, foreign investment practices, government procurement, intellectual property rights and, indirectly, environmental and labour standards (Bouzas 1995: 139).

Critical perspectives on NAFTA are evident:

'In North America regional economic integration has proceeded under entirely conservative auspices, rejecting high wages and continental regulation. Free trade undermines what is left of the mixed economy, which is seen as archaic and "protectionist" rather than deliberate and economically functional. NAFTA lacks even the embryonic safeguards of the EC: no regional development funds, no common regulations to prevent a "race to the bottom" in labor or environmental standards, and no movement towards democratic political and governmental institutions on a continental scale...NAFTA is merely one element of a larger problem: the disintegrating effects of globalization on our mixed economy and on our social contract.'

(Kuttner 1993: XIV)

NAFTA is also looked upon as a mechanism which is to eventually encompass the whole of Latin America, thereby enhancing the interests of the USA vis-à-vis other trade blocs in Europe (the EC) and the Far East. Negotiations tending towards a hemispheric regional free trade area were launched by the Enterprise for the America's Initiative in 1990 (Chudnovsky 1993) and at the Miami presidential summit of December 1994.

MERCOSUR is the other important trade bloc of the Western Hemisphere emerging to a great extent as a reaction to NAFTA. Important strides have been made since 1985 when the presidents of Argentina and Brazil expressed 'their firm political decision to accelerate their bilateral integration processes' (Ferrer 1996: 563). Formally established in 1991 with the signing of the Treaty of Asunción, it incorporated – apart from Brazil and Argentina, the original signatories – Uruguay and Paraguay. In 1996 Chile was also associated with MERCOSUR in a 4 + 1 relationship, after her accession to NAFTA was temporarily rejected. Apparently Bolivia is to follow suit.

MERCOSUR has the peculiarity of being an exclusively Third World trade and economic bloc. Yet, in terms of overall population, GNP and trade flows, as well as other social and economic indicators, MERCOSUR is one of the main economic blocs of the world.

Since 1991 intra-regional trade has been greatly liberalized and increased substantially, representing at present about 20 per cent of the overall trade of the total member countries. Advances have also been made towards the establishment of a common market. Nevertheless, important conflicts, points of negotiation and alternative plans persist with regards to the objectives and mechanisms whereby this regional grouping is to advance. These involve not only different business interests but also those of the numerous social actors of civil society as well.

ALTERNATIVE VIEWS OF MERCOSUR

MERCOSUR as a regional integration project is still in the making. At present MERCOSUR means different things to different people, implying different perspectives or visions concerning the very meaning of MERCOSUR itself.

According to one view, widely sustained by government officials in Argentina, MERCOSUR should be looked upon as simply one more step in a global liberalization process presently under way whereby 'the market' is to emerge as the main institutional setting and mechanism establishing necessary and sufficient rules for society as a whole. In line with liberalization trends and policies prevailing throughout Latin America including assorted 'structural adjustments' and the 'opening' of the national economies to world markets, it is assumed that MERCOSUR will create larger markets and therefore enhance free trade and capital movements.

According to Giarracca (1995: 1) 'as is usually presented in the media this integration vision is considered as undoubtedly a positive factor, essentially harmonious and liable to bring benefits to all. It tends to hide the social conflicts that these socio-economic processes inevitably induce' [my translation]. As a matter of fact, as Giarracca points out, analysts looking at MERCOSUR from a legal perspective, show a certain preoccupation because of the slowness with which the legal aspects required for the efficient solution of a series of conflicts are being considered. This is one area in which the market in itself will not solve many of the problems that have been emerging.

The end result of this process, according to this view, is that MERCOSUR will be eventually absorbed by NAFTA, thus leading to the formation of a continental American (North and South) economic bloc operating under the hegemony of the USA. This vision is compatible with the 'mainly trade' *(comercialista)* vision that is usually presented (Chudnovsky 1993: 495–498).

According to this view MERCOSUR is also looked upon as a mechanism that is to guarantee that the liberalization policies currently being implemented in member countries will not be reversed. As a matter of fact, this is one of the main reasons for the continued appeal MERCOSUR has for the defenders of a neo-liberal vision. Economic integration in itself is frequently considered by neo-liberals as anathema to overall liberalization measures. Only to the extent that MERCOSUR guarantees the continued existence of a relatively 'open' international system in line with wider domestic and international liberalization processes, will it apparently receive the support being accorded at present.

The World Trade Organization, more than MERCOSUR, has been given the role of maintaining certain (neo-liberal) rules of the game. As one author puts it:

> MERCOSUR is to have a positive effect to the extent that it is to concentrate on measures that will guarantee the multilateralization and liberalization of trade,...elimination of restrictions and subsidies,...maintenance of a low common external tariff, the reduction of (non-tariff) impediments to trade and the maintenance of a loyal international competitive framework.
>
> (Kesman 1996: 12)

233

It would not contribute to this vision if, via the maintenance of, for example, a high common external tariff, 'an import substitution industrialization strategy on a regional scale were enhanced' [my translation].

According to the neo-liberal vision MERCOSUR should emphasize intra-regional trade liberalization measures, reduce to a minimum the proposed common external tariff and other non-tariff impediments to free trade. Emphasis should thus be put on the 'trade creation' aspects of free trade zones and common markets, which would, presumably, contribute to revealing the comparative advantages of production in different countries or regions. This implies that limitations should be placed on 'trade diversion' (Viner) aspects of free trade areas. The free flow of capital and labour – according to neo-liberal prescriptions – should also be guaranteed as much as possible. Institutions should thus adapt to these prescriptions.

One wonders to what extent the adoption of global and national liberalization policies by the MERCOSUR member countries will contribute to a multilateralization of the world economy in which all countries and social and economic actors are to have more or less equal access to the benefits of trade and investments. Or as Shaikh (1994: 1) puts it:

> how does opening up a country to international competition through free trade affect its level of production and employment? Does free trade equalize competitive advantages, or does it worsen existing inequalities? Is *laissez-faire* the best way to participate in international trade, or is some degree of state support and management preferable?

Sometimes the means or instruments of public policy are confused with the objectives. While it is usually accepted that economic policy should contribute in general to the welfare of society, frequently it appears that the main objective of a policy is the liberalization and structural adjustment processes in themselves. Thus it is frequently assumed that any liberalization policy in itself would be beneficial for society as a whole.

None the less, prior to discussing this problem one can ask: to what extent does free trade effectively prevail in the world economy? The other question has to do with the impact of trade and capital liberalization measures forming part of the 'structural adjustments' being implemented at present on Third World economies and societies in general.

Luis Faroppa of Uruguay points out that despite the importance of the neo-liberal paradigm in the world today, since the 1980s measures have not tended towards increased free trade and the determination of comparative advantages world-wide. According to Faroppa, free trade and comparative advantages in conditions of perfect competition are not what prevail in the world today.

> Free trade...stopped being the best economic option given the massive diffusion,...of economies of scale, learning curves, the incorporation of technological innovations and certain business strategies, which until the late 1960s were considered to be exceptions to the rule.
>
> (Faroppa 1996: 19)

REGIONAL INTEGRATION IN LATIN AMERICA

According to Faroppa, the USA responded to competitive trade disadvantages *vis-à-vis* Japan and Europe and the export orientation of the Asian NICs by adopting restrictive and retaliatory measures. For example, the General Law on Trade and Competitivity of 1988 points out on the basis of certain unilateral interpretations what is to be considered disloyal trade. This leads to the establishment of temporal limitations on trade as well as diverse reprisal actions. Special unilateral trade concessions and agreements are sought, such as a certain organization of markets, compensatory rights and anti-dumping measures (ibid.: 20)

The EC also adopted a series of non-liberal measures such as exceptions and variable subsidies to imports under the Common Agricultural Policy, selective restrictions on imports, export subsidies, subsidies to sectors with problems and other trade restrictive measures. Korea, Japan and Taiwan also established important trade barriers. Furthermore, the tariff negotiations of GATT tended to privilege those sectors that were mostly of interest to the developed countries, while those 'sensitive' to the developed powers, mainly labour-intensive commodities, suffered the imposition of quotas, 'voluntary' restrictions on exports, guaranteed prices, anti-dumping measures and compensatory rights. Rather than visualizing an increase in the multilateralization of the world economy since the late 1960s, there seems to have been an increase in trade restrictions induced in large measure by the advanced capitalist powers, probably due in large measure to increased intercapitalist rivalry. As a consequence, since the late 1960s, the world economy has tended to become more unstable, as the previous hegemony of the USA in economic and financial matters has been put in question with the emergence as important world economic powers of Germany in Europe, and Japan in the Far East.

> The disintegration of the old order and the progressive emergence of a new one generated turbulence, disturbances and economic, financial, monetary and trade conflicts. All this elicited the creation of non-tariff barriers, special (tariff or tax) exemptions, quotas and 'voluntary' restrictions to exports, with the corresponding proliferation of international and regional conflicts.
>
> (ibid.: 20, my translation)

Thus the scenario which emerged in the world economy in recent years is not open and free trade as was to be expected. Non the less, it is one in which large multinational corporations reign supreme, and institutions are basically adapted to their needs. They are apparently the main beneficiaries of 'the market', in the world economy today. This is the context in which domestic liberalization policies concerning trade, foreign investments, and finances seems to be occurring in the MERCOSUR countries, in particular in present-day Argentina, and in Brazil in the wake of the application of the *Plan Real*.

But then there are other visions or paradigms that are presented with regard to MERCOSUR. One of these is the so-called 'industrialist' or *desarrollista* (developmentalist) perspective (Chudnovsky 1993; Porta 1996). According to this vision, economic integration should take on a more gradual and defensive course given the complexity of the numerous factors involved. This requires that negotiations be sustained by diverse sectoral interests, and that regional interests be defended *vis-à-vis* international interests. The 'rules of the game', according to this view, are varied, heterogeneous, and should be continously negotiated. A defensive vision of this economic bloc is usually presented, one permitting a more confrontative perspective with regards to overall globalization processes. In essence, it is the vision that appears to be prominent mainly among certain business and government circles in Brazil.

Thus the formation of MERCOSUR will require a long process whereby a series of agreements are to be reached between the different economic and social actors of member countries. Hence, there is a need to coordinate the policies of the member countries: macro-economic, industrial, financial, agrarian, technological, etc. (see Giarracca and Teubal 1995: 64). The main trend within this approach takes into consideration different business interests related to regional industrialization processes to the exclusion of other actors in civil society. Thus, emphasis is placed on trade and foreign investments, and the need to 'administer' the present regional integration process so as to take advantage of 'dynamic' competitive advantages which could favour local business interests, mainly the industrial ones.

This interpretation or vision of what MERCOSUR should be has much to do with how the economic integration process developed in Europe where a series of agreements and the coordination of policies were continously negotiated. According to this interpretation, emphasis should be placed on the medium and long run, on industrial restructuring, technological developments, and educational, scientific and cultural infrastructures. In this way, the pure market approach to regional integration would bring about excessively high economic and social costs, and therefore, should be avoided (Giarracca 1995: 3).

The need to coordinate policies arises when the internal economic space of MERCOSUR and certain interests associated with it tend to be consolidated. Coordinating policies would also increase the negotiating power of MERCOSUR in relation to the other trade blocs. Each of the member countries of MERCOSUR would thus be able to negotiate from a position of greater strength with the USA, Europe and Japan, or other areas of the Pacific.

A variant of this view states that an integration process also requires a certain commitment on behalf of the bulk of the social actors in civil society, many of whom so far have been excluded from this integration process. Integration processes have been discussed mainly in economic terms and are usually associated with the dominant business interests of member countries. But other social actors should also be considered if this integration process is to be legitimized. Labour, agrarian, cultural, legal matters, to mention only a few, will require not only the restructuring of certain parts of the productive structures but of the state apparatus and a series of other institutions as well.

The question which comes to mind is: how and to what extent could the formation of MERCOSUR become an opportunity for vast segments of the civil societies of member countries in that it could contribute to enhancing their rights and interests (see Portella de Castro 1995)? This aspect transcends the economic matters involving trade and foreign investments that have been prominent in most discussions concerning MERCOSUR.

These conflicting approaches to economic integration can thus also be related to the structural adjustment processes being implemented at present. Our focus is mainly on MERCOSUR and the alternative strategies that different approaches to the formation of this free trade area or common market are visualizing. The crux of the matter is not mainly the trade liberalization movement together with the establishment of a common external tariff for the region as a whole. As a matter of fact, previous regional integration movements, tended to focus partially on these matters. Nor is it only a question of creating an appropriate economic space for the purpose of attracting foreign investments – this apparently being one of the main objectives visualized at present (Guadagni 1995: 31–32). Surely attracting direct foreign investment flows following the expansion of the market, investing in one country with a view of increasing sales to a wider regional market, is of interest to certain corporate interests?

What does MERCOSUR mean to other segments of civil society? What about interests other than those business interests that already operate in the global economy? What about trade unions, medium and small-sized businesses, farmers and peasants, people in the professions? What about the other social movements in civil society: women, ecology, etc.? When consideration is given to these other social actors in society the focus on MERCOSUR changes somewhat.

DEVELOPING MERCOSUR

In the 1960s economic integration in Latin America was looked upon as a means to expand import substitution industrialization, confined by the limitations of the domestic market. What was visualized was a regional industrialization project that would encompass the whole of Latin America (Teubal 1961 1968). Nevertheless, the integration institutions that were established – the Latin American Free Trade Area (LAFTA), the Latin American Integration Association (ALADI) – never advanced beyond the adoption of certain trade liberalization measures.

In the 1970s and 1980s structural adjustments and economic restructuring became the main focus of economic policy. Import-substituting industrialization (ISI) began to be set aside as a 'regime of accumulation' and 'globalization' became an important force influencing policy issues.

The military coups in Brazil (1964), Chile, Uruguay (1973) and Argentina (1976) were important highlights in the development of the regional neo-liberal project. The emerging military regimes instituted the first deregulatory measures and adjustment policies tending towards a more 'open' economy. Thereafter, privatizations, deregulation (especially with regard to the flexibility of labour markets) and 'opening up' to the world economy became important aspects of 'structural adjustment' programmes. These did away with import substitution industrialization as a long-run development strategy. The adjustments required to reduce fiscal deficits and to pay the enormous foreign debt that had been accumulated became the main focus of macro policy (Teubal 1995, 1996a, 1996b).

These measures appeared in many respects complementary to the continental integration programme of the Initiative of the Americas, which proposed the establishment of a common North and South American economic bloc that would include the USA and Canada which previous Latin American proposals had excluded. Presumably a continental free trade area or common market would tend to favour mainly certain transnational corporations and banks of the USA.

MERCOSUR was thus approached as an alternative to a more inclusive economic integration programme encompassing the whole of the American continent. 'Since its inception MERCOSUR has been defined as a Brazilian and Argentinian response to the Bush Initiative, that had proposed extending trade agreements "from the Yukon to Patagonia"' [my translation] (Guilhon Albuquerque 1996: 15).

According to Guilhon Albuquerque, the creation of NAFTA did not change this perception. While it might be true that common strategic interests on the American continent exist and that these may be necessary for regional social and economic development and maintenance of peaceful relations, there are many impediments to the attainment of these overall objectives. According to this author, when approaching continental integration processes two main perceptions were present:

> one visualized the need to consolidate a continental economic bloc, in essence subordinated to the interests of the USA; the other required strengthening some of the sub-regional initiatives which would then permit a more effective process of negotiation or association to NAFTA.
>
> (ibid.: 15, my translation)

For historical reasons, the need to consolidate Brazilian–Argentinian relations, in both economic and political terms, became one of the main objectives of both countries' foreign policies despite conflicting views as to how they should cope with the superpowers, namely the USA. In recent decades the Brazilian government seems to have placed particular emphasis on strengthening sub-regional bonds in South America, and mainly with Argentina, as a means of maintaining her 'economic and political capacity to lead the sub Continent *vis-à-vis* the . . . USA or as an alternative to her' [my translation] (ibid.: 1996: 16). In this respect while Argentine diplomacy was much more pro-USA, Guido di Tella, the Minister of Foreign Affairs, joked about the need to maintain 'carnal relations' with the USA, it none the less gave priority to developing close economic and political relations with Brazil.

This is part of the background that helps explain some of the developments influencing Argentine–Brazilian relations in recent years.

In 1985 the governments of Argentina and Brazil signed an Economic Integration and Cooperation Programme [Programa de Integración y Cooperación Económica (PICE)] for the purpose of enhancing trade relations, industrial complementarity and technological cooperation, the latter mainly in the nuclear field. Eighteen bilateral protocols, including several annexes were signed. These were followed by an additional six protocols signed in the following two years. In 1989 a wider framework for the purpose of making these accords more permanent was established under the Treatise on Integration and Cooperation.

Both countries perceived the integration process as a means of becoming less dependent on fluctuations in the international market, boosting economic growth, bringing stability to bilateral trade, enhancing international negotiating capacity (i.e. in GATT) and attracting foreign investment (Ferrer 1991: 143).

In this phase integration assumed a gradual and selective bias. The PICE combined intensifying bilateral preferences accorded under the ALADI with sectoral negotiations, for the purpose of increasing intra-regional trade and industrial complementarity in some key branches of industry. Several of the protocols established mechanisms for a reduction of taxes or tariffs on specific trade products, the sequence and scope of the liberalization processes, as well as the norms that would protect these industries from disloyal competition or non-desired triangulations. At the time the areas where this methodology attained its most important results with regards to intra-regional trade were in capital goods, automobiles, and food (López and Porta 1995).

Global results seemed to have been quite successful although not as much as had been originally expected. Bilateral trade between Argentina and Brazil increased substantially in the late 1980s and expectations were that a new and more durable trade and production scenario would be established in the region.

Nevertheless while intra-regional trade increased in the late 1980s, Argentine–Brazilian integration processes were limited by the macro-economic instability and adjustment policies of that period. Many protocols remained ineffective, and the lack of coordination of industrial and technological policies that would enhance the dynamics of regional development were looked upon as important stumbling blocks (ibid.).

This was the scenario that prevailed in the early 1990s, when the governments of Argentina and Brazil, mainly for political reasons, decided to create MERCOSUR. Among the more immediate purposes of this new instrument of public policy was the intention to abandon the methodology of sectoral advances by changing to a scheme of greater generality.

In 1991 the Treaty of Asunción creating the Mercado Común del Sur (MERCOSUR) was signed. Member countries agreed to the establishment of a customs union in a period of no more than four years. A programme for the automatic liberalization of intra-regional trade was devised with the provision that it would be totally liberalized in a period of no more than four years. A common external tariff was also agreed upon. Certain benefits were accorded to the smaller countries of the union including more time for their automatic liberalization processes.

The formal establishment of MERCOSUR in 1991 had a significant impact on trade and regional integration processes. In agreeing to the formation of a customs union, the Treaty of Asunción transcended the free trade zones that had previously been negotiated. This meant that an automatic trade liberalization programme for intra-regional trade and a common external tariff would be defined in a period of no more than four years. For Argentina and Brazil this scheme would be completed by the end of 1994. While these measures were adopted rather rigidly, for example without contemplating asymmetries, regional, sectoral and macro-economic, subsequent negotiations and exceptions to the rule were adopted in many cases and the integration process proceeded quite successfully. The several safeguards that were also established gave greater flexibility to the whole process.

MERCOSUR: SOME BASIC DATA

Globally MERCOSUR has a total population of about 200 million inhabitants, the bulk of whom live in Brazil (158 million) followed by Argentina (34 million), Paraguay (4.4 million) and Uruguay (3.2 million). MERCOSUR also comprises most of the territory of South America, a total of 11.872 million square kilometers (see Table 10.1).

In 1995 total MERCOSUR GDP was estimated at $US981 billion which is quite high by Third World standards. More than two-thirds of total regional GDP belongs to Brazil, followed by Argentina. The GDP of Paraguay and Uruguay was relatively small in global terms. If income per capita is considered, Argentina stands out with the highest income per capita (more than $US8,000 per capita in 1995, though there is some question concerning government statistics on this matter), followed by Uruguay ($US5.000) and Brazil ($US4.300). In comparative terms Paraguay apparently has a much lower income per capita (though in the case of this country there is some question as to the magnitude of 'non-registered' income, which would imply a much higher income per capita).

In the early 1990s Argentina's GNP grew at an average of 5.3 per cent per annum, which was higher than the growth rates of Brazil, Uruguay and Paraguay. Nevertheless, Brazil and Paraguay in the 1970s and 1980s had grown much faster than Argentina and Uruguay who had suffered an important growth stagnation.

The value of MERCOSUR manufacturing production represented in 1993 about one-quarter of global GDP. The bulk of industry is located in Brazil followed by Argentina and Uruguay. Paraguay, in comparative terms, is hardly industrialized at all. Throughout the 1970s and 1980s Brazil developed a systematic industrialization policy. As a consequence Brazil has a dynamic industry sector related to certain 'modern' industries also associated with a greater export orientation of these. None the less, the share of manufacturing production of total GNP in Brazil is similar to that prevailing in Argentina and Uruguay (almost one-quarter of GDP). The average scale of production in terms of output or employment of Brazilian firms was much larger than in Argentina and Uruguay.

The MERCOSUR countries combined constitute a relatively important agricultural (including livestock) producer and exporter to the world economy. MERCOSUR agricultural production amounted to about $US64.5 billion in 1993, about 6.6 per cent of the regional GDP. For Brazil this ratio (agricultural production/GDP)

Table 10.1 MERCOSUR indicators

Concept	Unit of measure	Period	Argentina	Brazil	Paraguay	Uruguay	MERCOSUR
Total population	Million	1995	34.4	157.9	4.4	3.2	200.0
Area	thousand km²	1995	2767	8521	407	177	11872
GDP	billion $US	1995	280	678	8	16	982
GDP – growth rates	%	1991–95 average	5.3	2.6	3.2	3.9	3.8
GDP per-capita	$US	1995	8133	4345	1861	5015	4838
Agriculture production	million $US	1993	15330	46060	1660	1470	64520
Industrial production	million $US	1993	79000	164160	1590	3890	248640
Agriculture production/GDP	% (1986 prices)	1994	6.9	11.0 (92)	26.6 (93)	10.8	13.8
Industrial production/GDP	% (1986 prices)	1994	25.9	23.0 (92)	15.3 (93)	29.9	23.5
Exports	million $US	1995	20830	46500	1602 (94)	1913 (94)	70845
Exports/GDP	% (1986 prices)	1995	7.5	6.9	20.1 (94)	16.3 (94)	7.6
Imports	million $US	1995	19899	43300	2208 (94)	2786 (94)	68193
Imports/GDP	% (1986 prices)	1995	7.1	6.9	28.1 (94)	17.8 (94)	7.3
Balance of trade	millions of $US	1995	931	-3200	-606 (94)	-873 (94)	-3748
Current account – balance of payments	millions of $US	1994	-10074	-1451	-834	-258	-12617
Capital account – balance of payments	millions of $US	1994	10612	14836	344	413	26205
Foreign debt	billion $US	1994	75	151.5	1.3	8	235.8
Foreign debt/GDP	%	1994	26.6	23	16.2	52.1	24.0
Foreign debt/exports	%	1994	412	316	71	284	
Total interest payments/exports	%	1994	20.3	22.3	7.3	13.8	
Urban population	% of total population		87	77	49	89	78
Life expectancy at birth	years	1992	71	66	67	72	69
Birth rates	per 1000	1992	20	23	35	17	24
Infant mortality	per 1000 live births		29	57	36	20	36
Unemployment rate	%	1995	17.6	4.5	9.0 (94)	9.3	

Source: Instituto Nacional de Estadísticas y Censos, Instituto de Estudios Fiscales y Económicos and *Mercosur Journal* 1(4), Sept. 1996.

amounted to 11.0 per cent in 1992. In Argentina it was no more than 6.9 per cent in 1994 (7.3 per cent in 1995). This ratio increased to 10.8 per cent in Uruguay, for Paraguay in 1993 it amounted to 26.6 per cent, a proportion related to the latter country's lower degree of industrialization.

MERCOSUR's exports amounted to more than $US70 billion in 1995 or about 7 per cent of global GDP. Regional imports amounted to $US68 billion, a similar proportion of GNP. While total exports of member countries increased substantially in recent years, there are as yet great disparities with regard to the foreign trade ratios (FTR) (exports + imports/GDP) of the member countries. While the FTR of Argentina and Brazil amounted to between 15 and 16 per cent, that of Paraguay reached 60 per cent and for Uruguay it amounted to 35 per cent. Evidently, smaller countries are much more dependent on foreign trade than larger countries.

The combined foreign debt of MERCOSUR countries amounted to about $US 235 billion in 1994 representing 24 per cent of regional GDP. For Argentina foreign debt amounted to $US75 billion in 1994 representing 26.6 per cent of GNP; Brazil's foreign debt was about double that of Argentina (over $US151 billion in 1994) representing 23 per cent of GDP. Paraguay's foreign debt was comparatively much smaller (16.2 per cent of GNP) while that of Uruguay ($US8,075 million) represented 52.1 per cent of that country's GNP. Except for Paraguay, total foreign debt represented three and four times the value of each country's exports, though interest payments represented no more than 22.3 per cent of Brazilian and 20.3 per cent of Argentine exports.

Large social disparities also characterize MERCOSUR countries. The region as a whole is highly urbanized. More than 87 per cent of the total population live in localities of more than 2,000 inhabitants in Argentina. Urbanization amounted to 77 per cent of the population in Brazil and 89 per cent in Uruguay. Paraguay is the least urbanized of the MERCOSUR countries with only 49 per cent of its population living in urban areas. These trends also reflect the occupational structures of these countries, with Paraguay the country with the largest share of rural population, including an important peasant stratum.

Life expectancy in Argentina and Uruguay was somewhat higher than in Brazil and Paraguay. Birth and death rates of these two countries were also lower. Finally, unemployment in 1995 was much higher in Argentina than in other MERCOSUR countries.

In Table 10.2 some welfare indicators for the 1990s in comparison with the early 1980s are presented. As can be observed, the fall in income per capita for Argentina stands out in relation to how this indicator evolved in Brazil and Uruguay. None the less poverty rates are much higher, in comparative terms, in Brazil than in Argentina or Uruguay. A similar situation occurs with income distribution. In Argentina, as well, employment, real wages and social expenditures per capita have also fallen in recent years. These indicators denote that the social situation in Argentina has worsened substantially in recent years, though in the early 1980s it might have been better than in other MERCOSUR countries.

Table 10.2 MERCOSUR: welfare indicators

Country	Income per capita	Poverty rates (% of households)		Concentration of income in urban areas (Gini)[a]	Labour force employment (indices)[b]	Real wages (indices)	Social expenditure per capita (indices)
		Total	Urban				
Argentina							
1980	100	9	5[c]	0.365[c]	100	100	100
1990	72		16[c]	0.423[c]	88	77	75
1992	85		10[c]	0.408[c]	85	79	89
1994	95				72	78	
Brazil							
1979	100	39	30	0.493	100	100	100[d]
1990	98	43	39	0.535	94	116	125
1994	100				85	108	
Uruguay							
1981	100	11	9	0.379		100	100
1990	90		12	0.353		85	101
1992	101		8	0.301		91	118[e]
1994	108					96	

Source: CEPAL (1995).
Notes: [a] Estimated on the basis of the distribution of income per capita of households grouped by deciles.
[b] Percentage of non-agricultural labour force in formal activities.
[c] Greater Buenos Aires Area.
[d] 1980.
[e] 1991.

INTEGRATION STRATEGIES WITHIN MERCOSUR

MERCOSUR was set up in a period when a new 'regime of accumulation' as a consequence of the application of 'structural adjustments' had been developing throughout the region, although there were important differences between countries in the application of these programmes.

In this respect the case of Brazil stands out in relation to the other MERCOSUR countries. The military regime of that country, despite having destroyed the 'populist state' in the 1960s, increased the influence of the state apparatus over the economy. Funds were invested in infrastructures and foreign investments were oriented towards diverse areas of industry while protected markets for industry were maintained and an industrial exports strategy was sustained (Portella de Castro 1995: 2). Since the 1960s the industrial structure of Brazil has expanded and diversified, basically due to the development of metallurgical and chemical industries oriented to the domestic market which grew rapidly in the 1971–80 period. Traditional industries had more modest growth rates. In the 1975–80 period productivity increased at an average of between 3 and 3.5 per cent per annum for São Paolo industry. This occurred in the context of substantial protectionist barriers (Beckerman 1995: 12).

243

Industrial growth in the 1980s was somewhat slower, despite Brazilian industry's adaptation to a more 'outward-looking' strategy. Nevertheless, in world comparative terms a certain technological backwardness has characterized this industrialization process. The distance between modern and traditional industries grew in the 1970s due to the modernization of the former. In the 1980s this trend was reversed due to a certain stagnation of previously dynamic industries. Industries based on natural resources, energy and cheap labour catered increasingly to the world markets.

These policies extended import substitution in Brazil and had an important effect on industrial restructuring. Brazil emerged in the 1970s as an important Newly Industrializing Country (NIC) in many ways similar to those of South-East Asia. As Portella de Castro points out:

> These differences undoubtedly were reflected in negotiations tending towards the formation of the MERCOSUR in 1991, which was visualized as an integrated and protected trade area *vis-à-vis* other blocks. The motivations and nature of this Treaty, that ever since has been modified, probably constituted the last attempt in the region to strengthen a *desarrollista* model in opposition to the new configurations emerging in the international market.
> (Portella de Castro 1995: 2, my translation)

Therefore, in the case of Brazil, a strong entrepreneurial industrial bourgeoisie acquired an important power base in the 1970s. The *desarrollista* policies of the Brazilian government had much to do with the influence exerted by these sectors of the Brazilian establishment. Their power within the establishment continues to be important, having managed to forge an important export strategy and hence become important beneficiaries of MERCOSUR. MERCOSUR is seen as a wider market for their industrial exports and as a means for enhancing their regional power *vis-à-vis* Europe, the USA and Japan.

The case of Argentina is substantially different from that of Brazil. While industrialization in Argentina was begun several decades ago, and had consolidated itself substantially by the early 1970s, the military coup of 1976 established the beginnings of a new 'regime of accumulation' in which liberalization policies went counter to ISI and the alliances that had sustained this process in the 1950s and 1960s. Hence, policies based on the *concertación* or *pacto social* (social pact) as between labour unions and business interests, which benefited domestic market-oriented industries were set aside. These alliances tended to combine high domestic wages and domestic markets favouring the development of wages in goods industries. This alliance appeared as a threat to the more traditional establishment interests, the more conservative agrarian interests and foreign capital. The end result of this was a change in strategy which included a policy of deliberate de-industrialization. The economic and social basis of ISI policies had to be set aside, because – amongst other factors – they appeared to threaten traditional establishment and transnational interests.

Adjustments were begun and Argentina became substantially de-industrialized, while the power of finance capital increased and become one of the main beneficiaries, together with the large economic groups of these changes in policy. The importance assigned to industrialization in long-run strategies, in particular in relation to medium and small business, was minimized by succeeding governments, a situation that differed substantially from that prevailing in Brazil in the early 1990s when MERCOSUR was launched.

The 1980s were a 'lost decade' for Argentina. A series of indicators reflect the negative performance of her economy: GDP fell 9.4 per cent, industrial GDP 24 per cent, income per capita 24 per cent and investments by about 70 per cent. Unemployment began to rise, employment in industry fell 30 per cent and real wages in industry by 1990 had fallen 24 per cent in relation to the beginning of the decade. Income distribution also became more regressive in relation to the late 1970s.

While de-industrialization became the notion of the day, industrial structures became highly heterogeneous (Kosacoff 1995: 21–28) affecting some of the main traditional industries that had developed previously under import substitution strategies: light metallurgical industries, mechanical industries, textiles, wood products and non-metallic metal industries. Instead of restructuring industry and reorienting it towards world markets overall, macro policies went counter to this strategy.

Nevertheless, some basic industries did grow in the 1970–90 period: basic steel and iron products, the chemical industry, etc. Both these sectors represented some 30 per cent of industrial GNP in 1990. Finally there is agro-industry. Here the situation was quite heterogeneous: some agro-industries did not perform well – meat packing, sugar mills – others such as oilseeds and milk products were substantially expanded. Overall, the food industry increased its participation in industrial GDP from 21 per cent in 1970 to almost 27 per cent in 1990 (ibid.: 30).

At present Brazil is by far the most industrialized country of MERCOSUR with an industry which is also much more dynamic. Argentina has comparative advantages mainly in certain agro-industries, though Brasil is also an important exporter of fruit juice and oilseeds.

REGIONAL INTEGRATION PROCESSES WITHIN MERCOSUR

Economic integration of the MERCOSUR countries is based on the increased interaction of Argentina and Brazil. These two countries absorb 97.7 per cent of regional GNP, 98.0 per cent of industrial GNP, and 95 per cent of regional foreign trade. Thus, Argentinian–Brazilian relations constitute the basis of the MERCO-SUR economic integration process (Lavagna 1996: 556–564).

In this process two periods are usually considered. In the first phase (1985–91) when a series of sectoral negotiations and agreements were carried out between Argentina and Brazil which resulted in the signing of twenty-three sectoral protocols tending mostly to increase bilateral trade. Whether specifically due to these agreements, or because of other reasons, and despite the great disparity in macro-economic policies, intra-regional trade between Argentina and Brazil increased substantially. Exports by Argentina to MERCOSUR expanded fom $US667 million in 1985 to almost $US2000 million in 1991 when MERCOSUR was formally established. Brazilian exports to MERCOSUR also increased from almost $US 1000 million in 1985 to $US2300 million in 1991. The exports of Uruguay and Paraguay also followed a similar trend in this period. Intra-regional trade continued increasing thereafter. Argentine exports to MERCOSUR increased to $US4.8 billion in 1994, and those of Brazil reached almost $US6 billion in that same year. Throughout this period MERCOSUR increased its share of the exports of member countries. MERCOSUR absorbed only 8 per cent of Argentina's exports in 1985 while in 1994 she absorbed more than 30 per cent. MERCOSUR was comparatively less important to Brazil; none the less regional exports increased from 4.6 per cent of total exports in 1985 to 13.6 per cent in 1994. A much greater export dependency was denoted for Paraguay and Uruguay. For the former, MERCOSUR exports represented 27 per cent of total exports in 1985 and 52 per cent in 1994. For Uruguay the share of exports increased from almost 26 per cent in 1985 to 46.7 per cent in 1994. Regional exports of MERCOSUR countries represented 5.6 per cent of member country's world exports in 1985, and 19.4 per cent of these exports in 1994 (see Table 10.3).

Thus, if the share of intra-regional trade is given as an indicator of the degree of economic integration, then MERCOSUR has been advancing quite substantially towards this goal in the past decade. After the Ouro Prieto meeting of 1994 a more 'flexible' customs union was negotiated, and the need to coordinate macro-economic policies was put on the agenda in a much more forceful way (Lavagna 1996: 17). The question is, what policies are to be coordinated in the future and in response to whose interests in civil society?

LABOUR AND SOCIAL MOVEMENTS

Certain aspects of the economic integration process of MERCOSUR could create a series of social problems, for example, those related to employment in member countries. The rules of the game with regards to labour have not been negotiated regionally. This means that even less than NAFTA the safeguards required to avoid a 'race to the bottom' in matters concerning labour and social matters in general, have not as of yet been established.

The restructuring of industry in Argentina, to a large extent due to the 'opening' of the economy, led to an increase in imports, and contributed somewhat to a dislocation of activity. The different disputes with regard to productive regimes, for example, related to the automobile industry agreements, did not consider the possible dislocations which might emerge with regard to labour markets. Furthermore, 'each time more definitions regarding production regimes and labour regulations are being subordinated to the offer made to attract foreign investments' (Portella de Castro 1995: 5).

In this sense globalization of production as practised at present by large transnationals implies that the enormous power wielded by them permits greater facilities,

Table 10.3 MERCOSUR exports, 1980–93 (in $US million and as a percentage)

	Argentina		Brazil		Paraguay		Uruguay		Total	
	To MERCOSUR	MERCOSUR as percentage of total exports	To MERCOSUR	MERCOSUR as percentage of total exports	To MERCOSUR	MERCOSUR as percentage of total exports	To MERCOSUR	MERCOSUR as percentage of total exports	Total to MERCOSUR	MERCOSUR as percentage of total exports
1980	1,136,066	14.2	1,810,395	9.1	124,582	40.2	374,884	32.9	3,445,927	11.7
1981	892,131	9.8	1,702,040	7.4	131,820	44.6	296,987	24.4	3,022,978	9.0
1982	828,008	10.9	1,126,796	5.7	146,908	44.5	265,750	26.0	2,367,462	8.2
1983	522,184	6.7	991,916	4.6	88,414	34.2	220,553	21.1	1,823,067	5.9
1984	655,287	8.1	1,320,947	4.9	100,537	30.1	238,846	22.8	2,315,617	6.4
1985	667,331	8.0	989,109	3.9	81,959	27.0	229,034	25.8	1,967,433	5.6
1986	894,330	13.1	1,174,910	5.3	132,859	57.3	394,180	34.9	2,596,279	8.5
1987	768,209	12.1	1,305,274	5.0	127,158	36.0	340,319	27.0	2,540,960	7.5
1988	875,104	9.6	1,642,052	4.8	155,139	30.4	335,935	24.1	3,008,230	6.7
1989	1,428,472	13.9	1,367,982	4.0	388,057	38.4	525,702	32.9	3,710,213	7.8
1990	1,832,941	14.8	1,318,467	4.2	379,381	39.6	590,787	34.9	4,121,576	9.9
1991	1,976,700	16.5	2,308,670	7.3	259,451	35.2	551,500	34.4	5,096,321	11.1
1992	2,236,800	19.0	4,128,021	11.4	246,400	37.5	622,000	36.5	7,233,221	14.4
1993	3,683,967	28.1	5,395,235	14.0	276,283	39.8	698,800	42.5	10,054,285	18.6
1994	4,803,732	30.1	5,921,474	13.6	424,845	52.0	895,705	46.7	12,045,757	19.4

Source: Kosacoff (1995) INDEC, MERCOSUR: Sinópsis Estadística, Vol. 2, 1995, Buenos Aires.

not only over production units in the member countries (due to enormous access to capital and resources) but also over raw materials and labour sources. From the perspective of a large transnational the possibility of 'assigning' resources in a more 'efficient' way is one of the advantages of operating in this wider economic space. But this is not necessarily in the interests of each of the communities or of the labour market.

MERCOSUR represents an enormous labour market of more than 90 million people who none the less have differing characteristics in different countries and are highly segmented. In all of these countries 'structural adjustment' programmes have been applied so that the 'flexibility' of labour markets has been greatly expanded. This change in labour regimes induced real wage reductions, both direct and indirect. In all of the MERCOSUR countries employment in industry has fallen, in Brazil industry still represents about 30 per cent of the labour force; this percentage is much less in the other MERCOSUR countries. Unemployment in all its forms has also increased and remains at very high levels in the mid-1990s. In Uruguay, Paraguay and Brazil open unemployment affected 8–10 per cent of the labour force, in Argentina it has recently (1996) reached record levels: over 18 per cent. If underemployment and other measures of unemployment are also considered, these percentages increase substantially; in Argentina it is estimated that about one-third of the labour force suffers one or another form of unemployment. Real wages have also been falling although in some labour categories in particular Argentina has higher wages than Brazil. Finally it is estimated that about one-third of the MERCOSUR labour force is non-registered wage labour, i.e. does not receive the social benefits required by law. This also implies that their employers do not contribute the funds which by law they are obliged to contribute to the appropriate institutions of the state, and that labour protective laws are not being observed.

All these matters have induced to some extent the need to regulate and coordinate among the MERCOSUR countries the different laws and rules concerning labour. In this matter trade unions have an important say, and have begun to coordinate their actions between the different countries. A Coordinadora de Centrales Sindicales del Cono Sur (Coordinating Committee of Trade Union Federations for the Southern Cone Countries) has been established and in this organization the official federations of labour of MERCOSUR countries are represented.

CONCLUSIONS

MERCOSUR is still an open project. The path that is to be followed in the future is still open. The course that will eventually be taken will depend on many factors, but basically on political events and the prospects for social movements and how they operate in the near future. In this chapter, we have pointed out the problem between MERCOSUR as a neo-liberal project, as simply one more step towards the full liberalization of Latin American trade and capital movements in response to the corporate and political interests of the USA vs a more *desarrollista* and 'industrialist' project that would imply catering much more to certain regional interests.

Nevertheless economic integration has continued to advance. New rules of the game are being established between member countries and such factors as the increase in intra-regional trade reflects the importance this economic integration project has acquired. But as pointed out in this chapter, all this does not necessarily mean that the benefits of greater integration in the context of MERCOSUR will benefit civil society as a whole. An example of this is what is occurring with regard to the labour markets. Throughout MERCOSUR countries unemployment has increased as a consequence of the application of neo-liberal policies. Nevertheless the rules of the game in labour matters have not as yet been fully coordinated by the trade unions of the member countries. This is an example which points out the need to coordinate social policies, but more than that, the need to coordinate the actions of social movements throughout the MERCOSUR countries.

BIBLIOGRAPHY

Beckerman, W. (1995) *Growth, the Environment and the Distribution of Incomes*, Aldershot: Edward Elgar.

Bouzas, R. (1995) 'Preferential trade liberalisation in the Western hemisphere: NAFTA and beyond', in Jan Joost Teunissen (ed.) *Regionalism and the Global Economy: The Case of Latin America and the Caribbean*, The Hague: Fondat: 132–153.

Buxedas, M. (1995) 'MERCOSUR y TLC: convergencias, divergencias y negociaciones', in S. Cloquel and E. Santos (eds) *Argentina frente a los procesos de integración regional. Los efectos sobre el agro*. Rosario: Homo Sapiens Ediciones: 79–94.

CEPAL (1995) *15 años de desempeño económico. América Latina y el Caribe*, 1980–1995.

Chudnovsky, D. (1993) 'El futuro de la integración hemisférica: el MERCOSUR y la Iniciativa para las Américas', *Desarrollo Económico. Revista de ciencias sociales* 32(128): 483–510.

Faroppa, L. (1996) 'De la multilateralización a la regionalización', in Instituto Nacional de Estadísticas y Censos (INDEC), *MERCOSUR, Sinópsis estadística* 2: 18–31.

Fernández Jilberto, A. and Hogenboom, B. (1996) 'Mexico's integration in NAFTA: neo-liberal restructuring and changing political alliances', in A. Fernández Jilberto and A. Mommen (eds) *Liberalization in the Developing World: Institutional and Economic Changes in Latin America, Africa and Asia*, London and New York: Routledge: 138–60.

Ferrer, A. (1991) 'Argentina y Brazil: ajuste, crecimiento e integración', *Comercio exterior* 41(2): 135–44.

Ferrer, A. (1996) 'MERCOSUR: trayectoria, situación actual y perspectivas', *Desarrollo económico. Revista de Ciencias Sociales*, 35 (140): 560–75.

Giarracca, N. (1995) 'Globalización, integración regional y transformaciones en la agricultura argentina', paper presented to the Encuentro Regional de Sociología Agraria, Montevideo, 7, 8 December (unpublished).

Giarracca, N. and Teubal, M. (1995) 'Los pequeños productores cañeros y la integración económica con el Brasil', in M. Bekerman and A. Rofman (eds) *Integración y Sociedad en el Cono Sur*, Buenos Aires: Espacio Editorial: 61–84.

Guadagni, A. (1995) 'El MERCOSUR y los desafíos del futuro', text of a talk given at Fundación Omega, Buenos Aires, on 9 November 1995.

Guilhon Albuquerque, J.A. (1996) 'O MERCOSUL e a integração econômica no continente', in Instituto Nacional de Estadísticas y Censos (INDEC), *MERCOSUR: Sinópsis Estadística*, 2.

Kesman, C. (1996) 'El MERCOSUR y la multilateralización del comercio mundial', in Instituto Nacional de Estadísticas y Censos (INDEC), *MERCOSUR: Sinópsis estadística*, 2. 9–13.

Kosacoff, B. (ed.) (1995) *Hacia una nueva estrategia exportadora. La experiencia Argentina, el marco regional y las reglas multilaterales*, Buenos Aires: Universidad Nacional de Quilmes.

Kuttner, R. (1993) 'Forward', in R. Grinspun and M. Cameron (eds) *The Political Economy of North American Free Trade*, New York: St. Martin's Press: xi–xv.

López, A. and Porta, F. (1995) 'Nuevas modalidades de inserción international: el MERCO-SUR', in B. Kosacoff (ed.) *Hacia una nueva estrategia exportadora. La experiencia Argentina, el marco regional y las reglas multilaterales*, Buenos Aires: Universidad Nacional de Quilmes.

Porta, F. (1996) 'La integración de la Argentina en el MERCOSUR', in M. S. Portella de Castro, 'MERCOSUL, Mercado de trabalho e desafios para ação sindical regional', paper presented at the conference of the Latin American Studies Association, Washington, DC, September.

Portella de Castro, M. (1995) 'MERCOSUL, Mercado de trabalho e desafios para ação sindical regional', paper presented at the conference of the Latin American Studies Association, Washington, DC, September.

Shaikh, A. (1994) *Free Trade, Unemployment, and Economic Policy*, New School for Social Research, Graduate Faculty, Department of Economics, mimeo.

Tanzer, M. (1995) 'Globalizing the economy: the influence of the International Monetary Fund and the World Bank', *Monthly Review* 47(4): 1–36.

Teubal, M. (1961) 'Europa y Latinoamérica ante la integración económica', *Desarrollo económico. Revista de ciencias sociales*, 1(3): 97–122.

Teubal, M. (1968) 'The failure of Latin America's economic integration' in J. Petras and M. Zeitlin (eds) *Latin America: Reform or Revolution?*, Fawcett World Library.

Teubal, M. (1995) 'Exitos e fracassos dos ajustes neoliberais', *Tempo e presença*, 17: 284, Río de Janeiro: Nova Fase: 14–17.

Teubal, M. (1996a) 'Structural adjustment, democracy and the state in Argentina', in A. Fernández Jilberto and A. Mommen (eds) *Liberalization in the Developing World: Institutional and Economic Changes in Latin America, Africa and Asia*, London: Routledge: 52–60.

Teubal, M. (1996b) 'Modelli economici e crisi politica', *La Terra vista dalla luna. Rivista dell'intervento sociale*, 13.

11

THE POLITICS OF OPEN REGIONALISM AND NEO-LIBERAL ECONOMIC INTEGRATION IN LATIN AMERICA

The case of Chile and Mexico

Alex E. Fernández Jilberto and Barbara Hogenboom

INTRODUCTION

The political legitimation of neo-liberal restructuring, and of the political regime that it accompanies, towards civil society depends on the success in transnationalizing the economy. In the case of Mexico, entry into the North American Free Trade Agreement (NAFTA) has been very important in this respect. For Chile, association with the Mercado Común del Sur (Common Market of the South, MERCOSUR) and, possibly later on, entry into NAFTA seems to be the route followed. This chapter studies the regionalization process of both economies and the effects on the nature of the political regime and the relations between state and civil society.

Open regionalism is the new dominant strategy for the economic integration of Latin American countries. This neo-liberal approach to insertion into the world economy by means of regionalization constitutes a clear shift away from the variant of Keynesianism that had dominated in Latin America: import-substitution industrialization (ISI). Instead of a focus on national industrialization, efforts are now directed at industrialization on a regional scale. Open regionalism is the attempt to link the economic interdependency of the Latin American countries to liberalization and deregulation. This policy grants a fundamental role to market mechanisms in the assignation of resources in the production process. At the same time, open regionalism is directed at regulating and controlling the integration of Latin America in the globalization process, and improving the region's international competitiveness.

The consolidation of neo-liberal policies in Latin America, which in the 1980s were initiated by military regimes (Chile) or civil authoritarian regimes (Mexico), has coincided with fundamental political changes. The old populist political parties like the Partido Democrata Cristiano (Christian Democratic Party, PDC) and the

Partido Socialista (Socialist Party, PS) in Chile and the Partido Revolucionario Institucional (Institutional Revolutionary Party, PRI) in Mexico have been transformed into neo-liberal parties. Moreover, the shift of development model has profoundly affected the state form, relations between state and society, and civil society in Chile and Mexico, as well as in the rest of Latin America.

Depoliticization of the debate on development and economic policy; deepened transnationalization of the economy; consolidation of neo-liberal relations between state and civil society – these are all goals that are shared by the political and bureaucratic elites of Chile and Mexico. The political homogenization of these elites has been linked to profound changes in the ideology and state structure. This neo-liberal consensus enabled a fundamental economic restructuring and substituted Keynesianism, which for four decades had made up the basis of populism and ISI in Latin America. As opposed to current tendencies, populist elites combined the aspiration of self-sustained industrialization with nationalist policies, and attempted to stress the position of the state in the international political arena during the Cold War period through a strategy of non-alignment.

The former political elites' mission of a state creating society, politics and the economy was supported by different political regimes. The regime of Mexico was characterized by a state-party system with a political arena that was limited to a fractional struggle within the PRI. The system's relations with civil society took the form of corporatism, clientelism, patronage, and *caciquismo*, which conserved and reproduced the power structures embedded in the values of the Mexican revolution. In Chile, populism was to preserve the balance between democracy, participation and industrialization. This approach culminated in the governments of the 'Revolution in Freedom' headed by the PDC in the 1964–70 period, and of the 'Chilean Route to Socialism' of the Unidad Popular of 1970–73. The political arena was characterized by unrestricted participation of centre and left-wing, while the right was weak and lacked the capacity for electoral victory. Gradually, the right became more anti-democratic and authoritarian, as demonstrated by the military coup of 1973.

The radical transformation of the populist state into the neo-liberal state in Chile and Mexico was at the beginning a consequence of the external debts of both countries in the 1980s. The structural adjustment policy required by the International Monetary Fund (IMF) in return for new loans entailed in the long run a transfer of political sovereignty of the state to international economic organizations. In this context, both the old PRI bureaucracy and the military bureaucracy of the Pinochet regime lost control over their economic policy, and had to comply increasingly with the international requirements of neo-liberal restructuring.

In both countries, the old bureaucracy saw the dismantling of the economic and political model as external support for the rising neo-liberal technocracy. For the PRI this meant a shift of power in favour of the neo-liberal *técnicos*, and a virtual defeat of the populist *políticos*. The Mexican technocracy culminated under President Carlos Salinas de Gortari (1988–94), whose task it was to make the neo-liberal transformation irreversible through Mexico's entry into NAFTA. In Chile, the hegemony of the 'Chicago Boys' started during the military regime and could immediately count on the sympathy of the military bureaucracy. This bureaucracy saw neo-liberalism as a means of abandoning the concept of development based on industrialization, and instead focus on growth based on comparative advantages of primary products. With their strong anti-communist ideology, the military regime understood that a less strategic role of the industrial sector implied an equally less strategic role of the working class in politics.

The de-industrialization that followed the removal of protectionist measures has indeed produced a weakening of the labour unions' power. This process has been reinforced by the elimination of populist functions of the state, which previously functioned as regulator of social inequalities and as system of social integration and mobility. The privatization of education, social security and health put an end to the role of the state concerning the social and political demands of the labour move-ment. Simultaneously, the reduction of social functions of the state harmed the relation with the middle class, who had been strong supporters of the populist state. Numerous civil servants lost their jobs (e.g. 95,000 in Chile up to 1990 (Tironi 1990: 15)) and ended up in small entrepreneurship. As a result of these trends, the middle class started to identify themselves more with the labour movement.

The social segmentation that has been produced by the substitution of Keynesian populism by neo-liberalism has provoked instability of the state. Both in Chile and Mexico this has been expressed by a growing lack of legitimacy of the political regime. The PRI and Mexico's state-party system suffered a major crisis after the collapse of Salinas's political prestige linked to the assassinations of the president and the general secretary of the PRI in 1994. In the case of Chile, the political defeat of the dictatorship in the presidential referendum of 1988 and the presidential elections of 1989 were a result of the increasing social inequalities and the regime's incapacity to politically legitimate neo-liberal restructuring. The none the less con-servative and neo-liberal character of the successive civil regime can partly be explained by the authoritarian regime's position in the negotiations on the transition to democracy. While popular resistance was violently repressed, the military only negotiated with the centre-right opposition and restricted the future powers of the left-wing opposition. In the light of regime instability, the current political elites of Chile and Mexico have been stressing a rhetoric of pragmatism and realism, and a discourse of 'governability'. By means of the latter, they aim to create the political conditions to regain the confidence of international capital in their policy.

The structure of this chapter is as follows. First, we take a look at open regionalism and the recent flexibility of the labour market in Latin America, comparing these trends with earlier initiatives for regional economic integration. Next, we analyse the political transformation that accompanied the process of economic liberalization and regionalization in Chile and Mexico. The section on options for integration, then, describes the reasons for the regionalization paths as chosen by the two countries. The following section pays attention to the reaction of Chile's and Mexico's corporate sector, labour unions and environmental organiza-tions to the government integration strategies. Finally, in the conclusions, we discuss the prospects for further regionalization of Chile and Mexico, and the whole Latin American region.

OPEN REGIONALISM IN LATIN AMERICA

Neo-liberal restructuring in Latin America has been redefined and democratized through the concept of 'productive transformation with equity' of the United Nations Comisión Económica para América Latina (Economic Commission for Latin America and the Caribbean, CEPAL) (CEPAL 1990). This redefinition followed the enormous social costs of the structural adjustment policies of the 1980s implemented by dictatorial and authoritarian regimes which put a lot of effort in to defeating Keynesianism. With its new concept, CEPAL attempted to introduce a progressive social equity approach to decrease the economic inequalities ('social debt') that entailed the new development model. According to this concept, the main objective of regional development is growth contributing to income distribution in order to consolidate the democratization process, within a context of improving the environmental situation. Deepened insertion into the global economy, regionalization to regulate this insertion, and flexibility of the labour market have been presented as the major conditions for 'social equity'.

During the 1980s, the Gross Domestic Product (GDP) of Latin America grew by an annual 1.2 per cent, and went up to 3.4 per cent between 1990 and 1994. This growth was the result of Latin America's increased exports, which expanded from 14 per cent in 1980 to 21 per cent in 1990 and 23 per cent in 1994 (CEPAL 1995: 28). These figures support CEPAL's view that 'productive transformation with equity' can only be sustained by extending the economic integration of Latin America into the world market by means of a systematic policy of promoting exports and attracting external investments, while strengthening regional economic integration.

Open regionalism is the idea of regionalization and globalization of the Latin American economy as one inseparable process. Open regionalism is based on two pillars: first, on growing economic interdependency at the regional level, urged by various Latin American integration agreements which aim to increase competitiveness in the world market; second, on regionalization of national private capital elements that have been strengthened by the selling of public enterprises (CEPAL 1994). In addition, open regionalism serves as a strategy of regulation, and as a shelter against the protectionist tendencies of other regional economic blocs.

The trade strategies of Mexico and Chile have been inspired by open regionalism. This can be seen by the integration of Mexico into NAFTA, Chile's possible entry into this free trade zone, and their membership of the Asia Pacific Economic Cooperation (APEC). The creation of the MERCOSUR is another example of open regionalism in Latin America. Important elements for the success of the new integration model are privatization of public enterprises and liberalization of the labour market. These changes have been taking place within a depoliticized debate on economic development.

The consensus on the neo-liberal character of bloc formation in Latin America was previously legitimized by what has been called 'the new neo-liberal democracies' and the concept of the 'lost decade', referring to the sharp decline in development during the 1980s. The regional real per capita product of 1989, for instance, equalled that of 1976. Latin America faced the beginning of the 1990s with the effects of its external debt and the unsuitability of the composition of its exports with the structure of external demand. Added to this are its obsolete capital scheme and physical infrastructure, the incapacity to assimilate international technological changes, the deterioration of financial capacities of the countries, growing social inequalities, an enormous increase in unemployment and underemployment, inefficient and inaccurate exploitation of natural resources, and environmental decay.

Substitution of Keynesian integration

Latin American experiences with economic integration are not new (see Table 11.1). A contradictory and only partially successful attempt at regional economic integration was undertaken with the creation of the Asociación Latinoamericana de Libre Comercio (Latin American Free Trade Association, ALALC) at the beginning of the 1960s. Later on, in 1980, a similarly weak initiative was undertaken with the creation of the Asociación Latinoamericana de Integración (Latin American Integration

Table 11.1 Latin America: regional economic integration initiatives, 1960–94

Name	Year	Participants
Latin American Free Trade Association (Asociación Latinoamericana de Libre Comercio, ALALC)	1960	Argentina, Bolivia, Brazil, Chile, Colombia, Ecuador, Mexico, Paraguay, Peru, Uruguay and Venezuela
Central American Common Market (Mercado Común Centro Americano, MCCA)	1960	Costa Rica, El Salvador, Guatemala, Honduras, Nicaragua and Panama
Andean Group (Grupo Andino)	1969	Bolivia, Chile, Ecuador, Peru and Venezuela
Economic Community of the Caribbean (Comunidad Económica del Caribe, CARICOM)	1973	Small island states of the Caribbean[a]
Latin American Integration Association (Asociación Latinoamericana de Integración, ALADI)	1980	Argentina, Bolivia, Brazil, Chile, Colombia, Ecuador, Mexico, Paraguay, Peru, Uruguay and Venezuela
Common Market of the South (Mercado Común del Sur, MERCOSUR)	1991	Argentina, Brazil, Paraguay and Uruguay
North American Free Trade Agreement (NAFTA)	1994	Canada, Mexico and the United States

Note: [a] Antigua, Barbados, Guyana, Jamaica, Trinidad and Tobago, Grenada, Dominica, St. Lucia, St. Vincent, Montserrat, St. Kitts-Nevis-Anguilla, and Belize.

Association, ALADI). Both organizations were meant to deal with three problems. First, the formation of the European Economic Community (EEC) in 1957 was thought to pose the threat of closing the European market to Latin American agricultural products. Second, it was necessary to renew and extend the agreements on preferential goods between Latin American countries in order to take advantage of the most-favoured-nation clause that was confirmed by the General Agreement on Tariffs and Trade (GATT). Supported by article XXIV of the GATT, the creation of a free trade area was aimed at. Third, the stagnation and crisis of the ISI model became apparent in the early 1960s. Regional integration and thereby widening the internal market was perceived as one of the solutions to the crisis, as it was supposed to lead to regional industrialization in which each country would specialize in certain branches, reducing the costs of capital goods. This process would increase the profitability of capital and stimulate the process of accumulation, while also supporting state enterprises.

The crisis of models of Keynesian industrialization and the collapse of international Keynesianism was not simply the result of the failure of the early initiatives of Latin American integration. The 'new dependency' stemming from the strategy of multinational companies (MNCs) to evade Latin American protectionism also played a role in this respect. This strategy implied the installation of production processes at the heart of the economy in order to compete from within and profit from the protected market, thereby at times competing with national private capital. During this period only the parastatal enterprises were able to offer resistance to this competition by means of early internationalization, such as in the case of Chile's Corporación del Cobre (CODELCO) and of Petróleos Mexicanos (PEMEX).

The early introduction of neo-liberal restructuring in an authoritarian way during the 1970s (by the dictatorships of Chile, Argentina, Bolivia and Uruguay) and Mexico's debt crisis in 1982 fuelled the demise of Keynesian ideology. During the Cold War period, Keynesianism in Latin America had often been identified with international communism, most typically in the case of the military coup of US inspiration against President Joao Goulart in Brazil in 1964. The early neo-liberal tendency questioned the effectiveness of Keynesian-style regional policies that were labelled protectionist. Only in the middle of the 1980s, with the restoration of democracy in Brazil and Argentina, were the debates on regional integration reopened, giving way to the formation of MERCOSUR.

The first step to MERCOSUR was taken with the Programa de Integración y Cooperación Económica (Integration and Economic Cooperation Programme) between Argentina and Brazil in 1986. The major principles of the programme were gradualism, flexibility and balance: gradual opening of the economies, in order to regulate the social and economic costs of this process; flexible adjustment of the objectives to the real effects of integration; and keeping a balance between the various specializations of each economy for the sake of diversified international integration. In the eyes of the governments of Argentina and Brazil, this programme was a stabilizing factor in the democratization process following the end of the prolonged dictatorships. It was launched at a time when both countries were involved in anti-inflation actions.

In 1990 Brazil and Argentina decided to formalize the creation of a common market at the end of 1994, and in 1991 Paraguay and Uruguay joined the regionalization initiative. The latter gave rise to the Tratado de Integración (Integration Agreement) which officially created MERCOSUR. The agreement to establish a common market has several implications. First, goods, services and productive elements can circulate freely between the countries because of the elimination of customs rights and non-tariff barriers. Second, a common external tariff was established, and a common trade policy was adopted in relation to third states or groups of states. Third, coordination of macro-economic and sectoral policies has to take place between the participating nations. Finally, legislation of the participating countries were harmonized in order to strengthen the integration process. In August of 1994, an agreement was signed to form a customs union on 1 January 1995. The first economic results of MERCOSUR seem promising, as trade between the four participating countries nearly doubled between 1991 and 1993.

The creation of MERCOSUR came as a response to the international strategy of bloc formation. The participating countries aimed at improving their negotiation capacity with the USA and the EC, their principal commercial partners. Only under the regimes of Collor de Mello (Brazil) and Menem (Argentina) did MERCOSUR acquire a neo-liberal character. For Argentina, MERCOSUR has since then been considered a mechanism to consolidate its neo-liberal reforms and as a waiting-room for later entry into NAFTA. Relations of MERCOSUR with the USA have been formalized by agreements known as 'four plus one' that were signed in 1991. These agreements led to the formation of the Consejo Consultivo sobre Comercio e Inversión (Consultative Council on Commerce and Investment) of MERCOSUR. Negotiations with the USA, on participation in NAFTA among other things, will no longer take place by each individual country but through this joint council.

Mexico's entry into NAFTA is the other most far-reaching Latin American experience with open regionalism so far. From 1985 onwards, trade liberalization has been a central element of the Mexican economic policy. Participation was a logical step in the light of the historically considerable integration of Mexico in the US economy. The USA accounts for over two-thirds of Mexico's total external trade. Of even greater economic significance than trade liberalization, is the inclusion of free investment in NAFTA. During the ISI period, US MNCs first entered Mexico to produce for the internal market, but they have gradually started to dominate the Mexican export sectors. In the 1960s in particular US and Mexican liberalization policies on export manufacturing in the Mexican border region proved very effective. As the major recipient of US Foreign Direct Investment (FDI), Mexico has for the past twenty years received two-thirds of its FDI from its northern neighbour (Ortiz 1994: 163–5).

A first comprehensive framework agreement for US–Mexico trade and investment was drafted in 1985. Although President Salinas still (formally) rejected bilateral free trade when he took office in 1988, he approached President Bush with such a proposal in early 1990. The Canada–US Free Trade Agreement, which was implemented in 1989, had been the first step in consolidating North American free trade and can be taken as the precursor of NAFTA. Canada had no strong economic incentive to also participate in NAFTA as its trade relation with Mexico was marginal. To ensure that its interests *vis-à-vis* the USA were safeguarded during the negotiations, Canada nevertheless decided to participate. Besides, the possibility that NAFTA would eventually turn into a hemispheric agreement could not be ignored either. NAFTA came into force on 1 January 1994.

Regionalization and flexibility of the labour market

The current neo-liberal regionalization of the Latin American economy, in particular NAFTA and MERCOSUR, has been benefiting from the previous flexibility of the labour market (FLM). As part of neo-liberal restructuring, this flexibility initiated in the 1980s eliminated the minimum salary and thereby weakened the traditional Latin American state regulation of the labour market. The 1980s debate on FLM was not only accompanied by an anti-communist ideology, linking syndicalism to communism. It also supported the criticism on syndical corporatism, which had characterized the populist state under the ISI model. Equally, economic stagnation, inflation and unemployment have been attributed to state intervention, highly centralized salary negotiations, and trade union interventions in the management of enterprises. According to the proponents of neo-liberal restructuring, these were the causes of limited absorption of the expanding labour force, of insufficient adaptation to technological changes, and increased competition at the global market (Lagos 1994: 81). Conversely, critics of this view argue that the elimination of the minimum salary weakens the incentive to reduce production costs by means of technological innovation, and thus delays Latin American competitiveness in the global market based on modernization.

Various studies on Latin America have reported a significant loss of labour security and breaking of contracts between 1980 and 1989 (PREALC 1990). Simultaneously, the growth of the informal sector (6.7 per cent) more than doubled the growth of the formal sector (3.0 per cent). Various other indicators have confirmed the increased FLM in Latin America. The informal sector of the non-agricultural labour force grew from 16 per cent in 1980 to 22 per cent in 1989. Employment expansion in industrial and service enterprises with less than ten workers accelerated and accounted for 7.5 per cent in 1989, while employment expansion in medium and large companies only equalled 0.5 per cent that same year. This development is linked to the tendency of large companies to sub-contract basic components of production to small companies. In the public sector, the expansion of employment decreased from 4.5 per cent between 1950 and 1980 to 3.7 per cent between 1980 and 1989. The trend of salary flexibility produced an average one-third salary loss at the beginning of the 1990s compared with 1980.

In the case of Chile, the widely applied elimination of legal restrictions for dismissing workers, which was the final aim of FLM, has left employers with no more limitations than the derived costs of losing these workers (the payment of one extra month salary). This situation did not change significantly after the restoration of the democracy. The demands of labour unions for more protection of workers' rights, however, have formed one of the most discordant points between the Central Unitaria de Trabajadores (Single Workers Union, CUT) and the government of President Eduardo Frei with respect to Chile's entry into NAFTA and/or MERCOSUR.

In Mexico, by means of several pacts for economic stability, labour was forced to accept wage cuts and the abolition of constitutional social agreements. Between December of 1987 and May of 1994, the minimum salary increased 136 per cent, but the costs of basic goods increased 371 per cent (Heredia and Purcell 1994: 8). Workers in the *maquiladoras*, i.e. the export manufacturing sector at the border with the USA, suffered more than those employed in other manufacturing sectors. This relatively adverse situation can be attributed to the combination of a large surplus of manual labour with the international competition for *maquiladora* products. Moreover, ghost labour unions concluded collective contracts in which they renounced labour rights that are legally obligatory. Between 1977 and 1992, *maquiladora* workers experienced a constant decrease of purchasing power of a total of 45 per cent (Gambrill 1995: 543–5). In other sectors, this deregulation has been somewhat less extreme, but the effect of geographic relocation and annulment of collective contracts has been weakening unions in these sectors too. Many other companies went through a process of internal charge, which implies an adjustment of arrangements that leaves companies with more freedom of action *vis-à-vis* unions (Bizberg 1993: 177–180).

THE POLITICS OF ECONOMIC LIBERALIZATION

During the late 1980s and early 1990s, both Mexico and Chile went through a process of a consolidation of neo-liberal policy that formed the basis of the open regionalism approach. Despite various economic and political differences, let alone their geographic disparity, there are also several important similarities in the politics behind economic liberalization in these two countries. One of these similarities is the relative ideological homogeneity on neo-liberalism within Chile and Mexico. In the light of the socialist experience of the former and the revolutionary history of the latter, the uncritical adoption of the international neo-liberal ideology by the current political elites as well as the lack of political debate on this policy are remarkable. The absence of such a debate may be attributed to the success of national and international proponents of economic liberalization to depoliticize the issue of development, and to present their model as the only viable one.

Chile and Mexico also show similar tendencies with respect to the political role of the state and state–society relations. In both countries, there has been a striking state autonomy in the consolidation of neo-liberal restructuring. The influence on policy of social actors has been very limited and especially in the case of organized labour, state control has been tight. Interestingly, damage has been caused to the political legitimation of the political elites more by the socio-economic repercussions of neo-liberal restructuring than the restricted political leverage of groups within civil society.

The one major political difference between Mexico and Chile on economic liberalization involves continuity and change of policy and regime. In Chile, the transition from a military dictatorship to a civil democracy has left the former's economic policy basically untouched. In Mexico, conversely, the introduction and implementation of neo-liberal policy have been executed by the same party that previously adhered to populism and ISI. This section describes the main political features of regime change with policy continuity in Chile, and regime continuity with policy change in Mexico.

Chile's political transition

The electoral victory of the opposition candidate in the 1989 presidential elections put an end to the intention to continue the authoritarian regime and replaced the power of dictator General Augusto Pinochet (1973–90) with a right-wing civil political class. This change can be perceived as the ultimate alternative for regime continuity after the course of the 1988 referendum. The transition to democracy as initiated by President Patricio Aylwin should have produced a dismantling of not only the political regime but also the economic policy of the military dictatorship. The electoral victory of the democratic opposition organized in the Concertación de Partidos por la Democracia (Alliance of Parties for Democracy, CPD) consolidated the power of these parties, which had been supported by social mobilization. The alliance aimed to implement a strategy of negotiation with the military based on the acceptance of the institutional arrangements of the authoritarian regime. In other words, they tried to defeat the dictatorship by adopting its legality.

Next to the CPD, the more radical left-wing formed an important opposition movement. Its principal party, the Partido Comunista de Chile (Communist Party of Chile, PCCH), followed a confrontational approach of destabilizing the dictatorial regime. In line with its strategy of 'using all forms of struggle', the PCCH also used violence. However, the ineffectiveness of this strategy was shown by the failure of the intended assassination of Pinochet by the armed arm of the PCCH in 1985.

The CPD, on the other hand, demonstrated the effectiveness of their strategy with the defeat of the dictatorship in the 1988 referendum. General Pinochet had intended to continue his presidency until 1997 through this referendum. Although this failed, he was able to use the disintegration of the PCCH's political strategy following the unsuccessful assassination attempt. Instead of the planned destabilization of the new regime through popular pressure, the PCCH was integrated into the restricted political arena that had been formulated by the authoritarian regime itself.

The coming into being of these two types of opposition meant the rupture of the historical alliance between the PCCH and the Socialist Party of Chile (PSCH). This alliance went back to 1938 and had been the key to the political bond that enabled the triumph of the socialist government of Salvador Allende (1970–73). The crisis and division of the PSCH in 1979, based on internal factionalism and fed by the 1973 military coup, caused an ideological restructuring. The Marxist–Leninist line was replaced by a social democratic direction. Moreover, at the end of the 1980s the PSCH transformed itself into a neo-liberal party with a populist edge. This gave the PSCH the ideological legitimation necessary to participate in the CPD alliance dominated by the Partido Democrata Cristiano (Christian Democratic Party, PDC). This new alliance can be seen as a 'historic compromise' to gradually dismantle the heritage of the authoritarian regime while maintaining the neo-liberal policies of this same regime.

The first government of the democratic transition, which was installed in March 1990, defined four basic issues that needed to be tackled during its term: the human rights problems (political prisoners and missing persons); the definition of a new statute for the subordination of the military force to the civil government; reform and partial dismantling of the legal institutionality of the dictatorship; and the cancellation of the 'social debt' in order to minimize the negative social effects of the neo-liberal economic policy on social sectors with the lowest income.

The implementation of this fourfold policy required the democratic government to be able to neutralize the dangers of an authoritarian regression. This danger stemmed from the intention of the military bureaucracy, right-wing parties and businessmen to construct a *Pinochetista* political bloc directed at destabilizing the democratic regime. In the view of the new civil political class, the government's neutralization capacity depended to a large extent on maintaining the 'balance of macro-economic variables'. This balance had since 1985 favoured sustained economic growth and the prolonged social tranquility as characterized by a low level of labour conflicts. Politically, this was a clear message to corporate groups that still remained loyal to the military regime, and that during the campaign for the presidential elections of 1989 had supported the image of an eventual CPD government which would produce economic and social chaos. Stability, understood as economic growth, and governability were the two priorities of the transition government, in order to gradually but definitely dismantle the authoritarian enclaves. In the eyes of the CPD, the major threat for governability, however, was the populist tendency which came up as a means to satisfy the 'social debt'.

The systematic attempt to keep the populist tendency under control favoured technocrats in maintaining major elements of the dictatorial economic model. Conceptually, this development was expressed in the idea of 'growth with equity' that aimed to make growth, stability and income redistribution compatible while respecting the limits posed by the open market. In order to achieve this, a link was made between salary increases, productivity rises, reforms of labour legislation (without damaging the flexibility principle), and higher social budgets (financed by prudent tax increases). The new social budget was meant to diminish the poverty which affected nearly 5 million people (out of a total of 13 million) at the end of the Pinochet period. Nevertheless, each attempt to stress the differences between the old dictatorial and the new civil economic model was considered a threat to the climate of confidence in Chile's economic functioning. Apart from the government's aim to prevent any provocation of the corporate sector, it also attempted to not provoke the military bureaucracy regarding the continuity of General Pinochet's position as commandant and chief of the army.

The coexistence of the civil political class with the military bureaucracy was partly justified by the argument that the Chilean transition to democracy, in contrast to other Latin American experiences, had been directed by the dictatorial regime itself. The fact that the armed forces recognized and accepted their electoral defeat has been explained as the influence of democratic currents from within. Despite their electoral failure, the army maintained their powerful position by means of the earlier extorted conditions for transition. This prevented the civil government from introducing any fundamental changes within the army, including Pinochet's position. More than the fear of authoritarian regression, in the CPD and Aylwin's government, the conviction that any economic or political change would contribute to the cohesion within the military apparatus around Pinochet dominated their actions. In turn, this could only cause political destabilization and disarticulation of the economic functioning. As a result, the government renounced all intentions to force Pinochet to resign while simultaneously trying to diminish his protagonist role and political profile in the army. The aim was to leave him a strictly institutional role based on constitutional and legal norms, and prevent him from playing a role within the bloc of the armed forces.

The criteria used in the process of subordinating the military apparatus to the civil government formed the basis of the institutional reforms in Chile. The 1989 programme of the CPD government contains a plan for far more radical institutional reforms than have been implemented so far. The semi-presidential or nearly parliamentary system as proposed by this programme was limited by the same argument of 'political realism' that aimed at preventing a change in the climate of economic confidence and the recomposition of a political bloc for authoritarian regression. Given the 1980 Constitution, the government lacked a parliamentary majority for a radical political reform. In parliament, the government substituted its discourse on institutional reform for claims of democratic improvements, revindicating only partial changes of the authoritarian enclaves. The success of this strategy lay in the introduction of regional (provincial) governments, and the democratization of local politics. However, the situation of non-elected senators, the electoral system of the authoritarian regime, and the institutional role of the armed forces have all been conserved.

Major characteristics of the Chilean political system are the weakness of parliament and the presidency. Under the authoritarian regime, parliamentary and presidential duties were transferred to undemocratic state institutions. For a democratic regime, the capacity of the armed forces to interfere in political organs is unacceptable: they can designate four senators, two out of the seven members of the

Constitutional Tribunal, and half of the members of the Council of National Security. The Supreme Court of Justice, which is another state institution from the non-democratic period, can designate three members of the Senate and half the members of the Constitutional Tribunal. In addition, the electoral system directs disproportional powers to the board and leading circles of political parties while reducing the other members to mere ratifiers of party decisions.

The electoral law of the dictatorial regime has rendered Chile's multi-partyism into a *de facto* biparty system. Institutional arrangements have led to the construction of two electoral alliances, although there are eight political parties. The negotiations that lie at the basis of the electoral biparty system place major powers in the leading party elites at the cost of intervention on the part of civil society and social actors. Moreover, this system denies the principle of proportionate parliamentary representation, while favouring manipulation. Finally, the system assigns only two quotas (for two parties or electoral alliances) to an electoral district, and accepts no more electoral lists than available offices. This reduces the electoral process to nothing more than a simple ratification of decisions taken by the political bureaucracies of parties, who elect the candidates, and strengthens the 'party-cracy'.

The conservation of authoritarian characteristics has to coexist with the human rights policy of the democratic government based on the principles of 'truth, justice and reconciliation'. Instead of a genuine reform of the judicial system, justice for the victims of the authoritarian regime was handed out by means of an *ad hoc* legal arrangement, and by the sitting judges. This implied that the justice tribunals because of their alignment with the dictatorship could not offer guarantees of impartiality and effectiveness. This problem has led to the fragmentation of the Chilean legal regime. It has not only hampered the reconstruction of the constitutional state, but has in the end also favoured the formula of 'doing justice as far as possible'.

Deceptions and myths about the transition

Like each transition, the Chilean experience has given rise to a political mythology that seeks to constitute the transition as a paradigmatic example. This has happened even though the transition followed the pattern of a negotiated transition aimed at replacing the authoritarian regime while continuing its economic policy. Both the economic success (sustained economic growth for more than a decade, averaging an annual 6 per cent) and the political stability accompanying the transition process have led to the myth of a 'Chilean model' of transition to democracy. This myth has been cultivated by intellectuals, politicians and international officials of diverse ideological background. Some of them want to emphasize the virtues of structural adjustment policies. Others consider Chile proof of the idea that strong or authoritarian regimes hold better political conditions for accelerated growth than democratic governments. Others, again, present Chile as the prime example of the reconciliation of neo-liberalism and democracy.

All the debates on previous cases of democratization (in southern Europe during the 1970s, and in Brazil, Argentina and Uruguay in the 1980s) aimed to show the idea of political exceptionality. This exceptionality was used for political comparative advantage of these countries in their international political reintegration. The idea of exceptionality of Chile is encouraged by politicians who use it as an instrument for the consolidation of their weak power. At the same time, 'exceptionality' has improved the position of the new regime with respect to external economic support and foreign investment.

The economic reforms implemented by the military government were more than simply the result of structural adjustment. Based on the military anti-communist doctrine and neo-liberalism, the reforms brought about a comprehensive restructuring of the economy and the political system, which has been defined as a 'capitalist refoundation' (Garretón 1983). This concept signals that the authoritarian regime cannot be considered a mere restoration of the old social and economic order that preceded the socialist experiment (1970–73), but also as a radical project of neo-liberal modernization. The neo-liberal modernization project implied the substitution of the development model, the state form, and the relations between state and civil society due to an increased emphasis on economic calculation (Tironi 1990: 23). Consequently, this brought about the end of the discordant and contradictory 'Chilean democratic arrangement' that had dominated political life between 1930 and 1970. This arrangement had consisted of an expanding incorporation of marginalized social groups, industrialization directed at the internal market and supported by the state, and a constantly deepening democratic political system. One of the first deceptions was that the economic reforms were presented – both by the right and the left – as the direct consequence of the dictatorial nature of the military government. According to this interpretation, the right wanted to persuade others of the good of neo-liberal reforms and authoritarian governments in accelerating development. The left, conversely, found the interpretation supporting their criticism of neo-liberal restructuring by stressing its authoritarian character. In reality, the depth of the early economic transformation depended probably much more on the dictatorial regime's capacity to take a distant and independent stand regarding the economic and social groups who supported their policy. The restructuring of Chile's capitalism and its success were favoured by the deepening of the 'relative autonomy of the state', and not by the presence of traditional economic groups (industrial bourgeoisie, agricultural oligarchy and conservative middle classes) who supported the military government.

A second deception explained the start of the democratic transition as the result of the success of the economic reforms as implemented by the dictatorial regime. The economic reductionism that supports this explanation contradicts the symbolic validity of Chile's democratic traditions as the major obstacle for Pinochet to stay in power until 1997 (Martínez 1994: 46). In addition, the fact that the reconstruction of the political arena has meant the eradication of the electoral importance of the right who supported the authoritarian regime also contradicts this argument. The relative autonomy of politics with respect to industrial and financial groups who supported and profited from the dictatorial 'capitalist refoundation' puts into question the affirmation that the material forces of neo-liberalism irreversibly lead to democracy (which is the European Union's position with respect to Eastern Europe).

Another deception was the argument that the socializing reforms initiated in the period preceding the dictatorship (1970–73) formed a major obstacle for the neo-liberal restructuring process. Effectively, in 1973 a large share of the industrial, service and banking sector experienced state intervention. Large estates were completely eradicated by massive expropriations in the context of the agrarian reforms, while the large copper mining sector was nationalized. Exactly these conditions permitted the authoritarian government to reorient their policies towards modernization and liberalization of the economy, based on privatization of the highly centralized economy. From that point onwards, neo-liberal transformation could be initiated by the military political bureaucracy without opposition from the old capitalist classes who were seriously weakened in their material power after the socialist reforms of 1970–73. This political and economic weakness enabled the military regime to distance itself from simple restoration programmes as requested by these classes. In other words, the dictatorial state elite rather than the previous capitalist classes was the key to the 'capitalist refoundation' (ibid.: 47). The state-led capitalist revolution created room for a new generation of 'market businessmen' with an innovating and competitive character, who can operate without limitations by 'mass rebellion against capital'.

The limits of Chile's transition

The threat to the existence of the authoritarian regime did not come from the social actors or movements but the political parties who were organized in the CPD. The social actors had been devastated by the disintegration of the old social order in the change to a new neo-liberal order. This fragmentation, which was the most relevant characteristic of the democratic restoration, has been important for social stability and the return of the public confidence in Chilean politics. This tendency links up perfectly with the fact that the institutional transition was determined by the authoritarian regime.

Chile's democratic transition did not take place without or against the military bureaucracy but with their support. This second characteristic of the Chilean transition explains the success of the military in imposing neo-liberal reforms and *de facto* legitimizing an institutional system, which has been more effective than their previous policy of elimination of the political arena. After the military's political defeat, the democratic forces were not fit to impose a new Constitution and had to adopt the Constitution of the military regime. Based on the logic of the lesser evil, they chose the negotiation of cosmetic constitutional reforms. This measure, combined with the political defeat of the radical opposition in the 1980–84 period, was the main reason for the first transition government's ability to dismantle the authoritarian political regime.

265

The success of the military to impose a revolution from above contributes to the inability of the democratic system to produce a radical change of the political regime. This political reproduction has been supported by the *de facto* minority veto of the right, the actual power of enclaves of authoritarian power, the incomplete democratization of the right, and the neo-liberalization of the left (Moulian 1994: 35). The successful institutionalization of the dictatorial political regime as well as the achievements of their economic model cannot be explained by the insufficient democratization of the right alone. Equally important has been the left's acceptance of the two major ideological tendencies of the authoritarian period, namely the adoration of the market and the aversion to state-regulated activities. Consequently, Chile's left has ended up at the right of the PDC.

With respect to the democratic legitimization of neo-liberal policies, the PSCH has played a relevant role (Fernández Jilberto 1993). Both the party's participation in the government and its acceptance of the economic policy were essential to guarantee the constitution of 'neo-liberalism with a human face'. With this concept, the PSCH abandoned the critical discourse of the opposition of 1980–86, when authoritarianism was linked to the neo-liberal model and the end of the model was perceived as inherent to restoring the democracy.

The leftist movement, like the political centre, made an end to the 'party–movement–state' model (Touraine 1988b: 437) that had characterized the Chilean political arena since the 1930s and had reached its height under the socialist government. The redemocratization of the political system is now based on parties that are not only autonomous from the state but also from civil society. This situation feeds a consensus on neo-liberal reforms and a 'moderate pluralism' that, given the authoritarian heritage, always operates on the basis of the party bureaucracies' policy. Naturally, the autonomy of the political parties is based on the nature of the neo-liberal state inspired by the principle of the state's subsidiary role. Currently, the lack of wide-ranging social conflicts can be explained by the dominance of political processes, especially the recovery of citizenship and the restoration of the constitutional state.

Mexico's liberalization politics

The economic crisis of 1982 in Mexico contributed to the victory by the supporters of a fundamental restructuring of Mexico's economy based on neo-liberal principles. The economic restructuring initiated under President de la Madrid (1982–88) and deepened by President Salinas (1988–94) meant a new role for the Mexican state in the economy. The National Development Plans of de la Madrid and Salinas mention not only the need to rearrange and recover the economy in order to pass the critical stage, but also to make a shift away from the past through, respectively, 'structural change' and 'modernization'. De la Madrid's proposals were still rather moderate and were permeated by old-style nationalist populist discourse. He initially attempted to make a gradual move from the old to the new model because a sudden shift in economic control away from the state would entail widescale popular suffering. Halfway through de la Madrid's *sexenio* (six-year presidential term), however, a new economic crisis set in and internal and external pressure and support for an unambiguous introduction of neo-liberal policy intensified.

From 1985 onwards, Mexico's economic policy consisted predominantly of deregulation and liberalization, partly in relation to its entry into GATT in 1986. Many populist and nationalist regulations were aborted, subsidies were cut back, import restrictions limited, banking deregulated, and foreign direct investment stimulated. Finally, de la Madrid opted for an unorthodox approach of shock treatments to stabilize the economy, by means of an economic pact between the state, the business and agricultural sectors, and labour. In short, Mexico adopted an economic strategy that was more tightly linked to the requirements of its integration in the world market. These requirements were based on two classic ideas: economic stabilization, and growth by means of using comparative advantages. Low labour costs and geographical proximity to the USA are Mexico's two most relevant advantages, and of special importance in the exploitation of its cheap natural resources. These characteristics are compatible with the globalization of the world economy and with international neo-liberalism. Yet, in its dependence on cheap labour and natural resources for growth, Mexico remains more a Third World than a First World nation.

The economic restructuring programme required fundamental changes of the political system. The serious lack of political support for the PRI in the presidential elections of 1988 demonstrated that the state-party system needed to improve on its political legitimacy if it was to survive its economic policies. Mexico's economic crisis and the adjustment policy of de la Madrid had produced severe popular suffering. As well as harming the economic situation of millions of Mexicans, the government budget cuts entailed a significant decrease of resources to sustain the clientelist relations between government agencies and corporate organizations. As a result, the PRI's traditional links with and control over the electorate were weakened.

In the context of widespread popular discontent, Cuauthémoc Cárdenas (son of the charismatic populist President Lázaro Cárdenas of the 1940s) was able to organize a powerful left-wing opposition. This former *PRIista* founded the Partido de Revolución Democrática (Democratic Revolution Party, PRD) that was supported by many popular organizations and small political parties. On the right, the conservative Partido de Acción Nacional (National Action Party, PAN) also became stronger. With its neo-liberal economic ideas and its criticism of the undemocratic and centralist (Mexico City-dominated) PRI monopoly, the PAN found support principally among the middle class and economic elite in the Northern states. In the end, Cárdenas's populist call for social and economic justice and democratization rendered him more popular than Salinas. The latter was probably only able to win the presidential elections of 1988 by fraud, despite the huge resource base and media coverage of the PRI as compared with the opposition parties. Salinas officially won with 50 per cent of the votes: the lowest victory in the history of the PRI.

267

President Salinas aimed to continue and complete the economic restructuring process initiated by his predecessor. Compared to de la Madrid, Salinas's National Development Plan was far more explicit with respect to the neo-liberal character of his modernization project. The Plan maintains that ISI is exhausted and that the new economic strategy is to make use of opportunities offered by the external market in order to compensate for the lost dynamic of the internal market. Furthermore, the aim is to decrease the economic role of the state.

However, it was clear that for the sake of political legitimacy, economic liberalization had to be complemented by new populist discourse. Salinas's Development Plan states that both extreme liberalism and statism are rejected, while modernization is presented as politically neutral. In 1991, Salinas came up with the concept of new nationalism. The adjective 'new' is important here as it enables combining old values with new ones. New nationalism was explained as a new economic direction – internationally integrating the Mexican economy, especially with the rest of North America through NAFTA – for the old political purpose of development and solidarity. New nationalism complemented the concept of modernization and equally served to legitimize economic restructuring and state reform. In 1992, Salinas introduced the concept of *liberalismo social*, which was presented as liberalism with a human face. The concept forms the synthesis of two apparently opposite ideological concepts: neo-liberalism and populism. As such, it was a powerful political initiative to secure support from two clashing political sides within and outside the state–party system (Centeno 1994: 200–1; Rousseau 1992: 29–36).

The thrust of Salinas's political reforms was a combination of two, seemingly contrasting, changes: deconcentration and concentration. On the one hand, the undermined corporatist model that had secured sufficient popular support for the political system since the Mexican Revolution was partly replaced by more diverse state–society links. Instead of merely using the network in civil society of organizations based on sectoral dividing lines, Salinas opted to contact groups and organizations which had previously been ignored (e.g. in poor urban areas), and established social programmes that directly aided local communities. Simultaneously, local and state elections were less controlled from above, while the Catholic Church was allowed far more rights. On the other hand, Salinas's team consisted of a homogenous group of technocrats who further strengthened presidential power and decreased the interference of the PRI in state affairs.

The change in state–society relations under Salinas was a political necessity for three reasons. First, corporatist relations could not cover the increasing number of citizens outside the formal farmers', labour and middle-class structures: people working in the informal sector; migrants living in illegal slums in vastly expanding cities; workers who frequently cross the border with the USA in order to support their families in Mexico. The state–party system was not of relevance to these people who have the right to vote, and who started to become well organized in popular movements.

Second, the Mexican system of state corporatism had been weakened by the modernization policy, since the two were incompatible. Stabilization and adjustment gave way to a lack of state resources to sustain corporatist relations. Simultaneously, modernization implied a greater degree of exclusion and an end to the political compromise between the state, business circles and the working class. In order to carry out the economic restructuring programme and stay in power, the new political elite needed to establish new ties with civil society (Bizberg 1990).

Third, the new political elite needed to pacify and weaken the opponents of neo-liberal reform within the state–party system. This purpose was served by political reforms based on more plural relations between state and civil society. The old elite of *políticos* involved in corporatist relations lost their prominent position as these relations were of declining political importance. At the same time, *políticos* who were willing could join the modernization programme through jobs in the new clientelist institutions, thereby linking their faith to the success of the new elite's plans.

Salinas's extensive Programa Nacional de Solidaridad (National Solidarity Programme, PRONASOL or simply: Solidarity) was the most important initiative in the new state–society relations. State income from privatization was channelled to PRONASOL, providing for (a share of the) materials needed by local communities for welfare and development projects. Many projects involved direct support for groups hurt by the adjustment policy. By somewhat alleviating the situation of those most affected by the neo-liberal development model, PRONASOL helped to sustain this model (Bailey 1994: 97, 99; Dresser 1994: 144).

Under Salinas, organizations representing large companies were invited to become more involved in policy preparation. Like the other initiatives to extend political relations, this one also stemmed from the need for political legitimacy. With a middle class demanding price stability and a favourable exchange rate, and the poor wanting progress through economic growth, Salinas had to make his economic programme work. Confidence and the participation of the private sector's elite were essential ingredients, especially since this elite was to replace the state and the parastatal sector as the motor for growth (Castañeda 1993: 60).

Labour and farmers, on the other hand, experienced a declining political role. At the height of corporatist intermediacy, the largest representation organizations had had a double role. On the one hand, they channelled the main demands of their constituency to the decision-makers. On the other hand, they had been effective mechanisms of state control over these groups. Whereas this first, clientelist element was severely weakened, the latter remained largely in place. This was demonstrated most clearly by the social pacts for lower inflation and a stable economy, which the official unions accepted despite the burden to their own constituency. Salinas was disliked by leading labour bosses, but they had little room to manoeuvre since Salinas took a tough stand against labour resistance (Centeno 1994: 12, 64).

Presidential power and state autonomy

This brings us to the general point that presidentialism was deepened under Salinas. Presidential centralism has traditionally been a key element of the Mexican authoritarian system. Executive domination over the legislative and judicial powers is considerable, and most legislation comes from the presidential office. The President's power also lies in his authority to appoint officials and politicians at various levels, as well as the next presidential candidate for the PRI. During the Salinas *sexenio* the autonomy of the presidency and state bureaucracy increased. The union of the PRI and the state is still strong, but it seems that the balance of power has been gradually shifting away from the party towards the state bureaucracy. This notion, however, is tricky because one can hardly unravel the knots of the state–party system. A more evident development concerns the PRI losing its role as an intermediary agent for protest from below and for communication from above due to the weakening of corporatism (Centeno and Maxfield 1992: 71). Simultaneously, the party has been gaining more importance as the electoral basis for state policy.

The elite of technocrats who have dominated Mexico's political system since the 1980s, and especially under Salinas, have a high degree of ideological and occupational homogeneity. They see international integration and economic liberalization as the only economic solution for Mexico, and view neo-liberal restructuring as a logical and inevitable undertaking. By stressing the failure of the old model they decreased the possible role of the nationalist *políticos* who had earlier dominated the economic policy of ISI. The technocratic elite is highly educated, often in the USA, and includes many experts in economy. Technocrats have no corporatist experience, and little experience in grassroots organizations and/or local politics (ibid.).

Both political deconcentration and concentration fit the goal of a more autonomous state. The state reform that took place during the Salinas *sexenio* was technocratic, in other words, directed from above. The main instrument was bureaucratic control over economic and political resources. Instead of having the PRI recreate state–society links that were lost in the decline of corporatist mechanisms, the *Presidencia* became the leading institution in renewing these links. The new links, however, are *ad hoc* and flexible when compared with the corporatist structures. Like the economic restructuring process, the political reforms were headed by the presidency and top federal institutions, which could more easily distance themselves from traditional practices and populist forces. The increased autonomy of the state thus took the form of decreased party influence and less structural forms of state–society links.

The political effect of the changing state–party relation has been twofold. Internally, there has been a major struggle between the technocrats and the *políticos*. Even though there is still a lot of confusion with respect to the assassinations of two high PRI officials in 1994, these and other events have indicated growing tensions between the old and the new political elites. Next, in local and state electoral politics political liberalization has enhanced the opportunities of opposition parties *vis-à-vis* the PRI. Besides, on several occasions Salinas was willing to revise the official results of local and state elections when the opposition accused him of fraud and they made strong protests. In these instances, he rather risked deception of local

PRIistas than political unrest and his party being labelled undemocratic. However, in a centralist political system in which local governments have little authority and resources, and presidential power has further increased instead of decreased, the room to manoeuvre of local and state government remains very limited. Moreover, the fruits of political liberalization have not been equally distributed. The major party to the right of the PRI, the PAN, has profited, and gained several state and municipal elections. The left-wing PRD, conversely, experienced considerable repression during the Salinas *sexenio*.

In Mexico, the debate on economic liberalization versus a nationalist economic policy at first seemed exhausted with the accession to NAFTA and the electoral victory of Zedillo in 1994. The attempts to re-establish the former interventionist model that was identified with Cuauthémoc Cárdenas and the PRD had failed. Salinas was able to deepen the neo-liberal restructuring process by ending the supremacy of *políticos* over *técnicos*, neutralizing political and social demands through neopopulism, and opening future possibilities for *rapprochement* between the PRI and the political right that is represented by the PAN. The peso crisis, however, has shown that economic liberalization alone cannot solve Mexico's problems. Through increased deficits and the enlarged dependency on shock-sensitive foreign portfolio investments, liberalization has contributed to this crisis. Simultaneously, Mexico's new position in the world economy has undoubtedly contributed to finding a helping hand to stabilize the situation. The real costs of the crisis are nevertheless to be paid by the majority of Mexicans who have already experienced impoverishment due to the policies of de la Madrid and Salinas.

OPTIONS FOR INTEGRATION

Both Mexico and Chile have opted for open regionalism as a means to further expand national development, and have attempted to achieve greater regional and global economic integration through various means. As leading nations in neo-liberal restructuring in Latin America, it comes as no surprise that Mexico has been the first country of the region to arrange free trade with the USA while Chile was the next to be invited for consultations on future entry into NAFTA. Although the economic results of restructuring have been better in Chile than in Mexico (see Table 11.2), participation in NAFTA would not be as automatic for Chile as it has been for Mexico. As Table 11.3 shows, Chile's trade relations are far more diverse than those of Mexico, which were already greatly tied to the North American market prior to NAFTA. Chile's version of open regionalism is therefore considerably more open than the Mexican one. Compared to Mexico, Chile has more interest in economic integration with Latin American countries, the European Union (EU) and APEC. Although Mexico has also been active in extending trade relations outside North America and was for instance already an APEC member a year before Chile, it has less proportionally to gain from such trade links than Chile.

271

Table 11.2 Chile and Mexico: economic indicators as a percentage

Macroeconomic indicators	Chile		Mexico	
	1990	1994	1990	1994
Growth of GDP	3.3	4.1	4.4	3.5
Growth of exports	11.3	7.5	3.2	9.0
Investment (percentage of GDP)	19.8	22.1	18.9	21.9
Saving (percentage of GDP)	23.8	25.6	18.8	15.9

Source: CEPAL (1995)

Table 11.3 Chile and Mexico: exports as a percentage

Type of exports	Chile		Mexico	
	1985	1993	1985	1993
Exports of primary products	93.3	83.9	79.4	25.4
Exports of manufactures	6.7	16.1	20.6	74.6
Exports to North America	22.3	16.5	66.8	86.2
Exports to ALADI	14.4	19.8	2.6	3.1
Exports to Asia	20.6	28.0	10.1	2.5
Exports to EU	35.5	25.3	16.6	5.0

Source: CEPAL (1995).

Chile's options

Chilean economic growth of 8 per cent in 1995 is considered to be the result of the economic policy of the transition and the deepening of internationalization. Accordingly, the second transition government of President Eduardo Frei (1994–2000) intends to deepen the dismantling of authoritarian enclaves through an economic model that is politically legitimized by the democracy and to overcome the economic dilemma of continuity versus change. A major share of the success of the economic model has been identified with the external opening of the market and with the drastic and unilateral reduction of import tariffs to 10 per cent. Chile has difficulties with entry into NAFTA, which stem from the lack of Congressional support for US fast track authority[1] since the Republican majority, and the delay of negotiations due to the US presidential elections in 1996. With respect to MERCOSUR, Chile faces the impossibility of coming to specific agreements one way or the other (association or entry).

These recent integration problems have enforced the conviction of corporate groups and the Chilean government on the advantages of a unilateral and/or bilateral reduction of tariffs as the strategy for further internationalization of the economy. This strategy has been facilitated by the current economic stability. The government also argues that neither NAFTA nor MERCOSUR should limit Chile's freedom in commercial relations with other countries or regions, and its macro-economic policy. This attitude strengthens the possibility and desire to constitute a 'broad platform for business' between North America and the Southern Cone; between South America and the Pacific Asian area; and between the European Union and the Southern Cone. To achieve the latter goal, there is the problem of the negative position of the EU on formalizing bilateral bonds with Chile independently from MERCOSUR.

Given the high diversity of Chile's foreign trade partners, the country cannot escape an extremely liberal version of open regionalism. Its external policy has therefore been directed at simultaneously negotiating with several economic blocs (NAFTA, MERCOSUR, APEC, EU). Previously, there was wide consensus about this policy among the government, businessmen, and the Central Unitaria de Trabajadores (Single Workers Union, CUT). The 1990 Framework Agreement embodied this tripartite consensus on the Chilean integration in the global market as well as the political legitimacy of open regionalism. The creation of the Committee for Participation of the Private Sector in International Economic Relations in 1992 confirmed the tripartite consensus. However, debates on entry into NAFTA and/or MERCOSUR have split this consensus and have placed the labour unions opposite the government and private sector.

The Chilean interests that would be served by entry into MERCOSUR and NAFTA differ. MERCOSUR establishes a customs union, and a future common market with free circulation of goods, services and production factors. Chile is not aiming at entry into MERCOSUR, but aims at association for the sake of liberalization of trade with Argentina, Brazil, Paraguay and Uruguay. In this way, it can avoid the adoption of the common external tariff as used by the four member countries. The problem lies in that Chile's tariffs are lower and indiscriminate compared to those of MERCOSUR so that full integration would come at the cost of a loss of international competitiveness of the Chilean economy. Therefore, Chile would like to participate in the free trade zone without participating in the customs union. Association with MERCOSUR is of vital importance because of the fact that 42 per cent of Chile's manufacturing exports is directed at the MERCO-SUR member countries (Leiva 1994: 63). Added to this are the EU's refusal to strengthen its bilateral accords with Chile independently from MERCOSUR, and the fact that a substantial share of Chilean investments in Latin America (equalling nearly $US2 billion in 1995) go to the four incorporated countries.

The importance of NAFTA is based on the significance of the USA historically as Chile's principal trade associate. An advantage of NAFTA for Chile is that it is a free trade zone without a customs union. The political euphoria after the negotiations for entry into NAFTA, which was presented as a certificate of entry into the First World, ended in October 1995 as a result of the US Congressional decision not to provide President Clinton with fast track authorization. Confronted with this situation, the Chilean government may have to opt for a bilateral accord or insist on negotiations for NAFTA entry. The advantage of a bilateral agreement would be a negotiation framework that is not bound by the established NAFTA texts. In case of NAFTA entry, the only thing that Chile could negotiate is a list of exceptions, the pace of integration, and the application of phases of tax reduction and agrarian policy.

Studies of the advantages and disadvantages of Chile's entry into NAFTA support the Chilean government's preference for bilateral agreements (Aninat 1994: 8). They have supported the government's stance *vis-à-vis* the Treasury that immediate trade benefits of NAFTA membership would be limited. On the other hand, the high level of opening of Chile's economy puts the country in the position of being able to enter regional blocs without major structural adjustments. Among the benefits of integration are stable access to the North American market, which would reduce the actual risk of the Generalized System of Preference that favours Chilean products but is based on protectionist criteria and depends on US political willingness. On the other hand, the agrarian sector of Chile would suffer most from integration with the USA. The National Society for Agriculture has frequently claimed that Chilean entry into NAFTA without tariffs would produce a fall in basic grain (wheat, maize, rice and marigold) prices of between 11 and 26 per cent, while the profit margins would fall between 23 and 95 per cent.

Mexico's options

Trade liberalization was to reduce inflation and render Mexican production more efficient and competitive. The government approach in this respect was one of pragmatism: it opted for multiple negotiations. As global trade liberalization proved to move slowly and the threat of protectionism persevered, GATT membership in 1986 was only a first step. The most important next move was the decision to negotiate regional free trade with the USA and Canada. Predominantly, Mexico's entry into NAFTA consolidates its adoption of a neo-liberal development model and the integration of Mexico into the US economy, while also at the political– ideological level the agreement validates neo-liberalism and regionalization. The USA has not only been Mexico's largest trading partner, accounting for over two-thirds of Mexican trade, but is also crucial for foreign investment. An analysis of various studies on the possible economic effects of NAFTA supports the idea that for Mexico the impact of investment liberalization is going to be far more substantial than the impact of free trade (Ros 1992: 69–71).

Mexico's decision to participate in the North American free trade zone has sometimes been misunderstood as born out of necessity instead of free will. It has, for instance, often been argued that Salinas had little choice but to join NAFTA because of his disappointing trip to Europe in 1990, when Germany and France showed no interest in expanding trade with Mexico. Taken the historical importance of the USA as Mexico's major economic partner, however, a free trade agreement between the two is rather logical in times of liberalization. In addition, NAFTA membership has not stopped Mexico in promoting trade with other countries and regions.[2]

Salinas's eagerness to strengthen Mexico's economic ties and deepen liberalization through NAFTA had a higher purpose than merely regional integration.

For the sake of a continuous flow of foreign investment, Mexico wants to become a trusted and estimated member of the world economy. Joining NAFTA has been very important in this respect. The US and Canadian acceptance of Mexico as a fully fledged economic partner could serve as a global 'hallmark' for continuity and confidence. Mexico's entry into NAFTA showed the outside world the structural character of Salinas's reform policy, since a return to protectionist policy is impossible as long as Mexico participates in NAFTA.

Next to participation in NAFTA, Mexico has embedded its neo-liberal restructuring programme in various international deals and organizations. As of 1985, the Mexican government has made great efforts to act on the restructuring requirements of the World Bank and the IMF. In 1993, Mexico joined APEC, and in 1994 it was the first Third World country to join the Organization for Economic Cooperation and Development (OECD). Consultations with the EU on trade liberalization are still going on, but have so far only resulted in declarations of intent. All these initiatives show the genuine wish of Mexico's new political elite to become part of the international network for capitalist development and liberalized production and finance. Meanwhile, the success of most of these initiatives demonstrate the enthusiasm of international organizations for Mexico's change of development model, at least until the peso crisis.

Southward, even though only representing a few per cent of its trade relations, Mexico has also liberalized trade with many Latin American countries by means of integration initiatives like the ALADI, the Grupo de los Tres (Colombia, Mexico and Venezuela), and the Acuerdo de Complementación Económica Chile-México (Chile–Mexico Economic Completion Agreement). Next to the general motive of expanding economic relations, these and other partnerships have been based on the need for some diplomatic counterweight to NAFTA, and the expectation that NAFTA-enhanced investments in Mexico would expand its export capacity to Latin America (Guerra-Borges 1996: 158–9). On the one hand, increased efforts towards the USA and also Canada, combined with its increased extra-regional activities, seem to have come at the cost of Mexico's Latin American involvement. On the other hand, Mexico may become a stepping stone for the USA to the rest of Latin America and beyond. The USA has attached a new role to Mexico, namely, that of an intermediary platform; Mexico will become the means for the USA to enter other international spaces (Corro Barrientos 1991: 678–9). In spite of Mexico's recent economic and political instability and despite the fact that their markets were also harmed by the peso crisis, the other Latin American countries still look upon NAFTA as the neo-liberal materialization of Bolivar's ideal of panamericanism.

CORPORATE, LABOUR AND ENVIRONMENTAL POSITIONS

Political actors in Mexico and Chile have expressed similar concerns on economic integration. Major corporate organizations have applauded the policy of open regionalism, although the owners of small firms in Mexico have been worried about the effects of US competition under NAFTA. Labour unions have been concerned with the effects of economic internationalization on labour rights. Mexico's official unions were formally involved in NAFTA consultations but their interests were marginalized, while independent unions that criticized the governmental position had even less leverage. In Chile, the CUT also experienced marginalization in trade negotiations and has decided to therefore withdraw from its membership of trade commissions. Finally, both in Chile and in Mexico there have been environmental groups stressing the need to involve environmental protection in trade negotiations and trade agreements.

Political positions in Chile

In 1994, a rift in the tripartite consensus of Chile's corporate sector, CUT and government on the internationalization of the economy occurred. The consensus that had supported the parallel negotiations with various economic blocs (NAFTA, MERCOSUR, APEC) was broken on the part of the CUT after the private sector and the government had opposed the inclusion of social and labour clauses in NAFTA. A second rupture took place in March of 1996 when the consensus between various corporate groups was damaged. Agrarian entrepreneurs organized in the Sociedad Nacional de Agricultura (National Society of Agriculture) rejected the official Chilean proposals for entry into MERCOSUR. Businessmen organized in the Confederación de la Producción y el Comercio (Confederation of Production and Trade), conversely, accepted these proposals. With 42 per cent of Chile's exports going to the four member countries, and a market of 200 million consumers, these businessmen are anxious for a total tax reduction. The accords between Chile and MERCOSUR of March of 1996 stipulate a liberalization of 90 per cent of all trade within eight years, and a period of between fifteen and eighteen years to complete the tariff reduction of the other 10 per cent, containing mainly agricultural products. According to the National Society of Agriculture, the envisioned trade liberalization of agrarian products would cause the economic collapse of 200,000 Chilean farmers.

The Confederation of Production and Trade considers the strategy of open regionalism as the logical and coherent continuation of the unilateral economic opening of the military dictatorship in 1975. Entry into NAFTA or a bilateral accord with the USA would permit deepened integration by means of reciprocity of tariffs. It would also provide a possibility to put an end to non-tariff barriers that affect an important share of Chilean exports. Non-tariff barriers tend to be created in times when Chilean products reach an interesting position in the markets of the USA, Japan or the EU. Businessmen also expect that integration with North America would favour the liberalization of financial services. Moreover, NAFTA would be a mechanism to attract foreign capital. In a period of strong competition for international private capital as a result of privatization and deregulation in the whole Latin American region, this could be an important advantage.

Despite the general perception, entry into NAFTA would not produce drastic changes for Chile due to the already profound opening of its economy. Business sectors none the less expect a long-term foreign trade expansion to account for an additional 12 per cent of economic growth. The most significant effect would be produced by foreign investments, which would account for 2 per cent of GDP. This has to do with the high profitability that can be generated by capital, with which a 16 per cent increase of capital stock could be achieved. As a result, a 10 per cent growth in production and a 17 per cent increase in consumption would occur. The effect on the labour sector, according to the private sector, would be close to zero because of the already wide flexibility of the labour market in Chile (Aguero 1995: 26). In short, the Chilean private sector equates, rather uncritically, the model of Mexico's entry into NAFTA ('we do not need the three million meetings and four-hundred studies done by Mexico', ibid.: 6) with the argument that membership would consolidate the export of Chilean products to the North American market.

With respect to the dilemma of entry into NAFTA or bilateral free trade with the USA, corporate Chile repudiates clauses for labour and environmental protection as part of the trade agreement itself. If necessary, they would only accept the formula of parallel accords as designed for Mexico. The advantage of NAFTA is that its conditions are already known and are favourable to Chile's private sector, while encompassing simultaneous integration with three national markets. In the corporate view, the NAFTA structure of parallel environmental and labour agreements avoids any intention to re-establish a regulation mechanism of the labour market, and the Chilean Ley de Bases del Medio Ambiente (Law of Bases for the Environment) is perfectly in agreement with the principle of private enterprise. Therefore, Chile could accept the parallel agreements without any problems. Intents to substitute NAFTA entry with a bilateral agreement in the hope of changing the contents of the parallel accords would only hinder free trade and would negatively affect Chile's international competitiveness, Chile's private sector argues.

Chile's labour unions, especially CUT, do not want to limit the internationalization of the economy but strive for participation in the negotiations. Their aim is to protect the interests of workers and unions, and to make sure that Chile will ratify and comply with the international labour agreements it has signed. Economic integration processes may produce a lower level of employment security and more unemployment because of industrial closures and relocations. By stimulating competition of several products in the global market, economic policies may attempt to reduce production costs by means of lower salaries and greater mobility of production factors. This could negatively affect the national trade union structure, in the sense of less members and less power in negotiations. For Chile's unions, prevention of such developments has to be part of negotiations on MERCOSUR and NAFTA.

In 1993, the CUT presented a proposal to create a labour policy for regional integration at the Comité Privado para las Relaciones Económicas Internacionales (Private Committee for International Economic Relations). This proposal recognizes the necessity to continue with the bilateral or multilateral commercial strategy that is directed at full access to Chilean products on the international market. Deepened internationalization of Chile's economy is seen as the only long-term guarantee for economic growth and the improvement of equity and social justice. However, the consolidation of institutional democracy requires the incorporation of workers' interests in regional policies of economic integration.

The CUT thus opts for entry into NAFTA as long as there are guarantees to include the protection of workers' rights that counter the tendency of social exclusion which the neo-liberal model might otherwise consolidate. Without such guarantees, the CUT expects that NAFTA will maintain its character of favouring corporate and financial interests, while moving workers' rights to parallel agreements. Therefore, labour unions prefer the negotiation of a bilateral agreement with the USA instead of NAFTA, as the former would offer more possibilities to reach modifications of labour legislation on dismissals, collective negotiations, and training opportunities for workers in Chile. NAFTA does not offer such a minimum protection of labour rights.

The CUT's refusal to participate in the Chilean delegation to the Summit of the Americas in Miami in 1994 marks the break of the trade union movement with the economic integration of the government of President Frei. The CUT also decided to withdraw from all tripartite commissions on NAFTA and MERCOSUR because 'the workers have been marginalized in the discussion on all free trade agreements', especially on NAFTA (Manuel Bustos, CUT president, *El Diario*, 7 December 1994). This decision can be explained as a political repudiation of the government's extremely favourable attitude towards the private sector and its gradual disregard of trade union interests. According to the CUT, this marginalization stems from the alliance of the private sector and the CPD in international economic affairs, which favours the approach of attracting foreign investments based on cheap manual labour and the 'Asianization' of the economy (Manuel Bustos, *La Tercera*, 10 December 1994). The latter is shown by the government's refusal to consider social clauses and labour guarantees in the negotiations on NAFTA. The CUT's demands on this are consistent with the agreement it signed with the American Federation of Labour and Congress of Industrial Organizations (AFL-CIO), with which they have been actively pressurizing their governments.

The Chilean government has presented possible entry into NAFTA as part of a general effort towards modernization in favour of all social classes, especially low-income groups. It has in fact denied the identification of the government with corporate interests (Minister J.J. Brunner, *Las Ultimas Noticias*, 10 December 1994). The social clauses debate has placed the government between the trade union position that workers are legally unprotected *vis-à-vis* the private sector, and the corporate position that Chile's labour legislation is democratic, modern and compatible with the exigencies of a modern market economy. In the eyes of the trade unions, the government has been generally unwilling to comply with international regulations for labour security. It has, among other things, not ratified the International Labour Organization (ILO) convention's numbers 87 (union freedom and protection of right of unionism), 98 (collective negotiation), 154 (rural organizations), and 151 (workers' security and health, and working environment). Unions, therefore, expect that the Chilean government would not comply with NAFTA parallel labour clauses either.

With the lack of success in including labour and environmental issues in the negotiations with the Chilean government on NAFTA entry, the CUT has focused on a joint position with the US AFL-CIO, the Mexican Confederación de Trabajadores de México (Confederation of Mexican Workers, CTM) and the Canadian Labour Congress (CLC). In May 1995, they agreed to demand from their governments the recognition of respect for working conditions as laid down in the conventions of the ILO.[3] These demands implicitly show the need to create a code of conduct in order to regulate the activities of TNCs within open regionalism. In a joint declaration by the AFL-CIO with the Umbrella Organization of Central Unions of the Southern Cone in March 1994, it was repeated that international labour norms are confronted by commercial and financial interests that use globalization of production as an instrument to restrict workers' rights and ignore norms that regulate the production process. According to the CUT, in contrast with NAFTA which would not produce short-term unemployment, MERCOSUR can generate unemployment in agriculture and cattle breeding. This should be tackled by establishing unemployment insurance.

The Movimiento de Campesinos y Etnias de Chile (Movement of Farmers and Indigenous People of Chile, MUCECH) has also been highlighting the negative effects of open regionalism. This organization represents 250,000 small agricultural producers, poor farmers and indigenous families, and has been especially active with respect to MERCOSUR. It expects that the conversion of the agricultural sector will cause problems for the small producers of traditional crops in competing with the agricultural sectors of Argentina, Uruguay and Brazil. This competition might occasion a decrease in small agrarian ownership and accentuate the polarization process in this sector. The government has taken the position of extending the conversion pace to a period of fifteen years in favour of a list of exceptions for certain products.

In the open regionalism debate, Chilean ecologists have been more in favour of membership of MERCOSUR and entry of this bloc as a whole into NAFTA. In their opinion, it would be better to negotiate jointly for a NAFTA agreement that would incorporate the environmental and labour demands of the Southern Cone countries (*La Epoca*, 22 September 1995). For Chile this is most urgent as its foreign trade consists largely of primary products (see Table 11.3). This export situation stems from the Chilean export model which is based on low prices for natural resources, a lack of adequate environmental legislation, and low manual labour costs. The structure of the open regionalism negotiations as stimulated by Chile's government has placed the business sector in a dominant position. As a result, this sector has been able to impose its view on environmental policy.

Within this scheme, any agreement of trade liberalization would emphasize the pressure of foreign trade on Chile's natural resource base, and intensify monoculture production for the international market. This takes place in an international context of a surplus of natural resources supply and deteriorating prices.

Consequently, countries have to sell larger stocks of natural resources to finance the purchase of the same amount of manufactured goods. If Chile enters NAFTA, the pressure of the current export policy on the natural resource base would only be intensified. Chile's new environmental norms, which have been formulated in such a way as not to harm the competitiveness of producers, allow for such a compensation of lowered tariffs.

The threat of the transformation of environmental exigencies into tariff barriers is larger in the negotiation of a free trade agreement between countries with unequal environmental regulations. Chile faces being forced to greatly upgrade its environmental policy because of its high level of economic opening to the international market. This could in the short term mean a better quality of life in importing countries at the cost of the quality of life of Chile's inhabitants. The classic example is that of Chilean export fruit producers who have to comply with European environmental norms of recycling packaging while they are using pesticides and insecticides with Malathion in regions as densely populated as Germany. For Chilean ecologists it is thus vital that international environmental regulations are not only limited to demands on the final product, but also include production processes. Another issue in case of entry into NAFTA is the probability of industrial relocation to Chile, including the transfer of polluting production systems, and energy and natural resource-intensive processes.

The above-mentioned concerns for environmental deterioration are stressed by the general confusion over Chile's environmental legislation, and the ambiguity and insufficiency of its Law of Bases for the Environment. This law permits the start of productive processes before the results of the Environmental Assessment Study by the Comisión Nacional del Medio Ambiente (National Commission of the Environment) are known, provided that the firm involves an insurance company. This arrangement limits the regulating role of the state to that of a negotiator with insurance companies in case the economic activity which is already in operation receives a negative assessment. Moreover, the subjection of the Environmental Law to market mechanisms with respect to tradable emission rights that allow the productive sector the use of and negotiation over environmental sources such as the air will only worsen contamination, especially in densely populated areas.

Political positions in Mexico

Since the introduction of the economic restructuring programme, Mexico's private sector has been through a process of economic and political polarization. Where smaller companies have mostly been negatively affected by the programme, large national companies have in general profited. As the latter were the least vulnerable to foreign competition, they were the first to pick the fruits of the reforms. In addition, they received most of the government support in the form of financial assistance and the first choice of the privatized firms. Large companies, thus, quickly adjusted to the new opportunities, and are in the middle of a process of rapid transnational integration of productive and financial capital.

Mexico's business elite of large company owners was actively involved in the economic restructuring project and the preparation of entry into NAFTA. In contrast with the diminishing political leverage of small companies producing for the national market, the business elite's cooperation with the government has intensified as the technocrats turn out to be far more receptive to their demands than previously. The Consejo Coordinador Empresarial (Coordinating Business Council, CCE) in particular and the Consejo Mexicano de Hombres de Negocios (Mexican Council of Businessmen, CMHN) were very close to the Salinas administration. Headed by CCE, a new economic umbrella organization for foreign trade was created in 1990 to promote NAFTA. This Coordinadora de Organismos Empresariales de Comercio Exterior (Umbrella Organization of Business Agencies of Foreign Trade, COECE), which represents eleven large business organizations, has been criticized for over-representing big companies' interests. A central task of COECE during the preparation for entry into NAFTA was to handle the communications between the private sector and Mexico's negotiators. In addition, COECE assisted the Trade Ministry in providing information and drafting technical proposals. Although organizations representing major companies did play an influential role, the nature of genuine interaction was primarily informal, taking the form of close personal contacts between the Trade Ministry and key individuals in the private sector (Teichman 1993: 178, 188).

In general, Mexican opposition to NAFTA was limited and weak. Compared to the USA, Mexican groups criticizing the agreement were never able to organize a nation-wide debate or considerable popular mobilization on the issue. One of the reasons for this was the expectation that the most significant economic impact of NAFTA would come from its liberalization of foreign investment. This feature enabled the Mexican state to 'convince' official labour unions that NAFTA would be in their interest, as new investments would create jobs and higher wages. Next to the need for more funding, more jobs were exactly what Salinas needed, being faced with an 'overheated economy' and insufficient legitimation (Castañeda 1993: 65–6).

At first sight, NAFTA's effects on labour in Mexico indeed seemed promising. It was generally expected that in the short run the USA would lose some employment to Mexico and that increasing exports and investments would create new jobs. However, Mexico's experience with economic liberalization prior to NAFTA had shown that modernization feeds unemployment and harms labour rights. In addition, a study by the Office of Technology Assessment of the US Congress revealed that in Mexico (and in the USA) active labour and industrial policies were indispensable as market forces alone would not produce the social and economic rewards as promised by the heads of both states. According to this report, without fundamental changes of the relations between government, industry and labour, NAFTA will not accelerate development in Mexico (OTA 1992: 3).

The impact of NAFTA on Mexico's agricultural sector was generally estimated to be large and dramatic. In spite of certain new opportunities for the export of fresh fruits and vegetables to the USA and Canada, the overall prospect seemed negative. NAFTA is likely to cause many problems as Mexico's 20 million small agricultural producers will not be able to compete with USA and Canadian farmers (*La Jornada*, 12 August 1993: 40). After the destruction of many support programmes for farmers, the gradual end to agricultural import restrictions would particularly affect the small Mexican farmers. With the exception of maize, US agricultural subsidies are higher than Mexican ones, and US credits are cheaper (*Mexico and NAFTA Report*, 18 February 1993: 3). Consequently, 'regardless of whether the adjustment is gradual or immediate, liberalization contracts substantially the size of the rural labour force' (Levy and Van Wijnbergen 1992: 62). Estimates range from several hundred thousand to 2 or 3 million workers.

Another concern in Mexico was the possible environmental effect of NAFTA. First of all, NAFTA would evidently encourage and geographically expand the *maquiladora* industry. This industry has over the past thirty years been the main contributor to the devastating environmental degradation of that region. Second, there was the expectation that trade and investment liberalization would give rise to an accelerated 'selling out' of Mexico's natural resources. After having served for years as the symbol of Mexico's sovereignty, access to Mexican oil reserves was the major interest of the USA in NAFTA. The agreement also relaxes restrictions on the use of Mexican soil and water by foreign investors. Finally, there was concern that the rapid opening of the Mexican market to US and Canadian products and capital would run counter to efforts for sustainable development.

In Mexico there were a number of critical and moderate environmental organizations actively discussing NAFTA, predominantly located in Mexico City and the border region with the USA. Moderate groups accepted the dominant view of the necessity of economic growth through liberalization and regionalization, or at least perceived it as inevitable. They declared that economic integration with the USA and Canada should be accompanied by environmental restrictions. Critical organizations claimed that sustainable development requires not only environmental arrangements, but also democracy and social and economic redistribution. While the major moderate groups remained focused on environmental issues, critical environmental organizations worked on broader issues together with other kinds of non-governmental groups.

The most vocal network opposing NAFTA in Mexico was the Red Mexicana de Acción frente al Libre Comercio (Mexican Action Network on Free Trade, RMALC), which was created in 1991 by over a hundred non-governmental organizations (NGOs). A wide variety of NGOs cooperated in RMALC: labour unions, peasant organizations, environmental groups, organizations for development and social justice, human rights organizations and women's groups. One of the independent labour unions involved was the Frente Auténtico del Trabajo (Authentic Labour Front, FAT), which has been transnationally cooperating with the US United Electrical Workers. Through its various member organizations RMALC had a diverse grassroots base. Basically, RMALC considered NAFTA as a project that would only be profitable for a small elite at the cost of the majority of Mexicans and the degradation of Mexico's environment and natural resources. The Network's criticism of NAFTA was similar to the position of the PRD. Despite the considerable grassroots support of these and other political organizations and parties, and despite the various new links established with groups in the USA and Canada, the coalition of Mexican NAFTA opponents never gained momentum. The political elite used the strong rhetoric of NAFTA being favourable to all Mexicans, and critical groups had little political room and economic resources to mobilize a strong counter-movement.

CONCLUSIONS

Although the USA have announced that they will decide on Chile's entry into NAFTA after their presidential elections, the Chilean government is concerned that this project may be replaced by direct conversations between the USA and MERCOSUR. Such a change of US trade policy would be based on the slowness of the creation of the envisioned Free Trade Area of the Americas (FTAA). This area so far only incorporates Mexico, but according to the goals set at the Summit of the Americas in Miami in 1994, the FTAA should be operating by 2005. Canada's Trade Minister, Art Eggleton, has already criticized the loss of US leadership regarding the acceleration and creation of the FTAA as demonstrated by President Clinton's incapacity to obtain fast track authorization for negotiations with Chile (*El Mercurio Internacional*, 16–22 May 1996). Considering Chile's association with MERCOSUR and the latter's growing economic importance, one way of accelerating hemispheric integration would be direct negotiations between the USA and this southern bloc. In addition, US economic interest in MERCOSUR is substantial since Brazil forms Latin America's largest national market, and the GDP of Brazil and Argentina are respectively thirteen and four times larger than Chile's. Chile's association, the pact of Bolivia with MERCOSUR and the negotiations of this bloc with other Latin American countries might lead to the obsolescence of the idea of NAFTA as prelude to free trade from Anchorage to Tierra del Fuego. Instead, future economic regionalization in the Americas may take place through negotiations between NAFTA and MERCOSUR.

Ideologically, NAFTA extension would serve the proponents of neo-liberal restructuring in both Chile and Mexico. Chile's preference for entry into NAFTA has been based on the presentation of NAFTA (in Chile) as the ideological example of the triumph of neo-liberalism. Entry of Chile into NAFTA would also serve ideological purposes in Mexico in the sense of a symbolic reaffirmation of Mexico's cultural leadership in Latin America. Moreover, Chile's entry could give rise to somewhat more of a counterweight towards the USA and Canada within NAFTA. In this light we can also understand Mexico's interest in signing a trade agreement with Chile, whereas trade with Chile is practically irrelevant to Mexico. Yet, if the materialization of the FTAA is to take place through negotiations between NAFTA and MERCOSUR, Mexico wants to participate in the preparation process as a member of the collective of North American countries while Chile, with its current difficulties in achieving association of MERCOSUR, might risk remaining somewhat isolated from the hemispheric integration tendency.

National and international optimism on Chile's and Mexico's embrace of open regionalism has, among other things, been based on the assumption that political stability will be conserved despite the deepening of social inequalities since the introduction of neo-liberal policies in Latin America as a whole. So far, liberalization of the Latin American economy has been accompanied by increasing poverty. During the decade of the 1980s, for example, the number of poor people in the region doubled. Worsening social circumstances may in the medium term lead to the destabilization of the political regimes of both Mexico and Chile. If such a development results in political democratization, the nature of Latin American regionalization is likely to change. In contrast with the current domination of market mechanisms, we might envisage a form of regional integration that also includes concerns for labour rights, environmental protection and small-scale production.

NOTES

1. Fast track authority provides the US government with greater freedom in trade negotiations, as Congress gives up its right to amend certain parts of internationally negotiated agreements and can only vote on approval of an agreement as a whole. This authority was for instance assigned during GATT and NAFTA negotiations.
2. According to Castañeda (1993: 61), on the contrary:

   [t]he lack of European and Japanese funding was a false argument: the new Mexican team never really expected other areas to foot the bill for Mexico's recovery. The problem was that existing levels of funding from the United States were simply not substantial enough to finance higher levels of growth, infrastructure, trade and modernization, let alone Salinas' agenda for the poor.

3. These conventions include union freedom, right of collective negotiation, minimum age for employment, non-discrimination, equal salaries for men and women, and prohibition of forced labour.

BIBLIOGRAPHY

Agacino, R. and Echeverría, M. (1995) *Flexibilidad y condiciones de trabajo precario*, Santiago: PET.

Aguero, F. (1995) 'Chile y el NAFTA', *Estudios públicos* 57: 5–12.

Aninat, E. (1994) *NAFTA, ALC con USA y la estratégia económica comercial chilena*, Santiago: Ministerio de Hacienda.

Bailey, J. (1994) 'Centralism and political change in Mexico: the case of National Solidarity', in W. A. Cornelius, A. L. Craig and J. Fox (eds) *Transforming State–Society Relations in Mexico: The National Solidarity Strategy*, San Diego: Center for US–Mexican Studies.

Bizberg, I. (1990) 'La Crísis del corporativismo mexicano', *Foro internacional* XXX (4): 694–735.

Bizberg, I. (1993) 'Los efectos de la apertura comercial sobre el mercado laboral y las relaciones industriales en México', in G. Vega Cánovas (ed.) *Liberación económica y libre comercio en América de Norte*, México: El Colegio de México.

Bozzozero, L., Bodemer, K. and Vaillant, M. (1994)¿ *Nuevos regionalismos: cooperación o conflicto?*, Caracas: Nueva Sociedad.

Butelman, A. and Meller, P. (1993) *estratégia Comercial Chilena para la década del 90. Elementos para el debáte*, Santiago: CIEPLAN.

Castañeda, J. G. (1993) 'The clouding political horizon', *Current History* February: 59–66.

Centeno, M. A. (1994) *Democracy within Reason: Technocratic Revolution in Mexico* Pennsylvania: Pennsylvania State Press.

Centeno, M. A. and Maxfield, S. (1992) 'The marriage of finance and order: changes in the Mexican political elite', *Journal of Latin American Studies* 24(1): 57–85.

CEPAL (1990) *Transformación productiva con equidad*, Santiago: Naciones Unidas.

CEPAL (1994) *El Regionalismo abierto en América Latina y el Caribe, La transformación económica al servicio de la transformación productiva con equidad*, Santiago: Naciones Unidas.

CEPAL (1995) *América Latina y el Caribe. Políticas para mejorar la inserción en la economía mundial*, Santiago: Naciones Unidas.

Cerda Morales, A. (1995) *La integración comercial en América Latina en relación a la modernidad del estado y la gestión de la auditoria interna*, Santiago: Universidad de Chile.

Confederación de la Producción y el Comercio (1992) *Programa de estudios para el Acuerdo de libre comercio entre Chile y los Estados Unidos*, Santiago: PEPALC.

Coordinadora de Centrales Sindicales del Cono Sur (1993) *Carta de los derechos fundamentales del MERCOSUR: propuesta de los trabajadores*, Santiago: Coordinadora de Centrales Sindicales del Cono Sur.

Corro Barrientos, B. (1991) 'Apertura comercial de México y nueva proyección mundial de Estados Unidos', *Comercio exterior* 41(7): 676–81.

Cortázar, R. (1993) *Política laboral en el Chile democrático. Avance y desafíos en los noventas*, Santiago: Dolmen.

Dresser, D. (1994). 'Bringing the poor back in: National solidarity as a strategy of regime legitimation', in W. A. Cornelius, A. L. Craig and J. Fox (eds) *Transforming State–Society Relations in Mexico: The National Solidarity Strategy*, San Diego: Center for US–Mexican Studies.

Fernández Jilberto, A. E. (1993) 'Internacionalización y socialdemocratización de la política en Chile', in M. Vellinga (ed.) *Socio-Democracia y política en América Latina*, México, D.F.: Siglo XXI Editores.

Foxley, A. (1993) *Economía política de la transición*, Santiago: Dolmen.

Gambrill, M. (1995) 'La política salarial de las maquiladoras: mejoras posibles bajo el TLC', *Comercio exterior* 44 (7): 543–9.

Garretón, M. A. (1983) *El Proceso político chileno*, Santiago: FLACSO.

Garretón, M. A. (1995) *Hacia una nueva era política. Estudio sobre las democratizaciones*, Santiago: Fondo de Cultura Económica.

Guerra-Borges, A. (1996) 'México: integración hacia el sur', *Comercio exterior* 45 (2): 158–62.

Heredia, C. A. and Purcell, M. E. (1994) *La polarización de la sociedad mexicana: una visión desde la base de las políticas de ajuste económico del Banco Mundial*, Washington, DC: The Development GAP.

Lagos, R. A. (1994) '¿Que se entiende por la flexibilidad del mercado de trabajo?', *Revista de la CEPAL* 54: 81–95.

Larrain, S., Van Hauwermeiren, S. and De Wel, B. (1994) *Comercio y medio ambiente en Chile: preocupaciones del movimiento ambiental*, Santiago: Instituto de Ecología Política.

Leiva, F. (1994) *Los tratados de libre comercio*, Santiago: RECHIP.

Levy, S. and Van Wijnbergen, S. (1992) *Mexican Agriculture in the Free Trade Agreement: Transition Problems in Economic Reform*, Paris: OECD Development Centre, Technical Papers no. 63.

Martínez, J. (1994) 'Cuatro falacias sobre la transformación chilena', *Proposiciones* 25: 46–51.

Morales, J. and MacMahon, G. (1993) *La política económica en la transición a la democracia*, Santiago: CIEPLAN.

Moulian, T. (1994) 'Limitaciones de la transición a la democracia en Chile', *Proposiciones* 25: 34–45.

O'Brien, P. and Cammack, P. (1985) *Generals in Retreat: The Crisis of Military Rule in Latin America*, New Hampshire: Manchester University Press.

Ominami, C. (1986) *Le tiers monde dans la crise*, Paris: La Découverte.

285

Ortiz, E. (1994) 'NAFTA and foreign investment in Mexico', in A. M. Rugman (ed.) *Foreign Investment and NAFTA*, Columbia: University of South Carolina Press.

OTA (Office of Technology Assessment, US Congress) (1992) *US–Mexico Trade: Pulling Together or Pulling Apart?* Washington, DC: US Government Printing Office, ITE-545.

Pizarro, C., Raczynski, D. and Vial, J. (1995) *Políticas económicas y sociales en el Chile democrático*, Santiago: CIEPLAN/UNICEF.

PREALC (Programa Regional del Empleo para América Latina y el Caribe) (1990) *Empleo y equidad: Desafío de los 90*, Documento de trabajo 354, Santiago: OIT.

Ramos Arriagada, R. (1995) *Estructura empresarial, rol del estado y los tratados de libre comercio*, Santiago: Universidad de Chile.

Ros, J. (1992) 'Free trade area or common capital market? Notes on Mexico–US economic integration and current NAFTA negotiations', *Journal of InterAmerican Studies and World Affairs* 34(2): 53–91.

Rousseau, I. (1992) 'Le liberalisme social ou la politique du juste milieu?', *Problèmes d'Amérique latine* 5: 29–44.

Ruiz-Tagle, J. (1995) *La integración regional y el ingreso al NAFTA. Consecuencias para los trabajadores*, Santiago: PET.

Sociedad de Fomentos Fabril (1995) *Consideraciones eásicas a tener en cuenta antes del MERCOSUR y el NAFTA*, Santiago: SOFOFA.

Stepan, A. (1988) *Rethinking Military Politics: Brazil and the Southern Cone*, Princeton, NJ: Princeton University Press.

Teichman, J. (1993) 'Dismantling the Mexican state and the role of the private sector', in R. Grinspun and M. A. Cameron (eds) *The Political Economy of North American Free Trade*, New York: St. Martin's Press.

Tironi, E. (1990) *Autoritarismo, modernización y marginalidad*, Santiago: Sur.

Touraine, A. (1988a) *Actores Sociales y Sistemas Políticos en América Latina*, Santiago: PREALC/OIT.

Touraine, A. (1988b) *La parole et le sang*, Paris: Odile Jacob.

Vial, J. (ed.) *A donde va América Latina? Balance de las reformas económicas*, Santiago: CIEPLAN.

Zeitlin, M. and Earl Ratcliff, R. (1988) *Landlords and Capitalists: The Dominant Class of Chile*, Princeton, NJ: Princeton University Press.

12

TRADE LIBERALIZATION AND ECONOMIC INTEGRATION IN CENTRAL AMERICA

Oscar Catalán Aravena

INTRODUCTION

The crisis of the 1980s revealed the failure of the import substitution model in Central America which had inspired the successful regional economic integration of the 1960s and 1970s. The initial response to the crisis was to implement unilateral protectionist measures; later on unilateral stabilization and adjustment programmes were applied, with the consequent abandonment of the instruments of integration.

In the first half of the 1990s, the end of the Cold War made it possible to implement the peace agreements which the governments of the region had been proposing for the past decade. In economic terms, the regional situation came to be marked by apparently contradictory tendencies: on the one hand, the continuation and deepening of the structural adjustment begun in the 1980s, on the other hand, an evident willingness to resume the recently abandoned regional economic integration and to breathe new life into the Central American Common Market (Mercado Común Centro Americano).

At the international level, the post-Cold War period has also been marked by apparently contradictory economic tendencies: the globalization of the economies, and the expansion and consolidation of the large trade blocs which dominate international trade. It would appear that, despite the indisputable triumph of neo-liberal ideology on a world-wide scale, these strategic trade policies continue to dominate commercial policy in practice. The grouping of the industrialized countries in trade blocs would seem to support the idea that commercial liberalization does not lead to an economic optimum, and that the promotion of exports should be combined with deliberate and selective protection of strategic industrial sectors.

In Central America, the new impulse towards regional cooperation raises questions about the economic relevance of integration within a context of liberalization and reinsertion into the world market. The aims of this chapter are to grasp the logic of the renewed willingness to integrate in Central America, and to see to what extent the commercial opening up promoted by the structural adjustment programmes is in contradiction with, or is complementary to, the new regional economic integration.

In order to suggest answers to these questions, this chapter begins with a presentation of a conceptual framework to analyse the effects of regional economic integration. It then proceeds to analyse the former integration in the region, the relation between the new integration and structural adjustment, and the relation between this new integration and the accession to the North American market. This is followed by an evaluation of the effects of some of the main instruments of the integration agreements. The last section presents some final reflections.

REGIONAL ECONOMIC INTEGRATION: A CONCEPTUAL FRAMEWORK

To distinguish them from multilateral trade agreements, regional economic integration agreements are known in the literature as preferential trade agreements, limited to a group of countries. Preferential trade agreements can be distinguished according to the degree of economic integration they allow. *Free trade zones* are the simplest forms of economic integration, in which the member countries abolish tariffs on reciprocal trade while maintaining their own tariffs for imports from the rest of the world. *Customs unions* also eliminate tariffs on reciprocal trade between the member countries, but in addition they fix a common external tariff on imports from the rest of the world. *Common markets* are an advanced form of customs union: in addition to free trade between the members and a common external tariff, they eliminate or reduce restrictions on the movement of productive factors, workers and capital between the member countries. The common market can be reinforced through the coordination of fiscal, monetary and exchange policies.

According to the economic literature (Gillis *et al.* 1996: 531–534), preferential trade agreements can benefit the participants mainly through the emergence of *static gains* and *dynamic gains*. Static gains result from the increase in productivity due to the improved allocation of the productive factors. Dynamic or growth gains result from the incentives which arise for investments in production for export and in related industries.

The analysis of the static gains distinguishes between *trade creation* and *trade diversion*. Trade creation takes place when, by reducing or eliminating import tariffs between member countries, a trade agreement enables one of them to export more to another at the expense of the inefficient enterprises of the importing country. It is assumed that the displaced enterprises were only able to compete with imports thanks to protectionism. Since there is more trade in the new situation than in the past, it is described as one of trade creation. Although some inefficient enterprises in a country suffer, there are others which benefit considerably from the reduction in tariffs, so that the profits of the producers outweigh the losses. In addition, consumers benefit from lower prices and the greater choice.

In maintaining tariffs for the rest of the world, preferential trade agreements discriminate against non-member countries and can cause trade diversion by enabling a member country to export more to another member, displacing imports which previously came from a country which now has to pay tariffs.

Once the trade agreement comes into force, the consumers of the importing country will buy from the new exporter at a reduced price, due to the reduction or abolition of a tariff, but at a higher cost for the country in terms of foreign currency. Part of the revenue previously paid to the exporters from non-member countries is now paid to the exporters from member countries, who are less efficient producers. A preferential trade agreement is considered beneficial if trade creation outweighs trade diversion. The conventional theory considers the profits from trade creation as similar to the profits of the opening up of trade.

According to most scholars, the dynamic effects of economic integration outweigh the effects resulting from the increased efficiency of allocation. Integration agreements enable the market of the member countries to expand. In this way, economies of scale are now obtained in activities for which the domestic market of the country was too small. The enlarged market also facilitates *complementary agreements*, enabling the member countries to allocate larger-scale *infant industries* between one another. These complementary agreements make it possible to share the expenses of initiating activities on a larger scale, so that each member can benefit from the installation of strategic activities such as the petrochemicals industry, fertilizers, pulp and paper, and the basic metal industry.

The growth of markets through integration encourages competition between producers from the member countries, and thereby enhances efficiency. This can be especially important for industries whose scale of production means that they would monopolize the internal markets at inefficient levels of production without market integration.

In practice, one of the most striking characteristics of the patterns of integration is the growth of competition and the emergence of strong currents of *intra-industrial trade*: a large part of the increase in trade concerns similar products with very little differentiation. The member countries reciprocally export foodstuffs, footwear, cosmetics, metal products, capital equipment, and other products. The enlarged market enables firms to specialize: a firm can thus reduce the variety of its products in order to concentrate on producing less articles of better quality.

Now that with integration the national boundaries disappear and therefore the markets expand, for many firms more efficient regional trade patterns emerged with less transport costs. This intra-industrial trade reflects increased competition and a greater choice for the consumer. The dynamic effects operate in the long term by inducing increased investments, which in turn accelerate regional growth and restructure the economy, facilitating the rise of industries with export potential which could not have been initiated in any other way.

By applying the new growth theory, it is possible to demonstrate that the increased competition leads to higher levels of investment: a larger market implies bigger innovations and more investment in research and development (R&D). This is because of the increased profitability of the investments, improved opportunities for international cooperation, specialization in R&D, and increased efficiency of capital markets (Baldwin 1994, in Dijkstra 1996: 1).

Analysis of the static and dynamic gains makes it possible to understand how the reduction or elimination of tariffs at regional level and the maintenance of external tariffs can result in a growth in the markets. However, neo-classical theory easily shows that the alleged benefits of preferential trade agreements are in fact arguments in favour of free trade in general (Lal 1993: 358). The benefits of the preferential trade agreements are only a part of the benefits which can be obtained from multilateral free trade.

Using the concepts of consumer surplus and producer surplus, the modern theory of international trade (Krugman and Obstfeld 1996: 190–207) demonstrates that tariffs generate loss of economic efficiency through distortions in production and consumption. The net effect of a tariff on the national prosperity of a small country is thus negative (the consumer losses outweigh the benefits to the producers and the government). The theory only allows two exceptions in which protectionism is justified. The first is the so-called theory of strategic trade, based on the idea of the optimal tariff. This argument is not relevant to the developing countries, which are characterized by their inability to influence prices on the world market.

The second exception is more relevant to the developing countries. It concerns the regional version of the 'infant industry' argument which lies behind import substitution industrialization and the creation of a customs union in Central America in the 1960s. The idea is that a country with export potential requires temporary protection in order to be able to develop. Once the apprenticeship period is over, the protection can be removed. The individual markets in the developing countries are too small for many of the new industries, so this protection has to be organized at regional level.

The neo-classical argument can also be used to refute this variant of the infant industry argument. The application of tariffs which distort both production and consumption is not the 'first best' solution to stimulate potentially profitable new industries. The optimal solution in this case is the application of a subsidy to the producer. This has the same positive effect for the producer as a tariff, but it does not distort consumption, so that the loss of efficiency and welfare is less.

It is therefore not possible to justify the maintenance of preferential trade agreement tariffs within neo-classical theory. We find the explanation of the appropriateness and advantages of the preferential trade agreement in the application of an institutional economic framework to international trade.

According to the institutionalists, a market consists of a number of social institutions in which exchanges take place (Hodgson 1988, in Dijkstra 1996: 2). The exchanges imply contractual agreements and the exchange of property rights. Within this perspective, markets are not a natural system, but they have to be created. Within the international context, this means that the abolition of tariffs does not automatically bring about participation in international trade (North, in Dijkstra 1996: 3).

The existence of trade requires institutions to organize and legitimate the exchanges, especially at international level. Trade needs regulations or customs with regard to trade procedures, quality standards, units of measurement and legal procedures. In addition, there must be a minimum infrastructure to prevent the costs of exchange from becoming prohibitively high.

Particularly for the developing countries, the creation of institutions and the construction of an infrastructure are a complex task which is made easier if it is tackled regionally. Countries within the same region tend to have similar trading cultures and practices, which makes it easier to exchange information about products, prices, potential buyers and sellers at the regional level. It is also easier to establish agreements on legal procedures, harmonization of standards and regulations for the execution of contracts at the regional level. In short, the countries which need larger markets for their industrial development can obtain them more effectively through economic cooperation with a limited number of neighbouring countries.

To explain the advantages of regional integration, the institutionalist theory provides an additional argument based on the conduct of the enterprises. While neo-classical theory sets out from the idea that individuals and enterprises maximize the benefits and make rational choices, the institutionalists assume that rationality is socially induced and that behaviour of the individual and of organizations is largely determined by routine (Hodgson 1988, in Dijkstra 1996: 3).

According to the institutionalist approach, the new exports can be considered organizational innovations which enterprises can learn. These innovations should be understood as minor deviations from the familiar routines or as new combinations of existing routines (Nelson and Winter 1982, in Dijkstra 1996: 3). The more export activity comes to resemble the routine of selling on the domestic market, the greater the likelihood that it will be carried out successfully.

In addition to the reduced costs of transport, it can be supposed that export at the regional level is easier than export to distant countries because at the regional level there is a greater familiarity with the way of doing business, with the legislation, and with the cultural habits and tastes of the consumers. Furthermore, the quality standards are probably lower than for goods and services exported to the industrialized countries. When exports at the regional level have become a routine, this routine can be extended to other markets.

THE DYNAMIC OF ECONOMIC INTEGRATION IN CENTRAL AMERICA

In the late 1950s and early 1960s, the countries of Central America initiated a programme of regional economic integration under the name of the Central American Common Market (CACM). Although if one adheres strictly to the definitions, this attempt at integration did not rise above the level of a customs union, and the name CACM reflected the aspirations of the time: economic integration as a step towards making the old dream of the political reunification of the region come true.

The programme consisted of four main elements:

1 Free intra-regional trade of manufactured products, with the exception of agricultural goods and livestock, alcoholic beverages and tobacco.
2 A common external tariff on imports from outside the region.
3 Monetary agreements – such as fixed exchange rates, a common unit of currency (the Central American peso), and the establishment of a compensatory mechanism to facilitate intra-regional trade.
4 the establishment of a number of regional institutions – such as the Secretariat of the Economic Integration Treaty, the Central American Economic Council, and the Central American Bank for Economic Integration – in order to operationalize the programme.

The CACM is considered one of the most successful of all the attempts at integration among developing countries (Lizano 1994b: 4). Once the intra-regional free trade and the common external tariff had been set up, a sustained growth in regional trade was generated, rising from $US30 million in 1960 – 6.7 per cent of the total foreign trade – to $US300 million in 1970 – 26.1 per cent of total trade (Caballeros 1992: 134).

The increase in regional trade facilitated rapid industrial growth, which in turn breathed new life into general economic activity. The peak period of integration coincided with the establishment of the regional highway network, the regional telecommunications system, and the interconnection of the electricity supply. Furthermore, a regional financial system was set up to fund infrastructural works and to support the main productive sectors.

With the rise in the price of petrol at the beginning of the 1970s, imbalances occurred in the balance of payments, public funding and regional exchange. During this period, regional trade continued to expand, reaching a maximum of $US1250 million in 1978 (25 per cent of exports). Regional trade was still concentrated in textile products, food and industrial chemicals (Catalán Aravena 1981: 323).

The majority of the countries reacted to the crisis by unilaterally imposing non-tariff barriers, especially through the use of multiple exchange rates. The result was that the CACM common external tariff lost its relevance: in fact, the member countries proceeded to apply different implicit tariffs for imports from outside the region.

By the beginning of the 1980s, the imbalances in regional trade and finance had become uncontrollable. The management of the economic crisis was complicated by the fact that it was turning into a political crisis, even assuming the form of civil war in some countries. With the confrontation between the US government and the Sandinista government in Nicaragua, the countries in the region were subjected to strong external pressures to assume ideological alignments leading to the abandonment of the instruments of regional economic integration.

Regional trade dropped to its lowest level in 1986: a mere $US418 million, equivalent to 10 per cent of the total exports (Caballeros 1992: 137). The serious imbalances in regional trade and the collapse of the regional system of payments because of the accumulation of enormous debts, especially by Nicaragua (Edwards

1995: 156), paralyzed the integration institutions, paving the way for the abandonment of regionalism as a possible strategic instrument to tackle the foreign debt crisis. From the mid-1980s on, the response to the debt crisis was the unilateral implementation of stabilization and structural adjustment programmes.

In the 1990s the governments in the region took decisions aimed at adopting the instruments of economic integration once again. Unlike in the past, the current efforts to reactivate the CACM are not orientated towards protecting the industrial sector in order to develop the internal market. Since the financial crisis of the 1980s and especially since the reinsertion of these countries into the world economy initiated in the second half of the 1980s, a policy of inward-looking development and import substitution is regarded in the region as a stage which has been passed. Governments in the region no longer discuss the necessity and virtue of economic opening up; the discussion now is focused on how to obtain optimal insertion as rapidly and inexpensively as possible (Lizano 1994b: 3).

What is at stake now is an open regionalism which goes beyond the nostalgia for the years of accelerated growth through regional economic integration. The member countries of the CACM are joining forces to reduce the costs of opening up trade and to be able to increase exports as rapidly as possible. In this way regional integration is seen as a possible method of reducing the high social costs, and the consequent political cost, of structural adjustment. In addition, they are attempting to set up a regional platform to ensure better future conditions for the stable insertion of the region into the North American market.

A very important step was the signing in October 1993 of a treaty covering the free trade of goods and services within the region, the free movement of capital and labour factors, the coordination of economic policies, and the adoption of a common external tariff and a common currency (Dijkstra 1995: 1). These joint efforts have been accompanied by unilateral measures, such as the incorporation into GATT (Lizano 1994b: 4), which prove how seriously they are thinking about trade liberalization.

There are three striking characteristics of the new CACM which distinguish it from the original agreement signed in 1960. First, as well as the elimination of barriers to intra-regional trade, there is now a common external tariff ranging between 5 and 20 per cent. This tariff is significantly lower than the tariff structure which was in force up to the new agreement (Edwards 1995: 156), and is an indication of the clear shift towards policies of trade liberalization. Second, the new CACM set-up includes two new countries: Panama, which was not a party to the original agreement, and Honduras, which left the CACM in 1969 after the war with El Salvador. Third, the member countries of the CACM now implement active policies of diversification and promotion of exports.

Until at least the first half of the 1990s, the results of the structural adjustment programmes in terms of the restructuring and strengthening of the export sector have been mediocre. The price of adjustment in terms of economic recession, unemployment and social tensions has been high, without a sustainable solution to the balance of payments problem having being found. The exception is Costa

O. CATALÁN ARAVENA

Rica, which has applied a heterodox adjustment programme, in close collaboration with the World Bank, with a more gradual liberalization of the economy (Fürst 1992: 5).

Trade liberalization is done gradually if it is combined with the reactivation of regional economic integration, thereby producing dynamic effects. This gradual process of liberalization makes it possible for industries with export potential to survive and makes investment in industrial reconversion attractive. The emergence of new space for intra-industrial trade allows the survival and modernization of old firms with economies of scale and the creation of new ones. Through complementary agreements, it also allows the present consolidation at a competitive level of activities which are strategic for the development of the region. Because of these dynamic effects of economic integration, the impact of liberalization in terms of economic recession and unemployment is softened and the sustainability of the liberalization policies is strengthened.

As well as the dynamic effects mentioned above, the functioning of the customs union within a framework of accelerated trade liberalization means a low common external tariff, thereby considerably reducing the possibilities of trade diversion which existed in the past. Under these conditions, economic integration is not seen as an alternative to adjustment, but as a complement to it, allowing the consolidation of competitive industrial activities through the creation of intra-industrial trade.

The infant industry argument can now be applied within the context of the adjustment programmes. The liberalization of trade with neighbouring countries of the region grants industries a transitional period in which they can cut costs to increase international competitiveness (Dijkstra 1996: 2). The widening of the market with a low common external tariff enables economies of scale in industries with export potential without the risk of the occurrence of major trade diversions. In this way, with the growth of the market the opportunities for competitive industries to consolidate increase, the sites for industrial reconversion increase, and the process of industrial adjustment becomes more gradual.

In addition, the joint promotion of exports at a regional level allows new advantages such as risk diversification, the possibility of joint negotiations of the funding of investments, and cooperation with regard to the provision of infrastructure and research activities. To sum up, regional integration can facilitate structural adjustment programmes and make them more effective.

During the 1980s the economic crisis in the region had taken on social, political and military dimensions. In the case of El Salvador, Guatemala and Nicaragua, these conflicts led to civil wars which threatened to spread all over the region. Within this situation, the US strategy of offering preferential trading terms to its allies in the region through the Caribbean Basin Initiative achieved modest results and has the weakness of offering a temporary insertion into the US market (Lizano 1994b: 12).

The policy announced by President Bush in 1990 regarding the willingness of the USA to create a free trade zone from Alaska to Patagonia, with the present NAFTA as merely the first stage in this process, has been subsequently counteracted, especially by the US Congress. However, for the small Central American countries

294

interested in achieving a larger insertion in the international economy, incorporation in NAFTA appears a guarantee of stable accession to what has been their natural market since the end of the last century – the North American market.

The character of the large regional trading blocs has changed rapidly during the post-Cold War period. In Europe, the European Economic Community (EEC) has been transformed into the European Union (EU), increasing the number of its members and deepening its integratory links. In North America, the United States of America has widened the free trade zone it shares with Canada through the incorporation of Mexico into NAFTA. In Asia, trade, investment and aid from Japan dominate the economic relations between the countries of Eastern Asia and South-Eastern Asia, creating a *de facto* Japanese zone of influence despite the absence of a formal trade agreement. These new emergent commercial blocs have become as important as – if not more important than – the multilateral trade agreements covered until 1994 by the General Agreement on Tariffs and Trade (GATT), and subsequently by the World Trade Organization (WTO).

The emergence and strengthening of these large regional trade blocs create a good deal of uncertainty among those countries which do not belong to them. Due to the great potential for trade diversion and the unequal distribution of the dynamic benefits of these blocs, the non-participant countries have reason to be afraid.

For many developing countries, the fear that the formation of these blocs will lead to losses has been an incentive to establish new agreements which encourage South–South trade, as well as to try to find agreements allowing incorporation into one of the trade blocs of the North, either on an individual basis or as a group. Moreover, after the recent experience of the rise of a new protectionism in the 1980s which cancels out the positive effects of international trade agreements (Gillis *et al.* 1996: 529), there is a well-grounded fear that, at times of world recession, the large blocs may react by becoming fortresses of protectionism *vis-à-vis* the rest of the world, resulting in commercial marginalization of those countries that do not belong to the blocs.

The EEC and its successor, the EU, have not been noticeably more protectionist than the United States or Japan towards the countries of the region, although the preferential access given to exports from the former colonies in Africa and the Caribbean generates trade diversions which particularly affect the countries of Central America. With its incorporation into NAFTA, Mexico benefits from greater access to the North American market, and this too is at the expense of trade diversion from Central America.

Fear of becoming the big losers with the diversion of trade generated by the EU and NAFTA, and of having to assume a marginal position in world trade in the event of a future new round of protectionism, after the costly commercial opening up and structural adjustment, has led the governments of the region to breathe new life into CACM and to use this customs union as a platform to negotiate their incorporation into NAFTA.

Incorporation into NAFTA is thus seen as an instrument which makes it possible to improve access to the international market, which facilitates the recuperation of the losses resulting from trade diversion to Mexico, and which permits the stabilization of the region's participation in the world market, while avoiding the risks of marginalization during periods of resurgent protectionism.

Despite the enthusiasm of the Central American countries, the chances of entry to NAFTA in the near future are very low (Lizano 1994b: 8). However, it is obvious that by negotiating as a bloc, Central America can offer the NAFTA countries better opportunities for their exporters and investors than they could as individual countries. It is not realistic to expect the USA to be interested in bargaining with each of the small countries in the region separately. Besides, behind the US policies of quotas and limitations on trade are interest groups whose bargaining power in Washington is greater than that of the small countries of Central America.

THE STATIC ECONOMIC EFFECTS OF THE NEW INTEGRATION

Study of the consequences of the new integrationist pattern requires some statistical material to enable us to gauge the concrete impact of the main instruments on trade currents and other relevant macroeconomic variables. These effects can be studied on the basis of simulations of the development of the most relevant variables.

As far as these effects are concerned, the present section is based on the general equilibrium analysis of M. de Franco (de Franco 1993: 1–58). The results of this exercise should not be interpreted as forecasts, but as the probable effects that variation in the tariffs will have on the economy if the other variables remain constant.

To facilitate the analysis, the following factors are studied separately: the possible impact of the elimination of the barriers to intra-regional trade; the possible impact of the application of a low common external tariff; and the possible joint impact of these two measures.

The elimination of tariffs and the distribution of benefits

Despite the fact that the CACM stopped operations in the second half of the 1980s and that each country applied protectionist policies (tariffs, licences and quotas) aimed at limiting imports, the juridical framework of integration was not eliminated, nor were the tariffs officially re-established. The tariffs for intra-regional trade in force in 1992 fluctuated between 2 per cent in Costa Rica and 10 per cent in Honduras.

In addition to the tariffs, each country set up a system of licences, quotas and other protectionist practices which hamper trade (see Table 12.1). As these non-tariff barriers are equivalent to the application of tariffs, their effects can be considered similar to those of a tariff in the analysis.

Table 12.1 Tariffs (in percentages), licences and quotas in force in 1992 in Central America

	Tariff	*Non-tariff restrictions*
Costa Rica	2.0	Licences for 20 products
El Salvador	5.0	Licences for sugar and molasses
Guatemala	3.0	Licences for milk, beans, livestock quotas
Honduras	10.0	Licences for sugar, eggs, poultry
Nicaragua	8.2	Licences for sugar

Source: de Franco (1993).

The elimination of tariffs within the region should produce an equivalent reduction in the price of imports in local currency. The drop in the price of imports from Central America in relation to imports from the rest of the world causes the demand for imports from Central America to increase. With an average price reduction of 2.9 per cent, equivalent to the current average tariff, the demand for imports from the region can be expected to increase by 2.2 per cent.

However, while the prices of imports from the region drop in local currency, dollar prices for exporters from the region may increase because of the increased demand. As a result of the increase in the prices of exports, the decrease in the prices of regional imports in local currency is less than the tariff reduction.

The increase in the price of exports is due to the rigidness of the supply. As a part of the inputs used, even though it is a small one, is of regional origin, the drop in the price of imports from the region produces a slight reduction in the costs of production. This cost reduction generates a slight increase in production and employment. However, this increase in supply is not sufficient to meet the new level of demand (equal to the previous level plus the increase in demand resulting from the tariff reduction).

This difference between supply and demand generates an increase in the average price of exports. While the prices of imports in local currency diminish, there is an average increase in the dollar price of exports because of the increase in demand. In other words, the prices of imports from Central America in local currency are not reduced in the same proportion as the tariff reduction because of the increase in export prices.

The discrepancy between supply and demand is not only expressed in an increase in the prices of intra-regional exports, but it is also reflected in an increase in internal prices. This increase in internal prices is less than the increase in the prices of exports because internal prices are an average of the prices produced on the local market and of imports, and the prices of the latter are reduced because of the disappearance of intra-regional tariffs.

Traditional general equilibrium analysis supposes that small, open economies can sell all of their production at the same price and that they can import any quantity of goods without affecting their price. However, if a group of these economies forms a customs union, both the supply and demand curves will display rigidities because of the common external tariff. While the dollar prices of exports to Central America increase, the prices of exports to the rest of the world remain constant, leading exporters to prefer to export more within the region. While the prices of imports from Central America in local currency fall, the prices of imports from the rest of the world remain constant, which is why the consumers prefer imports from the region.

The internal increase in prices resulting from the elimination of intra-regional tariffs causes the real rate of exchange of exports to decrease. This appreciation of the national currency causes a decrease in total exports and an increase in total imports. This is because, although the price of exports to Central America increases, the price of exports to the rest of the world, which applies to the majority of exports, remains constant.

In the same way, although the prices of imports from Central America fall, the prices of imports from the rest of the world, which constitute the majority of imports, remain constant. The appreciation in the real rate of exchange leads to an increase of imports of the order of some 0.57 per cent and a decrease of exports of the order of 0.49 per cent. There is thus an increase in the balance-of-payments deficit, putting more pressure on the international reserves and the need for external funding.

Despite the deterioration in the balance of payments, with the simulations of de Franco, there is an increase in total trade, both with Central America and with the rest of the world, of 0.69 per cent. This net trade creation is produced although the increase in imports from the region is traded at higher dollar prices (trade diversion as a result of less efficient production in the region) than the price of imports from the rest of the world.

To sum up, the elimination of intra-regional tariffs has positive effects on welfare because it generates an increase in production and an increase in employment, and the creation of trade is larger than the trade diversion that is generated. The main disadvantage of the elimination of intra-regional trade barriers is the deterioration in the balance of payments.

Considering this deterioration in the balance of payments from the perspective of the saving-investment process, the elimination of tariffs means a reduction in government revenues which is larger than the increase in private savings generated by this measure. The budget of the government is affected by the reduction in tax revenues and by the increase in nominal expenditures due to the increase in prices caused by the elimination of tariffs.

The main cost of the elimination of intra-regional tariffs is the deterioration in the balance of payments. Moreover, this cost is not borne equally by the countries that are parties to the integration agreement. The distribution of the costs and benefits among the member countries can be analysed using the changes in the balance of payments of each country with respect to its partners in the region after the elimination of the tariffs.

A clear picture emerges from the static analysis of the effects of the elimination of tariffs: Costa Rica and Guatemala, the countries with the lowest tariffs, come out on top, while Honduras, Nicaragua and El Salvador, the countries with the highest tariffs (see Table 12.1) are the losers.

With the elimination of tariffs, Guatemala improves its position *vis-à-vis* El Salvador, Honduras and Nicaragua, while its position with regard to Costa Rica deteriorates. Weighing up the positive and negative effects, Guatemala has a net benefit of $US10 million. For Costa Rica, the elimination of tariffs would improve its position *vis-à-vis* all of its Central American partners.

With the elimination of tariffs, El Salvador improves its position *vis-à-vis* Nicaragua and Honduras, while its position with regard to Costa Rica and Guatemala deteriorates. The net result for El Salvador is a slight increase of $US2 million of its trade deficit. The situation of Honduras improves slightly *vis-à-vis* Nicaragua, while it deteriorates with regard to Guatemala, El Salvador and Costa Rica. The net result for Honduras is an increase in its deficit. The situation of Nicaragua deteriorates with regard to all of its partners, increasing its trade deficit by $US13 million.

In practice, the distribution of the results of the elimination of intra-regional tariffs is determined not only by the level of tariffs in force at the time of their elimination, but also by the capacity of the productive structures to respond to the incentives offered by the liberalization of trade within the region. The countries with a higher level of development (less rigid economic structures) and with lower tariffs will obtain greater benefits. Although all the countries benefit from the increase in production, employment and trade resulting from the elimination of tariffs, the balance-of-payments deficits of Honduras and especially of Nicaragua grow worse.

The low external tariff and the distribution of benefits

The reduction of tariffs on trade with the rest of the world was applied unilaterally in the region from the second half of the 1980s onwards within the framework of the structural adjustment programmes. Up to 1992 reductions in tariffs were normally applied in the context of exchange-rate appreciation, because the exchange rate was the favourite anchor of the stabilization programmes that were applied. In this context of exchange-rate appreciation, the reduction of tariffs to achieve the common external tariff agreed upon tends to aggravate the problems of the balance of trade (see Table 12.2).

The reduction in external tariffs applied to the rest of the world by the member countries to arrive at the common external tariff agreed upon directly reduces the price in local currency of imports from the rest of the world. As a result, because of the reduction in prices, the consumers and importers prefer goods from the rest of the world to national or regional goods. On average, the member countries would step up imports from the rest of the world by 8.6 per cent if they adopted an average common external tariff of 15 per cent.

To the extent that the majority of production inputs are imported from outside the region, the reduction in external tariffs reduces costs and has positive effects on production and employment. When the common external tariff averages 15 per cent

Table 12.2 Structure of tariffs applied by the CACM countries to the rest of the world (as a percentage)

Country	Pre-reform average	Legal average 1987	Range		
			1991	*1993*	*1995*
Costa Rica	52	26	10–50	5–30	5–20
El Salvador	48	23	5–35	5–25	5–20
Guatemala	50	25	5–37	5–20	5–20
Honduras	41	20	4–35	5–20	5–20
Nicaragua	54	21	5–20	5–20	5–20

Source: Saborio and Michalopoulos, in Edwards 1995.

the regional Gross Domestic Product (GDP) would increase by 0.32 per cent and employment by 0.57 per cent.

The fixing of the common external tariff at a low level produces a slight increase in internal prices because of the increase in internal demand for both tradable and non-tradable goods and services due to the increased income of workers and employers and to the reduction in the price of imports from the rest of the world. The greater demand for tradables can be satisfied by national production or imports, while the greater demand for non-tradables generates internal inflation to the extent that the supply is rigid in the short run.

As a large percentage of imports is from the rest of the world, the reduction of tariffs to achieve the low common external tariff significantly affects tax revenues, so that although prices increase slightly and public expenditure remains constant in real terms, a significant deterioration takes place in government finance.

The increase in internal prices combined with the drop in external prices brought about by the reduction of tariffs produces a deterioration in the real exchange rate, i.e. a real appreciation of national currencies, which stimulates imports and makes exports less competitive. Due to this deterioration in the real exchange rate, imports increase by more than 3 per cent and exports drop by more than 2 per cent. In this manner, the reduction in tariffs leads to an increase in the trade deficit and thereby to a drop in the international reserves and to an increased demand for external finance.

From the point of view of the saving–investment process, the establishment of a low common external tariff leads to a reduction in prices which facilitates a slight increase in private saving. This private saving does not compensate the strong reduction in tax revenues, so that a significant increase in external savings is required.

The reduction of the external tariff of the member countries produces benefits which are distributed in an unequal way because the initial external tariffs are unequal.

In the simulation carried out by de Franco, Guatemala obtains net trade advantages *vis-à-vis* its Central American partners: the liberalization increases its trade surplus with Honduras, El Salvador and Nicaragua, while its trade deficit with Costa Rica decreases.

El Salvador, which had pursued a liberal trade policy, experiences a minor reduction in the external tariff which does not significantly affect its trade position, and in net terms its deficit is slightly reduced: the deficits with Guatemala and Honduras are increased a little, but these increases are more than compensated by the reduction of the deficit with Costa Rica and the slight increase in the surplus with Nicaragua.

The reduction of the external tariff worsens the trade situation of Honduras in net terms: its deficit with Guatemala increases, its surplus with El Salvador is reduced, its deficit with Costa Rica stays the same, and its surplus with Nicaragua increases minimally.

In Nicaragua, the country with the most disadvantageous initial position because of its trade deficit with all of its Central American partners, the reduction of the external tariff hardly affects its trade position within the region. As a result of the policy of radical liberalization which was applied in the 1990s, the reduction in this country to bring it down to the common external tariff is very small. With the application of the common external tariff, the trade deficit with Guatemala, Honduras and El Salvador would increase very slightly, while the deficit with Costa Rica is reduced.

Costa Rica, the country with the most favourable initial conditions because of its trade surplus with the region of more than $US100 million, is also the country with the most protected economy in Central America. For this reason, the application of the common external tariff affects its trade position to a greater extent than its partners in the CACM. Although Costa Rica still maintains its trade surplus with its partners in the region after the application of the common external tariff, this surplus is reduced in every case.

The joint impact of the elimination of intra-regional tariffs and the common external tariff

For Guatemala, the combination of the elimination of the intra-regional tariff and the application of the common external tariff is favourable for its trade with all the countries in the region. In terms of trade, the proposed regional integration is favourable for Guatemala.

For El Salvador, the joint application of the proposed measures is neutral for the trade balance with the region, although the composition of its trade is altered: its deficit with Guatemala increases, its deficit with Honduras is transformed into a surplus, its surplus with Nicaragua increases, and its deficit with Costa Rica remains the same.

In the case of Honduras, the application of the reforms contemplated in the integration agreements leads to a deterioration of its trade position in the region. In the case of trade with Guatemala and Costa Rica, the initial deficit increases, and the surplus with El Salvador is transformed into a deficit. Only the trade position with Nicaragua is improved by integration.

Table 12.3 Trade balance of payments by countries in Central America, 1992 (in $US million)

	Base year 1992	Customs union simulation
Guatemala	129.3	147.2
El Salvador	−38.6	−38.4
Honduras	−30.6	−38.7
Nicaragua	−171.9	−187.9
Costa Rica	111.8	117.9

Source: de Franco 1993.

For Nicaragua, the country with the largest trade deficit in the region, the trade reforms increase this deficit by about 10 per cent. Nicaragua increases its deficit with all the countries of the region, and Guatemala and Costa Rica consolidate their role as creditors.

For Costa Rica, the application of the integration agreements enables it to increase its trade surplus by some 5 per cent. Although the trade surpluses with all of the countries in the region continue, its position *vis-à-vis* Guatemala is weakened, its position *vis-à-vis* El Salvador remains unchanged, and its position with regard to the weakest partners – Honduras and Nicaragua – is strengthened.

To sum up, due to the different initial situation within the region and in relation to the rest of the world, the static benefits of the increase in trade, resulting from the elimination of trade barriers in the region and the establishment of a low common external tariff, are distributed unevenly: the trade surpluses of Guatemala and Costa Rica increase, El Salvador would maintain its trade deficit with the region, and Honduras and Nicaragua would suffer a deterioration in their trade balance with the region (see Table 12.3).

Discounting their distribution, the integration agreements imply benefits for the region (see Table 12.4). The joint effect of the elimination of barriers to intra-regional trade and the application of a low common external tariff is an increase in the total trade of the region of the order of 5 per cent. This increase in trade entails an increase in production of almost 1 per cent and an increase in employment of 1.5 per cent. All of the countries in the region benefit from these increases in production and employment.

Due to the fact that the tariff reduction strengthens currency appreciation, the price the region pays for the increase in trade is the deterioration in the trade balance with the rest of the world, and therefore an increase in dependency on external finance. If the governments are not successful in elaborating policies aimed at reducing this appreciation, there is a risk that the trade imbalances may once again create political tensions between the member countries and that the enthusiasm for integration agreements may cool down.

The reduction of currency appreciation requires policies aimed at increasing competitiveness through increasing productivity in the region: development of the

Table 12.4 Simulation of the macro-economic effects of the customs union (as a percentage)

	Real GDP	Employment	Total exports	Total imports	Total trade
Guatemala	0.771	1.620	−1.615	5.242	3.160
El Salvador	1.472	2.371	−1.744	2.433	2.342
Honduras	0.348	0.707	−1.867	9.887	5.337
Nicaragua	0.534	0.766	−1.063	4.815	4.447
Costa Rica	0.635	1.027	−4.023	16.442	7.073
Central America	0.839	1.469	−2.645	8.875	4.742

Source: de Franco (1993).

physical infrastructure, development of human resources, and modernization of agriculture. In turn, this policy to increase productivity requires a restructuring of public expenditure. As in the past, regional integration agreements offer an adequate framework for the implementation of policies to increase productivity taking advantage of economies of scale and for the implementation of policies to restructure public expenditure in a more efficient manner and at a lower political cost.

CONCLUSIONS

Through the application of structural adjustment programmes, the countries in the region, like the majority of their Latin American neighbours, launched one of the most substantial trade liberalization operations in recent economic history. This commercial opening up was unilateral, in the sense that there was no reciprocal opening up on the part of the trade partners, either within or outside the region. This trade liberalization was imposed by the need to face up to the debt crisis in an international context of the maintenance of protectionism in the industrialized countries.

Despite the last round of multilateral GATT negotiations concluded in 1993, the commercial opening up of Central America has not found an international climate to ensure its sustainability. The industrialized countries maintain their protectionist practices, expressed principally in non-tariff barriers to trade – quotas, prohibitions, licences – which make access to those markets prohibitive in some cases.

From the review of the characteristics of the new integration it may be concluded that it has not been conceived as an alternative to the process of unilateral liberalization. Rather, it represents an effort to give a multilateral or reciprocal character to that liberalization. The countries involved are endeavouring to obtain concessions through negotiation which will facilitate access to the markets of their main trade partners.

With the application of a low common external tariff, the CACM countries have homogenized and deepened the commercial opening up in the 1990s. The liberalization of intra-regional trade created trade and new opportunities for development which buffer the recessionary effects of adjustment, rescuing activities which have competitive potential but require a period of adaptation to the new situation. In this sense, regional integration is an intermediate step to win time for the reconversion and consolidation of potentially competitive activities. The maintenance and development of these activities strengthen the sustainability of the reforms applied and reduces their social and political costs.

In addition, within the context of the maintenance of protectionism and fears of exclusion from trade during periods of recession, regional integration is seen in the region as an intermediate step to facilitate incorporation in NAFTA. Participation in NAFTA, besides allowing the recuperation of trade diverted by Mexico's recent admission, would enable a stable insertion into the world market.

Besides understanding its logic, it is important to know the possible economic effects of the proposed pattern of integration. After the recent reapplication of regional cooperation in 1993, regional trade immediately increased to almost $US1,000 million, amply surpassing the level of the previous decade.

Obviously, the process is such a recent one that the time has not yet come to evaluate the results. All the same, using the conceptual framework at our disposal, it is possible to suggest some of the pros and cons of the proposed scheme.

In the case of the CACM, the simultaneous application of a low common external tariff with the elimination of the barriers to intra-regional trade creates more trade than it replaces. This is a relevant conclusion because it means that the trade agreements in the region benefit the parties concerned with static gains. As a result, there are no grounds to support fears that integration would lead primarily to the emergence of internationally inefficient enterprises, which has been the main criticism levelled against the CACM in the past.

Trade creation is associated with increased efficiency due to the widening of the market and to the generation of additional economic growth. The additional growth of production and employment benefits the region as a whole. However, the analysis also suggests that, once they are made permanent, the measures reinforce the appreciation of the exchange rates and thereby worsen the general situation of the balance of payments in the region.

If we concentrate on the trade balance, the beneficiaries are Guatemala and Costa Rica, while El Salvador maintains its position and Honduras and Nicaragua would not stand to gain from the creation of trade. To sum up, the static effects of integration are not distributed equally, but there would be winners and losers. As the policy of integration increases the need for external funds, it should not be seen as the solution to the current balance-of-payments problems.

Under these circumstances, the adequate management of the balance-of-payments problems inevitably entails overcoming the present currency appreciation by means of measures to increase the competitiveness of the economies in the region. In countries with recent (hyper-) inflationary experiences, nominal devaluations are not sufficient to obtain a real depreciation of their currencies, as these devaluations are rapidly cancelled out by the re-emergence of inflation.

This means that what is needed is not the past exertions to make the labour market more flexible, but an improvement in the human capital of the region. In addition, it is necessary to promote public investment in infrastructure to make private investment more productive and to develop a programme of technological innovation, especially for agriculture.

An important part of the economic and social infrastructure of the region was created in the past, during the heyday of the CACM. This precedent reinforces the idea that there are excellent conditions at the regional level to efficiently tackle the execution of programmes orientated towards improving productivity with the modernization of the economic and social infrastructure of the region.

In the present circumstances, it is not realistic to imagine that infrastructural development programmes can be supported by an increase in public expenditure, as in the past. The funding of these programmes calls for the restructuring of public expenditure and of the tax systems. This restructuring would meet with less resistance and would be more efficient if it is applied within the framework of the coordination of macroeconomic policies at the regional level.

In balancing the advantages of integration, it is necessary to bear in mind that although it is certain that the static benefits are relatively modest, the important fact is that they generate efficient productive activities which would not have existed otherwise. Moreover, it should be realized that, although the empirical paragraphs of this chapter do not contain suggestions on the scale of the dynamic effects, in practice they should be much larger than the static effects.

The application of the regional peace agreements opened the way to the application of the regional integration agreements. However, political stability, and with it economic recovery, is still fragile in those countries in which the political polarization has not been overcome. At the present time these countries lack stable structures and rules of play to allow an efficient economic start.

Under these circumstances, the integration agreements can potentially make a major contribution to institutional development, especially in the relatively less developed and more politically polarized countries. The policies implemented in each country should have a place within the framework of the agreements signed with the other countries. In this way, these agreements form an important instrument for political and economic stability which prevents arbitrary decision-making and creates credible rules of play.

The association of economic integration with the period of economic prosperity preceding the crisis makes of the CACM an important instrument which will facilitate the modification of the rules of play in the countries or the application of policies which affect partial interests.

Given the importance of the integration agreements as a stabilizing factor and as a way of achieving institutional development, it is advisable that an image of equitable distribution of the benefits should be created in the region. To this end, special attention should be paid to mechanisms which generate a better distribution of the trade benefits, preferably through an increase in productivity rather than through redistributive mechanisms which increase the economic distortions and differences in productivity.

The potential advantages of integration are large, but there are also risks. If it is to be successful, the integration project must be able to count on extra investments.

Political and economic stability and the institutional development of the region are indispensable preconditions for this.

BIBLIOGRAPHY

Amsden, A. (1986) 'The direction of trade – past and present and the learning effects of exports to different directions', *Journal of Development Economics* 23: 249–274.

Caballeros, R. (1992) 'Reorientación de la integración centroamericana', *Revista de la CEPAL* 46: 133–45.

Catalán Aravena, O. (1981) 'De economische achtergrond van de Middenamerikaanse crisis', *Internationale Spectator* 35, 6: 319–328.

Catalán Aravena, O. (1996) 'Controlling hyperinflation and structural adjustment in Nicaragua', in A. Fernández Jilberto and A. Mommen (eds) *Liberalization in the Developing World*, London: Routledge.

Dijkstra, G. (1995) *The Benefits of Economic Integration: The Case of Central America*, Working Paper Series No. 207, The Hague: Institute of Social Studies.

Dijkstra, G. (1996) *Skill Intensive Exports from Latin America: A Case for Regional Integration?*, Development Economics Seminar Paper No. 96, The Hague: Institute of Social Studies.

Edwards, S. (1995) *Crisis and Reform in Latin America: From Despair to Hope*, New York: Oxford University Press.

Franco, M. de (1993) *¿Vale la pena la nueva integración centroamericana?: Un enfoque de equilibrio general*, mimeo, Managua: Instituto Centroamericano de Administración de Empresas.

Fürst, E. (1992) *Liberalización comercial y promoción de exportaciones en Costa Rica. Limitaciones y desafíos de la política de ajuste estructural reciente*, Serie Política Económica, Costa Rica: Universidad Nacional.

Gillis, M., Perkins, D., Roemer, M. and Snodgrass, D. (1996) *Economics of Development*, 4th edn, New York and London: Norton & Company.

Hamilton, N. and Thompson, C. (1994) 'Export promotion in a regional context: Central America and Southern Africa', *World Development* 22(9): 1379–1392.

Hodgson, G. (1988) *Economics and Institutions*, Oxford: Polity Press.

Krugman, P. and Obstfeld, M. (1996) *International Economics: Theory and Policy*, New York: Addison-Wesley.

Lal, D. (1993). 'Trade blocs and multilateral free trade', *Journal of Common Market Studies* 31(3): 349–358.

Lizano, E. (1994a) 'Integración económica y cooperación monetaria en el Mercado Común Centroamericano', *Integración Latinoamericana*, June: 23–31.

L. Zano, E. (1994b) 'Centroamérica y el Tratado de Libre Comercio de América del Norte', *Integración Latinoamericana*, October: 3–14.

Nelson, R. and Winter, S. (1982) *An Evolutionary Theory of Economic Change*, Cambridge, MA: Harvard University Press.

North, D. C. (1994) *Institutions, Institutional Change and Economic Perfomance*, Cambridge: Cambridge University Press.

Robson, P. (1993) 'The new regionalism and developing countries', *Journal of Common Market Studies* 31(3): 329–348.

Rodrik, D. (1995) 'Las reformas a la política comercial e industrial en los países en desarrollo: una revisión de las teorías y datos recientes', *Desarrollo económico* 35(138): 179–225.

Saborio, S. and Michalopoulos, C. (1992) *Central America at a Crossroads*, Policy Research Working Paper No. 922, Washington, DC: World Bank.

13

ASSOCIATION OF THE SOUTH-EAST ASIAN NATIONS' (ASEAN) FREE TRADE AREA (AFTA)[1]

The changing environment and incentives

Batara Simatupang

INTRODUCTION

Twenty-five years after the establishment of the Association of South-East Asian Nations (ASEAN) in 1967, the fourth summit meeting held in Singapore in January 1992 made a bold decision to create an ASEAN Free Trade Area (AFTA) to be completed in fifteen years (by the year 2008), starting from January 1993. Two years later the 27th meeting of the ASEAN economic ministers, advanced the completion target to the year 2003. Some members of the ASEAN proposed to advance the schedule to the year 2000, but this proposal was, however, rejected. It is generally acknowledged that ASEAN's accomplishments in the field of politics have been significant but, on the other hand, its achievements in the field of economic cooperations have been limited. Until a few years ago, an open discussion on economic cooperations was discouraged by ASEAN leaders. For instance, at the third ASEAN summit meeting in Manilla in 1987, the words 'free trade' were anathema for Indonesia, the largest member of ASEAN, which for long was the main obstacle to the progress of intra-ASEAN economic cooperations (Pangestu 1995: 38).

This chapter will examine the external and internal changing environment and incentives which encourage the ASEAN leaders to foster economic cooperation in the form of a free trade area (AFTA), its mechanism of implementation in the form of Common Effective Preferential Tariff (CEPT) for manufactured and processed agricultural products, the main problems confronting AFTA and its prospects. The chapter consists of four parts: the first part briefly outlines the main features and trends of the ASEAN economies, focusing on the dynamics of the economies, economic policies and structural changes. The second part examines the external and internal changing environment and incentives (shaping factors) leading to a breakthrough in the decision by the ASEAN leaders to create

AFTA. The third part deals with the mechanism of implementation of AFTA in the form of CEPT and other modes of economic cooperation such as sub-regional economic cooperation ('growth triangles') and investment links. The fourth part will discuss problems confronting AFTA like small intra-ASEAN and large extra-ASEAN trade, an expansion of AFTA with Vietnam (admitted in 1995), Cambodia, Laos and Myanmar (planned to be admitted in the near future), all four are low developed countries and in a process of transition to market economies; and a discussion on the prospects of AFTA. This chapter ends with a summary and conclusions.

MAIN FEATURES AND TRENDS OF SOUTH-EAST ASIAN ECONOMIES

ASEAN was formed in 1967 by five founding members – Indonesia, Malaysia, the Philippines, Singapore and Thailand. It is widely recognized that ASEAN was formed primarily for geopolitical and security reasons during the height of the Cold War in South-East Asia. Brunei, a tiny kingdom with a population of 280,000, rich with oil and natural gas, joined the association in 1984. Vietnam, a formerly centrally planned economy (CPE), which is in the middle of a process of transition to market economy, became the seventh member of the grouping in July 1995. It is planned that Cambodia, Laos and Myanmar will join ASEAN in the not very distant future. The planned ASEAN-Ten would then correspond to the geographical boundary of South-East Asia.

Economic liberalization, rapid growth and structural changes

Table 13.1 shows the size and the levels of economic development of the countries comprising ASEAN and that they are extremely diverse. Indonesia, the largest member with a population of 190.4 million – the world's fourth largest population – with an area covering nearly 2 million square km is huge, compared with the city–state of Singapore with only 2.9 million population covering an area of 1,000 square km. A comparison between Vietnam's GNP per capita of $US200, belonging to the group of low-income economies, and Singapore's GNP per capita of $US22,500, belonging to high-income economies, shows the large diversity in the levels of economic development of the members' grouping. In between these two extremes, the per capita GNP of the ASEAN members belongs to the group of lower and upper-middle income economies. Singapore, which has the highest income per capita in the region, is likely to gain most from tariff reductions under AFTA followed by Malaysia. Countries like Vietnam and Indonesia, which are much less developed, are likely to gain least. Unlike the relationship between the USA with Mexico and Canada in NAFTA, Singapore is small and has little to offer in exchange with other members of AFTA. The distribution of the gains in AFTA is likely to be uneven, the least developed countries are to bear the main costs of adjustment. This distributional conflict caused by the large diversity in size and

Table 13.1 ASEAN countries' basic economic indicators

	Indonesia	Malaysia	Philippines	Singapore	Thailand	Vietnam
Area (thousands of sq.km)	1.905	330	300	1	513	332
Population (mill) mid. 1994	190.4	19.7	67.0	2.9	58.0	72.0
Urban pop. (as percentage of total pop.) 1994	34	53	53	100	20	21
2000f	40	58	59	100	22	22
Labour force (mill) 1994	89	8	27	1	34	37
GNP p. capita $US 1994	880	3480	950	22500	2410	200
PPP adjusted 1994	3600	8440	2740	21900	6970	n.a.
GDP growth (in percentage)						
1980–90 (annual averages)	6.1	5.2	1.0	6.4	7.6	7.1
1990–94 (annual averages)	7.1	8.4	1.6	8.3	8.2	8.0
1995	8.1	9.3	4.8	8.9	8.6	9.5
1996f	7.8	8.5	5.5	8.0	8.3	9.8
1997f	7.7	8.0	5.7	7.5	8.0	9.9
Gross domestic saving (as percentage of GDP)						
1981–90 (average)	30.9	33.2	22.0	41.8	27.2	n.a.
1990–94 (average)	34.3	34.7	15.8	46.2	35.0	11.7
1995	36.0	37.2	14.7	55.6	34.2	19.1
1996f	37.4	37.5	16.1	55.9	35.0	21.1
1997f	38.5	38.0	16.9	56.4	35.0	22.0
Gross domestic investment (as percentage of GDP)						
1981–90 (average)	29.3	30.6	22.0	41.7	30.7	n.a
1990–94 (average)	32.5	34.9	22.7	35.6	41.1	18.0
1995	38.3	40.6	22.3	33.9	40.0	27.6
1996f	39.0	41.0	23.7	34.5	41.0	32.0
1997f	39.0	41.5	24.7	35.4	41.0	34.0
Trade in percentage of GDP (in 1994)	41.3	1675	55.8	289.7	69.6	52.7
Export growth (in percentage)						
1980–90 (annual average)	5.3	11.5	2.9	12.1	14.3	n.a.
1990–94 (annual average)	21.3	17.8	10.2	16.1	21.6	22.4
Changes in CPI (in percentage)						
1981–90 (average)	8.5	3.6	13.4	2.5	4.4	191.2
1990–94 (average)	8.6	3.8	11.7	3.1	4.8	34.4
1995	9.4	3.4	8.1	3.2	5.8	12.7
1996f	7.5	3.7	9.0	2.4	5.5	13.5
1997f	8.0	4.0	4.0	2.8	5.5	14.0

Source: *World Development Report 1996; Asian Development Outlook* (1996 and 1997).
Note: f = forecast.

levels of economic development of ASEAN member countries is a serious obstacle to successful economic cooperation. With a total population of 410 million, high growth of disposable income and rapid urbanization, ASEAN is potentially a large market for investors and business, if AFTA is successful.

According to the World Bank (1993) study, the ASEAN-Four (Indonesia, Malaysia, Singapore and Thailand) belong to the group of eight high-performing East Asian economies. With the exception of the Philippines, the average rate of growth of ASEAN economies during 1980–95 considerably exceeded the world growth average. The rate of gross domestic savings and gross investment has been high, accompanied by rapid growth of exports and with a growing share of higher value-added components in total exports. With the exception of Singapore, gross domestic saving was, however, short of investment, and this resource gap was funded by external capital inflows. Inflation has been low, amounting to a single-digit range in the ASEAN-Four during the period 1980–94 (see Table 13.1). High inflation in the Philippines was mainly due to the heritages of political instability during the Marcos and Aquino periods; while high inflation in Vietnam has been largely attributed to difficulties in coping with the problems of transition from CPE to a market economy. With political stability and economic reforms, the Philippines' economic growth in the last two years is approaching the high growth of its ASEAN neighbour and with rapidly falling inflation. Inflation in Vietnam is falling although it is still high by ASEAN standards. Despite a recent slowdown of export growth and widening deficits in the current account, ASEAN economic growth is forecast to remain buoyant in the near future due to sound economic fundamentals.

The combination of a prolonged world economic recession in 1980–83, a drastic fall of export prices of primary products produced by developing countries, the debt crisis and the high interest rates in the world financial market, affected developing countries (including the ASEAN ecoonomies) adversely. With the exception of Singapore, primary products formed a large share of the GDP and exports of ASEAN countries. Due to optimistic expectations that the world economy would soon recover, ASEAN countries (with the exception of Thailand which introduced stringent economic policies earlier) adopted expansionary counter-cyclical policies in the early 1980s. These policies, however, aggravated the unfavourable state of the economy (Chintayarangsan et al. 1992: 365). Fiscal deficits and deficits in the current account were growing rapidly while exchange rates were overvalued. The counter-cyclical policies were later abandoned. Average growth of GDP of the ASEAN economies during 1980–86 slowed down considerably, reaching its lowest point in 1985 when GDP in Malaysia, the Philippines and Singapore was falling and the growth rate of Indonesia was low.

In response to the highly unfavourable international economic conditions and slow economic growth during the first half of the 1980s which caused serious balance-of-payments pressure, the ASEAN countries adopted a package of macro- and micro-economic reforms which aimed to generate stable macro-economic relations and to stimulate investment in export-oriented industries. The tight fiscal and monetary policies which helped to keep prices stable and to ensure that a series of currency devaluations, introduced by Thailand (in 1981 and 1987), by Indonesia (in 1983 and 1986) and by Malaysia (since 1985 through a managed float), would improve export competitiveness. Reforms in the trade regimes and in industrial policies are crucial to the success of structural adjustment of the economy. Malaysia, Indonesia and Thailand pursued a strongly outward-looking strategy throughout the 1980s, taking measures by liberalizing import restrictions, strengthening export incentives, promoting foreign investment, particularly in export-oriented projects, adjusting foreign exchange rates to maintain competitiveness and liberalizing the financial system to promote savings and facilitate (foreign) investment. The timing was opportune since ASEAN's outward-looking strategy coincided with the huge flows of foreign direct investment to the ASEAN-Four from Japan, and later on from the East Asian NICs (Taiwan, South Korea and Hong Kong) following the appreciation of the yen and the currencies of the East Asian NICs. The process of production relocation due to comparative advantages and low cost of production has made the ASEAN countries profitable production platforms for both the domestic market and exports.[2] Since 1987 the ASEAN economies have regained the high growth trends.

Rapid growth in GDP of the ASEAN has been accompanied by rapid change in the structure of output and exports. Table 13.2 shows the rapid change in the structure of GDP of the ASEAN-Three (Indonesia, Malaysia and Thailand) in the last two decades. For instance, Indonesia's share of agriculture in GDP dropped from 37 per cent in 1975 to 17 per cent in 1994; while, on the other hand, the share of manufacturing rose from 11 per cent to 24 per cent during the same period. Table 13.2 also indicates that ASEAN countries have been transformed from agricultural to industrializing economies since the 1980s. Moreover, the direction of industrialization has shifted from import-substitution industries to export-oriented industries. Table 13.3 shows the rapid change in the structure of exports of the ASEAN-Five countries. The example of Indonesia again indicates the dramatic change in the structure of its exports within a relatively short period. If the share of manufactured goods in Indonesia's total exports was merely 2.3 per cent in 1980, it jumped to 35.5 per cent and 53.1 per cent in 1990 and 1993, respectively. On the other hand, the share of primary products (mainly oil) in Indonesia's total export dropped from 97 per cent in 1980 to 65 per cent and 47 per cent in 1990 and 1993, respectively. The share of resource-based (plywood) and unskilled labour-based products (clothing and garments) in Indonesia's total exports of manufactures is, however, still high compared to the share of those product groups in the manufacturing exports of Singapore, Malaysia and Thailand, where the share of exports of machinery (electronics) and means of transportation is relatively high.

Foreign direct investment and exports

Foreign direct investment (FDI), particularly from Japan and East Asian NICs (South Korea and Taiwan) since the mid-1980s, has played a crucial role in the success of the industrial strategy of outward orientation of the ASEAN countries. FDI has contributed substantially to improved export performance in manufacturing, competitiveness, product quality and labour productivity. According to a study

Table 13.2 Structure of the GDP of ASEAN economies

		Agriculture	Industry		Services
			all	manufacturing	
Indonesia	1975	36.8	27.3	11.1	35.9
	1985	24.0	36.0	14.0	41.0
	1990	22.0	40.0	20.0	38.0
	1994	17.0	41.0	24.0	42.0
Malaysia	1975	27.7	26.8	16.4	45.5
	1985	20.8	36.7	19.7	42.0
	1990	18.7	42.2	26.9	39.0
	1994	14.6	43.0	32.0	42.0
Philippines	1975	26.8	34.1	25.3	39.1
	1985	27.0	32.0	25.0	41.0
	1990	22.5	35.8	25.4	41.7
	1994	22.0	33.0	23.0	45.0
Singapore	1975	1.5	37.2	26.0	61.3
	1985	0.8	36.0	23.6	52.6
	1990	0.3	36.6	29.0	63.1
	1994	0	36.0	27.0	62.4
Thailand	1975	24.8	27.3	19.9	47.9
	1985	17.0	30.0	20.0	53.0
	1990	12.0	39.0	26.0	49.0
	1994	10.0	39.0	29.0	50.0
Vietnam	1975	n.a.	n.a.	n.a.	n.a.
	1985	n.a.	n.a.	n.a.	n.a.
	1990	n.a.	n.a.	n.a.	n.a.
	1994	28.0	30.0	22.0	43.0

Source: World Development Report (various years).

by M. Fry, the positive effects of FDI on investment, employment, economic and export growth which have been experienced by ASEAN countries are largely attributed to their adoption of open economic policies, accompanied by a less distorted financial system and trade regime (Fry 1993).

FDI flows into the ASEAN-Four (Indonesia, the Philippines, Malaysia and Thailand) during the colonial period and the early post-war period were largely associated with primary production. Starting from the early 1960s to the mid-1980s, the ASEAN-Four attracted large FDI for the import-substitution stage of industries, protected by high tariffs and other barriers (Yue 1993: 62). FDI flows since the mid-1980s were, however, typically motivated by the currency realignments, changes in comparative advantage at home and policy measures that opened up ASEAN economies. The sourcing of FDI in the ASEAN-Four has changed dramatically since the mid-1980s; Japan (earlier) and the Northeast-Asian NICs (South Korea, Taiwan and Hong Kong) have become the main source of FDI (ibid.: 77–87). FDI

Table 13.3 ASEAN-5: export structure as a percentage of the total

| SITC | | All food items | Agricultural raw materials | Fuels | Ores and metals | Manufactured goods | Of which | | | Unallocated |
| | | | | | | | Chemical products | Other manufactured goods | Machinery and transport equipment | |
		0 + 1 + 22 + 4	2 less (22 + 27 + 28)	3	27 + 28 + 68	5 to 8 less 68	5	6 + 8 less 68	7	
Indonesia	1970	19.6	34.8	32.8	11.4	1.2	0.5	0.3	0.3	0.3
	1980	7.6	14.1	71.9	3.9	2.3	0.4	1.4	0.5	0.1
	1990	11.2	5.0	44.0	4.4	35.5	2.4	31.6	1.4	–
	1993	10.8	4.2	28.2	3.5	53.1	2.2	45.9	4.9	
Malaysia	1970	12.6	50.0	7.3	22.6	6.5	0.7	4.2	1.6	0.9
	1980	15.0	30.9	24.7	10.2	18.8	0.6	6.7	11.5	0.3
	1990	11.7	13.8	17.8	2.1	54.2	1.7	16.4	36.1	0.4
	1993	9.4	8.7	10.3	1.2	69.7	2.1	23.3	44.2	0.6
Philippines	1970	44.0	25.8	1.6	21.0	7.5	0.5	6.9	0.1	0.1
	1980	35.9	6.1	0.7	20.6	21.1	1.5	17.4	2.1	15.7
	1990	24.9	4.8	4.9	6.1	39.0	3.4	22.1	13.5	20.4
	1993	15.6	1.5	2.0	4.5	41.6	2.3	20.7	18.7	34.8
Singapore	1970	16.4	28.3	23.2	1.6	27.5	2.7	13.9	11.0	3.0
	1980	8.1	10.3	28.9	2.4	43.1	3.4	12.9	26.8	7.2
	1990	5.2	2.6	17.9	1.6	71.7	6.6	17.6	47.5	1.1
	1993	5.0	1.4	12.2	1.5	78.5	6.4	17.3	54.8	1.5
Thailand	1970	52.3	24.7	0.3	14.6	4.7	0.2	4.4	0.1	3.3
	1980	47.0	11.2	0.1	13.6	25.2	0.7	18.6	5.9	2.9
	1990	28.7	5.1	0.8	1.0	63.1	2.0	41.4	19.8	1.2
	1993	21.9	4.0	1.1	0.5	71.1	2.8	40.6	27.7	1.5

Source: UNCTAD (1995).

Table 13.4 FDI in selected Asian countries, 1989–94 (in $US million)

	1989	1990	1991	1992	1993	1994	1989–1994
East Asian NICs	2,722	2,118	2,451	1,606	1,505	2,184	12,586
Korea	1,118	788	1,180	727	588	809	5,210
Taiwan	1,604	1,330	1,271	879	917	1,375	7,376
China	3,393	3,487	4,366	11,156	27,515	33,787	83,704
ASEAN-5	7,575	11,974	12,917	11,655	14,515	13,811	72,447
Indonesia	682	1,093	1,482	1,777	2,004	2,109	9,147
Malaysia	1,668	2,332	3,998	5,183	5,006	4,348	22,535
Philippines	563	530	544	228	763	1,126	3,754
Singapore	2,887	5,575	4,879	2,351	5,016	5,588	26,296
Thailand	1,775	2,444	2,014	2,116	1,726	640	10,715
South Asia	580	455	454	805	1,155	2,140	5,589
Bangladesh	–	3	1	4	14	11	33
India	350	165	148	344	600	1,314	2,921
Pakistan	210	244	257	335	346	649	2,041
Sri Lanka	20	43	48	122	195	166	595

Source: Asian Development Outlook (1996 and 1997).

occupies an important place in the export-oriented manufacturing, for example, about 70 per cent of FDI projects in Indonesia since the second half of the 1980s consisted of export-oriented projects (Soesastro 1996: 168). It has been estimated that by the early 1990s, foreign firms accounted for more than half of manufactured exports from the Philippines and Thailand, and over 80 per cent from Singapore and Malaysia (cited in Athukorala and Menon 1996: 80). This trade-investment nexus has created regional networks in which intra-industry and intra-firm trade is increasing. This trade-investment nexus has contributed to the rapid growth of ASEAN–East Asia trade and regional economic integration since the mid-1980s. The policies that have capitalized on FDI and trade links ignited a 'virtuous circle of development', i.e. an outward-oriented trade regime and appropriate investment policies have stimulated trade and attracted FDI, and these in turn have encouraged governments to sustain policies favourable to international linkages (Foreign Investment and Trade Linkages in Developing Countries 1993).

Since the late 1970s the ASEAN region has been one of the most attractive locations for FDI in the developing world. Despite the falling share of FDI flowing to developing countries, the share of ASEAN in the total flows of FDI going to developing countries increased from 9 per cent in 1980 to 22 per cent in 1992. Four (Singapore, Malaysia, Indonesia and Thailand) of the ten largest host developing countries to flows and stock of FDI in 1993 belong to the ASEAN grouping (UNCTAD 1995: 12). Table 13.4 shows the flows of FDI to ASEAN-Five and selected Asian developing countries during 1989–94. China and the ASEAN-Four are the two largest recipients of FDI flows to Asian developing countries. The rise of FDI flows to China has been dramatic, increasing from $US3.4 billion in 1989 to $US33.8 billion in 1994. This has caused great concern to the ASEAN countries because of the levelling-off of increases in FDI in the 1990s and the fear of FDI diversion away from ASEAN. It should be noted, however, that a significant part of the increase of FDI flows to China may be classified as 'round tripping', which actually means that part of domestic Chinese investment is recycled through Hong Kong in order to receive foreign investment incentive upon re-entry to China. A large part of FDI flows to China have originated from Chinese overseas (Hong Kong, Taiwan) and from large conglomerates owned by families domiciled in the ASEAN countries, of Chinese descent.

Foreign trade

The quantitative importance of foreign trade in the individual ASEAN economies varies significantly. For Singapore and Malaysia trade accounted for 290 per cent and 168 per cent, respectively, of GDP in 1994 while for the remaining members of the ASEAN, trade accounted for between 41 per cent (Indonesia) and 70 per cent (Thailand) of GDP in 1994. For the period 1980–94, the growth of exports exceeded the growth of GDP (see Table 13.5). ASEAN's major trading partners are the industrial countries. Japan, the USA and the European Union (EU) are the largest source of ASEAN imports and the largest export market. Japan is the largest source of import of capital goods and industrial intermediate goods, whilst the USA is the largest export market of manufactures for ASEAN. The share of ASEAN trade with North-East Asian NICs has grown significantly since the second half of the 1980s, largely reflecting the rapid growth of trade-investment links between East Asian NICs and ASEAN.

Intra-ASEAN trade has been relatively small[3] but it has been growing slightly in recent years. Intra-ASEAN imports accounted for only 17.6 per cent of total imports of ASEAN whilst intra-ASEAN exports accounted for only 22.6 per cent of total ASEAN exports in 1995 (see Table 13.5). ASEAN countries are not large customers of each other, since their major trading partners lie outside ASEAN region. Brunei, Singapore and Malaysia have individually a relatively high share of intra-ASEAN trade (over 20 per cent) of total trade, followed by Indonesia and Thailand (over 10 per cent); whilst the Philippines is the least integrated country with the ASEAN economy; its intra-ASEAN trade accounted only for by 8 per cent of its total trade (Menon 1996: Table 2.3). Nearly one-half of total intra-ASEAN trade was accounted for by Singapore, a city–state which is highly involved in trading and in entreport service for the region. Part of intra-ASEAN exports to Singapore is destined for re-export to outside the region.

The composition of intra-ASEAN trade is, however, changing rapidly, following the rapid industrialization of the region in the recent past. The importance of manufactures in intra-ASEAN trade has been growing rapidly. For instance the share of manufactured imports in total intra-ASEAN imports increased from 20 per cent to 58 per cent between 1981 to 1991, while the share of manufactured exports rose from 17 per cent to 56.5 per cent during the same period. A large part of the increase in intra-ASEAN trade in manufactures is attributed substantially to the rapid growth in intra-industry trade (ibid.). This process of change in the

Table 13.5 ASEAN external trade, 1970–95

	Percentage of ASEAN imports				Percentage of ASEAN exports			
	1970	1980	1990	1995	1970	1980	1990	1995
Intra-ASEAN	11.8	13.2	16.3	17.6	20.0	16.7	18.5	22.6
Japan	25.6	21.7	23.6	24.9	22.8	26.8	19.0	14.5
China	2.7	2.7	2.6	2.9	0.7	1.0	1.3	2.7
Asian NIEs–3	4.6	5.9	11.2	11.8	5.8	6.9	11.4	12.8
EAEC	44.7	43.5	53.7	57.2	49.3	51.4	50.2	52.6
Australia and New Zealand	5.0	3.7	3.1	2.6	2.5	3.0	2.2	2.1
United States	16.2	15.7	14.4	14.2	17.8	17.0	20.4	19.4
Canada and Mexico	1.1	1.0	1.1	0.8	1.1	0.6	1.2	1.0
NAFTA	17.3	16.7	15.5	15.0	18.9	17.6	21.6	20.4
EC	19.2	12.5	14.1	15.0	16.7	13.4	15.6	14.6
Rest of the World	13.7	23.6	13.7	10.2	12.6	14.6	10.4	10.3
Total	100.0	100.0	100.0	100.0	100.0	100.0	100.0	100.0

Source: International Monetary Fund (various years).

composition of intra-ASEAN trade reflects a trend from competition towards increasing complementarity within the ASEAN economies.

CHANGING ENVIRONMENT AND INCENTIVES

Attempts have been made by many developing countries over the past three decades to achieve regional preferential arrangements with the aim of promoting economic development but so far they have provided little benefits. The main reasons for the failure are lack of political commitment or will to implement economic cooperation programmes, very limited economic complementarity between the members, and inward-oriented industrial policies combined with macro-economic imbalances which made necessary economic adjustments extremely difficult. Most of the regional integration schemes took the form of a zero sum game (Langhammer and Hiemenz 1990; OECD 1993; Mytelka 1994: 23–32).

It is generally accepted that regional political stability and a peaceful environment, which are to a large extent attributed to ASEAN political cooperation and stability, have contributed to a favourable climate to pursue rapid economic development. But rapid economic development of the ASEAN countries, however, is due to national economic policies rather than the success of intra-ASEAN economic cooperation. So far, the results of ASEAN economic cooperation have been disappointing. The Preferential Trading Arrangements (PTA), introduced in 1977, grant tariff preferences for imports from ASEAN countries. The impact of PTA on intra-ASEAN trade was, however, negligible. Reasons for the limited progress included: great differences in tariff levels between member countries; a large list of irrelevant items (e.g snow ploughs); the 50 per cent ASEAN content (rules of origin) was too high to qualify for preference; a long exclusion list representing most intra-regional trade. Changes introduced at the third ASEAN summit in 1987 in order to make PTA work more effectively did not produce the desired results.

Regional industrial cooperation schemes, such as ASEAN Industrial Projects (AIP), ASEAN Industrial Complementation (AIC) and ASEAN Industrial Joint Ventures (AIJV) have produced meagre results (Pangestu *et al.* 1992: 335–338). Considerable variation in the level of economic development has led to serious problems with the distribution of costs and benefits of economic co-operation among the members; the less developed members of ASEAN fear that they will bear the main burden of the adjustments and enjoy the least benefits.

Despite the meagre results of the past ASEAN economic cooperation there is, however, a growing desire among the leaders since the late 1980s and early 1990s to expand intra-ASEAN economic cooperation. The changing internal and external economic environment has encouraged confidence among them to pursue ASEAN economic cooperation. It has been argued that under the new environment, improving and strengthening intra-ASEAN economic cooperation have become an imperative for the relevance and continuity of ASEAN as an international entity (ibid.: 333–334). The decision of Indonesia (which in the past strongly opposed far-reaching economic cooperation) to support the formation of a free trade area is decisive in getting AFTA off the ground.

> Indonesia, being the 'Big Brother' in the ASEAN family, tends to set the pace for the ASEAN. It is clear that AFTA can go only as far as or as fast as Indonesia would like it. This is not surprising, since Indonesia accounts for over one-half of the ASEAN market.
>
> (Ariff 1995: 57).

The changing environment and the expected benefits[4] arising from greater economic cooperation contributed to the decision of the summit meeting at Singapore in 1992 to establish the ASEAN Free Trade Area (AFTA).

Indonesia was an enthusiastic supporter of trade liberalization as testified by the adoption of the Bogor Declaration at the end of the APEC summit meeting held in 1994 and by a series of tariff reductions in the 1990s. But the mood seems to have changed since, and Indonesia has sent mixed signals on tariff protection. Contrary to expectation, Indonesia has granted tariff protection to the products produced by the petro-chemical project P.T. Chandra Asri. Indonesia insisted during the ASEAN economic ministerial meeting at the end of 1995 on exemptions from tariff cuts under the heading of 'sensitive list' products. This request will undermine the credibility of the AFTA programme which could lead to back-tracking.

The first of these changes in economic environment is to be found in the transition from inward-looking industrialization to the outward-looking industrial strategies of ASEAN economies, combined with trade liberalization in response to unfavourable world economies in the first half of the 1980s. The adoption of

317

economic reforms has improved the economic competitiveness of the ASEAN economies and this in its turn has enhanced self-confidence among the leaders. Tariffs and non-tariff barriers have been reduced unilaterally, so that tariff disparities among ASEAN member countries have been narrowed which in turn helps to facilitate regional integration. Rapid economic growth has accompanied far-reaching structural changes in production and exports, contributing to increased intra-industry and intra-firm trade in the region and hence making intra-ASEAN trade more complementary than competitive.

The second of the changes is related to the industrialization strategy adopted by ASEAN governments in the late 1980s and early 1990s which has underlined the requirement to attract FDI. ASEAN must compete with other regions or countries (Eastern Europe, China, Mexico and India) for scarce capital to prevent investment diversion. ASEAN governments are eager to ensure that ASEAN remains competitive as an investment location. It is expected that the formation of AFTA will improve the capability and the attraction of the region as a production location to foreign investors catering both to a larger free regional market and a global market.

> The greatest potential of AFTA in FDI promotion seems to lie in the sphere of efficiency-seeking investment, mostly of the export-oriented variety. Industrial restructuring through relocation of production activities and processing according to regional comparative advantage has become an important aspect of economic interdependence among the ASEAN countries in recent years. This process would be greatly facilitated by AFTA.
>
> (Athukorala and Menon 1996: 88).

It has been repeatedly stated that the rationale of AFTA would not be primarily to pursue a growing share of intra-ASEAN market in total trade but to improve ASEAN's competitiveness in the international market. In this context, the argument that the 'ultimate objective of AFTA is to increase ASEAN's competitive edge as a production base geared for the world market' (*AFTA Reader* 1993: 1) can best be understood.

The third group of factors favourably influencing the attitudes of ASEAN leaders towards regional economic cooperation is related to the development of international production networks which affects how business is done in ASEAN countries. As a result of technological progress which has cut the costs of transportation and improved communication networks, the choice of location of production is sensitive to production cost differentials, including those of wages. Successful implementation of AFTA will eliminate the barriers to intra-firm trade and trade in intermediate inputs, which will facilitate intra-regional production networks (Akrasanee and Stifel 1992: 36–37). In this context, AFTA is wholly welcomed, for example, by Japan 'since it enables many Japanese subsidiary companies located in ASEAN to procure intermediate goods from sources within the region more easily and at a lower cost as a result of reduction in tariffs' (Igusa and Shimada 1996: 159). The example of Matsushita Electric Company, the Japanese electric giant, which constructed its own horizontal business networks in the ASEAN region through affiliated joint-venture firms under the umbrella of its national trade marks in the 1980s, is an example of intra-firm trade. These firms were set up to interconnect production and marketing bases, and create identical networks in various locations beyond national borders in order to maximize their firm-level competitive advantage.

The fourth group of factors is related to the emerging new international environment at the end of the 1980s and early 1990s which affected the outlook of ASEAN leaders. The development of economic blocs in Europe (the EU was perceived as 'Fortress Europe') and in North America (NAFTA) has strengthened the fears of the ASEAN leaders of growing trade protection by others. The two blocs are important trading partners for ASEAN. Moreover, delays in the completion of the Uruguay Round Talks intensified the apprehension of the ASEAN leaders. Politically, ASEAN aimed to contain communism, particularly in South-East Asia. With the collapse of the international communist system and the settlement of Cambodian issue, ASEAN leaders feared that the organization would lose its legitimacy and become marginalized in international relations. Hence ASEAN needs a new cohesive glue to bind it together that would make ASEAN a serious negotiating partner. AFTA is supposed to be one of the means to bind the members together.

Finally, economic liberalization in the 1980s and in the 1990s in ASEAN countries has led to the emergence of stronger business interests. According to Linda Lim, as a result of economic liberalization the balance of economic power has shifted towards the private sector.

> Domestic liberalization also included privatization, deregulation and a general – if still gradual and partial – reduction in the role of governments and state enterprises in the ASEAN national economies. Instead, the economic balance of power shifted toward private enterprise, which in ASEAN has always tended to favour regional integration more than governments.
>
> (Lim 1996: 22–23)

Relationships between state and business interests are extremely complex and historically diverse in the individual ASEAN countries. Private business interests are of course not homogenous. Businesses operating behind tariff walls were wary of trade liberalization whilst those businesses which saw opportunities through opening external markets supported trade liberalization. Despite differences in the balance between state and private sectors in individual countries, the private sector in ASEAN countries in general has been pressing for an acceleration of the pace of ASEAN economic cooperation (Bowless and MacLean 1996: 337–9; Ravenhill 1995: 856). The ASEAN Chambers of Commerce and Industry (ASEAN-CCI), representing private business interests, have been generally more favourably disposed towards regional trade liberalization than government bureaucracies in the region.

COMMON EFFECTIVE PREFERENTIAL TARIFF (CEPT) AND OTHER MEANS OF REGIONAL ECONOMIC COOPERATION

Common Effective Preferential Tariff (CEPT)

As a free trade area AFTA entails a strong reduction or elimination of tariff and non-tariff barriers among member countries in a preferential fashion. Under the CEPT agreement, individual ASEAN countries, however, are free to pursue trade policies towards non-members; and unlike customs unions the question of common extra-regional tariffs does not arise. Attempts to raise tariff and non-tariff barriers against countries outside the region are not the aim of AFTA. It is widely regarded that AFTA will adhere to the principle of 'open regionalism'. As Professor M. Ariff, a Malaysian economist puts it, 'the cornerstone of AFTA is "positive" discrimination, acting in favour of its members but not against the rest of the world' (Ariff 1994). Discrimination on imports from non-AFTA members may, however, lead to trade diversion. The non-AFTA trading partners, like the USA, Japan and the EU would probably not hesitate to challenge AFTA at the World Trade Organization (WTO). In this context economists have argued that preferential trade arrangements are inferior to the multilateral trading system.

The Common Effective Preferential Tariff (CEPT) is the main instrument of implementation of AFTA. CEPT import items as a share of intra-ASEAN imports accounted for 37.2 per cent in 1990; but for individual countries, the share of CEPT import items varied considerably, ranging from 7.8 per cent for Indonesia to 60 per cent for Malaysia (Ariff 1995: Table 13.5). According to the original CEPT schemes, the objective of AFTA is to reduce tariff rates ultimately to between 0 per cent and 5 per cent within fifteen years, beginning from 1 January 1993. The agreement covers all manufactured products, including capital goods and processed agricultural products and in order to be considered as ASEAN products, at least 40 per cent of the contents must originate from a member state.

Tariff reductions are planned to proceed along two lines: the fast track for fifteen product groups[5] and the normal track for the remaining manufactured products. The fast track plans to accelerate the tariff reductions by reducing tariffs on items currently at above 20 per cent to between 0–5 per cent by the year 2003 and those currently at 20 per cent or below to 0–5 per cent by the year 2000. For the normal track tariffs currently above 20 per cent have to be reduced in five to eight years to 20 per cent and in another seven years (by 2008) to 0–5 per cent. Tariffs currently at or below 20 per cent have to be reduced to 0–5 per cent by the year 2003. Non-tariff barriers (NTBs) are to be removed on products within five years from the CEPT's start. Two types of exclusion are allowed. A general exception allows member states to consider permanent import restriction if they consider it necessary for the protection of their national security, public morals, protection of human life and health, etc. Member states may also exclude 'sensitive items' temporarily from the CEPT scheme which are sensitive to domestic industry, but these must be phased in later on.

There are many serious problems and issues involved in the implementation of the CEPT tariff reductions. Tariff reductions planned starting from January 1993 were delayed; technical details for the implementation of the agreement were not ready; industry lobby groups in various countries pressed for delays of the implementation of tariff reductions; the costs of adjustment should be spread out over time; and the use of the exclusion list as a protectionist loophole was widespread. The original transition period of fifteen years was considered too long. The ASEAN economic ministers meeting in October 1993 adopted a number of decisions in order to revive the stalled AFTA, such as an increase in the number of products included in the fast-track scheme.

The completion of the Uruguay Round Agreement in 1993 had a large impact on AFTA. It has been noted that 'the time frame for global liberalization is shorter under Uruguay Round (Agreement)...than under the original AFTA schedule' (Alburo 1995: 69). Moreover, unprocessed agricultural products are included in the Uruguay Round Agreement. After the completion of the Uruguay Round Agreement, the ASEAN leaders recognized the necessity of accelerating the implementation of AFTA and of expanding the items to be included in the CEPT scheme. The ASEAN economic ministers meeting in September 1994 decided to accelerate implementation of AFTA to be completed in 2003 instead of the original timetable of 2008 and to include unprocessed agricultural products in the CEPT scheme. In the revised CEPT the normal track is to be completed by 2003 in two steps: first, to reduce tariff rates above 20 per cent to 20 per cent by January 1998 and subsequently from 20 per cent to 0–5 per cent by January 2003; and second, to reduce tariff rates at or below 20 per cent to 0–5 per cent by January 2000. For the fast track to be completed, similarly there are two steps: first, to reduce tariff rates above 20 per cent to 0–5 per cent by January 2000; and second, to reduce tariff rates at or below 20 per cent to 0–5 per cent by January 1998.

Sub-regional cooperation zones: the 'growth triangles'

Recently several sub-regional or localized economic cooperation areas – known as 'growth triangles' – have emerged in Asia such as the Southern China Growth Triangle (Hong Kong, Taiwan and People's Republic of China), the Tumen River Area Development Programme from the North-East Asia region (Democratic People's Republic of Korea, Republic of Korea and Japan). The Singapore-Johor-Riau (SIJORI) growth triangle is the first growth triangle within ASEAN, and its success encouraged ASEAN leaders to plan the Northern Growth Triangle (the northern states of Malaysia, including Penang, southern Thailand and northern Sumatra) and the East ASEAN Growth Area (Brunei, Indonesia, Malaysia and Philippines). The idea of growth triangles is simple: 'three geographically proximate areas with different factor endowments and comparative advantages are linked in the form of an economically dynamic region' (Kumar 1994: 175; Tang et al. 1994: 1). It is further emphasized that political commitment by the leaders, and extensive cooperation between private and public sectors (i.e the provision of infrastructure, favourable administrative procedures and investment climate) are necessary for the success of the growth triangles.

The slow progress of ASEAN economic cooperation and trade liberalization was the main factor leading to the proposal of investment cooperation within the SIJORI growth triangle (Naidu 1994: 219). Initially, Indonesian participation in SIJORI was limited to Batam island. Indonesia originally aimed to develop Batam in the early 1970s as an entreport and export processing zone in competition with Singapore. In the 1980s Indonesia developed Batam as a logistic base for foreign oil companies. But progress was limited. A turnabout in Indonesia's policy towards Batam occurred when the Indonesian government began to look for cooperative development with Singapore to develop Batam. A meeting between President Suharto and Prime Minister Lee Kuan Yew in 1989 in Batam sealed the basic idea of cooperation with Singapore to develop Batam. Indonesia relaxed its investment regulations in order to attract investment to Batam (among others: 100 per cent equity ownership was allowed for the first five years of operation, foreign investment applications in Batam, and participation of private investment for the development of industrial estates and infrastructure in Batam). Under conditions of relaxed investment regulations and the strong support of Singapore government, reluctant Singapore enterprises and foreign MNCs based in Singapore have been encouraged to invest in Batam. By Indonesian presidential decree, issued in July 1990, the whole Riau archipelago became part of the SIJORI triangle area. An agreement between Singapore and Indonesia in 1991 stipulated that Bintan would supply Singapore with water.

The close economic links between Singapore and Johor date back to much earlier than the SIJORI triangle agreement of 1989, facilitated by a common history, proximity and a bridge linking the two territories. Johor is closer to Singapore with its international seaport and airport than the Malaysian capital Kuala Lumpur and other large seaports and airports. Traditionally, Singapore enterprises have invested in Johor to take advantage of lower land and labour costs. The Johor-Riau links remain undeveloped, mainly because of the lack of economic complementarity and lack of interest in both governments.

Comparative advantages arising from differences in factor endowments are complementary rather than competitive within each of the areas of the triangle. The rapid industrialization of Singapore and its economic restructuring in the 1970s and the 1980s have created a strong demand pressure on the limited supply of labour force and land. Costs of labour and land have risen fast in Singapore. Johor and Batam have advantages in low costs of unskilled or semi-skilled labour and land. Singapore's advantages lie in its skilled labour, its managerial and professional expertise, its developed capital market, transport and telecommunication networks. Singapore has attracted investment in capital-intensive, skill-intensive and high technology operations. With their advantages in low costs of labour and land, Johor and Batam have attracted labour-intensive and land-intensive investment from Singapore and other MNCs from other regions. With the relocation of unskilled labour-intensive and land-intensive activities to Batam and Johor, Singapore can concentrate its scarce resources on high value-added and high-technology activities and can maintain its competitive edge. The geographical proximity of the members of the triangle, combined with highly developed transportation and communication networks have contributed to low transaction costs, and facilitate monitoring and management of (joint) plants in Batam and Johor by key managers and investors from Singapore.

Foreign direct investments in Johor and Batam have grown rapidly. In Johor total FDI amounted to $M5,179 million (cumulative 1987–91 November). *Circa* 20–25 per cent of FDI flowing to Johor originated from Singapore, encouraged partly by liberalization in the Malaysian investment framework since 1986 (Naidu 1994: 226–234). Johor is the most important destination of Singapore investment in Malaysia, and long before the launching of SIJORI in 1989, Singapore had started to relocate industrial branches such as textile, electronics, rubber products, processed foods and wood products to Johor. The Johor state actively promoted the growth of the triangle by developing an infrastructure, such as a large number of industrial parks, and setting up an industrial training institute with the support of Singapore (Kumar 1994: 189–90). Labour, however, is becoming scarce in Johor and wages are rising rapidly.

In Batam total FDI reached $US1.6 billion (cumulatively) by end of 1993 up from only $US289 million in 1989. More than one half of the FDI in Batam originated in Singapore. Other countries like Japan, the USA and Taiwan are also active in Batam. One-half of the cumulative approved investment in Batam was allocated to real estate and tourist sectors. Industrial parks were set up in Bitan, modelled on Batam's industrial parks. More recently Taiwan machinery associations plan to set up a 25– acre assembling and warehousing centre; and its ocean shipping giant, Evergreen, plan to build a container dock and shipyard on Batam. Agribusiness (pig, poultry, and shrimp farming) has been developed on Bulan island. There is a plan to develop Singkep and Karimun as a major petroleum processing and shipyard centre. SIJORI has helped to attract foreign investment and to develop the relatively less developed economy of Riau. Batam's population has increased from a mere 7,000 in the early 1970s to 146,000 in 1993, a large part of them emigrants from other parts of Indonesia. The GDP of Batam has grown at an average of 14 per cent annually in recent years. A large number of tourists, mainly from Singapore, have visited Batam, Bintan and Johor (Yue 1995: 229–30).

Despite considerable economic achievements facilitated by the SIJORI triangle agreements, serious social and economic problems have cropped up. The infrastructure in Batam and to a less extent in Johor, has not kept up with the pace of economic growth and the issue of financing expensive infrastructure, so far, has not been solved satisfactorily. Labour, particularly in Johor, has become scarcer and more expensive than originally assumed. In Batam labour has to be imported from Java, making it more expensive. The engine of the SIJORI growth triangle is Singapore with its capital, skill, know-how and developed infrastructure; and the economic cooperation is perceived by Johor and Riau as 'unequal'. Indonesian and

Malaysian authors are becoming more concerned that 'neither Johor nor Riau, however, wish to remain the spokes to Singapore's hub' (Anwar 1995: 29), a concern which has encouraged nationalistic sentiments. Singapore has benefited most from the economic cooperation and the problem of finding a commonly accepted reasonable distribution of the benefits has haunted the relationship. Moreover, the preference of Singapore investors to affiliate themselves in business with Malaysian and Indonesian entrepreneurs of Chinese ethnic origins has led to the grouping being seen as a 'Chinese triangle' (Naidu 1994: 225), an issue which is sensitive both in Malaysia and Indonesia. Since most of the newly employed labourers in Batam are emigrants from Java, there is a feeling among the indigenous population of being marginalized in the development process.

Intra-ASEAN investment links

Like intra-ASEAN trade which is relatively small since trade is mainly oriented to extra-ASEAN countries, intra-ASEAN investment is also relatively small compared to total FDI. The relatively small intra-ASEAN investment has reflected the limited intra-ASEAN trade and investment links, since the major markets, sources of capital and technology are located outside the region. Intra-ASEAN investment to Indonesia accounted for only 2.2 per cent in 1967–87 and 3.9 per cent in 1989–91 of the total FDI. Malaysia which has the highest share of intra-ASEAN investment accounted for 16.8 per cent in 1982–87 and 12.6 per cent in 1989–91 of total FDI. Singapore is the main source of intra-ASEAN investment. The development of SIJORI encouraged the growth of intra-ASEAN investment (Yue 1993: 87–89). It is expected that in the future intra-ASEAN investment is bound to grow significantly.

Decisions by (joint) ASEAN enterprises investing in other ASEAN countries are motivated by a number of factors: first, different countries' comparative advantages based on resource endowments of labour, land and skills etc.; second, firms' competitive advantages which tend to have location-specific aspects; and finally, government policies encouraging intra-ASEAN investment. Thai enterprises' involvement in the aquaculture of freshwater shrimp in Indonesia has developed because suitable land in Thailand was exhausted, or Liem Sioe Liong's plan (an Indonesian conglomerate) and Robert Kuok (a Malaysian conglomerate) to jointly operate a large sugar plantation and sugar factories in South Sumatra are examples of intra-ASEAN investment based on comparative advantages in land and labour. Another example is the Malaysian company Sime Darby which invested in rubber, cacao and palm oil production in the Philippines taking advantage of its pioneering technology and world-wide marketing networks, while escaping the high costs of labour and land in Malaysia (Lim 1994: 145–146). There are a growing number of joint ventures between ASEAN businesses to exploit differences in the comparative advantages of individual countries. For many years, the Singapore government has encouraged unskilled and semi-skilled labour-intensive and land-intensive activities to be relocated to proximate areas. ASEAN investment in Vietnam, the new member of ASEAN, is quite significant, but only five years ago was non-existent.

The rapid growth of ASEAN economies during the past three decades has contributed to the emergence of several hundred big conglomerates, owned and run by business families of Chinese descent, living in ASEAN countries. Commercial and financial networks at national, ASEAN and at international levels (particularly with North-East Asia like Hong Kong and Taiwan) based on personal knowledge and mutual trust are among the main features of ASEAN Chinese-descended conglomerates. They are active in intra-ASEAN investment through joint business ventures with other conglomerates to develop specific projects or buying (listed) companies in another ASEAN country. The rapid development and liberalization of capital market in ASEAN capitals would help to facilitate intra-ASEAN investment. Further liberalization in investment regulation (for instance, national treatment for investment by ASEAN nationals, less bureaucratic obstacles) would stimulate intra-ASEAN investment. It would help to attract in particular intra-ASEAN investment by small and medium enterprises.

CONCLUSIONS

Intra-ASEAN trade has been relatively small, it accounts at present for only one-fifth of total ASEAN trade, and nearly one-half of it is attributed to Singapore. No big boost in intra-ASEAN trade is to be expected with the completion of AFTA. It is unlikely that CEPT exports will increase sharply under AFTA. Non-tariff barriers are still an important obstacle to intra-ASEAN trade. The main trading partners of ASEAN lie outside the region (North America, North-East Asia and Western Europe) and ASEAN's welfare depends on an open multilateral trading system. The share of manufactures has increased rapidly in intra-ASEAN trade and a substantial part of the increase in the trade of manufactures is attributed to intra-industry trade, reflecting increasing complementarity within the ASEAN economies. The dynamics of the ASEAN economies is expected to contribute towards growing intra-ASEAN trade. The formation of AFTA is expected to improve the attractiveness of the ASEAN region as a production location for foreign investors catering for export and domestic markets.

With the collapse of international communism and the settlement of the Cambodian issue, it seems logical from a geopolitical and economic perspective to include South-East Asian former CPEs (Vietnam, Laos, Cambodia and Myanmar) which are in the process of transition to market economies, as members of ASEAN. Vietnam became an ASEAN member in July 1995 and others which have the status of associate membership are expected to join ASEAN in the near future. In the protocol for accession to ASEAN, Vietnam has agreed to subscribe to all declarations, treaties and agreements in ASEAN. But membership in ASEAN will not make Vietnam automatically part of the AFTA. Vietnam needs a transitional period of three to five years between joining ASEAN and paticipating in AFTA. The protocol for the accession of Vietnam into ASEAN stated explicitly that Vietnam should prepare a list for tariff reduction effective on 1 January 1996 and ending with a 0–5 per cent tariff rate on 1 January 2006; phasing in products which are excluded temporarily in five equal instalments starting 1 January 1999 and ending 1 January 2003; and that a longer period is needed for phasing in agricultural products which are excluded temporarily (*Fifth ASEAN Summit* 1996: 101–102). Depending upon the speed of transition to market economies, loss-making state sectors and state trading companies in the former CPEs in Indochina occupy strong monopolistic positions which can limit their pace of integration with the rest of ASEAN. A substantial part of Vietnam's budget income came from import taxes and the planned cut of tariffs under AFTA agreement will create serious fiscal problems. With the major worry of budget deficits facing the Vietnamese economy, the government must increase its revenues, using a broader tax base and trying at the same time to reduce subsidies to loss-making and uncompetitive state-owned enterprises. Nguyen Manh Cam, Vietnam's foreign minister, reaffirmed the commitment of Hanoi to meet ambitious tariff reductions and urged the poorly performing state sector to become competitive (*Financial Times*, 6 December 1996).

The rapid growth of GDP of the ASEAN economies during the last two and a half decades has been accompanied by far-reaching structural changes. The changing internal and external environment and incentives encouraged the ASEAN leaders to set up the ASEAN Free Trade Area, despite the fact that economic cooperation efforts in the past were unsuccessful.

NOTES

1 I wish to thank Professor Michael Ellman for his helpful remarks on the draft of this chapter.
2 For extensive descriptions and analysis of economic reforms and structural adjustment in ASEAN countries during the 1980s, see Aziz (1990), MacIntyre and Jayasuriya (1992) and Chnitayarangsan *et al.* (1992).
3 Some observers noted that the low share of intra-ASEAN trade understated the actual level of intra-ASEAN trade because of widespread illegal trade (Ariff 1995: 61) between Singapore and neighbouring islands, smuggling between the South Philippines and Sabah or between South Thailand and Malaysia. Compare intra-ASEAN trade of *circa* 19 per cent to 41 per cent of intra-NAFTA trade and *circa* 60 per cent intra-EU trade.
4 For an extensive description and analysis of the changing internal and external environment and incentives contributing to the establishment of AFTA, see Langhammer (1992), Akrasanee and Stifel (1992), Naya and Imada (1992).
5 The fifteen product groups in the fast track are: vegetable oils, cement, chemicals, pharmaceuticals, fertilizers, plastics, rubber products, leather products, pulp, textiles, ceramics and glass products, gem and jewellery, copper cathodes, electronics, and wooden and rattan furniture.

BIBLIOGRAPHY

AFTA Reader (1993) 1(1): 1.
Akrasanee, N. and Stifel, D. (1992) 'The political economy of the ASEAN Free Trade Area', in P. Imada and S. Naya (eds) *AFTA: The Way Ahead*, Singapore: Institute of Southeast Asian Studies: 27–47.
Alburo, D. F. (1995) 'AFTA in the light of new economic developments', *Southeast Asian Affairs 1995* 35(1): 61–73.

Anwar, D. F. (1995) 'Sijori: ASEAN's southern growth triangle problems and prospects', *The Indonesian Quarterly* 22(1): 22–23.

Ariff, M. (1994) 'Open regionalism à la ASEAN', *Journal of Asian Economics* 5(1): 99–117.

Ariff, M. (1995) 'The prospects for an ASEAN free trade area', *The World Economy. Global Trade Policy* 1(1): 53–64.

Asian Development Outlook 1996 and 1997, Singapore and Oxford: Asian Development Bank and Oxford University Press.

Athukorala, P. C. and Menon, J. (1996) 'Foreign direct investment in ASEAN: can AFTA make a difference?', in J. L. H. Tan (ed.) *AFTA in the Changing International Economy*, Singapore: Institute of Southeast Asian Studies: 76–92.

Aziz, U. A. (1990) *Strategies for Structural Adjustment: The Experience of Southeast Asia*, Washington, DC: International Monetary Fund.

Bowless, P. and MacLean, B. (1996) 'Understanding trade bloc formation: the case of the ASEAN Free Trade Area', *Review of International Political Economy* 3(2): 319–348.

Chintayarangsan, R. *et al.* (1992) 'ASEAN economies: macro-economic perspective', *ASEAN Economic Bulletin* 8(3): 353–375.

Direction of Trade Statistics (various years), Washington, DC: International Monetary Fund.

Fifth ASEAN Summit (1996) meeting of the ASEAN heads of government, Bangkok, 14–15 December 1995, Jakarta: ASEAN Secretariat.

Foreign Investment and Trade Linkages in Developing Countries (1995), New York: United Nations.

Fry, M. J. (1993) *Foreign Direct Investment in Southeast Asia: Differential Impacts*, Singapore: Institute of Southeast Asian Studies.

Igusa, K. and Shimada, H. (1996) 'AFTA and Japan', in Tan, J. L. H. (ed.) *AFTA in the Changing International Economy*, Singapore: Institute of Southeast Asian Studies: 139–163.

Kumar, S. (1992) 'Policy issues and the formation of the ASEAN Free Trade Area', in P. Imada and S. Naya (eds) *AFTA: The Way Ahead*, Singapore: Institute of Southeast Asian Studies: 71–94.

Kumar, S. (1994) 'Johor-Singapore-Riau growth triangle: a model of sub-regional cooperation', in Myo Thant, Min Tang and Hiroshi Kakazu (eds), *Growth Triangles in Asia: A New Approach to Regional Economic Co-operation*, Singapore: Oxford University Press.

Langhammer, R. J. (1990) 'ASEAN economic cooperation: a stocktaking from a political economy point of view', *ASEAN Economic Bulletin* 8(2): 137–150.

Langhammer, R. J. (1992) 'Shaping factors and business conditions in the post-fourth ASEAN summit period in P. Imada and S. Naya (eds) *AFTA: The Way Ahead*, Singapore: Institute of Southeast Asian Studies: 1–22.

Langhammer, R. J. and Hiemenz, U. (1990) *Regional Integration among Developing Countries: Opportunities, Obstacles and Options*, Boulder, CO: Westview Press.

Lim, L. Y. C (1994) 'The role of the private sector in ASEAN regional economic cooperation', in L. Mytelka (ed.) *South–South Cooperation in Global Perspective*, Paris: OECD: 125–168.

Lim, L. Y. C. (1996) 'ASEAN: new modes of economic cooperation', in D. Wurfel and B. Burton (eds) *Southeast Asia in the New World Order*, Basingstoke: Macmillan: 19–35.

MacIntyre, A. J. and Jayasuriya, K. (eds) (1991) *The Dynamics of Economic Policy Reform in South-East Asia and the South-West Pacific*, Singapore: Oxford University Press.

Menon, J. (1996) *Adjusting towards AFTA: The Dynamics of Trade in ASEAN*, Singapore: Institute of Southeast Asian Studies.

Mytelka, L. K. (1994) 'Regional co-operation and the new logic of international competition', in L. K. Mytelka (ed.) *South–South Co-operation in Global Perspective*, Paris: OECD: 21–54.

Naidu, G. (1994) 'Johor–Singapore–Riau growth triangle: progress and prospects', in M. Thant, M. Tang and H. Kakazu (eds) *Growth Triangles in Asia: A New Approach to Regional Economic Cooperation*, Singapore: Oxford University Press: 218–242.

Naya, S. and Imada, P. (1992) 'The long and winding road ahead for AFTA', in P. Imada and S. Naya (eds) *AFTA: The Way Ahead*, Singapore: Institute of Southeast Asian Studies: 53–66.

OECD (1993) *Regional Integration and Developing Countries*, Paris: OECD.

Pangestu, M. (1995) 'ASEAN Free Trade Area (AFTA): an Indonesian perspective', *The Indonesian Quarterly* 23(1): 38–49.

Pangestu, M. et al. (1992) 'A new look at intra-ASEAN economic cooperation', *ASEAN Economic Bulletin* 8(3): 333–352.

Ravenhill, J. (1995) 'Economic cooperation in Southeast Asia: changing incentives', *Asian Survey*, 35(9): 850–866.

Soesastro, H. (1996) 'Policies towards foreign direct investment: new challenges facing Asian developing countries', *The Indonesian Quarterly* 24(2): 161–180.

Thant, M., Tang, M. and Kakazu, W. (eds) (1994) *Growth Triangles in Asia: A New Approach to Regional Economic Cooperation*, Singapore: Oxford University Press.

UNCTAD (1995) *Handbook of International Trade and Development 1994*, New York: UNCTAD.

Yue, C. S. (1993) 'Foreign direct investment in ASEAN economies', *Asian Development Review* 11(1): 60–102.

Yue, C. S. (1995) 'Progress and issues in ASEAN economic integration', in T. Kawagoe and S. Sekiguchi (eds) *East Asian Economies: Transformation and Challenges*, Singapore: Institute of Southeast Asian Studies: 265–305.

World Bank (1993) *The East Asian Miracle: Economic Growth and Development*, Oxford and Washington, DC: World Bank and Oxford University Press.

World Investment Report 1995. Transnational Corporations and Competitiveness (1995) New York: UNCTAD.

World Development Report (various years) Washington, DC: World Bank.

14

EXTERNAL LIBERALIZATION, REGIONALIZATION AND OPENNESS IN INDOCHINA'S ECONOMIC TRANSFORMATION

Carolyn L. Gates

Since the late 1980s, the Indochinese states of Vietnam, Laos and Cambodia have transformed their bureaucratically managed traditional economies into market-coordinated industrializing systems. Market reform in these countries has required fundamental changes in the internal institutions, organizations and structures embedded in their socio-economic systems. As Vietnamese analysts have remarked, shifting from central planning to the market 'was a radical renewal process, penetrating every aspect and relation of economic life in which general and partial reforms were closely connected and combined with each other and affected each other' (Nguyen Cong Nghiep *et al.* 1993: 74–5). To support the broad systemic and institutional changes required in their shift to the market, the three countries have rapidly opened their economies to international capitalist markets. Concretely, the Indochinese countries are liberalizing and restructuring their foreign trade and capital regimes, expanding regional cooperation, and opening themselves to the outside world, all of which are profoundly affecting their path of transformation.

In this chapter, I will explore the theme of economic transformation of Indochina, focusing on external liberalization and regionalization, which are institutionalizing a new economic openness. It will be argued that openness – through the rapid development of new structural links to regional and international markets – combined with essentially orthodox stabilization and adjustment measures have underpinned the positive performance of the Indochinese transitional economies. This successful formula, emerging gradually by trial-and-error experimentation, has reduced (expected) output losses, employment dislocations, and latent inflationary pressures that were experienced by the former Soviet Union and East European economies (FSUEE) (Kornai 1994) and developing economies undergoing more traditional structural change (Taylor 1993). Vietnam has benefited from a number of factors leading to these positive outcomes. One notable feature is a production structure that has been able to adjust quickly to international market demand after Vietnam initiated price liberalization and opened its doors to foreign trade and investment. This cushioned Vietnam from the kind of prolonged and severe transformational recession after it had introduced stabilization and structural reforms, as experienced by the FSUEE (Kornai 1994).[1] Thus, the economic structure of Vietnam has allowed it to take swift advantage of openness and market reforms, which has contributed to less burdensome market-adjustment costs.

Beyond the issue of outward-looking policies, the Indochinese and FSUEE objectives of and approaches to 'transition' differ in several ways. In contrast to the FSUEE which have adopted political and economic institutions to build democratic, free-market systems, the Indochinese countries have focused on developing their economies, bridging the wide economic gap between them and their neighbours (Ljunggren 1995: 2–4), and maintaining political stability. Further, they have accepted the market as a mechanism of coordination and resource allocation to be a necessary, if not sufficient condition, to move from a path of economic crisis to stabilization and development. Unlike the FSUEE, and indeed Cambodia, neither Vietnam nor Laos have repudiated their socialist goals: they continue to adhere to the ideal of building socialism.[2] Briefly stated, the strategic objectives of reform in Vietnam and Laos are the creation of market socialist economic systems that will sustain growth, while underpinning a 'renovated' Communist political system. By contrast, Cambodia seeks to reunite its society after decades of conflict by establishing a free market – that is, capitalist – economy and introducing more representative political institutions.

Market reforms in Indochina can be conveniently divided among those focused on (1) internal markets and structures; (2) external markets and structures; and (3) stabilization, which involves both internal and external dynamics. In practice, the three are interlinked and often overlap. Internal liberalization in the Indochinese economies has included the liberalization of prices and elimination of state procurement, direct subsidies to state enterprises and state trading monopolies. While few industrial state-owned enterprises (SOEs) have been privatized in Vietnam – with greater progress having been made in this respect in Laos and Cambodia – the vast majority of agriculture and services is now in the private sector. In addition, private manufacturing is becoming more competitive with the entry of new foreign and domestic private enterprises, although in Vietnam, the state sector continues to dominate industry. External liberalization in Vietnam, Laos and Cambodia has been extensive. First, the trade regimes have been liberalized and decentralized and tariffs are being rationalized and reduced. Second, attractive foreign direct investment (FDI) legislation has been adopted and FDI has increased significantly since the early 1990s. Third, realistic and market-based exchange rates have been established. In a related area, all three countries are seeking to institutionalize regionalization by joining organizations like the Association of South-East Asian Nations (ASEAN), ASEAN Free Trade Area (AFTA) and the Asia Pacific Economic Cooperation group (APEC). With regard to stabilization programmes, which have been supported by newly created indirect controls over macro economic balances, the three governments have sought to reduce fiscal deficits, control inflation, and manage external balances.

This chapter will focus on the external side of Vietnamese reform, although it will briefly discuss initial internal conditions with respect to central planning and reform.

Section two presents a brief overview of the internal mechanisms operating in the Indochinese economies during central planning and market reform. Section three will focus on external liberalization in Vietnam, Laos and Cambodia with specific reference to reform of the exchange rate, trade and foreign investment systems. The penultimate section examines the expansion of openness through institutionalized regionalization in Vietnam, which is likely to be followed by Laos and Cambodia in the near future. Finally, I will present concluding remarks.

The importance given to Vietnam in the 'Indochinese reform model' is apparent. This is due to Vietnam's dominance in Indochina, its longer experience with both socialism and reform, and more practically, to the fact that data and information are more available for Vietnam than for the other two countries. Although the basic economic and socio-economic structures of these countries diverge in some important ways (see Table 14.1 and Figure 14. 1), the three countries are united by a shared past: a common struggle against foreign domination and emerging nationalist aspirations; traditional agrarian economies; the adoption of Soviet-type socialism after revolutionary forces were victorious in 1975, which brought Vietnam and Laos (and Kampuchea/Cambodia in 1979) into the sphere of influence of Soviet planning and the Council for Mutual Economic Assistance (CMEA); and the inability to successfully adapt Soviet development strategies, which led to spontaneous or bottom-up adjustments and subsequently state-guided reform. In addition, the geographical location and outward-looking reform programmes of the three countries have brought an about-face of their external economic relations. They have shifted from the ideals of self-reliance and inter-dependent relationships with CMEA countries to pragmatic policies supporting trade with, and investment from, the capitalist world. Finally, they are (or soon will be) participating in regional organizations like ASEAN, AFTA, Pacific Economic Cooperation Council (PECC), the Greater Mekong Sub-region (GMS), APEC, and ultimately, the World Trade Organization (WTO).

Table 14.1 Socio-economic indicators of Vietnam, Cambodia and Laos, 1993

Indicator	Vietnam	Cambodia	Laos
GDP per capita (USS)	220	205	230
Real GDP growth rate (percentage)	8.1	4.1	5.9
Income ratio: highest 20 per cent to lowest 20 per cent (1989–1994)	5.5	22.5	4.0
Consume price inflation (percentage)	5.2	112.7	6.3
Debt-service ratio (percentage)	11.7	12.1	8.8
Life expectancy (years)	63	50	50
Infant mortality (per 1000 live births)	39	120	101
Adult literacy (percentage)	88	35	54
Urban population (percentage)	20	13	19
Population (millions)	70.9	9.2	4.6
Population growth rate (percentage)	2.0	2.5	2.9

Source: Economist Intelligence Unit (1996); Asian Development Bank (1996).

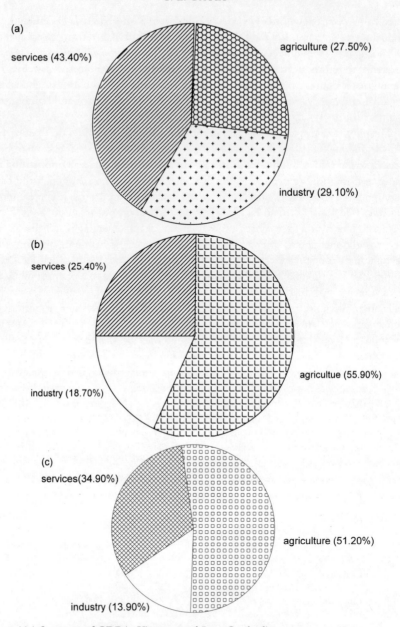

Figure 14.1 Structure of GDP in Vietnam, and Laos Cambodia
Note: 1995 for Vietnam and Laos, 1994 for Cambodia.
Source: Economist Intelligence Unit (1996); Asian Development Bank (1996).

CENTRAL PLANNING AND REFORM IN INDOCHINA: INTERNAL MECHANISMS

Central planning

The internal structures, markets and conditions of the Indochinese economies under socialist transformation were very distinctive from those of their advanced socialist allies in the Soviet Union and Eastern European countries. In contrast to highly industrialized, state-dominated economies in the FSUEE, the Indochinese economies were fundamentally traditional agrarian economies with informal but significant private sector activities. Further, compared to the centrally planned economies (CPEs) in the Soviet Bloc and even China, bureaucratic centralism was less firmly implanted in the Indochinese economies. This was partly due to their disparate economic structures and stages of development. But more importantly, central planning institutions and mechanisms, which were applied through flexible, decentralized and gradual methods in the three countries, existed only for a very brief period before market-oriented reforms were introduced. Thus, Vietnam, Laos and Cambodia have experienced very shallow penetration of central planning and management. For example, at its peak in Vietnam, central planning never touched more than a few hundred commodities in the economy.[3] By contrast, Soviet economic plans covered some 25 million commodities and China about 1,200 (Y. Qian and C. Xu, 1993 as cited by Sachs and Thye Woo 1994: 110). Nevertheless, they shared with more advanced CPEs a number of fundamental features of central planning: bureaucratic coordination, distorted relative prices, large state ownership, and direct control of macroeconomic balances (see de Melo *et al.* 1996: 400–401), which led to inefficient resource allocation, perverse incentive structures, stagnating (or declining) productivity and income levels and sluggish technical progress. On balance, however, because central planning was far less institutionalized in the Indochina economies, they have responded more quickly to market-oriented reforms.

Although Vietnam and Laos began experimenting with reform as early as the late 1970s when it became apparent that Soviet-type planning and control were failing, it was not until 1986 that both launched bolder market-oriented reform programmes to replace bureaucratic centralism and the old socialist strategies. At that time, Vietnam introduced *doi moi* ('renovation') and Laos, the New Economic Mechanism (NEM). After the Vietnamese occupation of Cambodia, its very first Five-Year Plan (1986–90) featured market-oriented reforms not dissimilar to those established in Vietnam and Laos.

Market reform

Vietnam's *doi moi* is frequently compared to Chinese reform, and the two show both similarities and differences. As in China, Vietnamese policy-makers viewed agrarian reform as vital because of its importance to the economy. Unlike China, at the outset of market reform, Vietnam did not target the agrarian sector as the primary

333

locus of change, nor can the achievements of Vietnam's marketization be primarily attributed to agriculture. This is because Vietnam began 'tinkering' with collective agriculture very soon after reunification to increase output, productivity and efficiency. Early changes in agriculture, like those in 1981 that introduced a contract system and granted increased autonomy to farming households, were intended to make collective organization work, rather than to overhaul the system. After the introduction of *doi moi*, the logic of earlier agricultural reform was extended, which in the latter period resulted in a fundamental restructuring of organizational management in this sector. Thus, with the enactment of Decree 10 in April 1988 – giving farmers the rights to sell their goods directly to the market and to greater security of land use and tenure – households became the primary unit of agrarian activities, thereby ending the dominant role of cooperatives in agricultural production and distribution under the old system. In clear contrast to China, Vietnam's agriculture was basically privatized in one 'big bang'.

> Vietnam made financial control and stabilization the key priorities in a shift to an increasingly open market economy, again in contrast to Chinese reform. Unless this field [the monetary and financial system] was controlled effectively and financial principles were improved, the matter of decentralisation of functions in production would not be carried out successfully, for if applied it would have the counter-effect of causing a disorderly situation, the pressure of inflation would be increased and currency credit would consequently not be controlled. So the process of the changed mechanism in Vietnam was started by strictly controlling the financial domain.
>
> (Nguyen Cong Nghiep *et al.* 1993: 76)

Improved financial control was initiated through a structural adjustment programme that liberalized prices, ended state procurement, and phased out the dual price system. A broad liberalization of prices (which excluded only a very few essentials) brought about a major realignment of relative prices, greater efficiency, and a reduction of state-financed subsidies to state producers. Complementing the structural adjustment programme was macro economic stabilization. The latter reduced fiscal deficits by slashing state subsidies and preferential credits to SOEs, holding rises of state employees' salaries to below consumer price inflation, and raising state revenues primarily from oil, foreign aid and investment. Second, it attacked hyperinflation by raising interest rates and reducing the growth of central bank credit. Third, it began to end the strong bias against export production and to realign international and domestic prices by unifying and devaluing the exchange rates. These initiatives were implemented in a big bang in 1989–90. Stabilization was particularly successful: the overall state budget deficit declined from −7.2 per cent of GDP in 1988 to −1.5 per cent in 1991; inflation declined from 308.2 per cent in 1988 to 36.4 per cent in 1990 (World Bank 1994, 1995); and the trade balance moved from a deficit of $US620 million in 1989 to a surplus of $US40 million in 1992.

Establishing financial control and stabilizing the macroeconomy composed the heart of Vietnam's early *doi moi* programme, but reform of the broader financial sector was slow and rudimentary. The first and most important reform of the financial system was the replacement of the unitary state bank by a dual banking system. The dual system was composed of the State Bank of Vietnam, which held regulatory, currency issue and other central banking functions; and four subsidiary commercial banks (agriculture, foreign trade, industry and commerce, and construction). However, the financial system, which constitutes little more than the banking sector, is still in the early days of reform. It continues to discriminate against the private sector and is inadequate to meet the financial intermediation needs of Vietnam's rapidly growing economy. A major constraint to financial deepening in Vietnam is the slow progress on privatization of state enterprises and the development of capital markets, notably, the long-awaited stock exchange.

Reform of state industrial enterprises has followed similar lines as that of agriculture with the extension of earlier measures (e.g., the 1981 A-B-C Plan for state industrial enterprises) to increase output, productivity and efficiency. But the pace and magnitude of change of state-owned industry have not kept up with the primary sector. In fact, state industrial enterprise reform lags behind virtually every other indicator of reform in Vietnam. Very little privatization (or 'equitization') of state industrial enterprises has been implemented, although the number of SOEs has declined by almost 50 per cent from 1991 to 1996 due to mergers and some liquidation. With the legalization of the private sector in 1988, 'bottom-up' privatization has occurred: joint-stock companies and private household enterprises have entered manufacturing and cottage production. Nevertheless, state enterprises have increased their dominance of industry in terms of capital and output, although state industry remains a comparatively small employer of labour. Thus, indirect privatization or growing out of the plan has not yet had an appreciable effect on Vietnamese industry, although official data do not reflect the important factor of partial internal privatization of SOEs (Gates 1995: 45–46). In contrast to industry, but similar to agriculture, the private sector is now thriving in the retail sector, petty commerce and consumer services.

The New Economic Mechanism in the Lao People's Democratic Republic (LPDR) was comparable to Vietnam's *doi moi* in that the leadership abandoned gradual adaptation of the centrally managed system with the adoption of market economic coordination (see Saignasith and Lathouly 1995: 154–209). Mirroring the reforms in Vietnam, they were designed to stabilize, decentralize and deregulate the economy, all of which were expected to improve overall performance. To stabilize the economy, policy-makers enacted extensive price and wage reforms whereby a unified price system was established for all goods with the exception of water, electricity, fuel, air transport and post and telecommunications; and the salaries of civil servants were adjusted to the new market conditions. They also reduced state procurement and state price-setting of agricultural goods; unified and devalued the exchange rate; raised interest rates; moved away from subsidized credit and enacted a two-tier banking system. Further, they reformed the fiscal system by shifting the largest burden of revenue mobilization from state enterprise surpluses to a tax-based system. Reformers also sought to shift the role of the state away from direct

C. L. GATES

control of the economy by establishing indirect controls over macroeconomic balances and a market environment that would encourage growth and development. Similar to agrarian reform in Vietnam, Laos has shifted production away from the cooperative towards family-based organization; and traditional agricultural land-use rights have been informally institutionalized by the reforms. By contrast, Laos has gone much further in state enterprise reform and privatization than Vietnam. Since 1988, the government has ended state subsidies to the SOEs, granted greater autonomy to their managers, and removed sixty-five primarily larger SOEs out of an estimated 400 (mainly small) SOEs by late 1994 (Pomfret 1996: 69). In addition, they have established policies to encourage the development of the private sector.

The timing, path and impact of reform in Cambodia have differed somewhat from that of Vietnam and Laos because of its recent past – the upheaval of the Pol Pot regime, overthrow of the Khmer Rouge by Vietnamese forces, civil war, and continuing political instability in the post-civil war period – during which much of its human, institutional and physical infrastructure was destroyed. Orthodox central planning/management had barely been inaugurated in Cambodia when market-oriented reform was introduced with its first Five-Year Plan (1986–90). Early reform recognized the realities of Cambodia: private sector activities were essential to prevent further devastation. In 1989, reform was intensified: price controls over a wide range of goods were eliminated; agriculture was decollectivized; private property rights were extended; measures to reform and privatize state enterprises were introduced; policies to encourage foreign direct investment were adopted; and a state monopoly over foreign trade was ended. But the 1985–91 reforms had limited effects because of flawed implementation, continuing political instability, and the fact that many reforms were only recognizing *de jure* what already existed on the ground (ibid.: 71). Nevertheless, the liberalization of prices and recognition of the private sector, combined with an expansion of domestic demand with the stationing of UNTAC forces in the early 1990s, led to rapid growth of small-scale, private production in goods and services. This, no doubt, was a major catalyst in moving the economy away from state domination. The reform process was reinforced in the post-1993 period with renewed efforts to stabilize the macroeconomy. Thus, the exchange rate was stabilized; inflation was slashed; and budget deficits were reduced. Nevertheless, threats to reform remain because of political instability, macro-economic volatility, and a perception that market development may not be in the interest of all Cambodians.

With such fundamental changes taking place in the Indochinese economies, how were they able to avoid many of the dislocations seen in the FSUEE? Beyond the factors of disparate structures and conditions discussed above, another element was instrumental in preventing protracted systemic shocks. That is the role of demand. Demand in the Indochinese economies, unlike that in the FSUEE, was sustained, and adjustment facilitated, by two important factors: the weight of the inefficient centrally controlled industrial sector was insufficient to paralyze growth in the rest of the economy; and the governments attacked inflation, thereby providing greater incentives to the private sector to invest in real assets and underpinning confidence in the economies.

336

External liberalization

Vietnam, Laos and Cambodia adopted market institutions and opened their economies to turn around their crisis-prone domestic economies. To take advantage of their well-placed geographical position in the most dynamic region of the world required a progressive dismantling of barriers to trade and exchange. This process was initiated as the governments began to liberalize and rationalize trade, capital and exchange rate regimes. Exchange reform was a key institutional change, as it realigned (overvalued) domestic and international relative prices to more realistic levels, thereby making Indochinese goods more competitive in international markets.

Exchange rate reform

A vital element of Vietnam's policy shift to encourage export production and to stabilize Vietnam's external balances has been exchange reform. In March 1989, Vietnam's system of multiple exchange rates, which greatly distorted the structure of relative prices and permitted hidden transfers and rents, was replaced by a unified system. During the same period, a series of currency devaluations brought the cross dong–dollar rate from VNDong 225/$US1 in early 1988 to VNDong 4,500/$US1 in mid-March 1989, which narrowed the margin between the parallel market and official rates to an average of 12.2 per cent in 1989 and 9.4 per cent in 1990. Between April 1989 and August 1991, the change in the market-based official exchange rate reflected the growth of inflation and developments in the parallel market. However, since September 1991, the official rate has ceased 'following the market', as the government has increased its influence in the foreign exchange market through foreign exchange trading floors and subsequently, the interbank foreign exchange market (Dodsworth *et al.* 1996: 36). Vietnam's management of the exchange rate has gradually improved since 1992, resulting in a fairly stable fluctuation within a band of VND10,500–11,000/$US1 in 1992–96. The government's October 1994 decision to remove the dollar from official circulation represents another effort to regain control over the financial system and to establish improved indirect controls over the macroeconomy.

Reforms of the exchange rate systems in Laos and Cambodia have followed a similar path as that of Vietnam. Pre-dating Vietnam's exchange rate policy reforms, the Lao People's Democratic Republic (LPDR) initiated a unification of multiple exchange rates in September 1987 and essentially completed it by July 1989. During those two years, the highly volatile currency was devalued from September 1987 under multiple rates of Kip 10–350/$US1 to a unified rate of Kip 700/$US1 in July 1989. In the 1990s, the official and parallel rates have narrowed to about 5 per cent. At the same time, an open exchange market has expanded with the dollar and Thai baht, as well as gold and silver bullion, circulating freely throughout the economy.

Because of highly unstable political conditions in Cambodia throughout the 1980s, the foreign exchange system was fragmented and barely institutionalized. With widespread smuggling and informal production, commercial and financial networks, Cambodia's parallel exchange market has played a dominant role in the economy. Since the late 1980s, its currency experienced 'free-fall' and was only

(a)

(b)

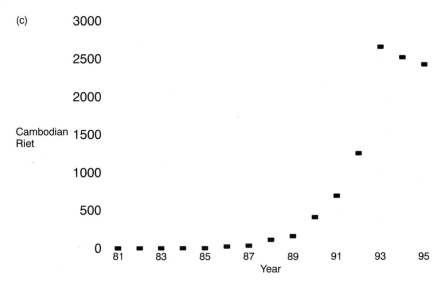

Figure 14.2 Exchange rates of Vietnam, Cambodia and Laos currencies, 1981–95.
Source: Asian Development Bank (1996: 376–377, 86–87, 190–191); *Asian Development Outlook* (1995, 1996: 257).

rescued through robust stabilization measures implemented in 1993–1994 by former Minister of Finance Sam Rainsy (Pomfret 1996: 73).

Foreign trade reform

Of the three Indochinese economies, Vietnam was the most integrated into the CMEA, but by the early 1980s, Laos and Cambodia were being incorporated into the system. The CMEA, which served a wide range of political and economic objectives of Socialist bloc members, was essentially an accounting system which planned and balanced import–export relationships among its members. Based on bilateral agreements between CMEA members, state bureaucracies of member countries monopolized imports and exports; and trade subsidies and multiple exchange rates were key features of the system. In Indochina, the CMEA increasingly dominated trade and assistance relationships; and all three accumulated large and persistent trade deficits with the grouping. This system effectively discouraged trade: exports were depressed by low procurement prices, overvalued exchange rates and an obligation to fulfil planned exports to CMEA before exporting to convertible currency economies; and imports were deterred by a system of licences and quotas (Dodsworth *et al.* 1996: 33). As integration evolved, the Indochinese countries became dependent upon the Soviet bloc for capital goods and many basic inputs like refined petroleum, fertilizer, cotton and steel. In return they exported mainly raw materials, agricultural goods, and low-quality consumer goods. At the same time, the three countries reduced their relations with convertible-currency

339

markets, although there appears to have been significant informal foreign trade carried out with non-CMEA regional economies by state and party cadres. Divorced from the notions of comparative advantage or consumer welfare, the CMEA system disconnected domestic prices from those of the international world market. This and a general distortion of internal and external relative prices affected production decisions and trade structures: at world prices, many goods were produced with negative added-value; and the production of labour-intensive goods, a comparative advantage held by all three countries, was not promoted.

Trade reform, initiated in the late 1980s, exposed the economies to new competitive forces and stimulated market-oriented restructuring. Specifically, it opened them to international market imports, providing them with more competitive technology and techniques. With improved inputs and techniques, they now can exploit their own comparative advantages like relatively low-cost labour, abundant natural resources and geographical location, through the growing opportunities to export to regional and international markets. Liberalized trade typically spawns strong effects on production decisions, export commodity structures, and patterns of commercial and financial relationships; and in the long run, it prompts fundamental technological change. Such effects are beginning to be seen in all three countries.

As political and economic instability grew in the Soviet bloc and as change erupted in the CMEA in the late 1980s, securing new trade partners became urgent for Vietnam and, to a lesser extent, the other Indochinese economies. To meet this challenge, the Vietnamese government introduced trade policies to expand non-CMEA commercial relationships, while attempting to protect the domestic economy from large trade-related adjustment costs. Thus, legislation was promulgated to protect selected local production against imports and encourage exports by liberalizing, decentralizing and rationalizing the trade regime. In 1989, a two-stage reform was established, whereby a new tariff regime was adopted that liberalized some imports, lowered most export taxes, and reduced quota restrictions on traded goods, although major non-tariff barriers remained in place. Tariffs remained high on luxuries and imported goods that could be domestically produced. In 1989, Vietnam's foreign trade system was also decentralized by abolishing the central state trading monopolies. And since 1991, all state and private enterprises that fulfil certain criteria have been granted direct trading access to foreign markets. Throughout the 1990s, the government has tried to build a firmer regulatory framework of trade to combat rampant smuggling and to balance the needs of the market, local industry and the state budget. However, comprehensive trade reform has only begun to be tackled since Vietnam joined ASEAN in 1995 with its agreement to comply completely by the year 2006 with trade rules set by AFTA. This requires a basic overhaul of Vietnam's trade and tariff regimes.

Reform of the foreign trade system in Laos has followed a similar trajectory and pacing as that of Vietnam. Since the late 1980s, Laos has undertaken significant reform of its foreign trade system, which is no longer monopolized by the state. In 1989, both the private and state sectors were given access to imports through licensed traders, composed of state, private and mixed companies. In March 1988, tariffs were rationalized, but coverage on imports was extended. The extensive system of import and export licensing was abolished in 1993, but tariffs and taxes/fees on imports have remained high and somewhat irrational despite efforts to streamline the system. The spread of tariff rates has been reduced from 0–200 per cent to 0–100 per cent and is now covered by eleven different bands (Saignasith and Lathouly 1995: 169).

Trade reform in Cambodia has been very rudimentary. Over the past decades of instability, the economy fragmented and smuggling became rampant. Therefore, the most urgent economic tasks in that country have been to rebuild production, enforce an institutionalized trade system, and expand formal commercial links that were destroyed in the previous two decades.

The progressive liberalization and rationalization of trade and the establishment of realistic exchange rates in the three economies have promoted micro-economic changes in production decisions, shifts in import–export structures and a diversification into labour-intensive exports. In Vietnam, they have encouraged exporters to expand production of competitive labour-intensive goods like garments, textiles, shoes and sandals (Figure 14.3). Furthermore, Vietnamese exports grew by 168 per cent during the liberalization period of 1989–95 (as compared to 97 per cent in the 1982–88 CMEA period) which have contributed to addressing its large external deficits. Vietnam's current account as share of GDP has moved from −9.8 per cent in 1989 to −6.1 per cent in 1995 (Table 14.2). Its trade balance improved greatly in the first years of stabilization, moving from a $US945 million deficit in 1982 to a surplus of $US40 million in 1992; but the trade deficit ballooned to $US1,905 million in 1995 (Table 14.3).

Similar reforms in Laos have prompted a surge in exports. Exports in 1995 had increased by a remarkable 451 per cent over 1989 – on average 64.4 per cent per annum – as compared with 45 per cent in the 1982–1988 period (Table 14.4). Moreover, textile and garment exports composed almost 18 per cent of total exports in 1993 (Figure 14.3), and this share is growing. Because its imports grew faster, however, its trade balance has continued to worsen: growing from −$US92 million in 1982 to −$US131 million in 1989 and −$US240 million in 1995 (Table 14.3). Nevertheless, its current account has improved from −18.6 per cent of GDP in 1989 to −12.6 per cent of GDP in 1994 (Table 14.2).

Table 14.2 Balance of payments on current account, Vietnam Cambodia end Laos, 1989–96 ($US million)

Country	1989	1990	1991	1992	1993	1994	1995	1996[a]
Vietnam	−584	−259	−133	−73	−1079	−836	−1061	−1318
Percentage of GDP	−9.8	−3.1	−2.2	−0.7	−8.3	−5.4	−5.8	−6.1
Laos	−135	−102	−78	−117	−144	−193	—	—
Percentage of GDP	−18.6	−11.7	−7.6	−9.9	−11	−12.6	—	—
Cambodia	−89	−50	−25	−45	−41	−175	—	—
Percentage of GDP	−6.2	−3.5	−1.3	−2.2	−1.8	−7.5	—	—

Source: Asian Development Outlook 1995 and 1996, Tables A15, A16.
Note: Forecasts.

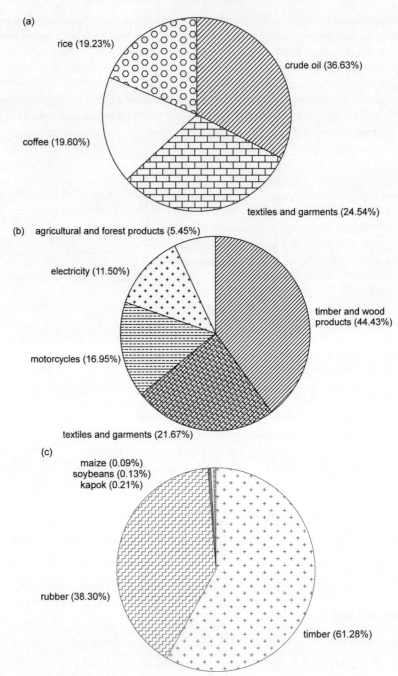

Figure 14.3 Exports from Vietnam, Combodia and Laos
Source: *Economist Intelligence Unit* (1996); Saignaith and Lathonly (1995: Table 14.7.11, Table 14.7.12).

Despite Cambodia's more difficult position (formal trade essentially ceased during the mid-1970s to early 1980s), its exports escalated by almost twentythree-fold in 1987–1995 (Table 14.4). Unlike Vietnam and Laos, its trade deficits have continually worsened from −$US116 million in 1987 to −$US332 million in 1995 (Table 14.3); and current account deficits as share of GDP have also climbed from −6.2 per cent in 1989 to −7.5 per cent in 1994 (Table 14.2).

Table 14.3 Balance of trade of Vietnam, Cambodia and Laos, 1982–95 ($US million)

Year	Vietnam	Laos	Cambodia
1982	−945	−92	—
1983	−910	−109	—
1984	−1095	−118	—
1985	−1158	−139	—
1986	−1366	−131	—
1987	−1601	−152	−116
1988	−1719	−91	−124
1989	−620	−131	−97
1990	−348	−106	−78
1991	−251	−113	−32
1992	40	−111	−178
1993	−444	−191	−188
1994	−900	−354	−236
1995	−1905	−240	−332

Source: Calculated from Asian Development Bank (1996: Tables 27 and 28).

Table 14.4 Annual merchandise exports and growth rates, Vietnam, Cambodia and Laos, 1982–95

Year	Vietnam		Laos		Cambodia	
	Exports (FOB $US million)	Percentage change per annum	Exports (FOB $US million)	Percentage change per annum	Exports (FOB $US million)	Percentage change per annum
1982	527	—	40	—	—	—
1983	617	17.08	41	2.5	—	—
1984	650	5.35	44	7.32	—	—
1985	699	7.54	54	22.73	—	—
1986	789	12.88	55	1.85	—	—
1987	854	8.24	64	16.36	36	—
1988	1038	21.55	58	−9.38	45	25
1989	1946	87.48	63	8.62	79	75.56
1990	2404	23.54	79	25.4	86	8.86
1991	2087	−13.19	97	22.78	253	194.19
1992	2581	23.67	133	37.11	265	4.74
1993	2971	15.11	241	81.2	283	6.79
1994	3600	21.17	300	24.48	490	73.14
1995	5220	45	347	15.67	856	74.69

Source: Calculated from Asian Development Bank (1996: Tables 27 and 28).

Although Vietnam expanded its exports to the CMEA in 1988 and 1989 after a number of years of stagnation, the 1990s have seen a strong shift to East Asian trade. Since the Sixth Party Congress in 1986, when Vietnam's leadership announced its about-face policy 'to participate in the international division of labour', it has increased its commercial ties with the Asia Pacific region, which now accounts for the majority of Vietnam's trade. In the 1985–94 period, Vietnam's exports to Asia grew from 24.7 per cent to 58.1 per cent of total exports. A similar trend in Cambodia can be seen with its exports to Asia expanding from 44.3 per cent of total in 1985 to 87.8 per cent in 1994. In the case of Laos, trade expansion with the region has been more modest because of its initial high base: 78.5 per cent of total trade in 1985 was with Asia Pacific, rising to 82.0 per cent in 1994. Thus, the principal trading partners of all three countries are now in Asia (Figure 14.4, Figure 14.5, Figure 14.6). This shifting direction of trade has supported a growing tendency

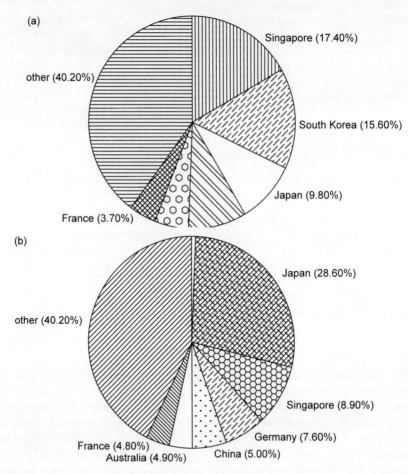

Figure 14.4 Origin and destination of Vietnamese exports and imports, 1994
Source: Economist Intelligence Unit (1996).

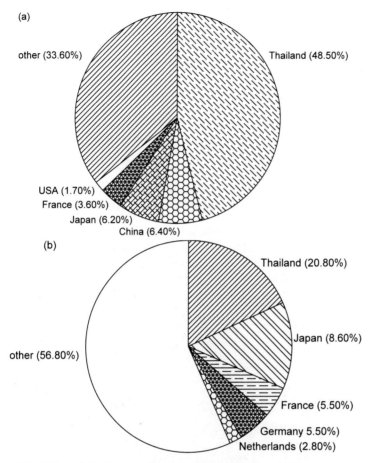

(a)

other (33.60%)

Thailand (48.50%)

USA (1.70%)
France (3.60%)
Japan (6.20%)
China (6.40%)

(b)

Thailand (20.80%)

Japan (8.60%)

other (56.80%)

France (5.50%)

Germany 5.50%)
Netherlands (2.80%)

Figure 14.5 Origin and destination of Laos, imports and exports, 1994
Source: Economist Intelligence Unit (1996).

towards East Asian regional economic cooperation. This in turn has begun to open
the countries to new international forces and globalization dynamics.

Foreign Direct Investment

The same trends of liberalization and regionalization have been evolving in the
Indochinese economies' non-trade flows. Direct investment is the most important
vehicle for foreign capital entry into these economies, as equity and other capital
markets either do not exist or are in primitive stages of development. In Vietnam,
Asian companies had invested almost 71 per cent of the $US23 billion of recorded
cumulative foreign direct investment (FDI) in Vietnam by the end of 1996 (*Vietnam
Economic Times*, December 1996: 13). The largest share of FDI originates from Japan
and the newly industrializing economies (e.g., Taiwan, Korea, Hong Kong, Singa-

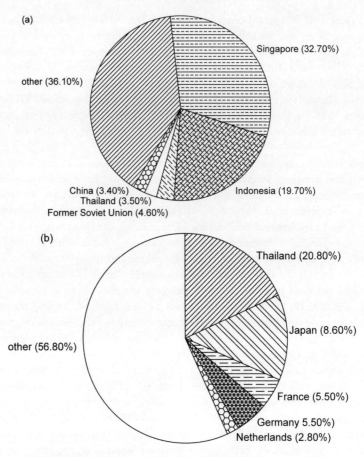

(a)

Singapore (32.70%)

other (36.10%)

China (3.40%)
Thailand (3.50%)
Former Soviet Union (4.60%)

Indonesia (19.70%)

(b)

Thailand (20.80%)

Japan (8.60%)

other (56.80%)

France (5.50%)

Germany 5.50%)
Netherlands (2.80%)

Figure 14.6 Origin and destination of Cambodian imports and exports, 1993
Source: Economist Intelligence Report (1996).

pore) with smaller but significant amounts originating from the remaining five ASEAN countries (that is, excluding Singapore). Most East Asian investors are seeking to relocate their labour-intensive manufacturing facilities to Vietnam where labour is abundant, cheaper and relatively well trained. This is a development which is likely to accelerate intra-trade in manufactures within the East Asian region. Reflecting this changing pattern of foreign investment is Vietnam's manufacturing sector, a recipient of 49 per cent of cumulative contracted FDI in 1996, as compared to 13 per cent in 1988–90.

From the earliest years of *doi moi*, FDI was envisioned as a primary mechanism to mobilize additional external resources for technological renovation and the capacity expansion of state enterprises and for upgrading the country's physical infrastructure. It is clearly playing such a role, particularly in providing capital to SOEs, as state subsidies have declined dramatically. Indicating the importance that the leadership attached to FDI, the Foreign Investment Law of December 1987 became a centrepiece of *doi moi*. Since that time, Vietnam's performance in attracting foreign capital has been impressive: by the end of 1996, contracted FDI amounted to $US23 billion; and 1995 showed the second largest increase in commitments (some $US7.5 billion or 85 per cent over 1994) since FDI began in 1988 (*Nhan Dan*, 3–4 March 1996). Balance of payments data indicate that actual FDI flows in Vietnam, 1988–95, have amounted to $US3,821 million (Table 14.6) as compared to contracted investment of $US18,438 million (Table 14.5), a realization ratio of 20.7 per cent.

While foreign companies invest in Vietnam as elsewhere according to their own interests and strategies, foreign capital flows into Vietnam have tended to reflect the economy's comparative advantage in labour-intensive production, its structural transition from the traditional sector of agriculture to modernizing industry and services, and high internal demand for infrastructure development. This is borne out by the changing composition of FDI in Vietnam: (1) the share of total foreign investment in agriculture declined from 21.9 per cent in 1988–90 to 2.1 per cent in mid-1996; and (2) the share of total FDI in industry (excluding energy) has grown from 13.2 per cent in 1988–90 to 49 per cent in 1996 (*Vietnam Economic Times*, December 1996:12; Le 1996: 67; Gates and Truong 1994: 6). Beyond the shift in composition and structure of FDI in these areas, there has also been high growth of foreign investment in infrastructure since 1994, a response to strong demand for infrastructure development and to improved FDI policy conditions for this sector.

These trends have been supported by a growing share of East Asian capital in total FDI. By mid-1996, about one-half ($US10 billion) of all committed FDI originated from Taiwan, Hong Kong, Singapore and overseas Chinese corporations.[4] East Asian investments have flowed into labour-intensive production (e.g. garments, textiles, shoes and leather goods); low-tech industries (e.g. assembly electronics, motorcycles); heavy basic industries (cement, chemicals, fertilizer, steel); infrastructure and energy projects; and property development. ASEAN investment in Vietnam, which has risen sharply since 1992, now accounting for some 17 per cent of total approved foreign investment, has generally followed East Asian patterns. The largest share of ASEAN investment has flowed to industry (particularly food processing), infrastructure and property development, and services. Currently, Vietnam is trying to integrate foreign investment policies into a larger industrial strategy. Its institutional environment, therefore, may be evolving towards a more level playing ground for foreign and domestic capital, reflecting the reality that both are essential to Vietnam's growth and transformation. Based on historical evidence, 70–80 per cent of all investment in Vietnam is likely to be mobilized domestically. Nevertheless, foreign investment accounted roughly for 20–25 per cent of aggregate economic growth in the 1988–95 period, and in the medium run, it is likely to continue to contribute a similarly important share to total growth.

The foreign investment institutional frameworks adopted by Laos and Cambodia are less complex than that of Vietnam, but they have followed its general lines. In

August 1988, Laos introduced a liberal foreign investment law that welcomed foreigners to invest via business contracts (which was removed in the March 1994 revision of the foreign investment law), joint ventures, and 100 per cent foreign-owned enterprises. The law guaranteed the security of capital against expropriation and permitted the repatriation of profits. From 1998 to July 1995, $US1,327.9 million of foreign investment commitments have been approved (Table 14.5), and the balance of payments data indicate that $US226.1 million have flowed into the country (Table 14.6). Initially, foreign capital was invested primarily in joint ventures, but since 1992, 100 per cent foreign-owned companies have gained favour. The preferred sectors of foreign investors in Laos have been manufacturing (particularly wood-based industries and garments) and banking.

Table 14.5 Contracted FDI, Vietnam, Cambodia and Laos, 1988–95
($US million)

Year	Vietnam	Laos	Cambodia
1988	371.8	2.7	n.a.
1989	582.5	41.5	n.a.
1990	839	90.4	n.a.
1991	1,322.3	155.5	n.a.
1992	2,165.0	259.6	n.a.
1993	2,861.0	245.4	n.a.
1994	3,765.6	207.5	n.a.
1995	6,530.8	325.3[a]	n.a.
1988–1995	18,438.0	1,327.9	n.a.

Sources: Laos: Committee for Planning and Cooperation, National Statistical Centre *Basic, Statistics about the Socio-economic Development in the Lao P.D.R., 1975–1995*: 97; Vietnam: Statistical Publishing House. *Statistical Yearbook 1995*: 51.
Note: [a] January–July 1995.

Table 14.6 Actual FDI, Vietnam, Cambodia and Laos, 1988–95
($US million)

Year	Vietnam	Laos	Cambodia
1988	—	2	109.6
1989	100	4	109
1990	120	6	94.2
1991	213	8	25.2
1992·	260	9	33
1993	300	59.8	54.1
1994	1048	60.1	69
1995	1780	77.2	101.7
1988–1995	3,821.0	226.1	595.8

Source: Asian Development Bank (1996: Tables 33) and 'Vietnam, Laos and Cambodia' (data derived from balance of payments statistics).

Cambodia's liberal 1989 foreign investment law has had to battle against large constraints on foreign investment: high political risks, an unstable macro-economic environment, and poor physical infrastructure and human capital. The stationing of UN troops in Cambodia with the UNTAC programme, which greatly increased effective demand and reduced perceived risks, at least in Phnom Penh, stimulated foreign investment in hotels, tourism and services. According to balance of payments data, cumulative disbursed foreign investment in Cambodia in 1988–1995 have amounted to almost $US500 million (Table 14.6).

REGIONALIZATION: INSTITUTIONAL COOPERATION

Vietnam, as compared to Laos and Cambodia, is on an advanced time path of regional institutional cooperation. Yet, all three share similar conditions *vis à vis* the region, and in the long run are likely to incur comparable benefits and costs from regional cooperation. Because Laos and Cambodia have not yet acquired membership in any significant regional organizations (although they are slated to join ASEAN in the near future), Vietnam's recent experience with integration into ASEAN and AFTA will be used here as a proxy for regional integration of all three states. Further, this section, which will only briefly mention ASEAN as a political and security organization, will concentrate on Vietnam's membership in AFTA as the focus of regional economic cooperation.

ASEAN was established in 1967 to meet regional security needs against perceived communist threats in Indochina, and by extension, Soviet and Mainland Chinese influence in South-East Asia. Second, it was a forum to defuse political hostilities and to encourage cooperation among the ASEAN members themselves. In ASEAN's early years, economic, social and cultural issues were minor areas of cooperation. It was only after the signing of the Paris Peace Accords that ended the conflict in Cambodia, and then the demise of the Cold War, that ASEAN made headway in remoulding its identity into a regional economic grouping, thereby expanding its traditional security and political *raison d'être*. With these changes, Vietnam became a serious contender for membership. This was bolstered by Vietnam's own market transformation and its goal to utilize ASEAN as a learning ground and easy entry point to the international market economy.

Vietnam's entry into ASEAN in July 1995 was a dramatic turning point in its relations with the region. Vietnam views its membership as a key mechanism to hasten integration into the world economy and entry into international economic institutions. Furthermore, the ASEAN Free Trade Area represents a manageable learning arena by which Vietnam can liberalize and rationalize its trade and tariff regimes, and potentially increase its international competitiveness (Chirathivat, 1996: 29–30). Vietnam's integration into AFTA will follow a step-by-step process over the next decade as it implements the Common Effective Preferential Tariff (CEPT), namely, by harmonizing its tariff, customs, and trade-related structures and procedures; reducing non-tariff barriers; and liberalizing its foreign exchange and payments regime.

Implementing the CEPT is the most difficult, but an essential task for Vietnam to acquire full membership in AFTA. Out of a total of 3,211 product lines that Vietnam trades, it initially submitted lists of 1,622 goods for tariff reduction and 857 CEPT tariff lines covering 18 sectors of Vietnam's economy, so as to meet its obligations under the CEPT agreement over the next decade (1996–2006). In addition to the items subject to tariff reductions that became effective on 1 January 1996, Vietnam submitted three other lists of goods subject to temporary exclusion from tariff reduction; full exclusion from tariff reduction (prohibited goods); and strategic or essential goods for Vietnam's economy. The lists cover two general categories, namely, manufactured goods and unprocessed agricultural goods. The CEPT scheme is complex, but its purpose – and the ultimate objective of AFTA – is simple: that is, to reduce tariff rates on all products traded among the ASEAN members to 0–5 per cent by 2003 for the ASEAN-6, with Vietnam to conform by 2006. Currently, more than 53 per cent of Vietnam's total tariff lines are found in the 0–5 per cent bracket, although some 17 per cent of them carry very high duties of 21–60 per cent. The Vietnamese government projects that by implementing tariff reduction over five stages, it will meet the January 2006 deadline for complete compliance with AFTA regulations. At that time, 70 per cent of Vietnam's total tariff lines (more than 2200 lines) will be included in the CEPT (Vu Tuan Anh 1996: 61). In addition, Vietnam must prepare a timetable to eliminate non-tariff barriers such as quantitative restrictions, foreign exchange restrictions, and non-transparent customs valuation procedures.

While integration into AFTA may bring Vietnam difficult adjustment problems, it could also bear significant benefits through greater foreign trade and investment. The adjustment constraints include the effects of trade liberalization on state revenues and competitiveness of domestic industries. Currently, trade-related tariffs and taxes compose about 25 per cent of state budget revenues in Vietnam. For the remainder of the decade, losses due to AFTA-related tariff and tax reductions are not projected to be large, but they are likely to become much more significant in the run-up to 2006. Regardless of the projected levels of trade creation, impact of restructuring tariffs, and effects of (a proposed) increase in taxes on domestic production (see 'Talking Trade', *Vietnam Economic Times*, July 1996: 14), it is highly probable that over the next ten years, tariffs and trade-related taxes will decline in their share of total state revenues. A second adjustment issue is whether Vietnam can compete with ASEAN products, after tariffs are reduced to the 0–5 per cent level. Some Vietnamese policy-makers argue that Vietnam will not be able to compete with even less-advanced ASEAN economies for many years. Hence, imported regional goods will flood Vietnam, eliminating many of its 'infant industries' and thereby aborting its industrial take-off. This ignores the current reality of extensive smuggling from the region, which is forcing many industries like textiles and garments, leather goods, electric products and others to operate essentially under free-market conditions. The most vulnerable industries to trade liberalization are those enjoying high and effective protection, many of which are politically privileged state industries producing goods like steel and cement. Following the line of the trade pessimists, the outlook for Vietnam's entry into capital-intensive and high-tech products is even worse, given the differential between advanced ASEAN and Vietnamese producers.

At the same time, AFTA deregulation may also bring with it improved access to regional and international markets. Vietnam stands to gain preferential access to more than 450 million regional consumers; and as its economy is more complementary to the other ASEAN countries, the gains could be significant. This preferential access could boost Vietnam's export production, leading to higher growth rates, increased economies of scale, and greater price competitiveness. Because ASEAN countries produce more technologically advanced intermediate and capital goods, Vietnam producers may also gain access to cheaper imported inputs (although it is likely that before that time, Vietnam will broadly liberalize many capital imports). Moreover, Vietnam is the only exporter of some agricultural goods in the ASEAN region, which will give it additional benefits (Forster 1996: 57). However, as it is not yet possible to forecast the level of trade likely to be created (as opposed to diverted) and the interaction between dynamic and static trade effects, the net effects of trade deregulation in Vietnam remain uncertain.

With membership in ASEAN/AFTA, Vietnam may also benefit from greater FDI from both ASEAN and non-ASEAN investors. The establishment of the ASEAN Free Investment Area, which aims to level the playing field between domestic and ASEAN-based investors, may encourage ASEAN members to invest in Vietnam (although currently foreign investors in Vietnam typically enjoy privileges not accorded to domestic investors). More importantly, non-ASEAN producers who wish preferential access to the ASEAN markets can gain that under the CEPT only by producing within ASEAN countries (with a 40 per cent local-content rule). This means that foreign capital could gain new incentives to invest in Vietnam: it could become not only a low-cost production base for export and domestic markets, but also a route to jump tariff walls in ASEAN. None the less, this could be a double-edged sword: a number of foreign investors have entered the Vietnamese market precisely because of its high protection. After AFTA regulations have been implemented, these foreign companies will no longer benefit from monopolistic or low numbers conditions; and consequently, many of them may become non-competitive, thereby ending the primary rationale for their operations in Vietnam.

CONCLUSIONS

The impact of external liberalization, regionalization and openness in the three Indochinese economies' reform and transformation processes cannot be quantified with any precision, not only because of very weak and often inconsistent data, but also because the effects of individual internal, external and stabilization reforms are difficult to isolate from each other. These reforms have worked by reinforcing each other; and where absent or neglected, they have created negative effects elsewhere in the economy. Thus, our conclusions are based primarily on qualitative evidence, supported by quantitative data wherever possible.

External liberalization has brought about important structural changes in all three Indochinese economies. Total foreign trade as share of GNP has grown significantly in Vietnam and Laos since the reforms: in Vietnam, this ratio has grown from 50.7 per cent in 1985 to 63.1 per cent in 1995; and in Laos, 13.2 per cent to 53.9 per cent, respectively. In Cambodia, no data are available for 1985, but it is unlikely that foreign trade represented even the small share that Laos showed for that period; by 1995, trade in Cambodia was 69.8 per cent of its GNP. Exports in all three countries showed strong growth in the 1989–95 period of external liberalization: 168 per cent in Vietnam (compared to 97 per cent in 1982–88); 451 per cent in Laos (compared to 45 per cent in 1982–88); and 981 per cent in Cambodia (no figures are available for the earlier period). This growth, however, has had mixed effects on the external balances of the different economies. Vietnam's current account deficit as share of GDP in 1989–95 has declined from −9.8 per cent to −6.1 per cent. Similarly, in Laos, this ratio in 1989–94 has improved, moving from −18.6 per cent to −12.6 per cent of GDP. However, in Cambodia, the current account deficit has climbed from −6.2 per cent in 1989 to −7.5 per cent in 1994. Moreover, as the growth rates of imports have tended to grow faster than those of exports in the three economies during the 1989–95 period, all have suffered rising trade deficits.

Foreign direct investment, which the three economies have sought to substitute partially for the loss of CMEA grants and preferential loans, has comprised an important part of the external liberalization process in Vietnam, Laos and Cambodia. In the 1988–95 period, data from the balance of payments (although it must be noted that balance-of-payments data do not fully reflect FDI flows) show that Vietnam was a recipient of $US3,821 million in FDI; Laos, $US226.1 million; and Cambodia $US595.8 million. In Vietnam, FDI represents 20–30 per cent of total investment and has generated 20–25 per cent of aggregate growth during the 1989–95 period. Data for Laos and Cambodia are insufficient to estimate these ratios, but there is little doubt that foreign capital is relatively important for both total investment and aggregate growth in the two economies.

Along with changes in investment and trade structures in the Indochinese countries came a shift in geographical focus from the Socialist bloc to East Asia. In the 1985–94 period, Vietnam's exports to Asia grew from 24.7 per cent to 58.1 per cent of total exports. In Laos, during the same period, the figures were 78.5 per cent to 82 per cent, respectively; and in Cambodia, 44.3 per cent in 1985 to 87.8 per cent in 1994. By 1995, some 70 per cent of contracted (accumulative) foreign investment in Vietnam and over 60 per cent in Laos originated from East Asia.

Following external liberalization and trade and investment regionalization, the three Indochinese countries are moving towards institutionalized openness via regional organizations. The most important example of this process is Vietnam's entry into ASEAN and the ASEAN Free Trade Area; and Laos and Cambodia are expected to join these organizations in the near future. All three countries are likely to join APEC and other regional and sub-regional organizations by the end of this decade. The effects of this process are unclear, but at this very early stage, they are likely to be more indirect: 'demonstration effects', 'learning-by-doing' in a small organizational arena, and adaptation to new external rules of the game that are less demanding than those of many international organizations. These effects cannot be quantified. Based on experience in other countries, however, these features can be reassuring to foreign investors, international capital markets and overseas donors, all of which comprise a growing source of financial capital, technology and knowledge for the Indochinese economies. Further, changes stimulated by such external forces will no doubt have spillover effects on internal agents, markets and structures. Direct effects, such as tight regional economic integration are unlikely, if the past evolution of intra-ASEAN trade and investment has any predictive power. Nevertheless, with the East Asian Tigers and some ASEAN economies rapidly moving up the economic ladder, it is likely that many will wish to continue or accelerate trends of moving labour-intensive and lower-technological activities to relatively cheaper production bases like Vietnam, Laos and Cambodia.

Finally, it is our contention that the rapid external economic adjustments of the three countries have supported economic transition by underpinning demand and employment during a period of major systemic and institutional change. To highlight what occurred in Indochina, we will digress a moment to discuss the very different situation in the FSUEE. In advanced centrally planned economies like those in the Soviet Union and Eastern Europe, demand typically outstripped supply – and sellers' markets dominated the economy – due to misaligned relative prices, perverse production and distribution incentives, and strategies and policies that depended on exceedingly high investment. After market coordination and institutions were introduced, the logic of the system changed swiftly: prices, incentives, management and policies shifted to support supply forces; and those shifts, which included large-scale redundancy of labour (adjusting to the real demand for labour in the firms and to decreasing demand for their output) undermined internal demand. Thus, the economies experienced a shock from the rapid shift from a sellers' to a buyers' market. Further, coordination was disrupted, as the economies moved from bureaucratic to market rules, thereby obstructing quick adjustment to the new situation. With the collapse of demand came responses that reinforced economic recession and constrained the accumulation of capital and other assets: persistent high unemployment, a sharp decline in labour productivity, rising inflation, a large decrease of domestic savings and thus a large contraction of investment. Facing a collapse of internal demand for their goods, the state industrial units in the FSUEE – the repository of a large share of the economy's capital – were unable to adjust quickly to the new conditions. This was in sharp contrast to the much weaker (but more flexible) non-state enterprises that operated under a very hard budget constraint: they shifted production, particularly the composition of output, towards rising foreign demand that emerged as a result of more realistic exchange rates and liberalization of trade and towards production of consumer goods that were demanded by the transitional domestic market. However, without reorientation to the new external and domestic opportunities by the major economic agents – the state enterprises – much capital remained idle, thereby reinforcing a vicious cycle of collapsed demand and recession. Demand in the FSUEE was further reduced by

Table 14.7 Annual change in Vietnamese output, employment and exports, 1989–92 (as a percentage)

	1989	1990	1991	Total		Average	Std.	Average	Std.
				1992	1989–1992	1989–1992	1989–1992	1990–1992	1990–1992
1. Gross Domestic Product	8.5	5.1	6	8.6	28.2	7.1	1.534	6.6	1.484
State	—	2.5	8.6	12.4	—	—	—	7.8	4.078
Excluding oil and state management	—	-7.7	3	8.8	—	—	—	1.4	6.834
Non-state	—	6.4	4.7	6.8	—	—	—	6.0	0.910
Agriculture	—	1.6	2.2	7.2	18.7	4.6	2.789	3.7	2.510
State	—	-23.2	2.3	2.2	—	—	—	-6.2	11.997
Non-state	—	2.4	2.2	7.2	—	—	—	3.9	2.311
Industry	-3.1	3.8	10.4	17.1	28.2	7.1	7.513	10.4	5.430
State	-2.5	6.1	11.8	20.6	36.0	9.0	8.412	12.8	5.965
Excluding fuel	-8.9	-0.5	6.7	16.1	13.4	3.4	9.201	7.4	6.797
Central	5.9	15.3	15.5	23.1	59.8	15.0	6.098	18.0	3.631
Excluding fuel	-5	5.8	8.3	17	26.1	6.5	7.846	10.4	4.800
Local	-13.9	-9.2	4.1	14.6	-4.4	-1.1	11.214	3.2	9.739
Non-state	-4.3	-0.7	7.5	9.5	12.0	3.0	5.689	5.4	4.413
Cooperatives	-36.1	-20	-41.4	-31.1	-128.6	-32.2	7.904	-30.8	8.739
Private	30.5	9.6	26.6	16.9	83.6	20.9	8.191	17.7	6.963
Services	19.1	10.8	8.3	7	45.2	11.3	4.706	8.7	1.577
State	—	2.1	7.4	7.5	—	—	—	5.7	2.522
Excluding state management	—	-7.8	8.9	8	—	—	—	3.0	7.669
Non-state	—	19.4	8.9	6.6	—	—	—	11.6	5.572
2. Total employment	1.6	5	2.2	2.7	10.3	2.9	1.287	3.3	1.219
State sector employment	-6.2	-10	-8.1	-5.4	-21.7	-7.4	1.781	-7.8	1.887
Government	-3.5	-4.2	-1.1	-2.8	-7.9	-2.9	1.151	-2.7	1.268
Central	-10.5	-10.3	9.9	-5	-6.4	-4.0	8.309	-1.8	8.551
Local	-1.4	-2.5	-3.9	-2.1	-8.3	-2.5	0.912	-2.8	0.772

State enterprises	−7.5	−13	−12.1	−7	−28.9	−9.9	2.675	−10.7	2.642
Central	−5.3	−8.2	−6.7	−3.9	−17.7	−6.0	1.599	−6.3	1.782
Local	−9.4	−17.3	−17.6	−10.5	−39.0	−13.7	3.772	−15.1	3.279
Non-state employment	2.8	7.3	3.6	3.6	15.1	4.3	1.748	4.8	1.744
Cooperatives	−6.3	−1.5	−6.2	—	—	—	—	—	—
Private	60.1	39.4	28.8	—	—	—	—	—	—
Agriculture and forestry	0.7	5.2	2.7	3.2	11.6	3.0	1.601	3.6	1.080
State	−5.2	−13.1	−10.7	−12	−31.7	−10.3	3.037	−11.9	0.981
Industry and construction	0.7	4.3	0.1	1.4	5.9	1.6	1.611	1.9	1.756
State	−8.3	−12.4	−15.5	−4.2	−29.1	−10.1	4.257	−10.7	4.767
Trade, transport and communications	15.8	4.4	2.4	1.1	8.0	5.9	5.821	2.6	1.357
State	−8.6	−14.4	−5.8	−8.5	−26.3	−9.3	3.138	−9.6	3.591
Education, health and science	−6.5	3.9	0.4	2.3	6.7	0.0	3.966	2.2	1.431
State	−2	−3	−3.1	−2.1	−8.1	−2.6	0.502	−2.7	0.450
Other	8.7	5.5	3.9	0.9	10.5	4.8	2.816	3.4	1.907
State	−6	−7.6	5	−5.1	−7.8	−3.4	4.946	−2.6	5.447
3. Merchandise Exports	87.5	23.5	−13.2	23.7	121.50	30.4	36.230	11.3	17.345

Sources: Calculated from International Monetary Fund (1995, tables 1, 10, 13, 14, 15): World Bank (1996: *Key Indicators of Developing Asian and Pacific Countries 1996*, tables 27, 28).

external factors: the collapse of the CMEA, the inability of large producers to adjust quickly to external (non-CMEA) demand or sell their rising inventory to international markets.

The story in Vietnam, Laos and Cambodia was quite different. As discussed previously, internal factors like 'non-CPE-type' structures and the short period of bureaucratic control over these economies were very important factors in facilitating a relatively rapid adjustment to market coordination. Analysis of Vietnamese data reveals positive performance in output, employment and exports during the critical transition years of 1989–92; similar data for Laos and Cambodia do not exist. Further, they show that despite the large and sometimes very abrupt systemic and institutional changes in Vietnam's economy during this period, internal and external demand expanded.

1. Gross Domestic Product, 1989–92, expanded at a robust average rate of 7.1 per cent per annum, falling to a low of 5.1 per cent in 1990.
2. Both the state and non-state sectors showed strong average annual growth in 1990–92 (data are unavailable for 1989) of 7.8 per cent and 6 per cent, respectively.
3. Expansion in the transition year 1989–92 was concentrated in industry (7.1 per cent average p.a.) and services (11.3 per cent average p.a.) with agriculture maintaining growth at an annual average of 4.7 per cent, exceeding that of a 2.2 per cent yearly increase in population.
4. The 2.9 per cent yearly average increase in employment, 1989–92, lagged output growth significantly, reflecting a systemic shift in the utilization of labour.
5. Employment in both government administration and state production declined dramatically, a yearly average over 1989–92 of −2.9 per cent and −9.9 per cent, respectively.
6. Employment in the non-state sector, which grew at an annual average in 1989–92 of 4.3 per cent, appears to have absorbed a large share of redundant state workers.
7. Merchandise exports grew at a robust pace during 1989–92 with an annual average of 30.4 per cent.

It is the last point that we would like to emphasize here. A cumulative growth of 121.5 per cent in Vietnam's exports over 1989–92 is remarkable, given that its foreign commercial markets, trade regime and structures were in a state of flux; and the CMEA was abolished during 1991 (when Vietnam's exports declined by 13.2 per cent). Analysis of aggregate export growth and disaggregated principal export commodities show that Vietnam (and anecdotal evidence indicates similar tendencies in Laos and Cambodia) has seized external export opportunities to support total demand for output and labour during the critical transition years. This trend has been underpinned by institutional changes to attract foreign capital, resulting in a flow of FDI into Vietnam of some $US700 million during 1989–92. While Vietnam did not receive multilateral loans to support structural adjustment and stabilization, as was the case with the Former Soviet Union and Eastern European countries, it was able to support its reform programme through foreign trade and investment, which likely had a more efficient outcome than that of official assistance funding.

In conclusion, the shift to openness, and concretely the establishment and expansion of trade and financial links with regional and international markets that the three economies have pursued throughout this decade, have supported a strong economic transition in Vietnam, with Laos and Cambodia following behind. External liberalization has combined synergistically with internal market and stabilization reforms to stimulate greater efficiency of the Smithian (allocative efficiency) and Keynesian (systemic efficiency to support demand) types, but they have supported Schumpeterian or adaptive efficiency (which is essential for long-run development) only in a very weak form. Finally, all three countries are still in the early stages of the transformation process: the path towards their objectives of developed market coordination and industrialized economies is long. Accelerated external liberalization, continuing regional cooperation and expanding openness can play key roles in achieving both.

NOTES

1 The briefer experiences of the three with socialist bureaucratic management and their earlier stages of economic development were two key factors resulting in very different economic structures and system dynamics from those operating in socialist economies like the Soviet Union and Eastern European countries. In great contrast to the latter, the three Indochinese economies have been characterized by a relatively low state share in total output and employment; small social welfare systems; comparatively large informal private sectors, which though illegal were nevertheless tolerated in order to fill in the large gaps of their economies; and highly underdeveloped central planning/management institutions and coordination structures. Their economies, which in many ways have more similarities with Third World countries than those of the Second World, were traditional in terms of organization, structure, technology and techniques. In fact, they are classic dual economies. Because Soviet-type development strategies were introduced for such a short period of time, the Stalinist strategy of extracting surplus from the agricultural sector to finance heavy industry was not very successful, even in the most industrialized of the three, Vietnam. After initiating agricultural reforms (especially in Vietnam), productivity and output increased, which was absorbed by rising domestic demand. This resulted in higher domestic savings and contributed to stabilizing the economies during transition. Unlike the FSUEE, agriculture has been the largest employer of labour and contributed either the largest (Laos and Cambodia) or a high share (Vietnam) of income to GDP. In Laos and Cambodia, industry has been very small and primitive, while Vietnam is still at an early stage of industrialization. All three economies are characterized by great capital shortages, labour surpluses, and underemployment in all sectors of the economy. Further, all show relatively low rates of productivity and slow technical change throughout the economies. Similar to economies undergoing market or traditional structural adjustment, all three have faced highly distorted relative prices which contributed to large and growing imbalances in the macroeconomy.
2 The leadership in Vietnam and Laos have explicitly blamed the Soviet socialist transformation model and inadequate approaches to implementing that strategy, not socialism *per se*, as the source of their failures.

3 Information provided by Vietnam's State Planning Committee (now merged in the Ministry of Planning and Investment) during interviews in October 1993.
4 Estimates from the Ministry of Planning and Investment, MPI (formerly known as SCCI), 1988–96. Not included in these data are the large number of small, unrecorded investments of Chinese origin (Taiwan, Hong Kong, China) in property and labour-intensive industries in southern Vietnam. Unofficial estimates of these investments are as high as $US1.5 billion.

BIBLIOGRAPHY

Asian Development Bank (1996) *Key Indicators of Developing Asian and Pacific Countries*, Singapore: Asian Development Bank, Economics and Development Resource Centre.
Asian Development Outlook (1995, 1996) Singapore: Oxford University Press for the Asian Development Bank.
Basic Statistics about the Socio-economic Development in the Lao P.D.R., 1975–1995, Vientiane, Laos: Committee for Planning and Cooperation, National Statistical Centre.
Chirathivat, S. (1996) 'ASEAN economic integration with the world through AFTA', in J. Tan (ed.) *AFTA in the Changing International Economy*, Singapore: Institute of Southeast Asian Studies.
Dodsworth, J. R., Spitäller, E., Braulke, M., Lee, K. H., Miranda, K., Mulder, C., Shishido, H. and Srinivasan, K. (1996) *Vietnam: Transition to a Market Economy*, Washington, DC: International Monetary Fund.
Economist Intelligence Unit (1995, 1996) *Country Report: Vietnam, Cambodia, Laos*, London: *Economist* Intelligence Unit.
Fforde, A. and de Vylder, S. (1996) *From Plan to Market: the Economic Transition in Vietnam*, Boulder, CO: Westview Press.
Forster, N. (1996) 'Vietnam and the ASEAN Free Trade Area', *Vietnam's Socio-Economic Development* 8 (Winter): 50–61.
Gates, C. L. (1995) 'Enterprise reform and Vietnam's transformation to a market-oriented economy', *ASEAN Economic Bulletin* 12(1): 29–52.
Gates, C. L. and Truong, D. H. D. (1994) *Foreign Direct Investment and Economic Change in Vietnam*, Copenhagen: NIAS (NIAS Report no. 20).
IMF (1995) *Vietnam: Statistical Tables*, Washington, DC: IMF Staff Country Report No. 95/93.
Kornai, J. (1994) 'Transformational recession, the main causes', *Journal of Comparative Economics* 19(1): 39–63.
Le, Q. P. (1996) 'ASEAN investment in Vietnam', *Vietnam's Economic Relations with ASEAN*, MA thesis, Griffith University, Queensland, Australia.
Ljunggren, B. (1995) 'Vietnam's second decade under *doi moi*: emerging contradictions in the reform process?', paper presented at an international seminar at the Centre for Pacific Asia Studies, Stockholm University, September 1995.
Melo, M. de, Denizer, C. and Gelb, A. (1996) 'Patterns of transition from plan to market', *The World Bank Economic Review* 10(3): 397–424.
Nguyen Cong, N., Dinh Van, N. and Le Hai, M. (1993) *Viet Nam: The Blazing Flame of Reforms*, Hanoi: Statistical Publishing House.
Nhan Dan, 3–4 March 1996.
Pomfret, R. (1996) *Asian Economies in Transition Reforming Centrally Planned Economies*, Cheltenham and Brookfield: Edward Elgar.
Qian, Y. and Xu, C. (1993) 'Why China's economic reforms differ: the M-form hierarchy and entry/expansion of the non-state Sector', paper presented at the conference on Transition of Centrally Planned Economies in Pacific Asia. Asia, Foundation, San Francisco.
Sachs, J. and Wing, T. W. (1994) 'Structural factors in the economic reforms of China, Eastern Europe and the Former Soviet Union', *Economic Policy: A European Forum* 10(1): 102–145.

Saignasith, C. and Lathouly, P. (1995) 'Transitional economy of the Lao PDR: current economic performance, progress and problems', in S. F. Naya and J. L. H. Tan (eds) *Asian Transitional Economies: Challenges and Prospects for Reform and Transformation*, Singapore: Institute for Southeast Asian Studies and San Francisco: International Center for Economic Growth: 154–209.

Statistical Yearbook 1995 (1995), Hanoi: Statistical Publishing House.

Taylor, L. (ed.) (1993) *The Rocky Road to Reform*, Cambridge, MA: MIT Press.

Tran, D. T. (1994) *Vietnam: Socialist Economic Development 1955–1992*, San Francisco: International Center for Economic Growth.

Tri, V. N. (1967) *Croissance Economique de la République Démocratique du Vietnam (1945–65)*, Hanoi: Editions en Langues Etrangères.

Tri, V. N. (1990) *Vietnam's Economic Policy Since 1975*, Singapore: Institute of Southeast Asian Studies.

Truong, D. H. D. and Gates, C. L. (1996) 'Vietnam's gradualist economic reforms', in A. E. Fernández Jilberto and A. Mommen (eds) *Liberalization in the Developing World: Institutional and Economic Changes in Latin America, Africa and Asia*, London and New York: Routledge: 72–95.

Vietnam Economic Times, July 1996; December 1996: 14.

Vu Tuan Anh (1996) 'Impacts of joining AFTA on Vietnam's economy', *Vietnam's Socio-Economic Development*, 5 (Spring).

World Bank (1993) *Viet Nam: Transition to the Market*, Washington, DC: The World Bank.

World Bank (1994) *Viet Nam: Public Sector Management and Private Sector Incentives: An Economic Report*, Washington, DC: The World Bank.

World Bank (1995) *Vietnam: Economic Report on Industrialization and Industrial Policy*, Washington, DC: The World Bank.

INDEX

DATE DUE

2/21/06			